The Tree Book

MICHAEL A. DIRR & KEITH S. WARREN

The
TREE
BOOK

Superior Selections *for* Landscapes, Streetscapes, *and* Gardens

TIMBER PRESS
PORTLAND, OREGON

Published in 2019 by Timber Press, Inc.
The Haseltine Building
133 S.W. Second Avenue, Suite 450
Portland, Oregon 97204-3527
timberpress.com

Printed in China
Text design by Adrianna Sutton
Production by Michelle Owen
Cover design by Jarrod Taylor

ISBN 978-1-60469-714-8
Catalog records for this book are available from the Library of Congress
and the British Library.

To our families,
with love, and to
those who plant trees,
with great appreciation

Contents

Introduction   8

Why We Wrote This Book   17

Origins of New Shade and   18
Ornamental Trees: The Roles of
Serendipity and Breeding

Provenance   31

Tree Sizes   33

Cultivar Names and Trademarks   33

A–Z Trees   35

Photo Credits   920

Index   921

Introduction

We love trees. For both of us, this love affair began early in life—with the deciduous monarchs of the Midwest (for Dirr) and the great coniferous rainforests of the Pacific Northwest (for Warren). We both spent our college years immersed in plants and began horticultural careers immediately thereafter, which we have each pursued for well over 40 years. One followed the path of an educator, as a university horticultural professor and researcher, and later, a plant breeder. For the other, the career path was in tree production as a nursery manager and researcher, and later, a tree breeder. Our paths began crossing some 30 years ago—university horticulture research meets commercial nursery production—and the flow of both ideas and plant materials has increased steadily ever since. Our horticultural thoughts often cross-pollinated each other, and soon the idea of co-authoring this book germinated. We both view trees as noble works of nature, we are humbled by their greatness, and we hope our works and words, in this book, will enhance and increase their presence in our society.

Whether walking through the redwoods of California, admiring the massive structure of a Midwest oak, or perhaps (having exited a hot freeway) pulling into the cool deciduous shade of a tree-lined street in an eastern city, we never cease to be amazed by the majesty of trees. The authors feel this every day and wonder if it is not so for everyone. Doubtless our bond with trees is unusually strong, as the two of us feel kindred spirit with trees, but it would be hard for us to understand someone who did not share a little of this feeling. At least to us, it seems to be a part of our humanity.

The advance of civilization has been largely about turning the wild environment into what is now called the "built environment," and we have to admit the conquest of nature has given us great creature comforts. But this comes at a price. At first, only a few voices, Henry David Thoreau, John Muir, and others, questioned the rapid conversion of wild to urban; today, organized environmental groups number in the hundreds, if not thousands, and are among the fastest-growing nonprofits. The world's first national park, Yellowstone, was created in 1872; today, the United States has 59 national parks, and the concept has spread to countries around the world. Some 15% of our planet (much of it ocean) enjoys some form of conservation protection. It is clear that as people have urbanized their world, they still need and cherish nature.

Forests reconnect us with nature.

Humans have certainly conquered the globe, living in every environment from the Antarctic ice to driest deserts. But conquest is almost always destructive, and populations prosper best in climates where trees are present. As civilization developed, trees were cut as a resource or cleared for agriculture. But soon after we did this, we realized we need trees, and we replant, selectively, to fill our needs. The woodsman cuts timber to make the lumber, then replants so the cycle can be repeated. The farmer clears for his crops, but then plants trees to break the wind and shade his house from the sun. As our urban centers have developed and grown, native trees are lost to houses, businesses, and endless miles of concrete. Then in our naked cities we feel the need for something natural, we miss the beauty, and so we plant our city streets, parks, and gardens with trees. People are attracted to a woodland environment, partly open with sunny meadows and partly closed with trees. We so often replicate this in our landscapes and city parks, partly open with grass and shrubs and partly closed in with trees for shade and screening. This seems to be where we want to live. We clear lots to build houses; then we plant trees for our homes.

Research at Yale University estimated that the Earth holds 6 trillion living trees. But the same 2015 study also determined that the Earth has suffered a 46% loss in its tree population since the dawn of human civilization, and that humans are the main driver of that loss. The world is currently losing about 15 billion trees per year. Tropical and boreal regions hold the largest portion of the remaining tree population, with the temperate zone holding only 22%. Clearly, widespread reforestation would be good for the planet. But what we do in our cities is disproportionately important. Planting trees in human population zones, especially in cities, has a multiplier effect on its benefits, as urban and residential trees mitigate so many human-caused adverse effects on the environment.

Beyond the aesthetic, trees bring us practical benefits. Environmental analysis confirms this, showing that deciduous trees on the south and especially the west side of a house can moderate the microclimate and greatly reduce energy consumption. As properly sited trees grow over time, their energy savings grow as well, making them incredibly cost-effective additions to the property. Mature trees add significantly to neighborhood home values, and research on the effect of tree loss due to the emerald ash borer has shown that crime rates and both respiratory and cardiovascular death rates have gone up with loss of the urban canopy.

A study led by Theodore Endreny, State University of New York, published

Trees shade the city and soften the harsh rectangles of our buildings.

Urban parks relieve stress, creating spaces for people to relax and enjoy their humanity.

in 2017, determined the value of trees to the world's largest cities, megacities with populations over 10 million. Urban trees added a mean value of $505 million (2017 dollars) to each city, or $1.2 million per square kilometer of tree cover. Economic value was gained by air pollution reduction, stormwater abatement, reduction of energy costs, and carbon emission reduction. Significantly, by far the greatest value was found to be from the health benefits derived from air pollution reduction. Trees significantly reduce dangerous air particulate matter smaller than 2.5 micrometers; these microscopic PM2.5 particles have an adverse effect on human health, notably to the respiratory and cardiovascular systems, and result in high health care costs and premature death. For health reasons, people need trees.

City managers have learned that trees shading pavement from the sun's ultraviolet light can make street surfaces last much longer. The foliage of trees traps particulates and creates cleaner air, as well as producing oxygen. And tree roots absorb great quantities of stormwater runoff, providing tremendous financial benefit to urban infrastructure. Many cities now plant trees and rain gardens to mitigate stormwater runoff as a less expensive alternative to enlarging pipes and to meet standards of clean water runoff. Urban heat islands, with their extensive hardscape areas and increased solar absorption, are many degrees hotter than the surrounding natural countryside. Our urban forests reduce these heat island effects; the more dense the forest, the more reduction is achieved.

Trees benefit people psychologically, too, in subtle ways that often go unnoticed. The presence of trees, the merest hint of a natural environment, somehow reduces stress, and stress reduction improves health. Long ago, John Muir wrote, "In every walk with Nature one receives far more than he seeks." Recent research by Roger Ulrich, Kathleen Wolf, and others who explore the interface between human psychology and nature has provided empirical evidence of this. The presence of trees and vegetation lifts moods and improves hospital recoveries after surgeries. Stressed brains find relaxation, depression is reduced, and concentration and creativity are increased by time spent in nature.

Trees and commercial districts are often in conflict. Trees may block store signs, damage and reduce the width of sidewalks, be expensive to install and maintain, and create potential liability. But again, research has shown that trees are beneficial to commercial districts. The perceived value of the merchandise is higher in stores that are in a well-planted retail area. Customers have been shown to be willing to drive a longer distance to access stores that are aesthetically planted and pay more for the goods found there. In short, trees pay for themselves and can increase the profits of a business. The key is to plan well and plant wisely.

Trees in the landscape are planted for a variety of reasons. To some developers it may be simply to meet the requirements of a city code (and too often the thinking is that the more cheaply done, the more profitable the project). To others it may be to create a great sense of place, an environment conducive to both mental and physical comfort. At its best, this could be a commercial district so well planted with large-caliper trees that it is immediately inviting and radiates a sense of class and heritage soon after construction. Or a new residential neighborhood whose canopy-covered streets create an instant feeling of cohesive community. Trees are planted for functional reasons—to create separation, to screen between properties, and to replace unwanted views with soft greenery. Trees frame views and provide the structural "bones" that define the landscape. Trees can soften the sounds of noisy streets, block the wind, and shade the sun.

People believe homes are more valuable when trees are present, and this is borne out by real estate sales, showing that landscaping, especially tree planting, is an investment that pays. Well-landscaped homes not only sell faster but for higher prices. Homeowners who plant trees aren't just improving the look of their residence; they also benefit financially.

City streets without trees are stark and uninviting.

Trees bring an inviting feel and additional business to a commercial district.

Houses become homes on tree-lined streets, and property values go up.

A well-landscaped garden can expand your sense of "home" beyond the walls of your house. A garden invites you out, educates you, entertains you, and certainly can exercise you. A garden is a place of relaxation, peace, and beauty, where nature is brought to you rather than you traveling in search of nature. A few trees can frame a sunny garden and create a more three-dimensional space, or many trees can be used to create a shady woodland garden. Surround your home with plants, and both your mind and body will benefit.

While the authors are consummate tree lovers, and we've observed that most people join us in our admiration of trees, we realize that some people are put off by the problems that trees can create. Tree lovers need to recognize this. We, too, have raked the leaves and even repaired the roof when the trunk has come crashing down. It often seems that everyone loves trees as long as they are on someone else's property. A tree in your distant neighbor's yard is a beautiful sight to see. A tree in your next-door neighbor's yard may be pretty but also the source of the leaves you rake, the lack of sun on your deck, or the cause of your fear of windstorms. A tree in your own garden can be a source of pleasure but also of work, expense, and potential liability. For these reasons, we put emphasis on education, teaching students and giving seminars to nursery and landscape professionals as well as the general public. We aim to spread the knowledge of horticulture and especially the characteristics of various species and cultivars with the goal that trees will be chosen and planted with careful, long-term consideration of the site.

And we have both pursued breeding and selection, developing better trees: better in the sense that they are not just valued for their beauty but are also more compatible and cooperative with

Gardens can be a relaxing retreat or a hub for recreation and entertainment.

the demands of humans. If we wish our urban forests to be more full, we need to plant trees that will not be objectionable by minimizing potential problems. The greatest threat to any tree is the property owner's chainsaw. Natural selection has already done its job of developing the best trees for the wild environment. But the human-altered environment is a much different place, and "survival of the fittest" has a very different meaning in the city. By selecting and breeding trees that property owners appreciate and find to be of lower maintenance, better structure, and less potential liability, our urban forests will grow. If species are chosen that are long-lived and healthy, the benefits multiply over time.

There may be cities that have requirements to plant annuals, perennials, lawns, and shrubs, but we don't know of them. Every city, however, seems to have some requirement for planting trees because of their value to the infrastructure. Too often, trees are planted simply to meet code requirements. Or planted with good intentions but little knowledge. As we drive our cities, wherever we go, we see dead and dying trees, trees that are butchered by pruning, and trees that are problems because they do not belong where they were planted. We see tree species and varieties that are poorly adapted to the climate and soils and that we know will have problems. We wish that the public was better educated and that better choices were made at planting. We would like to see trees look forward to time horizons of 100 years at planting rather than 10 years, which seems more common in practice. With age, trees reach noble stature and their benefits and beauty multiply with size. We urge you to choose wisely, plant carefully, and plant often.

ABOVE The invasion of *Pyrus calleryana*

RIGHT Breeding and selection brings reliable, improved urban performance, as in *Acer rubrum* REDPOINTE.

Our urban forests are facing great challenges. Our first dominant urban tree, the American elm, so common in the first half of the 20th century, was wiped out of our cities, years ago, by an imported fungus, Dutch elm disease. Green ash then became the dominant urban tree in the Midwest. Now it too is being eliminated, this time by an imported insect, the emerald ash borer. Invasive pests pose a huge and increasing problem to the vegetation of both cities and natural areas. There seems to be no end in sight to this assault. Accelerating world trade and faster transportation increase the likelihood that alien insects and diseases will cross borders. The next pest cannot be predicted, but we know it will come and change the makeup of our urban forest. Diversity of species and resistance are the best answers.

Diversity is our first line of defense. Urban forest geneticist Frank Santamour was an early champion of diversity in the urban forest. He proposed what has become known as the 10-20-30 Rule: that a city forest be made up of no more than 10% of one species, 20% of one genus, and 30% of one family. We knew Frank well; he was an inquisitive scientist who put this out for discussion, not as an authority who would want it to be a hard-and-fast rule. We certainly agree with the concept, but keep in mind that not all species, genera, and families are created equal. For example, *Sciadopitys verticillata*, native to a small area of Japan, is the only species in its genus, and *Sciadopitys* is the only genus in the family Sciadopityaceae. Compare that to the family Sapindaceae with close to 150 genera and 2,000 species. One of these genera is *Acer*, a worldwide genus of around 150 species. One of them, our common red maple, *A. rubrum*, is probably the most frequently planted (some would say overplanted) city tree. But *A. rubrum* spans a native range from the subtropical swamps of Florida to the frigid soils of southern Manitoba; it's a single species with a range perhaps a hundred times greater than the entire family Sciadopityaceae. With the tremendous native range of soils, climates, and geography that *A. rubrum* has conquered comes great genetic diversity, all held within a highly adaptable, single species.

The concept of embracing diversity in our urban planting is of great importance, but understand: the diversity in our plants doesn't adhere to strict percentage rules. Species designations are somewhat artificial lines we draw in the continuum of nature, so we need to look at the extent of diversity within species, genera, and families. Not all genera are equal. *Quercus* and *Acer*, our oaks and maples, are among the most diverse genera and are highly important urban trees that deserve more representation in our plantings than a strict percentage rule might dictate. We absolutely embrace horticultural diversity, but evaluate that in terms of true biological diversity and look beyond the names.

Scientists agree that our climate is warming and changing, although there is much argument as to what degree, and especially about future predictions. The danger this poses to our urban forests is mostly yet to be seen. We know already that our urban centers are heat islands that create their own local climate. Hard surfaces are hot surfaces, and the more exposed asphalt and concrete in a city, the hotter it is. When greenery transpires, it cools the environment and also increases the humidity. Our city centers are hot, and their air is drier than outer and more natural areas. Keep this in mind when considering varieties to plant: what may have been native to your local geography may no longer be appropriate for a downtown tree-pit environment in an expanse of concrete. Trees in forested areas benefit from the windbreak, the partial shading, and the humidity created by their green neighbors. In the city, a tree with genetic adaptation to heat, drought, flooding, soil compaction, high pH, and low humidity may have the key to long life. In breeding and selecting trees for urban landscapes, we keep this in mind. Often, trees from a hotter and drier climate will perform better in downtown areas, while native trees may be more suitable for residential and park settings.

Invasiveness is very difficult to predict and can haunt new plant introductions. We have seen this over and over. The current poster child of widespread invasiveness troubling urban forestry is probably *Pyrus calleryana* 'Bradford', a pear introduced by our prestigious USDA-ARS. Today, seedlings of 'Bradford' and similar *P. calleryana* cultivars have spread to become problematic throughout the Mid-Atlantic, central, and southeastern United States. We believe in placing more emphasis on plant selection within our own native species, as invasiveness from natives is much less likely. Selection for urban tolerance and improved form and appearance within U.S. natives is now producing many of our most promising new urban trees.

As trees are long-lived, potentially huge, and a valuable part of the city's infrastructure, breeding and selection should strongly emphasize the functional aspects of performance. Pest resistance, environmental tolerance, longevity, strength, and urban compatible form should be of utmost importance. Breeding and selection of improved cultivars gives us the ability to better our cities for the benefit of generations beyond our own.

Why We Wrote This Book

Tree references from national, state, and local perspectives are numerous. What is the secret sauce in this one? The answer lies in the DNA of the authors. For decades, Dirr lectured advanced gardeners and landscapers and listened to their questions and their hunger for knowledge, always wanting to learn about the best tree for a particular use. Warren walked his neighborhood and noted that in 15 blocks, not a single street tree was without problems. Either the choice of tree, its placement, or its maintenance was clearly wrong. Cracked and raised sidewalks, branches in pedestrian's faces, and diseased foliage were common. The authors realized that the planting of each tree is unique to the location and situation. No formula or list can prescribe the best tree for each site. This has to be done on location, at the site. The answer is education, spreading the knowledge of species and cultivars so the best decisions can be made. Knowing more about the vast potential palette of trees available will enable readers to choose the most suitable species and cultivars.

We intend this book to be both comprehensive in its scope and specific in its detail. And we wanted to provide the details that matter, the ones that are important in making planting decisions.

Here, we focus on the reality of plant use in landscape horticulture, from breeder to nursery, landscape architect to landscape installer, fine gardener to urban forester. We included trees that met one of three criteria: either 1) available in the trade and used in landscaping, 2) new, promising, and entering the trade, or 3) unknown or overlooked and worthy for breeding or adding to commercial production.

We first chose trees that make up the currently available landscape tree palette for use in the temperate northern hemisphere. Our base is North America but horticulture is global, and explorers and breeders spread plants among all continents, usually for the better (but sometimes not). The best cultivars have spread among continents, and this book should be useful in all countries across temperate climates.

We included the good and the bad. We praise the noble trees, discuss the relative merits of the mainstays of the landscape trade, and call the dogs for what they are. We feel that it is as important to say what not to plant as it is to suggest the best choices to plant. In general, we did not include old and out-of-date cultivars, those found only in arboreta, or cultivars named but never reaching significant nursery production, as too many futile searches for the unavailable only results in frustration. We do attempt to expand the diversity of trees in the landscape by including promising new varieties and suggesting species that could be explored for their potential in both breeding and production.

We intend this book to be a practical guide to the use of trees. It is heavily endowed with photographs, as pictures best convey form, texture, and appearance, so important in making landscape decisions. A book is portable, goes with you to the site, and is all-inclusive within its cover. While a computer is great for seeking out very specific information, we believe in the power of a book to encompass a subject within a framework of the authors' knowledge.

Nomenclature is always evolving. It follows the advances in the study of taxonomic relationships, as well as literature searches of historic name use. We have made this book as up-to-date as possible whenever nomenclatural changes seem solid and accepted but avoided changes that may be tentative. We have generally used the U.S. Department of Agriculture's GRIN database (Germplasm Resources Information Network) as our reference for species. For cultivar names, Dirr's *Manual of Woody Landscape Plants* and the European *List of Names of Woody Plants* were our best references.

Origins of New Shade and Ornamental Trees: The Roles of Serendipity and Breeding

The nursery world has moved from primarily seed-grown shade and ornamental trees to clonal (cultivar) material offering consistent uniform traits and reliable performance. Seedling blocks can be maddeningly inconsistent with the best trees tagged and sold from a given block (planting), the rest destined for lower prices and relegated to park grade. The industry had similar inputs for all, so arrived at the conclusion that cultivar trees with consistent superior traits were the future. Added to this equation are the landscape architects and designers who specify tree selections for large-scale projects, streets, campuses, parks, malls, stadiums, and urban development: they need uniformity and predictability. Assuming the trees are guaranteed by contract, all involved win when the installed trees survive and thrive. J. Frank Schmidt & Son Co., a major nursery, offered 342 vegetatively propagated cultivar trees and 69 seed-grown species (12 were oaks) in the 2016 catalog (i.e., 17% seedlings).

Seedling blocks can be maddeningly inconsistent.

Consistency on display, J. Frank Schmidt & Son Co.

The best-laid plans of landscape architects and designers require uniformity.

The financial advantages of uniform crops are obvious. Compound this with the Plant Patent Act of 1930, which allowed inventors to protect their intellectual property. To be patented, a tree (or any woody plant) must be discovered/found in cultivation (not in the wild), must be unique from any other tree of a given species, must be propagated asexually/vegetatively, and must maintain its desirable and unique traits from generation to generation. A plant patent requires a full botanical description of the plant and photographs. Anyone interested in the process should visit the uspto.gov site. A patent is effective for 20 years from the time of filing; the owner has sole rights to regulate production and may license other interested parties/nurseries to grow. The financial incentive involves a royalty fee per tree sold. The 69 species (seedlings) in the aforementioned example generate no royalty fees; many of the 342 cultivars do. Further, a patented tree offers value-added over a seedling tree of similar size and provides resources to sustain marketing and promotion.

The first (c.1947) patented tree was *Acer platanoides* 'Crimson King', a seedling of and significant improvement on 'Schwedleri'. 'Crimson King', with deep purple leaves, remains popular, especially in cool climates where the color is retained. The patent has long expired, the royalty stream dry, yet the selection is still grown and sold. A slightly different twist occurs with *A. rubrum* OCTOBER GLORY, patented in 1961 (PP2,116) by Princeton Nursery and the name trademarked (hence the all-caps typography); to grow and market the cultivar under that name, a $0.50 royalty is still attached and collected. The trademark name is forever assuming it is used correctly and renewed with the trademark office, and the plant is continuously sold and marketed. The patent law was changed in 2013, and the application is predicated on the first to

Acer platanoides 'Schwedleri' (left) and 'Crimson King'

Acer rubrum OCTOBER GLORY

file, not invent. If you're considering applying for a plant patent, hold the information close to the vest and move without announcing to the world what is in the works.

The current approach is to patent the introduction under a nonsense name and apply a selling or trademark name. For example, CHEROKEE BRAVE dogwood is listed as *Cornus florida* CHEROKEE BRAVE 'Comco No. 1'. This has muddied the nomenclatural waters and is certainly confusing to the customer when two names are applied to the same plant. The advantage is to the inventor who owns the trademark name and, even though the patent has expired and other parties can grow the tree, the trademarked name cannot be used without license. The royalty is still collected on CHEROKEE BRAVE, assuming the tree is sold as such. The advantage to the public is that the owner of the trademark has a vested interest and a responsibility to see that trees sold under the name are of high quality.

Enthusiasts may argue that no one has a right to patent a gift from nature. The restrictions granted by patents eliminate competition from growing the tree. But, whether technology or trees, the patent system spurs innovation and improvement. The patent and trademark costs are peanuts compared to marketing costs, stock build-up, and the time developing the new selection. Experience, wisdom, keen eyes, understanding a given species' characteristics and idiosyncrasies, and evaluation time and effort all factor into the final selection.

The American public is always seeking the new, whether an iPhone or tree. A plant buyer for a major chain of garden centers was asked why the industry introduces so many new plants each year. His response? "No customers come to the store and ask 'What's old?'"

Another debate with the use of clones is the lack of diversity owing to the restricted gene pool compared to seedlings. For example, many superior cultivars are selected from within the genome of *Acer rubrum*; it could be argued/contested that by planting multiple cultivars selected from Minnesota ('Autumn Spire', NORTHFIRE, 'Northwood', SCARLET JEWELL), New York ('Karpick'), Massachusetts ('Schlesingeri'), Kansas (BURGUNDY BELLE), South Carolina (SUMMER RED), and New Jersey (OCTOBER GLORY), the diversity is greater than seedlings produced from a local provenance in Bethel, ME.

Consider also the devastation wrought upon the ashes by emerald ash borer, the American elm by Dutch elm disease, and the American chestnut by the blight. Twenty-two *Fraxinus* species are U.S. natives, and unfortunately none are immune to the emerald ash borer. But with the intervention of breeders/selectors, several resistant cultivars of American elm can be planted, among them 'Princeton', 'Jefferson', 'Valley Forge', 'New Harmony', PRAIRIE EXPEDITION, 'St. Croix', and COLONIAL SPIRIT. And a long-term breeding effort has now produced a blight-resistant chestnut that is $^{31}/_{32}$nds *Castanea dentata* (American chestnut), having been back-crossed for generations to *C. mollissima*, a disease-resistant Asian species. Look for introductions in the future, with possible replanting in the native range.

Tsuga canadensis (Canadian hemlock) has been obliterated by the hemlock adelgid throughout the southern Appalachians. Ghostly gray skeletons mingle with the deciduous hardwoods, not a pretty sight. The U.S. National Arboretum, for over 20 years, has been breeding for resistance using *T. chinensis*, *T. sieboldii*, and *T. diversifolia*, all resistant species. The superior resistant clones of *T. caroliniana* × *T. chinensis*, similar in characteristics to *T. canadensis*, are now being tested for potential introduction. Authors observed them all and were impressed. Hemlocks, the most shade-tolerant needle evergreens, are readily pruned for hedges, make beautiful specimens, groupings, and tall screens. They are also an important food source for caterpillars, with 92 species reported to feed on their foliage. Purists will argue that the hybrids are compromised with foreign genes (*T. chinensis*); but since *T. canadensis* shows no resistance to the insect, these clones offer a partial solution to bringing hemlock back into cultivation.

Fraxinus pennsylvanica, showing the effects of emerald ash borer

Ulmus americana 'Princeton', looking good

Promising and impressive: *Tsuga* hybrids, USDA

The ultimate question is this: what are the origins of these introductions? The road to a new cultivar is rife with potholes, hairpin turns, drop-offs with no guardrails, countless miles, and a measure of good fortune. The origin of Keith Warren's *Quercus bicolor* AMERICAN DREAM 'JFS-KW12' affords an idea of the road traveled. What follows is his recounting of how it came to fruition, as filed with the patent office.

In 1998, I began a systematic program of selecting and evaluating improved seedlings of swamp white oak, *Quercus bicolor*. Between 1998 and 2005, I walked the cultivated nursery production rows of two-year-old trees in a nursery in Boring, OR. During this time, I walked dozens of rows and examined over 10,000 trees. From these, 66 trees with superior features were identified, selected, and transplanted for further study. These plants were all selected from trees that originated from seed of unknown, unpatented *Q. bicolor* trees. Of these 66 trees, 18 were chosen as finalists, assigned identifying numbers, and planted out into an evaluation block. I began propagating these 18 selected trees by chip budding on *Q. bicolor* rootstock and planting into small plots.

This particular invention, 'JFS-KW12', was first identified in late summer of 2002. My attention was first drawn to it by its vigorous growth habit, its large deep green glossy leaves, and its excellent branch structure. Further observation showed that it possessed much greater resistance to powdery mildew and oak anthracnose than typical seedlings of *Q. bicolor*. In January of 2003, I transplanted this original 'JFS-KW12' tree to a special evaluation row. In August of 2004, I began propagation of this new tree by chip budding to compare it to seedlings and to other promising selections of the species that I had identified.

Liriodendron tulipifera

The decision to introduce was made in 2009, with subsequent stock increase; it was offered for sale in the spring 2011 catalog, and in 2012 two-year-old trees were shipped to customers. As we write this, it is receiving plaudits nationwide, from Massachusetts to Georgia to the West Coast. Mike and Bonnie Dirr planted AMERICAN DREAM on the University of Massachusetts, Amherst, campus in memory of their beloved Susy as well as in their Georgia garden. Perhaps the highest accolade!

Thomas Jefferson said it most eloquently: "The greatest service which can be rendered any country is, to add an useful plant to its culture." Opportunities are available for such pursuits to all who love trees.

Owing to the kindness of nature, seeds offer the most logical opportunities for variation. For tree hunters, the tree that elevates its characteristics above the milieu is the goal. Species characteristics adhere to a bell curve, the majority fitting the "normal" middle area. At the tails of the curve reside the biological diamonds, which—when horticulturally polished—are the true treasures. In a nutshell, this is what Warren accomplished in developing AMERICAN DREAM. Of 10,000 seedlings evaluated, 66 fit the expectations, then 18, then *one*; the process initiated in 1998, mission completed in 2012.

A few other examples of the joys of looking under the tails of a bell curve? *Liriodendron tulipifera* is a tall, lofty, fast-growing, immense native tree. 'Little Volunteer' is about a third the size in all its parts and "fits" smaller landscapes. 'Arnold' ('Fastigiatum') is a columnar selection, ideal where space to spread is restricted. EMERALD CITY is a Warren selection of species size, but with improved branching, tighter crown, lustrous dark green leaves and increased cold hardiness (-30°F and greater).

Seedlings provide the greatest opportunity for new selections, but there are other processes which play important roles. Sports/mutations/chimeras are most often, or at least obviously, manifested in foliage variegation. Leaves may be yellow; white- or yellow-margined, with green centers; the reverse; or splashed, splotched, spotted, and streaked various colors. Occasionally, pink, rose, red, and/or purple leaf sports occur. These patterns are often unstable and may revert to green, white, yellow; require asexual (vegetative) propagation; and need to be evaluated to ensure stability of the characteristic. *Cornus kousa* is a model species for variegated foliage mutations. In one unusually prolific year, Warren tested nine "new" variegated selections received from various sources, hoping for commercial introduction; none was deemed good enough, as an even better one, 'Summer Gold' from Crispin Silva, arrived the next year, beating out the others to win a place in the Schmidt nursery catalog.

Traditional breeding is an important source of new trees, with universities, arboreta, and botanical gardens the principal practitioners; it is based on controlled crosses where the female and male parent are known. Open-pollinated refers to breeding from a known (usually) maternal parent, without absolute knowledge of the pollen parent, unless the species

Liriodendron tulipifera 'Little Volunteer'

Liriodendron tulipifera EMERALD CITY

Cercis canadensis 'Pink Pom Poms'

is self-fertile. Knowledgeable breeders use both approaches with the goal of producing superior genetics. Among other things in his distinguished 27-year career at the Morton Arboretum, one such man, George Ware, bred planetrees, *Platanus ×acerifolia*, including EXCLAMATION! and the newest, MONUMENTAL. Elwin Orton, Rutgers University, bred the spectacular disease-resistant flowering dogwoods of the Stellar series over a 48-year career. Richard Olsen, U.S. National Arboretum, and his staff are breeding *Catalpa*, *Chilopsis*, *Nyssa*, and *Tsuga*. Denny Werner, North Carolina State University, bred redbuds for 20 years, with 'Ruby Falls', 'Merlot', and 'Pink Pom Poms' the tip of the introduction iceberg. More are waiting in the wings. Many amateurs have contributed to the pool of useful trees, especially magnolias, notably in the development of yellow-flowered cultivars. The list of breeders and their accomplishments is a book unto itself and will need to wait for other authors to ferret out the numerous contributions.

For breeders to be successful, new sources of germplasm/genetics are paramount. If new traits (e.g., cold hardiness) are not available, breeding for same is akin to an endless cul-de-sac, for to expect anything different in the progeny is pure folly. Individuals, commercial firms, nurseries, universities, arboreta, botanical gardens—all source new genetics from the four corners of the world. *Cornus kousa* is at the limits of adaptability for cold tolerance in the Chicago area (-20°F). Imagine new collections from northern/mountainous regions of China, Korea, and Japan with increased cold hardiness, perhaps with hardiness genes to allow successful culture in zone 4. The Holden and Morris arboreta collected seeds from these three countries over a series of years. Recent laboratory studies showed the Japanese germplasm was hardy to -15°F, the Chinese to -22°F, and the Korean to -30°F. The reader might question how laboratory freeze data relate to equivalent low temperatures in nature. Authors have conducted laboratory studies using numerous woody species and cultivars with Orville Lindstrom at the University of Georgia; the data correlated closely with performance in the landscape, and the superior cold hardiness of the Korean provenance was confirmed during the polar vortex of 2014–15, when temperatures in northeastern Ohio hovered between -24.6 and -32°F. In August 2015, Tim Brotzman, Brotzman's Nursery, North Madison, wrote, "The other group of plants clobbered in all of northeastern Ohio were the Kousa dogwoods. Every nursery I have spoken to reports major damage and loss...I am pleased to say that a group of Holden/Morris seedlings collected in Korea in 1981 and 1983 were unfazed and flowered spectacularly."

The authors know at least one breeder who is utilizing the Korean cold hardy germplasm. Who would have thought a zone 4 *Cornus kousa* was realistic? The convergence of laboratory and field testing data showed unequivocally the superiority of the Korean material. Thirty-two years passed before this came to light.

Similar results were reported for *Cornus officinalis*, *C. mas*, *Parrotia persica*, and *P. subaequalis*. In fact, most *P. persica* were lost in all field locations, while a single *P. subaequalis* in a field

Parrotia subaequalis, fall color

Lagerstroemia 'TWILIGHT MAGIC'

location suffered only minimal tip dieback. The latter is a newer introduction from China now moving through the sharing/growing channels. In the Southeast it has proven heat and drought tolerant. The fall color is spectacular maroon to bright red in the Southeast, Midwest and New England. Warren reported slower growth in the Pacific Northwest but still with wonderful bright red fall color.

Kudos to the many individuals, institutions, and nurseries who collect evaluate, report and share the genetics. Our tree palette is richer, more diverse; the breeders are endowed with unique genetics; and time-tested, superior, sustainable trees are available to all.

Colchicine, oryzalin, and ethyl methanesulfonate are used to affect chromosomes by doubling or altering gene expression. Triploid plants are often (but not always) sterile. This is what makes seedless watermelon and bananas possible. Efforts to induce sterility in "weedy," invasive species like Callery pear, Norway maple, and lacebark elm involve doubling chromosomes, then crossing to a diploid (2N) to produce a triploid (3N), the latter sterile. Work at Oregon State University shows promise with Norway maple. Tom Ranney of North Carolina State University has developed a nearly sterile *Pyrus calleryana* using this technique, now introduced as CHASTITY 'NCPX2.'

Radiation (X-ray) is utilized to alter gene expression. The most transformational success of radiation is the purple-leaf crapemyrtle, *Lagerstroemia* DELTA JAZZ developed by Cecil Pounders, Mississippi State University and USDA. He used cobalt-60 to irradiate seeds of 'Sarah's Favorite'; a purple-leaf variant was the result. The trait is inheritable via traditional breeding, controlled or open-pollinated. Many new purple-leaf crapemyrtles, including those in the Magic, Delta, Ebony, and Black Diamond series, were derived from DELTA JAZZ. Breeding continues, and several tree types, including MOONLIGHT MAGIC and TWILIGHT MAGIC, are now in commerce.

The USDA-ARS maintains germplasm repositories across the country for all types of plants, including vegetables, flowers, berries, shrubs, and shade, ornamental, and nut trees. The concept is to preserve genetic resources in perpetuity. These germplasm resources are then available to scientists, breeders, and nursery producers. For example, the *Corylus* collection is maintained at Oregon State University, Corvallis. The U.S. National Arboretum Woody Landscape Plant Germplasm Repository (WLPGR) in Beltsville, MD, is charged with maintaining over 200 genera of priority woody plants of diverse origin. True to the mission statement, genera from *Acer* to *Zelkova* are represented with over 1,000 plants in the ground. Seeds of these plants are also preserved. The authors have visited on several occasions and were mightily impressed with the diverse and well-maintained germplasm. Further, we have been able to source material for evaluation, potential breeding, and introduction. The WLPRG is a collaborative effort of the government, public gardens, and individuals to broaden the genetic base of the 200 or so genera. The American nursery industry needs to become more engaged with WLPGR and make use of the tremendous resources. The authors are fond of *Aesculus*, particularly the noble *A. flava*, yellow buckeye. During a June 2016 visit, we spied an upright-columnar seedling of the species,

U.S. National Arboretum Woody Landscape Plant Germplasm Repository, Beltsville, MD

and our request for scion wood for grafting was graciously granted. This is a functional and dedicated government agency empowered to assist the nursery industry, breeders, and citizens.

Genetic engineering has the potential to produce new shade and ornamental trees, but current public attitude toward this technique holds its use back. Genes can be turned on, off, and inserted for unique traits; the system CRISPR-CAS9 enables geneticists to edit parts of the genome (genes that code for the plant) by removing, adding, or altering sections of the DNA sequence. If the genes that code for fruit development could be turned off, invasiveness would be a moot issue.

Tim Rinehart, USDA-ARS, reported no shade or ornamental trees have been genetically modified and introduced. However, a nut tree, the American chestnut (*Castanea dentata*), has been genetically modified; the transgenic result displays high resistance to the blight that killed an estimated four billion trees from Maine to Georgia. This represents a remarkable accomplishment, the result of 26 years of research involving a team of more than 100 scientists and students at the not-for-profit American Chestnut and Restoration Project. The researchers tested more than 30 genes from different plant species that could potentially enhance blight resistance. A gene from bread wheat turned out to be most effective at protecting the tree from the pathogenic fungus, *Cryphonectria parasitica*. This single wheat gene, OxO, inserted into the chestnut genome (which contains some 40,000 other genes) detoxifies the chemical the fungus uses to form the deadly stem cankers. The researchers noted the blight-resistant American chestnut is genetically 99.999% identical to wild-type American chestnuts. Before release of this non-patented 'Darling 54' transgenic chestnut, the trees must be shepherded through regulatory review by the U.S. Department of Agriculture, the Environmental Protection Agency, and the Food and Drug Administration, a process that may take three to five years; then the tree will be made quickly available to the public. Whatever the reader's philosophy/issues with GMOs, to think a gene from bread wheat could herald the return of the American chestnut is quite astonishing.

The most exhilarating aspect of tree prospecting? Taking advantage of any space where seedlings grow. We recommend the following for the best hunting.

- Forests
- Fields, fencerows
- River sides, lake sides, ocean sides
- Swamps, floodplains, river bottoms
- Ditches, embankments
- Road sides, city streets
- Cemeteries
- Campuses
- Parks (public, private, national)
- Golf courses
- Arboreta and botanical gardens
- Corporate landscapes
- Nurseries (seedling blocks)
- Heirloom gardens (Grandma's garden)
- Your front yard and backyard
- Google Earth

Herein we offer one rather humorous example of plant discovery. Dirr was lecturing in Columbus, OH, in January and mentioned Kentucky coffeetree and its variants. A city employee told him about an upright *Gymnocladus dioicus* in Goodale Park. Dirr scouts the entire park with no good fortune. Warren is advised about the tree, searches Google Earth, and locates the tree by its shadow. Tree exploration and discovery on Google Earth, who would have thought it possible?

By now, the reader is dazed, confused, and ready to hit the road, reconnoitering for trees. Before the royalty dollars are calculated, let's review the journey to introduction.

1) Think adaptability, i.e., can the selection be successfully grown in significant areas of North America and world? (*Ginkgo* potentially; *Franklinia* scarcely)
2) Discovery in nature or in cultivated habitat (the latter for patenting)
3) Permission to collect scion wood for propagation
4) Collection, shipping to capable nursery producers
5) Budding and/or grafting for evaluation; cutting propagation
6) Ease of propagation
7) Rate of growth—height, caliper
8) Canopy and branch structure development (strong/weak wood)
9) Flowering, fruiting
10) Summer foliage color
11) Fall color development as a young tree
12) Bark—thin, easily damaged in handling
13) Bark—color, texture, exfoliating
14) Disease and insect resistance
15) Heat, drought, soil tolerances
16) Ability to dig, store, and ship (no limb breakup)
17) Ease of transplanting for receiving/finishing nursery
18) Marketing (so customers know it exists and is available)

The upright-columnar seedling of *Aesculus flava*

As an example, in March 2007, the Dirrs discovered an upright-columnar *Quercus bicolor* in Virginia. Bud wood (scion wood) was sent to Warren. The steps just enumerated were followed and by fall 2009, a decision to introduce the tree was reached. The name BEACON 'Bonnie and Mike' was chosen, and it first appeared in the J. Frank Schmidt & Son catalog in 2011. This time frame was unusually fast. However, the parent tree was 20′ high, 4′ wide, and the budded trees displayed similar growth habits. What was unknown when the tree was "discovered" were the foliage characteristics: the new growth bronze, then lustrous dark green above, glaucous (silvery) below, turning a good yellow in autumn. Everything considered, a chance seedling discovery, with an aesthetic and functional persona.

Provenance

Provenance refers to the origin or source of something and, in plants, describes regional seed sources or ecotypes within species. In species with broad natural ranges, regional differences in appearance and adaptability are evident. Depending on gene flow and degree of isolation of the various populations, these differences can be minor or quite significant.

While provenance doesn't hold a place in the formal hierarchy of taxonomy and nomenclature, it can be of great importance in horticulture. While both appearance and adaptability can vary with provenance, it's the population's adaptability that is of greatest practical importance. It doesn't take much to imagine that a native red maple seedling from Minnesota is going to behave quite differently than one from Florida. Obviously, cold hardiness is the first thing that comes to mind, but features such as growth rate, heat tolerance, drought tolerance, wet soil tolerance, pH tolerance, timing of leaf emergence and dormancy, fall color, and insect and disease resistance may all vary.

It might seem logical that local seed sources would be considered best, but this is not always true. Local seed sources are naturally adapted to local conditions. For forestry, restoration work, and native plantings, local seed sources are indeed best. Both the U.S. Forest Service and private timber companies rely heavily on provenance for reforestation and track this information carefully. But city and landscape conditions are different. From the perspective of a tree, a great deal has been changed in the built environment. Root space is usually restricted, soils are altered (almost always for the worse), drainage is often reduced, and the urban heat island effect changes temperature and moisture availability. Trees from a more stressful provenance may outperform local sources when planted in urban conditions. For example, 'Patmore' ash, from the extreme northwestern edge of the species' range in western Alberta, was the most popular *Fraxinus* cultivar in the United States until emerald ash borer removed the genus from the landscape palette in much of the country. Not only a handsome cultivar, it proved to be widely adaptable to a broad range of climatic and urban conditions.

Quercus bicolor BEACON 'Bonnie and Mike'

In some markets, it is possible to purchase trees from a few selected provenances. But availability of local seed-produced trees is usually limited to local growers. Local seed sources are often unreliable from year to year. This causes uncertain availability of finished trees, and growers and landscaping businesses require steady availability. It would be beneficial to have more provenance-based nursery stock, but the realities of large-scale commercial production make this difficult. Local native plant nurseries are the best source of local seed sources, but you need to ask if the seed was wild-collected and local, as some natives have ranges across much of North America.

The nursery trade has moved strongly to cultivar production, and customers have embraced this, as cultivar production offers the reliability of known performance and lessens the uncertainty inherent in a dependence on local seed. Cultivar production is a practical way to provide provenance selection. Every cultivar has a provenance, although more often than not, the information has been lost because of movement of seed and tree before the cultivar was selected. Knowing the provenance of a cultivar can be valuable in understanding its adaptability. For example, among sugar maples, NORTHERN FLARE is from South Dakota, and UNITY is from Manitoba; both demonstrate cold hardiness. Provenance information gives strong hints at adaptability, but the location of a cultivar's commercial origin or introduction often has nothing to do with provenance. For example, FLASHFIRE came from a structured selection program in Oregon, where sugar maple is not native, but to optimize heat and drought resistance, it was purposefully derived from the Oklahoma Caddo seed source.

We encourage nurseries to make provenance information available when possible. Provenance is a powerful tool to use in tree improvement, and a greater emphasis should be placed on it by those breeding and selecting new cultivars as well as by those purchasing and planting trees.

Tree Sizes

We have endeavored to give our best estimate of mature tree sizes throughout this book, both for species and cultivars. First, for the purpose of this book, we chose 15′ as a rough lower limit to define a "tree" for inclusion, although we relented in a few special cases. In actuality, mature tree size will vary significantly according to climate and soil conditions. For example, redwoods may soar over 300′ in ancient stands in moist northern California coastal valleys, but in a residential garden in the West 100′ is more realistic, and in the East, where they are less well adapted, 50′ is more likely. Our tree size estimates are for average city landscape conditions at about 50 years of age. In stressful climates or in downtown planting pits, trees will mature to smaller sizes; in ideal climates and with park-like surroundings, they may be larger. A great many cultivars have been introduced recently, and for these, no 50-year-old specimens yet exist. We have used our experience and best judgment. Nursery catalogs may underestimate true mature size because so many cultivars are new. Some catalogs even give a 10-year projection for garden size. We take a longer view, as we wish our trees to grow to maturity and noble stature.

At times, we will verbally describe trees as small, medium, or large. When we do so, we are generally thinking of small trees as 15 to 30′, medium trees as 30 to 50′, and large trees as 50′ and greater. In constructs such as 20′ by 30′, height is first, then width.

Cultivar Names and Trademarks

Cultivar names are indicated by single quotation marks. Trademarks (™ and ®) are indicated by the use of all capital letters. Trademarks can change over time with registration and use. All cultivars have a 'Cultivar' name; some cultivars have a closely associated TRADEMARK.

A–Z

Trees

A

Abies alba
European silver fir

Evergreen conifer. Noble conical, church-spire-like habit, estimate 30 to 50′, to 100′ tall trees in ideal moisture-laden environment; slow-growing. Bark is light gray; checkered with maturity.

Foliage: Needles about 1″ long, shining dark green above, tip notched or pointed, 2 silver bands beneath, borne in 2 typically horizontal ranks; subject to late spring frosts. Young shoots are densely pubescent. **Flowers/seeds/fruits/cones**: Cones cylindrical, 4 to 6″ long, 1½ to 2″ wide, green-brown when young, reddish brown at maturity with exserted reflexed bracts. **Native range**: Central and southern Europe, primarily in the mountains of France, Switzerland, and Germany. **Adaptability**: Zones 4 to 6. **Landscape use**: Requires cool, moist climate, full sun, but a 50′ specimen of 'Pendula' continues to grow contentedly in the heavy clay soils of Spring Grove Arboretum, Cincinnati, OH. Large stately evergreen reserved for ideal climates. **Street tree use**: Limited to none. **In the trade**: Firs, in general, are not common in commerce, but are represented in major arboreta and botanical gardens. The Morton Arboretum, Lisle, IL, lists 18 species in its database. 'Pendula', with long weeping branches, the effect curtain-like, limp, with branches often brushing the main trunk, has prospered many years in the Midwest; originated as a seedling in France, c.1835.

Abies alba

'Pendula'

Abies balsamea
balsam fir

Evergreen conifer. Symmetrically pyramidal to narrow-conical in youth, more open with age, 45 to 75′ high; slow-growing. Bark gray, splitting into shallow, irregular blocks with maturity.

Foliage: Holiday-fragrant needles, 1″ long, glossy dark green above, 2 gray bands below, horizontally arranged with a V-shaped parting between, readily recognized by strong balsam scent of crushed needles. **Flowers/seeds/fruits/cones**: Cones dark violet (dull purple) when young, maturing gray-brown, oozing resin at maturity, 2 to 4″ long, 1 to 1½″ wide. **Native range**: Wide distribution from Alberta to Labrador, extending into the Arctic regions, south to Pennsylvania, Virginia, and West Virginia. Mixed with *Picea glauca* and *P. rubens* in Maine, growing along the shoreline. **Adaptability**: Zones 3 to 5. **Landscape use**: Requires cool, moist environment and suited only to the northern states. Acid, well-drained soils are paramount. Greatest use is for Christmas tree production, wreaths, holiday greens. **Street tree use**: No. **In the trade**: Several dwarf types; authors spotted an attractive light blue-green needle form in western Maine. Var. *phanerolepis* is considered a better option than the type and is common in the Northeast; it offers a slightly more compact habit, growing 45 to 75′ high, 20 to 25′ wide.

Abies balsamea

Abies cilicica
Cilician fir

Evergreen conifer. Tall, elegant, slender, tight-conical habit maintaining its lower branches into old age; 60′ high trees in Cincinnati, OH, are in remarkably pristine condition. Bark gray, becoming flaky and then furrowed with age.

Foliage: Needles, 1 to 1½″ long, shining bright green above, 2 narrow whitish bands below; arranged in V-shaped formation; from a distance canopy appears gray-green. **Flowers/seeds/fruits/cones**: Cones cylindrical, 7 to 8″ long, 2 to 2½″ wide, greenish, maturing reddish brown, bracts not visible, producing viable seeds, as spontaneous seedlings are common in unmowed areas in Spring Grove. **Native range**: Southern Turkey, northwestern Syria, Lebanon, where it forms pure stands or is mixed with *Cedrus libani* and other conifers. **Adaptability**: Should be better adapted to hotter, drier climates, given its nativity. Zones 5 to 6(7). **Landscape use**: A "better" candidate for heavy clay soils, although in the wild it grows on thin rocky soils, often limestone-based, in dry-summer mountain forests. Trees in Cincinnati are growing in high pH, clay soils. Still a fir, so no betting the farm on performance. Stately habit is maximized when utilized in groupings. **Street tree use**: No. **In the trade**: Sold as seed-grown.

Abies cilicica

A

Abies concolor

white fir

Evergreen conifer. Full and soft-appearing for a conifer, pyramidal form, fast-growing to 50′ or more in the landscape and over 100′ in its native habitat, 25′ in width. Bark gray, divided by furrows into ridges with maturity.

Foliage: Needles are light green, longer than most conifers, 1½ to 2½″ by 1/10″ wide, glaucous with a bluish white tint. **Flowers/seeds/fruits/cones**: Flowering cones are inconspicuous and reddish purple, developing into upright cones, generally 4″ tall. **Native range**: Mountainous terrain from southern Oregon to Utah and Baja California to New Mexico. **Adaptability**: Tolerant of extremes of heat, cold, and drought, thus has performed better than many *Abies* species when planted in urban landscapes. Performs well in the Midwest and across the East, as well as in its native Southwest. However, it doesn't like wet feet, so be sure to give it good drainage. Zones 4 to 7. **Landscape use**: A large landscape tree with a bluish tint, providing a softer-looking and faster-growing alternative to blue spruce. **Street tree use**: Large size and low-hanging branches preclude its use except for wide roadside areas. **In the trade**: 'Candicans' is the only cultivar likely to be found. It is a beautiful selection of the species, having long, soft, upturned needles of silvery blue. Fast-growing and densely pyramidal to 45′ by 25′, it gives the feeling of a soft, fluffy blue spruce.

'Candicans'

'Candicans'

Abies concolor

Abies concolor

38

Abies firma
Japanese momi fir

Evergreen conifer. Considered by C. S. Sargent to be the most beautiful Japanese fir, ascending 120 to 150′ in the wild. Never common, but 30 to 50′ high conical to broad pyramidal specimens occur in the Southeast, to 60 to 70′ in Mid-Atlantic and Northwest. A beautiful 25-year-old specimen at the University of Georgia is 20′ high and 12′ wide. Painfully slow by commercial standards, but worth the wait. Bark gray, then browner, flaky and furrowed with age.

Foliage: Needles to 1½″ long, dark green above, 2 gray-green bands beneath, stiff, prickly, the tips of the needle bifurcate (divided into a V-shaped notch), arranged in a comb-like, pectinate formation. **Flowers/seeds/fruits/cones**: Cones 3 to 6″ long, 1½ to 2″ wide, yellowish green in youth, grayish green to brown at maturity; noted cone production on a lone 15′ high tree on the campus of Georgia Southern University, Savannah. **Native range**: Most widely distributed fir in Japan, where it is found on moist and dry sites. **Adaptability**: No other fir we know possesses such heat and drought tolerances. Quality specimens grow from Boston to Raleigh, NC, and Mobile, AL. Old 70′ high plants have persisted at Longwood Gardens. Zones 6 to 9. **Landscape use**: Certainly the first choice for the Southeast. Its greater heat tolerance may be explained by its low-elevation distribution in Japan. Resists root rot and is used as an understock for other firs. **Street tree use**: No. **In the trade**: Uncommon, sold as seed-grown.

Abies fraseri
Fraser fir

Evergreen conifer. Narrowly and stiffly pyramidal, usually quite symmetrical, growing to 40′ in landscapes with a width of 20′. In prime natural settings can reach 70′. Moderate growth rate. Bark grayish brown when young, becoming more gray, fissured and scaly with age.

Foliage: Needles are deep green with a bluish silver tint, rather short, ½ to 1″ long, 1/24″ wide, soft-pointed, and curve upward on the twigs. **Flowers/seeds/fruits/cones**: Cones are borne on the top of the crown and held upright, about 2″ long and purple at first, becoming brown. **Native range**: Restricted to high elevations in the Appalachian Mountains from Virginia to north Georgia. It is the only true fir native to the southern Appalachians. Native stands are now under attack by the balsam woolly adelgid, which is reducing the tree's range and is a long-term threat to the species. **Adaptability**: Best adapted to cooler areas of the Piedmont through New England, northern Midwest, and Pacific

A

Abies firma

Abies firma

Abies fraseri

Northwest. While it likes cooler weather, it is more heat tolerant and usually a more successful landscape tree than the closely related balsam fir. Zones 4 to 7. **Landscape use**: Mostly living Christmas trees planted in yards. It makes an outstanding Christmas tree and a large industry has developed in Virginia and North Carolina, where millions of trees are produced annually. It's the Dirr choice for a Christmas tree every year. **Street tree use**: Low-hanging branches and pest susceptibility make it a poor choice. **In the trade**: Sold as seed-grown.

Abies grandis
grand fir

Evergreen conifer. Narrowly pyramidal and growing quickly to a grand scale (hence the common name). Reaches over 200′ in height in native stands near the Pacific coast, but is shorter in drier interior sites. Width is restricted to 25′. Bark dark gray-brown, fissured and checked with age.

Foliage: Needles are 1 to 2″ long, $\frac{1}{12}$″ wide, dark green with a prominently white underside, and flattened along the twig. **Flowers/seeds/fruits/cones**: The upright cones are unusually large and heavy and are held high on the tree. Warren grew up under grand firs and remembers from his childhood the sound of crashing cones falling to the ground from a hundred feet overhead, cut by squirrels. "Squirrel bombs." **Native range**: Pacific Northwest, from Vancouver Island to western Montana and north coastal California to central Idaho. **Adaptability**: It prefers cooler air temperatures, a Pacific Northwest–type climate, and well-drained soils. Zones 5 to 7, 8 near the Pacific. **Landscape use**: Chiefly used in native landscapes in its range, or retained in a woodsy landscape after construction. Grown as a Christmas tree because of its fast growth, and it occasionally enters the landscape as a living Christmas tree. **Street tree use**: Not a good choice because of low branches and dislike of poor drainage. **In the trade**: Sold as seed-grown.

Abies grandis

Abies grandis

Abies homolepis
Nikko fir

Evergreen conifer. Shapely, rather broad pyramid, clothed with branches to the ground; 30 to 50′ under cultivation, to 130′ in its native Japan. Slow growing.

Foliage: Needles, 1″ long, shiny dark green above, 2 chalk-white bands below, apices forked or notched, crowded on the upper sides of the branchlets, pectinate below. **Flowers/seeds/fruits/cones**: Cones 3 to 4″ long, 1½″ wide, dark purple maturing pale to purplish brown. **Native range**: Japan in mid-elevations. **Adaptability**: Succeeded in Canton, GA (north Georgia) and Wilmington, NC (coastal), but best in cooler climates. Zones 4 to 6. **Landscape use**: An enigma, as often misidentified; landscape jury is still deliberating. Reportedly tolerant of atmospheric pollution. **Street tree use**: No. **In the trade**: Available. Closely related to *A. firma* and forms the hybrid *A. ×umbellata* (mitsumine fir).

Abies homolepis

Abies koreana
Korean fir

Evergreen conifer. Slow-growing, small-statured, densely compact, of neat, uniform habit. Possibly the most attractive fir but somewhat fickle under cultivation; 15 to 30′ in height constitutes a successful plant. Bark pale gray in youth, darkening and becoming blocky with age.

Foliage: Needles ½ to ¾″ long, shining dark green with gleaming white bands beneath divided by a thin green midrib, radially arranged on vigorous shoots, loosely so on others. **Flowers/seeds/fruits/cones**: Cones are exceptionally elegant, produced on wee plants, 2 to 3″ long, 1″ wide, bright violet-purple to blue, maturing purplish brown, often abundant and spectacular. **Native range**: South Korea, Jeju Island, where it grows with other conifers and hardwoods in the subalpine forest of mountain summits. **Adaptability**: Not heat/drought tolerant; do not be tempted if your garden is southeastern/southwestern zone 7 and higher. The species and several cultivars have succeeded in zone 4,

A

Abies koreana

'Silberlocke'

Abies koreana

'Silberlocke'

'Silberlocke'

at the Minnesota Landscape Arboretum. Zones 5 and 6.
Landscape use: Specimen plant only, a small conifer for
restricted space. Certainly one of the most unique firs.
The beautiful jewel-like cones are more beautiful than the
flowers of many angiosperms. Requires excellent drainage.
Street tree use: No. **In the trade:** Available. Most cultivars
are slow-growing and compact. 'Silberlocke' ('Horstmann's
Silberlocke'), with the lower side of needles turned up, is the
most common. Grown as a spreading shrub, but can reach
30′ as a conical tree.

Abies lasiocarpa
subalpine fir

Evergreen conifer. Beautiful dark green regiments of weather-dwarfed subalpine firs lead to the alpine zone of the Mountain West. Tightly and very narrowly pyramidal, symmetrical and spire-like when undisturbed, but sometimes artistically contorted at the base by snow load, then straight above the snowpack level. Moderate growth rate, reaches a height to 60′ but usually shorter due to harsh mountain conditions. Bark smooth and gray with resin blisters on young trees, becoming rougher and scaly with age.

Foliage: The needles are dark green to glaucous bluish green, arranged fully around the twig but oriented upward toward the top side, ¾ to 1½″ long by ⅟₁₆″ wide. Needles appear more loosely arranged than on the similar noble and silver firs, which often occupy the same slopes at lower elevations. **Flowers/seeds/fruits/cones**: Cones are held upright, high on the tree, purple-gray maturing to brownish and usually 3 to 4″. **Native range**: Mountains of western North America, from the Coast Range of southeastern Alaska to the Yukon, south through the Rockies to the mountains of northern California and scattered alpine locations in Arizona and New Mexico. Var. *arizonica* is found in the southern part of the range, mostly Arizona and New Mexico. **Adaptability**: Happiest in the mountains, but adaptable to landscape use in cooler locations throughout the West with adequate moisture. Zones 3 to 6, 7 in the cool-summer West. Probably 4 for the more southern var. *arizonica*, which is the better form for lowland use, as it is more heat tolerant. **Landscape use**: Hiking the mountains of the Northwest, there is nothing more beautiful than alpine meadows near the tree line, interlaced with scattered clumps of subalpine fir, as the forest gives way to mountain tundra. In former years, subalpine fir was frequently collected from fragile areas for landscape use, but fortunately this is now restricted. The trees are of absolute beauty and great character in their native habitat, but when brought to lowland landscapes, they widen and open in shape and may lose some of their glaucous sheen, although the variety and cultivar listed here work well. Great for your mountain cabin. **Street tree use**: Narrow enough for an accent or grouping at the entrance to a mountain town, but a straight row would look out of place. **In the trade**: Available; mostly seed-grown from local sources.

A

Abies lasiocarpa

var. *arizonica* (corkbark fir). Usually marketed as a distinct variety, and horticulturally there is good reason for this. Thanks to its southern provenance, it shows much better heat tolerance and, when used in a hot city landscape, it is more likely to be successful.

'Compacta'. A selection of corkbark fir, it features beautiful bluish foliage and is more compact in size, 10' to perhaps 15', like a small, soft blue spruce. A desirable and successful garden plant. 'Glauca Compacta' is probably a synonym.

'Compacta'

'Compacta'

Abies nordmanniana

Abies nordmanniana
Nordmann fir, Caucasian fir

Evergreen conifer. Elegant, aristocratic, perhaps the handsomest *Abies* species for the adventuresome gardener; broad pyramidal habit with branches slightly arching and blanketing the ground; 40 to 60' under cultivation, to 200' in the wild. Bark as shown.

Foliage: Needles, ¾ to 1½" long, lustrous dark green, almost black-green, 2 white bands beneath, appear notched or rounded, densely arranged, pointing forward and overlapping above, pectinate below. **Flowers/seeds/fruits/cones**: Cones 5 to 6(8)" long, 1¾ to 2" wide, cylindrical to tapered at apex, greenish initially, reddish brown at maturity. **Native range**: Western Caucasus, northern Turkey. Forms pure stands or is mixed with *Picea orientalis* and other trees. Grows in the cool, humid Black Sea mountains at elevations above 6,000'. **Adaptability**: Reasonable heat tolerance; handsome specimens in Hillsborough, NC, Winchester, TN, Crestwood, KY, and Braselton, GA. Zones 4 to 6. **Landscape use**: More common in cultivation than generally thought, principally because it is misidentified as another *Abies* species. Grown as a Christmas tree in cooler climates. **Street tree use**: No. **In the trade**: Sold as seed-grown. Subsp. *equi-trojani* (subsp. *bornmuelleriana*), native to northwest Turkey, may prove more adaptable; beautiful specimen at Swarthmore's Scott Arboretum.

Abies nordmanniana

Abies pinsapo
Spanish fir

Evergreen conifer. Broad pyramidal habit, stiff secondary branches extending outward and turning up at their ends. Habit is distinctly different from all others hercin. Slow to moderate growth rate, 20 to 30(40)′ under cultivation, 100 to 150′ high in the wild. Bark grayish brown, developing deep ridges and furrows with maturity.

Foliage: Needles, ½ to ¾″ long, dark green, radiating from all sides of the branchlets creating a bottlebrush effect, pale bands below. **Flowers/seeds/fruits/cones**: Cones are 4 to 6″ long, 1½″ wide, cylindrical, greenish yellow or reddish brown in youth, yellowish to purplish brown at maturity. Have not observed cones on cultivated trees. **Native range**: Mountains of southeastern Spain, northern Morocco and northeastern Algeria. **Adaptability**: Excellent for limestone soils and certainly adapted to acid situations, as trees on Long Island and Raleigh, NC, are prosperous. Zones 6 and 7. **Landscape use**: Unique architecture and needle arrangement make for an engaging garden guest. **Street tree use**: Utilized as such in southern Spain. **In the trade**: 'Aurea' with yellow-tinged needles and 'Glauca' with blue-gray needles are occasionally available.

Abies pinsapo

A

'Aurea'

'Glauca'

Abies pinsapo

'Glauca'

Abies procera
noble fir

Evergreen conifer. Narrowly pyramidal, straight and symmetrical, moderately fast-growing to 100′ with a width of 25′, can exceed 200′ in the wild. Bark gray and smooth with resin blisters when young, then gray-brown, breaking into plates.

Foliage: Beautiful glaucous blue-green needles curve neatly upward and somewhat stiffly along the twigs, making the trees stand out in the forest with a silver-blue sparkle. Needles ¾ to 1½″ by 1⁄16″ wide. **Flowers/seeds/fruits/cones**: Cones are very large, about 7″, standing upright on the top of the tree, greenish yellow maturing to brown. **Native range**: Cascade Range and coastal mountains from Washington to northern California. **Adaptability**: Best in the cool Pacific Northwest; will grow in New England. Well-drained soil is essential. Zones 4 to 7. **Landscape use**: This is the premier Christmas tree in the West and annually graces the Warren living room. Most landscape plantings result from the sale of living Christmas trees, which are sold as seedlings but are quite uniform in appearance, reducing the need for cultivars. **Street tree use**: No; it is low-branched and susceptible to wet compacted soils. **In the trade**: Mostly sold as seed-grown. 'Glauca' is a full-sized selection with nice silvery blue-green foliage and large cones that are an attractive purple in spring. Not to be confused with the sprawling, low-growing 'Glauca Prostrata' (sometimes listed as 'Glauca', prostrate form).

Abies procera

'Glauca'

Abies procera

Abies procera

Acer barbatum. See A. *saccharum* subsp. *barbatum*

Acer buergerianum
trident maple

Deciduous. Medium-sized tree, 20 to 30(40)′ with oval-rounded outline and clean, uniform branching. Shapes run the gamut from upright broad-columnar to rounded. Branches are strong and resist wind, snow, and ice damage. Pretty winter silhouette and the gray-brown-orange scaly bark are worthy attributes.

Foliage: Leaves 3-lobed (hence the common name), 3 to 4″ long and wide, emerge rich bronze to purple, maturing glossy dark green with potential for yellow, orange, and red fall color. Foliage emerges early (late March zone 8) and persists into November. Remains clean throughout the seasons with no serious diseases. **Flowers/seeds/fruits/cones**: Greenish yellow flowers appear with emerging leaves followed by the ¾ to 1″ long samara. Fruit is often produced in abundance, persisting into late fall-winter. **Native range**: China and Korean peninsula. Although consistently a medium-sized tree in U.S. cultivation, Roy Lancaster noted 100′ trees in China. **Adaptability**: Trees have prospered from Boston to Atlanta to East Lansing, MI. Plant does not harden (develop dormancy) sufficiently in the Pacific Northwest and may be injured by early fall freezes. Zones 5 to 8. **Landscape use**: For general landscape plantings, it requires only well-drained, preferably acid soil and full sun. Increasingly popular in the Southeast. **Street tree use**: Yes. **In the trade**: The bulk of nursery-produced trident maples are seed-derived and not particularly uniform. Several cultivars are in commerce, and the authors envision increased acceptance with upright-columnar, uniform oval-rounded habits, less fruit, and consistent orange-red fall color. Current breeding work is aimed at developing sterility, thus fruitless cultivars.

A

Acer buergerianum

Acer buergerianum

Acer buergerianum

Acer buergerianum

AERYN

BLOOD MOON

AERYN

BLOOD MOON

'Angyo Weeping'

AERYN 'ABMTF'. Uniform canopy, lustrous dark green leaves, yellow-orange-red fall color, 35 to 40′ by 25 to 30′.

'Angyo Weeping'. Prominently weeping as a young specimen, less so with age, developing a semi-pendent character. Leaves are larger than those of the species, fall color yellow to orange. Branches build on each other, developing into a 20 to 25′ high and wide canopy. More susceptible to limb breakage from wind.

BLOOD MOON 'Rusty Allen'. Compact with a pyramidal-oval outline in youth, more rounded with age; emerging foliage orange-red-purple, dark green at maturity, fall color varies, yellow, orange, red, often all colors intermixed; estimate 20 to 30′ high, similar spread; pretty addition to the woefully small list of trident cultivars.

VALYNOR 'ABFSS'. Tight vertical branch angles, develops a more compact, upright oval habit. Fall color is orange-red. Estimated to mature at 35 to 40′ tall, 15 to 20′ wide.

VALYNOR

Acer campestre
hedge maple, field maple

Deciduous. Rounded shape, spreading to upright-spreading branch structure, overall medium texture, 30 to 35′ tall and wide is typical, but with time and the right location it can double that, with a slow-but-steady growth rate. Bark slightly orange-brown and very corky when young, then dark gray, ridged and furrowed.

Foliage: Leaves 2 to 4″ long and wide, rounded, with 5 irregularly blunt lobes and undulate margins, smaller and slightly finer-textured than most maples, milky sap in petiole. Yellow fall color. **Flowers/seeds/fruits/cones**: Greenish yellow flowers with the first leaves, hardly noticeable, can self-pollinate. Abundant seed crops (1½″ samaras) scatter in the wind. **Native range**: Most of Europe, from England to the Near East. **Adaptability**: Grows well from New England through the central Midwest, mid-Georgia to Oklahoma, and in the West from Vancouver, BC, through the California central valley and mild sites of the interior. It takes heat and is more drought resistant than most maples but is slow in the Southeast. Powdery mildew is increasingly problematic in areas of high summer humidity. Zones 5 to 8. **Landscape use**: Tough in the landscape, resistant to high pH soil, tolerant of urban and drought conditions. It won't win any beauty contests, but hedge maple is as functional as they come. Branch structure is strong, and rarely is breakage observed. It can set considerable amounts of seed with age but has not shown invasive tendencies. Small leaves are less of a problem at leaf fall. We see them lining a bank parking lot and think of it as a business-minded tree: it grows so slowly, there are virtually no maintenance costs; it stays small, so there is little risk of liability for storm breakage; it is long-lived, so there is no depreciation. A great conservative choice, just like you want your bank to be: always solid, always there, always reliable, but otherwise not interfering with your life. On the other hand, plant it in your front yard, and think "Boring!" Leave this species to corporate landscapes, or use it if you want a tough tree for a tough site. **Street tree use**: A great city tree. It doesn't particularly mind the tree pit environment, the concrete rubble in the soil profile, or the roadside salt. With minimal pruning, it can be used under utility wires. **In the trade**: The species, when seed-grown, is variable and often rather wide-spreading; we like the more upright cultivars as they provide uniformity.

'Carnival'. Very pretty leaves, variegated white and green, with pink tints that show on the spring new growth. As it ages, the white portions of the leaf can be larger than the green, giving it a captivating yet ghostly appearance from a distance. Best in cooler climates; occasional branches revert

Acer campestre

Acer campestre

'Carnival'

JADE PATINA

METRO GOLD

METRO GOLD

to green. Unfortunately, it is so slow-growing that, while it grows decently in the nursery, trees planted out in a garden seemed frozen in size. You would have to live a long time to see a 15′ tree.

'Elsrijk'. Well suited as a street tree, this Dutch selection is frequently seen in Europe but not in the United States. The crown is oval but densely branched, tighter and slightly more compact and with smaller leaves than the species, making it more appropriate for narrow streets, to 30′ by 30′. Has shown some resistance to powdery mildew.

JADE PATINA 'Bailee'. Upright oval to broadly oval, with attractively lobed, clean green foliage. It has better cold hardiness than typical seedlings, although still rated zone 5, and has shown resistance to frost cracking. 35′ tall, 25 to 30′ wide.

METRO GOLD 'Panacek'. One of the narrowest of the hedge maple cultivars. Selected in a nursery row for its narrow upright crown, it maintains this shape well in the landscape and produces nice golden fall color. It makes a great street tree, 35′ high, 20′ wide.

'Nanum'

QUEEN ELIZABETH

QUEEN ELIZABETH

'Nanum' ('Compactum'). Diminutive in every way. Dwarf and globose in shape, its leaves are also much smaller than the species. Fine-textured, thin branches create the dense canopy. It makes an interesting formal statement in the garden and serves where space is limited, growing to 10′ by 10′.

ST. GREGORY

QUEEN ELIZABETH 'Evelyn'. Similar to METRO GOLD in shape and height but gets a little wider, growing 25 to 30′ in width. Upright oval with excellent branching characteristics. It features dark green foliage and uniform appearance as a street tree. It is slightly less hardy than other cultivars, to zone 6. Heavy seed production in the Southeast.

ST. GREGORY 'Stgrezam'. Described by the originator as upright-columnar and only 12 to 15′ wide, but our observations are that it is more wide-spreading, more open and oval, with less foliage density, a disappointment. We think 35′ by 30′ is realistic. It claims better cold hardiness than typical of the species.

STREETSIDE 'JFS-Schichtel2'. The narrowest of the cultivars. Upsweeping branches form a narrow oval crown ideal for street use. Selected in western New York, where hedge maple often shows cold damage, this is a cold hardy and reliable selection. To 35′ tall and 18′ wide.

Acer capillipes
red snakebark maple

Deciduous. Upright-spreading tree, usually low-branched, medium texture, moderately slow growth rate, to 30′ tall, 25′ wide. Bark beautifully striped, vertically, green and white.

Foliage: Leaves, 2 to 4″ long and 2 to 3″ in width, simple, broadly elliptic, with a small single point or lobe on each side, giving them a slightly squared look and interesting landscape texture. Foliage emerges reddish and becomes dark green in summer. Fall color is a good mix of yellow, orange, and red, depending on the individual tree. **Flowers/seeds/fruits/cones**: Small flowers appear in spring in chain-like, greenish white, pendulous racemes. Chains of samaras follow in summer, and the wings take on a red tint. **Native range**: Japan. **Adaptability**: It's a little touchy in the garden, like all the snakebark (striped) maples. Prefers

A

Acer capillipes

Acer capillipes

Acer capillipes

STREETSIDE

a moderate climate. We have observed that it may be more heat tolerant than other snakebarks. Zones 5 to 7. **Landscape use**: Beautiful in the woodland garden in all seasons. Spring flowers and red-tinted new growth initiate the season. Red shoots and petioles complement the dark green summer foliage. The striped bark adds interest, standing out in the winter and providing a softer feeling throughout the year. Give it partial shade and frequent moisture. **Street tree use**: No; can sunscald, doesn't like reflected heat, drought. **In the trade**: Uncommon, sold as seed-grown.

Acer circinatum
vine maple

Deciduous. Upright-spreading, generally multi-stem small tree, usually with an artistically irregular form. The form is variable based on seed source and growing condition. In the Olympic rainforest, trees arch up and then bend to touch the ground, and then repeat, in serpentine form, like giant green anacondas; this sprawling behavior gave rise to the "vine" of the common name, but this is a product of that rainforest environment as much as genetics and not to be expected in the landscape. In hot, dry sites in the Cascades, they grow short, stiff, and bushy. Typical landscape plants are informally upright and slightly open, fine-textured, slow-growing to 15′ tall, 12′ wide. Bark stays green and smooth for a long time, stems look attractively jointed at the node, eventually turning grayish green.

Foliage: Elegant is the best descriptor. Small, rounded, palmately lobed and veined green leaves resemble Japanese maple but are not as deeply cut, 2 to 3″ in diameter, with 7 to 9 lobes. **Flowers/seeds/fruits/cones**: Small greenish white flowers appear in spring as the tree leafs out, with deep red sepals subtending the corolla. Delicate and attractive up close when in flower. Paired samaras with nearly opposite wings appear in summer. **Native range**: Pacific coastal strip from southeastern Alaska to northern California; it is restricted to the moist side of the mountains and extends only slightly into the drier east side. **Adaptability**: Well adapted to its native Pacific Northwest haunts, it likes cooler weather and moisture, although it can stand periodic drought, and fall colors are best in a soil that dries a bit in summer. It also grows well in the similar climate of northern Europe. Zones 5 to 8 in the West; doesn't like the humid heat of the East. **Landscape use**: Frequently used in the Northwest, a darling of the native landscape crowd. Always informal in appearance, every plant creates a different shape. Usually grown from seed, which adds to its charming variability. Small enough for the urban landscape, growing in full sun to deep shade. Its sprawling stems appear jointed at the nodes, and the stems snake upward in a zigzag pattern. We think this is a species with a great deal more potential. It shows greater resistance to drought and

Acer circinatum

Acer circinatum

verticillium wilt than *A. palmatum*. Selections from exposed high ridges in the north could extend its cold hardiness, while selections from northern California could give greater heat tolerance. Breeders, take notice. **Street tree use**: No, as it is usually multi-stem and even single-stem trees tend to be wide. Development of more upright cultivars (e.g., THREE CHEERS) may change this. **In the trade**: Mostly sold seed-grown, but cultivars are becoming more common. We list here only those of more tree-sized proportions.

'Monroe'. Elegant cutleaf foliage, deeply dissected with strong serrations, on a plant that is slightly smaller than the species, probably 10′ high and wide.

'Pacific Fire'. Noted for its fiery coral-red stems, which intensify in the winter. Rows of young plants are spectacular in the nursery. Vigorous new growth is most highly colored,

'Pacific Fire'

'Pacific Fire'

and the stems need full sun to develop the best color. Cut back each year to push new growth for the best appearance; when growth slows on mature plants, the bright colors fade to insignificance, and you will wonder what's so special about it. Summer foliage is slightly lime-green, fall color is yellow. Reaches 15′ high, 12′ wide.

PACIFIC PURPLE 'JFS-Purple'. Leafs out green in spring then takes on a bronze tint. As summer comes on it develops a dark purple color that stays with it until fall, when orange and reds take over. A little smaller and more compact than the species, 12 to 15′ high and wide.

'Sunny Sister'. Slightly smaller than the species, upright-spreading and rounded, selected for the apricot tint of its new spring foliage, which becomes light green in summer. Yellow to orange fall color, to 12′ with equal width.

THREE CHEERS 'HSI2'. Strongly upright and moderately tight in form, twice as tall as wide, with a stiff, straight trunk. It loses the artistic irregularity of the species, but its narrower form makes it good for small gardens and a possible breakthrough small native street tree for the Northwest, probably to 15′ tall, 8′ wide.

PACIFIC PURPLE

Acer cissifolium
ivy-leaved maple

Deciduous. Upright-spreading tree, usually low-branched, developing a rounded head which becomes broader. Moderately fast-growing when young, slowing with maturity, to 25′ in the garden with a similar width. Medium texture. Bark smooth, lightly dimpled, gray.

Foliage: Trifoliate, which is quite unusual for a maple. Leaves 5 to 7″ long with each leaflet 2 to 4″. The foliage resembles vines of the genus *Cissus* (hence the epithet). Spring foliage and shoots emerge with a reddish tint, then slowly turn green in summer. Fall color mostly yellows and orange, with occasional tints of red. **Flowers/seeds/fruits/cones**: Dioecious. Flowers tiny, yellow, produced in chain-like racemes. Female trees produce ornamental samaras, which develop seedlessly in the absence of a pollinator. **Native range**: Japan. **Adaptability**: It likes a moderate climate with reasonable moisture. Tolerant of heat, it will grow in the Southeast. Testing for cold hardiness has been limited, but likely zones 5 to 8. **Landscape use**: Rarely grown. In the landscape, it's all about its foliage. The unusually shaped leaf is complemented by the pinkish red color of the new growth, making it a "what's that?" plant. You'd never guess it's a maple. **Street tree use**: A little too broad and low-branched; use it in the garden. **In the trade**: Uncommon, seed-grown, but its unique appearance is making it better known, and availability is increasing. The closely related *A. henryi* is sometimes considered a subspecies; it is difficult to tell them apart.

Acer cissifolium

Acer cissifolium

Acer davidii
David's maple

Deciduous. Upright-growing to 35′, usually somewhat loose and open, perhaps because it favors partial shade. Width is typically 15 to 20′, and branching is lax yet graceful, upright and then spreading or weeping at the tips. In a climate where open-grown trees are possible, it will be more fully branched and broadly oval. Moderate growth rate. Bark smooth, bright, light green striped vertically with white.

Acer davidii

Acer davidii

Acer davidii

'George Forrest'

Acer davidii

Foliage: Leaves are ovate to elliptic, cordate at the base, occasionally with a small side lobe, 3 to 6″ long and 2 to 3″ wide. Foliage is soft green in the shade, darker green in full sun. Fall brings a delightful assortment of pastels: soft yellows, apricots, and orange tints mixed in the canopy. **Flowers/seeds/fruits/cones**: Flowers small, yellow, held in pendent racemes in spring after leaves emerge. Short chains of light green samaras develop in summer and redden slightly if they ripen in full sun. **Native range**: Central and western China. **Adaptability**: Like most other snakebark maples, this needs a Goldilocks zone: not too hot, not too cold, not too wet, not too dry. We have observed it self-seeding around Chapel Hill, NC. **Landscape use**: In the right location, it can be long-lived and beautiful. Its most noteworthy ornamental feature, its green and white striped bark, really looks best in the shade. Sun-exposed bark will discolor yellow at the least. Three lovely David's maples grow in a shaded ravine alongside Warren's deck, where they have been happily situated for over 25 years. The clean bright green foliage drapes overhead, filtering the summer sun, and they are at their best in the fall with pastel foliage colors and the verdant colors of the trunk, accentuated by rainfall. Elegant, with four-season appeal. **Street tree use**: Limited, may easily sunscald and canker with intense exposure. **In the trade**: Available.

'George Forrest'. A faster-growing, large, upright, arching form with pendulous tips. Leaves are deeper green with a red petiole and reddish new shoots. We estimate 30′ tall, 25′ wide.

'Serpentine' A slightly smaller tree, upright and graceful, with purplish green bark with white striations, to 20′ by 15′.

Acer ×freemanii
Freeman maple

Deciduous. Large, upright-spreading tree, pyramidal when young, becoming a full oval, moderately coarse in texture, fast-growing to 60′ or more with a width of at least 40′. Bark smooth and silvery gray when young, then splitting vertically and becoming fissured, eventually darker, charcoal-gray and roughly fissured. Bark splits into vertical fissures at an earlier age than *A. rubrum*, perhaps because of faster growth. These summer growth cracks are harmless, and they rapidly fill with new bark tissue. They should not be confused with damaging frost cracks, which originate with extreme weather in winter and are much slower to heal.

Acer ×freemanii

Foliage: Palmate leaves, medium green, intermediate in size between red and silver maple, 3 to 5″ long and wide. Provides a bold look and gives a somewhat coarse texture to the tree. **Flowers/seeds/fruits/cones**: Generally dioecious, but sometimes polygamo-dioecious (mixed sex). Flowers are produced in early spring before the leaves, yellowish red and moderately showy. Male and female trees sporadically produce flowers of the opposite sex, making "seedless" selections difficult to be sure of. It is very difficult to draw the lines between red, Freeman, and silver maple; the best single characteristic seems to be the length of the samara wing. Silver maple samara wings are at least twice as long as red maple wings; in *A. ×freemanii*, the wings are intermediate in length. **Native range**: This hybrid species occurs with some frequency in nature where the ranges of red and silver maple overlap through the northeastern and north-central United States and adjacent areas of Canada. Freeman maple represents a fascinating case of first-generation (F1) hybrid trees occurring in nature, as well as established populations where genetic introgression has occurred and natural populations self-perpetuate with varying degrees of mixed appearance. **Adaptability**: Grown throughout most of the country except the most southern regions or areas with high soil pH. Freemans usually develop a slightly deeper root system than pure red maples, which gives them an advantage in drier climates. Zones (3)4 to 8, depending on cultivar. **Landscape use**: Fast-growing with attractively shaped oval canopies and excellent fall color, they are among the most popular and widely grown landscape trees. But fast growth gives rise to the same potential for branch breakage that plagues silver maple. Watch for narrow crotch angles, and prune out at a young age to avoid later storm damage. **Street tree use**: Highly adaptable to city streets, surviving compacted wet soils, periodic drying, and adverse conditions. As soil pH is often higher in street plantings (because of concrete and construction rubble) than in surrounding residential soils, this needs to be watched. **In the trade**: All available plants are cultivars. The relative length of their wings seems to be a very good indicator of the overall degree of silver vs. red maple genetics; in other words, Freeman cultivars with the longest samara wings (e.g., AUTUMN FANTASY) look and act much like a silver maple. Because the cultivars are similar and intergrade with those of red maple and the parentage of some is controversial, Freeman cultivars are listed under *A. rubrum*.

Acer ginnala
Amur maple, ginnala maple

Deciduous. A small, bushy tree, to 20′ with a spread of 15′ for single-stem trees, 20′ if multi-stemmed. Fine-textured. Fast-growing when young, then it slows down after it exceeds 10′. Bark is fairly smooth, gray-brown.

Foliage: Small sharply pointed leaves have a deeply cut single lobe on each side; 1½ to 3″ long and 1 to 1½″ wide. Dark green, slightly lustrous, and held on fine branches. Bright fall colors, usually red, orange-red, and red-purple. **Flowers/seeds/fruits/cones**: Small yellow-white flowers, held in panicles as the leaves emerge in spring. Fragrant. Samaras develop in summer and often have showy red

Acer ginnala

Acer ginnala

wings that dry tan-brown with maturity. Samaras can be ornamental in summer but then look untidy as they brown and begin to fall, prolifically produced. We are hoping for the development of seedless cultivars, as there is some concern about invasiveness in the northern Midwest and Northeast. **Native range**: China, Manchuria, Korea, Japan. It is closely related to *A. tataricum* and sometimes treated as a subspecies thereof. But its native range is separated from that of *A. tataricum* (western Asia), and its horticultural appearance, size, and use differ, so we treat them as separate species. **Adaptability**: Highly adaptable, this tree seems to grow almost anywhere and is a staple in the harsh climate of the upper Midwest and Plains. Tough, drought resistant, cold hardy yet tolerant of heat, takes full sun but also tolerates shade. It prefers acid soils but will tolerate some alkalinity. Susceptible to verticillium wilt in wet ground. Zones 3 to 8. **Landscape use**: Highly varied, as it can fill the role of a small upright-spreading tree or a broadly spreading multi-stem plant. Used singly or massed, as a specimen or a screen. Its toughness makes it favored for commercial sites. **Street tree use**: Low branching prevents its being a good street tree, but it is quite functional in mass plantings at highway interchanges or other broad, spacious roadside locations. **In the trade**: Available.

'Flame'

BEETHOVEN. See *A. tataricum*

'Flame'. Developed by the USDA. Because it is seed-grown, it is somewhat variable, but more consistent than open-sourced seedlings. Form is typical of the species, but fall color is significantly better, bright red. 20′ by 20′.

RED NOVEMBER

RED NOVEMBER

RED NOVEMBER 'JFS-UGA'. Selected in Georgia, where it showed heat tolerance and strong growth, but has also proven hardy in North Dakota. Lighter green, longer leaves and an upright-spreading branch habit, good as a tree form or multi-stem. Impressive bright red fall color comes on a week or so later than typical, early November in both Georgia and Oregon. 20′ by 20′.

'Ruby Slippers'. Named for its bright red samaras, but this cultivar is outstanding in many more ways. Stronger growing and more upright than the species or other cultivars, it develops a form that might be used on streets, or in gardens where a high canopy is desired. Its greater vigor also produces larger leaves, but foliage and shoots align with the type in appearance. Essentially, it's a more robust, more upright selection and our first choice for a tree form of this species. May reach 25′ tall, 15 to 20′ wide. Red fall color.

'Ruby Slippers'

Acer glabrum
Rocky Mountain maple

Deciduous. Upright-growing tree, forms an oval canopy to 25′ or more, with a spread of 15′. Variable; western river valley populations may grow twice that tall, while dry-climate mountain populations can be almost shrubby. Fine-textured and moderately fast-growing. Bark smooth, gray, lightly fissured with age.

Foliage: Leaves are typically palmate, 3-lobed (sometimes 5-lobed) and reminiscent of a small, coarsely serrate, strongly veined red maple leaf, 1½ to 4″ in length and width. Some trees show leaves that are deeply dissected to virtually trifoliate. Foliage is dark green and leaves are spaced along the branch at a little more distance than typical, adding to the openness and fine texture. **Flowers/seeds/fruits/cones**: Small greenish yellow flowers emerge in clusters in spring just after the leaves. Samaras follow in summer, at first reddish then ripening to brown by fall. **Native range**: Much of western North America, on the coast from southeastern Alaska to northern California and continuing south through the Sierras. Also in the interior from British Columbia south through the Rockies to the peaks of Arizona and New Mexico. This great range of climatic variation hints at diversity. **Adaptability**: In its native habitat, Rocky Mountain maple usually occupies rocky slopes with seepage, indicating that it likes moisture but also good drainage. In nursery production, it has been a little touchy to handle and can be difficult to transplant. Once established, it will grow in shade or full sun. With its broad geographic range, adaptability is related to provenance. Zones (4)5 to 8 in the West, likes cool weather and is virtually unknown in the East. **Landscape use**: Most is inspired by the desire for native plants. Popular in communities near the Sierras and the Rocky Mountains. Shoot growth is usually purple-red, and young branches maintain this color through the winter, providing color. Some individuals show very bright red coloration. **Street tree use**: Potential within its native range; cultivar development would increase that potential. **In the trade**: Sold as seedling-grown trees. Warren has made and trialed several improved selections, but reliability in nursery production has been difficult to achieve. The most important subtaxa follow.

var. *diffusum*. Occurs from eastern California to Utah with smaller leaves and whitish twigs.

var. *douglasii*. Pacific Northwest from coastal Alaska through Washington and Oregon to western Montana. It often shows very red new-growth twigs and can grow quite tall in moist environments.

var. *glabrum*. The type, large-growing, with red twigs, in the Rocky Mountains. Exhibits drought tolerance. It is the most common form in commerce and landscape use.

Acer grandidentatum
bigtooth maple, Wasatch maple

Deciduous. Small rounded tree, upright-spreading form, rather slow-growing to 25′ tall and wide. Often multi-stemmed, with moderately fine texture. Bark smooth, grayish brown, finely fissured with age.

Foliage: Small palmate leaves with 5 lobes, 2½ to 4½″ long and wide. Closely related to sugar maple, but leaves are smaller, reflecting the low humidity and dryness of the Mountain West, where it is native. Deep green foliage takes on colors of yellow, orange, and red in the fall. High-intensity sunlight and summer drought bring on intense reds in the canyons of the Rockies. **Flowers/seeds/fruits/cones**: Inconspicuous yellow-green flowers emerge in small clusters in spring just after leaf out. Samaras form

Acer glabrum

Acer grandidentatum

in summer and ripen to brown in the fall. **Native range**: Canyons in the mountains of the interior West, from southern Idaho and western Montana to Arizona and west Texas. The most extensive populations are in the Wasatch Mountains of Utah. **Adaptability**: Tolerates drought, cold, rapid temperature shifts, and the drying winds that characterize its native range. Avoid over-irrigating or planting in wet soils. Zones 4 to 8. **Landscape use**: An increasingly important landscape tree in the difficult climate of the Mountain West, especially popular in Utah and Colorado. Its virtues are being noted elsewhere for important characteristics: in addition to its tolerance of tough climates, it is smaller and more delicately textured than sugar maple. Homeowners are often disappointed by fall color in their gardens; they see the bright reds in the native mountain canyons, but find yellows when grown in their garden. This is a product of the landscape environment. Intense sunlight, cool nights, and drought help create the beautiful colors noted in nature. The irrigated yards and more fertile flatland soils of our city landscapes keep the trees green and growing, but this also mutes their colors. Look for selections made to give more reliable bright colors in the urban setting. **Street tree use**: A little low-branched to be ideal, but with pruning for clearance and a wider planting strip, it can make a good small street tree. HIGHLAND PARK and MESA GLOW are the best cultivars for this purpose based on upright shape. **In the trade**: Seedling plants tend to be slower growing, rounded, and are often grown multi-stem or low-branched. Cultivars have been selected for faster growth, more upright, tree-like habit, and better fall color.

CANYON TREASURE 'Orbit'. Selected for extreme cold hardiness in North Dakota from a large group of seedlings mostly of Utah origin. This was the only seedling to survive the zone 3 conditions of the Northern Plains. Slower growing than other cultivars and rounded in shape; can produce orange fall colors. Perhaps not as refined in appearance as other selections, but if you are choosing strictly for cold hardiness, this is your tree. 20′ tall, 15′ wide.

HIGHLAND PARK 'Hipzam'. Appears to be a hybrid (*A. grandidentatum* × *A. saccharum*), originating from seed collected from a mixed planting in a New York park. It displays intermediate characteristics: faster growing than bigtooth, more upright, and with excellent red fall coloration in landscape settings. But it may not be as environmentally tolerant as true bigtooth in the Mountain States, and its leaves are larger, more similar to sugar maple. Its nice upright pyramidal form and moderate size suggest street use, to 35′ tall and 20′ wide.

'Manzano'. A selection from the Manzano Mountains of New Mexico, emphasizing drought resistance. It is seedling-grown, so trees are variable. Leaves are larger than typical bigtooth and tend to be marcescent (hang on when brown), like the Caddo source of sugar maple. Provenance is a disjunct population; it may be more related to Caddo sugar maple than to bigtooth. Typically 35′ by 25′.

MESA GLOW 'JFS-NuMex 3'. Selected for drought tolerance in testing at New Mexico State University from seed sources ranging from the mountains of New Mexico to west Texas. Foliage is typical, the form is more upright, and the growth is a little faster. In Oregon testing, it has proven to be the most reliable of the true bigtooth maples for red fall color. It holds strong promise for urban landscape and street tree use. We rate size as 28′ tall, 18′ wide.

ROCKY MOUNTAIN GLOW 'Schmidt'. The first and most widely planted introduction, selected from a Utah seed source. Faster growing than the species and develops an oval to broadly oval canopy. Used as a small urban tree throughout most of the country as well as being a frequent and reliable landscape component in the Mountain States. Fall color brings on nice orange colors. 25′ by 15′.

CANYON TREASURE

'Manzano'

MESA GLOW

ROCKY MOUNTAIN GLOW

MESA GLOW

A

Acer griseum
paperbark maple

Deciduous. Upright-spreading with a rounded crown. Moderately slow-growing in the West, definitely slow in the East, to 25' high and 20' wide. Fine-textured. Usually grown tree form but also makes a wonderful multi-stem, emphasizing its highly ornamental bark. Bark is universally acclaimed, exfoliating in paper-thin layers (hence the common name) of coppery orange-brown.

Foliage: Leaves are 3 to 5" long and trifoliate, each leaflet 2 to 2½" long and 1" wide, dark green with a pale to glaucous underside. Spring foliage red-tinted; fall color usually very bright, from orange-red to deep red. **Flowers/seeds/fruits/cones**: Flowers small, yellowish, inconspicuous, appearing in clusters as leaves expand. Samaras follow in summer and ripen to brown in the fall. **Native range**: Central China. **Adaptability**: Tougher than previously thought. Had been viewed as being rather delicate, adapted only to moderate climates, but this impression may have been created by its

rarity and high price. Propagators have been highly successful recently (improved seed sources may be part of the story), and the species is now widely available. It grows well on the West Coast from central California to coastal British Columbia, on the East Coast from southern Maine to Georgia and inland to the Great Lakes. Takes heat and reasonable drought. We have observed this tree prospering on the street in dry 100°F heat and in other cases surviving a verticillium wilt attack and growing to healthy maturity, an unusual accomplishment among the maples. It seems slower growing in the East, perhaps because of heat load from the warm humid nights. Hybrids with *A. maximowiczianum* are in the trade, grow faster in the East, and expand the adaptability. Zones 5 to 8. **Landscape use**: Beautiful, breathtaking, distinctive, eye-catching, noble—how many adjectives can we use? The list goes on and on. The tree has many great features, but first among them is the bark, exfoliating over a long period of time, different for each seedling tree grown. These peeling layers stay temporarily attached and catch the sun, giving the trunk a translucent orange glow. Multi-stem plants are all about the bark and can be spectacular. Foliage is fine-textured and unusual, with leaves that are both darker green and smaller than most

Acer griseum

Acer griseum

maples. Branch structure ends in fine twigs. Bright fall color adds to the seasonal beauty. Winter can be its best season because of the exposure of the entire tree's bark. Plant as a prominent specimen for a "wow" response from your neighbors. **Street tree use**: Increasingly used for this purpose, especially as urban density increases and planting strips are squeezed smaller and smaller. In the West, it is valued for its resistance to summer drought. Small and moderately slow-growing, it can be used in narrow planting strips with less chance of quickly outgrowing its location and causing sidewalk damage. Select well-grown, upright-oriented trees with a straight central leader, as low branches will need to be removed for vehicle clearance. **In the trade**: Mostly sold as seed-grown. Warren has made a couple of selections of true *A. griseum* (one still unnamed) suitable for street use, but most available cultivars are hybrids with *A. maximowiczianum*. Authors have observed many incarnations of the hybrid; most are attractive small trees. Some of the original hybrids were developed by Sid Waxman, University of Connecticut; these trees are extant, with the original 'Cinnamon Flake' (now more than 40 years old) 30′ by 30′ and still beautiful. In Georgia, fall color develops in mid to late December. Leaves are quite frost resistant, withstanding low to mid 20s. The hybrids grow faster in eastern and midwestern climates, but the bark is less impressive than that of *A. griseum* itself. If you want the best-looking bark, plant true *A. griseum*.

Acer griseum

BRONZE TABLET 'AROY'. Bright bronze exfoliating bark on young branches, healthy summer foliage, red shades in autumn, a second-generation seedling of *A. griseum* × *A. maximowiczianum*. Will probably reach 25′.

'Cinnamon Flake'. *A. maximowiczianum* hybrid with darker green foliage, tighter, finer flaking cinnamon-brown bark than GINGERBREAD. The branch surface appears pleated like corduroy bark. Rounded canopy and orange-red fall color. 30′ tall and wide.

Acer griseum

'Cinnamon Flake'

'Cinnamon Flake'

CINNAMON GIRL

CINNAMON GIRL 'Molly Fordham'. Perhaps the best of the *A. maximowiczianum* hybrids with a good growth rate, more upright habit, proven heat tolerance, and a deep brownish orange flaking bark. Orange-red fall color. 20 to 30′ tall, 15 to 20′ wide.

FIREBURST 'JFS-KW8'. A true *A. griseum* selection, it removes the variability inherit in seed-grown trees of the species. Selected for a straight trunk, an upright oval crown with a good central leader, outstanding orange-brown exfoliating bark that peels in thin, colorful sheets, and bright red fall color. Good dark green summer foliage holds into the fall before coloring. The straight leader and upright form make it a better choice for street use or a garden tree form, as seed-grown trees are often variable or crooked. We expect 28′ tall and 15′ wide.

GINGERBREAD 'Ginzam'. *A. maximowiczianum* hybrid. Vigorous grower with larger leaves and cinnamon-brown flaking bark. Orange-red fall color. Upright oval habit, 25 to 30′ tall, 15 to 20′ wide.

'Girard's Hybrid'. The first of the *A. maximowiczianum* hybrids. Cinnamon-orange to cinnamon-brown flaking bark with foliage typical of *A. griseum*. Orange-red fall color. Broadly oval to rounded, to 25′ by 20′.

SHAVED CHOCOLATE 'KLMEE'. Cinnamon, curling-flaking bark, clean summer foliage, vibrant red fall color. Parent tree is 16′ by 6′, but could reach 25′ height, 15′ width.

CINNAMON GIRL

FIREBURST

'Girard's Hybrid'

FIREBURST

FIREBURST

GINGERBREAD

Acer henryi

Henry maple

Deciduous. Upright-spreading, developing a rounded to oval head, moderately fast-growing when young, maturing to 30' with a spread of 20 to 25'. Branch structure is slightly open, more coarse-textured in winter, but the unusual foliage gives it medium fine texture in summer. Bark smooth, green with a brown tint when young, becoming gray with age.

Foliage: Trifoliate foliage, very similar and hard to distinguish from *A. cissifolium*, attractive and quite different from most maples. Young shoots and leaves are red in spring, more so than *A. cissifolium*, making it an eye-catching tree early in the season. Leaves 5 to 7" long with each leaflet 2 to 4". Foliage matures to a deep green, turning shades of yellow-orange (occasionally bright red) in the fall. **Flowers/seeds/fruits/cones**: Dioecious. Small yellow flowers are produced in chain-like racemes. Female trees produce ornamental samaras, which develop seedlessly in the absence of a pollinator. **Native range**: Central China. **Adaptability**: Not as tough as its widely distributed and rather wild-growing cousin, *A. negundo*. It likes a fairly moderate climate without extremes but will take Georgia heat. Zones 6 to 8. **Landscape use**: Much more refined in appearance and of a smaller size than *A. negundo*, it is an attractive garden tree, especially in spring when the new growth emerges and lights up the landscape, shrimp-pink to red. Highly textured trifoliate foliage is a curiosity to the uninitiated. Fall colors can be excellent but vary by individual tree. We love the texture of this tree; it's a real favorite of ours. But it's a little touchy, and we have seen healthy-looking plants go downhill. It's not quite ready for widespread nursery production, but we are hopeful that cultivar selection will eventually make it more practical. **Street tree use**: Usually a little broad; probably not a good candidate until upright cultivars are developed. **In the trade**: Still rare, sold as seed-grown. May have more of a landscape impact when successful cultivars surface. We expect to see more of this species and have evaluated a few selections, but difficulties in vegetative propagation have forestalled their introduction.

Acer henryi

Acer henryi

Acer henryi

Acer japonicum
fullmoon maple

Deciduous. A worthy small tree where adapted. Restrained, well-groomed, slow-growing to 20 to 30′ high and wide, but usually smaller under cultivation. We consider it coarser in texture than *A. palmatum*, and certainly it has fewer cultivars, yielding the landscape floor to the bounty of Japanese maple selections.

Foliage: Leaves emerge early and are susceptible to late spring frosts. At their best, they are soft green, changing to rich yellow and crimson in fall. The rounded leaf outline results from the 7 to 11 lobes, the lower often overlapping. Leaves are 3 to 6″ across, larger than those of *A. palmatum*. Fall color is late to develop, mid-November in zone 8. Mature foliage is quite frost resistant, surviving 25°F and still coloring well. **Flowers/seeds/fruits/cones**: Flowers are an afterthought, developing before or with the leaves; purplish red with yellow anthers, ½″ wide in long-stalked nodding corymbs. Refined and beautiful on close inspection. Fruits (the wings) are red-purple and held upright, usually above the foliage, at maturity. **Native range**: Japan, growing in the understory of mixed forests. **Adaptability**: Zones 5 to 7(8). **Landscape use**: Culture comparable to *A. palmatum* except requires more shade in the heat. Even in shade, fall color is respectable. **Street tree use**: No. **In the trade**: Available.

'Aconitifolium'. Leaves with deeply cut sinuses and filigree lobes. Typically, a small tree, 15 to 20′, but references list size to 50′. One of the best of the Asiatic maples for fall color, producing glorious orange, red, and crimson from Chicago to Atlanta to Portland.

'Aureum'. One of the yellow-leaf cultivars. Prefers a cool climate and protection from direct sun. Color fades in the heat. Striking accent plant. Often listed as a cultivar of *A. shirasawanum*. 10 to 20′ high.

'Ed Wood #2'. An attention-getter, 'Aconitifolium' on steroids, more vigorous with coarser texture and comparatively huge leaves, which are similarly deeply dissected and give a tropical impression. Lovely orange to orange-red fall color.

'Vitifolium'. A worthy and reliable small tree, with iridescent yellow, orange, red, and purple fall color, large 6″ wide leaves, and strong rounded habit. Leaves are cut about halfway from tip, not as deep as 'Aconitifolium' or as finely textured. Grows 20(40)′.

A

'Aureum'

'Aconitifolium'

'Aconitifolium'

'Ed Wood #2'

'Ed Wood #2'

'Vitifolium'

Acer leucoderme. See *A. saccharum* subsp. *leucoderme*

Acer macrophyllum
bigleaf maple

Deciduous. A very large and very fast-growing tree, to 70′ or more in height with a spread of 60′ and a very heavy trunk. Attains massive size in West Coast rainforests. Upright-spreading branches form an upright oval to broadly rounded crown. Big and strong, it is definitely bold and coarse-textured in appearance. Bark smooth, gray, staying smooth for quite a while, then becoming charcoal-gray and fissured. Native trees in their natural habitat are often heavily moss-covered and support aerial crops of licorice ferns. Visit the Hoh rainforest in Olympic National Park to see a moss-garden jungle growing mostly on bigleaf maple.

Foliage: The epithet means "big leaf," its common name is bigleaf, and yes, it has big leaves! Deeply cut palmate leaves are huge by maple standards, 8 to 12″ long and wide, but occasional leaves can be twice that size. Mildew is sometimes seen on young trees in the shade, but not on older trees in the open. Nice yellow fall color. **Flowers/seeds/fruits/cones**: Flowers in spring as leaf buds open. The long pendulous racemes of light yellow flowers say "hello, spring" to the woods of the Pacific Northwest, where bigleaf maple is abundant in river valleys and low woodlands. **Native range**: Moist coastal lands and at low elevation in the mountains from British Columbia to central California, always occurring in areas with Pacific Ocean influence. **Adaptability**: It likes a moderate maritime climate and is best in its native range. Will grow in the Mid-Atlantic, but there are better choices for that area. **Landscape use**: An obvious choice in the Pacific Northwest for native landscapes, but only if you have plenty of space. Most commonly used for restoration plantings. Keep a distance from your house; prolific and large-winged seeds clog gutters, and large (and often wet!) leaves are heavy to rake. It likes moist soils and is quite flood tolerant, yet withstands summer drought. **Street tree use**: Look elsewhere. It is attempted on streets

Acer macrophyllum

Acer macrophyllum

'Seattle Sentinel'

Acer macrophyllum

in its native range, but get ready for concrete repair. Its fast growth and massive, buttressed trunk mean damage to sidewalks and roads. **In the trade:** Mostly sold as seed-grown. The narrow and upright 'Seattle Sentinel' may have street tree form, but it is going to do the same damage to the hardscape. Plant, in parks and big yards, where roots have room. Its fast growth and narrow crotch angles invite storm damage. You are probably better off with a seedling. 60' tall or more, 20' wide.

Acer mandschuricum

Manchurian maple

Deciduous. Exquisite, refined tree, upright-spreading habit, more open canopy than *A. griseum*, *A. triflorum*, and *A. maximowiczianum*, but equally beautiful, especially in fall color. Seedlings grow quickly, reaching 4 to 6′ in a season in Georgia; moderate rate of growth with age. Largest tree known to authors is a 40′ specimen in the Arnold Arboretum. Bark is smooth, similar to American beech.

Foliage: Leaves composed of 3 leaflets, each 2 to 3½″ long with sharp serrations, medium to dark green, on an elongated red petiole, to 4″ long. Glabrous (without hairs), which separates it from *A. maximowiczianum*. Fall color is spectacular orange to red; leaf drop (abscission) complete. **Flowers/seeds/fruits/cones**: Flowers are greenish yellow, often produced in 3s, and coincide with emerging leaves. Fruit a schizocarp, each samara 1 to 1½″ long. **Native range**: Eastern Siberia, Manchuria, northeastern China, Korean peninsula. **Adaptability**: Adaptable and trouble-free. Zones 4 to 7. **Landscape use**: A pest-resistant species deserving of greater use. At its maximum fall color expression, the best of the trifoliates. Issue has always been one of availability. **Street tree use**: Potential. **In the trade**: Sold as seed-grown. No cultivars to date, but we are hopeful.

Acer mandschuricum

Acer mandschuricum

Acer maximowiczianum
(A. *nikoense*)
Nikko maple

Deciduous. Lovely, slow-growing, vase-shaped to rounded-canopied tree, 20 to 30′ high and wide. Bark is smooth, gray, somewhat rough with age. Slow-growing.

Foliage: Leaves in 3s, 2 to 5″ long, entire or with a few serrations, medium green above, glaucous and soft pubescent below, turning yellow, red, and purple in autumn. Typically, not as vibrant as other trifoliates in fall. **Flowers/seeds/ fruits/cones**: The yellow flowers, ½″ wide, are borne in 3s, on drooping pedicels in May with the developing leaves. The fruit is a 1 to 2″ long densely hairy samara with a hard, bony exterior. **Native range**: Japan and central China. Now rare in the wild. **Adaptability**: Slightly more cold hardy than *A. griseum*. Zones (4)5 to 7. **Landscape use**: Another garden-worthy trifoliate maple, offering adaptability, attractive disease-resistant foliage, beautiful fall color, and smooth gray bark. Excellent garden or park tree. **Street tree use**: Possible in favorable climate if pruned up for clearance. **In the trade**: Available. Our observations indicate the several hybrid cultivars between this and *A. griseum* are faster growing than either parent (hybrid vigor), more heat tolerant, with reliable red to red-purple fall color and a cinnamon-stick exfoliating bark. See *A. griseum* for a listing of these hybrids.

Acer maximowiczianum

Acer maximowiczianum

Acer miyabei
Miyabe maple

Deciduous. A large shade tree, moderately fast-growing to 50′ height and 40′ width, forming a broadly oval canopy, medium-textured. Bark is rough, somewhat corky, fissuring at an early age, becoming very rough and brownish gray.

Foliage: Leaves are medium size for a maple, 3 to 5″ in length and width, green, palmate, generally 5-lobed, and similar in appearance to closely related *A. campestre* but slightly larger and with a smoother and more lustrous surface; it too contains milky sap in the petiole. Fall color yellow. **Flowers/seeds/fruits/cones**: Small yellow-green flowers appear in upright corymbs of 10 to 15 as leaves emerge in spring. Samaras follow in summer and ripen to yellow-brown in the fall. **Native range**: Northern Japan. **Adaptability**: Known in the nursery and landscape trades mostly from its first cultivar, STATE STREET, it has proven to be highly adaptable. Nursery-grown trees shipped around the country have found success in a wide variety of climates and soils. From the hot South to the cold North, wet soil or dry, acid to slightly alkaline, this tree has succeeded. Zones 4 to 8. **Landscape use**: Rarely has a "new" tree had such widespread success; it looks like it will be a very reliable urban tree. Use wherever a large shade tree is desired. Although it resembles *A. campestre* in many ways, this is a significantly larger tree. The summer foliage is of high quality, the fall color is good, and the winter branch structure is robust. **Street tree use**: City streets are welcoming this species as a substitute for Norway maple where Norway has been overplanted or limited by invasiveness. Similar in size, shape, color, and texture, it brings the diversity of a little-known and little-used species to the urban forest. It is proving to be one of the better trees for withstanding the rigors of urban street life, where its moderately fast growth and sound branch structure are appreciated. **In the trade**: Available.

RUGGED RIDGE 'JFS-KW3AMI'. A selected seedling of STATE STREET. The parent tree from which the seed was picked was growing near *A. campestre*, and it may well be a hybrid. Its name reflects its rugged, corky bark. Darker green foliage than STATE STREET and yellow fall color. Tested cold hardy in zone 3. 45′ tall, 35′ wide.

STATE STREET 'Morton'. Selected from a planting of several mature trees of the species growing at the Morton Arboretum. Larger and more upright, it is the finest tree in the arboretum group. Smooth leaves are lighter green than RUGGED RIDGE but are moderately lustrous and quite handsome. Nice yellow fall color. Upright-growing, developing a strong branch structure. It has proven to be widely adaptable: growers all over the United States report good performance, North, South, East, and West. A great urban tree, which we recommend. 55′ tall, 40′ wide.

Acer miyabei

Acer miyabei

RUGGED RIDGE

RUGGED RIDGE

A

STATE STREET

STATE STREET

Acer negundo

boxelder

Deciduous. Fast-growing with an upright-spreading habit, forming an irregularly rounded crown. The canopy can be somewhat open; the coarse branch structure combines with compound leaves to give the tree an overall moderately coarse-textured appearance, often with considerable dead twigs. Seedling trees grow to 40 to 50′ in both height and spread, but all cultivars are more compact, usually 25 to 40′. Bark smooth and green when young, then gray-brown, becoming lightly ridged and fissured.

Foliage: Leaves pinnately compound, 6 to 8″ long, with 3 to 5 (occasionally 7) leaflets, light to medium green in color. Leaflets 2 to 4″ long and 1½″ wide, often hanging with a bit of a droopy appearance. Fall color dull to decent yellow. **Flowers/seeds/fruits/cones**: Dioecious. Male and female flowers are quite different. Male flowers are corymbs consisting of multiple anthers hanging from long filaments, looking like reddish yellow clusters of many strands of thread; female flowers are in pendulous racemes and look a little more solid. Samaras develop in long, light green chains in summer, then ripen to brown and hang unattractively in fall. **Native range**: Much of eastern North America, from central Canada to New York and from Florida to Texas, with scattered distribution from California through the Rocky Mountains to Colorado in the West, usually following streams, and with widely scattered populations ranging south to Central America. With such a wide geographic distribution and disjunct populations, it is no surprise that many subspecies exist. **Adaptability**: Highly adaptable, it seeds heavily, reproduces rapidly, and grows quickly: all characteristics of a weed, and indeed, it is sometimes considered a weed tree. But it is redeemed by its cultivars, which are generally well-behaved, refined ornamentals that

Acer negundo

Acer negundo

fill a need. **Landscape use**: Choose a cultivar, as they are much improved over seedlings. Male trees are preferred because they are seedless. The seeds are a maintenance nuisance and can attract large numbers of boxelder bugs. Popular as a shade tree in dry climates for its toughness. **Street tree use**: Found on city streets in harsh climates, and if the right cultivar is used in the right location, it can be a good choice. **In the trade**: Available.

var. *californicum*. A California native, with very pubescent foliage. Flowers on the male tree are brighter red than typical. Seedling-grown trees are frequently sold for restoration purposes in that state. Locally adapted, it is easy to transplant and establish.

'Flamingo'. A variegated selection featuring bright pink margins on its new growth which become white in summer. It is very pretty in the nursery and when young, as vigorous young trees push new growth well into the summer, and the pink margins on the new leaves are quite effective. However, as the tree ages the pink becomes less and less noticeable, and on a mature tree you might not even see it. Male, 25′ by 25′.

'Kelly's Gold'. Unlike the variegated cultivars, the entire leaf of this tree is yellow. When young, and in spring, the bright yellow foliage is striking. As the tree ages, less new growth is seen, and the tree appears more yellow-green. In Georgia heat, the leaves are completely green in summer. Foliage may burn in intense sun. 25′ by 25′.

'Sensation'. A cultivar that really gets it right. To begin with, the branch habit and form are much improved over the species. More compact and with stouter branches, it grows to a smaller size with a stronger structure and a more upright oval form. This is a boxelder that can be used as a street tree. Foliage emerges with a reddish bronze tint and becomes deep green in summer; then in the dog days of August, a slow transition to bronze-purple begins, eventually brightening to red. Fall color does not come on all at once; leaves seem to gradually and individually turn red. While not a spectacular flash for a week like some trees in fall color, it is attractively colored and pleasing for a transitional month or two. Male and therefore seedless, a great landscape selection for the harsh climates that appreciate boxelder. 30′ tall, 25′ wide.

A

'Kelly's Gold'

var. *californicum*

'Flamingo'

'Sensation'

'Sensation'

'Variegatum'. Our choice among the variegated cultivars. It combines creamy white and green foliage with a more refined growth habit, producing a rounded tree of 30′ by 30′. Its foliage holds up better in the heat than most variegated trees, still bright and effective in August. Long chains of seeds are quite ornamental, light green through the summer, and are sterile: they don't carry the risk of invasiveness or weediness, and they drop before they ripen to the ugly brown of the species. Interestingly, the wings of the seeds (samaras) are green and white variegated like the foliage. 'Aureomarginatum' and 'Aureovariegatum' are similar variegated forms, but with yellowish margins; both female; but neither seems to perform as well as 'Variegatum'. 25′ by 25′.

'Variegatum'

'Variegatum'

Acer nigrum. See A. *saccharum* subsp. *nigrum*

Acer palmatum
Japanese maple

Deciduous. Overwhelmingly variable genetically, but a garden treasure in every manifestation. Most commonly 15 to 25′ high and wide, with some specimens ascending 40 to 50′. Refined, fine-textured foliage and stems and restrained habit allow it to blend unobtrusively into any garden nook, cranny, and open space. Slow to moderate growth.

Foliage: Leaves 2 to 5″ long and wide, 5 to 9 lobes, margins finely serrated, dark green. Spring foliage (emerging leaves) are susceptible to late spring freezes; however, mature foliage is remarkably freeze tolerant to at least 25°F. Fall colors in glorious yellow, orange, and/or red develop late, with colorful leaves still present in zone 8 in late November, early December. **Flowers/seeds/fruits/cones**: Flowers, red to purple, refined, exquisitely jewel-like, borne in arching-pendulous inflorescences with the emerging foliage. Close inspection is the only way to fully appreciate their beauty. Fruits are 2-winged schizocarps, green to red-purple, and showy into fall. **Native range**: Japan, China, Taiwan, Korea, growing in the understory. **Adaptability**: Adaptable to any soil as long as not wet. Authors have never observed iron chlorosis due to high pH conditions. Zones 5 to 9 with proper cultivar selection. Nothing to date has been successful in zone 4, although hybrids with *A. pseudosieboldianum* offer potential. A seedling tree in Wisconsin that survived -37°F without injury is being propagated for distribution. **Landscape use**: The dominant small ornamental tree for much of the United States and coastal Canada. Excellent in sun or shade. Easily transplanted as a container-grown or balled-and-burlapped plant. In the Deep South (zones 8 and 9), high shade, under pine trees, is recommended. The red-purple leaf cultivars hold their color more vividly in the North (zones 5 and 6). To date, no cultivars remain red-purple in the South. **Street tree use**: Typically too low and wide for traffic clearance. The very narrow

A

Acer palmatum

Acer palmatum

Acer palmatum

'Arakawa'

'Twombly's Red Sentinel' might be considered. 'Glowing Embers' and 'Sango-kaku' have been used with great success as street trees in Spartanburg, SC; still performing well 10 years after planting. **In the trade**: Cultivars—many too small to be considered in this treatment, among them the laceleaf weepers of the Dissectum Group—are akin to a 1,000-piece jigsaw puzzle, overwhelming at first glance, but with study and patience, coalesce to a manageable number. Several of the best and time-honored tree-sized cultivars offered by U.S. retailers follow.

'Arakawa' (rough-bark maple). Vigorous, upright-spreading, green foliage, with a rounded top. Grown for its distinctive bark, which develops cracks and fissures at an early age, then warty and ancient-looking. Prune to display the trunks. Red fall color, 20′ by 20′.

'Bihou'. Soft green summer leaves develop yellow-apricot hues in autumn. Stems are beautiful yellow-orange in winter. Estimate 15 to 20′ in height. Site in partial shade.

'Bloodgood'. The standard (and considered by many to be the most cold hardy) purple-leaf type. Foliage color is diminished in warm climates. Red fruits are attractive. Vigorous form reaching 25 to 30′ in height and width. 'Bloodgood' is not completely uniform in characteristics and is represented by more than one clone.

'Butterfly'. Green and white variegated foliage, developing pink and red fall color. Will reach 15 to 20′ high with 10 to 15′ spread.

'Bihou'

'Crimson Prince'. Red-purple foliage and deep red stems in winter. Habit is upright-spreading, arching. 15 to 20′ high and wide.

'Bloodgood'

'Butterfly'

'Bloodgood'

'Butterfly'

'Crimson Prince'

'Emperor I'

'Fireglow'

'Glowing Embers'

'Hefner's Red'

'Hefner's Red'

'Katsura'

'Katsura'

'Emperor I'. Deep red-purple early-season foliage. Typically leafs out 2 weeks later than 'Bloodgood', thus avoiding spring frost damage. 15 to 20' high and wide. Said to have better red-purple color in the heat.

'Fireglow'. Brighter red foliage than most red-leaf cultivars and develops pronounced bright red fall color. Grows more slowly than 'Bloodgood'. 15 to 20' high and wide.

'Glowing Embers'. Small dark green leaves, turning orange-red in fall. One of the most heat- and drought-tolerant cultivars. Discovered as a chance seedling in the University of Georgia Botanical Garden in 1979. Original tree now 25' by 30'.

'Hefner's Red'. More restrained in habit, superior red-purple leaf color and a better choice for hot climates. Estimating 15 to 20' high and wide.

'Katsura'. One of the most beautiful spring foliage trees, with orange-red tipped lobes, yellow centers. The leaves then become yellow, maturing green in summer, to glorious yellow-orange in autumn. Strong growing tree, reaching 20 to 25' in 15 years in zone 8. Habit is vase-shaped with a dome-shaped canopy.

'Koto No Ito'. Elongated, narrow, almost thread-like green leaves, unique among tree-sized A. palmatum cultivars. Mixed with the thready segments are occasional normal, fully developed leaves. Fall colors are a blended yellow, orange, gold. Grows 15 to 20' high and wide. Authors have measured a 25' by 25' specimen at Virginia Tech.

'Moonfire'. Deep red-purple leaves that turn crimson in fall. Develops an upright habit in youth, more spreading with maturity. Touted as holding leaf color better in heat, but this is debatable. 15 to 20' high and wide.

'Koto No Ito'

'Koto No Ito'

'Nuresagi'

'Moonfire'

'Nishiki-gawa' (pine bark maple). Much like 'Arakawa', but develops corky, warty, ancient-looking bark at a young age, later cross-checked on a stout branch structure, like a giant bonsai. Red fall color, 20′ by 20′.

'Nuresagi'. A fast-growing, red-purple, 7-lobed leaf selection, the emerging leaves covered with silver pubescence. The foliage color persisted to midsummer in the Dirr garden (zone 8) without any foliage necrosis/burn during the hottest summer on record. Fall color is consistent red. Quite impressive in youth, upright in habit, maturing 18 to 20′ high, 10 to 12′ wide. In production, 3 to 4′ shoot increases are reported. Slows down in the garden, 12 to 16″ on the plant in Dirr garden, even in the heat. An heirloom cultivar, appearing in nursery catalogs c.1882.

'Osakazuki'. Large, bright green foliage belies the fact that the chilly days of fall produce brilliant red fall color, perhaps the most vivid of any *A. palmatum* cultivar. Develops a rounded canopy, eventually 20′ by 20′. Fall color varies from vivacious orange-red to eye-catching red from year to year; consistently brilliant red in the Warren garden in Oregon.

'Nuresagi'

'Osakazuki'

'Osakazuki'

'Oshio-Beni'

'Ryusen'

'Oshio-Beni'. Orange-red spring foliage maturing green-purple in summer, then brilliant red in autumn. Fast-growing in zone 8, with 15-year-old trees now 25′ high.

'Ryusen'. A true weeping form, easily manipulated to become a graceful, 15′ high weeper. Must be staked to develop a leader. The lateral branches decurve to form a slender fountain. The soft green leaves develop yellow, orange, sometimes kisses of red in fall. Seedlings of 'Ryusen' segregate to a 1:1 ratio of weeping:normal. The logical goal is to breed purple-leaf weepers.

'Sango-kaku' ('Senkaki'). This time-honored coral bark maple remains the classic by which all coral/red-stemmed introductions are judged. Brilliant coral-red young stems simply electrify the winter landscape. The most vibrant color occurs on first- and second-year stems. Large branches and trunks develop amber colors. Emerging foliage is green

'Sango-kaku'

'Sango-kaku'

'Suminagashi'

'Seiryu'

'Shishigashira'

tinged with red, light green in summer, yellow-gold-pink in fall. Authors have observed 30′ high trees. Vase-shaped habit in youth and old age. Tolerant of heat, drought, and full sun in zone 8.

'Seiryu'. To our knowledge, this is the only dissected-leaf tree-form Japanese maple, eventually 20′ by 20′. Superb and especially reliable in hot climates, where outstanding performance is not guaranteed. Develops yellow-orange to red-purple fall color. A purple-leaf tree type with the dissected foliage would be a worthy addition to gardens. Fast-growing in youth.

'Shishigashira'. Deeply cut, crinkled dark green leaves turn gold-rose-crimson in autumn. Develops an upright habit, 15 to 20′ high.

'Suminagashi'. Ranked in the top 10 of tree-form Japanese maples by David Freed, Garden Design Nursery, Georgia, purveyor of an immense selection of the cultivars. Emerging 7(9)-lobed leaves are purple-red, deep maroon in summer, and bright red in fall. Vase-shaped habit in youth, eventually broadening, 10 to 15′ high and wide. Ideally, site in partial shade, as coloration is better retained.

'Seiryu'

'Seiryu'

'Tsukasa Silhouette'

'Trompenburg'

'Twombly's Red Sentinel'

'Trompenburg'. Develops finger-like lobes, as the leaf margins decurve and roll under each other. The early foliage is deep red-purple, greenish in summer, red again in fall. Described as one of the larger Japanese maples, to 30′, but those we observed are consistently under 30′ high.

'Tsukasa Silhouette'. Possibly the most upright cultivar with green foliage turning red in autumn. Estimate 15 to 20′ high, 6 to 8′ wide. Named and introduced by Don Shadow, Winchester, TN.

'Twombly's Red Sentinel'. Deep red-purple leaves turn red in fall. Develops a strong upright vase shape, 15 to 20′ high, 6 to 8′ wide. Considered one of the better forms for retaining the red leaf color.

Acer pensylvanicum

striped maple, moosewood, snakebark maple

Deciduous. Never large in stature, 20 to 30′ high with an upright-spreading, eventually rounded canopy. Slow-growing. Woodsy denizen, always in the shadows of the behemoths, but resplendent in its glowing fall color and green bark with white striations.

Foliage: Large, goosefoot-shaped leaves, to 8″ long, almost as wide, 3-lobed at the apex, pinkish tinged at emergence, maturing bright green, then yellow in fall. Certainly easy to identify in its native haunts, as nothing else is remotely comparable in leaf and bark. **Flowers/seeds/fruits/cones**: Principally dioecious. Yellow to yellow-green flowers are borne in 4 to 6″ long racemes and shrouded by the large leaves. Fruit is a samara, ½ to 1″ long. Often fruits are hollow, i.e., no sound seed. **Native range**: The only snakebark maple native to North America. Authors have tracked this species from Georgia to Nova Scotia. Prevalent in north Georgia and North Carolina in the Appalachians. **Adaptability**: Zones 3 to 7. **Landscape use**: Beautiful small tree, but fickle under cultivation. Best in cultivated situations that parallel the native habitat: moist, well-drained soils, cool climate, minimal disturbances, shade. Any mechanical damage to bark opens the window to decline via canker. Have not been able to keep any snakebark alive for any time in Athens, GA. This and other snakebarks do well in partial shade in the cool-summer Pacific Northwest. **Street tree use**: Not recommended; trunks very susceptible to sunscald from reflected heat, even in favorable climates. **In the trade**: 'Erythrocladum' has spectacular bright coral-red young stems. With size, trunks are yellow-amber-brown and very attractive. Grows to 20′ with a strong vase-shaped outline.

Acer pensylvanicum

Acer pensylvanicum

'Erythrocladum'

Acer pictum (A. *mono*)
painted maple

Deciduous. The tree grows to 40′ with an equal spread, forming a broadly vase-shaped branching structure with a broadly rounded crown. Moderate growth rate, medium texture in the landscape. Bark gray-brown, then gray and fissured with age.

Foliage: Leaves are dark green, somewhat glossy, palmate with 5 shallow lobes that are more equally sized than is usual in maples, although its widespread native distribution leads to variability in leaf shape. Leaves 3 to 5″ in length and width. Petiole with milky sap. Fall color is yellow to orange. **Flowers/seeds/fruits/cones**: Yellow-green flowers appear in corymbs with the leaves in spring, and 1″ long samaras follow in summer. **Native range**: Japan, Korea, Manchuria and west to north-central China. **Adaptability**: Fairly adaptable, having been grown successfully in the Northeast and Mid-Atlantic areas, west to the north-central states, and on the West Coast. Zones 5 to 8. **Landscape use**: A very lovely medium-sized tree with a branch structure suited to most residential lots, but it's had little opportunity to prove its virtues, as it is both rarely produced by nurseries and rarely seen in the landscape. If it could speak, it would say, "Try me." **Street tree use**: Rarely used, but its medium-sized vase-like structure might work. **In the trade**: Usually seed-grown when found. What some authors list as subsp. *mono* is the most common form.

CANYON SUNSET 'KLMSS'. Green summer foliage turns nice shades of gold and burnt orange in the fall. 30′ tall, 25′ wide.

'Usugumo'. Of the several variegated (and rather obscure) named cultivars, this is the most likely to be found. The tree has green and white speckled foliage with prominent veins. Matures to a smaller size than the species, 10 to 15′, and rated zone 6.

Acer pictum

Acer platanoides
Norway maple

Deciduous. Fast-growing to 50′ or more with a spread of 40′, moderately upright with a strong branching structure, and forming a broadly oval to rounded crown. The tree presents a bold and moderately coarse-textured landscape appearance. Bark smooth and gray-brown when young, soon becoming rough, eventually dark gray with shallow furrows and ridges.

Foliage: Leaves are large, 4 to 7″ in length and width, palmate, and classically "maple" in appearance. They hold a handsome dark green color through summer. In autumn, the foliage takes on yellow coloration and at its best can present a very clear, bright yellow. The petiole contains milky sap. **Flowers/seeds/fruits/cones**: Flowers are yellow to slightly yellow-green, in corymbs, large and bright, held on naked branches, quite showy in spring. Samaras follow in summer and despite their 1½ to 2″ size, their light green coloration hides them in the foliage until fall when they turn yellowish, then brown and become more obvious. **Native range**: Europe, from southern Norway east to central Russia and from northern Spain east to the Caucasus Mountains. **Adaptability**: Highly adaptable, shade tolerant and sun tolerant, growing in a range of soils from wet to droughty and from acid to moderately high pH. Its native range indicates that both heat tolerance and cold hardiness can be found within its genome, and this is borne out in the landscape. Zones 4 to 7 in the East, through zone 8 in the West. **Landscape use**: In the landscape, its great success is also its downfall. Its broad adaptability has led to its being planted widely and then planted even more heavily because of its reliability—then criticized for being overplanted. Its seeds can be carried by the wind from city plantings into the natural environment, where it has become invasive, mainly in areas of the U.S. Northeast and adjacent Canada. In warmer and drier climates, invasive tendencies have not been noted, and it is still a popular city tree. The best advice is to check locally, as invasiveness has everything to do with the local climate. Where invasiveness is a problem, it should not be used. In the right locale, it does make a great shade tree. Its large leaves and broad spread cast a wonderful shade in the summer heat of an urban garden. **Street tree use**: Its broad adaptability and urban tolerance make it among the most reliable of street trees. Urban foresters value it because it is so successful in surviving on the street, but sometimes they may be at odds with those in the same city whose task is to protect the natural environment. Fortunately, plant breeders are working toward a seedless cultivar to satisfy both sides of the issue. But since it is already so heavily planted in many cities, diversification calls for less use of this popular species in the future. **In the trade**: Available.

Acer platanoides

Acer platanoides

A

'Cleveland'

'Columnare'

'Cleveland'. Slightly compact and a little tighter than the species, it is a nearly full-sized tree that grows to a broad upright oval form that is appropriate for street use, 40′ tall, 30′ wide.

'Columnare'. Like the name says, columnar Norway maple is just that, vertical growing. It's also slower growing, about two-thirds as fast as the species, making a dense column of foliage. Expect 35′ in height with a width of 15′.

CONQUEST 'Conzam'. A purple-tinted tree with a compact upright shape. It grows more densely than 'Crimson King' but faster than 'Crimson Sentry', and it is lighter in foliage color than either: red-purple in spring, becoming more dull and reddish bronze in summer. Expect 40′ by 35′.

'Crimson King'. The standard by which other purple-foliage maples are compared. Deep dark purple leaves, glossy and beautiful in spring. The dark foliage suffers more than green leaves in heat, so growth slows or shuts down in the heat of summer. It makes a slightly open structured, oval tree that matures about a third smaller than the full-sized green cultivars, 40′ tall, 30′ wide.

CONQUEST

'Crimson Sentry'

'Crimson King'

'Crimson Sentry'

'Crimson Sentry'. Densely compact, this is the tightest-growing cultivar of the group, upright oval in shape. At first, it appears to promise a columnar form, and sometimes it has been promoted that way, but as it matures it widens considerably and should be thought of as a very dense broad oval, which eventually can even become globe-shaped. Purple in spring, becoming more bronze in summer heat. Watch for powdery mildew, as this is the most susceptible of the cultivars. Expect 20′ tall, 15′ wide.

'Deborah'. One of the best of the lighter purple forms. This is a full-sized tree, broadly oval in form like the species, but with reddish purple foliage that becomes more greenish bronze in summer, yet it maintains a nice bright appearance. More cold hardy than most, into the milder portion of zone 3. 50′ tall, 40′ wide.

'Drummondii' ('Silver Variegated'). Bright and shining, there is a reason everyone seems to call it 'Silver Variegated' instead of its true cultivar name. The center portion of the leaf is silvery gray-green, and the broad margin is bright creamy white. Broadly oval and nearly full-sized, a mature specimen nearly glows in the landscape due to its brightness. Occasionally a branch will emerge that has reverted to green and should be pruned out, more of a problem when it occurs high on the tree. 35′ tall, 30′ wide.

'Deborah'

'Drummondii'

'Drummondii'

EMERALD LUSTRE

'Emerald Queen'

'Emerald Queen'

EMERALD LUSTRE 'Pond'. This full-sized tree is green and rounded in shape, with better documented cold hardiness than typical. Not as symmetrically shaped as some other selections, but great to use when you need to take advantage of its zone 3 rating. To 50′ tall and wide.

'Emerald Queen'. The standard of comparison among the green-foliaged Norway maples and the most popular. Fast-growing, strongly upright with especially dark green foliage, this cultivar develops symmetrically into an upright oval. Excellent uniformity and shape for street use. 55′ tall, 40′ wide.

'Eurostar'. Selected in Europe for its excellent structure. Broadly pyramidal to oval. Maintains a single, straight leader. Branches at strong 45° angles without weak narrow crotches. Low maintenance because of its form, 50′ by 40′.

'Fairview'. Similar to 'Deborah' in its reddish purple foliage that becomes bronze in summer, it differs in being more strongly upright and symmetrical in form and is probably a little faster growing. A good street tree form to 50′ tall, 40′ wide.

'Globosum'. The classic round-headed tree. Formal, oh so formal-looking, it's ideal for a business plaza or a central landscape feature. Green foliage, compact and dense, it grows to 15′ in height with a spread of 20′, looking like a broad lollipop.

'Fairview'

'Globosum'

PARKWAY

'Royal Red'

PRINCETON GOLD

PARKWAY 'Columnarbroad'. Named for its ideal application: it is a great street tree for use on parkways and wider streets. Green foliage, upright with a dominant central leader and a little tighter in form than the species, it grows pyramidally, eventually becoming more oval in shape, about 40′ tall, 25′ wide.

PRINCETON GOLD 'Prigo'. Bright yellow foliage is this cultivar's claim to fame. Brilliant yellow in spring, it brings tremendous brightness to a landscape. As summer progresses, it turns a little more lime-green, and some leaves may bleach toward whitish. It can burn in full sun, but it usually holds up surprisingly well. Rounded and slower growing than fully green forms, to about 30′ height and spread.

'Royal Red'. Dark purple, very similar to 'Crimson King', and virtually impossible to tell apart, but it claims greater cold hardiness and can be used a little farther north. 40′ tall, 30′ wide.

'Schwedleri'

'Summershade'

'Schwedleri'. An older cultivar, very common and widely planted in the past. Reddish purple becoming more bronze-green in summer, it is much like 'Deborah' and 'Fairview' (which have largely replaced it), only a little looser and more irregular in form. To 50′ by 50′.

'Silver Variegated'. See 'Drummondii'

'Summershade'. Fast-growing, lighter medium green in color, and broadly rounded in shape. Formerly popular in the Northeast for its heat resistance, but the market there has largely turned away from Norway maples because of invasiveness. Seen on the streets but now rarely produced. 45′ by 45′.

'Superform'. Selected for its classic, symmetrical, broadly oval form, clean green foliage, and good branch structure. Straight-growing, making a classic street tree. With proven hardiness, it is favored in the North. To 50′ by 40′.

'Superform'

Acer pseudoplatanus

planetree maple, sycamore maple

Deciduous. Large tree, 40 to 60′ high, seldom at its genetic best, except on East Coast and occasionally in Midwest. Upright-spreading branches form an oval to rounded outline. Mature trees observed in Europe are impressive with dense rounded canopies. Bark, grayish, reddish brown to orange-brown, exfoliates in irregular-shaped scales. Moderate growth rate.

Foliage: May be confused with Norway maple at times, 3- to 5-lobed, 4 to 7″ wide, dark green above, grayish white below. Petiole base when broken lacks the milky sap of Norway maple. Fall color is dirty yellow at best, most leaves falling green. **Flowers/seeds/fruits/cones**: Fragrant yellow-green flowers occur after leaves are fully developed in upright panicles up to 6″ long. When pollinated, the entire infructescence becomes pendulous. Fruits often develop showy red wings. **Native range**: Europe, especially mountainous regions; western Asia. **Adaptability**: Adaptable to both alkaline and acid soils, exposed sites and maritime conditions. Not at all suited to the South. Requires cool continental climate. Zones 4 to 7. **Landscape use**: A species with no landscape ubiquity in North America. Utilized more in Europe, but then principally via the cultivars. Some invasiveness noted in moist soils of the Pacific Northwest and Northeast. The greater the heat, the less likely to thrive. **Street tree use**: The species and 'Atropurpureum' make decent street trees. **In the trade**: The variegated cultivars offer a spectrum of mottling, streaks, dashes, and dots in shrimp-pink, yellow, cream, and purple permutations. Can be infatuation at first sight.

Acer pseudoplatanus

Acer pseudoplatanus

'Atropurpureum'

'Atropurpureum'

'Brilliantissimum'

'Esk Sunset'

'Atropurpureum' ('Spaethii'). Leaves dark green above, rich purple below, purplish red samaras, and large size. The most common form in U.S. cultivation, this old 1883 cultivar comes partially true-to-type from seed, so variation in foliar traits will occur.

'Brilliantissimum'. Shrimp-pink new leaves, then pale cream to yellow-green, maturing off-green. Slow-growing to 20′, but an absolute knockout in early spring. 'Prinz Handjery' is similar but slightly larger, with leaves tinged purple below. Foliage of both may burn in summer sun.

'Esk Sunset'. Leaves unfurl pink, then speckled, streaked, and blotched salmon-pink, green, and yellow-white on upper surface, purple-red on underside. May cause ophthalmological indigestion. Foliage may burn in summer sun. Slow-growing; 20 to 30′ high.

A

Acer pseudosieboldianum
Korean maple

Deciduous. A small tree, upright-spreading to widely spreading, often multi-stem, loose in form, lax at branch tips. Form is similar to Japanese maple except slightly more open and stiff, a little more erratic, and coarse, not as graceful. Medium texture, moderate growth rate to 20′ high and wide. Bark is smooth, thin, becoming gray with age.

Foliage: Green, palmate with 7 to 9 lobes, occasionally 11, leaves slightly larger than Japanese maple, 3 to 5″ long and wide. Serrate to irregularly and deeply serrate margins, slightly lacy in appearance, but not as delicate as a Japanese maple. Fall colors orange to red and purple-red.
Flowers/seeds/fruits/cones: Flowers are reddish purple, opening with the leaves in spring and somewhat hidden but

Acer pseudosieboldianum

Acer pseudosieboldianum

attractive up close. Fruit winged samaras, green turning brown with maturity. **Native range**: Korea, northeastern China and adjacent Russian Far East. **Adaptability**: This plant is all about cold hardiness, with documented survival below -40°F. Populations in the Russian Far East may possess even greater cold hardiness. It has somewhat greater drought and low-humidity tolerance than Japanese maple. Finding success in the north-central United States. Zones 3 to 8. **Landscape use**: This little tree has earned its place in the landscape in areas where winters are too cold for Japanese maple, where it makes a great substitute; it possesses a similar beauty, and its fall colors can be very good. Expect more landscape use as cultivars are developed. **Street tree use**: No, too wide-spreading. **In the trade**: Mostly sold as seed-grown, both tree form and multi-stem. As well as the straight species, hybrids with Japanese maple are increasingly available; they are more graceful than the species and are great choices for zone 4 gardeners.

ARCTIC JADE 'IslAJ'. Broadly upright and somewhat irregularly spreading, slightly stiff and open, larger leaves, orange-red fall color. *A. pseudosieboldianum* × *A. palmatum*. Zone 5.

NORTHERN GLOW 'Hasselkus'. Upright-spreading to broadly spreading, good density with foliage resembling Japanese maple, reddish in spring, green in summer, and good orange to red fall colors, to 20′ by 20′. *A. pseudosieboldianum* × *A. palmatum*. Zone 4.

NORTHERN SPOTLIGHT 'KorDak'. Upright-spreading, somewhat irregular and open, a true *A. pseudosieboldianum*, probably better cold hardiness than the hybrids but slower growing, not as refined, and less attractive, proven in North Dakota to -40°F. Orange to orange-red in fall, to 20′ by 20′. Zone (3)4.

NORTH WIND 'IslNW'. Upright-spreading to broadly spreading, improved density over the species, foliage reddish in spring, green in summer, then good orange-red fall colors, to 20′ by 20′. *A. pseudosieboldianum* × *A. palmatum*. Zone 4.

ARCTIC JADE

ARCTIC JADE

NORTHERN GLOW

NORTHERN GLOW

NORTHERN SPOTLIGHT

NORTH WIND

NORTH WIND

A

Acer rubrum

red maple

Deciduous. Following the decimation of American elm by Dutch elm disease and concerns of invasiveness surrounding Norway maple in some climates, our native red maple has emerged to become America's most popular street tree, and we see more red maples going into the ground than any other species. While not as grand or majestic as some, it is beautiful and above all practical. Outstanding cultivars abound, introductions that are easy to transplant, reliable, and available in a number of street-friendly shapes. The species itself is quite variable in habit over its extensive range, generally upright oval when young, becoming rounded, often irregular in nature, but the cultivars bring uniformity. Branch structure is pyramidal in youth, then more upright-spreading. Medium texture. Fast-growing, 40′ by 40′ is typical in cities (60′ tall for *A. ×freemanii* types), one-third larger in natural stands. Bark gray-brown when young, then smooth and a lovely silvery gray for many years as it builds diameter, eventually becoming darker gray with vertical ridges and shallow fissures.

Foliage: Palmate, green, 3- to 5-lobed leaves, lobes acute. Leaves 2 to 4½″ long and wide. Foliage colors brightly in the fall to shades of yellow, orange, and reds. **Flowers/seeds/fruits/cones**: Dioecious, but polygamo-dioecious trees are not uncommon. Flowers in late winter to early spring before the foliage emerges on bare branches, effectively brightening the landscape. Individual flowers are small but impressive en masse. Female flowers bright red, male flowers appear more yellowish orange because of the bright yellow anthers. Small red samaras appear quickly and ripen to tan about a month after the spring foliage emerges, scattering in the wind. Samaras are small, average 1″ in length, thin and not woody, so they disappear in a lawn or break down

Acer rubrum

Acer rubrum, interveinal chlorosis on high pH soil

Acer rubrum

quickly without creating mess. **Native range**: Widespread in eastern North America, Newfoundland to southern Manitoba, Florida to eastern Texas. Variable with habitat from medium-sized "swamp maple" in the wetlands of the Deep South to large upland trees in the North. **Adaptability**: Quite adaptable as its geographic range would hint, very tolerant of compacted wet soils, tolerant of heat, and reasonably tolerant of drought. After being used to seeing these in dry city soils and well-drained nurseries, it was enlightening to take a swamp tour in Louisiana and see them in dense stands, alongside bald cypress, with roots systems under 3′ of water for most of the year. The incredible genetic adaptability and diversity provides horticulturists with an

opportunity to make selections adapted to a great many locales and landscape situations. Its main weakness is intolerance to high pH soil, which induces manganese deficiency and results in leaf chlorosis. Acid soil keeps trees green all summer, but high pH will cause yellowing. Some cultivars have been developed that are much more tolerant of high pH. **Landscape use**: An extremely popular urban tree; a good choice in moist acid soil. Widely used, largely thanks to abundant improved cultivars that feature a variety of attractive forms along with reliable and brilliant fall color. One of the best trees to brighten landscapes in the fall. Columnar forms are useful for screening or as an accent; rounded and spreading forms make good shade trees. **Street tree use**: Frequently used, some say overused, but there is a reason for such popularity: it is easy to grow, easy to transplant, handsome, and reliable. Not as long-lived as an oak, but fast growth makes it quickly effective. Selected cultivars provide some of the best upright and columnar forms available; these are compatible with streets and narrow locations. **In the trade**: We list both the cultivars of *A. rubrum* and hybrid *A. ×freemanii* here as they incrementally intergrade in both genetics and appearance, are imperfectly separated, and function as a cultivar group for landscape choice.

'Armstrong'. Fast-growing with fastigiate branching and a columnar to narrow oval form. This is an industrial-strength maple. It performs better than other narrow red maples in difficult sites, especially in soils that are dry and urbanized, and can grow to a large size in a small concrete cutout with minimal sidewalk damage. On better soils and with decent moisture, it can be excessively vigorous and become much wider than expected. The leaf is reminiscent of a small silver maple. Probably *A. ×freemanii*,

Acer rubrum

'Armstrong'

'Armstrong'

ARMSTRONG GOLD

ARMSTRONG GOLD

ARMSTRONG GOLD

but we have raised seedlings of 'Armstrong', and all look more like *A. rubrum*, indicating there is not much silver maple in its genetics. Fall color is usually a weak yellow, sometimes orange-red. Looser in form, wider, and more vigorous than 'Bowhall' or ARMSTRONG GOLD, 'Armstrong' is a good choice on difficult street sites where its vigor is controlled by poor soils and dryness. The tree listed as 'Armstrong Two' has been shown to be identical to the original 'Armstrong'. Both male and female flowers are produced. 50′ tall, 20′ wide.

ARMSTRONG GOLD 'JFS-KW78'. Tightly columnar with better density and a more compact shape than 'Armstrong', this seedling of 'Armstrong' represents a significant improvement over the original. Leaves are smaller, form is tighter, and fall color is usually a better golden-yellow to orange. It is a narrower, more refined, finer-textured tree. While 'Armstrong' often becomes loose and spreads with age, ARMSTRONG GOLD stays tight and presents a neater appearance. Smaller leaves and smaller overall size give it a closer resemblance to *A. rubrum* than to *A. ×freemanii*. Female. 40′ tall, 12′ wide.

AUTUMN BLAZE 'Jeffersred'. For years this cultivar epitomized *A. ×freemanii* in the eyes of the nursery and landscape trade. Indeed, it is a perfect 50/50 mix of the features of the two parent species. Like silver, much faster growing and larger than a true red maple; like red maple, a little finer branching and truly bright red fall color. Upright oval in shape with a good central leader when young, it unfortunately develops multiple strong upright branches with narrow crotch angles, and we have observed major storm breakage, a feature of its silver maple side. Landscape and street trees need early corrective pruning to avoid later

AUTUMN BLAZE

AUTUMN BLAZE

troubles. Reasonable tolerance to high pH and bright red, early fall color are among its best features. Very popular because of its quick landscape impact and fall color. Male and female flowers produced. 60′ tall, 40′ wide.

AUTUMN FANTASY 'DTR 102'. Although clearly an *A. ×freemanii*, this cultivar is much more like its silver maple parent than others. The only evidence of red maple parentage is its bright red fall color. Looser in form than AUTUMN BLAZE, it is at least as fast-growing. A good choice for hot, dry climates, where it colors well, its leggy form is held in check by reduced growth, and where most water-loving red maples will not perform, with good performance in the Southeast and in California. Open in branch habit, coarse in appearance, and broadly oval to round in shape. Female, 55′ tall, 45′ wide.

'Autumn Flame'. Very early fall color and fine-textured foliage define this tree. Quite round in shape and maturing to a smaller size than most cultivars, this tree has proven to have good cold hardiness but also good adaptability to heat. Fall color is generally a reliable bright red. A great cultivar, too often overlooked. Male, seedless, 35′ by 35′.

A

'Autumn Flame'

AUTUMN FANTASY

'Autumn Flame'

AUTUMN RADIANCE. Upright oval becoming rounded in form with early fall color. Moderate growth rate. One of the more reliable forms for a good bright red throughout the canopy. Female, 40′ tall, 35′ wide.

'Autumn Spire'. A Minnesota selection with excellent cold hardiness as its claim to fame. Upright oval in form with a good central leader and the earliest fall color of all commercial cultivars, a good red. Its northern heritage causes it to stop growing in early summer, which means slower overall growth. Use where cold hardiness is the prime criterion; in warmer climates there are better choices. Male, seedless, 40′ tall, 30′ wide.

'Bowhall'. Where it can be grown well, this is often the first choice among the columnar red maples. Unfortunately, it seems to be the touchiest of these cultivars, disliking anything other than moist acid soil. It is the first red maple to show chlorotic, yellow foliage as soil pH rises. Roots often do not like city soils. Be sure of your soil before planting: it needs to be acidic and well drained, with adequate moisture.

'Bowhall' (chlorotic)

'Autumn Spire'

'Bowhall'

'Bowhall'

'Brandywine'

Tightly upright, narrower than 'Armstrong' and very uniform in shape with bright orange-red fall color. Female, 40′ tall, 15′ wide.

'Brandywine'. Pyramidal to upright oval in shape with deep red to purple-red fall color that comes on toward the end of the season. Has shown good adaptability in the South, displaying greater heat tolerance. Male, seedless, 40′ tall, 30′ wide.

'Brandywine'

BUILT TO LAST

'Columnare'

BURGUNDY BELLE

CELEBRATION

BUILT TO LAST 'ARNOG'. Selected in Georgia and adapted to the heat of the South. Very similar to OCTOBER GLORY, but a little faster growing and more heat tolerant. Broadly oval to rounded, red to red-purple fall color; 40′ by 30′.

BURGUNDY BELLE 'Magnificent Magenta'. Introduced in Illinois from a parent tree growing in Kansas, this cultivar's Midwest heritage hints at its performance: it tolerates higher pH soils and drought better than most red maples. Leaves are smaller than most, giving a finer-textured appearance. Fall color is a little later than most, turning a deep red to burgundy; has colored well in the South. Rounded form, 40′ tall, 35′ wide.

CELEBRATION 'Celzam'. Broadly pyramidal to broadly oval in form, fast-growing, but maintains a central leader better than most *A. ×freemanii* cultivars. Foliage closely resembles silver maple, but shows some orange tints in the fall. Performs well in city sites. Male and female flowers, 55′ tall, 35′ wide.

'Columnare'. Truly columnar, with a narrow, cylinder-like form. Parallel upright branches ascend straight toward the sky. Slow-growing in the nursery and particular about soil. Fall color is usually deep and dark red or maroon-red. A large tree is an impressive sight. Female, 40′ tall, 12′ wide.

'Fairview Flame'. Broadly pyramidal to broadly oval in form with midseason fall color, similar to the species. Fall color is a good orange-red, but not the brightest. Male, seedless, 40′ tall, 30′ wide.

FIREFALL 'AF#1'. A deliberate *A. ×freemanii* cross between 'Beebe' silver maple and 'Autumn Spire' red maple, it captures the cutleaf foliage of 'Beebe' and combines it with cold hardiness and red fall color from 'Autumn Spire'. Upright-spreading in habit, it becomes rather leggy as it grows showing its silver maple side. Male, seedless, 50′ tall, 35′ wide.

'Florida Flame'. As the name hints, this selection was made in Florida and is well adapted to the Deep South in sites that have enough water to help it tolerate the heat. Attractive dark green summer foliage, yellow to red in the fall. Not recommended in the North. It has consistently frozen in Oregon trials due to lack of fall hardening. Rounded, 40′ tall, 35′ wide.

'Halka'. Selected as a yellow fall color red maple, an alternative to the orange and reds that dominate commercial availability. Fast-growing, large and broad, with a rounded shape, 45′ by 45′.

'Karpick'. Compact, it's fairly narrow when young, but then it broadens with age to become a dense oval. A good egg-shaped street tree form and very dense, but not as

A

'Fairview Flame'

'Florida Flame'

'Halka'

'Marmo'

'Karpick'

narrow as truly columnar cultivars, and its widest portion is low, where traffic must pass. Fall color yellow to orange. Male, seedless, 40′ tall, 25′ wide.

'Marmo'. A fast-growing *A. ×freemanii* hybrid with strong upright growth, it widens to become oval to broadly oval with age. Despite heavy upright branching, it seems to have good branch strength, which resists storm damage. Fall color is only average and never seems very bright, a mix of yellows, oranges and some reds, 60′ tall, 45′ wide.

MATADOR 'Bailston'. *A. ×freemanii*, very close in appearance to AUTUMN BLAZE and we can't see the difference, but it is reported to have better cold hardiness. Red fall color, 60′ tall, 40′ wide.

'Morgan'. Faster growing than most red maples with an upright oval form and good branch angles. Slightly open, giving it a more informal or native appearance. Wider branch angles result in less susceptibility to storm damage. Larger leaves than most with orange-red to solid red fall color, 50′ tall, 40′ wide.

'New World'

'New World'

MATADOR

'Morgan'

'New World'. Strongly upright in habit becoming narrow oval in form and flaring slightly at the top, it has the shape of a great street tree. It has been eclipsed by narrower, more columnar forms, but it should not be forgotten. Nice orange fall color. Male, seedless, 45′ tall, 25′ wide.

NORTHFIRE 'Olsen'. Broadly oval to round in form. Vigorous, but open and leggy when young. A Minnesota selection with good cold hardiness. Fall color yellow and copper-orange to red. Female, 45′ tall, 35′ wide.

A

NORTHFIRE

'October Brilliance'

'Northwood'

OCTOBER GLORY

'Northwood'. One of the first cold hardy Minnesota source selections and still perhaps the best, it is faster growing than 'Autumn Spire' and forms a full, broadly oval canopy that tends toward round with age. Fall color is average, very pleasant and reliable although not the brightest, a good orange. Male, seedless, 45′ tall, 35′ wide.

OCTOBER GLORY

REDPOINTE

REDPOINTE

REDPOINTE

'October Brilliance'. Upright and slender when young, it widens to broadly oval with age. It leafs out late in spring, avoiding frost. Fall color is red, sometimes tinted purple-brown, a little dark. Male, seedless, 40′ tall, 30′ wide.

OCTOBER GLORY 'PNI 0268'. This has been the standard choice for the South, generally outperforming other cultivars in the heat and providing reliable fall color, although

REDPOINTE and SUMMER RED are now contenders there. Broadly rounded in shape with nice glossy summer foliage, it turns red late in the season, one of the last to color ("November Glory" might have been a better name). In a good year, fall color can be spectacular. In the northern half of the United States, there are better choices as cold hardiness (zone 5, but just barely) is a bit less than most cultivars. Female, 40′ tall, 40′ wide.

'Red Rocket'

RED SUNSET

REDPOINTE 'Frank Jr.'. Becoming the top choice among the red maples, this has rapidly become the most popular of Warren's introductions and the top-selling tree at J. Frank Schmidt & Son nursery. Strongly pyramidal with a straight and dominant central leader and radiating branches, it has an ideal shape, good vigor, and strong structure. Unlike other cultivars that suffer chlorosis at high soil pH, it has succeeded at higher pH levels, including some soils above pH 8.0. Highly sought-after for China's limestone soils, and now becoming popular in Europe, its acceptance has been rapid and shows its broad adaptability. Very uniform with an ideal street tree form. Reliable, tolerant of heat and cold, with bright red fall color that comes on early. Female, 50′ tall, 30′ wide.

'Red Rocket'. Narrow, tightly upright, and with reliable red fall color, this is a good choice for narrow streets. Its only drawback is that it has the slowest growth rate of the columnar red maples, taking longer for nurseries to get to size and for a street planting to impress. Minnesota source, zone 3, a good columnar choice for the cold North. Male, seedless, 40′ tall, 15′ wide.

RED SUNSET

REGAL CELEBRATION

RED SUNSET

SCARLET JEWELL

RED SUNSET 'Franksred'. The standard of comparison among the red maples, it has dominated the market for 40 years and become one of the most widely planted shade and street trees, for good reason. Broadly oval in form with good density but a slightly more relaxed look, dark green glossy foliage, and bright red midseason fall color. It nicely combines the uniformity and bright colors of a cultivar with the more informal grace of the species. Very reliable, it is a go-to tree in the northern half of the United States, giving way to OCTOBER GLORY for dominance in the South. Female, 45′ tall, 35′ wide.

REGAL CELEBRATION 'Jefcel'. *A. ×freemanii*, discovered and introduced in Manitoba, it is extending the range of Freeman maples into zone 2. Shows improved pH tolerance. Rounded crown to 40′ tall, 30′ wide, we suspect larger in milder climates, red fall color.

'Scanlon'. Identical to 'Bowhall', which was the original name.

SCARLET JEWELL 'Bailcraig'. Upright pyramidal, slightly stiff and open in youth becoming broadly oval. A faster-growing, cold hardy Minnesota selection, zone 3. Fall color is average but comes on early, orange to rusty red, then defoliates early, 45′ tall, 35′ wide.

SCARLET SENTINEL 'Scarsen'. *A. ×freemanii*? A wonderful growth habit for a street tree or in a parking lot: stiffly upright and flaring outward high above the street, narrow but not columnar and widest at the top, providing shade and impact with minimal interference to traffic below. Its weakness is unreliable fall color; expect the "scarlet" of its name every few years, more often yellow to orange. Female, 50′ tall, 20′ wide.

SCARLET SENTINEL

SIENNA GLEN

'Schlesingeri'

SIENNA GLEN

'Schlesingeri'. Certainly the oldest red maple cultivar and still one of our favorites. Vigorous upright-spreading form, wide at top, with informal architecture and wide crotch angles. Lovely orange-red fall color comes on early. Male, seedless, 45′ tall, 35′ wide.

SIENNA GLEN 'Sienna'. A Minnesota selection of *A. ×free-manii*, chosen for a strong form and cold hardiness. Pyramidal in youth, it becomes tall and broadly oval as it ages. Its names hint at rusty orange fall color, but it sometimes

'Somerset'

SUMMER RED

SUMMER SENSATION

SUMMER RED

A

surpasses this in brightness. May become a little too vigorous and leggy in warmer climates, but has good form in the
North. 50′ tall, 35′ wide.

'Somerset'. This is a solid red maple, the result of a cross of
OCTOBER GLORY and 'Autumn Flame'. Pyramidal in youth
becoming broadly pyramidal then oval with a medium
growth rate and well-behaved branch structure. Deep red
fall color. Male, seedless, 45′ high, 35′ wide.

SUMMER RED 'HOSR'. Selected for the maroon red tint
of its new growth, this South Carolina selection is a good
choice in the southern states. Cold hardiness may limit in
the North, and the tree has shown top dieback from fall
freezes in Oregon. Probably safe in zones 6 to 9 in eastern
states. Broad oval in shape, unique spring foliage color, and
yellow to orange fall color make it a good choice for warmer
climates, 45′ tall, 40′ wide.

SUMMER SENSATION 'Katiecole'. An Ohio selection and
better adapted to northern states. Purple-red new growth
is even deeper in color than SUMMER RED. Glossy foliage is
beautiful through the first half of summer, then begins to
fade and stress in the heat of August, orange-red to deep red
in the fall. Oval to rounded form, slightly loose in habit, 40′
tall, 35′ wide.

SUMMER SENSATION

'Sun Valley'

'Sun Valley'. A little slower growing with smaller leaves than most, this combines to make a fine-textured tree with a more refined habit and less chance of outgrowing its site. A hybrid of RED SUNSET and 'Autumn Flame'. Orange-red to bright red fall color in the North, a little less intense in the South. A great choice if slower growth and smaller size are your criteria. Male, seedless, 40′ tall, 30′ wide.

'Sun Valley'

Acer saccharinum
silver maple

Deciduous. Large, strongly upright then spreading, broadly oval but wider on top, often becoming moderately vase-shaped. Coarse in texture and fast-growing, easily to 60′ high and 45′ wide, larger in favorable conditions. Bark smooth and gray when young, soon becoming ridged and furrowed, eventually fairly rough and a little shaggy.

Foliage: Leaves large, 3 to 6″ long and wide, palmate, with 5 main lobes, sinuses deeply cut, medium green above and glaucous silvery white below, flashing in the wind and earning the tree its "silver" moniker. Reliably yellow, often quite bright, in the fall. **Flowers/seeds/fruits/cones**: Usually monoecious but polygamo-dioecious and dioecious trees occur as well, an interesting mix. Small reddish orange flowers decorate twigs early in spring, before foliage emerges, much like red maples. Samaras are large, over 2″ long, light green maturing to tan in early summer. Their size makes them a bit messy in the landscape. **Native range**: Eastern North America, Maine to Minnesota and Georgia to Oklahoma. **Adaptability**: Highly adaptable, native to river bottoms and thus tolerant of wet compacted soils, but also fairly drought resistant. Prefers acid soils but is slightly more tolerant of higher pH than red maple, although it too can become chlorotic. Both cold hardy and heat tolerant. Not a fussy tree, it tolerates poor soils and difficult sites. Zones (3)4 to 9. **Landscape use**: Appreciated for its fast growth and quick size, but these attributes become its main liabilities over time as its wood is rather brittle and breakage becomes an increasing problem. Potential storm damage causes us to recommend it be sited away from homes and streets. Roots are aggressive. Parks, natural areas in its native range, and broad roadside areas are good locations. Useful in difficult sites in urban settings in harsher climates where more desirable trees will not thrive. **Street tree use**: Not recommended because of the breakage potential and sidewalk damage. **In the trade**: Available.

'Silver Cloud'. A cold hardy selection from Manitoba, Canada, zone 3, with upright-spreading form developing a broadly oval to round canopy. Recommended for cold prairie locations. Yellow fall color. 50′ by 50′.

'Silver Queen'. The most popular cultivar, upright oval with a slightly more controlled branch structure than seed-grown trees, fewer heavy branches with narrow crotch angles, and probably a little less tendency to breakage...but still, not next to your house. Yellow fall color. Male, seedless. 60′ tall, 45′ wide.

Acer saccharinum

Acer saccharinum

'Silver Queen'

'Skinner'. Upright pyramidal in form with a good central leader and somewhat subordinate, horizontal to weeping branches. Attractive cutleaf foliage gives it a fine-textured, lacy appearance. Yellow fall color. 50′ tall, 40′ wide.

Acer saccharinum

'Silver Queen'

'Skinner'

Acer saccharum

sugar maple

Deciduous. Ah, the noble sugar maple. Always beautiful, long-lived and carrying the grace of age in the proper soil and climate. Upright rounded with a strong branch structure, maintaining broad lower branches that are upsweeping when grown in the open, broadly oval and becoming round with age. Slow to moderate growth rate to 50 to 60′ height with a 45′ spread. It can be much taller in forests, but urban settings rarely allow such time. Bark is gray-brown when young, then gray with age, furrowed and scaly.

Foliage: Palmate leaves, simple, moderately large, 3- to 5-lobed, margin entire, medium to dark green. Leaves 4 to 7″ long and wide. Leaf surface varies geographically and with cultivars from slightly pebbly to smooth to somewhat glossy. Leaves occasionally marcescent, persisting brown after fall color ends. We have noted this in Caddo seed sources and 'Legacy'. **Flowers/seeds/fruits/cones**: Pendulous corymbs of many very small, yellowish flowers appear before the leaves in spring and persist as the tree begins to leaf out, a lovely sign of spring. Samaras, 1 to 1½″, are usually rather sparse and develop slowly over the summer and mature brownish in the fall. **Native range**: Taxonomically diverse, the native range of this species depends on how you choose to classify a closely related group of species or subspecies. In the traditional, fairly restricted view of the species, it is native to eastern North America from Nova Scotia to southern Manitoba and from Georgia to eastern Kansas. Closely related *A. nigrum*, *A. barbatum*, *A. leucoderme*, *A. grandidentatum*, and the "Caddo" maple of Oklahoma are all regarded as subspecies by various authors and would extend the range considerably. We choose to treat these separately. **Adaptability**: Usually thought of as a tree that prefers cool moist soils and not too much heat, shade tolerant but best in full sun. But sugar maple can surprise, with healthy trees sometimes seen in the Plains and dry interior West, where you might not expect; and healthy trees live on the hot University of Georgia campus. Soil moisture is key, not too wet, not too dry, and a small amount of landscape watering extends its range. One thing is certain, the species does not like an intensely urban environment: compaction, road salts, and trunk damage are limiting. You will see happier trees in residential landscapes than on downtown streets. The provenance of the seed source of various cultivars hints at their regional adaptability. Several cultivars have been selected from the disjunct population growing in Caddo County in west-central Oklahoma. Others were selected at the western edge of the Midwest population, and still others from the South. The Caddo location sees extreme heat and frequent drought and seems to give extra adaptability to urban stress, where heat reflected from concrete brings on similar stress in climates that are otherwise milder. Zones

Acer saccharum

Acer saccharum

Acer saccharum

APOLLO   APOLLO   'Arrowhead'

4 to 8. **Landscape use**: An ideal shade tree, with strong structure, moderate growth, a range of shapes provided by cultivars, and roots that are less aggressive than some other maples. Fall colors can vary from beautiful to spectacular; it's hard to go wrong in full sun with a well-chosen cultivar, most of which were selected with fall color in mind. It is a climax species in the forest, surviving in shade, but give it sun to develop the best fall color. **Street tree use**: Good as long as wide planting strips with decent soils are provided. Avoid where road salt is heavily used. Better on more residential streets. Not well adapted to small tree pits and lots of reflected heat from concrete. In short, a nice street tree when the location is properly selected. **In the trade**: Available.

APOLLO 'Barrett Cole'. Uniquely narrow and densely upright, making a very symmetrical, conical form. Branches radiate outward; it is narrow because branches are short, not because they are upright, so crotch angles are good. Ideal for tight locations. Landscape architects should learn this tree; its unique form and appearance make a great impact on a site. Dark green foliage changes to bright yellow-orange to red in the fall. Slow-growing to 30′ by 10′.

'Arrowhead'. More upright than most, strong central leader, forming a pyramidal shape that becomes somewhat narrow oval with age. This is a full-height sugar maple with a width of about half to two-thirds of its height. Yellow-orange to red fall color, 55′ tall, 35′ wide.

AUTUMN FAITH 'Hawkersmith 1'. Slower growing, dense and compact, upright when young becoming oval in shape, with nice dark green summer foliage and bronze-red fall color that comes on later than most. Has shown good heat and drought tolerance. Matures to a smaller size than most cultivars. 35′ tall, 25′ wide.

AUTUMN FEST 'JFS-KW8'. Strongly upright in form with a dominant central leader, this tree is easier to grow in the nursery and landscape. It is relatively fast-growing and forms a more upright, full-sized oval. The form is appropriate for street use or landscapes, giving more clearance than the rounded cultivars. Fall color is bright orange-red to red, grows to 55′ tall, 35′ wide.

'Autumn Splendor'. A selection from the Oklahoma Caddo seed source. Dark green glossy foliage with a good growth rate and a rounded form. Foliage resists heat and leaf tatter. Fall color is usually a good orange to orange-red, 45′ tall, 40′ wide.

BELLE TOWER 'Reba'. This is a narrow upright selection, almost columnar in form, from a southern Tennessee seed source. Well adapted to the South and other hotter areas. The form is nice for street use where soils are appropriate. Fall color yellow-orange, 45′ tall, 20′ wide.

'Bonfire'. Perhaps the fastest-growing of the sugar maple cultivars, it is pyramidal in youth, becoming broadly oval

AUTUMN FAITH

AUTUMN FEST

AUTUMN FEST

A

'Autumn Splendor'

BELLE TOWER

'Bonfire'

'Caddo'

'Caddo'

FALL FIESTA

with age. Seems to prefer the cooler climate of the Northeast and upper Midwest. Fall color is orange to red, 55′ tall, 45′ wide.

'Caddo'. Not a clone, but a unique seed source, Oklahoma provenance. Sometimes sold as a seed-grown tree under this name. Heat resistant but more susceptible to wet soil. 45′ by 45′.

COMMEMORATION. Broadly ovate in form becoming rounded, this cultivar has especially glossy, thick leaves and has nice yellow to orange fall color, 45′ tall, 40′ wide. Foliage resists leaf tatter. Similar to 'Legacy', shows heat resistance and best in zones 6 to 9.

CRESCENDO 'Morton'. An Illinois introduction, with darker leaves that show some heat resistance. Broadly oval in form. It develops orange-red to bright red fall color. 50′ tall, 40′ wide.

'Endowment'. Strongly upright habit, becoming narrow oval, one of the narrowest full-sized sugar maples, a good form for street use. Fall color is yellow to orange-red, 50′ tall, 20 to 25′ wide.

FALL FIESTA 'Bailsta'. With a well-behaved, moderate growth rate and slightly compact form, it still matures to a full-sized tree. Form is upright with a good central leader, becoming broadly ovate. Fall color comes on with mixed yellows, oranges, and red. 50′ tall, 40′ wide.

FLASHFIRE 'JFS-Caddo2'. Another selection from the Oklahoma Caddo source, known for heat and drought resistance. Dark green summer foliage resists heat and leaf tatter and looks good through the season. Oval, becoming broadly oval in shape. Fall color is early, bright fire-engine red. Colors well in the South as well as in the typical northern locations, 45′ tall, 40′ wide.

GREENCOLUMN. See *A. saccharum* subsp. *nigrum*

COMMEMORATION

'Endowment'

CRESCENDO

FALL FIESTA

FLASHFIRE

FLASHFIRE

'Green Mountain'

'Green Mountain'. The longtime standard for sugar maple cultivars. It has been the dominant player in the field since it was introduced, and for good reasons. It has proven hardiness, good urban tolerance, and a broadly oval shape with upsweeping branches, eventually becoming round. Fall color can be excellent, a reliable reddish orange to bright red in northern locations, but yellow-orange in the South. 50′ tall, 45′ wide.

HARVEST MOON 'Sandersville'. A selection from the sandhills of Georgia, may be a hybrid with subsp. *barbatum*. Unlike *barbatum*, it grows to the typically large size of a sugar maple. Broadly oval in shape, its fall color follows *barbatum*, orange. 50′ tall, 40′ wide.

HIGHLAND PARK. See A. *grandidentatum*

'John Pair'. Another selection from the Oklahoma Caddo seed source, this tree is slower growing and matures to a smaller size than the others. Globe-shaped, expect about 30′ by 30′ in size. Foliage is especially glossy green in summer but is quite susceptible to powdery mildew. Fall color is bright red.

'Green Mountain'

HARVEST MOON

'John Pair'

'John Pair'

'John Pair'

A

Acer saccharum, CONTINUED

LEGACY

LEGACY

MAJESTY

'Newton Sentry'. Rarely sold, but included because of its oddity and confused history. As close as you can come to a living telephone pole. Probably the most columnar of all maples, it is extremely skinny with short stubby lateral branches. Orange-red in fall. Very confused in the trade and often sold under the incorrect name 'Monumentale'. For years, Arnold Arboretum had the labels of this tree and 'Temple's Upright' reversed, and propagules were distributed. The Arnold trees are now corrected; a correctly labeled tree exists at the Hoyt Arboretum in Portland. To 60′ tall, 15′ wide.

NORTHERN FLARE 'Sisseton'. Selected at the western edge of sugar maple's range in South Dakota and tested for cold hardiness in North Dakota, this tree is tough and reliable in the Northern Plains. Broadly ovate in shape, it grows well with a strong central leader and develops orange-red to red fall color. 50′ tall, 40′ wide.

OREGON TRAIL 'Hiawatha 1'. Selected in eastern Kansas along the Oregon Trail, it has thick dark green leaves and a rounded shape. Quite heat resistant. Orange-red to red fall color. 45′ by 45′.

POWDER KEG 'Whit XLIX'. Selected in Oklahoma, this cultivar is one of the nicest we have seen from the heat resistant Caddo seed source, especially symmetrical, upright oval form when young, and becomes more rounded with age. Dark green foliage and a nice orange-red fall color. 50′ by 40′.

LEGACY. This tree is the most popular sugar maple in the South, where it is well proven and reliable. Foliage is smooth and glossy, resists heat and leaf tatter. Broadly oval in shape. It is less cold hardy than many cultivars, probably best in zones 6 to 9. Fall color comes on late, reddish orange in the North and yellow-orange in the South. 45′ by 45′.

MAJESTY 'Flax Mill'. A fast-growing selection maturing to a broadly oval form, it is a vigorous tree that is well adapted to northern states and rated to zone 3, although 4 might be safer. Orange-red fall color. 55′ tall, 45′ wide.

'Newton Sentry'

OREGON TRAIL

POWDER KEG

STEEPLE

'Sugar Cone'

STEEPLE 'Astis'. Upright-growing, narrow ovate to oval in form with a good density and maintaining a central leader. Dark green foliage, heat resistant, a southern selection from Georgia, but performs well to the north. Fall color is yellow to orange. Original tree now measures 60′ tall, 30′ wide.

'Sugar Cone'. Compact, dense, and narrowly ovate, this semi-dwarf tree is slow-growing and will not outgrow its place, eventually maturing to about 25′ and 15′ wide. Dark green in summer with good orange-red fall color.

'Sweet Shadow'. Deeply lobed, cutleaf foliage combine with a more upright habit to give this tree a finer-textured, lacy appearance. Long upright branches tend to be somewhat leggy but develop a more vase-shaped form, widest at the top. Very attractive in fall with orange fall color. A very different sugar maple, light and informal, favored by the authors. 50′ by 35′.

'Temple's Upright'. Strong central leader with ascending branches, like a typical sugar maple in structure, but significantly narrower, forming a narrow oval shape. Dark green in summer with reddish fall color. Often (or even usually) incorrectly sold in the trade under the name 'Newton Sentry' (see our earlier discussion). If it looks like a telephone pole, it's 'Newton Sentry', not 'Temple's Upright'. To 50′ tall, 25′ wide.

UNITY 'Jefcan'. Selected in Manitoba from northern Minnesota seed, this probably has the best-documented cold hardiness of the sugar maple cultivars, resisting frost cracking and dieback. Thick dark green leaves and a good growth rate. Broadly oval in shape, it has good yellow-orange to orange-red fall color that develops early. 50′ by 40′.

'Sweet Shadow'

'Temple's Upright'

A

UNITY

'Wright Brothers'

'Wright Brothers'. Selected in Ohio and popular there as a fast-growing, tough, cold hardy sugar maple, upright-spreading becoming broadly oval to round in shape. It is resistant to leaf scorch and frost cracking. Fall color is bright, comes on later than most, yellow to orange and red. 50′ by 45′.

Acer saccharum subsp. *barbatum* (subsp. *floridanum*)

Florida sugar maple

Deciduous. Variable in habit from oval to rounded; in fact, a friend mentioned it is not a nurseryman's tree (i.e., it does not form a respectable shape without extensive pruning). Trees in the wild reach 60′ and greater; the National Champion is 96′ high, 71′ wide. Those we witnessed under cultivation were always smaller, 20 to 30′ high. Slow-growing.

Foliage: Summer foliage is similar to the type in size and lobing but cupped in outline, with a glaucous underside. Fall foliage yellow, orange, and red, often all colors interspersed through the canopy. Leaves tolerate extreme heat and do not scorch. Leafs out earlier than sugar maple, often in full canopy by early April in zone 8. **Flowers/seeds/fruits/cones**: Yellow-green flowers appear before the leaves, adding an early spring glow to an otherwise gray-brown landscape. In full flower, the first week of March 2017, in Athens, GA. Fruit is 2-winged schizocarp, i.e., smaller version of sugar maple. **Native range**: Found throughout the Southeast from Virginia to Florida, Louisiana, southeastern Missouri, Arkansas, Oklahoma, and Texas, as an understory tree, but nowhere common. **Adaptability**: Zones 6 to 9. **Landscape use**: If domesticated, by improving uniformity of habit and fall color, it would prove a great sugar maple alternative in the Southeast. It flowers about 2 weeks earlier and fall colors 2 weeks later than sugar maple. A useful tree for woodland planting, under pine trees, and in naturalistic plantings. Tolerates heat, drought (once established), full sun, and heavy shade. Prefers well-drained soil. **Street tree use**: Potentially good, especially if upright cultivars are developed. Authors observed trees in planting pits along streets that did not develop leaf scorch. **In the trade**: Only as seedlings, which populations are totally unpredictable in habit, growth rate, and fall color. Attempts to develop superior cultivars have yet to succeed.

Acer saccharum subsp. *barbatum*

Acer saccharum subsp. *barbatum*

Acer saccharum subsp. *leucoderme*

chalkbark maple

Deciduous. Small tree, 25 to 30′ high and wide, more commonly low-branched or multi-stemmed in the wild. More uniform habit than subsp. *barbatum* with ash-gray (not white) bark that gives minimal credence to the common name. Slow-growing.

Foliage: The 3- to 5-lobed, mid-green leaves are smaller, to 4″ high and wide, than subsp. *barbatum*, medium green, lighter green below and with a persistent soft pubescence. Variation in fall color, from yellow and orange to red, is maddening and akin to subsp. *barbatum*. **Flowers/seeds/fruits/cones**: Flowers are similar to subsp. *barbatum* and occur before leaf emergence. **Native range**: North Carolina to Georgia, Florida panhandle, Louisiana, eastern Oklahoma and Texas, on drier upland woods, always in the understory. **Adaptability**: Zones 5 to 9. **Landscape use**: Pretty, fall-coloring small tree deserving of greater use. Displays significant heat and drought tolerances. **Street tree use**: Potential. **In the trade**: Seedling material. Reliable fall color is consistent among seedlings. Uniform cultivars would give it commercial legs.

A

Acer saccharum subsp. *leucoderme*

Acer saccharum subsp. *leucoderme*

Acer saccharum subsp. *leucoderme*

Acer saccharum subsp. *nigrum*
black maple

Deciduous. Similar to the straight species in most characteristics and, at times, difficult to separate with assurance. Oval to rounded in outline. Leaves are cupped/clasped, and petioles develop a leaf-like stipule at point of attachment to stem. Since nothing is absolute in biology, this is the best authors can offer for separation. Slow-growing, 50 to 60′ tall and 45′ wide.

Foliage: Large, dark green leaves, to 6″ long, on 5″ long petioles, result in a semi-cascading appearance. Fall color is a consistent yellow to yellow-gold. **Flowers/seeds/fruits/cones**: Flowers yellow, before leaves, similar to sugar maple. Beautiful in early spring, and the flowers are borne in significant quantities to produce quite a show. **Native range**: Varies with authority but overlaps with sugar maple, occurring in Quebec and New England to New York, West Virginia, Kentucky west to South Dakota, Iowa, Kansas, and Arkansas. **Adaptability**: Considered more adaptable to hot, dry, high pH soils than sugar maple. Zones 4 to 8. **Landscape use**: Based on Kansas and Iowa research, black maple is slower growing and more susceptible to leaf tatter (caused by dry winds) than the best sugar maple cultivars like 'Caddo', COMMEMORATION, and LEGACY. One constant with black maple is the consistent fall color, yellow to soft golden apricot. Bright oranges and reds do not occur based on the authors' experiences. Size approximates sugar maple, 60 to 75′ high. **Street tree use**: Potential. **In the trade**: Limited. 'Greencolumn', selected from a native population in Iowa, develops a broad-columnar outline with a central leader, reaching 65′ by 25′; considered zone 4.

Acer saccharum subsp. *nigrum*

'Greencolumn'

Acer tataricum
Tatarian maple

Deciduous. A small tree with an upright-spreading growth habit and a broadly oval shape. Some trees may become as broad as tall. More tree-like than the closely related *A. ginnala* and presents a more solid appearance with a medium texture. Moderate growth rate, reaching 20 to 25′ in height with a 20′ width. Bark smooth, thin, gray-brown when young, becoming gray with shallow fissures.

Foliage: Leaves are small, 2 to 4″ long by 1½ to 2½″ wide, ovate, and medium green with a rough texture. Leaves have a serrate and irregularly wavy margin, not lobed with frilled margins like *A. ginnala*. **Flowers/seeds/fruits/cones**: Flowers perfect, appear in spring with the foliage on upright short panicles, creamy white and not especially impressive. Samaras, 1″ long, become bright red in June and hold color until late summer, an ornamental feature. They brown as they mature and fall. **Native range**: Central Europe, southeast Asia and east into Russia. **Adaptability**: A tough tree,

'Greencolumn'

tolerant of heat and drought as well as high pH soils. Cold hardy and favored in cold, windy, harsh climates where tree choices are more limited. Popular in the High Plains. Zones 3 to 7, 8 in the West. **Landscape use:** In the High Plains and Intermountain West this is a reliable performer. In moderate climates and wet soils, there are better choices. In harsh climates, excels in one way where others fail: it lives. It can be grown multi-stem, low-branched, or tree form. Generally, choose this species when you want tree form; choose *A. ginnala* when you want a multi-stem. **Street tree use:** Makes a good small street tree if pruned up to an appropriate height. Upright-growing cultivars are best for the purpose, as seedlings are variable. **In the trade:** Sold as seed-grown trees, both tree form and multi-stem. Improved cultivars are recommended for their predictable forms.

BEETHOVEN 'Betzam'. An upright grower, forming an oval canopy. Although introduced as *A. ginnala*, this cultivar appears closer to *A. tataricum*, having the broader leaf and more upright and robust habit of that species, and possibly is a hybrid. Yellow-orange to orange-red fall color, 25′ tall, 15′ wide.

HOT WINGS 'GarAnn'. Selected for its bright red samaras, which are quite showy through the summer, this small tree tends to spread more than others, at least as broad as tall, forming a rounded crown. It makes a good multi-stem form as well as a tree. Yellow to red in the fall, 20′ tall, 25′ wide.

PATTERN PERFECT 'Patdell'. Selected as a tree form, it grows vigorously but we find that it also spreads rather wide. Consider it broad oval to rounded in form. Samaras become bright red, fall color is orange-red, 25′ by 25′.

HOT WINGS

Acer tataricum

Acer tataricum

HOT WINGS

RUGGED CHARM

RUGGED CHARM 'JFS-KW2'. The best street tree form, it's the most upright and refined of the cultivars. Somewhat compact and narrower in habit and grows into a upright oval shape. Samaras are bright red, fall color is yellow-orange to bright red, 30′ tall, 15′ wide.

Acer tegmentosum

Acer tegmentosum
Manchurian striped maple

Deciduous. Oval to rounded tree reaching 20 to 30′ high. Rich green to green-purple stems developing vertical white fissured patterns on second-year stems. Bark is brighter green than *A. pensylvanicum*, otherwise similar.

Foliage: Pale to rich green leaves, 4 to 6″ long, two-thirds as wide, typically 5-lobed (compared to 3-lobed of *A. pensylvanicum*), provide a bold texture. Leaves emerge early and can be injured by frosts. Fall color is yellow but not as vivid as that of *A. pensylvanicum*. **Flowers/seeds/fruits/cones**: Yellow-green flowers in 3 to 4″ long pendulous racemes open with the developing leaves. Each samara 1 to 1½″ long, forming a wide-angled schizocarp. **Native range**:

'Joe Witt'

China, Manchuria, Korea, Russia. **Adaptability**: Requires acid, moist, cool environment. Grows well in cool summers. Zones 4 to 7, 8 in the Pacific Northwest. **Landscape use**: Pretty small tree requiring the same cultural conditions as *A. pensylvanicum*. Best utilized in a woodland garden. Mechanical damage on the thin bark is the portal to decline. **Street tree use**: No, trunk susceptible to sunscald. **In the trade**: Limited.

Acer tegmentosum   'Joe Witt'   'White Tigress'

'Joe Witt'. More prominent white bark on young branches in the winter months. Grows 15 to 20′ by 10 to 15′.

'White Tigress'. Branches and trunk conspicuously streaked with blue-green and white, bears up to 6″ long leaves with 5 taper-pointed lobes, matte green turning yellow in autumn. Same size expectations as 'Joe Witt', but authors recorded a robust 25′ high and wide specimen at Mount Holyoke College. Probably *A. davidii* × *A. tegmentosum*. A brief note of caution: all snakebarks are suspect in heat and drought. 'White Tigress' offered promise, but succumbed to canker and tip borer in the Dirr garden (zone 8); likewise for 'Joe Witt'.

Acer triflorum
three-flower maple

Deciduous. Lovely small tree, 20 to 30′ high and wide with sturdy upright-spreading branches forming a dense, full canopy. Bark is ash-brown to golden amber, loose, peeling, and vertically fissured. Slow-growing.

Foliage: Trifoliate leaves, dark green above, glaucous below, each leaflet 2 to 3″ long, turning orange to red in autumn. Magnificent fall color, often long-persistent but late, usually mid-November in zone 8. **Flowers/seeds/fruits/cones**: The yellow-green flowers are borne in clusters of 3 (hence the common name). Flowers open with the leaves. The fruit is a 1 to 1¼″ long samara, the hard nutlet covered in bristly pubescence. **Native range**: Manchuria, northern China to Korea. **Adaptability**: Demonstrated adaptability from

Acer triflorum

Acer triflorum

Acer triflorum

Minnesota to Maine to Georgia, where two trees in the Dirr garden baffle most visitors. Zones 4 to 8. **Landscape use:** One of our favorite small maples, offering cultural tenacity and multi-season aesthetics. If more readily available, would be a staple in gardens and urban settings. Best in full sun and moist, acid, well-drained soil. Consistent fall color from year to year, even in the Southeast. In terms of performance and adaptability the authors rate the trifoliate maples in the following order: *A. triflorum*, *A. griseum* × *A. maximowiczianum* hybrids, *A. griseum*, *A. maximowiczianum*, and *A. mandshuricum*, although in the West, *A. griseum* has proven surprisingly reliable and *A. triflorum* slower growing. **Street tree use:** No. **In the trade:** Available but uncommon.

ARTIST ETCHING 'CROY'. Light buckskin-tan exfoliating bark extending to the smallest branches. Yellow to gold fall color on a small rounded crowned tree.

'Jack-o-Lantern'. Consistent orange-red fall color. Tree grew 15′ in 15 years in the North Dakota State University Arboretum. No iron chlorosis developed in moderately alkaline soils. Based on geographical origin, it should be zone 3 hardy.

Acer truncatum

Acer truncatum

Shantung maple, purpleblow maple

Deciduous. A small to medium-sized tree, upright-spreading in form with a broadly vase-shaped branching structure and a rounded crown. Moderate growth rate to 25′ tall, 20′ wide. Bark as shown.

Foliage: Palmate leaves are typically 5-lobed, like a 5-pointed star, 2½ to 4″ in length and width. Curiously, leaves on juvenile trees have more complex lobes with additional points. Foliage is glossy and very attractive, deep green in summer. Fall colors are typically bright red but range from yellow-orange to purple-red. In Oregon, we usually see purple-red; in Georgia, yellow. **Flowers/seeds/fruits/cones**: Bright yellow flowers form in spring; they emerge with the leaves and are held in the young foliage in small upright corymbs. Greenish samaras follow and hold until fall, when they turn brown. **Native range**: Northern China and Korea. **Adaptability**: Quite adaptable, reasonably cold hardy, and tolerant of a variety of soils from acid and moist to alkaline and dry. Heat and drought tolerant and therefore valued as an urban-tolerant tree in hotter parts of the United States. The straight species does extremely

Acer truncatum

Acer truncatum

Acer truncatum

CRIMSON SUNSET

CRIMSON SUNSET

well in the southern Midwest and Southeast; we have seen healthy plants as far north as the Minnesota Landscape Arboretum and University of Maine, but cold hardiness may depend on seed provenance. Hybrids, common in the trade, are adaptable and reliable. Zones 4 to 8. **Landscape use**: Use it as a beautiful small spreading tree in the landscape, larger and faster growing than Japanese maple but smaller and slower growing than red maple. The species tends to grow with a flaring habit, forming a rounded crown above a broadly oval to vase-shaped form. Hybrids with *A. platanoides* have slightly larger leaves, are more upright, straighter, and more centrally dominant with a stronger leader and a more tree-like form. The straight species is more of an ornamental plant because of its usually low-branched, spreading form and delicate texture. The hybrids make better shade trees because of their size, 30 to 35′ in height. **Street tree use**: The hybrid cultivars are popular street trees; the straight species is a little too low-branched and spreading. **In the trade**: Seed-grown trees available. Cultivars divide between selections of true *A. truncatum* and hybrids, both first and advanced generations.

'Akikaze Nishiki'. Variegated creamy white and dark green foliage; pattern is erratic, some leaves much more variegated than others, may have instability. Smaller than the species, probably 15′. A true *A. truncatum*.

CRIMSON SUNSET 'JFS-KW202'. Deep purple leaves on an upright-growing, dense and compactly branched, full-sized tree. Upright oval form. Glossy foliage holds color well all summer in most climates with the exception of the high-altitude Mountain States. More heat tolerant than *A. platanoides* 'Crimson King' and with better summer and fall foliage. Has tolerated -33°F in North Dakota, probably the most cold hardy of the cultivars. Rusty orange-red fall color, 35′ tall, 25′ high.

'Fire Dragon'

MAIN STREET

MAIN STREET

NORWEGIAN SUNSET

'Fire Dragon'. Selected for bright red fall color and drought resistance in Texas. A true *A. truncatum*, fine-textured with smaller leaves, less of a central leader tree and more spreading in shape, 25′ tall, 20′ wide.

'Golden Dragon'. Golden yellow fall color, main leaf lobes with additional pointed minor lobes, a Texas selection of true *A. truncatum*, 25′ tall, 20′ wide.

MAIN STREET 'WF-AT1'. Broadly oval, symmetrical in form, with good vigor and growth rate. Selected in North Carolina for growth habit and fall color, it has proven to be the best of the true *A. truncatum* trees tested in Oregon with good cold hardiness and a more formal form. Excellent with consistent orange-red fall color in the Dirr garden (zone 8). Fall colors bright red in Oregon, 25′ tall, 20′ wide.

NORWEGIAN SUNSET 'Keithsform'. Fast-growing, upright oval becoming broadly oval. Glossy dark green foliage, a first-generation hybrid with larger leaves than true *A. truncatum*. Good heat resistance, makes a good shade or street tree with its faster growth and central leader form. Very nice pumpkin-orange color at Halloween time in Oregon, 35′ tall, 25′ wide.

A

141

NORWEGIAN SUNSET

PACIFIC SUNSET

PACIFIC SUNSET

RUBY SUNSET

PACIFIC SUNSET 'Warrenred'. Upright-spreading in form with fast growth and a good central leader when young, spreading to become more rounded with age. Maturing a little shorter than NORWEGIAN SUNSET. Makes a good landscape or street tree. A first-generation hybrid with larger, glossy leaves. Fall color orange-red to bright red, 30′ tall, 25′ wide.

RUBY SUNSET 'JFS-KW249'. Compact, symmetrical, and dense with upright oval growth when young becoming broadly oval with maturity. An advanced-generation hybrid, with the look of a more formal, bolder true *A. truncatum*. Dark green and glossy in summer, the foliage turns orange-red to bright red in fall. Expected to mature to 25′ tall, 20′ wide.

URBAN SUNSET 'JFS-KW187'. "Urban" for its strongly upright, central leader with moderately compact upsweeping branches, which makes it a natural for street tree use. Narrow pyramidal to moderately narrow oval in form, reaching a height of 35′ with a 20′ spread. An advanced-generation hybrid with smaller leaves that mimic true *A. truncatum*. Glossy green in summer turning deep red in fall.

URBAN SUNSET

Aesculus californica
California buckeye

Deciduous. Rounded to broad rounded habit, composed of coarse branches, maturing at 20 to 30′ in height and width. Beautiful species in foliage and flower, but not well suited to cultivation beyond its native range. Slow-growing. Bark is smooth, pale to light silver, reminiscent of American beech bark. Almost a ghostly aura when leafless.

Foliage: Lustrous dark green leaflets, typically 5 to 7, each to 6″ long, sharply serrated, typically abscise in heat/drought of summer. If provided ample moisture, leaves may persist into fall. **Flowers/seeds/fruits/cones**: Flowers in May-June, white, fragrant, held in upright to slightly arching panicles up to 8″ long. Beautiful foil to the dark foliage. Fruit is large, the largest of the commonly cultivated species, to 3″ wide, a pear-shaped to rounded, smooth, light brown dehiscent capsule housing 1 to 3 large, dark brown seeds. Authors collected several fruits from an East Coast garden, each close to the size of a tennis ball. **Native range**: California,

URBAN SUNSET

Aesculus californica

143

Aesculus californica

Aesculus ×carnea

Aesculus ×carnea

occurring naturally on dry soils in canyons and gullies, where it drops its leaves in July-August. **Adaptability**: Zones 6 to 8, 9 on the West Coast. Several East Coast public gardens have notable specimens with a 15′ high, 20′ wide, low-branched tree at Norfolk Botanical Garden. **Landscape use**: Would prove both beautiful and functional for small landscapes if it weren't so persnickety about cultural conditions. Foliage, flower, and bark offer multi-season beauty. Might be useful to hybridize with other buckeyes, particularly *A. pavia*. **Street tree use**: No, too low and wide. **In the trade**: 'Blue Haze' is a free-flowering selection with a bluish cast to the foliage. 'Canyon Pink' grew for several years in Athens and, indeed, flowers held their pink coloration; blooms early to mid-May in Raleigh, NC.

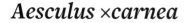

Aesculus ×carnea
red horsechestnut

Deciduous. At its best, a splendid flowering tree, rounded to broad-rounded, coarse-textured, 30 to 40′ high. A common occurrence in English gardens, less so in the United States, but absolutely beautiful when in flower. Growth is slow. Bark is brown-black, with age becoming scaly, platy.

Foliage: Compound palmate foliage, lustrous dark green, composed of 5 to 6″ long, doubly serrate leaflets that turn, at best, yellow in autumn. Leaves are susceptible to blotch/anthracnose and are often brown, crispy, and mutilated by late summer. At its purest, foliage is unique, bold, and beautiful. **Flowers/seeds/fruits/cones**: The greatest dividend resides in the rich pink to red flowers, carried in panicles to 10″ long, rising like plump candles at the end of the stems;

'Briotii'

A

'Fort McNair'

'Briotii'

they open in May in zone 5, persisting for 2 weeks, and are favored by hummingbirds. Fruit is the typical leathery capsule 2 to 2½″ across, sprinkled with prickly spines, dehiscing to release 1 or 2 large, shiny dark brown seeds. Squirrels love the seeds and will glean them in short order. Anyone enthused about growing any aesculus from seed should collect, sow (cover to diameter of seed), and protect from critters. Root radicle germinates immediately; shoot typically the following spring. **Native range**: Hybrid species between the American *A. pavia* and the European *A. hippocastanum*. **Adaptability**: Zones (4)5 to 7(8). **Landscape use**: Superb park, large area, campus, and golf course tree, and one that every arboretum should include. Sun and moist, well-drained soils, low or high pH, support good growth.

The blotch/anthracnose has developed in August in Raleigh, NC. **Street tree use**: Utilized in Salt Lake City, UT, where trees appeared quite healthy; certainly, less leaf blotch than *A. hippocastanum* mixed in same street planting. **In the trade**: Available.

'Briotii'. Deeper red flowers in 10″ long inflorescences. An old cultivar, said to have originated in the mid-1800s. Unfortunately, some plants sold as 'Briotii' do not match the original description, being lighter in flower color. 30′ by 30′.

'Fort McNair'. Lighter pink flowers and greater resistance to the leaf blotch; however, it is still susceptible. Selected from the grounds of Fort McNair, Washington, DC. 30′ by 30′.

'O'Neil's Red'. Close to pure red flowers in 10 to 12″ long inflorescences. Possibly the best cultivar but limitedly available. Worth pursuing! It too is susceptible to the leaf blotch. 30′ by 30′.

Aesculus flava

Aesculus flava (A. *octandra*)
yellow buckeye

Deciduous. Large tree, 60 to 75′ high, upright oval to
oval-rounded with immense secondary branches, coarse-
textured. Arguably the best large buckeye/horsechestnut
for large-scale planting because of reliable performance and
resistance to leaf blotch and anthracnose. Moderate growth
rate. Three-year-old seedlings flowered and fruited in the
Dirr garden. Bark is smooth, gray in youth, with maturity
a combination of gray and brown with large, flat, smooth
plates and scales covering trunks.

Foliage: Compound palmate leaves, generally 5(7) leaflets,
to 6″ long, a third to half as wide, finely serrate, dark green,
turning yellow to pumpkin-orange in autumn. Emerging
leaves often deep bronze to purple before maturing green.
Of the native American tree buckeyes, this offers superior
foliage. **Flowers/seeds/fruits/cones**: The yellow flowers,
tinged green, in 6 to 7″ long, 2 to 3″ wide panicles, open
in May. Effect is muted as the flowers blend with the foliage. Fruit is the typical dehiscent, pear-shaped to almost
rounded, smooth, 2 to 3″ long, light brown capsule, usually
containing 2 brown seeds. **Native range**: Common species

Aesculus flava

in the southern Appalachians to 6,000′ elevation, consistently in the understory and on well-drained ridges, slopes,
moist coves, and along streams. Extends from Pennsylvania
to Tennessee, north Alabama, north Georgia, to Ohio and
Illinois. **Adaptability**: From Minnesota to Georgia and from
coast to coast, it displays remarkable adaptability. Successful in North Dakota. Zones 4 to 8. **Landscape use**: As good
as genetically possible in a stately, majestic, noble buckeye.
Its native habitat belies its heat, cold, drought, and soil

Aesculus flava

Aesculus glabra

Aesculus flava

tolerances. Fast-growing, strong-wooded, semi-majestic in all seasons, it is worthy of greater use. Never on the tip of anyone's tongue when spinning favorite trees. The authors urge greater consideration. **Street tree use**: Certainly potential, but suspect the large fruits and seeds would prove a litter issue. **In the trade**: 'Homestead' (*A. flava* × *A. glabra*) is even more resistant to foliar disease, with yellowish red flowers and red fall color; upright-rounded habit, 30 to 40′ high and wide.

Aesculus glabra
Ohio buckeye

Deciduous. State tree of Ohio, and the Ohio State University mascot masquerades as an anthropomorphic buckeye. With maturity, the tree morphs into a low-branched, rounded to broad-rounded canopy with branches bending toward the ground, then arching back up at the ends, forming a thick, dense canopy. Landscape size approximates 20 to 40′ in height, although trees may reach 60 to 70′. Growth is moderate. Bark is ashy-gray, corky-warty and on large trunks furrowed and scaly.

Foliage: Leaflets 5 (rarely 7), each to 6″ long and about a third as wide, finely serrated, forming a compound palmate leaf; very early leafing, bright green to bronze-purple-green when unfolding, dark green with maturity, on occasion

Aesculus glabra   var. *arguta*

Aesculus glabra

'Autumn Splendor'

'Autumn Splendor'

EARLY GLOW

A

EARLY GLOW

pretty pumpkin-orange-red in fall. Regrettably, subject to leaf blotch and anthracnose, so may appear a bit shabby entering late summer–fall. **Flowers/seeds/fruits/cones**: Flowers similar to A. *flava*, greenish yellow, in 4 to 7″ high, 2 to 3″ wide panicles, and lost in the shuffle of the foliage in May. The spiny, 1 to 2″ long, broad-obovoid capsule contains 1 or occasionally 2 dark brown seeds. **Native range**: Pennsylvania to Nebraska, Kansas, and Alabama. Observed along streams, typically in the understory. **Adaptability**: Considerably more cold hardy than the native range reflects, easily zones 3 to 8. Several selections from North Dakota attest to zone 3 adaptability. **Landscape use**: Best use for this pretty tree is naturalized situations approximating its native conditions, i.e., deep, moist, slightly acid soils. Authors have observed in higher pH soils without signs of chlorosis. **Street tree use**: Minimal. **In the trade**: Limitedly available.

var. *arguta*. The southwestern edition of the species, smaller in all its parts, 15 to 20′ high, with more refined leaflets, 7 to 9(11). Low-branched, wide-spreading habit, the fruits smaller and perhaps spinier than those of the species. It too is susceptible to foliar maladies. Zones 4 to 8.

‘Autumn Splendor’. An A. ×*arnoldiana* hybrid, a cross of A. *flava* with A. *pavia* and probably A. *glabra* as one contibuting parent. Smaller than the species, round-headed, with similar yellow-green flowers. Selected in Minnesota for clean foliage and maroon-red fall color. In the South, does not achieve the vibrant fall color.

EARLY GLOW ‘J. N. Select’. Form similar to the species but shows better late-season foliage quality and produces very early, bright red fall color. It develops very few seeds. The original 30-year-old tree was 30′ by 20′. Found at Johnson Nursery, Menomonee Falls, WI. Zones 3 and 4.

LAVABURST ‘LavaDak’. An upright oval form with compact crown of bright green, more disease-resistant foliage, developing orange-red in autumn, 25 to 28′ high, 14 to 18′ wide, zones 3 to 6. From North Dakota State University.

PRAIRIE TORCH ‘Bergeson’. A hybrid with dubious parentage but characteristics similar to A. *glabra*. Round-headed tree, 30′ by 30′, clean dark green summer foliage with beautiful red fall color. From North Dakota State University; in NDSU trials it grew faster than most buckeye accessions in the first 10 to 15 years. Zones 3 to 7.

Aesculus hippocastanum
common horsechestnut

Deciduous. Large upright oval to rounded tree, massive in structure, very coarse in texture, the grandfather of the *Aesculus* family and widely planted in colonial America. Landscape maturity 50 to 75′ in height, slightly less in spread. Moderate grower. Bark is dark gray to brown; on large trunks becoming platy, exfoliating, and exposing orangish brown inner bark.

Foliage: Largest leaves (leaflets to 10″ long) of the commonly cultivated *Aesculus* species, dark green at maturity, yellow to brown fall color. Certainly impressive but tremendously susceptible to the fungal foliar diseases blotch (pathogen: *Guignardia aesculi*) and anthracnose (pathogen: *Glomerella cingulata*). Trees are infected by summer and often rendered brown by fall. **Flowers/seeds/fruits/cones**: Flowers, each with 4 or 5 petals, white with a yellow blotch at the base, becoming reddish with maturity, are

Aesculus hippocastanum

'Baumannii'

Aesculus hippocastanum

'Baumannii'

borne in up to 10″ long, 4″ wide panicles held principally upright, like candles on a Christmas tree, in May. Showy in flower and for that reason, commonly planted, particularly throughout the Midwest and Northeast. The spiny brown dehiscent capsules, 2″ wide, contain 1 or 2 shiny black seeds.

Native range: Debatable, but listed as mountainous areas in Greece, Albania, and Bulgaria. **Adaptability:** Quite adaptable in cultivation, and certainly, at its best in cooler climates. In the South, growth is slow due to high temperatures; a plant has persisted on the University of Georgia

'Baumannii'

campus for over 40 years but is only 20′ high. Zones 4 to 7. **Landscape use**: For parks, arboreta, campuses, commercial grounds, golf courses, and large areas, it has a place. In the great gardens of Europe, notably Versailles, it is an integral design element. Trees are pleached (pruned) to maintain formal shapes and uniform sizes, a tactic rarely employed in American gardens. Best adapted to acid, well-drained soils. Authors have observed outstanding specimens in Boston, Salt Lake City, UT, and Urbana, IL, a testimonial to its tenaciousness. In Europe, leaf miner and bleeding canker have disfigured and resulted in dieback and death, respectively. **Street tree use**: Be careful. Seeds are often so abundant, the ground underneath the tree appears to be covered with large black marbles. **In the trade**: Not common. 'Baumannii', the most common of the many introductions, is handsome and impressive in flower, particularly so because the flowers are double and produce no fruit. Discovered by A. N. Baumann as a branch sport on a tree near Geneva in 1820, it is a large tree, easily reaching 60′ in height.

Aesculus indica
Indian horsechestnut

Deciduous. Immense tree, paralleling A. *hippocastanum* in stature, leaf size (texture), and flower quality. Often described as oval-rounded in habit, but the bulk of the trees authors encountered are rounded to broad-rounded, ultimately 50 to 60′ high. The gray-brown bark is largely smooth, but fissured longitudinally and horizontally into irregular patterns.

Foliage: New growth emerges bronze-green, lustrous dark green in summer, developing yellow, salmon, to orange-red fall color. Leaves, composed of 5 to 8 leaflets (each to 12″ long), lend a tropical, *Schefflera*-texture. For foliage alone, the species is worth considering. **Flowers/seeds/ fruits/cones**: Flowers (May-June), in 12 to 16″ long, 4 to 5″ wide, erect cylindrical panicles, are awe-inspiring at their best. Each flower 1″ long, white, 4-petaled, with upper pair blotched yellow and red at base, the lower pair shorter, pale rose. Overall effect is pink to pinkish rose. Fruit capsule,

Aesculus indica

'Sydney Pearce'

Aesculus indica

2 to 3″ wide, rough but not spiny, contains 1 or 2 brown seeds. **Native range**: Northwestern Himalayas. **Adaptability**: Zones 7 and 8. Small trees grow in Raleigh, NC, and Athens, GA; best suited to coastal Pacific Northwest into British Columbia. **Landscape use**: A stately tree at its genetic best but seldom observed in the United States. Like other *Aesculus* species, it is adaptable to varied soils as long as well drained. Remarkably well adapted to high pH (limestone) soils. **Street tree use**: Acceptable and utilized for this purpose in England. **In the trade**: Seldom available. 'Sydney Pearce' has deeper pink flowers, in tighter panicles, more freely produced. A small plant in the Dirr garden maintained reasonable foliage but never flowered. Will rival the species in size at maturity.

Aesculus pavia
red buckeye

Deciduous. Lovely, small flowering tree for bringing a sparkle to the early spring landscape, 20′ high and wide, rounded in habit, low-branched and slow-growing. Bark is gray, smooth.

Foliage: Since all *Aesculus* species have compound palmate leaves, there are only so many ways to pronounce them different, but the foliage, composed of 5 to 7 irregularly and often doubly serrate leaflets, to 6″ long, on *A. pavia* emerges as early as late February–early March in zone 8 (Athens) and meshes well with trilliums, hepaticas, and other spring ephemerals. Young leaves chocolate-red-purple, maturing lustrous dark green with no appreciable fall color, yellow at best. **Flowers/seeds/fruits/cones**: One of the prettiest

Aesculus pavia

Aesculus pavia

native spring-flowering trees, flowers in up to 8″ long panicles as the leaves are developing. Immense variation in flower color, from diluted green-yellow-pink to light rose-pink to brilliant red. The 2″ wide subglobose to ovoid, smooth, gray-brown, dehiscent capsule holds 1 or 2 shiny deep brown seeds. Authors have grown many seedlings with

Aesculus pavia

Aesculus pavia

2- to 3-year-old plants developing flowers. **Native range:** Virginia to Florida, Louisiana, and Texas. **Adaptability:** Observed in coastal sands of South Carolina and Alabama, to clay-based soils of Piedmont, consistently lurking in the shadows. Zones 4 to 8(9). **Landscape use:** A great small native tree for wood edges, understories, and naturalistic areas. Dig a hole, insert a seedling or larger plant, and the floral dividend is forever. This and A. *parviflora* make superb companion plants in a woodsy environment. In Athens, GA, flowers may open in late March. The foliage is subject to leaf blotch and anthracnose; by late summer, trees may be partially to completely defoliated. **Street tree use:** No. **In the trade:** The species hybridizes with A. *flava*, A. *glabra*, and A. *sylvatica*, so flower colors vary enormously. 'Atrosanguinea', 'Humilis', and 'Splendens' (formerly afforded species status, as A. *splendens*) produce consistent red flowers. Logical to buy the trees when in flower; similar red flowers will be available. Even more satisfying: collect seeds and start your red buckeye nursery.

Aesculus turbinata
Japanese horsechestnut

Deciduous. Built along the same lines as A. *hippocastanum* and, from a distance, easy to confuse. A large tree with coarse-textured foliage, reaching 80′ or more. The species is sparsely represented in U.S. arboreta, the largest, 40′ high, at the Arnold Arboretum. Slow-growing.

Aesculus turbinata

Aesculus turbinata

Aesculus turbinata

Foliage: Leaves are compound palmate, with 5 to 7 dark green, crenate-serrate leaflets, each to 14″ long. Similar to *A. indica* in texture. Not as susceptible to blotch and anthracnose; at the JC Raulston Arboretum it fared better than *A. ×carnea* and 'Briotii'. Still, no resistance guarantees, and seedling trees may be as seriously infected as *A. hippocastanum.* **Flowers/seeds/fruits/cones:** Flowers are yellow-white, each with a red blotch, borne in up to 10″ long panicles in May-June. Usually 2 to 3 weeks later than *A. hippocastanum.* The broad pear-shaped capsule fruit has a bumpy exterior, but no spines like *A. hippocastanum.* The brown seed is 1″ wide, the hilum (eye) covering nearly half the surface. **Native range:** Japan. **Adaptability:** Adaptable like other *Aesculus* species, but difficult to procure commercially. Zones 5 to 7. **Landscape use:** A collector's species with better foliage manners than *A. hippocastanum.* An *Aesculus* collection is a worthwhile endeavor for parks, campuses, and large areas. Most tree species in the genus are early leafing, April-June flowering, with richly textured foliage. Certainly easy to grow from seed, which should be planted as soon as collected. Good project for Master Gardeners, third-grade science projects, and inquisitive naturalists throughout the United States. **Street tree use:** In Japan. **In the trade:** Seed-grown trees, no cultivars.

Ailanthus altissima

Ailanthus altissima

tree-of-heaven

Deciduous. Possibly misnamed as it is a mischievous invader of any fallow space from sidewalk cracks to open fields. On its best behavior, a large, 40 to 60′ high, upright-spreading, somewhat coarse-textured outline, especially in winter with its chubby branches. Will sucker and form recalcitrant colonies. Exponentially fast-growing. Smooth gray bark with shallow vertical fissures.

Foliage: The compound pinnate dark green leaves are composed of 13 to 25, 3 to 5″ long leaflets. Early spring foliage emerges bronze-purple. Leaves die off green in autumn, occasionally with a hint of yellow. **Flowers/seeds/fruits/cones:** Dioecious. Yellow-green flowers are borne in long panicles in June. The male flowers have a vile odor; female flowers, scentless. This presents a conundrum for any type of selection. A male tree stinks, and the female produces bushels of yellow-green to orange-red samaras, the latter spawning the next generation of thuggish seedlings. **Native range:** China, but naturalized over much of the United States. **Adaptability:** This is among the most adaptable and culturally tenacious species on the planet. Remarkably adaptable to salt, grime, soot, air pollution, low and high pH, heavy clay soil, sandy soil, low oxygen tensions in soil. In the East and Midwest, simply gaze out the car window in any city, and an ailanthus will be staring back. Not as prevalent

Ailanthus altissima

in the South. Zones 4 to 8. **Landscape use:** What to do? We have observed large trees with excellent traits but have yet to witness any significant commercial interest. Perhaps an enterprising breeder will induce sterility. **Street tree use:** Nothing official but makes itself at home in any abandoned spot of soil in urban environments. **In the trade:** A few cultivars (variegated leaf, red-fruited, semi-pendulous habit) are mentioned in literature. Interestingly, perusing nursery catalogs from 100 years ago, we found it was once popular, with a number of named cultivars, long gone because of invasiveness. 'Purple Dragon' offers attractive purplish young foliage, spring into summer, maturing to green.

Albizia julibrissin

mimosa, silk-tree

Deciduous. Fine-textured, typically multi-stemmed tree, 20 to 30′ high and wide, with light to deep pink, powder-puff summer flowers. A terrible weed species in the Southeast, obnoxiously invasive, developing shoots from roots; seeds are produced in prodigious quantities, further contributing to macro-aggression.

Foliage: Bipinnately compound leaves to 20″ long and greater, each falcate-shaped leaflet only ½″ long, dark green, often dying off green. Beautiful, refined, delicate texture seldom available in a relatively cold hardy species. **Flowers/seeds/fruits/cones**: Flowers, shades of pink, composed of long pink stamens, appear in wispy heads during summer. Flowering occurs over a long period, starting in May with a smattering of flowers in August (Southeast). The 5 to 7″ long light straw to gray-brown pod matures in fall, persisting into winter. Not attractive and a sterile selection would be welcome. Seeds (shape of small beans) need only be soaked for 24 hours in water and sown. Germination is rapid.

Native range: Iran and central China, Taiwan, but escaped over much of the eastern and southern United States. **Adaptability**: Adaptable to alkaline and acid soils. Zones 6 to 9. **Landscape use**: A pretty, small, flowering tree for summer color. Requires full sun for best performance. Highly invasive in the Southeast, much less so in the West. We have seen no invasiveness in the cool Pacific Northwest, where it succeeds in the landscape while the climate prevents invasion. **Street tree use**: Possible, but low branch development and heavy fruit set are liabilities. **In the trade**: Several new cultivars have brought renewed landscape life to the species. All cultivars are fertile and produce copious quantities of pods. In fact, seeds from the purple-leaf cultivars produce a smattering of purple-leaf seedlings.

CHOCOLATE FOUNTAIN 'NCAJ1'. A weeping purple-leaf hybrid, estimated to reach 15 to 20′ by 15′. Pretty addition to American gardens. Derived from crossing 'Ishii Weeping', a green-leaved weeper, with 'Summer Chocolate'.

Albizia julibrissin

Albizia julibrissin

'Summer Chocolate'

Alnus cordata

MERLOT MAJIK 'Nurcan 10' ('Fine Wine'). Vibrant red-purple leaves, the color persisting through the summer, even in the heat of the Southeast. Considered an improvement on 'Summer Chocolate'.

OMBRELLA 'Boubri' and 'Flame'. Deeper pink flowers but otherwise similar to the type.

'Pendula' (probably same as 'Ishii Weeping'). A strong weeping form with green foliage and rich pink flowers. Fruits are produced in abundance. Approximately 15′ by 15′.

f. *rosea* ('E. H. Wilson'). The most cold hardy form of the species with similar habit, foliage, and bright pink flowers. A large specimen grew at the former Case Estates, Weston, MA, attaining mature size without winter damage.

'Summer Chocolate'. The first maroon-purple leaf selection offered in U.S. commerce. Masato Yokoi discovered it in the wild in Japan. Tree in Georgia trials is 20′ by 20′. Flowers are pink-white, not deep pink.

Alnus cordata
Italian alder

Deciduous. Fast-growing, upright and uniformly pyramidal, with a dominant central leader, forming a loosely pyramidal shape at maturity. 50′ tall, 25′ wide.

Foliage: Leaves are heart-shaped (cordate), resembling a broad linden leaf, but smoother, dark green, and quite glossy, 2 to 4″ long and slightly less in width. **Flowers/seeds/fruits/cones**: Male catkins are yellowish, 3 to 4″ long, and hang from bare branches in early spring. Female flowers are in small insignificant catkins that develop into 1″ long brown cones in the fall. **Native range**: Southern Italy and Corsica. **Adaptability**: Quite tolerant of poor soils, wet or dry, high pH, heat and drought, but also more tolerant of cold than its native range might indicate. A good choice in warm areas with lower rainfall. Zones 5 to 8. **Landscape use**: Useful as a fast-growing, nitrogen-fixing tree on dry difficult sites, especially in higher pH soils, but also tolerant of moist acid soil. In form, it resembles *Tilia cordata* from a

Alnus cordata

Alnus glutinosa

'Imperialis'

distance, but up close you will appreciate its lustrous foliage. **Street tree use**: Has potential in the right locations. Used thus in Europe. Alders tend to have weak wood, so consider wind and snow load. **In the trade**: Sold as seed-grown.

Alnus glutinosa
black alder, common alder

Deciduous. Pyramidal when young becoming loosely pyramidal to broadly ovate in shape. Sometimes grown multi-stem, in which case it spreads more widely. Moderately coarse-textured, fast-growing, 50′ by 35′.

Foliage: Broadly oval to broadly obovate leaves are very dark green and slightly glossy, 2 to 4″ in length and width. Leaves hold on the tree late in fall and usually drop without coloring. **Flowers/seeds/fruits/cones**: Male catkins are 2 to 4″ long and reddish brown, held on bare branches early in spring. Female flowers are in very small catkins. Seeds develop in small ½″ long brown cones, in the fall. **Native range**: Europe, western Asia, and northern Africa. **Adaptability**: Very adaptable, perhaps too much so. It does well on infertile soils, as it fixes nitrogen. Tolerates standing water but is not so happy in dry soils. It has become invasive in the upper Midwest and Northeast and is a threat to wetland areas. **Landscape use**: Considerable in Europe, where it is native. Has been used in North America for its adaptability to waterlogged sites, but its invasive potential argues against this. **Street tree use**: Tough enough but—considering invasiveness and the potential for branch breakage and considerable twig shedding—not recommended. **In the trade**: Sold as seed-grown, tree form or multi-stem. Cultivars are rare. 'Imperialis' has deeply incised foliage, the leaves resembling cutleaf birch. Pyramidal with thin, gracefully arching branches, giving a much lighter impression than the species, to 30′ tall, 20′ wide.

Alnus glutinosa

Alnus glutinosa

Alnus glutinosa

Alnus glutinosa

Alnus incana
gray alder, white alder

Nomenclatural note: This is a confusing circumpolar species complex, encompassing the northern hemisphere and consisting of three to six subspecies (in North America, both subsp. *rugosa* and subsp. *tenuifolia* formerly held species status). We cover the subspecies that are in horticultural use and let the taxonomists figure out the rest.

Deciduous. Variable, a medium-sized, generally pyramidal tree. The subspecies vary, some smaller and often multi-stemmed. Bark is gray to brown, smooth.

Foliage: Variable over range, usually dark green, broadly elliptical to broadly ovate leaves with a coarsely doubly serrate margin, 2 to 4″ in length and slightly less in width. **Flowers/seeds/fruits/cones**: Male catkins are 2 to 4″ long and held on branches in spring before leaves emerge. Female catkins are visually insignificant, developing into ½″ cones holding seeds in the fall. **Native range**: The type, subsp. *incana*, is native to Europe except for the most western part. Subsp. *rugosa* is native to northern North America from Virginia to the eastern Yukon. Subsp. *tenuifolia* is native to the mountains of western North America, from interior Alaska, south through the Rocky Mountains and the Cascade and Sierra Nevada mountains of the western states. **Adaptability**: Adapted to cooler, and let's face it, just plain cold climates. And wet. Fixes nitrogen, will grow in low-fertility soils as long as plentiful moisture is available. Tolerates flooding. Zones 1 to 6, depending on subspecies and seed source. **Landscape use**: Valuable in colder climates and difficult, wet sites. In North America, usually used in native landscapes. Subsp. *incana* appears more often in formal landscapes. **Street tree use**: Possible in the right climate. **In the trade**: Sold as seed-grown and European cultivars.

subsp. *incana* (European gray alder). A moderately large tree, pyramidal to oval, 50′ tall and 40′ wide. Dull green foliage. 'Aurea' is smaller, 25′, with yellow-orange twigs and orange-brown bark. 'Laciniata' is 35′ with cutleaf foliage. 'Pendula' is 20′ and weeping.

subsp. *rugosa* (speckled alder). Grows near water, in thickets, makes a single-stem or multi-stem tree 15 to 25′ tall. Bark is polished brown with lenticels forming speckles on the trunk (hence the common name). Leaves broadly ovate, sharply and irregularly toothed. Used in natural landscapes and wetland remediation, where it is a good choice because of its ability to fix nitrogen. Leave abscise green without fall color.

subsp. *rugosa*

subsp. *tenuifolia*

subsp. *tenuifolia*

subsp. *tenuifolia* (mountain alder). Used as a small landscape tree, either single-stem or multi-stem, especially in the Rocky Mountain communities and interior West, as long as soil is moist. It makes an excellent addition to the native landscape. Single-stem trees grow to an upright broad oval, 30′ tall, 15′ wide, while multi-stems are more spreading and irregular, to 25′ wide. Native to high mountain areas where soils are wet, especially along streambanks and meadows. Grayish brown trunks are attractive, and foliage can be quite nice.

subsp. *rugosa*

Alnus rubra
red alder

Deciduous. Strongly upright, pyramidal in form, often loose and open. Lower branches typically abscise and drop in shady locations. Moderately coarse texture, very fast-growing to 60′ high with a 30′ spread. Silver-gray bark. As more desirable eastern hardwoods have become rare for timber harvest, red alder has become very important and valuable to the furniture industry, as its wood can be attractively stained to imitate many species.

Foliage: Medium green leaves are broadly ovate to oval, doubly serrate to dentate, 3 to 6″ in length and 2 to 3½″ in width. Little fall color; leaves usually drop while still greenish yellow. **Flowers/seeds/fruits/cones**: Male catkins are unusually large, cylindrical, 4 to 6″ long, reddish and attractive, held on bare branches in early spring. Female flowers are in small inconspicuous catkins, which develop into woody brown cones, oval, about 1″ long. **Native range**: Pacific Northwest maritime strip from southeastern Alaska through northern California. **Adaptability**: A pioneer species in its native habitat, it often takes over the landscape after logging, especially in moist soils, where it fixes nitrogen and grows rapidly. Easy to grow in the Pacific Northwest, often becoming weedy. Needs a moist climate to thrive. **Landscape use**: Frequently used as a restoration species in its native range, where it performs that task exceedingly well. Rarely planted in ornamental gardens or commercial landscapes, as it is short-lived and a bit messy. It can be an attractive tree where landscapes merge into wild areas, its lighter trunks making an attractive entrance to a conifer woodland. Brittle wood and frequent limb breakage preclude its use near homes, where wind may cause damage. **Street tree use**: Not appropriate. **In the trade**: Sold as seed-grown.

Alnus rubra

Alnus rubra

Alnus rugosa. See A. *incana*

Alnus ×spaethii
Spaeth alder

Deciduous. Upright pyramidal becoming loosely pyramidal with age. It has a good central leader with branches that become horizontal. Medium texture, fast-growing to 50' high, 25 to 30' wide.

Foliage: Dark green, glossy leaves are sharply serrate, 4 to 6" long, 2 to 3" wide. They hold on the tree in the fall with little fall color developing. **Flowers/seeds/fruits/cones**: Male catkins, 2 to 3" long, hang from bare branches very early in spring, brownish yellow in color. Female flowers are insignificant, held in small oval catkins. Seeds mature in the fall in cone-like strobiles. **Native range**: A nursery hybrid of the eastern Asian A. *japonica* and western Asian A. *sub-cordata*. **Adaptability**: Quite adaptable and highly valued in Europe for its urban tolerance, wind resistance, and general freedom from pests and disease. Tolerant of wet soils and drought. Zones 4 to 7. **Landscape use**: More of a functional, utilitarian tree than a beautiful ornamental, it is used extensively in Holland and to a lesser extent across northern Europe. Almost unknown in North America. **Street tree use**: Widely utilized in Holland, mostly in tough sites. It would make a good addition to North American streets, especially on wet windy sites near the coast. **In the trade**: Usually cutting-propagated as a clone; sometimes listed as cultivar 'Spaeth'.

Alnus tenuifolia. See A. *incana*

Amelanchier arborea
downy serviceberry, juneberry

Deciduous. Upright-spreading tree with rounded crown; often multi-stem and more informal in habit, 20 to 30' tall and wide. Fine-textured in appearance, slow-growing.

Foliage: Distinctly pubescent on new emerging foliage, which appears grayish white over green. Leaves are small, elliptical and become green in summer. Fall color is yellow-orange to bright red. **Flowers/seeds/fruits/cones**: White flowers in pendulous racemes 2 to 4" long appear as the leaves are emerging. Summer fruits are ¼ to ⅜″, purple-blue, edible and sweet. **Native range**: Eastern North America, Maine to Iowa, and Florida to Louisiana. **Adaptability**: Broadly adapted; see comments under *A. ×grandiflora*. Zones 4 to 9. **Landscape use**: Like *A. ×grandiflora*, it is useful in many situations, especially if a naturalistic look is desired. Usually grows a little more tree-like and slightly larger than *A. ×grandiflora*. **Street tree use**: When grown as a single-trunk tree form and properly pruned, it can be used on residential streets, although adequate branch clearance can be difficult to achieve. **In the trade**: Sold as seed-grown. PINK DAMSEL 'Tift County' is pink in bud and light pink in flower. Fine-textured appearance, leaves narrower, branches a bit more slender and lax in form, 15′ tall and wide. Selected as a native in southern Georgia, well adapted to the hot South, susceptible to early freeze in the North; zones 6 to 8. Most other cultivars are *A. ×grandiflora* hybrids.

Amelanchier arborea

Amelanchier arborea

PINK DAMSEL

Amelanchier arborea

PINK DAMSEL

Amelanchier ×grandiflora

apple serviceberry

Deciduous. Upright and irregularly spreading small multi-stem trees, sometimes grown as oval to rounded single-stem trees. Fine texture, slower growing, 15 to 20′ tall by 15′ wide as single-stem and up to 20′ wide as multi-stem.

Foliage: Small ovate leaves, 1 to 3″ in length, half that in width, finely serrate, green to bronze in spring, lightly pubescent on the underside. Nice fall colors, yellow-orange, orange-red, or bright red. **Flowers/seeds/fruits/cones**: White 5-petaled flowers appear in 2 to 4″ pendulous racemes as the leaves emerge in spring, typically flowering very heavily and turning the whole plant white. A beautiful spring sight. Flowers faintly malodorous. Summer fruit is ¼ to ⅜″, purple-blue, an edible pome. **Native range**: A naturally occurring hybrid of *A. arborea* and *A. laevis*, both native to eastern North America. Taxonomy of the genus is extremely complex and not well understood, and botanists spend careers trying to figure out the reproductive strategies of the species, hybrid swarms, and apomictic populations. For horticultural purposes, vegetatively propagated tree-sized cultivars dominate, classified as either *A. ×grandiflora* or *A. laevis*. **Adaptability**: Broadly adapted, can be grown throughout most of the United States, preferring reasonable moisture and acid soils but can do well in drier soils with slightly elevated pH. Zones (4)5 to 8(9), depending on cultivar. **Landscape use**: Multiple uses as specimens, groupings, or screens but often best used naturalistically in gardens, created naturescapes, or along the edges of woodlands or creeks. The growth habit tends to be irregular and provides that relaxed, "native" look. Rust (common) and possibly other leafspots can disfigure the foliage but not so much that it is noticeable at a distance. **Street tree use**: No, too low and spreading. **In the trade**: Available.

'Autumn Brilliance'. The most popular *A. ×grandiflora* cultivar and more vigorous than most, producing a stronger plant, generally multi-stem but will also grow into a small single-trunk garden tree, 20′ tall, 15′ wide. Clean white flowers in spring and good orange-red fall color.

A

'Autumn Brilliance'

'Autumn Brilliance'

'Princess Diana'

'Ballerina'

'Cole's Select'

'Princess Diana'

'Ballerina'. A selection from Holland of uncertain parentage; expect to find it listed under multiple species names. More upright than most, fine branches are upright and flaring, with an overall broad oval shape reaching 20′ tall, 15′ wide. Red fall color.

'Cole's Select'. Very similar to 'Autumn Brilliance', foliage may be slightly more glossy, orange-red fall color, 20′ tall, 15′ wide.

'Princess Diana'. Slightly smaller and more spreading than 'Autumn Brilliance', selected in Wisconsin for nice white flowers, good cold hardiness, and very bright red fall color, to 15′ tall and wide.

'Robin Hill'. Features pink flowers, although we have to admit they are rather pale pink and may fade to white. Slow-growing but more upright than others, it can make a good small single-stem tree to 20′ tall, 15′ wide. 'Rubescens', with pale pink flowers, is similar.

'Robin Hill'

Amelanchier laevis

Allegheny serviceberry

Deciduous. Growth habit and form are similar to the other *Amelanchier* species, but this is usually the most tree-like of the group, growing slightly larger and producing the most refined, tree-like cultivars with the most upright, formal shapes. Trees are upright oval to rounded in shape, and multi-stem forms are upright-spreading. Fine-textured, moderate growth rate. Trees reach 30′ by 25′, multi-stem to 25′ by 25′.

Foliage: Leaves emerge in spring with distinct coloration: purplish bronze to orange-bronze. This characteristic can be used to differentiate *A. laevis* from other species. By summer, the leaves have turned completely green and it becomes much more difficult to identify. The spring leaf color makes it the prettiest *Amelanchier* species at this time. Leaves 1½ to 3″ long, broadly ovate. **Flowers/seeds/fruits/cones**: Flowers are white in pendulous racemes, 4 to 5″ long, and appear as the leaves are emerging. Racemes are typically longer and looser-appearing than the other species, and petals are long elliptic, making individual flowers appear star-like. Summer fruits are ¼ to ⅜″, purple-blue, edible and sweet. **Native range**: Eastern North America, Newfoundland to Michigan and Georgia to Kansas. **Adaptability**: Broadly adapted; see comments under *A.* ×*grandiflora*. Zones 4 to 8. **Landscape use**: Most often seen as an isolated specimen but useful in many situations, especially when a natural appearance is desired. More vigorous and seems to have better resistance to rust and powdery mildew than other species. **Street tree use**: Upright-growing cultivars make good small street trees, the best in the genus for this purpose. **In the trade**: Sold as seed-grown, but care should be taken: seed sources are unpredictable, especially among a group of species with taxonomic difficulty. Vegetatively propagated cultivars dominate because of their predictability.

'Cumulus'. A narrow upright form, oval in shape, among the most tree-like and suitable for street use, growing to 30′ tall and 20′ wide. Yellow-orange to orange-red fall color.

LUSTRE 'Rogers'. Upright oval form, somewhat open, to 30′ tall, 25′ wide. Foliage is dark green with a nice gloss; fall color is orange-red.

'Snowcloud' ('Majestic'). Upright oval form, quite tree-like, narrower than the species, good for street use, to 30′ tall, 20′ wide. Orange-red fall color.

SPRING FLURRY 'JFS-Arb'. Upright oval, relatively narrow, maintains a good leader, a good street tree form, growing to 30′ tall, 20′ wide. Could be used as a substitute for *Pyrus calleryana* where that species is invasive. Profuse flowering in spring, orange to orange-red fall color.

A

Amelanchier laevis

Amelanchier laevis

'Cumulus'

LUSTRE

'Snowcloud'

SPRING FLURRY

SPRING FLURRY

A

'Snowcloud'

Amelanchier lamarckii

juneberry, snowy mespilus

Deciduous. Upright-spreading to spreading, somewhat lax. In flower and leaf, most closely resembles *A. laevis*, but in growth habit, more similar to *A. ×grandiflora*. Fine-textured, moderate growth rate, 15 to 20′ in both height and width.

Foliage: Bronze-orange over green in spring becoming green in summer. Leaves 1½ to 3″ long, broadly ovate. Red to orange fall color. **Flowers/seeds/fruits/cones**: Racemes of white flowers. Summer fruits are ¼ to ⅜″, purple-blue, edible and sweet. **Native range**: An enigma for taxonomists, can be thought of as a microspecies, or a seed-source cultivar, discovered in Europe but derived from North American *Amelanchier* germplasm that was taken to Europe in the 1700s. The resulting apomictic population is *A. lamarckii*. **Adaptability**: Broadly adapted; see comments under *A. ×grandiflora*. **Landscape use**: Widely used in Europe, it is especially nice when grown multi-stem in a naturalized landscape. **Street tree use**: No, too wide-spreading.

Amelanchier lamarckii

Amelanchier lamarckii

In the trade: Sold as seed-grown. The genus is often apomictic; in simple terms, this means it can produce seed asexually, therefore all seedlings are virtually identical and show no recombination of traits. Because it is apomictic, seed-grown trees are very uniform.

Araucaria araucana

monkey puzzle tree

Evergreen conifer. Talk about a tree that gets attention: even the least horticulturally inclined can't fail to notice a monkey puzzle. Its unique form and texture identify it at first glance. Pyramidal, with a strong single trunk, a dominant leader, radiating branches that sway downward then swoop up like heavy, dark green ropes, eventually forming a broad pyramidal shape with a rounded crown. Usually quite symmetrical. Can reach 70′ tall or more with a 35′ spread. Coarse in texture, medium growth rate.

Foliage: Very dark green leaves are closely packed, spiraling around each branch, 1 to 2″ long, stiff and densely set, sturdy at the base and tapering to very sharply pointed tips. Scary to look at and even scarier to touch. You would be a foolish monkey to try to climb through these. **Flowers/seeds/fruits/cones**: Usually dioecious. Male flowers are in 4″ long,

Araucaria araucana

Araucaria araucana

Arbutus ×andrachnoides

Arbutus ×andrachnoides

'Marina'

broad catkins; in the second year the females mature into 5 to 8″ thick, spiny pineapple-shaped cones that weigh several pounds. Not a tree to take a nap under! **Native range**: Chile and western Argentina. **Adaptability**: Limited by cold hardiness but does well in the mild, coastal climate of western North America and the similar climate of Great Britain. Also grows in the Southeast. Zones 8 to 11. **Landscape use**: A curiosity. Or a tree that makes a statement, if that's the kind of statement you want to make. It does have a unique beauty. Dark and stiff rope-like branches give it a prehistoric appearance yet carry a graceful sway and flow with the strong directional orientation of the foliage. Definitely attention-getting as well as imposing. Good for those who want their home to look like a Victorian natural history museum. **Street tree use**: Not recommended; a falling cone could take out a car, its spiny branches could shred one. **In the trade**: Sold as seed-grown. Selection of a male cultivar would eliminate the hazard of the heavy seed cones.

Arbutus ×andrachnoides

hybrid strawberry tree

Broadleaf evergreen. Upright-spreading, usually with multiple low branches forming ascending trunks. The twisting trunks are beautifully covered with exfoliating orange-brown bark. Broadly rounded crown. Fine-textured, moderately slow-growing to 30′ with a similar spread.

Foliage: Leaves 2 to 4″ long, elongated oval to long ovate, with sharp-pointed fine serrations, dark green, thick. Glossy and attractive. **Flowers/seeds/fruits/cones**: Flowers are small, urn-shaped, in clusters, white to ivory, present from late fall through early spring. **Native range**: A naturally occurring hybrid of *A. andrachne* and *A. unedo*, both from southern Europe and Asia Minor. **Adaptability**: Appears a little more adaptable than its parent species. Needs a Mediterranean climate with well-drained soils, dry in summer, and likes an acid soil, but experience in Britain shows it can tolerate a higher pH as well. Zones 7 to 10. **Landscape use**: An all-season evergreen with exfoliating cinnamon-colored bark, attractive all year, and pendent flowers through the winter. **Street tree use**: Only in a wide planting strip to allow for the spreading branches and with careful attention to water and soil drainage. **In the trade**: Most commonly represented by 'Marina', which offers improved vigor, growing to 40′ in height and width. Leaves are a little larger than the species, bronze when young, then glossy green; flowers tinted rosy pink. Easier to grow than most plants in the genus, this cultivar is especially popular in the San Francisco area.

Arbutus menziesii
Pacific madrone

Broadleaf evergreen. Quite upright with a single trunk or multiple ascending trunks, forming a vase-shaped canopy overhead with a rounded top. Medium coarse in texture, moderate growth rate. Quite variable in mature height based on site conditions; 50′ is typical with a spread of 25′, but height can exceed 100′. Its bark is incredibly beautiful, exfoliating from roughened cinnamon to satiny smooth orange. Its open form highlights the bark, which is clearly visible high into the canopy.

Foliage: Large oval dark green leaves, 3 to 6″ long and half as wide, thick with smooth surface and an entire margin. **Flowers/seeds/fruits/cones**: Small white urn-shaped flowers appear in spring in clustered 6″ panicles. Bright red fruits, ⅓″, are ornamental from late summer into the winter. **Native range**: Pacific coast of North America from southwestern British Columbia to southern California. **Adaptability**: Despite its large native range, this is a picky plant: conditions have to be just right. It wants a Mediterranean climate with a coastal influence, definitely well-drained soil with the right mycorrhizae. Grow it within its native range. Zones 7 to 9. **Landscape use**: An incredibly beautiful tree where it succeeds. Susceptible to phytophthora root rot, cankers, and leafspots; too much summer water will kill it; it prefers neglect and needs air circulation. The twisting, tall sinewy trunks are of great beauty, their orange-brown colors reflecting the sunlight and accentuated by shadows. In his youth, Warren lived in a community where madrones lined the bluff along a boulevard overlooking Puget Sound. You could never tire of looking at the orange glow of madrone trunks at sunrise or sunset, truly a sight to see. If it is native in your garden or neighborhood, cherish and protect. If you want to plant it, conditions and climate must be just right, and a little good luck will help. Very difficult to transplant. **Street tree use**: Not recommended, street soils are not suitable. **In the trade**: Sold as seed-grown; not common, difficult to produce.

Arbutus menziesii

Arbutus menziesii

Arbutus unedo
strawberry tree

Broadleaf evergreen. Shrubby when young, becoming a broadly oval small tree to 15' high and 10' wide. Slow-growing. Bark as shown.

Foliage: Leaves elliptical to narrow obovate 2 to 4" long and ¾ to 1" wide, thick glossy dark green with a serrulate margin. **Flowers/seeds/fruits/cones**: Clusters of small white urn-shaped flowers appear in the fall. The fruit develops slowly and becomes ornamental almost a year later when the ¾" globose fruits ripen to bright orange-red then strawberry-red and hold in winter. They are edible, but the flavor doesn't live up to the strawberry name. **Native range**: Mediterranean region, Spain to Asia Minor with an isolated population in Ireland. **Adaptability**: Reasonably adaptable, which is as good as it gets in this touchy genus. Well-drained soils are important but nowhere near as essential as for madrone. Well adapted to the West Coast; can be grown in the Southeast if soils are sharply drained. **Landscape use**: Grow it as a tree, not a shrub. It may be cute and bushy when small, but it will outgrow its shrub proportions and needs pruning to establish a clean trunk. It makes a nice small garden tree. The fruit will impress your neighbors and garner frequent "What's that?" questions. **Street tree use**: A little small for this purpose, difficult to create a clean trunk tall enough for traffic. Plant a little back from the traffic and it's fine. **In the trade**: Sold as seed-grown for tree form. Most cultivars are dwarf selections.

Arbutus unedo

Arbutus unedo

Arbutus unedo

Arbutus unedo

Asimina triloba

common pawpaw, custard apple

Deciduous. A favorite native small tree or suckering, colonizing thicket-forming large shrub; always variable over the native range. Grows 10 to 20′ high, greater in deep, moist, well-drained, alluvial soils along streams and rivers. Size 30 to 40′ under ideal growing conditions. Terrific species for understory planting and is typically found there in nature. Fast-growing. Bark is dark brown with grayish areas when young becoming rough and slightly scaly with maturity.

Foliage: We love the large, slightly droopy leaves, to 12″ long, lustrous dark green, turning glorious soft to deep yellow in autumn. Without question, one of the best understory species for yellow fall color; at its best, the yellow is so rich it appears bug lights have been installed.
Flowers/seeds/fruits/cones: Dioecious. Before the leaves emerge, fuzzy dark brown globose, ¼″ wide buds open to lurid purple, 6-petaled flowers, 2″ wide, on ¾″ long, downy,

Asimina triloba

Asimina triloba

Asimina triloba

Asimina triloba

recurved pedicels. Quite easy to miss the April-May flowers as the color and timing reduce the potency. Edible, bloomy (waxy), greenish yellow, maturing brownish black, 2 to 5″ long berry fruits ripen in fall. Fruits are odd shapes, from elongated (banana-like) to rounded. Taste is similar to banana, the flesh, when ripe, with a custard consistency. Seeds, typically 2 to 3 per fruit, are 1″ long, dark brown, flattish to bean-shaped. **Native range**: New York to Florida, west to Nebraska and Texas. In southern Appalachians, it is common in rich hardwood forests and river bottoms, almost universally as an understory tree. **Adaptability**: Prefers deep, moist, fertile, slightly acid soils to maximize growth in sun or shade. Zones 5 to 8. **Landscape use**: Terrific tree for naturalizing with existing woods, either as an edge or understory element. A degree recalcitrant in the transplanting process, so logical to choose small container-grown trees. Small bare-root seedlings or grafts (cultivars), transplanted to a 3-gallon container, will develop 4 to 6′ height with a solid root system in a single growing season. These plants can be readily planted and will prosper. Shoots will develop from the roots of established trees. If left, a colony develops, just as in nature. **Street tree use**: No. **In the trade**: Kentucky State University, Frankfort, conducted an extensive research program to develop a commercial industry in the lower Midwest, upper South; recommendations from the program follow. Many more cultivars selected for fruit quality are available from specialist fruit growers. Need to listen to experts about the best.

ALLEGHENY ('2-9'). Complex flavor with citrus overtone, firm custard-like texture, quite seedy.

'Overleese'. Rich butterscotch flavor, melts in the mouth.

POTOMAC ('4-2'). Sweet rich flavor, firm texture, medium yellow color, large (to 1 lb.) fruit, few seeds.

RAPPAHANNOCK 'Aidfievate'. Refreshing taste, firm texture, symmetrical fruits.

SHENANDOAH 'Wanserwan'. Sweet fruity flavor, smooth custardy texture, pale green skin with glaucous waxy bloom.

'Sunflower'. Thick texture and butter-colored flesh, yellow skin, few seeds.

SUSQUEHANNA 'LERfiv'. Sweet rich flavor, firm buttery texture, large (to 1 lb.) fruit, skin greenish yellow speckled with black dots, very few seeds.

WABASH '1-7-2'. Creamy smooth, sweet, flavorful, medium-firm texture, green skin, yellow to orangish flesh.

Azara microphylla
little-leaf azara

Broadleaf evergreen. Pretty small tree or large shrub, 10 to 20′ high and wide, suited only to West Coast gardens. Common in English gardens. Slow-growing.

Foliage: Leaves are densely arranged in a planar fashion on the fine branches. Each lustrous dark green leaf is ½ to ⅝″ long, resulting in a refined texture. **Flowers/seeds/fruits/cones**: The chocolate-vanilla-fragrant, apetalous, green-sepaled flowers are composed of numerous mustard-yellow stamens. Flowers appear in leaf axils in late winter to early spring and continue over an extended period. The effect is

Azara microphylla

'Variegata'

somewhat masked as the flowers are obscured by the foliage, being produced on the underside of the shoots. **Native range**: Chile and Argentina. **Adaptability**: Limited by cold hardiness, as with most South American genera. Zones (8)9 to 10, West Coast. **Landscape use**: Worthy espalier, container, or small accent plant that should be sited in partial shade, well-drained, moist, and fertile soil. **Street tree use**: No. **In the trade**: 'Variegata', green-centered leaves with yellow-cream margins, is a pretty change of pace. Slightly slower growing than the species and subject to reversion; remove any green shoots that develop. Noted reference to a 22′ high plant in Ireland.

B

Bauhinia ×blakeana

Bauhinia variegata
orchid tree

Tardily deciduous. Slender-trunked flowering tree, 20 to 30′ high and wide, loose, open, with wide-spreading arching branches. Fast-growing. The genus is most closely related to *Cercis* among hardy trees. Approximately 150 species, primarily from Brazil and India, are recognized.

Foliage: Unique, butterfly-shaped leaves cleft at apex and base, light to medium green, persisting into winter (zone 9), gradually abscising into spring. **Flowers/seeds/fruits/cones**: Spectacular, fragrant, orchid-shaped, 5-petaled flower, 4 to 5″ long, pale purple to white, open in January-February to April. Flowers develop on old wood, so avoid pruning in summer-fall. Fruits are flat, sharp-beaked black pods, to 12″ long, which usually persist through winter. **Native range**: India and China. **Adaptability**: Only for the warmest regions of the country, zones 9 to 11. **Landscape use**: Pretty garden specimen, border addition, park or container tree for warm climates, producing beautiful floral show in a slow time of year. Authors have observed in the Leu Gardens, Orlando, FL, but have seen nowhere else. Requires little more than well-drained soil and full sun, although will flower in partial shade. Displays high drought tolerance. Trees tend to lean and often require staking. Supple branches are subject to storm breakage. Considered invasive in south Florida. **Street tree use**: Possible with structural pruning and certainly utilized for the purpose in warm-climate urban areas. **In the trade**: *B. ×blakeana*

Bauhinia variegata

(Hong Kong orchid tree) is slightly less hardy but offers 5 to 6″ wide flowers and a range of flower colors from reddish to orchid-pink, starting in late fall, progressing into spring. Develops an umbrella-like canopy, to 20′ high and wide. The gray-green foliage is evergreen to semi-evergreen.

Betula albosinensis
Chinese paper birch

Deciduous. Pyramidal in youth, eventually gracefully rounded, a 40 to 60′ high tree with rich orange-red to orange-brown bark, peeling in sheets the thickness of tissue paper, each successive layer with a waxy glaucous bloom. It may sound too good to be true, but it is as described. Fast-growing in youth; slowing with age. For a non-white-bark birch, this species is among the best for effect.

Foliage: The lustrous dark green, doubly serrate leaves, 2 to 3″ long, half as wide, have 10 to 14 vein pairs. Fall color is yellow, similar to that of most *Betula* species. **Flowers/ seeds/fruits/cones**: Flowers, before the leaves, the female in upright aments (catkins), male in pendulous aments. Birches are part of the spring awakening with their pretty yellow-green-tawny-brown catkins. Fruit is a small winged nutlet, produced in prodigious quantities, maturing in autumn. **Native range**: Central and western China. **Adaptability**: Best adapted to the Pacific Northwest. Not adapted to hot, dry conditions; we have never observed a single tree under such conditions. Zones 5 and 6, to 8 in the maritime Pacific Northwest. **Landscape use**: Unfortunately, not common in American gardens. An impressive specimen birch, more imposing and aesthetic in the winter garden because of its beautiful bark. Requires cool, moist climate, well-drained soil and full sun. **Street tree use**: Could serve if trained as a single-trunk specimen. **In the trade**: Uncommon but worth the effort to procure. Most are seed-grown, so bark qualities will vary. All the many European cultivars were chosen for their bark.

Betula albosinensis

Betula albosinensis

'Fascination'

Betula alleghaniensis

'Bowling Green'. Honey-colored, peeling bark.

'China Rose'. Rich copper-red bark with little white bloom; 33′ by 26′.

'China Ruby'. Bark cream-white, flushed gray and pink, maturing coppery red.

'Chinese Garden'. Darker, pinkish bark.

'Fascination'. Bark becomes quite reddish brown and then peels to reveal light pinkish white. Slower growing, it forms a loose pyramidal shape to 30′ tall, 20′ wide. Good golden yellow fall color.

'Kansu'. Multi-colored copper and pink bark.

'Pink Champagne'. Smooth, peeling, pale pink bark, softened by a persistent white bloom (wax), reaches 50′ by 33′.

'Red Panda'. Beautiful copper-pink (pinkish red) bark.

var. *septentrionalis*. Larger statured, with yellow-orange to orange-gray to orange-brown exfoliating bark. A Great Plant Pick by Seattle's Elisabeth C. Miller Botanical Garden, which reflects top performance in the Pacific Northwest.

Betula alleghaniensis
yellow birch

Deciduous. Beautiful native birch, resplendent in a golden yellow mantle in fall foliage. Pyramidal in youth, rounded at maturity, ascending to over 100′ in nature but under cultivation in the 60 to 75′ range. Fast-growing. The wood is extremely valuable, being utilized for tool handles, veneers, furniture, cabinets, flooring, and doors. The bark on young stems and branches is yellowish or bronze, semi-exfoliating in loose papery permutations. Mature bark is gray to red-brown, breaking into large, ragged-edged, grayish to blackish brown plates. Old trunks still show papery traits. The exfoliating bark is a method to separate *B. alleghaniensis* from *B. lenta*.

Foliage: The dull dark green leaves, to 5″ long, doubly serrated, turn beautiful yellow in autumn. All birches bear their leaves singly on current year's shoots and in pairs on short shoots emanating from older stems. The effect is similar to butterfly wings when spread. **Flowers/seeds/fruits/cones:** Flowers and fruits are as described under *B. albosinensis*. This species is difficult to separate from *B. lenta*, but has larger fruiting catkins, 1 to 1½″ long and ¾″ thick. Young stems, when bruised, emit a faint wintergreen odor. **Native range:** Extended distribution from Canada to high

Betula alleghaniensis

Betula alleghaniensis

Betula alleghaniensis

elevations (6,000′) of the southern Appalachians into Georgia and Tennessee. Common in rich woods of mountain slopes and ridges in rocky, infertile, inhospitable locations. **Adaptability**: Zones 3 to 7. **Landscape use**: Magnificent cool-climate birch for specimen use in large areas. Requires cool, moist, acid, well-drained soils. It is resistant to bronze birch borer. A pity that the horticultural community has not embraced it (or selected superior cultivars). **Street tree use**: Certainly feasible, but river birch and the white-bark species dominate U.S. and Canadian commerce. **In the trade**: Seldom available, unfortunately. No known cultivars.

Betula lenta

sweet birch, cherry birch, black birch

Deciduous. What is written about *B. alleghaniensis* could be dittoed for *B. lenta*. Habit is pyramidal in youth, gently spreading at maturity, averaging 40 to 50′ tall and wide under landscape conditions. Trees reach 80′ and greater in the wild. Like *B. alleghaniensis* a cool-climate species, but may exhibit greater heat tolerance. Stems emit the odor of wintergreen when bruised. The glistening gray bark is ringed with horizontal lenticels, similar to cherry (hence one of the common names). Mature bark is gray to brownish black, breaking into large, thin, irregular scaly plates. The bark does not exfoliate/peel like that of *B. alleghaniensis*.

Foliage: Autumn entices the glossy dark green leaves, to 6″ long, to don the glorious cloak of golden yellow. Fall color in the Dirr garden lasted almost 2 weeks from the first wisp of yellow to the golden coronation. Foliage has remained pristine in zone 8, showing no evidence of birch leafspot, leaf miner, or premature defoliation. **Flowers/seeds/fruits/cones**: Flowers and fruits are typical for birch. Fruiting catkins 1″ long, ½″ wide, smaller than those of *B. alleghaniensis*. Collect seed (actually winged nutlet) when the entire structure is brown. Seeds require light (sow on top of medium) or 15 to 30 days of cold-moist stratification. Seedlings grow 5′ in a single season. **Native range**: Maine to Georgia and Alabama, west to Ohio. Akin to *B. alleghaniensis*, it occurs in cool mountainous regions of the Southeast to 6,000′ elevation. **Adaptability**: Zone 3 to higher elevations of zone 8 in the Southeast. **Landscape use**: Just a beautiful birch, but allied to *B. alleghaniensis* as far as minimal landscape use. Requires similar cultural conditions and grows in similar habitats. **Street tree use**: The authors believe our native North American birches, especially this and *B. alleghaniensis*, which are borer resistant, deserve greater respect as park, campus, commercial, golf course, and street trees. **In the trade**: Subsp. *uber* (roundleaf birch), which occurs in

Betula lenta

Betula lenta

subsp. *uber*

Betula lenta

a restricted area in the floodplain of Cherry Creek, Smyth County, Virginia, is an exciting anomaly. Besides growing at lower elevations than typical *B. lenta*, it is smaller, 20 to 30(40)' high and wide, and has a shiny dark green, rounded leaf. In Georgia, all seedlings grown from subsp. *uber* have shown remarkable heat and drought tolerance. The 4-year-old tree in the Dirr garden showed no leaf necrosis (browning) or stress during the hottest summer

on record in Athens and under intense drought. It is 18' by 10', perfectly pyramidal-conical with upswept branches; its lustrous dark green leaves turn brilliant golden yellow. This tree produced viable seed in the third year. Seeds sown fresh germinated sparsely; seeds mistakenly stratified for 4 months germinated in great numbers. It is being propagated for introduction.

Betula nigra
river birch

Deciduous. Single-stem trees are quite pyramidal in youth, eventually losing their central leader and becoming spreading with an irregularly rounded crown. Multi-stem trees are upright-spreading and flaring with several irregularly rounded tops. Young plants branch heavily with slender branches giving a fine-textured appearance both when dormant and in foliage. Fast-growing to 40' by 35', a little wider for multi-stem and clumps. Bark, which exfoliates in strips of creamy tan, pinkish orange, orange-brown, and darker brown, is at its best when the trunk is 2 to 8" in diameter. As the trunk gets larger, the bark tends to darken, eventually becoming rather charcoal-colored (hence the epithet).

Foliage: Leaves are medium green above, grayish green below, ovate with an angular appearance and coarsely serrate, 1½ to 3" long, 1 to 2" wide. Fall color is a nice buttery yellow; fall colors seem to develop better in the South and West than in the upper Midwest and Northeast. **Flowers/seeds/fruits/cones**: Monoecious. Male catkins are 2 to 3" long, slender, yellow-brown, and appear just before the leaves. Female catkins are small at flowering stage but enlarge with seed, which ripens quickly and is shed in spring. **Native range**: Eastern United States from Massachusetts to southeastern Minnesota and northern Florida to eastern Texas. **Adaptability**: Broadly adaptable, both heat tolerant and relatively cold tolerant, well adapted to wet soils.

Betula nigra

Betula nigra

Betula nigra

It prefers moist acid soils and can suffer under both drought conditions and high soil pH, which causes chlorosis. Drought will cause extensive interior leaf drop. Zones (3)4 to 9. **Landscape use**: This has become the most frequently used birch in American landscapes, largely because it is, by far, the most resistant species to bronze birch borer. Like other birches, it can be susceptible to leafspot, leaf miner, and aphids, but the borer is the scourge of the genus and this species' resistance is its claim to fame. As city trees have come to be under more and more stress, bronze birch borer has expanded its range and its impact on white-bark birch species. In response, the nursery and landscape trade has made a significant shift to river birch. The development of improved cultivars has made river birch more aesthetically pleasing in the landscape. Most commonly used as a multi-stem tree or planted in clumps where its beautiful young bark is shown off to the best advantage. **Street tree use**: Not commonly used as such, a little messy, often shedding fine branches and developing a wide-spreading form. **In the trade**: Widely sold as seed-grown, especially in clumps, but improved cultivars are becoming more dominant and are recommended.

CITY SLICKER 'Whit XXV'. Selected at the western edge of the species range in Oklahoma, it has shown heat resistance and the best drought resistance of the cultivars. Its foliage is quite lustrous because of surface waxes, which impart the drought resistance. Our current favorite river birch for most uses, 35' tall, 25' wide.

DURA-HEAT 'BNMTF'. Selected in Georgia and favored in the Deep South, it is quite heat resistant. Leaves are very dark green and a little smaller than typical, giving it a very fine-textured appearance, and foliage holds well all through the late season, when others may defoliate because of stress. 40' tall, 30' wide.

FOX VALLEY 'Little King'. Introduced in the Chicago area, this is a small and densely compact river birch. Curiously, it stays quite small, almost shrubby, in Chicago, but in mild climates, the plants elongate much more and seem only slightly dwarfed. We estimate 10' by 10' in Chicago, but we observe 15 to 20' in Oregon, the Mid-Atlantic, and the Southeast.

HERITAGE 'Cully'. Discovered in a St. Louis suburb and tested and introduced by the great plantsman Earl Cully in Illinois, this selection is noted for cold hardiness and a beautiful light-colored trunk with bark that peels in large attractive layers. This cultivar has been planted in huge numbers and has become the standard of comparison among river birch. Large growing, maintaining ornamental bark quality to a greater trunk diameter than most, it is well adapted to much of the country. A proven favorite, to 40' by 40'.

CITY SLICKER

DURA-HEAT

B

DURA-HEAT

DURA-HEAT

FOX VALLEY

HERITAGE

HERITAGE IMPROVED

NORTHERN TRIBUTE

'Shiloh Splash'

HERITAGE

TECUMSEH

'Summer Cascade'

HERITAGE IMPROVED 'Cully Improved'. Of questionable origin, it was discovered as a tree at the JC Raulston Arboretum that may have been mistakenly labeled as HERITAGE. It is a worthy river birch but not very different from typical seedlings and, in our opinion, inferior to the original HERITAGE. 40' by 35'.

NORTHERN TRIBUTE 'Dickinson'. An important addition and the only true zone 3 river birch, selected in North Dakota; it has shown good adaptation to the drought and high pH soils found in that state. We hope it expands the role of the species in the Plains states and regions with high pH. 35' by 30'.

'Shiloh Splash'. A variegated birch with leaves that are creamy yellow in spring, then white along the margins and green in the center. The lack of chlorophyll slows its growth and makes it a dwarf, growing only to about 15', rounded in shape. Reversions to green foliage are frequent and need to be pruned out.

'Summer Cascade'. A lovely weeping birch, faster growing than most weeping trees, but fine-textured and quite graceful. Easily pruned into a variety of shapes, from a formal, symmetrical umbrella to an irregular artistic form, to 10 to 15' tall and wide, depending on training.

TECUMSEH COMPACT 'Studetec'. A very practical landscape plant, this semi-dwarf, spreading form matures to about half the size of the species, making it very garden-friendly, about 20' tall and 20 to 30' wide. A great form for limited space with the wonderful bark of the species.

Betula occidentalis
water birch

Deciduous. Usually multi-stemmed, a shrubby small tree growing to 15 to 20' in height and width. Fine texture, moderate growth rate. The bark can be outstanding, coppery brown to mahogany and shiny, with prominent light-colored horizontal lenticels, reminiscent of some of the Japanese cherry cultivars.

Foliage: Leaves are small, usually about 1½" long, very broadly ovate to almost round. The small leaves combined with delicate branching give this plant a very fine-textured appearance. Yellow fall color. **Flowers/seeds/fruits/cones**: Monoecious. Yellowish brown male catkins emerge just before the foliage, female catkins ripen seed in spring. **Native range**: Western North America from Alaska south to California and the Rocky Mountains and extending east into the northern Great Plains, especially in Canada. Most commonly found along watercourses in cold dry areas. **Adaptability**: It does well in irrigated landscapes in the Intermountain West. Limited use outside of its native range. Zones 4 to 7, but could extend to 2 with Canadian or Alaskan seed sources. **Landscape use**: Mostly used in native landscapes. It wants to grow as a multi-stem, so don't fight it; its fine branching looks good this way. Deserves more attention. **Street tree use**: No, too small and shrubby. **In the trade**: Sold as seed-grown, uncommon.

Betula papyrifera
paper birch

Deciduous. Pyramidal when young, eventually broadening and developing an upright oval and somewhat open habit at maturity. Moderately fast growth rate to 50' high, 35' wide. The trunk and branches tend to be thicker and sturdier than other birch species. A medium-textured tree. Showy white bark.

Foliage: Leaves are ovate, medium green and large for a birch, with a light pubescence on the underside, 2 to 4" long and two-thirds as wide. The large leaf size along with the stout branch structure imparts a more solid appearance than other birch species, which are typically fine-textured. Fall color can be excellent, usually a reliable yellow to golden. **Flowers/seeds/fruits/cones**: Monoecious. Male catkins are preformed in summer at the end of twigs, slender, about 1" long, then expand to 4" in spring, brownish at first, becoming yellow and ornamental as pollen ripens. Female catkins develop seed that ripens in late summer. **Native range**: Northern portion of North America, from Newfoundland to Alaska, Pennsylvania to Washington, often growing in river

B

Betula papyrifera

Betula papyrifera

Betula papyrifera

PRAIRIE DREAM

valleys. The widest east-west distribution of all North American birches. **Adaptability**: As its native range indicates, it is restricted by dryness and prefers cooler temperatures and cooler moist soils. In U.S. landscapes it is restricted by heat and drought stress. Zones 2 to 6 in the East, to 8 in the cool maritime Pacific Northwest. **Landscape use**: Probably the best white-bark birch for this purpose. All white-bark birch species are susceptible to bronze birch borer, but paper birch is the most resistant of these, and cultivars have been developed for increased resistance. Heat and drought stress spur

borer attack, so cultivars that are selected to be more stress resistant likewise achieve functional borer resistance. Proper site selection within a landscape is important, as trees situated in low-stress spots tend to resist borers. The slightly open, upright habit of the tree and the stout nature of its trunk and branches show off the white bark well. Best when used as a clump, but also makes a good single-stem tree. **Street tree use**: Not a good candidate because of the additional stresses of that environment. **In the trade**: Commonly sold as seed-grown, both single-stem and clump form, and

RENAISSANCE OASIS

RENAISSANCE OASIS

as improved cultivars. All in the RENAISSANCE series were selected for resistance to bronze birch borer. Don't consider them immune, just more resistant than seedlings. Moisture and low stress are still important.

PRAIRIE DREAM 'Varen'. Selected from a western North Dakota seed source, this is one tough paper birch. Pyramidal to upright oval becoming broadly oval in habit, to 40′ tall and 25′ wide, with white bark and dark green summer foliage changing golden yellow in fall. Drought and cold tolerant, zone 3.

RENAISSANCE OASIS 'Oenci'. Broadly oval in form with a more rounded crown, it develops a very nice, clean, chalky white bark at an early age. It can be used single-stem, to 50′ by 30′, or will form a broadly spreading clump. Nice golden yellow fall color.

RENAISSANCE REFLECTION 'Renci'. Upright and pyramidal, maturing to a somewhat narrow oval, 50′ by 25′, it makes an excellent single-stem tree or can be used in upright-growing clumps. The bark is slower to whiten and never looks quite as clean as RENAISSANCE OASIS.

RENAISSANCE UPRIGHT 'Uenci'. The narrowest of the RENAISSANCE series, it forms a narrow pyramid with a strong central leader and slightly glossy foliage, 50′ by 20′.

RENAISSANCE REFLECTION

Betula pendula
European white birch, silver birch

Deciduous. Quite pyramidal when young, it becomes broadly oval to irregularly upright oval with age, with gracefully weeping branch tips. All the main structural branches are strongly upright-spreading, but the smaller branches reverse this pattern, and the thinnest branch tips weep back toward the ground. It presents a fine-textured appearance. Fast-growing to 50′ tall, 30′ wide. Bark seems to be affected by sun intensity. We have noted that bark tends to be dirty white to gray in Britain, while in the U.S. Midwest and East, it is clean white. We have similarly observed decent white bark in western Oregon, but in the dry intense sunlight of arid eastern Oregon, the bark is at its best, beautifully and intensely bright white.

Foliage: Leaves dark green, deltoid, small, 1 to 3″ long, ¾ to 1½″ wide. Fall color is medium yellow, nice, but never as rich as paper birch. **Flowers/seeds/fruits/cones**: Monoecious.

Small male catkins develop in late summer on branch tips and elongate as the spring leaves emerge, becoming yellowish. Female catkins appear in spring and ripen in late summer. **Native range**: Europe, especially northern, from Britain to Russia. **Adaptability**: Formerly widely adaptable in North America, but bronze birch borer has greatly restricted its suitability. As discussed at *B. papyrifera*, cool, stress-free sites give trees the best chance. The bronze birch borer is a native North American pest and provides a good example of a non-native tree having no inherent resistance to a pest with which it did not coevolve. Zones 2 to 6 in the East, to 8 in the cool maritime Pacific Northwest. **Landscape use**: Only in areas where bronze birch borer is not present. In North America, the cool coastal regions of the Pacific Northwest have been a safe haven for this species, but recently it has been seen dying in Portland. **Street tree use**: Not recommended because of twig drop and borer susceptibility. **In the trade**: Available.

Betula pendula

Betula pendula

'Dalecarlica' ('Cutleaf'; cutleaf weeping birch). A wonderful graceful form with a very straight, slender trunk, fine branches radiating upward at neat 45° angles, a very narrow pyramidal form, and pendulous branch tips, reaching 45′ tall and 25′ wide. Bright white bark. Leaves are deeply incised (hence the common name).

'Fastigiata'. Very narrow and upright with ascending, wavy branches that frequently cross as they grow. A truly fastigiate form, 40′ tall and 15′ wide. Impressive when young, but the tree may lean or branches open up with weight over time.

PURPLE RAIN 'Monle'. Purple foliage, bright in spring and fading to dull bronze in summer, to 35′ tall and 20′ wide.

'Purpurea'. Purple foliage, bright in spring, rather dull in summer. Several purple-foliaged birch cultivars have been developed, all quite similar. 35′ by 20′.

'Youngii'. If ever a vote was held for the most graceful tree ever created, this certainly would be in the running. The trunk ascends, then arches, and fine branches weep beautifully back to the ground. It may be formally trained with a single central stem and radiating branches, forming an umbrella-like head, or it may be allowed to develop a wilder and more naturally branched arching form, with multiple curving branches producing the final weeping splay of twigs. A large multi-stem form graces the corner of Warren's garden in Oregon with curtains of fine twigs hanging to the ground, 15′ tall and 20′ wide.

B

Betula pendula

'Dalecarlica'

'Fastigiata'

187

'Purpurea'

'Youngii'

PURPLE RAIN

'Youngii'

Betula platyphylla
Asian white birch

Deciduous. Upright pyramidal when young becoming oval and somewhat open in habit when mature. Medium fine texture, moderately fast-growing to 45′ with a 30′ spread.

Foliage: Dark green, ovate leaves are 1½ to 3″ long and two-thirds as wide. Fall color is yellow but not as impressive as paper birch. **Flowers/seeds/fruits/cones**: Monoecious. Male catkins are brown at first then elongate and become yellowish in spring when pollen is present, just as the leaves emerge. Female catkins mature seed in summer. **Native range**: Japan, Korea, adjacent Manchuria. **Adaptability**: A cold hardy, adaptable species but susceptible to bronze birch borer, which can be a fatal flaw where the pest is present. Zones 4 to 7. **Landscape use**: Use caution, as this is a confused and confusing plant in the North American nursery and landscape trade. The first introduction, 'Whitespire', was welcomed as a borer-resistant cultivar of *B. platyphylla*, and the trade assumed the species was resistant to the pest. However, 'Whitespire' is now recognized as a selection of *B. populifolia* (and *B. platyphylla* remains susceptible to the borer). **Street tree use**: Not recommended. **In the trade**: Avoid seed-grown plants, unless you are sure of the source.

'Crimson Frost'. A hybrid with *B. pendula* with dark purple foliage in spring, white bark, and a narrow pyramidal form, 40′ tall and 25′ wide. Foliage goes dull bronze in late summer and the form becomes open. Largely replaced by ROYAL FROST, which we prefer.

B

Betula platyphylla

Betula platyphylla

'Crimson Frost'

DAKOTA PINNACLE 'Fargo'. Very narrow pyramidal and dense, almost columnar in form, fine-textured and an impressively tight-growing tree to 35′ by 15′. Nice white bark and very dark green foliage. Its narrowness and density make it a striking specimen. A North Dakota selection, rated zone 3.

PARKLAND PILLAR 'Jefpark'. Discovered as a sport of DAKOTA PINNACLE, it shares the same features except it has an even narrower form, truly columnar, 40′ by 10′. Good as an accent or in a row as a screen.

PRAIRIE VISION 'VerDale'. A large-growing broadly pyramidal tree reaching 50′ height, 30′ width. Selected in North Dakota for tolerance to stress, especially cold, and is rated zone 3. The original tree has shown resistance to bronze birch borer for 30 years, but this has yet to be confirmed over wider geographic areas.

ROYAL FROST 'Penci 2'. A hybrid with paper birch, its purple spring foliage becomes bronze in summer. Its early spring color is not as dark as 'Crimson Frost', but color holds better through summer and the tree seems more stress tolerant. 40′ by 25′.

DAKOTA PINNACLE

PARKLAND PILLAR

PARKLAND PILLAR

PRAIRIE VISION

Betula populifolia
gray birch

Deciduous. A smaller birch, with a narrow somewhat open pyramidal habit, becoming irregularly upright oval, narrower than most. Moderate growth rate, to 30′ high and 15′ wide. Presents a fine-textured appearance. Bark is grayish white.

Foliage: Leaves are dark green, triangular with an elongated acuminate tip, smooth and slightly glossy, 2 to 3½″ long and 1½ to 2¼″ wide. Attractive foliage. Yellow fall color. **Flowers/seeds/fruits/cones**: Male catkins are 3″ long and appear with the leaves. Female catkins mature seed in the fall. **Native range**: Northeastern North America, from Nova Scotia to eastern Ontario and south to Delaware. **Adaptability**: A tree for cooler areas, as indicated by its nativity. Best in its native range. It is happy on poor sandy and gravelly, acid soils. **Landscape use**: Used in native landscapes and for restoration purposes, it grows easily in the Northeast, where conditions are to its liking. It has been overlooked by the landscape trade because its bark is a little dull compared to *B. pendula* and other exotic species. However gray birch has better resistance to bronze birch borer than the exotic white-barked birch species. While no match for the borer resistance of *B. nigra*, it ranks with *B. papyrifera* in having moderately good field resistance in the right environment. **Street tree use**: Not recommended. **In the trade**: Sold as seed-grown, or as 'Whitespire Senior', a vegetative cultivar introduced from a birch planting in Madison, WI, where the original tree survived without damage while adjacent trees showed damage or death from bronze birch borer. Pyramidal in form with dark green leaves and yellow fall color; bark is whiter than typical of the species, not quite equal to *B. pendula* but preferable because of its improved borer resistance. Note that 'Whitespire' has been sold as seedlings of the original tree, which have questionable borer resistance, and the name 'Whitespire Senior' was established for the true tissue-cultured clone of the original. Be sure to specify the "Senior" version. 40′ by 25′.

B

ROYAL FROST

Betula populifolia

Betula populifolia

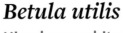

Betula utilis
Himalayan white birch

Deciduous. Upright oval becoming broadly oval, usually more full and symmetrical than most birch species. Medium texture, moderately fast growth to 45′ high and 30′ wide. The bark of the type is off-white to orange-brown, usually in the range of pinkish tan-brown; subsp. *jacquemontii* has the whitest bark of all the white-bark birches, and most commercial cultivars were derived from it.

Foliage: Leaves are broadly ovate, 2 to 4″ long, three-fourths as wide, very dark green. The density of the foliage and its rich dark color give the tree a more solid appearance than most birches. Fall color is a decent yellow. **Flowers/seeds/fruits/cones**: The brown catkins enlarge as leaves emerge in spring and become long, yellow, and ornamental as pollen is dispersed. Female catkins ripen seed in early fall. **Native range**: Himalayas from Afghanistan east through western China. Subsp. *jacquemontii* occupies the western half of the range; subsp. *utilis*, the eastern half. **Adaptability**: Like most birches, it likes cooler temperatures and moisture, suffering in hot, dry areas. Originally and wrongly believed to have some resistance to the bronze birch borer, the tree should be avoided in places where the borer is active. Quite susceptible to Japanese beetles. The best trees are seen in the low-stress, cool maritime Pacific Northwest, Britain, and northern Europe. **Landscape use**: Used equally as single-stem trees and as clumps. Cultivars of subsp.

'Whitespire Senior'

Betula utilis

'Doorenbos'

'Doorenbos'

'Jermyns'

WHITE SATIN

jacquemontii make particularly striking specimens, the dark green foliage adding additional contrast to the white bark. **Street tree use:** Not common, but in a borer-free locality, the faster-growing and more upright cultivars could be used, if soils are good. **In the trade:** In the United States, almost exclusively sold as clonally produced cultivars from tissue culture. In Europe, grafting is more common. We don't have confidence in nomenclatural differentiation of the cultivars between subsp. *utilis* and subsp. *jacquemontii*, so they are grouped together.

'Doorenbos'. The most widely grown selection and in our opinion the best, at least as a single-stem form. Stronger growing, upright oval, and very symmetrical with finely formed, slightly glossy, very dark green leaves, to 40′ by 30′. A truly beautiful tree, presenting a more formal appearance than typically found in the genus. This Dutch selection is nomenclaturally confused; it is often sold in Britain as 'Snow Queen' and in the United States as 'Jacquemontii' or simply *B. jacquemontii*. Under any name, it is the go-to cultivar.

'Grayswood Ghost'. Pyramidal to upright oval with good symmetry, moderately fast-growing, slightly glossy dark green foliage, bark brownish on young trunk becoming a very good clean white as the tree gains size, to 40′ by 30′.

'Jacquemontii'. See 'Doorenbos'

B

193

'Jermyns'. The most vigorous form we have grown, upright and loosely pyramidal becoming broadly pyramidal to 40' by 40'. Not as symmetrical as 'Doorenbos' and more open. Nice white bark but not as smooth as some of the other cultivars. It presents a more informal appearance.

'Silver Shadow' Upright-spreading, a little slower growing than other cultivars, with more informal branching but developing a symmetrical, broadly oval crown at maturity, 35' by 35'. Its form would make a good multi-stem or clump. With slower growth, bark may take a couple more years to turn white, but at maturity it becomes very smooth and pure white.

'Snow Queen'. See 'Doorenbos'

WHITE SATIN 'Madison'. Selected in Madison, WI, from a documented seed source in Yunnan of subsp. *utilis* origin. Upright pyramidal in habit, becoming oval, it has good white bark and yellow fall color, to 40' by 30'. It showed bronze birch borer resistance in its original location, but propagated plants in more stressful locations have succumbed. May be a little more resistant than other cultivars, but still use caution in borer land.

Butia capitata
pindo palm, jelly palm

Evergreen. Authors consider this among the most aesthetic of hardy palms. The habit is elegant, broad-rounded with gracefully arching fronds. Size 15 to 20(25)' high, about half this in spread. Growth is slow to moderate, with plants reported 15' high in 12 years. The red-brown trunk is thick, stout (1 to 1½' in diameter), densely covered with the remains of old leaf bases.

Foliage: Fronds light green, gray-green, bluish green, occasionally glaucous blue, typically 3 to 6' long, but extending to 10' long, with leaflets up to 2½' long, descending from the spiny midrib and forming a less-than-perfect V shape. **Flowers/seeds/fruits/cones**: Monoecious. Cream-yellow to reddish flowers in inflorescences up to 3' long. Fruit is an oblong-rounded drupe, 1″ wide, orange-yellow, edible with a sweet pineapple flavor, produced in great abundance, blanketing the ground upon abscission. **Native range**: Brazil, Uruguay, in grassland, dry woodlands, and savannas. **Adaptability**: Zones 8 to 11, but trees were largely uninjured at 11°F along coastal Georgia and are reported growing in Washington, DC, and British Columbia on the West Coast. **Landscape use**: An important landscape species in the southern tier of states into California. The species meshes

with small properties, containers, raised planters, as an accent or specimen. It is utilized in parking lot islands, which attests to heat and drought tolerances. Easy to transplant and prospers in sandy, well-drained soils; withstands maritime environments, full sun to partial shade. In shade, plants are more graceful, with larger fronds. **Street tree use**: Used as such where adapted. **In the trade**: Sold as seed-grown. It has hybridized with *Syagrus romanzoffiana* (queen palm) to produce the handsome sterile ×*Butyagrus*.

Butia capitata

Callistemon viminalis
weeping bottlebrush

Broadleaf evergreen. The bottlebrushes are eastern Australian and Tasmanian natives suited only to the warmest parts of the United States. All possess narrow-linear leaves and masses of showy stamens, both anthers and filaments, borne in bottlebrush fashion along the shoots. The weeping bottlebrush is appropriately named, with its round-headed, arching shoots. The entire tree is elegantly fine-textured and fast-growing, 20 to 25′ high and wide.

Foliage: Grass-green linear leaves, typically 2″ long (to 6″), develop a bronze tint in cool weather. **Flowers/seeds/fruits/ cones**: Bright red inflorescences, to 8″ long, 1 to 2″ wide; the thread-like stamens are the delicate and showy parts, lending the refined appearance. Flowers open most profusely in summer and sporadically throughout the year. The effect is long persistent, and a tree in full flower is quite remarkable. The growing point (meristem) does not abort after flower production but grows on beyond the inflorescence to produce further stem, leaf, and flower. Fruits are button-like capsules, adherent to the stems and persisting for several years. **Native range**: Australia. **Adaptability**: Not cold hardy, best in zones 9 to 11. **Landscape use**: As a small specimen or accent element, it is superb. Disney, Orlando, has utilized this effectively near ponds. Graceful garden element where adapted. Requires full sun and well-drained acid soil. **Street tree use**: Potential. **In the trade**: 'Boyette' has an extreme weeping habit and year-round flower production. 'Red Cascade' with pendulous branches, abundant rose-red flowers, grows 20 to 25′ high, 15′ wide.

Callistemon viminalis

Callistemon viminalis

Calocedrus decurrens
(Libocedrus decurrens)
incense cedar

Evergreen conifer. Stiffly upright, forming a very narrow pyramid, almost columnar in shape, dense and formal. One of the narrowest large conifers; it is sometimes called "pencil cedar" because it has served as the favored wood for making pencils, but the name is also fitting for its growth habit. Medium texture, moderate growth rate to 80′ tall and 15′ wide. The gray-brown to reddish brown bark presents an interesting texture, peeling in plates when young and becoming ridged and deeply fissured with age.

Foliage: Rich medium green, scale-like leaves, ¼ to ½″ long, are closely appressed, making flattened sprays of foliage. Individual pairs of opposite leaves are arranged to appear whorl-like, with the edge pair flaring at the tips, making the foliage noticeably distinct and easy to separate from other cedars. The green foliage color holds well through the winter. **Flowers/seeds/fruits/cones:** Monoecious. Yellow-green pollen cones, very small, are produced on branch tips. Female cones are ellipsoid, about 1″ length, yellow-brown to orange-brown at maturity, generally with 4 to 6 scales that flare outward with curled tips to release the ⅓″ wide seeds. **Native range:** Drier mountains of the West, from the Cascades of northern Oregon through the Siskiyou and Marble Mountains and the Sierra Nevada to northern Baja California. **Adaptability:** Adaptable, very tolerant of drought and poor soils, but needs reasonable drainage; soggy soils should be avoided. Full sun. At home all through the western United States, short of desert conditions, and will adapt to the South, East, and Europe as well. Zones 5 to 8. **Landscape use:** Perfect when grouped as a tall evergreen screen. Or use it as a fine-looking specimen in the well-maintained garden, a bright green exclamation point. Its drought tolerance and general toughness suggest use in unirrigated industrial and commercial sites. A tree that should have more use. **Street tree use:** One of the better conifers to consider for the purpose. The narrow form is appropriate, and it can be pruned up for clearance, revealing the beautiful trunk; just avoid locations where roadside drainage creates excess wetness. Often used in freeway and roadside plantings in the West, its drought adaptability making it long-lasting and maintenance-free. **In the trade:** Mostly sold as seed-grown; seedlings are fairly uniform.

'Aureavariegata'. Variegated, with alternating and contrasting sprays of completely green and completely yellow foliage, like random splashes of gold paint on the tree. Interesting and unusual for sure, but beautiful? Well, that's in the eye of the beholder. 30′ tall, 15′ wide.

'Berrima Gold'. Soft to bright yellow with a hint of orange in summer, turning tawny orange in winter. May hold more yellow in the interior than 'Maupin Glow'. 25′ tall, 12′ wide.

'Maupin Glow'. Wow, we've been impressed when we have seen this; pure yellow and so bright. A little more greenish in the interior, narrow in form, a little slower growing than the species, bronzing some in winter. Few bright yellow plants resist burning as well as this selection. 25′ tall, 10′ wide.

Calocedrus decurrens

Calocedrus decurrens

'Aureavariegata'

'Berrima Gold'

Calocedrus decurrens

Calocedrus decurrens

'Maupin Glow'

Camellia japonica

Japanese camellia

Broadleaf evergreen. Without equivocation, one of the great winter-flowering small trees or large shrubs. Somewhat stiff and stodgy in habit, usually a dense pyramidal to oval, but when meshed with finer-textured, shade-adapted evergreens, results in a pleasing composition. Some literature reports 30 to 40′ high, but we asked two prominent camellia breeders about the largest *C. japonica* they'd ever witnessed, and both mentioned nothing larger than 20 to 25′ in height, which confirms our experience. Growth is slow.

Foliage: Leaves are leathery, lustrous dark green, to 4″ long, their serrations tipped with black glands; they maintain their rich color throughout the seasons, particularly when provided dappled shade. New growth is shiny rich to bronzy green. If plants never flowered, the foliage alone is more beautiful than most broadleaf evergreens. **Flowers/seeds/fruits/cones**: Renowned for the winter-flowering effect, initiating in November, with various cultivars producing spectacular displays into April. The numerous hybrids offer increased cold tolerance and every conceivable flower color, shape, and size. Flowers are categorized as single, semi-double, anemone, peony, rose form double, and formal double. These translate to number of petals with singles least, formal doubles most. The true species flower of *C. japonica* is single, red, solitary at the end of branchlets, stalkless, 2½ to 4″ wide, with numerous yellow stamens. Flowers are borne from the leaf axils along the length of the previous season's shoot and abscise intact. Fruit is a shiny, green, eventually brown, dehiscent capsule, housing 1 to 3 brown seeds. Seeds germinate readily using a 24-hour hot water soak followed by planting. **Native range**: Japan and China. Grown and hybridized worldwide where adaptable.

Adaptability: Zones 7 to 9(10) are safe. Trees with trunks 20″ across were killed to the ground in Athens, GA, after back-to-back cold winters, with a low of -3°F. This climatic disaster triggered breeding and selection for cold tolerance. **Landscape use**: A woodland site is the ideal, one with light overhead shade and moist, well-drained, acid to neutral soil laden with organic matter. Flowers discolor after hard frosts; overhead protection (e.g., from pines) mitigates damage. Flower buds are numerous; even if injury occurs, there will be another floral wave. Plants are most often available as container-grown specimens and are extremely easy to transplant. Always supply supplemental water during extended dry periods. Scale is possibly the most serious pest. **Street tree use**: No. **In the trade**: David Parks, Camellia Forest Nursery, Chapel Hill, NC, recommends the following tree types (greater than 15′ high). 'Kumagai', 'Lady Clare', 'Professor Sargent', 'Royal Velvet', and 'Tama no Ura' are all zone 7 selections of the species. The hybrids 'High Fragrance', 'Lavender Prince II', 'Rose Twilight', 'Scarlet Temptation', and 'Tiny Princess' are equally hardy.

Camellia japonica

Camellia japonica

Camellia japonica

Carpinus betulus
hornbeam

Deciduous. Moderately slow but steady growth rate creates a strong, upright-spreading branching habit and broadly oval crown. Medium fine texture. 50′ by 40′, but this is a long-lived tree, so larger sizes can be achieved with age. Bark is cold silvery gray, sometimes smooth or sinewy-looking, very attractive.

Foliage: Leaves are dark green, ovate to oval, 2½ to 4″ long, half or slightly more as wide, and prominently veined, with the veins forming parallel ribs that create an interesting corrugated texture. Foliage tends to be clean and problem-free, except for occasional mites under hot, dry conditions. Fall color is not the brightest but can be a nice yellow. **Flowers/ seeds/fruits/cones**: Monoecious. The catkins are not particularly ornamental, males 1½″ long, females 1½ to 3″ long, forming short chains with prominent bracts in summer as seeds are formed. Fruit is a small nutlet, less than ¼″, maturing in fall. **Native range**: Europe, extending slightly into western Asia. **Adaptability**: Very adaptable, quite well suited to the urban environment. Tolerant of drought and a wide range of soil conditions; not particularly sensitive to acidity or alkalinity; prefers full sun but tolerates shade. It withstands abuse, including heavy pruning for shape. Zones 4 to 8. **Landscape use**: Widely used in city landscapes for centuries. In Europe, it is often pruned into hedges or formed into a variety of ornamental shapes. In the United States, the species is usually seen as a cultivar, most frequently 'Fastigiata', which is commonly used as a large screen or street tree. Seedling trees are variable in form but still make fine single specimens. Nothing bright and flashy about this tree, but it is solid, tough, and generally quite healthy. **Street tree use**: An excellent street tree, frequently used, especially the cultivars with narrower shapes. **In the trade**: Sold as seed-grown, but seed-grown trees tend to be quite variable and are usually used for hedging or sheared for shape. Most individual trees used in landscapes and on the streets are cultivars.

'Columnaris Nana'. An amazing little plant, but as slow as slow can be. Very dense, very compact, and upright oval, growing only a few inches per year; it might reach 10′ in 25 years if you push it.

'Cornerstone'. Although quite upright when young, this cultivar broadens to become round-headed, making a shorter and more rounded tree than 'Fastigiata', to 30′ tall and 25′ wide.

EMERALD AVENUE 'JFS-KW1CB'. A standout for its rich green foliage in the heat and dryness of late summer, this cultivar develops an upright, narrow oval habit with a dominant central leader and a shape that is ideal for street use, with better branch angles and spacing than 'Fastigiata'.

Carpinus betulus

Carpinus betulus

Carpinus betulus

'Columnaris Nana'

EMERALD AVENUE

Carpinus betulus

EMERALD AVENUE

'Fastigiata'

'Fastigiata'

'Fastigiata'

Trunk is stout and branch structure is particularly well formed. Nice yellow fall color. 40′ tall, 25′ wide.

'Fastigiata'. Long a standard for urban planting, this cultivar has proven itself for over a century. It is quite narrow and almost columnar when young, but don't be fooled: it broadens significantly with age to become distinctly egg-shaped or perhaps wider. Central leader holds many close-spaced, radiating branches, which look good at first but can become too dense if not thinned, developing included bark. Watch out for narrow crotch angles. The wood is strong, and with proper branch spacing, splitting is not a problem. Typical city size is 40′ by 30′, but a tree in the arboretum at Wageningen showed us that with over 100 years and favorable soil, it can double that size.

'Frans Fontaine'. Quite upright, a loose, moderately narrow oval. Has been promoted as being narrower than 'Fastigiata', but our observation is that, with age, it can widen. In a well-irrigated, park-like setting, this selection becomes loose and more spreading on top than 'Fastigiata'; but in a more stressful, commercial setting with slower growth, it stays a tighter, narrow oval. A nice tree and a good street form, strongly upright but more oval than columnar, 40′ by 25′.

'Globosa'. Slower growing and rounded in form, dense, with wide-spreading branches, perhaps reaching 20′ by 20′. We have observed heavy seed set on these.

'Frans Fontaine'

'Globosa'

'Pendula'

'Frans Fontaine'

'Pendula'. A weeping form, broad, full, symmetrical, dome-shaped, weeping to the ground. It can be made more interesting by pruning, opening it up to show some of its structure. More than one clone has been sold under this name, but plants in commerce now seem uniform. Slow-growing, eventually reaching 20′ tall and 30′ wide.

'Pinocchio'. Upright and pyramidal but more loosely so than 'Fastigiata', and with less density, which could be a benefit, to 40′ by 25′. It lacks the formality, but its more open form may result in a stronger structure; still, watch for narrow crotch angles.

Carpinus caroliniana

Carpinus caroliniana

American hornbeam, ironwood, musclewood

Deciduous. Upright-spreading, often low-branched, forming an irregular, broadly rounded crown to 25' high and 20' wide, usually fine branched or even twiggy, and presenting a fine-textured appearance. Shade-grown trees will be taller and more open; in full sun they become dense. Rather slow-growing. Its bark is thin, smooth, and cool gray, covering a sinewy trunk, which gives rise to its occasional but descriptive common name of musclewood.

Foliage: Dark green, ovate to long ovate, 2 to 4½" long, about half or less in width, and prominently veined. Foliage is medium green in summer; fall colors range from so-so to excellent, yellow to scarlet. Seedling fall colors will be variable; cultivars selected for fall color bring consistency. Some trees hold brown foliage into the winter; others defoliate cleanly. **Flowers/seeds/fruits/cones**: Monoecious. Male catkins are 1 to 2" long and appear as leaves emerge, much like birch, yellowish brown, bringing interest in spring. Female catkins are small at flowering time but then elongate to 2 to 4" long as seeds mature inside winged bracts. Fruits are tiny

Carpinus caroliniana

Carpinus caroliniana

FIRE KING

FIRE KING

nutlets. **Native range**: Eastern North America, from Nova Scotia to Minnesota and Florida west to Texas and south into Mexico and Central America, usually along watercourses. **Adaptability**: An adaptable tree, except for being hard to transplant. Once established, it is durable. It likes rich, moist soils but will survive in tougher urban situations, growing a little more slowly. Tolerant of acid and alkaline soils; likes partial shade but handles full sun. Zone rating will depend on seed source or cultivar, but the wide-ranging species certainly has the ability to encompass zones 3 to 9. **Landscape use**: Most often used in naturalized settings or as a small native landscape tree within its range. It presents an informal appearance in the garden and blends well with adjacent woodlands. **Street tree use**: Makes a good small street tree if upright cultivars are chosen. Seedlings are too variable in form for reliability on the street. **In the trade**: Seed-grown trees are commonly sold and excellent for naturalized situations. Several sources are working on cultivars with more predictability and consistency, so expect additional introductions.

FIRE KING 'JN Select A'. Selected from a small group of nursery trees that survived a particularly cold Wisconsin winter, when others did not. Among these cold hardy survivors, this was selected for orange-red fall color, fast growth, and a broadly oval canopy that becomes rounded. At 20 years, the original was about 20′ by 20′.

FIRESPIRE 'J. N. Upright'. Selected in Wisconsin for upright form, fall color, and good cold hardiness, this is the slowest-growing cultivar, making a smaller, finer-textured, dense oval tree. Nice red fall color in the North, but not developing in the South. At 25 years, the original tree was 15′ tall, 10′ wide.

NATIVE FLAME 'JFS-KW6'. Features a good central leader and upright growth habit, a moderately fast growth rate, darker green, neatly shaped summer leaves, and bright orange-red fall color. Leaves drop cleanly in the fall rather than holding and turning brown. Upright oval, a little narrower than the species, to 30′ tall and 20′ wide.

FIRESPIRE

NATIVE FLAME

NATIVE FLAME

PALISADE

RISING FIRE

PALISADE 'CCSQU'. A Georgia selection chosen for its strongly upward growth habit and narrow oval form, among the narrowest of cultivars, staying tight, 25 to 30′ tall, 10′ wide. As a southern selection, it is probably less cold hardy but more heat tolerant, and fall color hasn't impressed, tending toward a fair yellow.

C

RISING FIRE

Carpinus japonica

Carpinus japonica

RISING FIRE 'Uxbridge'. Quite narrow and upright, this is a northern selection, discovered in Ontario. It shows good cold hardiness and a tight, narrow oval form to 30' tall and 15' wide. It looks like an excellent small street tree. We have been very impressed by its fall color, the brightest and most consistent scarlet-red we have seen.

Carpinus japonica
Japanese hornbeam

Deciduous. Its growth habit alone makes this small tree garden-worthy. It forms a broadly rounded crown, typically low-branched, with branches that radiate like ribs on a traditional Japanese fan. Slow-growing to 20' by 20'. Fine-textured in appearance. Bark gray, smooth to finely fissured.

Foliage: Leaves are wonderful, long ovate with an acuminate tip, longer and narrower than other *Carpinus* species, 2½ to 4", and about a third as wide, neatly serrate, and very crisply veined, which gives them a highly textured look. Medium to dark green. Fall color is yellowish but nothing special. **Flowers/seeds/fruits/cones**: Monoecious. Male and female catkins appear in spring with the leaves; the females develop nutlets within the 2 to 3" long, densely packed, pendulous chains of bracts, looking much like hops. **Native range**: Japan. **Adaptability**: A little touchy, compared to the other, more adaptable species in the genus. It can be hard to transplant and establish; it seems to prefer moist soil and probably would be best in a cooler climate or with partial shade. **Landscape use**: Should be more widely planted. If you're after texture in the landscape, this is your little tree; the fan-like form is unusual and combines with the corrugated look of the heavily veined foliage. It makes a nice understory plant in the woodland, or use it along the edge of a garden, partially shaded in hotter areas or full sun in a cool climate. Zones (4)5 to 7, 8 in the cooler, coastal West. **Street tree use**: No, too wide-spreading. **In the trade**: Sold as seed-grown; seedlings are fairly consistent.

Carya aquatica

water hickory

Deciduous. A sleeper in the magical world of *Carya*, an afterthought even to those who love hickories, but recently surfaced as the one hickory that could be readily transplanted (which may sound like hooey, but it's the principal reason *Carya* species are not common in commerce). Finer-textured than most hickories; in youth gracefully pyramidal; at maturity upright-spreading, 50 to 70′ high. Moderate growth rate. Bark is light brown, splitting into plate-like scales.

Foliage: 7 to 15, usually 9 to 11, narrow, dark green leaflets, 3 to 5″ long. Fall color, often golden yellow on hickories, is usually more yellow-green on this species; however, trees at the USDA-ARS germplasm repository in Beltsville, MD, developed a most beautiful uniform birch-yellow in early November 2015. **Flowers/seeds/fruits/cones**: Monoecious. Male flowers in drooping catkins, females in few-flowered spikes developing with the leaves in April-May. Hickories are wind-pollinated and self-fertile, so another seedling is not needed to facilitate fruit development. Fruit a nut, 1 to 1½″ long, broad-oval, 4-winged along the seams, splitting the entire length or nearly so, the seed bitter. **Native range**: Reasonably common in swamps and river bottoms from Virginia to Florida, west to southern Illinois, eastern Oklahoma, and Texas. **Adaptability**: Probably the most adaptable *Carya* species and will prosper in heavy clay soils. Zones 6 to 9. **Landscape use**: Essentially unknown as a landscape element and just now gaining momentum. Select Trees, Athens, GA, trialed the species for many years, regularly spading trees around their nursery; every tree survived. They developed a protocol to root cuttings, thus assuring uniform plants. For parks, golf courses, campuses, any expansive area, water hickory would prove effective and beautiful. The National Champion is 100′ by 61′, so choose wisely when planting. **Street tree use**: Doubtful. The nuts are large and messy, so urban/suburban use is minimal. **In the trade**: Small containerized trees are readily transplanted and recommended. The authors love hickories, but the transplanting difficulties for most species preclude wholesale/extensive use.

C

Carya aquatica

Carya aquatica

Carya aquatica

Carya glabra
pignut hickory

Deciduous. Develops a regular, oval head of slender contorted branches, which are thinner, finer-textured than, for example, *C. ovata*, resulting in a finer-textured outline. Growth is moderate, 1 to 2′ per year. Trees average 50 to 60′ in height, 25 to 30′ wide. Bark is tightly woven into diamond-shaped patterns by the crisscrossing, gray-brown, rounded ridges. Young trees have a smooth bark and bear no resemblance to a hickory.

Foliage: Compound pinnate, smaller and more refined than most hickories, typically with 5 (to 7) dark green leaflets, the terminal the longest, to 7″ long, each leaflet sharply and uniformly serrated. Fall color is a rich golden yellow. Foliage remains clean through leaf drop; in the wild, this and other hickories (pecan, an exception) are less prone to foliage diseases. **Flowers/seeds/fruits/cones**: The seeds are quite astringent; the nuts subglobose, ¾ to 1¼″ wide, with 4 suture lines from base to apex. **Native range**: Relatively common over most of eastern North America, from Maine to Ontario, south to Florida and Texas, with tall tapering trunk and narrow crown in mixed association with other hardwoods. Home-based along hillsides and ridges in well-drained, dry to reasonably rich soils. **Adaptability**: Zones 4 to 9. **Landscape use**: Certainly, if native in an area, preserve and treasure. Beautiful as a lone specimen but finicky about transplanting. **Street tree use**: No. **In the trade**: Sold as seed-grown. Unfortunately, will never prove major-league commercial but worth collecting nuts and growing your own or purchasing small seedlings from a hardwood seedling nursery.

Carya glabra

Carya glabra

Carya illinoinensis

pecan

Deciduous. Contrary to the common literature's description of habit, trees develop a broad, almost flat-topped crown, composed of vase-shaped branches, with a large relatively short trunk. Outline is impressive, coarse in texture, unique in the genus. Bark is gray-brown to brown-black, becoming scaly with age. Pecans are behemoths, reaching over 100' (in the landscape, 60 to 70' high, 40 to 60' wide is common); growth is fast. Throughout the Southeast, trees literally shroud and shade older homesteads. In November, typically around Thanksgiving, casual nut gatherers with their sticks and buckets glean the tasty thin-shelled nuts under and around isolated trees. Fascinating where trees pop up, as the squirrels had no defined planting plan and willy-nilly buried nuts for future eating. Hence, seedlings almost become pestiferous. The tap root on a seedling is forever, making removal by hand-pulling a back-breaking activity.

Foliage: The 11 to 17, lustrous dark green leaflets, serrate to doubly serrate, each 4 to 7" long, are falcate in outline, curved or scythe-shaped along their length. The entire leaf stretches to 20" long, the largest of North American hickories. On occasion leaves develop a pleasing soft yellow fall color but more often abscise owing to disease (scab) or simply turn brown. **Flowers/seeds/fruits/cones**: Floral characteristics are similar to those mentioned under *C. aquatica*. We surmise that few people have noticed the flowers of this or any *Carya* species. Flowers arise from the previous year's wood, open with the leaves in April-May, are green, and blend with the emerging leaves. Fruit a fascinating oval shape, with 4 slight ridges, splitting to expose/release the ovoid-shaped, thin-shelled nut, possibly the most delectable of all temperate nut trees. Nuts can be cracked by hand, and the sweet-meated seeds eaten raw. Fascinating that the kernel (seed) develops most rapidly in September. If weather is cloudy and rainy, harvests are significantly less. **Native range**: Follows waterways from Indiana, Iowa, to Alabama, Texas, and Mexico, often in deep soils, where the tap root may reach depths of 4' and greater. Amazing that Georgia is the nation's leading producer, yet the tree has no native roots therein. **Adaptability**: Zones 5 to 9. **Landscape use**: Transplant in the dormant season, provide supplemental irrigation, and enjoy the harvest. Pecans are prized for all manner of culinary uses, as entire recipe books attest. Plain, chocolate-coated, cinnamon, roasted, brittle, in pies—writing about it makes us hungry. Authors have observed newly established orchards, each tree forlorn, with the dignity of a broom handle; in 5 to 10 years, trees are producing nuts, and 50-year-old orchards are still productive. **Street tree use**: No. **In the trade**: We asked pecan breeder and researcher Darrell Sparks, University of Georgia, for the best of the many available cultivars. For the northern homeowner, he suggests 'Green River', 'Major', 'Peruque', and 'Striking Hardy Giant'. For the southern homeowner, he suggests 'Elliott' (small nut size) first, then 'Tom' for a slightly larger nut; if a yet bigger nut is desired, then 'Gloria Grande', 'Huffman', 'Sumner', 'Tanner', and 'Whiddon'.

C

Carya illinoinensis

Carya illinoinensis

Carya ovata

shagbark hickory

Deciduous. The patriarch of *Carya* species almost inspires love at first sight, with its earthy steadfastness, a certain Yankee rigidity. Few native trees are more magnificent than a lone shagbark hickory, straddling a hillside, resplendent in fall color. Where open-grown, it develops a straight, cylindrical trunk with an oblong crown of ascending and descending branches, certainly a testament to sturdiness. Trees ascend 60 to 80′ in height, less in spread. Authors observed trees in forest (close proximity) settings, with the powerful trunks ascending 30 to 40′ before a branch was evident. Growth is slow. Easy to identify because of the bark: on young trees, it is smooth, gray-brown; on mature trees, it is muscular, shagging characteristically into elongated beef-jerky-like strips, free at the base or both ends.

Foliage: This and *C. glabra* have the fewest leaflets of North American *Carya* species, typically 5 in *C. ovata*, rarely 7, the entire leaf to 14″ long. Summer foliage is deep dark yellow-green, the cool days of autumn triggering rich yellow to golden brown tones. Foliage is quite frost resistant, with autumn colors remaining effective after 25°F. **Flowers/seeds/fruits/cones**: Flowers are similar to those of *C. aquatica* and, no doubt, seldom noticed by passersby. The nut is 4-ribbed, rounded, 1 to 2″ wide, its husk splitting at base to expose the thick angled shells. The seed is sweet and edible. Cracking the shell and extracting the seeds are adventures; for the time-pressed, shelled nuts are available on the Internet. **Native range**: Quebec to Minnesota, south to Georgia and Texas, on drier upland slopes and deep well-drained soils in lowlands and valleys. **Adaptability**: Zones 4 to 8. **Landscape use**: Deserves wholesale planting for conservation, wildlife, naturalizing, and nut production. If only...transplanting was without difficulty. Authors have purchased seedlings and transplanted to containers, with subsequent growth slow and frustrating. In an Oregon nursery trial, we planted out 12″ seedlings in field rows. Three years later, the adjacent maples and oaks were 10 to 15′ tall. The shagbark hickories were all alive and well...and still 12″ tall. Hardly a recipe for profitable nursery production! Roots are coarse, the taproot may extend 2 to 3′ deep. Fruits are messy, with both husks and nuts falling over an extended

Carya ovata

Carya ovata

Carya ovata

Carya laciniosa

C

Carya laciniosa

Carya laciniosa

period. **Street tree use**: No. **In the trade**: Available. Closest candidate for confusion is the similar *C. laciniosa* (shellbark hickory), but its leaves are composed of 7 to 9 leaflets, only occasionally straying to 5. It further differs in having pubescent orange-brown stems and oval fruit to 2″, with 4- to 6-ribbed nuts. In nature, *C. laciniosa* tends to inhabit wet bottomlands, even those covered with water for extended periods.

Castanea dentata
American chestnut

Deciduous. The story goes that a squirrel could travel from Maine to Mississippi over the canopies of American chestnut. The blight, introduced c.1904 along the East Coast, eventually spreading through the entire native range, changed that story line. The loss was tragic and should remind all who love trees that a single pathogen can alter the balance of nature. Perhaps the greatest loss was the reduction in nuts, which were used by animals and humans (the lyric "chestnuts roasting on an open fire" refers to the fruit of this species). A reasonable question to ask—what does American chestnut become with age? The authors have never observed a storied specimen, described reaching heights of 100′ with massive, wide-spreading branches, and a deep broad-rounded crown; but isolated trees have been bypassed by the disease, and for a reference point, the National Champion is 106′ by 70′ in Multnomah Co., OR. Like other climax species (oaks, maples, hickories), chestnuts are shade tolerant with the ability to regenerate from the forest floor to nobility. When hiking in the southern Appalachians, we've seen regenerated stump sprouts

Castanea dentata

Castanea dentata

Castanea dentata

Castanea hybrid, ³¹⁄₃₂nds American chestnut

that occasionally bear a few fruits; but eventually, the fungus reinfects the small trunks, and the large, irregular, elongated cankers become evident. The American Chestnut Foundation supports breeding for resistance, with back-crossed trees now as high as $^{31}/_{32}$nds American and surviving canker. The idea is to replant parts of the native range to re-establish the "species."

Foliage: Beautiful, lustrous dark green leaves, to 10″ long, with bristle-tipped, sharp serrations, turn yellow-green, yellow to golden brown in fall. Foliage is frost resistant in the range of 25 to 28°F. **Flowers/seeds/fruits/cones**: White flowers obvious in bloom time and odor. Indescribably stinky, inspiring passersby to fasten clothespins to their noses. Much later to flower than most deciduous trees, opening in June, in large-flowered spicate panicles at the ends of shoots. The porcupine-spiny fruit, 2 to 3″ wide, splits at maturity to release 2 or 3 brown-black, edible nuts. **Native range**: Difficult to pinpoint, but Maine to Michigan, south to Alabama and Mississippi is cited. **Adaptability**: Authors have observed trial blocks of American chestnut hybrids from Maine to Georgia. Zones 4 to 8. **Landscape use**: Certainly, the hope for afforestation, reforestation, and backyard gardeners resides in the hybrids. **Street tree use**: No. Fruits are terribly messy, the burs with their spiny exteriors, borderline lethal. **In the trade**: In the future, not too distant, we think. For up-to-date information, visit the American Chestnut Foundation website.

Castanea dentata

Castanea mollissima
Chinese chestnut

Deciduous. Rounded to broad-rounded, with a low-branched trunk. Resistant to the blight, but with neither the nobility nor sense of place of the American chestnut, it will always languish in the footnotes of chestnut lore. As with the American chestnut, malodorous flowers and late flowering are the prime indicator of its presence. Potential to grow 40 to 60′ high and wide, usually less under cultivation. Bark is gray-brown to brown and strongly ridged and furrowed.

Foliage: Leaves, to 8″ long, are similar to those of *C. dentata* except with pubescence on veins below and on the petiole. **Flowers/seeds/fruits/cones**: Monoecious. Flowers are white, the staminate (male) on top, and usually 3 female in a prickly involucre (modified leaf) toward the base, the entire paniculate inflorescence to 8″ long and wide, in June. The involucre splits at maturity into 2 to 4 valves, containing 1 to 4 rich chestnut-brown, ¾ to 1½″ wide edible nuts. The litter caused by the burs (spiny involucres) and actual nuts is substantial, with both falling over an extended period. **Native range**: Northern China and Korea. **Adaptability**: Zones 4 to 8. **Landscape use**: Resistant but not immune to the blight. Best reserved for out-of-the-way places, removed from human activities. Observations support the species' ability to grow in any well-drained, acid soil, ideally in full sun. This and *C. crenata* (Japanese chestnut) are useful for breeding blight resistance into American chestnuts. Orchards of these hybrids (as well as *C. mollissima*) bear fruits in 4 to 5 years. The hybrids display accelerated vigor, and trees in the Georgia test block reached 15′ in 5 years, bearing heavy quantities of nuts. **Street tree use**: No. **In the trade**: Sold as seed-grown.

Castanea mollissima

Castanea mollissima

Castanea mollissima

Castanea sativa

Spanish chestnut, European chestnut

Deciduous. Crown is oblong to rounded, massive, dense, and imposing. Splendid and noble tree as observed in Europe with a massive trunk, rich cinnamon-brown, deeply ridged and furrowed, the ridges spiraling. The bark alone is reason to grow the species. Unfortunately, it is susceptible to the blight and is restricted in the United States; authors have yet to observe a single tree here. Fast-growing, which is reflected in annual 2 to 3′ long growth extensions, even on older trees. Valuable tree for timber and is coppiced for stakes and poles.

Foliage: Leaves akin to *C. dentata*, to 9″ long, lustrous dark green, soft yellow-brown in autumn. **Flowers/seeds/fruits/cones**: Flowers are greenish white, July (England), in terminal panicles. Fruiting structures similar to *C. mollissima*, house from 1 to 5(7), ¾ to 1¼″ wide nuts. Nuts are produced

Castanea sativa

Castanea sativa

only in hot summers. **Native range**: Southern Europe, western Asia, northern Africa. **Adaptability**: Zones 5 to 9. **Landscape use**: Certainly not a tree for the residential landscape, but prominent in European parks, gardens, and estates; authors have observed magnificent specimens at Petworth House in West Sussex and Mottisfont Abbey in Hampshire, England. **Street tree use**: None in the United States. **In the trade**: 'Albo-marginata' has leaves with cream-white margins and green centers.

Catalpa bignonioides

southern catalpa

Deciduous. Broadly rounded with an irregular crown of short, crooked, thickish branches. Smaller than *C. speciosa*, landscape size approximates 30 to 40(60)′ in height, although the National Champion in Dallas is 56′ by 71′. Growth is fast. Bark as shown. Catalpas, in general, receive a bad rap for their coarse texture and messy fruit. Even most tree lovers (present company included) give them short shrift. But they do have good qualities. All are adapted to a wide variety of climates and soils, and breeding at the U.S. National Arboretum by Richard Olsen portends a great future with compact habits, pink flowers, reduced fruits.

Foliage: The large rounded leaves, to 10″ long, are medium to dark green, seldom with more than a hint of yellow-green in fall. Texture is certainly coarse, but this and its catalpa cousins are among the few large-leaf, cold hardy trees adaptable in zones 4 to 9. A larva, the catalpa sphinx, will shred the leaves to hail-damage proportions. The sphinx makes excellent fish bait, and catalpa orchards are planted for this purpose in the Southeast. The foliage holds no magic and in late summer–early fall may appear tatty and tired. **Flowers/seeds/fruits/cones**: A shout-out to the flowers, each white, with 2 ridges and rows of yellow spots and numerous purple

Catalpa bignonioides

Catalpa bignonioides

'Aurea'

'Nana'

spots on the tube and lower lobe, borne in massive 8 to 10″ wide terminal panicles in late spring–early summer. The floral display is powerful and comes at a time when most large trees are nothing but green. The ugly green icicle-like fruit, a thick-walled, to 15″ long capsule, splits (dehisces) upon drying to release fringed seeds, which in our experience germinate virtually 100% without pretreatment. Without question, seeds move ("float"), and baby catalpas (all species) occur in the strangest of places. **Native range**: Georgia, Florida, Alabama, Mississippi, possibly Louisiana. **Adaptability**: We have discovered it far from its native haunts. Zones 4 to 9. **Landscape use**: We love the species and understand the need for sterility, certainly retaining flower but producing no fruit. The fruits drop from fall to spring, seeds still attached to the interior capsule wall, so cleanup is continual. Utilize in open, sunny areas in any well-drained soil. An isolated tree or grouping of 3 to 5 is effective. **Street tree use**: Possible but limited, as cleanup is a "forever" problem. **In the trade**: Available.

'Aurea'. The most common and worthy of several cultivars. New leaves are beautiful yellow, holding color into summer, then diminishing to yellow-green. The yellow leaves really jump, particularly on cloudy days in Europe. In the Dirr garden, the foliage is green by midsummer. Flowers are similar to the species, borne on purple stalks, contrasting vividly with the yellow foliage. As an aside, seeds produce a mixture, about 1:1 of yellow:green seedlings. Estimate mature landscape dimensions 20 to 25′ high and wide.

'Nana'. Historical (1850) selection of dense, bushy rounded outline that rarely, if ever, flowers. Often grafted on a standard to produce a mushroom-headed small tree. Forms a head 10 to 15′ wide. Most often sold on the West Coast under the incorrect name of *Catalpa bungei*.

'Variegata' and 'Kohnei'. Cream-yellow and yellow-margined foliage types, respectively. Neither overwhelm, and variegation is diminished/lost in the heat. 15′ high and wide.

Catalpa ×erubescens
hybrid catalpa

Deciduous. A hybrid species (*C. ovata* × *C. bignonioides*), representing individuals primarily smaller in stature than the parents. The largest tree authors observed was 30′ by 30′ at Hillier Arboretum, Hampshire, England. Develops more fine-textured branching structure than the parents. Fast-growing.

Foliage: Leaves are broad-ovate to slightly 3-lobed, heart-shaped at base, pubescent beneath, and up to 10″ long. Beauty resides in the unfolding purple new growth, which turns to medium green with maturity. Fall color, similar to all *Catalpa* species, is yellow-green. **Flowers/seeds/fruits/cones**: The white flowers are smaller than those of *C. bignonioides*, more numerous, stained with yellow and minutely spotted with purple. Flowers open in June-July and are quite showy. Fruit is similar to the parents, perhaps intermediate in length. **Native range**: Hybrid species. **Adaptability**: Not adequately defined, but zones 5 to 8 are safe. **Landscape use**: Originated c.1874 from seed of *C. ovata* and raised by J. C. Teas, Bayville, IN, but has occurred at different times and places around the world, resulting in several named selections. **Street tree use**: Possible, but fruit litter is problematic. **In the trade**: Available and worth considering, as it and all catalpas are remarkably climate- and soil-adaptable across the continent. We believe they will become more prominent with the demise of American elm, American chestnut, and American ash species, and ongoing breeding programs at the U.S. National Arboretum portend superior cultivars. In 'Purpurea', new leaves emerge blackish purple, maturing dark green. Flowers are borne in inflorescences 12″ high and 8″ wide, the peduncle and pedicels dark purple. Size is estimated at 45′ by 40′.

C

'Purpurea'

'Purpurea'

Catalpa speciosa
northern catalpa

Deciduous. Beautiful, on occasion majestic species. Immense trees from Wiscasset, ME, to Tulsa, OK, the majority irregular in outline, some as wide as high, but most taller than wide. The National Champion in Vanderburgh, IN, is 78′ by

Catalpa speciosa

Catalpa speciosa

Catalpa speciosa

81′. Texture is coarse in winter and leaf. Fast-growing. Bark is gray-brown on old trunks, ridged and furrowed.

Foliage: The foliage, to 12″ long, medium green, is little differentiable from *C. bignonioides*. **Flowers/seeds/fruits/cones**: Each flower is 2″ long, 2″ wide, the tube bell-shaped, lobes spreading and frilled at their margins, lower with yellow spots and ridges but less freely purple-spotted than *C. bignonioides*. The upright panicles, to 8″, open in May-June, about 2 weeks earlier than *C. bignonioides*. The capsular fruit, to 20″ long, ½″ wide, contains numerous fringed seeds, those of *C. bignonioides* being tufted. Persistence, messiness, quasi-invasiveness are similar to *C. bignonioides*. **Native range**: Restricted, southern Illinois to northern Tennessee and northern Arkansas. **Adaptability**: Far ranging in adaptability from Maine to Florida, East Coast to West Coast. It has what we term "species ubiquity," meaning it will succeed in differing climates and soils (except permanently wet), acid or alkaline, and extremely hot conditions. Zones 4 to 9. **Landscape use**: Well suited to large properties, parks, golf courses, campuses, and cemeteries. For absolutely miserable soils, this would be a respectable nurse tree to stabilize and reduce erosion, increase organic matter,

HEARTLAND

HEARTLAND

Cedrus deodara

and mitigate rainwater runoff. **Street tree use**: Not unless rendered sterile. **In the trade**: Like its southern cousin, much neglected, but there is hope for improved selections. HEARTLAND 'Hiawatha 2' is a narrower introduction with more uniform branching, upright oval habit, dark green summer foliage, yellow-green fall color. Flowers and fruits are similar to the species. Estimate 50′ by 25′.

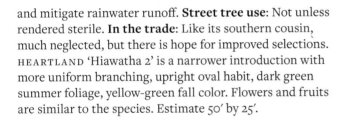

Cedrus atlantica. See *C. libani* subsp. *atlantica*

Cedrus deodara

deodar cedar

Evergreen conifer. Combines wonderfully large size with delicate elegance that never leaves it despite its mass. A pyramidal conifer with a strong central leader and branches that radiate outward horizontally, sweeping slightly down, then up, and weeping at the tips. Very full and fluffy and appearance when young, more broadly pyramidal, even rounded to flat-topped with age, graceful, and artistic. Moderately fine texture, fast-growing to 70′ high, 40′ wide in favorable sites. Bark brownish gray, furrowed and checked, quite attractive on mature trees.

Foliage: The longest needles of the genus, 1 to 2″, borne singly on current season's growth. Soft bluish green year-round. **Flowers/seeds/fruits/cones**: Monoecious. Male cones are upright, 2″ long, and shed prodigious clouds of yellow pollen in the fall. Female cones are upright, quite large, thick, looking like little barrels, averaging 4″ long by 2½″ wide, impressive in appearance and ornamental value, even if a bit messy when shed at maturity. **Native range**: Western Himalayas in Afghanistan and northern Pakistan. **Adaptability**: Narrow climatic adaptability, preferring a cool but mild and moist climate. At its best in the cool maritime Pacific Northwest, where older park and campus trees can easily exceed 100′ height, and in the similar climate of northwestern Europe. In the eastern United States, summer heat stress reduces its size, and cold winters limit areas of adaptability; but it does very well in the Southeast, where it matures to a more rounded 60′ by 60′. For seedlings, figure zones 7 and 8, 9 in the maritime West Coast. Cultivars selected for cold hardiness extend the range into zone 6 and even 5. **Landscape use**: An outstanding large and

Cedrus deodara

'Albospica'

Cedrus deodara

graceful conifer, reaching impressive size. Give it plenty of room. With lower branches intact, it fills landscape space and presents a swath of handsome foliage at eye level; prune them away, and the broad-spreading canopy can be lovely overhead. Despite its potentially massive size, it is always soft in appearance because of its nodding tips. Great for parks, roadsides, campuses, or larger gardens. The listed cultivars generally have slower growth rates and lesser mature sizes than seed-grown trees and are more suitable for most landscape settings. **Street tree use**: Not appropriate, given the broad spread of its lower branches; however, it can be wonderful for roadside plantings were space allows. **In the trade**: Seed-grown trees are commonly sold and are reasonably uniform. Many ornamental cultivars have been developed, variously emphasizing foliage color, increased cold hardiness, or form. All tend to be smaller than the species. Only tree-sized cultivars are listed; many fine dwarfs also exist.

'Albospica'. Silvery white new growth contrasts nicely with the dark green older foliage, a white-on-green appearance. It is especially nice up close in spring. As the tree matures and produces less new growth, the white become less noticeable. Less cold hardy, grows to 30′ tall, 20′ wide.

'Aurea'

'Aurea'. Rich golden yellow new growth in spring, fading to cream-yellow tips on soft green inner foliage later in the season. A little smaller than the species at 40′ tall and 25′ wide, becoming flattened at the top, a full form with softly nodding branch tips. A little more tender than the species, definitely needs a cool mild climate.

'Bracken's Best Cedar'

'Devinely Blue'

'Bush's Electra'

'Devinely Blue'

'Bill's Blue'. Upright pyramidal, a little stiffer than most but still graceful, blue-green needles, to 40 to 50' tall, 25' wide.

'Blue Ice'. Pyramidal with silvery blue foliage, moderately dense but still soft in appearance. Moderate growth, slightly compact, 40' tall, 20' wide.

Cedrus deodara, CONTINUED

'Gold Cone'

'Karl Fuchs'

'Bracken's Best Cedar' ('BBC'). More compact in appearance than the species because it is full and dense, but reaching nearly full size. Graceful with weeping branch tips and bluish green foliage, 50 to 60′ tall, 25′ wide.

'Bush's Electra' ('Electra Blue'). Slightly compact, narrow, and more upright than the species, with branches that curve upward rather than droop. Wonderful bright blue foliage, grew well in the Dirr garden. Can be used in narrower spaces than the species, probably to 40′ tall, 15′ wide.

'Crystal Falls'. Broadly and erratically pyramidal, interesting and unpredictable, shorter than the species, with silvery blue-green foliage and an open form with distinctly weeping branches. 30′ by 30′.

'Devinely Blue'. A small graceful selection with the bluest foliage we have seen. It forms a soft pyramid with down-sweeping branches. Often sprawling in form. Sometimes listed as 6′ maturity, but we have seen nicely grown 8 to 10′

pyramids in a nursery, so we think it has potential to make 15′ with semi-pendulous branches. Named for Bill Devine.

'Eisregen'. A cold hardy selection, zone 5. Upright, slightly stiff and open when young becoming artistically irregular with weeping tips when older, creating a naturalistic alpine look, to 30′ tall, 15′ wide. A beautiful plant; blue-green foliage is especially nice. One of our favorites, it fits a smaller garden and adds blue foliage and mountain character.

'Gold Cone'. Bright golden new growth in spring, the color holds well all year without fading, while the interior foliage is more blue-green. Nicely pyramidal and upright with a narrower shape, to 30′ tall and 15′ wide, and brighter golden foliage through the season than 'Aurea'. Performs well in the South.

'Karl Fuchs'. Cold hardy selection, zone 6 at least, possibly zone 5. Stiffer form, quite upright, a bit thin and open, becoming graceful with age. Striking blue needles, moderate

222

MYSTIC ICE

'Sander's Blue'

MYSTIC ICE

'Sander's Blue'

growth rate, it matures a little smaller and narrower than the species, around 40′ tall, 20′ wide. A specimen in the Dirr garden was the neighbor's favorite plant. This became evident when a giant *Quercus nigra* plummeted to earth,

making a direct hit on the 'Karl Fuchs'. After cleanup, Dirr was continually asked, "When will you replant that blue evergreen?" Please note, no one knew the identity!

'Shalimar'

'Silver Mist'

'Kashmir'. Blue-green needles, graceful pyramidal form, slightly pendulous branches, moderately improved cold hardiness, we've seen it given both zone 6 and zone 7 ratings.

'Mountain Aire'. Slightly narrow, fast-growing, upright with somewhat layered growth, stiff straight leader but branches with weeping tips, green foliage, 50 to 60′ tall, 20 to 30′ wide.

MYSTIC ICE 'CDMTF1'. Narrowly pyramidal with stiffly radiating, rather short and densely spaced branches. Foliage is bluish gray-green. Makes a prominent accent plant, 40′ tall, 15 to 20′ wide.

'Sander's Blue' ('Blue Velvet'). Distinctly blue spring foliage, becoming more blue-gray later in the season. Form is more open than the species, branches stiffer yet with weeping tips. Beautiful foliage, but form is sometimes a little awkward, not as full as other cultivars, growing to 40′ by 20′. Performs well in the South.

'Shalimar'. Upright pyramidal, moderately bluish needles, form tends to be more open and irregular than most and more spreading, slightly erratic but that makes it interesting. Selected for greater hardiness than typical of the species, usually rated to zone 6.

'Silver Mist'. A broad and bushy pyramid, slow-growing, with silvery white new growth. Short and fat, it will take a long time to get to 10 to 15′ in both height and spread.

'Snow Sprite'. A wonderful little tree, the shoots come out ivory-white in spring, turn creamy yellow in summer, then bluish in the fall. It is especially nice against a dark background. Small and compact, forming a garden-sized, irregularly mounded pyramid, eventually 15′ tall, 10′ wide.

STERLING FROST 'Grester'. Upright, rather stiffly so for *C. deodara*, with blue-green needles. Pyramidal to 40 to 50′ tall, 20 to 30′ wide.

'Snow Sprite'

STERLING FROST

WYNDIMERE 'CDMTF2'. Broadly pyramidal and full in form with branches that weep at the tips. It presents a soft and graceful appearance, bluish gray-green foliage, 40′ tall, 30′ wide.

Cedrus libani

cedar of Lebanon

Evergreen conifer. Young trees are narrowly pyramidal and strongly upright with a dominant central leader, or sometimes multi-trunked from near the base. As they age they develop broad-spreading, layered-looking tops with many heavy limbs which nearly equal the leader in height, eventually 60′ high and spreading at least as wide. Fine-textured and moderately fast-growing. Bark gray and fissured, sometimes separating into small blocky plates.

Foliage: Stiff, bright rich green needles, shorter than those of *C. deodara*, ¾ to 1½″ long, borne singly on current season's shoots. **Flowers/seeds/fruits/cones**: Monoecious. Male cones are erect, 2″ tall, shedding yellow pollen in the fall. Female cones develop into barrel-shaped cones, 4″ tall and 2½″ wide. **Native range**: Turkey, Syria, Lebanon. **Adaptability**: Very drought tolerant, but also does well in moist but not soggy soil, preferring good drainage. Tolerant of both acid soils and some alkalinity. The most cold hardy species in the genus. Adapted to a Mediterranean climate, it does well

C

Cedrus libani

Cedrus libani

'Glauca Pendula'

subsp. *stenocoma*

in zones 5 to 9 near the ocean on the West Coast but more limited, zones 5 to 7, in the East. **Landscape use**: An imposing tree in the landscape because of its unusually broad spread and the strength of its heavy trunks and branches. A large tree is impressive from a distance, even more so from underneath its canopy. The seed-grown species is best left to campuses and large estates; narrower cultivars are suitable for home gardens. **Street tree use**: No, too wide-spreading but appropriate for broad roadsides and interchanges. **In the trade**: Sold as seed-grown as well as grafted cultivars.

'Glauca Pendula'. A tall slender tree with an ascending single trunk, vertical at first and then arching, generally with short pendulous branches hanging close to the trunk but also developing occasional long, wild, and more upright branches that create an interesting irregular form, 50′ tall and 25′ wide. Green with a slight bluish tint.

subsp. *stenocoma*. Frequently sold because of increased cold hardiness, to zone 5, a moderately narrow pyramid that tends to stay single-trunked and maintains its pyramidal shape at maturity, not broadening on top like typical trees of the species, dark green needles, 50′ by 25′.

Cedrus libani subsp. *atlantica*
(*C. atlantica*)
Atlas cedar

Evergreen conifer. Magnificent, noble needle evergreen requiring time and space to attain its artistic traits. In youth, somewhat open, stiff, with a central leader and pyramidal outline. With age, becoming flat-topped, dense, with horizontally spreading branches that sweep the ground. Reaches 40 to 60′ high, 30 to 40′ wide and greater. Moderate growth rate. Trunks become massive, gray-brown, with a rough texture, often visible only when walking under the canopy.

Foliage: Needles are 1″ long, dark green to the most delicate powder-blue. Needles are borne singly on the current season's shoots and in clusters of 20 to 35(45) on the short shoots of older branches. **Flowers/seeds/fruits/cones**: Monoecious. The 2 to 3″ long, ½″ wide male cones shed clouds of yellow pollen in autumn. The glaucous green to purple female (seed) cones, 2 to 4″ long, 2″ wide, mature in 2 years, turning rich tan-brown, with cone scales abscising through fall-winter. **Native range**: Atlas Mountains of Algeria and Morocco. **Adaptability**: From Boston to Atlanta, to the Pacific Ocean, this and its cultivars will prosper, zones 6 to 8, 9 on the West Coast. Through many years of observation, cold hardiness equates with -5 to -10°F; plants were eliminated at -20°F. **Landscape use**: Like its *Cedrus* brethren, a cherished and revered needle evergreen for large estates, campuses, parks, golf courses, commercial grounds. Performs admirably in well-drained, acid, clay-based soils in full sun. Best to move as container or balled-and-burlapped material. Consider tip pruning young plants to allow them to gain density. Without question, a superb accent and focal point in any suitable landscape. Memorable trees dot the English countryside, no more so than at Bodnant Gardens, Wales, where ancient trees by the water lily garden speak to its inherent nobility. **Street tree use**: Too large, but fastigiate clones might have a place. **In the trade**: Difficult to separate from the type, but to be sure, most of the bluest needle forms in cultivation have arisen within the genetic plasticity of this subspecies. Glauca Group is the umbrella for blue-needled cultivars, which are more common in cultivation than green-needled types.

C

'Aurea'

'Glauca'

Cedrus libani

Cedrus libani subsp. *atlantica*

'Glauca'

'Glauca Fastigiata'

'Aurea'. Graceful, golden yellow needle form reaching 20 to 40′ by 20 to 30′. The yellow-gold needles become green in the heat of summer, remaining so until the new spring flush.

'Glauca'. The commonly sold blue atlas cedar, a stable clone. Stiffly pyramidal with a central leader, it broadens to a slightly broader pyramid with a rounded top with age. Striking blue needles, 50′ tall, 30′ wide.

'Glauca Fastigiata'. Columnar-pyramidal, densely branched form with pretty blue-green needles, growing 40 to 50′ by 15 to 20′.

'Glauca Pendula'. A pendulous type, often staked and weeping uniformly, or left to wander into a more wild form; grows 15 to 20′ high and wide.

'Horstmann'. A blue form, similar to 'Glauca' but slower growing and more compact in form, to 25′ tall, 15′ wide.

'Glauca Pendula'

Celtis laevigata

sugarberry, sugar hackberry

Deciduous. Upright-spreading, forming an oval crown that becomes rounded to vase-shaped with age. Branching dense and a bit twiggy. Form resembles an American elm but not as graceful, and on a slightly smaller scale. Moderately fast-growing to 50′ height and 40′ spread, presenting a medium texture. Bark is blue-gray and beech-like when young, becoming curiously corky-warty on some trees, while others stay relatively smooth.

Foliage: Leaves are long ovate with a long acuminate tip, 2 to 4″ long and about half as wide. Leaf base is variable from asymmetrically acute to oblique. Leaf appearance is quite variable, from dark green, glabrous, and rather smooth and glossy to textured and lightly pubescent. Susceptible to nipple gall, but less so than *C. occidentalis*. **Flowers/seeds/fruits/cones**: Polygamo-monoecious, having male, female, and perfect flowers. Flowers inconspicuous, very small, greenish yellow, appearing in axils with the leaves. The fruit is a drupe, rounded, about ⅜″, turning orange-red to purplish or blue-black, each containing a single stony seed, enjoyed by birds. **Native range**: Southeastern Virginia to Missouri and Florida to central Texas. Local populations are variable and have sometimes been classified as subspecies; hybridization with *C. occidentalis* is common in Arkansas and Missouri, with broad introgression creating intermediate types. **Adaptability**: Usually a tree of moist acid bottomlands, even swamps, but its range in the West extends into areas of higher pH and drier soils. Zones 5 to 9. **Landscape use**: An interesting tree, which we believe has more

C

Celtis laevigata

Celtis laevigata

Celtis laevigata

landscape potential hidden in its genome. Used in the South as park or residential shade tree, mostly from local seed sources. Not commonly used in the larger commercial trade because seedling variability among various provenances creates unpredictability of form, appearance, and function. Its resistance to witch's brooms is an advantage over common hackberry. **Street tree use**: Where well adapted in the South, it can make a good large street tree, and its elm-like form is suitable. Susceptibility to damage from ice and snow suggests caution farther north. **In the trade**: Sold as seedlings, but know your source and check the appearance of trees. Sugarberry's variability and hybridization with common hackberry presents opportunities for breeders, and northern provenances especially hold potential. The few cultivars have been difficult to propagate thus far.

'All Seasons'. Selected in Illinois with cold hardiness to zone 5 and a full oval crown with heavier branching that is less twiggy than the species, 50′ by 40′. Smooth gray bark when young, developing wartiness with age.

'Magnifica'. A hybrid with *C. occidentalis*, described under that species.

ULTRA 'Ulzam'. Introduced as a common hackberry, we think its appearance is closer to a sugarberry, having the smooth, blue-gray young bark, dark green leaves, and spreading twiggy branches of this species when young. Possibly a hybrid, but we'd use it where sugarberry is adapted until proven. It matures to a rounded shape, 50′ by 45′.

Celtis occidentalis
common hackberry

Deciduous. Upright-spreading, becoming somewhat vase-shaped, developing a rounded crown, like a smaller, less refined version of an American elm. 60′ high, 50′ wide. Moderately fast growth rate, medium coarse in texture. Bark is light brown and rough on young trees, differentiating it from the young smooth gray bark of *C. laevigata*. Bark becomes darker gray-brown and corky-rough with age.

Foliage: Wins no beauty contest when viewed up close, but quite acceptable from a distance. Leaves are light to medium green, ovate to long ovate, serrate, dull-textured, rugose, 2 to 4½″ long and one-half to two-thirds as wide. Yellow fall color. **Flowers/seeds/fruits/cones**: Polygamo-monoecious. Flowers are very small and insignificant, appearing with the leaves in spring. Fruit, a ⅜″ orange to dark purple drupe, ripens in the fall. **Native range**: Southern Quebec to southern Manitoba, and Georgia to Oklahoma, but primarily a tree of the Great Plains. **Adaptability**: One word always comes to mind with hackberry: tough. Cold hardy, heat tolerant, adapted to high pH soils, and tolerant of flooding.

Celtis occidentalis

Celtis occidentalis

Celtis occidentalis

230

Celtis occidentalis

'Chicagoland'

Despite its toughness, it can be tricky to transplant, so do so carefully. An excellent tree for the rigors of the Midwest and Plains. Seems happier in a challenging climate than in a mild one. Zones 3 to 9. **Landscape use:** Never the first choice for an ornamental garden in a mild climate, but a utilitarian green tree that will survive harsh climates and questionable sites. We are not encouraging mistreatment, but this tree can take parking lots, tree pits, construction rubble, and road salts. Nipple gall and witch's broom may detract from appearance. Young trees are occasionally a little ungainly, but with age and maturity they become quite handsome, bordering on majestic. Use for parks, commercial sites, and roomy backyards. **Street tree use:** A good large street tree, especially within its native range. **In the trade:** Mostly sold as seed-grown. Cultivars provide more reliable forms, but propagation difficulties limit their availability.

'Chicagoland'. Quite vigorous, more so than the species, and also more upright. Central leader is strong and form is good; although leggy when young, it becomes a nice upright oval and then broadens, 50′ tall and 35′ wide.

'Delta'. A cold hardy selection from Manitoba. Its form is upright-spreading, roughly elm-like, with a rounded crown, 45′ by 40′.

'Magnifica'. More refined-looking than *C. occidentalis*, this hybrid has a good growth rate and improved insect resistance, apparently picked up from its second parent, *C. laevigata*. Develops a broadly oval to vase-shaped crown. A fine choice for city use, and a good street tree, to 50′ by 40′.

'Prairie Pride'. Selected for thicker, darker green foliage, the leaves are also longer than typical. It develops a rounded crown that is a little more compact than the species, 40′ by 40′.

PRAIRIE SENTINEL 'JFS-KSU1'. A fastigiate form that fills the role of a tightly columnar tree for narrow street use in tough climates. Discovered in the hot, dry plains of western Kansas, its adaptability to the difficult prairie climate makes it well suited to the challenges of city streets. Truly tight and narrow in form, to 45′ high and 12′ wide.

'Prairie Pride'

Celtis sinensis
Chinese hackberry, Japanese hackberry

Deciduous. Upright-spreading, eventually vase-shaped, similar to common hackberry but smaller in scale, to 40′ high and 35′ wide. Moderate growth rate. Bark is attractive, gray, smooth at first, becoming roughened to corky with age.

Foliage: Dark green, thick and glossy, 2 to 4″ long and half or more as wide, serrate, the most attractive foliage in the genus. Leaves are ovate with an acuminate tip. Leaf base is asymmetrically acute or rounded to oblique. Yellowish green in the fall. **Flowers/seeds/fruits/cones**: Flowers in the early spring, greenish and small, inconspicuous. Fruit, a drupe, ⅜″, orange-red, with a single stony seed. **Native range**: Korea, China, Japan, Taiwan. **Adaptability:** Adapted to a warm climate, especially with moist soils, but landscape plants will survive moderate drought. Not nearly as cold hardy as the other *Celtis* species listed here, zones 7 to 9. **Landscape use**: It makes a handsome shade tree, its foliage being especially deep green and lustrous, a bit like a small elm with especially nice leaves. Used successfully in California and Florida, but caution: it has become invasive in riparian areas of Australia. **Street tree use**: Has been used

PRAIRIE SENTINEL

Celtis sinensis

nicely as such in California; where the climate is right, it is appropriate. **In the trade**: Sold as seed-grown, variable in form. 'Green Cascade' is a graceful weeper with the glossy dark green foliage of the species and a smooth gray-barked trunk. Stake to the height you want, then allow to weep. Tends to be sculpturally irregular in its weeping form, 15′ tall and 20′ wide.

Celtis sinensis

'Green Cascade'

'Green Cascade'

Cercidiphyllum japonicum
katsura

Deciduous. Pyramidal when young, becoming oval to broadly oval or rounded with branches that first ascend and then flare outward in graceful arches. Elegant in form at all ages; presents a medium fine texture. Typically 50′ high and 40′ wide, but under ideal conditions it can grow much larger. Moderately fast-growing. Bark smooth and gray-green when young, soon becoming rough, gray, and shaggy.

Foliage: Lovely, leaves opposite, broadly heart-shaped with a wavy, crenate margin, 2 to 4″ in length and width. Soft green, often with a bronze tint in spring, and almost always a bluish tint in summer. The fall foliage carries the scent of burnt sugar and brings back those childhood memories of the smell of cotton candy machines. Fall colors come in beautiful pastels, mixing yellows and pinkish tints of apricot-orange, never blazingly bright but always soft, with elegant beauty. **Flowers/seeds/fruits/cones**: Dioecious, flowering in spring before the leaves. The purple-tinted flowers are small and of minor landscape significance but are quite interesting up close. Seed pods look like cute miniature green bananas, ¾″ long, in clusters maturing in fall. **Native range**: China, Japan. **Adaptability**: Likes moderate conditions with even moisture. Not too cold, not too hot, and definitely not too dry, but it's also not a tree for soggy soil. Foliage may be damaged by spring frosts. Subject to sunscald when young, so avoid low humidity, windy dry sites, and concrete heat reflection on the lower trunk. Tolerant of elevated pH as well as acidic soil. Individual

C

Cercidiphyllum japonicum

233

Cercidiphyllum japonicum

Cercidiphyllum japonicum

'Amazing Grace'

'Amazing Grace'

Cercidiphyllum japonicum

trees are sometimes much tougher, as specimens are happily growing in Colorado, Maine, North Dakota, and other difficult climates. Zones 4 to 8. **Landscape use:** An absolute favorite of the authors, it presents a gentle and understated elegance yet can grow to noble proportions. Beautiful both young and old and when viewed both near and far. Perfect in parks and excellent for commercial plantings and residential gardens where size allows. Its foliage presents a soft appearance both by its heart-shaped form and fall colors, which are never bold yet always strikingly beautiful. But be sure to give this tree special attention in siting, as it wants good soil and moisture. **Street tree use:** Generally not recommended because of its susceptibility to sunscald and drought, but in cooler climates it can work well. We have seen successful street tree plantings in Seattle and Portland. **In the trade:** Most frequently sold as seed-grown. We hope to see tougher cultivars; some have been selected for unusual form and leaf color.

'Amazing Grace'. A graceful weeper with an arching growth habit, quickly forming a mound, wider than tall. In Oregon nursery trials, it was faster growing than other weepers at a young age. Found by Theodore Klein in the small nursery of Jesse Elliott in Indiana, it was distributed years before it received the name. Trees in the trade as 'Pendulum' are sometimes the same clone. A good specimen that will need ample room for spread, to 15′ by 25′.

'Boyd's Dwarf'. Smaller but similar in form to the species. Loosely oval, growing to 20′ by 20′, fall color yellow to pinkish orange.

CLAIM JUMPER 'HSI1'. Yellow foliage selection. Leaves are soft yellow in spring, and new growth holds this color through summer. Inner foliage may green up, and tips bleach whitish and can burn, so avoid hot, dry sites. From a distance it displays a soft yellow color through the season. Newly introduced, probably to 20′ by 20′.

HANNAH'S HEART 'Biringer'. Narrow and tightly upright, more compact and slightly slower growing than the species, nice density, to 30′ by 20′. Very appealing in appearance with brighter green foliage than usually seen in the species.

'Heronswood Globe'. Compact, globe-shaped, growing to 15′ in height and spread, best produced as a top graft. Leaves

CLAIM JUMPER

HANNAH'S HEART

'Morioka Weeping'

'Morioka Weeping'

are smaller than the species to match the scale of this plant, fine-textured and cute.

'Morioka Weeping'. Upright-growing and ascending, yet always weeping. This graceful plant is the most popular of the weeping katsuras, reaching greater heights than the others and creating a specimen that is taller than wide, to 35′ by 25′. Multiple branches may ascend, trunk-like, each producing a weeping section of the tree. Always artistic in form, fountain-like from above. Formerly classified as *C. magnificum* 'Pendulum', but DNA analysis has placed it in *C. japonicum*.

f. *pendulum* ('Pendulum'). For 400 years, weeping forms have been cultivated in Japan, where they are known as shidare-katsura. Trees sold under this name are shorter in stature, more mounded in form, with smaller leaves and finer-textured branching than 'Morioka Weeping'. To 15′ tall and 20 to 25′ wide.

'Rotfuchs' ('Red Fox'). Deep purple spring foliage is truly eye-catching. Upright-growing, slender and rather weak-stemmed, slowly producing a pyramidal tree. Leaves are smaller than the species, and the tree is less dense. In

f. *pendulum*

f. *pendulum*

'Rotfuchs'

'Rotfuchs'

'Strawberry'

summer, the green chlorophyll pigment increases, and the foliage turns more bronze in color, often looking dull and tired. An exciting tree when you first see it, especially in spring, but it may disappoint as it ages. Probably will attain half the size of the species, 25 to 30′ tall and 15′ wide.

'Strawberry'. Selected for red-tinted spring foliage, it is similar in form to the species, growing to a full-sized oval tree, 50′ by 40′. The soft red new growth is attractive in spring, then goes green in summer, followed by a nice apricot-orange fall display.

'Tidal Wave'

Cercis canadensis

'Tidal Wave'. Ascending but never really upright, it spreads, arches, and weeps. A little open at first, it eventually seems to fit between 'Amazing Grace' and 'Morioka Weeping' in form. 15 to 20′ tall, 30′ wide is probably typical, but the original tree was about 25′ by 50′ at 27 years of age.

Cercis canadensis

eastern redbud, Canadian redbud

Deciduous. Without equivocation, one of the best small flowering native trees, truly a harbinger of spring. Trunk divided close to ground, branches spreading, forming a flat-topped to rounded crown, (15)20 to 30′ high and wide. Medium growth rate in first 5 to 10 years, slowing with maturity. Bark is black to brownish black with orangish inner coloration.

Cercis canadensis

Foliage: Leaves heart-shaped, 3 to 5″ wide, with 5 to 9 palmate veins, radiating from the cordate base; emerging leaves suffused red-purple, maturing dark green, occasionally rich yellow in autumn. **Flowers/seeds/fruits/ cones**: Flower rosy pink to red-purple, before leaves, lingering after leaf emergence, long-lasting, frost tolerant to 20 to 25°F. Bee activity is intense when trees are in flower (March–early April in zone 8; month later in Boston); the trees appear to be humming and vibrating from their activities. Fruits (pods), 3″ long, ½″ wide, produced in abundance, brownish black, persisting, rather raggedy, into winter, which a segment of gardeners finds objectionable. **Native range**: Massachusetts to Florida, west to Nebraska, Oklahoma, Texas, and Mexico. **Adaptability**: Tolerant of many soil types as long as well drained, acid to neutral; full sun for maximum flowering; canker can be a problem. Zones (4)5 to 9. **Landscape use**: The authors

Cercis canadensis

are apostolic advocates for increased use, as single specimen, grouping, woodland edges, color (focal point) accent. Every city, town, municipality, and garden should enthusiastically embrace redbuds; they add seasonal ornamental attributes to landscapes, rewarding with expressive and much-anticipated spring flowers, elegant and artistic

Cercis canadensis

'Appalachian Red'

'Pink Pom Poms'

branching structure, clean dark summer foliage, and respectable yellow fall color. **Street tree use**: Serviceable but low-branched, needs pruning for clearance. **In the trade**: Available and spectacular new cultivars (via selection in the wild and controlled breeding) have expanded the palette. They are presented by feature; if not otherwise noted, plants share the species habit and flowers are some shade of pink, rose, or lavender.

Green foliage

'Appalachian Red'. Abundant deep red-purple buds and richly pigmented deep rose-pink flowers.

'Pink Pom Poms'. A major advancement with deep rose-pink double flowers and sterility (no fruits). The foliage is thickish, leathery, lustrous dark green, owing to the subsp. *texensis* 'Oklahoma' parent. Beautiful in the Dirr garden.

C

'Royal White'

'Tennessee Pink'

subsp. *texensis* 'Oklahoma'

'Appalachian Red'

'Royal White'. The most cold hardy white-flowered form with glistening milk-white flowers.

'Tennessee Pink'. Vigorous, reliable, with pure pink flowers. A proven doer in the Dirr garden.

subsp. *texensis* 'Oklahoma'. Smaller (15′) than the species with lustrous undulating leathery dark green leaves, deep rose-purple flowers, and zone 6 hardiness. Possibly more heat and drought tolerant, derived as it is from an Oklahoma seed source.

Purple foliage

BLACK PEARL 'JN16'. Dark purple foliage holds color well in the heat, more so than 'Forest Pansy'. Compact growth with shorter internodes, we expect a rounded form and a smaller mature size, probably 15 to 20′ tall and wide.

BURGUNDY HEARTS 'Greswan'. A relatively new introduction from Greenleaf Nursery, OK, with maroon foliage.

'Forest Pansy'. The first (1947) pigmented foliage introduction and still the most popular. Shimmering red-purple (maroon) foliage fades in the heat of summer in Georgia, but is vibrant in Oregon and cooler climates. It is an important source of genes for the modern purple-leaf introductions. Less cold hardy than the species, considered zone 6.

'Merlot'. More vigorous with shinier foliage than 'Forest Pansy', one of its parents (the other is subsp. *texensis* 'Texas

'Forest Pansy'

BLACK PEARL

'Forest Pansy'

'Forest Pansy'

'Merlot'

White'). In the Dirr garden, it did not impress to the degree of 'Forest Pansy'. In Oregon, it looks better in early summer with its glossier foliage, but 'Forest Pansy' wins out in the end by maintaining its purple color with less fading in the summer sun.

Variegated foliage

These grow quite contentedly in the Dirr garden, but in Oregon's sunny, low-humidity summer, all variegated forms, including 'Silver Cloud', burn badly.

'Alley Cat'. Discovered in an alley in Louisville, KY, by Alan Bush. Produces its variegated foliage when grown from seed. Considered by some experts to be better than 'Floating Clouds', which has a similar variegation pattern.

'Floating Clouds'. Leaves emerge green, become white and green spotted/streaked and hold the pattern through summer. Vigorous grower, has quadrupled in size compared

'Alley Cat'

'Floating Clouds'

'Silver Cloud'

'Silver Cloud'

'Hearts of Gold'

to THE RISING SUN in 6 years. Will be wider than tall at maturity so plan accordingly (Dirr did not). Seeds produce true-to-type seedlings, i.e., all with green-white leaves.

Yellow to gold foliage
Cultivars with yellow foliage are slower growing than the green, purple, and variegated leaf types, based on observations in the Southeast. Both listed here grow in the Dirr garden and are at their best for foliage color from April to June; in Oregon, the yellow foliage color stays in the cooler summer weather, but perhaps because of less chlorophyll, they are disappointingly weak growers.

'Hearts of Gold'. Uniform yellow foliage turns green in heat.

THE RISING SUN 'JN2'. The best in our opinion, with orange new growth, turning yellow, then green. High summer heat accelerates the yellow fading to green. Leaves are spotted with dark green chlorophyll blotches, a trait permitting separation from the uniformly yellow leaf of 'Hearts of Gold'.

THE RISING SUN

'Minnesota Hardy'

NORTHERN HERALD

Cold hardy

'Minnesota Hardy' ('Northland Strain', 'Northern Strain', 'Minnesota Strain'). Seed-grown from reliably cold hardy sources, so expect some seedling variation. This is the only redbud offered for sale in St. Paul, and many specimens are extant and thriving at the Minnesota Landscape Arboretum, Chanhassen. At Coastal Maine Botanical Gardens in Boothbay, this is the only redbud that thrived.

NORTHERN HERALD 'Pink Trim'. A clone, discovered near Bismarck, SD. It is more upright-growing, slightly compact, and wonderfully heavy flowering. North Dakota State University is introducing the plant. Should prove cold hardy in zone 4. Strong grower in zone 7.

Weeping habit

CAROLINA SWEETHEART 'NCCC1' and WHITEWATER 'NC2007-8'. Both variegated but not vigorous growers, the latter with graceful, slender weeping branches. CAROLINA SWEETHEART, with stunning white, pink, rose, purple young leaves, loses color in summer. It is not a true weeper, but the thin stems are semi-arching, lending a graceful, refined habit. Foliage of both cultivars will burn in Oregon's low-humidity sun.

CAROLINA SWEETHEART

LAVENDER TWIST 'Covey'. Among the first weeping introductions. Green-leafed. Develops a stiff, cascading habit similar to 'Ruby Falls', one of its children. From Tim Brotzman, North Madison, OH.

PINK HEARTBREAKER 'Pennsylvania Pride Pink Heartbreaker'. A vigorous green-leaf weeper, faster growing and with a wider arching form than LAVENDER TWIST.

WHITEWATER

LAVENDER TWIST

PINK HEARTBREAKER

LAVENDER TWIST

'Ruby Falls'. Stiffly branched with strongly descending shoots that skirt the ground. Beautiful red-purple new growth holds color into summer better than 'Forest Pansy' in the Dirr garden.

subsp. *texensis* 'Traveller'. Thick-textured, shiny dark green, undulating-surfaced leaves and more compact weeping habit than LAVENDER TWIST. Authors observed specimens trained with a central leader and others as cascading hummocks. Essentially fruitless.

'Vanilla Twist'. A white-flowered weeper, otherwise quite similar to LAVENDER TWIST. From Tim Brotzman, North Madison, OH.

'Ruby Falls'

'Ruby Falls'

subsp. *texensis* 'Traveller'

subsp. *texensis* 'Traveller'

'Vanilla Twist'

SUMMER'S TOWER

'Ace of Hearts'

'Ace of Hearts'

'Little Woody'

Upright habit

SUMMER'S TOWER 'JN7'. An upright vase-shaped form. Good potential for street tree or tight areas.

Compact habit

'Ace of Hearts'. Small heart-shaped leaves, a 10 to 15′ multi-stem shrub but can be trained to form a single trunk. Flowers are smaller than the species but produced in abundance.

'Little Woody'. Undulating, rough-surfaced leaves, larger than those of 'Ace of Hearts'. 10 to 15′ high and wide.

Cercis occidentalis
western redbud, California redbud

Deciduous. A pretty native redbud for drier, hotter regions of the western United States. Typically a small tree, 15 to 20′ high and wide, with variable, irregular outline, but often shrubby and staying smaller. Slow to moderate growth.

Foliage: Blue-green, somewhat leathery leaves, 2 to 3″ across, rounded, notched to rounded at apex, cordate at base, do not inspire. There have been references to good red fall color on stressed trees, but we have seen only yellow-green to yellow fall color on *Cercis* species. **Flowers/seeds/fruits/cones**: Flowers, typical for most of the genus, appear on previous season's growth and larger branches/trunks in late winter–early spring. Colors range from pink to magenta. The fruit is a 4 to 6″ long, glabrous, flattish

Cercis occidentalis

Cercis siliquastrum
Mediterranean redbud, Judas-tree

Deciduous. Spectacular species, forming a rounded crown in the 15 to 25′ high and wide range. Trees are quite dense, more so than *C. canadensis*. In Europe, 30 to 40′ high trees are extant. Bark is brownish black with orangish coloration peeking through the cracks and fissures.

Foliage: The rich reddish bronze-purple emerging leaves are beautiful, maturing a matte blue-green. Leaves are 2 to 4″ long, to 5″ wide, with an indented apex and pronounced cordate base; their undulating surface imparts a unique texture. **Flowers/seeds/fruits/cones**: Flowers 3 to 6 in a cluster, opening before the leaves in April-May, and persisting until the leaves have fully matured. Effective display for an extended period, especially during cool springs. Fruit, 2 to 4″ long; young pods are purple-tinged with color persisting into summer. Pods mature brown and are long persistent. **Native range**: Southern Europe and western Asia (eastern Mediterranean). **Adaptability**: Redbuds, in general, adapt well to higher pH soils, and this species is no exception. Maximally reserved for Mediterranean type climates, although authors observed pretty specimens (particularly 'Bodnant') in England. A fine specimen prospered for many years at the JC Raulston Arboretum, Raleigh, NC. Zones 7 and 8. **Landscape use**: Full sun, well-drained soil, and an English manor garden suit it well. **Street tree use**: No. **In the trade**: Available. We love the flowers, foliage, habit, and see potential for breeding with our native *C. canadensis*.

reddish pod, aging to light brown and persisting into winter. **Native range**: Arizona, Utah, Nevada, California, and Oregon. Naturally found at elevations to 4,500′ and on dry slopes, canyons, ravines, and streambanks; authors observed rather scraggly specimens on dry slopes in California with *Aesculus californica*. **Adaptability**: To our knowledge has not been domesticated like eastern redbud; certainly it is not commonly cultivated. Many West Coast plants from similar habitats do not perform well in the Midwest, East, and Southeast. Zones 7 to 9, 10 on the West Coast. Mature plants are hardy to 10°F. **Landscape use**: Useful for West Coast gardens, although difficult to compete with the many cultivars of *C. canadensis*, which are also adapted to western gardens with proper siting. For use as a small tree, especially in water-restricted areas, it has a home. California literature reports it tolerates acid and alkaline conditions and clay-based soils. Authors have not observed a single tree in eastern gardens. **Street tree use**: Potential. **In the trade**: No cultivars extant, which is odd considering the multitude of variation within *C. canadensis*. DNA analysis shows the two species are distantly related. Perhaps hybridization using the many beautiful *C. canadensis* cultivars would yield selections better adapted for western gardens.

f. *albida* ('Alba'). It and 'White Swan' produce white flowers. The foliage of f. *albida* is pale green. Typically the white-flowered forms of all redbuds lack anthocyanins, so emerging leaves are always pure green with no hint of red or purple.

'Bodnant'. Spectacular, with deep rose-purple flowers in abundance on a vigorous round-headed tree. The most common representative of the species in cultivation.

Cercis siliquastrum

Chamaecyparis lawsoniana
Port Orford cedar, Lawson falsecypress

Evergreen conifer. The species is a magnificent pyramidal to conical tree with massive, buttressed trunk, short ascending branches, drooping at the tips and ending in flat sprays. Behemoth in size, with specimens over 200′ high in the wild. Difficult to estimate landscape size as every cultivar is different. Cultivarism is a common thread throughout the conifer world, especially so with this genus; a visit to Bedgebury Pinetum, Kent, England, was punctuated with the collection of 285 *C. lawsoniana* cultivars. Bark is silver-brown to reddish brown, fibrous, divided into thick, rounded ridges separated by deep irregular furrows, 6 to 10″ thick on old trees.

Foliage: The needles (scales) overlap producing a soft-textured foliage spray, gray-green to deep green, with indistinct white markings below. **Flowers/seeds/fruits/cones**: The staminate "flowers" are pink to crimson; the pistillate, steely blue. The 8-scaled cones, ⅓″ wide, are bluish green, maturing reddish brown. Cones are produced in great numbers. **Native range**: Limited, southwestern Oregon and isolated locales in northwestern California. **Adaptability**: In the eastern United States, has not been hardy in Maine; does not survive the heat, humidity, and wet soils of the Southeast; and the many cultivars do not prosper, primarily due to heavy wet soils. In the wild, the species suffers from a phytophthora root rot. Realistically, suited only to the West Coast, zones 6 to 8(9). **Landscape use**: At its genetic peak, *C. lawsoniana* is a splendid landscape plant. In English gardens, it thrives on neglect. Prefers moist, acid, well-drained soils in full fun to partial shade. Utilize in groups, as a screen and hedge, as it responds well to pruning. Appears more windfirm than, for example, Leyland cypress. **Street tree use**: Limited to none. **In the trade**: Oregon State University has recently developed a rootstock that is resistant to *Phytophthora lateralis*, the scourge of the species. This resistant rootstock has made Port Orford cedar once again a viable landscape plant. If you plant it, be sure it is on resistant rootstock.

'Oregon Blue'. Lovely blue foliage, softly held on a dense, pyramidal frame; 'Pembury Blue' and 'Blue Surprise' are similar.

'Sullivan'. The only cultivar that receives attention in the eastern United States. It has survived well in the Midwest and Upper South; foliage is green, habit loose.

Chamaecyparis lawsoniana

Chamaecyparis lawsoniana

Chamaecyparis lawsoniana

'Oregon Blue'

Chamaecyparis lawsoniana cultivars

Chamaecyparis nootkatensis.
See *Cupressus nootkatensis*

Chamaecyparis obtusa
hinoki falsecypress

Evergreen conifer. Many horticulturists have never observed the species because its many cultivars dominate commerce. In its finest form, *C. obtusa* is an immense, broadly conical tree, exceeding 100′ high in the wild. Moderate growth rate, soft-textured foliage, so densely borne on the more compact cultivars that the bark is seldom evident, but it is beautiful, a rich reddish brown, on mature trees shedding in

Chamaecyparis obtusa

'Aurea'

Chamaecyparis obtusa

long, slender strips. In its native Japan, the timber is highly prized, and the species is commonly used in afforestation.

Foliage: The branchlet sprays, fern-like in outline, are soft to the touch, shining dark green above, with waxy white X/Y-shaped markings below. Foliage remains dark green through the seasons. Many cultivars (e.g., 'Gracilis') have more rounded sprays, borne in tufted configuration; quite easy to separate these from the cultivars of *C. pisifera*. **Flowers/seeds/fruits/cones**: The male cones are yellowish; the female solitary. The ⅜″ globose cones comprise 8 to 10 scales, ripening orange-brown and often produced in great numbers. Cones are larger than those of *C. pisifera*. **Native range**: Central and southern Japan, in mixed conifer forests on mountainsides and ridges. **Adaptability**: Adaptable once established and more heat tolerant than would be projected based on native habitat. Less cold hardy than *C. pisifera*; authors consider -20°F the lowest temperature for survival. Zones 5 to 8. **Landscape use**: In Oregon, these are go-to trees where a graceful small/medium conifer is desired. In the Southeast, the Atlanta area is suitable for successful culture. To predict the ultimate size on the misapplied "dwarf" conifers, which, with years, reach tree status, is foolhardy. For example, in Athens, GA, 'Crippsii' has proven rock solid in full sun, reasonably well-drained, acidic soils,

'Compacta'

'Fernspray Gold'

'Crippsii'

reaching 15 to 20′, with yellow foliage retention fluctuating but persistent year-round; on Cape Cod, it ascends 50′ high. **Street tree use**: Certainly could be utilized. **In the trade**: Available.

'Aurea'. Golden yellow foliage on a full-sized pyramid, like the species but bright and colorful in the landscape. 'Confucius', 'Goldilocks', 'Melody', and many others have similar bright yellow foliage.

'Compacta'. Dense and more compact, slightly slower growing but eventually plan on 25′, with fresh dark green foliage.

'Crippsii'. In cultivation for over 100 years. A broad pyramid, branches spreading, branchlets broadly frond-like, tops decurving, rich golden-yellow new growth changing to green within the plant, yellowish at ends of sprays even in summer, 30 to 50′ tall, one of the better choices from Massachusetts to Georgia for performance and retention of yellowish coloration.

'Fernspray Gold'. Arching sprays of foliage are indeed somewhat fern-like in appearance and bright golden yellow. Slow-growing and more compact but eventually will reach 15′. It adds unique texture and color to the landscape.

'Gracilis'

'Graciosa'

'Verdoni'

'Filicoides' (fernspray falsecypress). Will ascend 20′ or more and becomes more open than 'Crippsii'. The branches are encased in tight, dark green, fern-like, soft-textured needles. Quite unique texture and readily available.

'Gracilis' (slender hinoki cypress). This form has historically been common in the trade. Well named, tall, slender, slightly open and graceful. Dark green, eventually 30 to 40′ in the landscape. 'Gracilis' has rounded sprays and often reverts to the species type with broad, feather-like sprays. Authors have observed these reversions on old trees in Newport, RI.

'Graciosa'. Compact and slow-growing with attractive bright green foliage sprays, it eventually will meet our 15′ standard to gain tree status.

'Verdoni'. Yellow foliage, similar to 'Aurea' but warrants mention as an improvement. New growth shows a hint of orange, and its foliage is less likely to burn in the sun. Usually rated smaller, but we think it can reach 15′.

Chamaecyparis pisifera

Sawara falsecypress, Japanese falsecypress

Evergreen conifer. Similar to *C. obtusa* in habit, the species develops a broad-conical outline, reaching 150′ high with a trunk 6′ in diameter in Japan, where it grows in the wild at elevations to 5,000′; at best, 50′ high is a robust specimen under cultivation. Growth is moderate. The reddish brown bark is shed in long strips, moderately ridged and graying with age. Like *C. obtusa*, an extremely important timber species in Japan and extensively planted by foresters.

Foliage: Soft-textured, shiny dark green, fern-spray foliage. The lower surface of the sprays bears the whitish X/Y-shaped markings, similar to *C. obtusa*. The individual scale tips are sharper compared to the rounded apex of *C. obtusa*. **Flowers/seeds/fruits/cones**: Reproductive structures are similar to *C. obtusa* except the (4)6(8)-scaled, globose, yellowish brown cone is smaller, ⅙ to ¼″ wide. **Native range**: Central Japan, primarily Honshu and Kyushu, where it occurs in mixed conifer forests in rocky, wet places on slopes and valleys. **Adaptability**: Zones 4 to 8. Authors observed the cultivars of this species are more cold hardy and heat tolerant than those of *C. obtusa*. The species is thoroughly represented by numerous cultivars at the Minnesota Landscape Arboretum, Chanhassen, zone 4, while *C. obtusa* and cultivars are absent. **Landscape use**: The species is limitedly represented in the United States, primarily in arboreta. North and south, trees require full sun, moist, acid, well-drained soils with supplemental moisture in periods of drought. The cultivars add summer and winter color, unique shapes and textures, and are not troubled by insects and diseases. All withstand pruning and, like *C. obtusa*, function as hedges, screens, accents, and specimens. **Street tree use**: No. **In the trade**: A staggering number of cultivars, most small buns and meatballs, are in American commerce; they are categorized by foliage type, including those that are normal representatives of the species (i.e., with flattened, soft-textured sprays).

'Filifera'. Green foliage, with branches becoming stringy and cord-like. Forms a formidable tree to 50′. 'Filifera Aurea', with golden yellow needles, will exceed 20′ high.

'Plumosa'. Foliage similar to the species but more ferny and airy, because the needles stand out at a 45° angle to the stem. 'Plumosa' may grow 50′ or more; the golden form 'Plumosa Aurea', 20 to 30′. This cultivar appears more often

Chamaecyparis pisifera

'Filifera'

253

Chamaecyparis pisifera

'Squarrosa'

'Squarrosa'

'Squarrosa'

'Filifera Aurea'

in zone 8 as an established tree than any other *C. pisifera*. During a recent visit to an Oconee County, GA, garden, the authors noted stray seedlings, all similar to 'Plumosa', germinating willy-nilly.

'Squarrosa' (moss falsecypress). Soft-textured juvenile foliage is borne in billowy tufts, typically silvery glaucous blue. Many cultivars have similar traits, 'Boulevard' the most common, reaching 15 to 20′ high. Authors noted 'Squarrosa' specimens 60′ high.

Chamaecyparis thyoides

Atlantic white cedar

Evergreen conifer. Habit is softly conical-pyramidal in youth, the crown more open in old age with lower trunk devoid of foliage. Estimate 40 to 50′ high, 10 to 20′ wide. Bark is ashy gray and stringy in youth, becoming prominently ridged and furrowed on large trunks. The rot-resistant wood is used for furniture. At the University of Georgia, 50 cultivars were amassed for testing and possible introduction. Accessions were sourced from Maine to Alabama with great anticipation. Although well adapted to container culture, where water and fertility were optimum, not a single clone persisted over time in the field. Why the disappointment? In the wild, the species occurs in swamps. When exposed to extended drought, plants simply languish and die.

Foliage: Irregularly arranged, usually not flattened in sprays, soft-textured, green, bluish green to blue, developing off-color bronze-brown in cold weather. The Georgia goal was to find selections that maintain the summer color through winter; one of the best greens was 'Rachael', which grew 20′ by 13′ in 11 years in Georgia trials. **Flowers/seeds/fruits/cones**: Staminate cones yellow to red, prolific; female, sporadic, bloomy green to blue-purple, $\frac{3}{16}$ to $\frac{1}{4}$″ wide, globose with 4 to 6 scales. **Native range**: Eastern United States in swamps; primarily along the Atlantic coast from Maine to Florida, to Alabama and Mississippi. **Adaptability**: Cold hardy to zone 4 and extending to zone 9. Authors have theorized that hybrids between this and *C. obtusa* or *C. pisifera* would embody the best traits and make splendid evergreens for wet and dry conditions. Much work remains to support our theory. **Landscape use**: The UGA project was exciting and witnessed unimaginable variation, but nothing that would advance horticulture acceptance. For naturalizing in wet areas, it is worthy. Must have continuous moisture in the garden. **Street tree use**: No. **In the trade**: Foliage forms, including the aforementioned 'Rachael', are available. 'Rubicon' ('Red Star') sports juvenile blue-green summer foliage, turning plum-purple in winter, on a compact, dense, columnar tree; authors recorded 20 to 25′ high. 'Variegata', with yellow splotches and specks on a conical tree, is rather pretty. Foliage bronzes in cold weather. Estimate height to 20′.

Chamaecyparis thyoides

Chamaecyparis thyoides

'Variegata'

Chilopsis linearis

Chilopsis linearis

Chilopsis linearis
desert willow

Deciduous. Rather willowy, unkempt, slouching, arching, splaying small tree or large shrub, the redeeming quality the fragrant, rainbow-esque white, pink, rose, lavender flowers with purple markings. Habit is loose and open, and large populations of seedlings grown in Georgia reflected this. Grows 15 to 25′ high, 10 to 15′ wide, with a tree over 60′ found in the wild. Extremely fast-growing. Roots are thick and rope-like.

Foliage: The rich green leaves, 6 to 12″ long, to ½″ wide, indeed resemble willow (*Salix*) foliage (hence the common name). No appreciable fall color; leaves abscise green to yellow-green. **Flowers/seeds/fruits/cones**: Large flowers, 1 to 1½″ long and wide, develop on new growth of the season from spring into summer, serving as a nectar source for bees. Flowers are attractive but seldom borne in numbers that provide the "wow" factor. One-year-old seedlings will flower. Foliage drops early in fall, exposing a mixed bag of narrow, 6 to 12″ long, ¼″ wide, capsular fruits, containing numerous winged-fringed seeds. Note well... seeds germinate without pretreatment, as readily as green beans. **Native range**: Southern California to Texas, south to Mexico. **Adaptability**: Well adapted to alkaline, dry, well-drained soils. Zones 7 to 10. **Landscape use**: Certainly tenacious and serviceable as a small tree in harsh climates. Requires full sun for best flowering. Does not appreciate excessive water, as was evident with container-grown seedlings in Georgia. The U.S. National Arboretum crossed this with catalpa; the resulting hybrids are under evaluation. Authors have walked the test plots and were impressed with the many variations. In Oregon, the species can flower beautifully, but the long days of that higher latitude mean the plant grows too late into the fall, and while it may succeed for a year or two, an early hard freeze will eventually take it down. **Street tree use**: No, too wide-spreading.

In the trade: A profusion of cultivars for flower color have been introduced, including 'Alpine' (white/amaranth), ART'S SEEDLESS 'Shelly's Nuts' (pink-rose), 'Barranco' (lavender), 'Bubba' (burgundy), 'Burgundy' ('Burgundy Lace'; burgundy-pink), 'Dark Storm' (dark pink-magenta), 'Desert Amethyst' (dark lavender), 'Hopi' (white with yellow throat), 'Lois Adams' (lavender-magenta, fruitless), LUCRETIA HAMILTON (dark purple), 'Marfa Lace' (pink-rose), 'Mesquite Valley Pink' ('Pink Star'; pink), 'Regal' (lavender), 'Rio Salado' (deep burgundy), ROYAL PURPLE (purple), 'Tejas' (rose-pink/amaranth), TIMELESS BEAUTY (burgundy-lavender), WARREN JONES (pink), 'White Star' (white), and 'White Storm' (white).

Chionanthus retusus

Chionanthus retusus
Chinese fringetree

Deciduous, tardily so in warm climates, dropping most leaves by late December, early January. An Asian relative of *C. virginicus*, equally meritorious, but lacking the cold hardiness of that native species. Relatively slow-growing, a 20 to 25′ tree with a broadly rounded to spreading habit is more typically found in the landscape. Bark is noticeably pretty when young, exfoliating to various degrees in gray to cinnamon colors, at maturity ridged and furrowed, furrows black, ridges flat and gray; a variable trait, with 'China Snow' bark resembling this description, 'Arnold's Pride' less so.

Foliage: Enlightening to describe foliage, for 'Arnold's Pride' and 'China Snow' appear to have originated from different planets. The former with 6 to 8″ long, narrow-elliptic, duller green leaves compared to the rounded, leathery, 2 to 3″ high and wide, lustrous, polished dark green foliage of the latter. Both have been cultivated at the University of Georgia for over 30 years, with the latter clearly superior for ornamental traits. On occasion, beautiful yellow fall color develops on 'China Snow', as late as December in zone 8.
Flowers/seeds/fruits/cones: A foolproof method to separate *C. retusus* from *C. virginicus*: the former flowers on new growth of the season, the latter on second-year stems. Also, *C. retusus* flowers slightly later than *C. virginicus*, late April, early May in zone 8. The snow-white flowers are held in 2 to 3″ high, 2 to 4″ wide panicles, the overall effect a fleecy dome of snow. Flowers are effective for an extended period. Sexes are essentially separate, and the ½″ dark blue drupes, ripening September through October, occur only on female plants. Fruits persist longer than those of *C. virginicus*, and this may be related to bird preference. Fruit production is, at times, profuse, with fruits more visible because of being borne on the terminals. **Native range**: China, Korean peninsula, Japan, in mixed forests, thickets, and along rivers.
Adaptability: From Boston to central Florida to the West Coast, the species has displayed its mettle. Hardiness is

Chionanthus retusus

open to question with zones 6 to 8 most suitable. Authors wonder, given native range, whether introduction of new genetics, especially Korean provenance, would allow for increased cold hardiness. We would like to push zone 5, but -15°F killed plants to the ground. **Landscape use**: Parallels *C. virginicus*. Observations signal to us that this is more tolerant of heat, drought, and full sun. Plants on dry berms, slopes, in commercial settings, have prospered. Groupings of 3, 5, or 7 provide a powerful landscape element throughout the seasons. At Callaway Gardens, Pine Mountain, GA, mature specimens, now over 50 years old, have survived the heat and drought that debilitated many woody plants in the collections. **Street tree use**: Potential. Fits under utilities, but pruning needed for clearance. **In the trade**: Available, and we hope to see more cultivar selections and controlled breeding in the future. Of the approximately 60 *Chionanthus* species, the two herein are the hardiest; however, a South American taxon, *C. pubescens*, with deep pink-rose flowers, might make a great breeding partner. Seedlings of the latter are growing at the University of Georgia.

'Arnold's Pride'. Described throughout the previous text. A 30 to 35′ high specimen still resides at Boston's Arnold

Chionanthus retusus

Chionanthus retusus

Arboretum, the seed collected by E. H. Wilson in 1901. Magnificent flower and produces heavy crops of dark blue fruits. This would be the authors' first choice for street tree planting.

'Ashford'. Upright habit, golden tan exfoliating bark, grows 30' by 20'. Introduced by Rich Hesselein, Pleasant Run Nursery, and named for the home where his children were born. Zone 6.

'China Snow'. A leathery (close to plastic) leaf selection named by the great Don Shadow. Low-branched tree or multi-stemmed shrub, reaching 15 to 20(25)' high and wide. Habit is rounded to broad-rounded, the canopy as tight as an army bed sheet. One could bounce a quarter off the impenetrable foliage.

'Confucius'. A large tree form, vase-shaped with a rounded canopy, the parent tree 30' high and 25' wide; somewhat similar to 'Arnold's Pride' but not as shapely and sturdy in branch structure. A new male introduction from the U.S. National Arboretum. Foliage lustrous dark green, larger than 'China Snow' but similar to 'Arnold's Pride'.

SPIRIT 'CRN10'. Attractive small ornamental tree with fleecy white flowers and gray-brown exfoliating bark, leathery dark green foliage, turning shades of yellow in late fall; 10 to 20' high and wide. A female, produces copious quantities of bluish fruits.

'Tokyo Tower' ('Ivory Tower'). Its broad applicability brings a smile to all chionantho-philes. Foliage and flower (yet to observe fruit) is similar to 'China Snow', but the habit is distinctly upright-columnar, 15' by 6'. A tremendous plant for areas where lateral space is limited. Might be grown

SPIRIT

single-stemmed, as it naturally branches low, the laterals ascending and almost paralleling the central axis. Bark is light brown/tan and exfoliates in small flakes, curls, and sheets. Slow to produce flowers; did so in its sixth year in the Dirr garden, at a size of 14' by 5'. Based on growth in Dirr garden, 25' might be attained in 10 years.

'Tokyo Tower'

Chionanthus virginicus
white fringetree

Deciduous. Superb native small tree or large shrub, 20 to 30′ high and wide, usually smaller under cultivation, with newer clonal selections providing uniformity and superior ornamental features. Extremely variable in all its characteristics and row-run seedlings may disappoint. Slow-growing. Bark is rather smooth, on ancient trunks textured and pebbly, with gray beech-like coloration.

Foliage: Leaves range from anemic yellow-green to lustrous emerald-green, from narrow-elliptical to broad-ovate, 4 to 8″ long, a third to half as wide, margins entire, and glabrous to woolly-mammoth hairy on the lower surface. Seldom given kudos for fall color, may be expressed as a golden shroud or tacky off-yellow. Since foliage is a 6- to 7-month proposition, purchase in leaf. **Flowers/seeds/fruits/cones**: Typically dioecious. Flowers are among the most beautiful of all woody plants, white, borne in 6 to 10″ long and wide fleecy panicles in April-May. Petals emerge green and open porcelain-white with a slight sweet fragrance. Flowers do not brown as they age but abscise, forming a fine-textured carpet. The ½″ long, egg-shaped, waxy, dark blue fruits ripen in August-September. Fruits are held in drooping panicles and shrouded by the foliage. On close inspection, they are reminiscent of Concord grapes. Birds are fond of the fruits and can strip a plant in short order. **Native range**: New Jersey to Florida, west to Missouri, Oklahoma, and Texas. Nowhere common, found as an understory tree (lone or in isolated colonies) in upland hardwood and pine

'Tokyo Tower'

Chionanthus virginicus

Chionanthus virginicus

Chionanthus virginicus

'Emerald Knight'

forests, rock outcrops, savannas, flatwoods, and shrub bogs. **Adaptability**: Habitat reflects its tenaciousness under cultivation, and venerable old specimens in New England and the Midwest attest to its persistence. Successfully cultured far outside its native range, from Maine to Minnesota to West Coast. Zones 4 to 9. **Landscape use**: For specimen plant use, in groupings or in a border, the species shines. For everyday garden employment and enjoyment, it fills many niches. Performs well in full sun to partial shade, with abundant floral production. Even young seedlings, 2 to 3 years old, produce significant flowers. This translates to a short juvenility period before the onset of sexual maturity, i.e., flowers and fruits. The species is easily transplanted as container or field-grown material; some references say otherwise, but authors experienced no transplanting issues. Easy plant to maintain as pruning, except to shape, is seldom required. Prune after flowering so as not to remove flower buds. Flowers develop on previous season's wood and initiate slightly before or as the new shoots are developing. Superb choice when showcased against an evergreen background like hemlock, pine, southern magnolias. **Street tree use**: Would serve as a small street or urban tree, but we have yet to witness such applications. **In the trade**: Cultivars are few, owing to difficulty of vegetative propagation via cuttings and grafting; however, both methods are successful, relying on clonal selection (easy to root) and the skill of the propagator.

Dirr Clone. Now being produced by Pleasant Run Nursery in New Jersey. The most vigorous tree form and the fastest grower under nursery production. Dark green leaves, larger than those of SERENITY, 'Spring Fleecing', and 'White Knight', turn golden yellow in fall in Athens. Displayed heat and drought tolerance in zone 8 for over 20 years. A male, so no messy fruits if utilized in trafficked areas. Expect 15′ tall and wide in 15 years.

'Emerald Knight'. Glossy dark green foliage, upright habit, a male selection. Reportedly will reach 15 to 20′ in height, slightly less in width; however, a Georgia nursery reported height and width the same.

PRODIGY 'CVSTF'. Narrow, shiny, leathery dark green leaves, clouds of white flowers, abundant blue-purple fruits, and a rounded habit. This selection was introduced based on ease of rooting from cuttings from a large seedling population of native southern provenance. 10 to 15′ tall and wide.

PRODIGY

SERENITY

SERENITY 'CV1049'. Compared to typical seedlings a broader, denser canopy with outstanding vigor and showy white flowers; dark green foliage, yellow fall color; 20′ by 20′.

'Spring Fleecing'. Pretty tree, a male. Another shiny, narrow-leaf, heavily flowered selection from North Carolina. Flowers almost too heavily as a young rooted cutting. Principal reason for selection was ease of rooting via cuttings. 10 to 15′, less in spread.

'White Knight'. Prolifically flowering male introduction from Maryland. A 3′ high plant in the Dirr garden flowers so profusely that subsequent vegetative growth is reduced. In fact, a Tennessee nurseryman mentioned the slow rate of growth of this and 'Emerald Knight', making them commercially suspect. 12′ by 15′.

C

×*Chitalpa tashkentensis*

chitalpa

Deciduous. A low-branched or multi-stemmed small tree, shrubby and rounded. Fast-growing, medium texture, 20 to 25′ tall and wide. Bark smooth, light gray, eventually developing vertical splits.

Foliage: Leaves simple, long ovate to lanceolate with an acuminate tip, margin entire, pubescent below, medium green, dull surface, 4 to 6″ long and a third as wide. Quite susceptible to mildew with humidity. We have not seen any fall color. **Flowers/seeds/fruits/cones:** This is where the tree shines. Large, full racemes of 15 to 40 flowers form on new growth during the summer months. The individual flowers, about 1″ across, are trumpet-shaped with petals fused at the base and flaring with 5 wavy reflexed tips, the lower lips of the flower more highly colored, from white to pink to lavender, a bit orchid-like in appearance, and most have a yellow throat. The tree is sterile, so it will continue to flower through the summer. **Native range:** A bigeneric hybrid of *Catalpa bignonioides* (U.S. Southeast) and *Chilopsis linearis* (U.S. Southwest and northern Mexico). **Adaptability:** Best adapted to the dry air and heat of the Southwest, and popular in California to Arizona. Both authors craved this plant for its flowers. But in Georgia's humidity, it succumbed to heavy mildew, and in Oregon, all cultivars tested were dieback shrubs: they did not harden in the fall and suffered from the first hard freeze. We are hopeful that breeding work at the U.S. National Arboretum or by others will extend the climatic range of this plant. Zones (6)7 to 9. **Landscape use:** In the right climate, they are beautiful, long-flowering small trees or large shrubs, great garden ornamentals. Flowers are wonderful close-up for their detail, and the racemes are heavy enough to be equally effective at a distance. **Street tree use:** No, too low and spreading. **In the trade:** Sold only as cultivars.

'Morning Cloud'. Flowers white to pale pinkish with the corolla throat streaked purple, 25′ by 25′.

'Pink Dawn'. Light pink flowers; throat pale yellow streaked with deep magenta, 25′ by 25′.

SUMMER BELLS 'Minsum'. Flowers white with a light lavender margin; throat light yellow with purple streaks, 25′ by 25′.

'Morning Cloud'

×*Chitalpa tashkentensis*

Cinnamomum camphora
camphor tree

Broadleaf evergreen. Upright-spreading with a heavy trunk and a broadly rounded crown, becoming globe-shaped and then wider than tall. Moderate growth rate, presenting medium-textured foliage on a bold, coarse-textured trunk, to 50′ high, 60′ wide. Bark gray, strongly ridged and furrowed.

Foliage: Smooth glossy dark green leaves, ovate to slightly obovate, with a smooth margin and an acute to acuminate tip, 1½ to 4″ long and one-half to two-thirds as wide. New growth has a reddish tint in spring. Leaves hold until the new foliage emerges, then drop. Fragrant when crushed, smells of camphor. No fall color. **Flowers/seeds/fruits/cones**: Small yellowish white flowers are borne in panicles in spring, fragrant, profuse enough to be attractive en masse. Fruit a ⅓″ rounded drupe, black, in late fall; can be messy, seeds may grow. **Native range**: China to northern Vietnam, Japan, Taiwan. **Adaptability**: A tree for warmer climates, thrives in Florida along Gulf Coast to southern Texas, and quite happy in California. Adaptable, pH and drought tolerant. Limited by cold weather, zones 9 to 11. **Landscape use**: A large spreading tree for residences with room for it, commercial areas, and roadsides. Roots are aggressive, and fruit is messy over hard surfaces. Caution: invasive in Florida, along the adjacent Gulf Coast, and Australia. Widely used in California but seems much less problematic there. **Street tree use**: Survives but the trunk becomes quite large, the canopy wide-spreading. Needs room, and not many modern streets have it. **In the trade**: Mostly sold as seed-grown. MAJESTIC BEAUTY 'MonProud' is a more compact version of the species, slower growing and smaller maturing, with a symmetrical form, its size more appropriate for garden use, 20 to 25′ high with equal spread. We would like to see work toward sterile cultivars.

Cinnamomum camphora

Cinnamomum camphora

Cinnamomum camphora

C

Cladrastis delavayi (*C. sinensis*)

Chinese yellowwood

Deciduous. One of those special trees that all aficionados aspire to cultivate. The foliage and flowers are beautiful, and assuming it was nursery-friendly, the species would be grown and sold in quantities. Largest tree referenced was a 33 to 38′ high and wide specimen in England. Moderate growth rate.

Foliage: Late to emerge in spring. Large, 3 to 5″ long, 1 to 1½″ wide leaflets, 9 to 13(17) per compound pinnate leaf, bright green above with rusty pubescence on lower midrib and petiole. Leaflet shape resembles that of *Styphnolobium*. Fall color is similar to *C. kentukea*. **Flowers/seeds/fruits/cones**: Fragrant, blush-white, lavender to pinkish flowers are borne in 12″ long, 9″ wide erect, terminal panicles in June-July, each flower with lavender-pink on the keel, yellow blotch on the standard. Bees are frequent visitors, and the entire tree, when in flower, appears to be vibrating as bees move from flower to flower. The pods are shorter than *C. kentukea*, to 3″ long, ½″ wide, flattened and smooth. **Native range**: Western Sichuan, China, in moist woods to 8,200′ elevation. **Adaptability**: Authors believe the zone 5 to 7 range does not translate to success. Although a respectable tree grows at the Sarah P. Duke Gardens, Durham, NC, most attempts in the Southeast have met with disaster. Certainly worth considering in the Pacific Northwest. Coastal British Columbia to San Francisco provide the best conditions for success. **Landscape use**: Unquestionably, a beautiful flowering tree, but fickle as to climatic expectations. Authors project a mild climate, neither too cold nor hot, with reasonable moisture, are requisites. **Street tree use**: No. **In the trade**: We have hope for the future. The lone cultivar, 'China Rose', with deeper pink flowers, was tested in the Southeast without success; it was killed below the snowline after –24°F.

Cladrastis kentukea (*C. lutea*)

American yellowwood

Deciduous. A signature joy of our careers was to experience the species growing along the Little River in Tennessee's Great Smoky Mountains National Park; doubtful it will ever become mainstream, but in flower—literally dripping with white rain—it was the envy of all species in the park that day. Trees are 30 to 50′ high and wide, with a pretty canopy of shimmering leaves. An Achilles' heel is the sharp branch angles, which lead to breaking/splitting; however, many half-century specimens continue to deport themselves in

Cladrastis kentukea

Cladrastis kentukea

Cladrastis kentukea

Cladrastis kentukea

'Perkins Pink'

elegant fashion. Moderate rate of growth. Beautiful, smooth, silver-gray, beech-like bark adds to the allure, bringing a bit of sparkle to the winter landscape.

Foliage: The (5)7 to 9(11), egg-shaped, 2 to 3″ long, entire-margined leaflets emerge bright yellowish green, maturing bright green, teasing autumn with beautiful yellows. The leaflets often abscise early, with the rachis (central stalk)

extant, dressing the tree in soft cream-yellow porcupine quills. Certainly one of our most beautiful native species for foliage. **Flowers/seeds/fruits/cones**: Fragrant, white, pea-shaped flowers are held in cascading, often branched, 8 to 14″ long, 4 to 6″ wide panicles in May-June. Truly spectacular and unrivaled among large trees when in full regalia. Flowering is cyclic, alternating abundant, then light, or in 3-year cycles. Provides excellent bee pasture; they swarm the tree when in flower. Fruit is a 2½ to 4″ long, ½″ wide, flat pod with 4 to 6 seeds. Pods persist into early winter. Seeds given a 180°F water soak will germinate when sown. **Native range**: Scattered native range, nowhere abundant, from North Carolina, to Missouri, to Oklahoma. Occurs in rocky coves of mountains, limestone cliffs and ridges, rich hardwood forests to 3,400′ elevation. **Adaptability**: Adapts to acid and higher pH soils. Suitable for zone 8 with proper siting and much more cold hardy (zone 4) than reflected in its southern heritage. Has proven hardy in Minnesota and Maine. Just mentionably, at Yellowwood State Forest in southern Indiana nary a yellowwood is to be found. **Landscape use**: For residential use, parks, campuses, or any large area. Requires well-drained, moist, clay-based soil. Full sun for maximum performance but adapted to partial shade. Has suffered in extended droughts of the Southeast, with leaf margins turning brown. **Street tree use**: Perhaps too fragile for street tree, urban applications. Maybe, in a favorable climate. **In the trade**: Available. Few cultivars are listed.

'Perkins Pink' ('Rosea'). Beautiful pink-flowered introduction with traits otherwise similar to the species. Seedlings produce true-to-type with pink flowers.

'Summer Shade'. Improved foliage, although the few trees we observed varied little from the species. Princeton Nursery introduction.

Clerodendrum trichotomum

harlequin glorybower

Deciduous. A sleeper small tree, blending with the spring greens, until *kaboom*—fragrant white flowers in summer, followed by blue fruits nested in the red-rose-purple, star-shaped calyx. Certainly, nowhere common in commerce, but authors run into trees on both coasts, with reasonable frequency in Oregon and Washington gardens, where it is reliable. Elsewhere, it's often a dieback shrub, seldom reaching 10′, but does form a 15(20)′ tall tree. Be leery of suckering as the species will form aggressive colonies. Fast-growing.

Foliage: The dark green foliage, when bruised, gives off an odor that is difficult for the olfactory sense to digest ("stinky" to peanut buttery are common conclusions). Leaves are pubescent, especially below, large, often to 9″ long. Fall color is at best yellow-green, and a hard freeze turns leaves Kraft-bag brown. Typically leaves die off green. **Flowers/seeds/fruits/cones**: The individual flowers are white, very fragrant, 1 to 1½″ long, tubular at the base, spreading into 5 narrow lobes at the mouth. The cymose, 6 to 9″ wide inflorescences develop on the new growth of the summer, subtended by the large leaves. Flowers open over an extended period of time, with the pretty pea-sized bright blue drupe subtended by the leathery-plastic 5-lobed calyx, developing with and after flowering. The fruit color is exquisite, and very few hardy woody plants offer anything similar. **Native range**: China, Japan. **Adaptability**: Adaptable to sun and moderate shade, in acid or higher pH soils. Hardiness ratings are questionable, and observations support zones 7 to 9. Even as a dieback plant, flowers will be produced on the new growth, yet instead of a tree, the end result is a suckering shrub. **Landscape use**: Beautiful when integrated into an herbaceous or perennial border. For fragrant late-summer flowers, colorful fruit display, it is worthy. Requires moisture in droughty conditions and well-drained soil. Will run; authors observed suckering shoots 15 to 20′ from the parent plant. **Street tree use**: No. **In the trade**: Usually sold both as cutting and seed-grown material. Several cultivars are listed.

'Carnival' ('Variegata'). Leaves develop vivid yellowish margins, but unfortunately the plant often reverts to green. It has a propensity to sucker like the species, the shoots, developing from roots, almost always green. Readily available.

'Purple Haze'. Dark purple emerging foliage, eventually green. Hardier than the species.

Clerodendrum trichotomum

Clerodendrum trichotomum

Clerodendrum trichotomum

Clethra barbinervis

Japanese clethra

Deciduous. Truly one of the most beautiful summer-flowering small trees for colder climates where *Lagerstroemia* and *Vitex* are not hardy. Overall texture unique, artistic, and the plant readily identifiable. Gray, orange, brown, exfoliating bark initiates on 2″ and thicker branches. Authors have observed sufficient *C. barbinervis* to understand that bark qualities range from blasé to hooray; in the finest seedlings, bark is exquisite, paralleling the best *Stewartia pseudocamellia* for effect. Habit is upright-spreading, with a rounded canopy; largest plants we encountered were 20′ high with a similar spread.

Foliage: Leaves, oval to obovate, sharply and prominently serrate, are clustered at the ends of the branch, creating a whorled effect. They emerge bronze-purple, maturing lustrous dark green, 2 to 6″ long, 1 to 2¼″ wide, developing, on occasion, bronze-red to maroon fall color. Variation in fall color is maddening, and selection for vivid, reliable fall color clones is a worthy pursuit. **Flowers/seeds/fruits/cones**: The ⅓″ wide white flowers are held in 4 to 6(8)″ long terminal racemose panicles in July-August. Borne in great profusion with the foliage as a backdrop, they are extremely effective. Authors noted fragrance varies from slight to quite sweet, again offering opportunities for improvement. Fruit is a 5-valved, dehiscent capsule, green, maturing brown, ⅓ to ½″ across, persisting into winter. Seeds are tiny and will germinate immediately upon sowing with no pretreatment. **Native range**: Japan, South Korea. **Adaptability**: Successful in Massachusetts, Maine, and Connecticut, where it grows with abandon. Zones 5 to 7, but flexible enough to survive 4 and 8. **Landscape use**: Authors experienced single- and multi-stemmed plants, both styles effective where utilized as accents, specimens, in borders and woodland gardens. Requires moist, acid, well-drained soils, full sun to moderate shade. **Street tree use**: Potential when grown as a standard, also functional in large raised beds and containers. **In the trade**: Available. Breeders, selectors, nursery producers have yet to maximize the true potential of the species by incorporating its best traits (i.e., flower, fall color, bark) into a cultivar—a goal for the authors, as the genetic variation is obvious on plants in cultivation. 'Variegata' has pretty bronze leaves maturing green, speckled, streaked, and swirled with white. Seedlings the authors grew from *C. barbinervis* × *C. fargesii* produced striking orange-red fall color.

C

Clethra barbinervis

Clethra barbinervis

Clethra barbinervis

Cornus
dogwood

Dogwoods are an essential component of North American landscapes, occurring naturally in the temperate northern hemisphere, with two species in South America and one in Africa. The taxonomy is not well defined, and the genus was for a time subdivided into *Cornus*, *Swida*, *Chamaepericlymenum*, *Benthamidia*, *Cynoxylon*, and *Dendrobenthamia*. Sound confusing? It was! A few botanical gardens followed these changes, and their labels reflected these passing names. Thankfully, *Cornus* is current, still dominates, and is used herein.

For those who love plant identification, the genus displays similar leaf morphology: the impressed veins emanate from the midrib and parallel the margin, which is entire on all dogwoods. Additionally, when a leaf is torn in half, a rubbery, stringy compound stretches from the veins, similar to a rubber band. All but two species have opposite leaves. Many of the approximately 60 species are shrubs, with *C. florida*, *C. kousa*, and *C. nuttallii* the major white-bracted, deciduous tree types. Within these and via hybridization, numerous cultivars have been introduced. Few tree species match their flowers, fruit, fall color, and bark for year-round beauty. In recent years, evergreen tree species (*C. capitata*, *C. elliptica*, *C. hongkongensis*) and cultivars with showy white bracts have surfaced in the Southeast and Northwest; they flower later than the closely related *C. kousa*, their flowers are poised on short peduncles, rising above the shiny, rich green foliage.

The dogwoods are an important economic driver in the American nursery industry, with Tennessee, Oregon, and North Carolina the leading producers. The disease issues discussed in this preamble could impact sales, but so far the passion for dogwoods and an infusion of resistant selections keeps demand for them high. Particularly in zones 5 and 6, *C. kousa* and its hybrids have become more popular than ever, owing to their disease resistance.

Of the several diseases that have manifested themselves over the past 30 years, anthracnose (pathogen: *Discula destructiva*) and powdery mildew (pathogens: *Erysiphe pulchra*, *Microsphaera pulchra*, *Phyllactinia guttata*) are the most serious. The anthracnose, initially described c.1980 in the eastern United States, induces cankers, injures branches, promotes epicormic sprouts, and eventually kills the tree. The mildew appears as a gray powdery residue on the foliage, causing distorted, malformed leaves. Fortunately, degrees of resistance to the diseases are inherent in the genome of *C. florida*, and resistant selections exist. *C. nuttallii* is also susceptible to anthracnose. *C. kousa* is slightly affected and was utilized to breed anthracnose and mildew

resistance into the Stellar series, *C. ×rutgersensis*; and later, with *C. nuttallii*, to produce the *C. ×elwinortonii* series. To date, the authors have not observed anthracnose or mildew on *C. elliptica*, even on seedlings growing next to heavily mildew-infested seedlings of *C. florida*.

In the 1990s, when anthracnose was percolating throughout New England and the Mid-Atlantic, the University of Tennessee led a research effort to select resistant types from the wild, from nursery seedlings, and via breeding. The resulting cultivars of the Appalachian series (discussed under *C. florida*) are anthracnose and/or mildew resistant. Several of the old reliable *C. florida* cultivars (e.g., CHEROKEE BRAVE, 'Cherokee Princess') are also highly mildew resistant. Our best advice is to keep the dogwoods culturally healthy and vigorous. Stressed dogwoods are also subject to increased susceptibility to borers and cankers.

Dogwoods should be a part of every landscape where they can be successfully grown. We believe spring would not be the same without a flowering dogwood, whether *C. florida*, *C. kousa*, *C. nuttallii*, or their hybrids. Add to this the newer evergreen dogwoods and hybrids for zones (7)8 to 9, and the palette of large-bracted choices is expanded.

Cornus alternifolia
pagoda dogwood

Deciduous. Wonderful native but susceptible to stem blight/canker; few large trees are evident in cultivation. Develops a layered, stratified branching structure, at maturity wider than high, 15 to 25′ in height. The pretty red-purple

Cornus alternifolia

young stems and older slightly ridged and furrowed bark provide off-season color and texture. Growth rate is slow to moderate.

Foliage: Alternate leaves, dark green, 2 to 5″ long, have 5 to 6 vein pairs and occasionally develop reddish purple fall color. This latter trait is seldom consistent, with most trees minimally colorful. **Flowers/seeds/fruits/cones**: Flowers dance in syncopated orchestration across the tops of the horizontal branches, each yellowish white, 2½″ flat-topped inflorescence persisting 7 to 10 days in May-June. Flowers are profuse, and the overall effect is quite striking. Authors noticed, on close nose-to-nose confrontations, the flowers are sickeningly fragrant. We love the fruits, bloomy, globose to ⅓″ wide, ripening in a defined sequence, from green to red to blue-black at maturity. Excellent feathery-friend food, not long persistent; after abscission, the colorful pinkish red pedicels and peduncle are more evident. Delicate, lovely color when contrasted with the dark green foliage. **Native range**: Newfoundland to Minnesota, south to Georgia, west to Florida, Alabama, Mississippi, principally in the mountains. In north Georgia, it is abundant along mountain roadsides, proliferating in well-drained, acid, gravelly/rocky soil. Typically, an understory plant in broadleaf and coniferous woods; moist to dry habitats. Several floras list it as rare, but authors observed it in quantity from Maine to Georgia. **Adaptability**: Cold hardy to zone 3, following the mountains into zone 7. **Landscape use**: Ideally, utilize as an understory plant in native plant gardens. Can be a specimen with proper cultural conditions; site on the north side of structures or in pine-mediated shade. Provide well-drained, acid soil and even moisture. The Warren garden included one for 10 years or so, but it gradually declined. It seems to be touchy outside of its native habitat, and even there it is short-lived. **Street tree use**: No. **In the trade**: The authors have *never* observed the species at a retail garden center. Only a few of the several pretty cultivars are available, but nowhere common.

‘Argentea’. With silver to cream-margined leaves, smaller and more shrubby than the species, growing 10 to 15′ high and wide. Introduced c.1900 and still the most common variegated form of the species.

Cornus alternifolia

Cornus alternifolia

‘Argentea’

GOLDEN SHADOWS

BIG CHOCOLATE CHIP 'Bichozam'. Develops an upright rounded habit, 25′ by 25′, more vigorous than the species, with burgundy fall color, chocolate stems and branches.

'Black Stem'. A robust tree to 25′ with purplish black stems.

GOLDEN SHADOWS 'Wstackman'. Yellow-margined, green-centered leaves, mature leaf margins turn cream-white; quite colorful but diminished in heavy shade; trends to a shrubby habit. 'Goldfinch' appears similar.

PISTACHIO 'Piszam'. Burgundy-red new leaves mature lustrous dark green. Cream-yellow flowers are held on mint-green stems. Develops a rounded habit, 20′ by 20′.

Cornus controversa
giant dogwood

Deciduous. Upright-spreading becoming wide-spreading, forming a horizontally layered structure, the layering becoming the dominant feature of its form. Moderate growth rate to 30′ tall, 40′ wide, although we have seen trees to 50′. Medium in texture. Bark dark gray, lightly ridged and furrowed.

Foliage: Leaves are large for a dogwood, 3 to 6″ and half or more as wide, broadly ovate with an acuminate tip, smooth except for prominent parallel veins arcing across the surface. Leaves are particularly clean and trouble-free, resisting anthracnose and powdery mildew. Bright medium green in spring, darker green in summer, and a wonderful mix of fall colors, from yellow-orange to orange-red and purplish, all on the same plant. **Flowers/seeds/fruits/cones**: Very large, flat-topped cymes of tiny white flowers are quite showy in May-June. Round fruits, less than ¼″ wide, follow in summer and turn blue-black as they ripen. Favored by

Cornus controversa

Cornus controversa

JUNE SNOW

JUNE SNOW

JUNE SNOW

birds and small in size, they disappear into grass or planting beds but could put purple stains on a hard surface. The broad, highly branched pedicels take on a bright red color as the fruit ripens, and they remain on the tree as coral-like ornamental features after the fruit drops. **Native range**: Japan, China. **Adaptability**: Zones 5 to 8. **Landscape use**: A tree of four-season interest, with early spring leaf out, late

spring flowering, summer foliage quality, late summer fruit, later summer bright pedicels, fall color, and winter layered structure as highlights. The four seasons just morphed into seven, but such is this tree: always of interest, and one of our absolute favorites. A great specimen or tree for the broad border. **Street tree use**: No, too wide and low spreading. **In the trade**: Almost always sold as a cultivar.

'Janine'. Variegated foliage, yellow on the broad margin and green in the center. Layered growth habit of the species, slower growing with smaller flower heads, 20′ by 20′. Partial shade suggested.

JUNE SNOW 'June Snow-JFS'. Green-leaved and full-sized, this cultivar really gets it right. Unlike the variegated forms, this is a strong-growing tree with a bold appearance. Flower heads can be nearly the size of salad plates. The form is full and artistically layered, the foliage is healthy and does not burn. Outstanding fall color. Tougher than others, it performs well in the South and on both coasts; it has even done well in the harsh climate of Colorado. Tall enough to limb up for garden clearance below, it earned its place in the Warren's front yard. A winner and the authors' favorite, to 30′ tall, 40′ wide.

JUNE SNOW

'Variegata'

Cornus elliptica

Cornus elliptica

'Variegata' (wedding cake tree). Layered form and white-variegated foliage (white margin, green center). The white color is almost ghostly against a dark background. Very slow-growing to 20′ by 20′. Provide partial shade and have patience, it's worth it.

Cornus elliptica (*C. angustata,* *C. kousa* var. *angustata*)

Chinese evergreen dogwood

Broadleaf evergreen. Oval to rounded tree with arching, cascading branches, creating fine-textured persona. In the Southeast, it is reasonably common to encounter trees 30′ high and wide. Growth is slow. Bark smooth, gray to grayish brown.

Foliage: Emerging leaves are soft green; the mature upper surface is glossy dark green, lower pale to glaucous, with sandpapery gray pubescence. Vein pairs, 3 or 4 on each side of the midrib. The oblong to elliptic to lanceolate leaves are 2½ to 4″ long, ¾ to 1½″ wide. Leaves were always on the small side on trees authors observed. Leaves turn bronze-purple (maroon) in cold weather, persisting to

various degrees depending on temperatures. **Flowers/seeds/fruits/cones**: Floral bracts emerge green, open white, shaped like *C. kousa* bracts, each 1 to 2″ long, ½ to ⅘″ wide. The cream-white bracts contrast beautifully with the rich green foliage. Bracts are narrower than and do not overlap like those of most *C. kousa* or *C. capitata*. Flowers open May-June (zone 8) and are effective for a month or more. Fruit is a syncarp of drupes, globose, ¾ to 1″, red, ripening in October-November, persisting into December. **Native range**: Southern China. Found in forests, slopes, streamsides at 1,000 to 7,000′ elevation. **Adaptability**: Definitely a species requiring favorable habitat for any measure of success. Several references speculate it requires more heat than available in England or the Pacific Northwest to flower well. In Oregon, the species is semi-evergreen, and the leaves look ratty in winter; it would be better if they fell. Plants survive to 0°F, but may drop most of their foliage. Zones (7)8 to 9. **Landscape use**: Use as a small specimen tree, in a grouping, or in a border. Trees perform best in partial/dappled shade or on the north and east sides of structures in moist, acid, well-drained soils and with wind protection.

EMPRESS OF CHINA

EMPRESS OF CHINA

LITTLE RUBY

LITTLE RUBY

Surprising to experience so many trees in the Southeast. **Street tree use**: Probably not. **In the trade**: Available, as are two other evergreen species. A few separatory characteristics, based on examinations of living material and the literature, may be traced in the cultivars. *C. hongkongensis* (*C. omeiensis*, *C. capitata* subsp. *omeiensis*; Hong Kong dogwood) has bronze new growth, smooth lower leaf surface. Leaves of *C. capitata* (Himalayan evergreen dogwood) are dull gray-green above, whereas both *C. elliptica*

C

and *C. hongkongensis* have a glossier upper leaf surface. All have foliage that turns bronze-maroon-purple in winter; retained to various degrees based on cold. All have floral bracts that open lime-green, maturing white. The bracts of *C. capitata* are broad ovate to rounded, almost overlapping at their edges, with a short, narrow point at the apex; both *C. elliptica* and *C. hongkongensis* have narrower ovate, usually non-overlapping bracts, the apex long extended. All have aggregate fruits, similar to those of *C. kousa*, the drupes globose to rounded, raspberry to rose-red.

EMPRESS OF CHINA 'Elsbury'. Authors have grown seedlings with all manner of habits, leaf retention, and tardiness to flower. Most take 5 to 7 years before flowering, whereas this introduction flowers profusely as a young plant in a 3-gallon container, providing consistent and reliable flowering. Foliage is shiny dark green, the flowers held on a 1½ to 2″ long peduncle, rising above the foliage, the latter a perfect high-resolution contrast to the milk-white floral bracts. Trees to 20′ high and wide are known. *C. elliptica* cultivar.

LITTLE RUBY 'NCCH1'. Single to double pink-rose bracts, red new foliage, and bright red to maroon fall-winter foliage. Trends toward a shrub, but with *C. kousa* 'Satomi' × *C. hongkongensis* 'Summer Passion' genes, it could be fashioned

273

into a small tree. Adaptability is predicted in zone 6b to 9, 10 on the West Coast. From the breeding program of Tom Ranney, NCSU.

'Mountain Moon'. Listed as a selection of *C. capitata*, but the lone plant in Athens, GA, was more closely allied to *C. elliptica*. Supposedly, the flowers are 5 to 6″ across, but in a decade of observation in Athens, flowers were consistently 3½ to 4″ across, the showy bracts shaped like *C. elliptica*, not *C. capitata*; and leaves are lustrous, not dull as in *C. capitata*. Tree reached 20′ high, 15′ wide.

'Summer Passion'. Seed-grown cultivar introduced by Piroche Plants, Pitt Meadows, BC. It did not fare well in Athens, GA. The young leaves flush red, maturing glossy dark green. The underside of the leaves, glabrous and smooth, places this with *C. hongkongensis*.

'Mountain Moon'

'Mountain Moon'

Cornus florida
flowering dogwood

Deciduous. For the authors, to choose between this or *Cercis canadensis* would require the wisdom of Solomon. In truth, we love both. *C. florida* is the premier four-season tree, in flower, fruit, fall color, winter silhouette. Stature 20′ high and wide constitutes successful garden husbandry, with trees in the wild ascending 30 to 50′. Forms a rounded to broad-rounded outline, often flat-topped, with horizontal branches, resulting in a layered/stratified appearance. The red-purple stem and grayish older branches are pretty in the dormant season. Growth rate is slow to moderate. Classic bark pattern ("alligator hide") provides instant recognition of larger trees. Bark is a grayish brown. Considered a short-lived garden tree, subject to many maladies (anthracnose, mildew, borers), but with proper cultivar selection and planting/maintenance practices, it will outlive the gardener.

Cornus florida

Cornus florida

274

Foliage: The 3 to 6″ long, 1½ to 3″ wide leaves range from medium to dark green, dull to glossy, with 6 or 7 vein pairs, becoming red to red-purple in autumn. Selections with purplish new foliage (CHEROKEE BRAVE) and multiple variegation patterns/colors are common; both summer and fall color are worth considering when purchasing. One hundred and eighteen caterpillar species depend upon the foliage for sustenance. **Flowers/seeds/fruits/cones**: On the Georgia campus (zone 8), a lone seedling is always in flower by late March, with full expression in April, effective for 2 weeks and longer; and a few trees are in full regalia in early May. Translating, that means one might plan for 4 to 6 weeks of flowering. The emarginate (indented) white bracts, each 2″ and longer, borne 4 together, subtend the true greenish yellow fertile flowers, the precursors of the fruits. The flowers appear on naked branches, often persisting (a tad forlorn) through the maturation of the leaves. Certain trees assume the aura of a billowy cumulus cloud. Fruit, seldom given publicity, is an ovoid, glossy red, ⅓ to ½″ long drupe, ripening in September-October; it provides important nutrition for the birds. More than 40 bird species eat the fruits and flower buds. Interesting to note that certain trees are stripped clean as fruits ripen, while others retain fruits into late fall after leaf abscission. **Native range**: Maine to Florida, west to Ontario, Texas, and Mexico. An understory tree, along wood edges, fencerows, and open fields in deep, moist soils to well-drained upland areas. **Adaptability**: Zones 5 to 9 with proper selection of cold- and heat-adaptable cultivars. Northern provenances, Ontario and others, offer promise of increased cold hardiness. Bailey Nurseries, St. Paul, MN, is focused on breeding selections with flower buds reliably hardy to zone 4 (to -30°F). **Landscape use**: As a lawn, border, woodland, naturalizing tree, plant many and often. A cultivar exists for every garden situation. In fact, at the Augusta National Golf Club, home of the Masters, hole 2 is designated pink dogwood, hole 11 is white dogwood; for a tree, this is the greatest recognition that can be bestowed. In a cultural nutshell...provide moist, acid, well-drained soil, partial shade to full sun (yes, full—assuming supplemental water), keep vigorous with half-rate late-winter fertilizer, mulch (to control weeds, maintain moisture, avoid compaction), and protect from mechanical injury (mowers, weed-eaters). A Kentucky study quantitatively showed mechanically injured dogwood trees suffered greater borer infestation than healthy trees. In the Pacific Northwest and other cool and moist climates, full sun and air circulation are important to avoid anthracnose. **Street tree use**: No limits, but street tree plantings typically suffer unless adequate space and moisture are provided. In Athens, GA, too many decrepit, straggly, unkempt, and feeble dogwoods suffer from street tree–itis. **In the trade**: In the United States, no other flowering tree outsells *C. florida* and cultivars. Small seedling trees are inexpensive and planted in spades will reward abundantly, as a percentage always survives and thrives. Kudos to a great native!

White flowers

Appalachian series. From the University of Tennessee. Should be first choice, especially in residential gardens, for clean foliage and consistent red to red-purple fall color. Absolute cold hardiness is not known, but zones 6 to 8 are safe. Plants were selected for mildew and/or anthracnose resistance: 'Appalachian Blush' (powdery mildew resistant,

Cornus florida

Cornus florida

'Appalachian Blush'

C

'Appalachian Joy'

'Cherokee Princess'

'Appalachian Mist'

'Appalachian Snow'

'Cloud 9'

white bracts with hint of pink), 'Appalachian Joy' (powdery mildew resistant, 4 to 8 overlapping white bracts), 'Appalachian Mist' (powdery mildew resistant, stiff slightly overlapping white bracts), 'Appalachian Snow' (powdery mildew resistant, large white floppy bracts), and 'Appalachian Spring' (anthracnose and powdery mildew resistant, smaller white bracts). Note, 'Appalachian Spring', selected in Maryland's Catoctin Mountain Park, is the only tree in the trade with proven resistance (not immunity) to both anthracnose and powdery mildew; it is also the only member of the series

not patented, as it was found in the wild. In Georgia trials, 'Appalachian Blush' and 'Appalachian Joy' have been free of the diseases and sport large glossy leaves and excellent red-purple fall color.

'Cherokee Princess'. One of the best for abundant white flowers, slightly glossy green foliage, and resistance to spot anthracnose and canker. Along with 'Appalachian Joy', this has been the best performer in the Dirr garden.

276

'Appalachian Spring'

'Cherokee Princess'

'Cloud 9'. Showy white overlapping bracts, flowering profusely when young. In Kansas trials, it was rated one of the most cold hardy. Spreading habit, 15 to 20′ high and wide. 'Barton' is the same as 'Cloud 9'.

SPRING GROVE 'Grovflor'. Often produces 2 or 3 terminal flowers buds with individual flowers to 5″ wide. Parent plant was 22′ by 32′ at 45 years of age. Survived −26°F and flowered. Spectacular in flower and worth pursuing.

Double white flowers
'Pluribracteata'. Robust, vigorous tree of upright oval outline with shiny dark green leaves, highly resistant to spot anthracnose. The double flowers are beautiful, opening later than the typical species. A splendid, 25′ high, 15′ wide specimen that grew on the University of Georgia campus exceeded the accolades just given.

'Welch's Bay Beauty'. About 7 sets of whorled bracts, each flower 4½ to 5½″ across. Holds leaves late in the season, developing red-purple autumn color. Selected in the South and best in zones 7 to 9.

Pink flowers
The pink cultivars are not as cold hardy as the better whites and typically open 3 to 7 days later. Best in zone 5b and higher (warmer).

CHEROKEE BRAVE 'Comco No. 1'. We rate this at the pinnacle of the pink ladder. Mildew resistant bronze-red-green young leaves, reddish pink bracts with a white center, and vigorous growth. Excellent performance in the Dirr gardens, Bonnie, Mike, and daughter Katie.

'Cherokee Chief'. A legacy cultivar with rich ruby-red flowers and reddish new growth. More susceptible to bract spotting, but one of the best "pinks" and is still widely available.

'Prairie Pink'. From Wichita, KS, with light pink to pink-blush flowers, and possibly the most cold hardy f. *rubra* taxon. Leaves are thicker than typical, reflecting its resistance to the prairie heat and wind, glossy dark green, turning orange-red to purple-red in fall. Upright-spreading developing a rounded crown, 20′ high and wide. A plant in the Dirr garden has performed admirably.

CHEROKEE BRAVE

'Cherokee Chief'

'Prairie Pink'

'Cherokee Chief'

f. *rubra*

RAGIN' RED 'JN13'. Flower color is deeper than others in the pink group, close to red. New foliage is maroon-red in spring, greener in summer, then burgundy fall color develops. Shows resistance to mildew. To 25′ tall, 20′ wide.

f. *rubra*. The precursor of the many pink, rose, and red selections, numbering over 30. Not a clone. It is the most widespread pink form in commerce, often sold as 'Rubra'. Lovely soft pink bracts.

Variegated foliage

Whether with white or pink flowers (bracts), these types are numerous and appear more prone to leaf and bract spotting. Ask a local nursery about the best option for your region.

CHEROKEE DAYBREAK 'Daybreak'. One of the best, with white-margined leaves and white flowers.

f. *rubra*

CHEROKEE DAYBREAK

RAGIN' RED

CHEROKEE DAYBREAK

CHEROKEE SUNSET

CHEROKEE SUNSET

FIREBIRD

CHEROKEE SUNSET

'First Lady'

CHEROKEE SUNSET 'Sunset'. Pinkish red new growth, maturing green with broad yellow margin, pink-red to purple fall color, and red flowers.

FIREBIRD 'Fircom 2'. A variegated sport of CHEROKEE BRAVE with red, pink, cream margins, the foliage remaining pristine in full sun; 20 to 25' high and wide. Flower color is similar to CHEROKEE BRAVE, pink with a white center.

'First Lady'. White flowers, yellow-green foliage, resistant to spot anthracnose and canker. In zone 8, much of the variegation is lost.

Cornus kousa

kousa dogwood

Deciduous. Upright at first, soon losing its central leader and spreading to become broadly vase-shaped. Branches tend to be elegantly layered, with age it can be broader than tall. Moderately slow-growing with a fine-textured appearance, to 20 to 30′ high and wide. Bark can be a wonderful ornamental feature of this species, with age exfoliating and developing a beautiful mosaic pattern of grays, warm tans, and orange tones.

Foliage: Dark green, 2 to 3½″ long, half as wide, smooth with a satiny sheen, ovate with smooth margins and a gracefully acuminate tip; the foliage is as elegant as the tree's form. Fall color is yellow-orange, orange-red, or bright red, always attractive. Resistant to anthracnose and powdery mildew, which are so troublesome on *C. florida*. **Flowers/seeds/fruits/cones**: What we view as the flower is actually a star-shaped assemblage of 4 creamy white bracts surrounding a densely packed center umbel of the tiny, yellow, true flowers. Flowering occurs 2 to 3 weeks later than in *C. florida*. The inflorescence is 2 to 4″ across, and the white bracts have an advantage over typical flower petals, as they are more substantial and tend to last for at least a few weeks. As the bracts age they sometimes take on slightly pinkish margins; a true pink that does not fade has been an elusive goal in kousa dogwood breeding. Bumpy red aggregate fruit, 1″. **Native range**: Japan, Korea, China. **Adaptability**: Likes a moist, acid, well-drained soil and a little humidity in the air. Does well in the temperate climates along the West Coast, East Coast, and through the Southeast, but becomes stressed in the more extreme climates of the Plains and Mountain States. Overall, it's slightly more cold hardy than *C. florida*, but depends on the individual seed source or cultivar. Zones 5 to 8. **Landscape use**: Comes close to being the ultimate garden tree. Small and elegant with

Cornus kousa

Cornus kousa

Cornus kousa

Cornus kousa

Cornus kousa

C

'Akatsuki'

CHAMPION'S GOLD

'China Girl'

all-season appeal, it fits well into most landscapes and tends to be problem-free in favorable climates. Flowering comes later than the early spring burst of most trees, providing welcome beauty in late spring or early summer. Rich green summer foliage is among the nicest of small trees, and the fall color is not far behind red and sugar maple in intensity. Fruits, the size of ping-pong balls, hang like Christmas ornaments in early autumn, strange-looking but beautiful in their own way, and thankfully edible, in case your kids decide to sample one. We have tasted—not our favorite flavor, but worth trying for a little adventure. Winter form is elegant, fine-textured and layered. **Street tree use**: No, too low and wide. **In the trade**: Widely sold as seed-grown, usually as subsp. *chinensis*. A great many cultivars have been developed, more than are justified, often being only slightly different from the species, or selected for having variegated foliage but with uncertain quality otherwise. Both authors have made selections in this species, but we have not introduced them, believing that a new cultivar must be better, not just different. The following cultivars have white flowers (bracts) unless otherwise stated.

'Akatsuki' ('Pretty Sunrise'). A smaller growing, more delicate plant with variegated foliage. Leaves are white and green with the margin becoming pinkish red in the fall. Flowers are white with a pink tint but smaller than the species. Very pretty, but somewhat weak growing. Foliage may curl or burn in full sun. 15′ by 15′.

'Big Apple'. Vigorous green-leaved variety selected for its large fruit, which may reach 1½″ in diameter. The weight of the fruit gives the tree a more spreading shape. 20′ by 20′.

CHAMPION'S GOLD 'Losely'. Green spring foliage changes to bright gold in late summer. In transitioning, the outer foliage turns yellow while the inner foliage remains green, giving the tree a bicolor appearance. Pink, orange, and red fall colors follow. The summer yellow color develops well in the hot Midwest, not so in the cooler Pacific Northwest. Rounded form. 20′ by 20′.

'China Girl'. An excellent green-leaved selection of the species, having good foliage quality, vigorous growth, moderately upright form, and heavy early flower display. A good choice where a typical kousa form is desired but adds reliability and heavy flowering. 25′ by 25′.

subsp. *chinensis*. Much has been made of the supposed superiority of this subspecies, but there is little botanical difference, as the species varies over its geographic range. It

CROWN JEWEL

'Gold Star'

C

does have thicker, slightly larger leaves and heavier flowering. This is often the taxon you are said to be getting when buying seedling *C. kousa*, but that is doubtful, unless you are purchasing seed directly from a Chinese source. Nurseries typically collect seed from their best-looking, most reliable plants, and actual provenance is usually mixed or lost.

CROWN JEWEL 'Madison'. As summer heats up, the leaves take on a bright yellow color, beginning at the leaf base and progressing slowly toward the tip; green in spring and early summer, a mottled green and yellow mix in late summer, and a red and yellow mix in fall. Interesting and attractive. Performed poorly in heat of Georgia. Color change needs the right climate and is not seen in Oregon. 20′ by 20′.

'Empire'. Very narrow and upright. The original tree was 33′ tall and 4′ wide at 20 years. We expect typical landscape trees to be 20 to 25′ tall and 4 to 6′ wide. Broad bracts.

GALILEAN 'Galzam'. An excellent rendering of the traditional green-leaved kousa. Leaves are larger than typical, smooth and substantial, the plant is more vigorous, and flowers have unusually broad creamy bracts, making them more impressive. Good cold hardiness. 25′ by 25′.

'Gold Star'. Variegated, bright yellow center and dark green margins, the opposite of most variegated dogwoods and with more intense colors, giving a very different appearance. We have seen some reversion. Foliage holds up well in the heat of the summer. 15′ by 15′.

'Greensleeves'. Fairly upright for a kousa with good dark green foliage with wavy margins, large bracts, heavy flowering, one of the best of the traditional forms. 20′ by 20′.

GALILEAN

'Greensleeves'

'Greensleeves'

HEART THROB

HEART THROB

MANDARIN JEWEL

'Lustgarten Weeping'

'Milky Way Select'

'Milky Way Select'

'Milky Way Select'

HEART THROB 'Schmred'. Flowers with rose-pink, broad, rounded bracts are prolifically displayed and more long-lasting than most. Spring foliage carries a slight purplish tint, fall color is red. Rounded form. 20′ by 20′. Indistinguishable from 'Satomi'.

'Lustgarten Weeping'. Of the several weeping forms of kousa dogwood, we feel this is the most graceful. It needs to be staked to reach a desired height, and then it will weep to the ground. Moderate flowering, but flowers are well displayed along arching stems. Yellow to purple-red in fall. 15′ by 15′.

MANDARIN JEWEL 'Madi II'. Selected for unusual yellow-orange fruit; when fully ripe and pumpkin-orange, it stands out against the foliage more than the typical red fruits. But this tree is a beauty in other ways: flower bracts are very neatly formed and star-like; foliage is high quality, dark green. 20′ by 20′.

'Milky Way'. A confused and confusing "cultivar." It started as a vegetatively propagated group of 15 different, but superior, stock plants. Later, seedlings of these were widely sold. It is best looked at as a seed source cultivar. Generally nice, but not recommended because of variability. 20′ by 20′.

'Milky Way Select'. A recommended improvement over the original. In an attempt to end the confusion of 'Milky Way', a single superior seedling from the 'Milky Way' group was chosen and cloned in tissue culture, and thus predictability was returned. An excellent tree with typical kousa form, very heavy flowering with clean bracts, excellent orange-red fall color, and abundant bright red fruit. One of the best for resistance to anthracnose and powdery mildew. 20′ by 20′.

PROPHET

SCARLET FIRE

PROPHET

SAMARITAN

'National'. One of the most upright cultivars, with a narrower vase shape. Foliage is dark green and of high quality. Heavy flowering, strong growing, 25′ by 18′.

'Pam's Mountain Bouquet'. Broad bracts are partially or fully fused in over half the flowers, giving a solid, squared look. Impressive bloom, a little later to flower than most. Spreading, 15 to 20′ tall, 20′ wide.

PROPHET 'Propzam'. Features outstanding foliage quality, with leaves that are thicker, darker green, and cleaner than typical seedlings. Flowers are substantial with broad bracts, but perhaps not as prolific as some cultivars. Fall color is usually orange. More rounded and less layered in shape. 25′ by 25′.

RADIANT ROSE 'Hanros'. Pink flowers with broad bracts, very similar to 'Satomi' and hard to distinguish from it. Introducer says flower color holds longer in summer and leaves are slightly larger and darker. 20′ by 20′.

'Red Steeple'. Narrow and upright. Foliage carries a red tint that lasts most of the summer, fading to green in heat. Bracts are red-tinted on the margin. We estimate 20′ tall, 6 to 8′ wide.

SAMARITAN 'Samzam'. One of the best variegated dogwoods and our choice among white variegated forms for the Midwest. Its creamy white and green to gray-green foliage brightens up a landscape. Displays heavy flowering and good form, resists burning, and has proven cold hardiness to at

RADIANT ROSE

'Summer Fun'

'Satomi'

'Summer Fun'

SCARLET FIRE

least zone 5; we enjoyed the beautiful plant at Coastal Maine Botanical Gardens. 18′ by 18′.

'Satomi' ('Miss Satomi'). The standard among the pink variegated kousa dogwoods. Probably sold under several other names. Rose-pink bracts are rounded; floral display is long-lasting in cool climates in late spring and early summer, but color quickly fades to nearly white in hot climates. Leaves have deeply indented parallel veins, which gives

the foliage a corrugated, textural look. A little smaller and slower growing than the species, becoming broadly rounded to spreading. 20′ by 20′.

SCARLET FIRE 'Rutpink'. The best pink of the kousa dogwoods, very close to a bright true pink, really a color breakthrough. Bred in New Jersey, it develops and holds its pink color in the heat better than 'Satomi' and others, which are bright in cool cloudy weather but fade to pinkish white where summers are hot. Georgia's heat proved too much for a good pink, but in Oregon's cool spring, bract color has been intensely pink. Flowers heavily at an early age. Moderate growth rate. 20′ by 20′.

'Snow Tower'. Narrow form with tighter, more upright branching. If pruned up, could be used in narrower sites. Large flowers hold well. 20′ tall, 10′ wide.

'Summer Fun'. The brightest of the white variegated kousa dogwoods and our choice among these for the Pacific Northwest and other cool and mild climates. The leaf margins are especially broad and are a cleaner white than others. Brighter and more vigorous than similarly variegated SAMARITAN and 'Wolf Eyes' but has shown some leaf burn in hot areas of the East. 20′ by 20′.

'Summer Gold'

'Summer Gold'

'Summer Stars'

'Sunsplash'

'Temple Jewel'

'Summer Gold'. Bright yellow and green variegated foliage, with the yellow margins changing to pinkish red in the fall. Good growth rate and form, faster growing than 'Sunsplash', our first choice among the yellow variegated kousa dogwoods. 18′ by 18′.

'Summer Stars'. Slower growing, with finer-textured foliage; leaves have a wavy margin and prominent veins. Flowers are a little small but quite prolific and long-lasting. More bushy than most, making a small spreading tree. 15′ by 15′.

'Sunsplash'. Bright yellow and green variegated foliage, similar to 'Summer Gold' but considerably slower growing. A little later to develop fall color, pinkish red along the margin. 15′ by 15′.

'Temple Jewel'. A subtle and elusive variegation. Green and light yellow variegated, the pattern the reverse of most, with the darker green portion along the margin. The central portion is a faded yellowish green, softer, not as bright as other variegated dogwoods. The variegation shows best in spring; the leaves become more solid green in summer. 20′ by 20′.

'Teutonia'. European selection with large, broad-bracted flowers. Considered impressive for its bright orange-red fall color. 20′ by 20′.

'Tri-Splendor'. Variegated foliage that changes through the seasons. Creamy white and green in spring, becoming more yellowish in summer, and then almost completely green later on. Some reddish autumn tints. A very interesting progression of foliage color from spring to fall, soft and subtle. Never as brightly colored as other variegated cultivars, but beauty is in the eye of the beholder, and we like its gentler effect. 18′ by 18′.

'Weisse Fontaine' ('White Fountain'). A vigorous upright-growing cultivar. The branches become heavy with flowers with time and arch, inspiring the name. 20′ by 20′.

'Temple Jewel'

'Tri-Splendor'

'Wolf Eyes'

'Wolf Eyes'

'Wolf Eyes'

'Wisley Queen'. Propagated from a very large, broadly vase-shaped to rounded, arching tree at RHS Wisley. The original tree is truly impressive. Broad-rounded overlapping bracts. 25′ by 25′.

'Wolf Eyes'. Variegated cream-white and gray-green with a distinctly wavy leaf margin. The leaves tend to curl upward in summer. Similar to SAMARITAN and 'Summer Fun', and we would give the nod to those two variegated cultivars as having better foliage. 15′ by 15′.

Cornus mas

corneliancherry dogwood

Deciduous. Beautiful small tree, 20 to 25' high and wide, or large multi-stemmed shrub that heralds the spring gardening season. Quite dense in habit, usually rounded to broad-rounded, with numerous, relatively fine-textured, interlacing branches. In Europe, it is often pruned into a dense hedge. Flower buds open in February-March, Athens, GA. We noted all manner of variation among seedlings in density/abundance of flowers and believe a superior selection for such would be useful. Growth is slow. Bark is rather pretty, with age scaly, flaky, gray-brown to rich brown, but not as exfoliating as that of *C. officinalis*. Species has been in fruit cultivation for 7,000 years.

Foliage: Leaves are quite variable in gloss and green-ness, most often dark green. Each leaf 2 to 4" long, ¾ to 1½" wide, with 3 to 5 vein pairs on each side of midrib. Foliage abscises late. Fall color is muted reddish purple at best; more often leaves die off green. **Flowers/seeds/fruits/cones:** The vivid, mustard-yellow flowers appear on naked branches in February-March, each flower only ⅙" wide, borne in great numbers in stalked umbels. Flowers persist for 3 weeks and longer because of the cool weather. We have never noticed emerging flower buds or flowers damaged by cold. Quite an amazing plant. The bright cherry-red, oblong drupaceous fruits, ½ to ¾" long, ripen in July-August, camouflaged by the foliage. Fruits are sour and acid (trust us), but in Europe, particularly the Caucasus, many selections have been made for fruit qualities, and the "cherries" are utilized in jams, jellies, pies, and for syrups. Oregon's Northwoods Nursery and other specialty fruit and nut nurseries offer these fruiting types. Ideally, plant several clones to ensure cross pollination and abundant fruits.

Cornus mas

Cornus officinalis

Cornus officinalis

Cornus mas

Cornus mas

'Golden Glory'

C

'Kintoki'

'Kintoki'

'Variegata'

'Spring Glow'

'Golden Glory'

SAFFRON SENTINEL

Native range: Central and southern Europe. **Adaptability**: Along with closely related *C. officinalis*, a virtual iron-clad performer from the coast of Maine to north Georgia to the West Coast. In the Deep South, the flowering response is not as profuse. Zones 4 to 8, but is not reliably cold hardy in Minnesota. The Chicago area is the northern limit for maximum performance, which suggests zone 5, not 4, is safer. **Landscape use**: Remarkably adaptable tree for almost any site except permanently wet. Acid, high pH, clay-based—all are acceptable soils. Handles full sun and moderate shade. May sucker and form large thickets. Usually not the case, and most *C. mas* exist as multi-stemmed, low-branched trees. May be grown as a single-stemmed small tree. Uses are multifaceted—specimen, container, border, around buildings to soften expanse of brick/concrete. On the University of Georgia campus, 15 to 20′ specimens have performed admirably for over 40 years. **Street tree use**: With pruning, narrower forms would make pleasant small street trees, considering stress tolerance. Still, the species is best adapted to colder areas. **In the trade**: Wealth of cultivars

are known, with few in everyday commerce. 'Aurea' (yellow foliage), 'Flava' (bigger, sweeter, yellow fruit, based on our sampling), and 'Variegata' (white leaf margin, green center) offer color variations. Dirr tested fruiting types 'Pioneer', REDSTAR 'Vidubetskii', and 'Elegant'; all proved mediocre and were heavily browsed by deer. The Morton Arboretum will be introducing a selection with vibrant red fall color.

'Golden Glory'. The standard for many years. Habit in youth is upright, eventually broad-oval, with abundant yellow flowers. Foliage is glossy dark green; inconsistent and minimalist red-purple in fall. Originally selected in the Chicago area, hardy in zones 4 and 5.

SAFFRON SENTINEL 'JFS PN4Legacy'. A new release, very upright and narrow in form, tighter than 'Golden Glory', and with dark green glossy foliage of the highest quality. Its form makes it realistic for use as a street tree, or in a garden where headroom below the branches is desired. We estimate 20′ tall, 12′ wide.

SAFFRON SENTINEL

'Spring Glow'

SAFFRON SENTINEL

'Spring Glow'. Shiny, mirror-surfaced dark green leaves and numerous flowers at a young age. Probably the best selection for zones (6)7 and 8. Not as cold hardy as 'Golden Glory'. From the JC Raulston Arboretum, Raleigh, NC.

C. officinalis (Japanese cornel dogwood), a deciduous species native to Japan and Korea, is closely allied to *C. mas* and often difficult to separate. Similar small tree/large shrub status, 20 to 25′ high and wide. Yellow flowers before those of *C. mas* with fruits ripening later. Bark is more showy, prominently exfoliating, even on 1 to 2″ wide branches, in shades of gray, orange, and brown. Zones 5 to 8. 'Kintoki' is a superior selection with abundant early flowers (early February in Dirr garden) on a smaller-statured framework; its flowers seem just a touch brighter and larger than those of *C. mas*. At -25 to -30°F in northern Ohio, 'Kintoki' was killed to the ground, whereas *C. mas* cultivars were untouched.

Cornus nuttallii

Pacific dogwood

Deciduous. Strongly upright, with one or more strongly
ascending trunks, developing an upright oval habit, not
layered like *C. florida* and *C. kousa*. Moderately fast-growing,
medium coarse in texture, to 45′ high, 20′ wide.

Foliage: Medium to dark green, smooth-surfaced, ovate,
similar but usually a little larger than leaves of *C. florida*,
3 to 6″ long and 2 to 3″ wide. Fall colors yellow-orange to
pinkish red. Foliage is susceptible to anthracnose, especially
in the shade. **Flowers/seeds/fruits/cones**: The flowering
inflorescence is similar to *C. florida* but significantly larger,
as much as twice the size, with 4, 6, or 8 large white oval
bracts surrounding the dense central umbel of tiny true
flowers. Flowering occurs in May in most of its native range,
and surprisingly, a second flowering often occurs in August,
not as heavy as the May display but perhaps more notable
because it is unexpected. **Native range**: West coast of North
America from British Columbia to northern California, with
additional distribution extending into the Sierra Nevada.
Adaptability: A touchy plant. It likes the climate and soils
of its native range. Zones 7 to 9. **Landscape use**: A beautiful
tree in its native habitat or in the backyard of the developed garden. Give it moist acid soil, but be sure it is sharply
drained and does not receive summer irrigation. Soggy soil
during the summer will kill it. **Street tree use**: Not recommended due to soil and drainage issues. **In the trade**: Difficult to transplant, therefore many nurseries and landscapers
avoid growing it. Sometimes sold as seed-grown, more often
as a cultivar, and increasingly as one of the new Rutgers
hybrids (see next entry), which have greatly increased landscape tolerance.

'Colrigo Giant'. Vigorous, upright, with a strong trunk and
especially large flowers, to 7″ wide. 50′ tall, 20′ wide.

Cornus nuttallii

Cornus nuttallii

'Goldspot'

'Eddie's White Wonder'

'Goldspot'

'Eddie's White Wonder'. A hybrid of *C. nuttallii* and *C. florida*, but most similar in appearance to *C. nuttallii* and used as such in landscaping. Tall and oval, with large flowers. More adaptable because of its hybrid parentage and grafting on *C. florida* rootstock, which is more tolerant of irrigated gardens. 45′ tall, 20′ wide.

'Goldspot'. Features beautifully gold-splashed foliage, as if someone took a paintbrush and flicked dots and splatters of bright yellow onto the dark green foliage. As a true *C. nuttallii* cultivar, it often has a second flowering in late summer. 40′ tall, 20′ wide.

Cornus ×rutgersensis / Cornus ×elwinortonii
Rutgers hybrid dogwoods

Deciduous. Breeders at Rutgers University have developed a series of hybrid dogwoods using the genes of *C. kousa*, *C. florida*, and *C. nuttallii*. Elwin Orton spent nearly 50 years working with this group. The hybrids seem to take a year or two longer to come into heavy flower production compared to *C. florida* and *C. kousa*. They flower with the foliage, after *C. florida* and before *C. kousa*. Improved resistance to anthracnose is probably the most important characteristic of these hybrids. They also have better resistance to powdery mildew than *C. florida*, but not always as good as *C. kousa*. **Landscape use:** The hybrids combine the characteristics of their parents but represent a distinct group of trees to consider for landscape use. They are best viewed as individual cultivars, as each is different. As a group, they tend to be more vigorous, more disease-resistant, and more dense than their parents, with greater landscape adaptability. Curiously, their form tends to be more solid and lacks some of the aesthetically pleasing layered branching of *C. florida* and *C. kousa*. **Street tree use:** Like other dogwoods, not a good choice for most street situations. **In the trade:** Available.

Cornus ×rutgersensis
These are hybrids of *C. kousa* and *C. florida*. They tend to be slightly more vigorous than the parent species, grow to a slightly larger size, have broadly oval to rounded forms, have good resistance to anthracnose, and show good cold hardiness. All have white bracts unless indicated and are rated zones 6 to 8, but are worth trying in zone 5b. Many in this Stellar series are similar, so if you want a short list, we consider AURORA, CELESTIAL, and STELLAR PINK the best.

AURORA 'Rutban'. Bracts are very round and broad, giving the bloom a very substantial appearance and holding up better in windy weather than most dogwoods.

AURORA

AURORA

CELESTIAL

'Celestial Shadow'

'Celestial Shadow'

Upright-spreading in form with rounded crown, to 24′ high and 20′ wide. One of the best.

CELESTIAL 'Rutdan'. Bracts are broad and substantial, holding up in the wind, similar to AURORA. Foliage is handsome and shows good disease resistance. Attractive upright-spreading form with rounded crown, 20 to 25′ tall and wide. Along with AURORA, our favorite white in the series.

'Celestial Shadow'. Originated as a nursery bud sport of CELESTIAL. Bright yellow and green variegated foliage is excellent, one of the best of the variegated dogwoods, and bright red fall colors are outstanding. To 20′ by 20′.

CONSTELLATION 'Rutcan'. Vigorous and more upright than others in the series but also more leggy and open in form, 25′ tall, 20′ wide. Bracts are long and somewhat narrow and are often twisted by the wind. We have been disappointed; there are better cultivars in this group.

CONSTELLATION

RUTH ELLEN

STELLAR PINK

HYPERION

HYPERION 'KF111-1'. Vigorous, slightly coarse and open in form compared to others in the series. Flowering has been sparse when young but dense with age. To 20′ by 20′.

RUTH ELLEN 'Rutlan'. A little slower and more wide-spreading than others in the series, and blooms have somewhat narrower bracts. We feel it's not up to the standard of the others. Mildew susceptible. 18′ by 22′.

SATURN 'KF1-1'. Nice, broad overlapping bracts. A little slower growing. Shows some susceptibility to powdery mildew. To 20′ by 25′.

STARDUST 'Rutfan'. A broad-spreading tree, the shortest and widest of the group. Has shown some graft incompatibility and is rarely grown. Mildew susceptible. To 12′ by 20′.

STELLAR PINK 'Rutgan'. Pink flowers are lovely in cool, cloudy spring weather but fade to almost white in hot sun. Depending on your climate, consider it a wonderful soft pink or a white with barely a pink tint. It's pretty in either case, but you will like it better if you live in a cool area. Broadly rounded in form, with good flower density, 20 to 25′ tall and wide.

STARDUST

ROSY TEACUPS

VARIEGATED STELLAR PINK

STARLIGHT

VENUS

VARIEGATED STELLAR PINK 'KV10-105v1'. A variegated sport, or bud mutation, of STELLAR PINK. Certainly sounds appealing, but in our observation, the foliage tends to be slightly distorted and wrinkled-looking, not as attractive as other variegated dogwoods. Similar light pink flowers, may reach 18′ by 18′.

Cornus ×elwinortonii

These are hybrids involving *C. kousa* and *C. nuttallii*. They are vigorous, have the largest flowers, are more upright, and grow to the largest size, but are somewhat less cold hardy. Fall colors are good orange-reds to red. Zones 6 to 8, 9 along the West Coast.

ROSY TEACUPS 'KN144-2'. The pink flowers are wonderful, close to a true pink in color and held upright on the tree. Unfortunately, flowering has tended to be sparse in Oregon trials, and the foliage has shown more powdery mildew than seedling *C. kousa*. A backcross, with more *C. kousa* than *C.*

nuttallii in its pedigree; vigor, size, and form are more similar to *C. kousa*, 25′ by 25′.

STARLIGHT 'KN4-43'. A great look-alike substitute for the difficult to grow *C. nuttallii*. The fastest-growing of the hybrids, strongly upright and very vigorous, developing an

STARLIGHT

VENUS

VENUS

upright oval shape and reaching 30 to 40′ in height, half that in width. Flowers a week before VENUS; large flowers have white bracts that spread 4 to 5″.

VENUS 'KN30-8'. Wow. Huge flowers, by far the largest we have seen among dogwoods, quite floriferous and truly impressive in bloom. The 4 broad bracts can easily stretch over 6″ in diameter. A vigorous plant with an upright oval form becoming rounded, a little open and leggy when young but filling in with age, to 30′ by 30′. Zone 6, possibly to 5b.

C

Corylus avellana
European hazelnut, filbert

Deciduous. Commercially grown for its nuts, the species and its orchard cultivars have little to offer in the landscape. Several ornamental cultivars are too small and shrubby or disease-susceptible for inclusion. We list the species briefly here for the one new introduction that merits attention as a small deciduous landscape tree: 'Burgundy Lace' features attractive maroon-purple new growth of its cutleaf foliage. Resistant to eastern filbert blight. It bears edible hazelnuts if a compatible pollinator is nearby. Typically a spreading multi-stemmed tree, it can be grown as a low-branched single-stem tree if suckers are controlled. 20 to 25′ tall and wide.

'Burgundy Lace'

Corylus colurna
Turkish filbert

Deciduous. Densely pyramidal-conical to oval outline, ascending 40 to 50′ and greater, two-thirds as wide, maintaining central leader into middle age. Growth is moderate. Rather pretty bark, flaking, scaling, pale brown to gray-brown, exfoliating and exposing orange-brown inner bark. The exfoliating trait develops on young branches, persisting on mature trunks, adding color and texture to the dormant season.

Foliage: Leaves are large, to 6″ long, half as wide, prominently serrate to quasi-lobed, with a cordate leaf base, dull yellow-green to lustrous dark green. One very handsome specimen resided in the oval on the Ohio State University campus; its leaves were thick as leather, mirror-surfaced polish, and black-green. Fall foliage is, on the best of days,

Corylus colurna

Corylus colurna

yellow, often green upon abscission. **Flowers/seeds/fruits/cones**: Male flowers in 3″ long brown catkins, dangling, worm-like, in March; the female virtually inconspicuous, with 2 or 3 red styles protruding from the bud scales. Wind-pollinated; the male catkins release clouds of pollen. The ½″ wide nuts are enclosed in a deeply incised, fimbriated involucre, which is about twice the length of the fruit, ripening in October; nuts are hard-shelled and smaller than cultivated filberts. Seeds are edible but not considered as tasty as those of *C. avellana*. **Native range**: Southeastern Europe, western Asia. **Adaptability**: Remains difficult to assess the species' environmental toughness. Literature is rich with accolades about ubiquitous adaptability, but John C. Pair of Kansas State University tested numerous tree species for the hot, dry, windy Plains states, and this failed miserably. Zones 4 to 7. Injured at -30°F in Orono, ME. Grows well in the West, but authors have yet to experience the species in zone 8 of the South. **Landscape use**: We have encountered magnificent trees in public gardens, cemeteries, and arboreta, but nowhere is the species common in urban areas. Pretty specimen tree where space is available, considered heat and drought tolerant once established. Where American elm, American chestnut, and American ash are (or have been) under siege, perhaps this is a useful addition. **Street tree use**: Perfect habit for this purpose. In Germany, it is highly rated for this use. **In the trade**: The nuts have a complex dormancy that may require several cycles of warm and cold, but *Corylus* species are now produced via tissue culture, so propagation excuses should no longer apply. Authors have observed the results of breeding efforts by Shawn Mehlenbacher, Oregon State University, including beautiful *C. colurna* × *C. fargesii* trees; J. Frank Schmidt & Son is evaluating. 'Te Terra Red' has deep red-purple leaves, maturing dark green, and red-purple involucres with conspicuous frilly margins; forms a small tree or large shrub 20 to 25(30)′ high.

Corylus fargesii

Corylus fargesii
Farges filbert, hazelnut

Deciduous. The next great street, lawn, park, campus, golf course, urban, and collector species, so surmise the authors. Introduced in 1996 from China and slowly climbing the recognition ladder as a species with great promise. Trees over 100′ high were noted in China, logical to estimate 40 to 60′ by 30 to 40′ under cultivation. Develops a *Tilia cordata*–like pyramidal-oval outline as a young tree and has maintained this shape on 40′ high trees. Initially the captive of botanical gardens, its virtues were extolled by tree aficionados, leading to a breakout from museum prison. The Morris Arboretum shared seed with the authors, the resultant seedlings grow quickly (easily 4 to 5′ per year); several planted out to the Dirr garden have shown remarkable heat and drought tolerance. Magnificent exfoliating bark, every seedling different, described by some as yellow to copper-brown and gray. From our perspective and experiences, it resembles the bark of *Betula nigra*, only more elegant. Impressive early exfoliation. Year-old seedlings show exfoliation by the end of the growing season, 2-year-old branches likewise, with color a shiny, rich copper-brown, rivaling *Acer griseum* but significantly faster growing.

Foliage: For starters, the foliage looks nothing like a corylus, 2 to 4″ long, oval in outline, coarsely toothed, with an oblique base. The medium to dark green leaves may develop yellow fall color. In Schmidt production/trial areas, the foliage was dark green with no scorch in late August after one of the hottest summers on record in the Portland area; it has also weathered the vagaries of zone 8 weather in the Dirr garden, remaining healthy into autumn. **Flowers/seeds/fruits/cones**: The male catkins, to 4″ long, rich red-brown, elongate in March, while the ½″ wide globose nut, enclosed in a yellowish, hairy, 2″ long beaked involucre, ripens in fall. The shells are steel-casing hard, and germination under the best conditions may occur over 3 to 4 years. Seeds are edible and much loved by pesky squirrels. We are interested in the level of dental insurance squirrels carry. **Native range**. China, growing in open woodland among rocks in sandy silt loam soil along streams. Our gardens are indebted to the Morris Arboretum, U.S. National Arboretum, Arnold Arboretum, Morton Arboretum, and others for collection efforts there in the 1990s and early 2000s. **Adaptability**: Resistant to eastern filbert blight. Has proven successful from Boston to Georgia to the West Coast. Hardiness in the -20 to -25°F range. Minnesota research determined stem hardiness to -20°F. This is a laboratory test with first-year stems measuring LD50 (lethal dose 50), when 50% of tissues are killed. **Landscape use**: Without question, a transformational introduction that we hope will grace gardens for centuries. Our early observations indicate full sun and acid (and even high pH) soils with adequate moisture are sufficient. Propagation has been the limiting factor, for cuttings are difficult to root and seeds

Corylus fargesii

Corylus fargesii

recalcitrant to germinate. The species has been successfully tissue cultured, and small plants have so many branches, it appears to be a shrub. **Street tree use:** We believe it possesses the moxie to become a major element in residential urban environments. **In the trade:** Tissue culture propagation has been successful. The Morton Arboretum is tissue culturing its best *C. fargesii*, one with uniform habit and superior exfoliating bark, for eventual introduction. Oregon nurseries have a separate tissue-cultured line already in production, which should be available very soon.

Corymbia citriodora (*Eucalyptus citriodora*)
lemon-scented gum

Broadleaf evergreen. Very tall, quite upright, open branching and spreading to a vase-shaped crown. Older trees are often devoid of branches on the lower half of their trunks, bare to high above, the foliage appearing clumpy at the end of branches. Medium-textured, fast-growing, to 90′ by 40′.

Bark is very smooth, exfoliating in patches of gray and coppery tan, at times presents as bright chalky white.

Foliage: Juvenile leaves ovate, green. Mature leaves lanceolate, quite long, 3 to 8″, yellowish green. Strongly lemon-scented. **Flowers/seeds/fruits/cones:** Small white clusters of filaments flowering sporadically through the year, followed by small green seed capsules that mature to brown. **Native range:** Australia. **Adaptability:** Needs a hot climate, frost-free or very close to it. Tolerant of a range of soil conditions. May show freeze damage at 28°F. Zones 10 and 11. **Landscape use:** A very impressive tree. Tall is the word, as a mature specimen towers overhead, its slender trunk accentuated by the bright white bark. Form is a little elm-like. Trunk is supple when young and may need staking for a while. **Street tree use:** Good form for the purpose. You can count on the lower trunk becoming bare, so there will be plenty of clearance below. **In the trade:** Sold as seed-grown.

Cotinus obovatus
American smoketree

Deciduous. The Europeans have long admired and grown this U.S. native for its spectacular fall color. Develops an oval to round-headed canopy, in the 20 to 30′ high range. Tendency to form multiple trunks, so requires staking to develop single-trunk status. Moderate growth rate. Easily identified by the bark, gray to gray-brown with mature trunks becoming scaly, reminiscent of the scales on a fish. Quite eye-catching and little else in the tree world compares.

Foliage: Blue-green to dark green leaves, oval-elliptic in outline, 2 to 5″ long. The range of fall colors, from yellow and orange to red, often intermingled, is astounding and parallels the fall colors in *Fothergilla ×intermedia* 'Mt. Airy'. Few native tree species produce such a spectacle. **Flowers/seeds/fruits/cones:** Small yellow-green flowers open in April-May and are largely lost among the pubescent cotton-candy inflorescences (panicles). Panicles may be green or with a red-purple blush, 6 to 10″ high, three-fourths as wide. Showy parts of the "flower" are actually soft brush-like pubescence that covers the pedicels and peduncle of the inflorescences. Opportunities exist for selection of deeper panicle color. Fruit is a kidney-shaped, ¼″ wide drupe that is sparsely produced and matures in autumn. **Native range:** Occurs naturally in restricted localities in limestone-based soils in Tennessee, Alabama, and the Edwards Plateau of Texas. On the Cumberland Plateau, near Winchester, TN, populations literally spring from crevices in the rocky soils. **Adaptability:** The rocky outcrops where it grows in the wild attest to its heat and drought tolerances. Best suited to higher pH, well-drained soils, although it is adapted to acid soils. Hardy to -40°F, with reports in the literature of its

Cotinus obovatus

Cotinus obovatus

C

Cotinus obovatus

surviving -50°F without injury. Authors noted the species growing at the Minnesota Landscape Arboretum, Chanhassen; and for many years, a plant prospered on the University of Georgia campus. Zones 3 to 8. **Landscape use**: Fine small specimen tree that has yet to establish a toehold in American gardens. Authors have not observed serious insect issues, but it is highly susceptible to verticillium wilt; it may need well-drained soils to avoid this. Authors observed damage from ice storms. May suffer breakage from wind. **Street tree use**: Minimal unless pruned as a standard. **In the trade**: Available.

'Candy Floss'. Green foliage turning yellow to purple, then scarlet in autumn. Produces massive fluffy pink inflorescences. *C. coggygria* 'Daydream' × *C.* 'Flame'.

COTTON CANDY 'Northstar'. Small, oval-rounded tree, 18′ by 15′, with pink inflorescences and brilliant red fall color. Zone 3a.

'Flame'. Large pink inflorescences in summer, brilliant orange-red fall color. *C. coggygria* × *C. obovatus*. Authors recorded a 25′ by 20′ tree.

'Grace'. Vigorous hybrid with light purplish leaves turning green then red in fall. Produces large purplish pink inflorescences. 20′ by 20′.

'Grace'

Crataegus crus-galli

cockspur hawthorn

Deciduous. Upright-spreading when young, becoming horizontally spreading, wider than tall, to 20′ high and 30′ wide. Grown both single-stem (usually low-branched) and multi-stem. Medium fine texture. Nasty thorns are up to 3″ long and very sharp. Bark is grayish brown, lightly fissured into scaly plates, but with those thorns, who wants to get close enough to look?

Foliage: Dark green, glossy leaves are attractive, oblong-obovate, glabrous and finely serrate, 2 to 3″ long and 1″ wide. Fall color is nothing special, a decent bronze-red to purplish. **Flowers/seeds/fruits/cones**: About a month after leaf emergence, May in most climates, small white flowers (½″ across) occur in flat corymbs to 3″ wide, effective en masse but with an unpleasant odor. Fruit, a round pome-like drupe, about ½″ wide, usually deep red to maroon, ripens in the fall. **Native range**: Eastern North America; Maine to southern Ontario and Florida to Texas. **Adaptability**: A tough little tree, tolerant of heat, drought, wet soils, and varying soil pH. Insects and foliar diseases can be a problem. Zones 4 to 8. **Landscape use**: For this, we need to make a clear distinction between the species (seed-grown) and the vegetatively propagated thornless cultivar 'Inermis'. Although attractive, seedling plants are a scary proposition, heavily armed with military-grade thorns. They certainly can discourage intruders, but you would never plant one if you knew that you would have to be the one to prune it. On the other hand, 'Inermis' is an excellent small tree and is quite reliably thornless. Cedar-hawthorn rust can disfigure the fruits. **Street tree use**: No, too low-branched, but very tolerant of street conditions and good in wide roadside

Crataegus crus-galli

'Inermis'

Crataegus crus-galli

'Inermis'

areas. Use only the thornless cultivar near wheeled equipment, as thorns can easily pierce tires. **In the trade**: Sold as seed-grown, usually multi-stem, or the cultivar.

'Inermis'. A highly successful cultivar, it truly duplicates the species, yet completely eliminates the thorns. A lesson in evolution: those nasty seedling thorns have a purpose, as we have seen the bark chewed off entire nursery rows of the thornless cultivar in a matter of a day or two by rabbits when the ground in frozen. Summer foliage is very glossy and attractive. Rounded in form, 20 to 25′ tall and wide. Occasionally sold as CRUSADER.

C. ×prunifolia 'Splendens'. A hybrid of *C. crus-galli* and *C. macracantha*. A smaller spreading tree with a full complement of long nasty thorns, but nicely decorated with prolific, bright red fruit in the fall, 20′ by 20′.

Crataegus laevigata
English hawthorn

Deciduous. Upright-spreading, then wide-spreading with a rounded, arching top. Branching pattern is dense with many crossing branches and a fine twiggy appearance. The cultivars tend to be a little more upright and oval, 20 to 25′ high and 20′ wide. Moderately fine-textured appearance, moderate growth rate. Bark grayish brown, lightly checked and flaking off in small pieces.

Foliage: Medium green leaves are on the small side, 1 to 2″ long and 1 to 1½″ wide, incised halfway to the midrib with rounded lobes, and dull to slightly glossy. Fall color is drab. **Flowers/seeds/fruits/cones**: Flowers are white, ⅝″ wide, malodorous in May, in slightly domed 3″ corymbs. Fruit is a pome-like drupe, ¼ to ½″ wide, red. **Native range**: Europe, northern Africa. **Adaptability**: Like other hawthorns, it tends to be quite adaptable to soil pH, tolerant of hot and cold weather, wet and dry soil. Zones 4 to 7 in the East, to 8 in the West. **Landscape use**: An adaptable small flowering tree for gardens and commercial sites, looking its best in spring flower and with fall fruit. Summer appearance is nothing special, a dense green tree. Hawthorn leafspot fungus can defoliate it in wet weather, and fireblight is a concern. Winter appearance is dense and twiggy with a rather confused-looking branching pattern, every limb armed with small thorns. Warren remembers as a boy, playing football in the front yard, with hawthorns along the street. An errant kick or pass and, psssss...thorn meets football, thorn wins, end of game. **Street tree use**: It is certainly tolerant of streetside soils but can be a little too wide-spreading, and thorns make pruning to a narrower shape unpleasant. The more upright cultivars are occasionally used. **In the trade**: Almost exclusively sold as cultivars, much improved over the species.

'Autumn Glory'. Has the finest foliage of the group, glossy and a little darker green and crisp-looking. Bright white flowers in spring followed by long-lasting very bright red fruit, larger than other cultivars, ovoid, ½″ in diameter by ⅝″ long. Has some resistance to leafspot. Fireblight susceptible but good in the Pacific Northwest, where the disease is rare. 20′ by 20′.

'Autumn Glory'

'Crimson Cloud'

Crataegus laevigata

'Paul's Scarlet'

'Paul's Scarlet'

'Crimson Cloud'. A curious tree to grow, its new growth tends to zigzag and curve but somehow the tree develops quite an upright branching habit with reasonably good structure. The top of the tree tends to arch, keeping the curving habit of the new shoots. The leaves are small, glossy, and more resistant to the leafspot that is so troublesome on 'Paul's Scarlet', making it a better choice. The small flowers are bright red with a white center, beautiful up close. Fruit is on the small size, decreasing messiness, ¼″ wide, red. 25′ tall, 18′ wide.

'Paul's Scarlet'. An old cultivar with incredible flowers but a significant disease problem. The flowers are fully double, like tiny pom-poms, deep rose-pink, creating a beautiful spring display. Unfortunately the foliage is highly suscepti-ble to hawthorn leafspot, and in wet spring or early summer weather the tree can completely defoliate. Rather upright in form with an arching top. Fruit is sparse, deep red, ⅜″ wide. 22′ tall, 20′ wide.

'Rosea Flore Pleno'. Very similar to the more popular 'Paul's Scarlet' but with lighter rose-pink double flowers. Similar susceptibility to leafspot. 20′ by 20′.

'Rosea Flore Pleno'

Crataegus ×lavalleei
Lavalle hawthorn

Deciduous. A rather tight, upright, inverted cone when young, it becomes oval, sometimes irregularly so, and eventually rounded with age. It has good density and branch form without being twiggy like so many hawthorn species. Medium in texture and growth rate to 25′ by 20′. Bark is dark gray, flaking off in patches to expose brown beneath.

Foliage: Glossy dark green, oval, finely serrate and substantial in thickness, giving the impression of being evergreen, although it is not. The foliage tends to resist rust and the leafspot so common in other hawthorn species. Leaves hold late in the fall and then turn coppery red to deep purple. **Flowers/seeds/fruits/cones**: Clusters of white, ¾″ wide flowers occur in flat 3″ wide corymbs in late May. Fruit is a ¾″ wide pome-like drupe, rounded to slightly ovoid, held in tight clusters, ripening in the fall and holding into early winter, orange-red then deep red. **Native range**: A garden hybrid of *C. crus-galli* (eastern North America) and *C. mexicana* (Mexico). **Adaptability**: Adaptable, excellent on the West Coast and quite acceptable in the East. Zones 4 to 8, 9 in the West. **Landscape use**: Its foliage gives it a bold, solid feel in the landscape. Can be used singly but is often planted in rows or groups, or as a screen. In mild climates, both the glossy green foliage and the red fruit hold into December, and considering the season, it makes you think of Christmas holly. **Street tree use**: It has been used as such and when young its form is compatible, but with age it becomes too wide-spreading for all but the widest strips. **In the trade**: Almost exclusively sold as a single cultivar, 'Carrierei', which is as just described. In the United States, it is almost always called Lavalle, 25′ by 20′.

'Carrierei'

'Carrierei'

Crataegus ×mordenensis
Morden hawthorn

Deciduous. Two hybrid cultivars of *C. laevigata* 'Paul's Scarlet' and *C. succulenta* were developed by the Morden Research Station, Manitoba, and are favored in the Northern Plains for their cold hardiness. Leaves are a little larger than *C. laevigata* and coarsely serrate rather than lobed. **Adaptability**: Zones 3 to 6. **Landscape use**: Similar to *C. laevigata*. Good choices for cold climates. **Street tree use**: A little wide for the purpose, but sometimes used. **In the trade**: Available as the cultivars, both of which are very susceptible to leaf disease in the Southeast.

'Snowbird'. Upright-spreading form, slightly narrower than 'Toba', with small pure white double flowers that stay white as they age, in clusters, reminiscent of bridal wreath spirea. Fruit red, ⅜″. 22′ by 20′.

'Snowbird'

Crataegus phaenopyrum

'Toba'

'Toba'. Upright-spreading form, becoming somewhat rounded, with clusters of small white double flowers that age to a good pink, providing a surprise spring color change. Fruit red, ⅜". 20' by 20'.

Crataegus phaenopyrum

Crataegus phaenopyrum
Washington hawthorn

Deciduous. Upright-spreading habit developing an upright oval shape with a rounded crown as a tree, or wide-spreading as a multi-stem, somewhat densely branched, armed with 1" thorns, moderate in growth rate and medium texture, to 25' high and 20' wide as tree form, 20' by 25' as multi-stem. Bark gray, exfoliating in patches to reveal brown.

Foliage: Attractive, dark green with a nice gloss, leaves are deltoid overall and shallowly 3-lobed, 1½ to 2½" long and three-fourths as wide. Fall color orange to reddish purple. **Flowers/seeds/fruits/cones:** Small white flowers are clustered in corymbs, flowering in late May, somewhat fragrant. Attractive clusters of orange-red to red ¼" wide fruit, coloring up in September and holding into the winter, then taken by birds, persistent enough to not be messy. **Native range:** Mid-Atlantic to Missouri and Arkansas. **Adaptability:** Quite adaptable, native to the Southeast but it has proven to be cold hardy considerably farther north, even Ontario. Tolerant of variety of soils, acid to elevated pH, wet and dry. Does better in the heat of the South than other hawthorns. Zones 4 to 8. **Landscape use:** One of the most popular hawthorns, used singly or in groups. Its form is more graceful than English hawthorn, and the tree is at its best in the fall, when colorful leaves and vibrant fruit create a bright spot in the landscape. The often abundant fruit is lovely against a backdrop of snow. **Street tree use:** Occasionally chosen for its soil tolerance; it's a little wide-spreading, but is more upright with better clearance than most of the genus. Thorns remain a concern. **In the trade:** Sold as both seed-grown and vegetatively propagated cultivars. Seedlings are typically sold as a multi-stem. Tree forms are almost always one of the two cultivars, which are very similar. Thorns are more prolific and longer on seed-grown plants.

"Washington Tree"

'Winter King'

C

WASHINGTON LUSTRE 'Westwood I'. A good tree form, more upright than seedlings, with glossy foliage, fewer thorns, and early persistent flowers. Very similar to "Washington Tree," we compared and couldn't see the difference. 20 to 25′ tall and wide.

"Washington Tree." The most common selection in commerce is a long-grown, unnamed cultivar that nurseries refer to as "Washington Tree." A budded (grafted) selection with greatly improved characteristics over seedlings. Good upright tree form, glossy foliage, nice flower display, fewer thorns, good orange-red fall color. 25′ tall, 20′ wide.

'Winter King'

Crataegus viridis

green hawthorn

Deciduous. The species is upright-spreading, dense, rounded. But in the landscape it is entirely known by the single cultivar 'Winter King', which is more angular and spreads to a broad vase shape. Medium texture, moderately fast-growing to 20′ high, 25′ wide. Bark silvery gray, exfoliating in strips, exposing orange-brown.

Foliage: Dark green leaves are irregularly serrate, some leaves developing a set of shallow lobes at the base, 1½ to 3″ long and two-thirds that in width. Foliage holds up well with better disease resistance than most hawthorns. Yellow to bronze-red fall color. **Flowers/seeds/fruits/cones**: Small white flowers in corymbs in May. Bright orange-red, ⅜″ wide fruit develops in the fall and holds into winter. **Native range**: Maryland to Illinois and Florida to Texas. **Adaptability**: Its wide use by the landscape industry attests to its adaptability. Tolerant of a variety of soils; cold hardy but also one of the best hawthorns in the heat of the South. Zones 4 to 8. **Landscape use**: 'Winter King' is the king of the hawthorns, by far the most popular and widely used of all hawthorn cultivars in the United States. An excellent specimen tree for residential gardens and commercial

'Winter King'

sites, it is beautiful, tough, and reliable, with few thorns. High-quality summer foliage. Its striking branching habit, most evident in winter, is very angular, like a well-organized latticework. Silvery gray bark adds to its visual impact in winter. Fruit retention is good. Less susceptible to problems that plague other hawthorn species. **Street tree use**: Too wide-spreading, but good for wide roadside plantings. **In the trade**: Exclusively represented by its single cultivar, 'Winter King', which is as just described.

Cryptomeria japonica
Japanese cedar

Evergreen conifer. Lofty, imposing, conical to pyramidal needle evergreen, maintaining this outline into old age, often losing lower branches along the way. In Scotland, massive trees between 200 and 300 years old are more open yet awe-inspiring, particularly as the peeling, stringy reddish brown bark becomes more visible. Older trees develop "poodle tails" at their ends, the internal branches sparsely clothed with needles. Moderate to fast growth rate. The species is the largest, most popular timber tree in Japan, where it's listed to 200′ high with 13′ trunk diameter. Authors have never observed anything close to 100′ in the United States, where landscape size averages 50 to 60′ high, 20 to 30′ wide. Phenomenal 60 to 70′ specimens are common in the landscapes of many of the mansions on Bellevue Avenue in Newport, RI; their proximity to the ocean suggests a measure of salt tolerance, especially from aerial deposits.

Foliage: Rather dense, the ¼ to ¾″ long, shiny dark to blue-green needles persisting for 4 to 5 years. Depending on severity of winter, the needles remain green or take on a bronzy hue. Certain cultivars (e.g., 'Elegans') turn muddy brown to red-brown in cold weather; some people enjoy the color change, but most desire the bright, rich dark green color year-round. **Flowers/seeds/fruits/cones**: Monoecious. Male cones are small and brown, clustered at the ends of branches, opening in March, evident throughout fall-winter, spewing a cloud of yellow-brown pollen when brushed. Apparently, the pollen affects hay fever sufferers. Female cones terminal, to 1″ wide, round, comprise 20 to 30 scales, each with 3 to 5 seeds. Cones initiate green, then yellow-green to brown, carried into winter, dehiscing and releasing the seeds. **Native range**: China and Japan, primarily in the mountainous regions of Japan where annual rainfall averages 100″. **Adaptability**: Zones 6 to 8 with good success; well adapted to Pacific Northwest. **Landscape use**: Along with 'Green Giant' arborvitae and Leyland cypress, a major tree-type screening evergreen for zones 6 to 8. Culturally, the species prefers well-drained, rich, deep, light, permeable, acid soil with abundant moisture. Site in an open sunny area, ideally. Light shade is tolerated; trees planted beneath high-canopy loblolly pines have prospered. Once established, trees fend for themselves very well. Based on success in the Southeast, the species is more heat and drought tolerant than would be expected based on its native habitat. In its finest form, a noble conifer when used as a single specimen or in groupings as an extended screen between properties. Not happy as a hedge plant, needs to be

Cryptomeria japonica

Cryptomeria japonica

'Araucarioides'

'Black Dragon'

'Black Dragon'. Slow-growing, dense and upright. Bright green new foliage becomes deep dark green as the summer progresses and holds this outstanding color through the winter. In the Southeast numerous unsightly male cones are carried through the winter months. Matures at less than 10′ but included as a Warren favorite.

'Cristata'. Cockscomb-like needles randomly interspersed throughout the canopy. Often considered dwarf, authors observed a 60′ high tree at Oregon's Iseli Nursery. Appeared a degree worse for wear compared to 'Radicans' and 'Yoshino'.

'Gyokuryu'. Starts garden life as a dwarf conifer and 15 years later is 20′ high and 10′ wide. The pretty dark green needle color is largely maintained through winter. This has been a great doer in zone 8 and has the potential to reach 40′. As small plants resemble evergreen birds-nests, who knew?

'Radicans'. Blue-green needles and, to our eyes, denser in habit compared to 'Yoshino'. This observation held true on plants in Athens, GA. Also it does not discolor in winter to the degree of some 'Yoshino'. Grows 40 to 50′ high.

free to roam. **Street tree use**: Certainly could be utilized, and several Southeast growers remove lower branches to 5 to 6′ with that in mind. **In the trade**: Available, as are a few large tree-type cultivars.

'Araucarioides'. A novelty cultivar with whipcord-like branches and more open habit. May reach 30′ and greater.

'Cristata'

'Cristata'

'Gyokuryu'

'Radicans'

'Rein's Dense Jade'

'Rein's Dense Jade'. A more compact version of 'Yoshino', reaching 20 to 25′ by 15′, with dark green needles, the color maintained year-round. Resulted from a witch's broom that developed on 'Lobbii'. We recorded an outstanding, 30′ high specimen at Iseli Nursery.

'Radicans'

'Rein's Dense Jade'

'Sekkan'

'Sekkan'

C

Cunninghamia lanceolata

'Yoshino'

'Glauca'

'Sekkan' ('Sekkan Sugi'). Cream-yellow new growth, maturing green. Pretty color element in spring and though listed at 20 to 30′ high, authors noticed a 60′ high specimen at Iseli. Even in Oregon, when observed in late August, the needles were green.

'Yoshino'. The most common tree type in cultivation with dark green needles and a tight, dense, conical habit. A report from John Ruter's Tifton, GA, trials noted 27′ high and 18′ wide plant in 10 years. In authors' minds and observations, the 'Yoshino' epithet umbrellas more than one clone. The best 'Yoshino' is dense pyramidal-conical in youth to 30 to 50′ or so, becoming wider and looser with age and size.

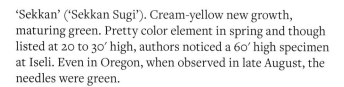

Cunninghamia lanceolata
China-fir

Evergreen conifer. Habit is somewhat stiff, pyramidal, developing broad pyramidal outline, with branches more widely spaced in old age and dead brown needles persisting in the interior; it is not unusual to experience a huge pile of abscised shoots and needles at the base of the trunk to the drip line. Grows over 100′ and higher in the wild. In the Southeast, the species surfaces in the most unusual places, particularly old homesteads in and near small towns, the trees 60 to 80′ tall and still ruggedly handsome (some would argue this). Bark scales in long irregular strips exposing the reddish inner bark. Bark becomes distinctly ridged and furrowed on large trunks, the ridges flat, mostly gray and stringy, the furrows brown.

Foliage: The sharp-pointed needles (pin-prick apices) to 2½″ long, ⅛″ wide, range from bright medium green to bluish green, becoming duller, and bronze-green in winter. Undersides of needles with 2 broad silver-gray bands. Needles persist 5 years or more and may remain another 2 years when dead/dried. Readily identified by a simple handshake with a shoot. Ouch! **Flowers/seeds/fruits/cones:** Male reproductive cones in terminal clusters; female terminal, developing a globose, 1½″ broad, artichoke-shaped, shiny brown, persistent cone. **Native range:** China. **Adaptability:** Zones (6)7 to 9. Long-forgotten trees in abandoned home sites, still robust but tatty, reflect the species' adaptability.

'Glauca'

×*Cupressocyparis leylandii.*
See *Cupressus* ×*leylandii*

×*Cupressocyparis notabilis.*
See *Cupressus* ×*notabilis*

×*Cupressocyparis ovensii.*
See *Cupressus* ×*ovensii*

C

Cupressus arizonica var. *glabra* (*C. glabra*)
Arizona cypress

Evergreen conifer. Develops a narrow to broad pyramidal habit, more graceful than *Cryptomeria*, *Cunninghamia*, *Thuja*, and others, with fine-textured, semi-pendent branches. Moderate to fast-growing, 40 to 50′ by 25 to 30′ is reasonable in the Southeast. *Cupressus* is a mixed bag as far as agreed species count and taxonomic purity; *C. arizonica* now includes *C. glabra*, one of the described differences being the bark—gray to dark brown, ridged and furrowed in the former; in the latter, reddish brown, smooth, peeling in thin curly plates. One might well ask how to identify young trees.

Foliage: Needles (scales) light green, gray-green, blue-green to blue, closely overlapping, flattened to the branchlet, superposed in 4 rows, soft to the touch and fragrant when bruised. The branches resemble stereoisomers from your chemistry days (i.e., they are shaped like small leafless trees). **Flowers/seeds/fruits/cones**: Monoecious. Male cones are small, yellowish; female with 6 to 8 peltate scales (shaped like a soccer ball), globose, and 1″ wide. Cones persist closed after maturing in the second year and are rather unsightly. **Native range**: California, Arizona, and Mexico, depending on how broadly the species is defined. **Adaptability**: In the wild, the species (in the broadest sense) grows on dry, rocky mountainsides (Mt. Lemmon, AZ). Certainly an excellent needle evergreen in the hot, dry areas of the Southwest. Trees have a presence in the Southeast and Pacific Northwest but may be short-lived. Zones 7 to 9. **Landscape use**: Often utilized for screening. Excellent as a specimen plant and in groupings. Elegant at its genetic

Old trees at the former USDA Bamboo Station, Savannah, GA, possibly date from its 1919 founding. **Landscape use**: Might prove a difficult sell in today's garden center market. One touch and—ouch, so placement far away from activities is logical. Certainly a specimen evergreen and useful in groupings of 3 or 5. Can be pruned into old branches and the main trunk and regenerate shoots. Branches and root systems are extremely windfirm. We have read many prescriptions for culture, but believe any well-drained soil, sun or partial shade, serves it well. If propagated via cuttings, they should be collected from vertical shoots. **Street tree use**: No. **In the trade**: Scarce. 'Glauca', a pretty glaucous blue-needled form, is occasionally offered. The soft powder-blue of its emerging new growth is diminished in winter but still noticeable. Slower growing than species and perhaps slightly more cold hardy, 30 to 40′ high. The related *C. unicanaliculata* (Sichuan China fir) has soft-textured, blue-tinged needles that develop purplish hues in cold weather. It is a dense, broad-based pyramid in youth, potentially 15 to 25′ high. Estimated adaptability is zones 7 and 8. New spring growth is susceptible to late frosts.

Cupressus arizonica var. *glabra*

Cupressus arizonica var. *glabra*

'Blue Pyramid'

'Blue Pyramid'

best; tatty under less-than-ideal cultural conditions. Species requires full sun and should not be crowded by other evergreens, as foliage is quickly shaded out. Plants have a stringy, sparse root system and are subject to wind-throw; authors observed large 12′ high, balled-and-burlapped plants, all staked to keep them upright. Choose small container-grown plants to ensure transplanting success. Provide acid to higher pH, clay-based to sandy, well-drained soil. Heat and drought tolerant once established. For all this, venerable, majestic, mature specimens are largely absent from the Southeast, being more at home in the Southwest into California. **Street tree use**: Not suitable. **In the trade**: Available.

'Blue Ice' and 'Blue Pyramid'. Blue foliage and more tightly pyramidal than the species. Estimate 20 to 30′ high, 6 to 8′ wide, in 10 to 12 years for both. They were trialed at the University of Georgia Horticulture Farm but declined over the 15-year test period and removed. 'Blue Ice' is slower growing than 'Blue Pyramid'.

'Blue Ice'

'Limelight'

'Carolina Sapphire'

'Carolina Sapphire'. Airy in habit and quite elegant, the most popular clone in the Southeast, common in groupings, screens, and as a lone specimen. Needles are more gray to silver-green-blue than 'Blue Ice' and 'Blue Pyramid'. A looser, open, billowy tree, 25 to 30′ high, 10 to 15′ wide.

'Limelight'. Wider than other cultivars, with yellow to lemony green foliage, the needles becoming greener with maturity. Pretty color element! Reaches 15 to 20′ high.

'Raywood's Weeping'. The character of *Sequoiadendron giganteum* 'Pendulum' with a curvilinear leader and secondary branches like a lion's mane. Foliage is gray-green, perhaps gray-blue. Ascends 15 to 20′ high, estimate 3 to 4′ wide or wider, depending on how trained.

'Silver Smoke'. Silver-gray foliage, upright symmetrical pyramid becoming looser and more open with age; reddish bark peels on larger trunks, 15 to 20′ high, 10 to 15′ wide.

'Raywood's Weeping'

Cupressus ×leylandii

Cupressus ×leylandii

Cupressus ×leylandii (×*Cupressocyparis leylandii*)
Leyland cypress

Evergreen conifer. The most important large screening/ hedging evergreen of the 20th century and still a landscape force in the 21st. Several spontaneous hybrids originated in Wales in 1888 and again in 1911. They were then planted on the estate of C. J. Leyland, and the rest is history. We are not sure who or when it was introduced into the United States, but no conifer has ever traveled faster into commerce and landscapes. Numerous names have been assigned to this taxon, with DNA work confirming that it is the result of hybridization between two *Cupressus* species, *C. macrocarpa* × *C. nootkatensis*, the hybrids retaining the foliage character of the latter. Remarkably beautiful in their spire-like, conical, columnar-pyramidal habits. Dense and solid-looking, they lack the more open, graceful forms of the parent species. Growth is extremely fast and with reasonable care, even on mediocre soils, 2 to 3′ in height per year is guaranteed. We estimate ultimate landscape size 60 to 70′ in height, spread variable, 8 to 25′, but trees can scrape the sky, ascending 130′ and greater, as at Bedgebury Pinetum, Kent, England. Bagworms find the foliage particularly digestible; other problems include wind-throw and needle canker diseases. In spite of all, Leyland cypress remains an important element in contemporary landscapes, and the many cultivars offer breadth of size, growth rates, and foliage colors. In the South, it is among the precious few tall, narrow, fast-growing screening needle evergreens, as well as a part of the Christmas tree industry. Bark is grayish, fibrous, peeling in thin strips, eventually shallowly ridged and furrowed.

Foliage: Needles in tree-shaped flattened sprays, soft-textured, green to gray-green, to bluish green, holding color

Cupressus ×leylandii

'Gold Rider'

in winter. **Flowers/seeds/fruits/cones**: Cones are spherical, ½ to ¾″ wide, 8 scales, each flattened, with a flattened conical point on the face; size is intermediate between the parents, seeds are fertile. **Native range**: Hybrid origin. Known only in cultivation. Nature was on her game when she spirited these two North American species together to Wales and allowed them to marry, unfettered by the intervention of humans. **Adaptability**: The species is highly salt tolerant, excellent in coastal environments, and displays wide adaptability to sand, clay, acid, alkaline soils. Zones 6 to 10. Authors recorded healthy plants from Cape Cod to Orlando to the West Coast. **Landscape use**: Virtues include specimen, grouping, screen, and hedge. Leyland is amenable to heavy-handed pruning and can be maintained at any size for decades. Prune only on young growth, as needleless branches and trunks will not produce new shoots. As long as well-drained, best to site it in full sun, but can hold its own in light shade. Root systems are sparse/stringy; successful transplanting is best with container-grown plants, although balled-and-burlapped material is available. **Street tree use**: Roadside plantings, yes; but not suggested as street trees. Trees planted under utility wires quickly impinge, resulting in ongoing pruning battles. **In the trade**: Many, although difficult to discern what is sold, as the larger-growing types are simply listed as

C. ×leylandii. Many were trialed at the University of Georgia and observations are presented here. Numerous yellow- to gold-needled selections, in particular, have been introduced; they arose as branch sports and were introduced willy-nilly without serious evaluation. 'Castlewellan', 'Fern Gold', 'Gold-conda', 'Gold Rider', and 'Robinson's Gold' have been trialed in the Southeast, with 'Gold Rider' the best for color retention. Unfortunately, 'Gold Rider' is susceptible to phomopsis tip blight, which kills sprays, leaving an unsightly patchwork of gold/browns. 'Castlewellan' is still popular in the West, but in Georgia lost all yellow needle coloration over time, even on new growth. The question was raised: can prolonged heat and sun "turn off" the genes for yellow-gold pigment production? All the yellow-gold types are slower growing yet still capable of 50′ and greater.

EMERALD ISLE 'Moncal'. Bright green (dark green) needles in flattened sprays. It is more dense in habit and smaller than the typical form in commerce. Reported to be canker resistant. Grows 20 to 25′ by 6 to 8′, but authors expect larger.

'Green Spire'. Dense, narrow, columnar, with rich green needles; this was raised in 1888 at Haggerston Castle (clone 1).

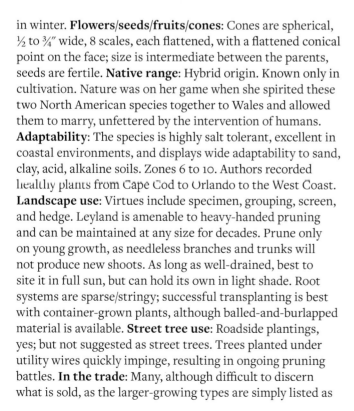

'Naylor's Blue'

'Haggerston Grey'. Slightly more open than 'Leighton Green', the green needles with a gray cast, although closer to blue-green, 1888 (clone 2).

'Leighton Green'. A tall columnar form with a central leader and rich green foliage; consistently produces cones; raised in 1911 (clone 4); in actuality there is little difference in foliage color between this and 'Haggerston Grey'.

'Naylor's Blue'. Forms a broader pyramidal-columnar outline, still distinctly upright; branches are more loose and irregular; the needles pretty glaucous bluish green; slower growing than 'Green Spire', 'Haggerston Grey', and 'Leighton Green'; it performs well in the Southeast; reports from south Georgia indicate over 2½′ height increase per year over a 10-year period; estimate 40 to 50′ by 15′.

'Silver Dust'. Produces white-speckled and -streaked sprays. Grows slower than 'Green Spire', 'Haggerston Grey', and 'Leighton Green', yet has averaged 2′ per year.

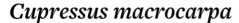

Cupressus macrocarpa
Monterey cypress

Evergreen conifer. Golfers who watch the Pebble Beach Open have knowingly (or not) noticed the Monterey cypresses thrusting their outstretched limbs toward the Pacific Ocean. Trees are shaped by the fierce ocean winds, with their crowns flattened and leaning. Habit in youth is variable, from steeple-like to broadly conical, at maturity broad, open, and flat-topped with massive trunks. Estimate 30 to 40(50)′ high with specimens exceeding 100′.

Foliage: Needles are rich dark green, maintaining the color through the winter. **Flowers/seeds/fruits/cones**: The 8- to 14-scaled cones average 1″ wide and are borne singly or in pairs on short, thick stalks. **Native range**: Restricted,

Cupressus macrocarpa

'Aurea'

'Donard Gold'

'Goldcrest'

'Wilma'

'Donard Gold'

occurring on the headlands at the mouth of Carmel Bay, Monterey County, CA. **Adaptability**: Zones 8 to 9(10). At Strybing Arboretum, authors observed massive trees (and eventually a massive stack of logs) infected by a canker (pathogen: *Seiridium cardinale*). The species is extremely susceptible. **Landscape use**: For areas of the West Coast, perhaps worth considering. It likes the coastal climate and is a good choice anywhere near salt water in the Pacific Northwest and in mild areas inland; a century-old specimen surprises us in Ashland, OR, where dry 100°F summer days and winter freezes are common, but normally we would plant in a more temperate location. Remarkably fast-growing and salt tolerant, its greatest pragmatic fame is as a parent of Leyland cypress. Immense trees, superior to those in their native habitat, are common in Ireland, Australia, and New Zealand and have apparently avoided the canker. The numerous gold and yellow foliage cultivars are pretty accents and container plants; they are often sold as the latter in the East and Southeast, where they do not survive for any length of time. Authors do not know of a single plant in the Southeast. **Street tree use**: No, the trunk tends to be quite large for the height. **In the trade**: For reference purposes only, the following are but a few of the gold and yellow foliage cultivars: 'Aurea', 'Conybearii', 'Donard Gold', 'Goldcrest', 'Golden Cone', 'Golden Pillar', 'Lutea', and 'Wilma'.

Cupressus nootkatensis
(Chamaecyparis nootkatensis)
Nootka falsecypress, Alaska yellow cedar

Evergreen conifer. Among the most beautiful of North American needle evergreens with a conical crown composed of numerous drooping branches with long, pendulous flattened sprays. Elegant and refined in texture and considering its Pacific Northwest native range, well adapted to gardens. Will grow 40 to 60' high under cultivation, half that in spread, considerably smaller in the eastern United States. Fast-growing. Bark is shredding, ridged and furrowed, gray-brown.

Foliage: The foliage is soft-textured, varying from soft green to shining dark green. The color remains vibrant in cold weather. The leaves have no white markings on the lower surface and emit an off-odor when crushed. **Flowers/seeds/fruits/cones**: Male cones are red; female globose, glaucous, ⅓ to ½″ wide, with 4 to 6 scales, the tips of the scale with a sharp point. Cones mature in the second year. **Native range**: Pacific Northwest from Alaska's Kenai Peninsula through British Columbia to the Siskiyou Mountains of extreme northwestern California. For unknown reasons, wild populations are decreasing. **Adaptability**: DNA molecular sequences confirm its placement in *Cupressus*, which makes this the most moist-climate and northerly distributed (native and in gardens) taxon in the genus, as most are warm-climate and dry-soil species. In the wild it occurs on wet peat-type soils to rock outcrops, an indication of its greater landscape adaptability than typical *Cupressus*. Zones 4 to 7 in the Southeast, to 8 in the West. Does well in the Chicago area but is absent from Minneapolis–St. Paul (zone 4) landscapes. **Landscape use**: One of the most stately evergreens and for specimen use, there are few rivals. Large groupings make a powerful statement. Moist, acid, well-drained soils in full sun maximize performance. **Street tree use**: No. **In the trade**: Several cultivars available in American commerce.

Cupressus nootkatensis

Cupressus nootkatensis

Cupressus nootkatensis

'Glauca'

'Green Arrow'

'Glauca'. Blue-green foliage, grows to a dense pyramidal form, presenting a more solid appearance, to 40′ with a 20′ spread.

'Glauca Pendula'. Very dark, blue-green needle color and weeping habit. Most branches sweep downward, but occasional branches arch stiffly upward, hunchback-like and a bit eerie, like a perch for Poe's raven. Grows to 40′ by 15′.

'Green Arrow'. Maintains a central leader with deep green, slighty blue-tinted foliage. May reach at least 30′ high and is quite narrow, only 4 to 5′ wide, but we would not be surprised if it expanded with age. Does not fill in to the degree of the dense form of 'Pendula'.

'Pendula'. Beautiful, graceful, elegantly arranged pendulous branches and rich green foliage. More than one clone is in the trade under this name, which is understandable as the species itself always has weeping tips. The most common clone is a more solid pyramid, rich but pleasantly soft in color, with branches that first sweep slightly upward then weep gracefully. It grows to 45′ with a spread of 20′. Has withstood -30°F. A second clone is much narrower, a strong central leader with branches that hang close to the trunk and flare out at the tips, growing to 40′ tall and 10′ wide. Both are lovely, but we prefer the fuller form.

'Strict Weeping'. Just that, with central leader and curtain-like draping green foliage. With age, it can send up additional nearly vertical branches making it more multi-stem in appearance and considerably wider. Such a magnificent sculptural specimen sits at Iseli Nursery. Plan on at least 35′ by 10′.

'Van den Akker'. A very narrowly weeping form, similar to 'Strict Weeping' in form and size, maybe just a bit narrower and usually with darker green foliage.

'Variegata'. Yellow-splashed green foliage on a moderately dense pyramid, to 35′ by 15′.

Cupressus nootkatensis, CONTINUED

'Green Arrow'

'Pendula'

'Glauca Pendula'

'Pendula'

'Variegata'

'Strict Weeping'

'Van den Akker'

'Strict Weeping'

Cupressus ×*notabilis*
Alice Holt cypress

Evergreen conifer. Another hybrid (*C. arizonica* var. *glabra* × *C. nootkatensis*), this time dating to the 1950s, derived from seed of the maternal species at Leighton Hall. The crown is dense conical with gently arching sprays and upswept sinuous branches. Slower growing and more open-crowned than *C.* ×*leylandii*, yet still reaching 60′ in height, 10 to 15′ in width. One of the original trees reached 75′ in 57 years. Bark is reddish to purplish brown, peeling in vertical lines or scales.

Foliage: Needles in slightly flattened sprays, dark gray-green (glaucous green) with thin wax evident at the base of the needles. **Flowers/seeds/fruits/cones**: Cone is spherical with 6 to 8 scales, each with a flattened, triangular point on the face, purple-brown at maturity with a bluish white waxy bloom. **Native range**: Hybrid origin. Known only in cultivation. **Adaptability**: The maternal parent theoretically imparts high heat and drought tolerances based on its central Arizona native habitat. Zones 7 to 9. **Landscape use**: Scant landscape information is available. It would serve the same functions of *C.* ×*leylandii* without the gargantuan size. We noted a single reference that reported it as an attractive tree, fast-growing, as well as displaying good drought tolerance. Best transplanted as a container-grown plant. The introduction history provides pause for reflection. The original seedlings, two from seed collected in 1958, were raised at the Forestry Research Station at Alice Holt Lodge, Surrey, UK. One tree was removed in the early 1980s, the other in 2013. Our question: which one was introduced? **Street tree use**: No. **In the trade**: Rare, largely superseded by superior cultivars of *C.* ×*leylandii* ('Green Spire', 'Haggerston Grey', 'Naylor's Blue') and increasingly by *C.* ×*ovensii*.

Cupressus ×*notabilis*

Cupressus ×*ovensii*
Westonbirt cypress, Murray cypress

Evergreen conifer. Another rather mysterious hybrid (*C. lusitanica* × *C. nootkatensis*) clone, originating from seed collected in 1961 from *C. lusitanica* growing in Westonbirt Arboretum, England. The seedlings were raised by Howard Ovens in his nursery in Wales. It has gained a significant foothold in the Southeast because of finely dissected bluish green sprays, foliar disease resistance, and fast growth: in

Cupressus ×*ovensii*

Georgia trials it gained 3′ per year, and in south Georgia, a 7-year-old tree was 37′ high. A Christmas tree grower in Georgia, Bill Murray, promoted this as an improvement over *C. ×leylandii*, and it was christened *C. ×murrayana* (Murray cypress). We examined the tree early in its promotion and determined it a rename of *C. ×ovensii*. Habit is more open, graceful, and broad than *C. ×leylandii*. Ultimate size predicted greater than 60′ high, 15′ wide.

Foliage: Needles, in slightly flattened sprays, loosely attached to stem, finer-textured than *C. ×leylandii*, bluish green. **Flowers/seeds/fruits/cones**: Cone is spherical, 4 to 6 scales, ⅓″ long, each with a low triangular point on the face; otherwise smooth, purple-brown at maturity with a white waxy bloom. **Native range**: Hybrid origin. Known only in cultivation. **Adaptability**: Zones 6 to 8. **Landscape use**: Certainly a useful needle evergreen for screens, grouping, hedges, and Christmas trees. The fastest-growing hybrid treated herein, with increased cercosporidium needle blight resistance. Has performed admirably in sandy and heavy clay soils as long as well drained. Best transplanted as a container-grown plant. There are three *C. ×ovensii* in the Dirr garden, two of which are staked to keep them upright until established. **Street tree use**: No. **In the trade**: As a single vegetatively propagated clone. No cultivars to date, but with increased use, someone will discover a sport!

Cupressus sempervirens Stricta Group
Italian cypress

Evergreen conifer. In cultivation, the species is represented principally by the upright-columnar cultivars of the Stricta Group, members of which may reach 50′ high and be only 2 to 4′ wide. The wild form is seldom encountered and differs in having a conical to spreading crown and more horizontal branches.

Foliage: Green or blue, depending on cultivar. Soft to the touch. Color retained throughout the year. **Flowers/seeds/fruits/cones**: Cones average 1″ wide, spherical to oblong, with 10 to 12 scales; they are produced in abundance, remaining on the tree for years. **Native range**: North Africa, northeastern Mediterranean to Iran. **Adaptability**: Ubiquitous in the coastal Southeast into California. Likes a Mediterranean climate and does well even in the wet winter/dry summer Pacific Northwest if given full sun. Zones 8 to 10. **Landscape use**: Strictly vertical structural elements and effective when well grown, the green/blue subjects catching the eye and carrying it to distant points when planted in rows. Any 3′ by 3′ space is prime real estate. Best utilized in dry climates. Excess moisture spells doom; well-drained clay or sandy soils are requisites, as is full sun.

Cupressus sempervirens

Cupressus sempervirens

Trees are often staked especially in youth, as root systems are sparse. Common in the Southeast but almost universally afflicted with canker, which induces patches of dead needles throughout the narrow canopy; in the Athens, GA, area, all plants have or will contract the canker, as well as producing cones in great numbers, which often causes the branches to splay. **Street tree use**: Certainly narrow enough, a striking statement on any street. **In the trade**: Available.

'Glauca'

'Swane's Gold'

TINY TOWER

'Stricta'

'Stricta'

'Glauca' ('Glauca Stricta'). A tightly columnar blue form, otherwise similar to 'Stricta', 50′ tall and 6′ wide. Increasingly dominant in the trade because of its color.

'Stricta'. The original tightly columnar form, deep green with a blue tint, 50′ by 6′.

'Swane's Gold'. A narrow form with golden green foliage. Not as rigidly columnar as 'Stricta' and probably maturing slightly shorter.

TINY TOWER 'Monshel'. A compact columnar form, blue-green, growing at about half the rate of 'Glauca' and 'Stricta' and maturing half the size.

C

Cydonia sinensis. See
Pseudocydonia sinensis

D

Davidia involucrata

'Lady Sunshine'

'Sonoma'

Davidia involucrata
dove-tree

Deciduous. Dove-tree is every gardener's dream small to medium-sized flowering tree. Unfortunately, it is stubbornly fickle under cultivation. Develops a broad pyramidal habit in youth, similar to a linden, becoming more rounded with maturity. The largest the authors have observed was 40′ in height. A 20 to 30′ high specimen is more realistic and even this is rare although reported to 65′ high in the wild. Slow to moderate growth rate. Bark is quite attractive, developing scaly, exfoliating plates and orange to brown coloration.

Foliage: The large (to 6″ long) almost rounded, dark green leaves have large marginal serrations with long pointed teeth. Leaves are deeply veined, creating a corduroy pattern. Foliage persists late in fall and is often rendered brown by frosts. Authors have never observed respectable fall color, although red is mentioned in English literature. **Flowers/ seeds/fruits/cones:** In flower, with the tissue-paper white bracts shimmering in the slightest breeze, it has no rival; hence, the allure. The actual flower is inconspicuous, but it is framed by a pair of showy bracts, the lower 7″ by 4″; the upper 3 to 4″ by 2″ wide, produced in May, after the leaves have fully matured. Remarkably exquisite, the envy of all flowering trees, but not consistent from year to year. Further, seed-grown trees may not flower until 10 years of age. Flowers (bracts) arch from the shoots, mingled with the large leaves, and are better viewed from under the canopy than from afar. The 1½″ long, ridged, leathery-coated drupe, green to russet to purple-tinged, borne on a 2″ long peduncle, is reminiscent of a dangling damson. Fruits ripen in fall,

Davidia involucrata

with a smattering persisting into winter. The sharply ribbed endocarp contains multiple seeds. Germination is fraught with difficulty. **Native range**: China. **Adaptability**: Best adapted to coastal central and northern California, through the Pacific Northwest. Performs well in the Mid-Atlantic and New England. In the South, it is subject to canker issues. Zones 6 and 7. **Landscape use**: As a specimen it is unsurpassed. Requires moist, acid, well-drained soil, rich in organic matter, full sun to partial shade, and a measure of good fortune, for optimum success. The various Dirr gardens have nothing to show for at least five attempts. Heat, drought, and heavy soils render it compost. **Street tree use**: No. **In the trade**: Not readily available. In recent years, collectors have introduced several variegated and purple-leaf cultivars from Japan. The variegated types ('Lady Dahlia', 'Lady Sunshine', 'Aya Nishiki') have yellow/cream margins or centers.

'Iseli Fastigiate'. Narrow, strongly upright form, developing an upright oval canopy, 25′ by 12′.

'Sonoma'. The best selection, as young trees are precocious with the largest bract to 10″ long. This cultivar has performed reasonably well in the Southeast, although many have been lost to drought and heat.

'Iseli Fastigiate'

Dermatophyllum secundiflorum
(*Sophora secundiflora*)

Texas mountain laurel

Broadleaf evergreen. A native species that most gardeners would embrace for its artistic habit, small size, and spectacular fragrant flowers. Typically 15′ high with potential to 25′. Growth is slow and pruning should be minimally practiced to limb up and produce shapely specimens. Bark is gray-brown.

Foliage: Compound pinnate, 4 to 6″ long, composed of 7 to 9 oblong or obovate, emarginate (notched) leaflets, each 1 to 2″ long, rich glossy green to dark green. **Flowers/seeds/fruits/cones**: Flowers blue-violet, rarely white, fading as they age, fragrant, each 1″ long, borne in a 2 to 6″ long terminal wisteria-like inflorescence in February-March; flower buds initiate in August of the previous year. Fruits are brownish gray, constricted, thick pods, 6 to 9″ long; the red seeds, ½″ wide, are poisonous, containing the alkaloid cytisine. **Native range**: Texas, New Mexico, northern Mexico. **Adaptability**: Zones 8 to 10(11). **Landscape use**: Uses are many including accent, background screen, informal hedge, in courtyards, containers, and groupings. It must be sited in full sun and well-drained alkaline, limestone soils. In Georgia trials, it was quick to perish because of heavy, acid soils. Root rot is often cited as the limiting cultural factor. Great plant for mesic or desert urban landscapes. **Street tree use**: We have observed it in San Antonio, TX, where it was a beautiful and effective street tree. **In the trade**: Propagation is a challenge. Seeds represent the best avenue of success, requiring acid scarification. Vegetative propagation is difficult; the pretty 'Silver Peso' ('Silver Sierra') is limited because of this issue. Its silver-gray foliage is described as being highly resistant to the larvae of pyralid moths.

Dermatophyllum secundiflorum

Dermatophyllum secundiflorum

'Silver Peso'

Diospyros virginiana

common persimmon

Deciduous. Massive genus with 175 species, this being the most cold hardy, to at least -20°F. Variable in habit, slender oval to rounded crown, to a suckering mass of shoots, similar to sumacs. If it were not an American native, it would be tagged invasive. Authors observed entire fallow fields being assimilated into a persimmon nursery. Deer, raccoon, opossum, skunk, and foxes are equal opportunity distributors of the seeds. Size, when in tree mode, 30 to 60′ in height, 20 to 30′ wide. Tremendously fast-growing, a seedling becomes a 20′ high tree in 7 years. Pretty bark on large trunks/branches, dark gray, brown, to black, prominently broken into scaly, squarish blocks. The wood is dense, hard, strong, close-grained and has been used for golf club heads, billiard cues, flooring, and veneer.

Foliage: Leaves emerge pale, dusty green, mature dark green, often lustrous, developing yellow, orange, red, to purple fall color, no two trees alike. Leaves 2 to 5″ long, 1 to 2″ wide, oval to ovate with entire margins. A leafspot is ubiquitous, inducing blackish lesions, variable in severity from year to year, more aesthetically displeasing than injurious. **Flowers/seeds/fruits/cones**: Dioecious. The flowers escape the notice of most people, as they open after the leaves mature, the smaller male borne in 3s; the larger female singularly, in May-June. They are greenish white to white, fragrant, 4-lobed, the lobes recurved, and shaped like blueberry flowers. Trees develop flowers in 3 to 5 years from seed. Flower stalks persist and are evident in the axils of buds; 3-count equals male; the thick one equals female. The fleshy yellowish to pale orange berry, 1 to 1½″ wide, subtended by 4 persistent calyx lobes, ripens typically after frost and persists into November-December. The fiber-laden flesh is astringent and, if eaten before ripe, causes puckering. Pulp is utilized for pudding, cakes, and breads. Fruits contain 2 to 8 large, flattish, brown-black seeds. **Native range**: Extensive, from Connecticut to Florida, west to Kansas and Texas. Found in dry to wet habitats, usually in

D

Diospyros virginiana

Diospyros virginiana

open areas, as not very shade tolerant. A pioneer species devouring any abandoned field. **Adaptability**: Zones 4 to 9. **Landscape use**: Prospers in sand, silt, clay, moist, dry, acid, high pH, and full sun. Considered somewhat difficult to transplant, but container-grown plants provide success. Once established, the tendency to sucker from roots and form thickets is problematic. For wildlife habitat, impossible soils, and soil stabilization, the species is a lock. The fruit is gaining acceptance as an edible. **Street tree use**: We do not envision the species ascending to common use as a street tree. Its remarkable resiliency fosters the idea for a male clone (no fruit) with clean summer foliage, richly imbued with red-purple fall color. **In the trade**: Many cultivars for fruit qualities have been introduced with 'Early Golden' (early ripening), 'John Rick' (excellent flavor and firmness), and 'Killen' (good flavor and firm fruit) receiving plaudits. MAGIC FOUNTAIN 'JN5' is a weeping introduction with a strong pendulous secondary branching structure. Must be staked to develop a central leader. Lustrous dark green foliage and produces fruits. Serves as an unusual accent plant and performed well in the Dirr garden. Estimated size is 20 to 30′ high, 5 to 10′ wide.

Diospyros virginiana

E

Elaeagnus angustifolia
Russian olive

Deciduous. Low-branched or multi-stem and broadly spreading, rather open, forming an irregular to moderately rounded crown. Young trees are quite thorny, much to the dislike of nursery workers. Medium fine texture. Fast-growing to 20′ tall and 25′ wide. Bark gray, rough and fissured into irregular fibrous-stringy ridges and strips.

Foliage: Silvery gray new growth, gray-green older leaves. Leaves are oblong-lanceolate, ½″ wide and up to 3″ long. The foliage itself gives a fine-textured appearance, but with age and in high humidity or rainy sites, leaves may abscise from disease. **Flowers/seeds/fruits/cones**: Small yellow flowers, fragrant, ⅜″ long, appear along new shoots in May but are largely hidden by the silver foliage. Silvery yellow ovoid fruit, ½″ long, follows at the end of summer. Edible, used for sherbet in Asia. **Native range**: Southern Europe to central Asia. **Adaptability**: As tough as they come. Thrives on poor and alkaline soils, in drought, extreme heat and cold. Not as happy in humid climates. Zones 2 to 7. **Landscape use**: Let's start with the bad. This plant is invasive in 31 states. And in the states where it is not invasive, mostly the South, there are many more desirable trees from which to choose. Yes, it is a tree that will take the cold, dry, tough sites of the High Plains and Intermountain areas; it does well there and is commonly used, but still it invades, especially along sensitive watercourses. Think twice before planting, as it has become an environmental problem in too many areas. We wish it had been left in Russia. **Street tree use**: Not appropriate, too low and wide. **In the trade**: Sold as seed-grown, both tree form and multi-stem.

Elaeagnus angustifolia

Elaeagnus angustifolia

Elaeocarpus sylvestris
blueberry tree

Broadleaf evergreen. This rare taxon, the most cold hardy of the 60 or so species in the genus, has prospered for 16 years in University of Georgia trials, the leaves partially browning in one winter, with no stem kill and complete regrowth the following spring-summer. This lone tree has flowered and produced copious quantities of fruits with no evidence of invasiveness; it is 20′ high, 10′ wide, densely foliated and pyramidal in outline. Expect 20 to 30′ in height by 10 to 15′ wide, although listed to 50′ in wild. Growth is slow. Bark is gray, smooth surfaced on the 10″ wide trunk of the University of Georgia tree.

Foliage: Obovate to oblanceolate, leathery, margins crenate, 2 to 5″ long, ¾ to 3″ wide, glabrous, emerging bronze-green, maturing glossy dark green, abscising leaves often turning red. **Flowers/seeds/fruits/cones**: Flowers 5-petaled, ½″ long, white, fragrant, campanulate, each petal divided into 10 to 12 segments in upper half, appearing fringed, borne in 2 to 3″ long, 8- to 18-flowered racemes and hidden among the leaves, June-July in Athens. Fruit is an ellipsoidal drupe, ½″ long, ⅓″ wide, blue, with a fleshy exterior and a hard, thick, bony endocarp with 3 sutures, ripening in summer. Fruit is rather pretty, but, like the flowers, embedded with the foliage. **Native range**: China and Taiwan, where it grows in evergreen forests at elevations of 1,000 to 7,000′. **Adaptability**: Zones 8 to 10, but has survived zone 7 conditions. No foliar damage following a low of 6°F. **Landscape use**: A beautiful broadleaf evergreen tree of restrained habit with pretty foliage. Effective as a specimen and in groupings, although fruits are a nuisance. The plant is often tightly pruned during production and can be maintained as a topiary specimen. Has shown high heat and drought tolerances and never flinched during its tenure at the University of Georgia. Provide moist, acid, well-drained soils in full sun, although moderate shade is acceptable. Seeds are difficult to germinate, requiring extended warm-cold stratification period. Plants are typically grown in containers in the nursery trade. **Street tree use**: Potential, but fruit litter would prove objectionable. **In the trade**: Occasionally offered as seed-grown material, most notably in Florida and southern California into maritime Pacific Northwest. The closely related *E. decipiens* (Japanese blueberry tree) is quite similar but not as cold hardy.

Elaeocarpus sylvestris

Elaeocarpus sylvestris

Elaeocarpus sylvestris

Emmenopterys henryi

Henry emmenopterys

Deciduous. Considered the collector's holy grail because of slow-to-develop flowers, cultural difficulty, and minimal commercial presence. Even at specialist nurseries, it is woefully under-represented. So why bother? The flowering 20 to 30′ specimens at the Scott Arboretum and U.S. National Arboretum inspire covetousness. Truly a sight to behold, one the authors have enjoyed too rarely. Trees develop a rounded, spreading canopy, 30 to 50′ high at landscape maturity. Growth is slow to moderate. Bark, smooth, gray on young branches, gray to copper-brown and broken into plates and scales on mature trees.

Foliage: The beautiful elliptic-ovate to oblong-ovate foliage is sufficient reason to grow the species. Leaves, to 6(9)″ long, half as wide, entire, emerge bronze and mature lustrous dark green. The bright red petiole, to 2″ long, positions the leaves at a 90° angle to the stem in an opposite arrangement. Authors have never observed fall color, as leaves are rendered crisp by the first fall freeze. Emerging foliage is extremely sensitive to cold. **Flowers/seeds/fruits/cones**: Flowers occur only on older specimens in 8″ by 10″ terminal panicles in June-July on the current season's growth. The white flowers are funnel-shaped with one of the calyx lobes enlarging into a 2″ by 1½″, white bract. Fruit is a ribbed, spindle-shaped capsule, 1½″ long, ⅝″ wide, ripening in fall. **Native range**: China. **Adaptability**: Zones (6)7 to 8. Observed mature trees only in Europe, a few small specimens in the Mid-Atlantic states. A plant grew for many years in the University of Georgia trials but never flowered; an early April drop to 25°F killed it to the ground. It did resprout but, more than a decade on, still had not flowered. A small tree grew well in Warren's garden in Oregon for a few years until an early fall freeze took it out. **Landscape use**: If *E. henryi* were easy to grow, it would be a part of many gardens. Speculating on culture: an even climate, without early fall or spring freezes, would prove best. Soils should be moist, acid, well drained. European references note the species tolerance to high pH soils (chalk). Surprisingly, once established in the University of Georgia trials, it withstood heat, drought, and full sun, the foliage as pristine as iceberg lettuce. Authors believe there is genetic plasticity in the species that would permit early-flowering selections. In flower, it is similar to *Pinckneya bracteata* (fevertree), housed in the same family, and possibly could be hybridized. As a specimen tree, the one-of-a-kind the neighbor covets, *E. henryi* is worth the effort. **Street tree use**: No. **In the trade**: Rare.

Emmenopterys henryi

Emmenopterys henryi

Eriobotrya japonica
loquat

Broadleaf evergreen. Quite architectural. Bold, coarse-textured, rounded, 15 to 25′ high and wide. Growth is slow to moderate. Bark, seldom touted, is patchy, quilty, exfoliating in gray, brown, and deeper colors; when specimens are limbed up and grown as small trees, this pretty feature is highlighted.

Foliage: The broad obovate, corrugated, leathery-textured leaves, 6 to 9(12)″ long, 3 to 4″ wide, are lustrous dark green above, covered with grayish brown pubescence below. The parallel veins are deeply ribbed, ending in prominent coarse marginal teeth. Foliage color is consistent throughout the year, when protected from winter sun and wind. **Flowers/seeds/fruits/cones**: Flowers open over an extended period, as early as September, typically November to January. The dirty (off) white (yellowish white), fragrant, ¾″ wide flowers are borne in 3 to 6″ long terminal panicles, the effect not overwhelming. The pedicels and peduncle are covered with dense brown pubescence. If flowers are not injured by cold, the yellow to orange, pear-shaped to oblong fruit, to 2″ long, matures in spring. The fruit is edible with sweet, soft-textured flesh and a large seed. **Native range**: Japan and China. **Adaptability**: Adaptable to extremes of soil, heat, drought, and salt-laden environments. Zones 8 to 10 but has survived 6°F in Georgia when plants were sufficiently hardened going into fall. At -3°F, a large University of Georgia plant was killed to the ground but regenerated from the base. A zone 7 designation (cold hardy between 0 and 10°F) is merited if the plant is established and growth has matured. **Landscape use**: From our observations, the species is culturally flexible from sand to clay, acid to high pH, moist to dry (once established), and full sun to moderate shade. Displays moderate salt tolerance and is utilized in Atlantic coastal landscapes where hardy. Also functions

Eriobotrya japonica

Eriobotrya deflexa

Eriobotrya japonica

Eriobotrya deflexa

'Variegata'

Erythrina crista-galli

as a large shrub and an espalier. **Street tree use**: Utilized as such in the South and West. **In the trade**: 'Golden Nugget' (abundant, flavorful, pear-shaped, yellow-orange fruit), 'Hatsushimo' (chlorophyll-deficient new leaves, gradually developing flecks of green, eventually completely green), and 'Variegata' (white-margined, green-centered leaves). The closely related *E. deflexa* (bronze loquat) is similar, usually a large shrub, but with leaves that have rounded teeth (serrations) and are glabrous (no pubescence) beneath at maturity. The emerging leaves are copper-red, eventually green (not as lustrous or dark as *E. japonica*). It is utilized in California as a street tree, and a Florida reference points to its being short-lived and fireblight susceptible, as is *E. japonica*; however, the authors have never witnessed fireblight on *E. japonica*. Hybrids of *E. deflexa* and *Rhaphiolepis indica* include 'Coppertone' with enhanced spring foliage coloration (copper-red) and pale pink flowers. A new genus, ×*Rhaphiobotrya*, now houses the hybrids. They make pretty small trees or large shrubs, the foliage smaller and finer-textured than the *Eriobotrya* parent. *E. deflexa* is native to China, Vietnam, and Taiwan; adapted to zones 8 to 10, with the hybrids more hardy, to zone 7.

Erythrina crista-galli
cockspur coral-tree

Deciduous. A pretty flowering tree but certainly not common; authors remember only a single 20′ tree in Houston. Habit is rounded with rather coarse-textured branches. Growth is slow to moderate, with the largest U.S. tree on record at 32′ in height. Trunks are often irregular, twisted and contorted. Bark on large trunks is ridged and furrowed, with gray, flattish ridges and brown furrows.

Foliage: The leaves comprise 3 leaflets, each to 6″ long, half as wide, bright green, dying off same in fall. Nasty, razor-sharp hooked prickles on leaflet, midrib, and stem.

Erythrina crista-galli

E

Flowers/seeds/fruits/cones: Flowers, borne in 16 to 24″ racemes, are spectacular, brilliant crimson, warm pink to wine-red, produced on the new growth of the season in summer and continuing into fall. Removing spent flowers encourages rebloom and reduces fruit production. The legume fruit, 3 to 8″ long, constricted between the seeds, each seed ½″ wide, rounded, and brown. **Native range**: Brazil, Bolivia, Paraguay, Argentina, and Uruguay. **Adaptability**: Adaptable to any well-drained soil and full sun, but temperatures below 20°F result in damage, and a report from San Diego noted 14°F killed trees to the ground. Zones 9 to 11, 8 with trepidation. **Landscape use**: Hardiness limits use as a specimen and small landscape element. Suited only to Florida, the warm Gulf Coast, into California. Requires heat and long growing season to ensure prolific flower production. **Street tree use**: Used, but low-branched and spiny. **In the trade**: The species and cultivar 'Red Lights' are sold.

Eucalyptus cinerea
silver dollar tree

Broadleaf evergreen. A smaller rounded tree, low-branched or multi-stem. Medium fine texture, moderately fast-growing to 30′ by 25′. Bark is fibrous and reddish brown.

Foliage: Both juvenile and mature leaves are silvery blue-green. Juvenile leaves are round, like silver dollars. Juvenile foliage may persist into the mature tree and is often encouraged by pruning; this growth is prized by the florist trade. Mature leaves are lanceolate, 3 to 4″ long. **Flowers/seeds/fruits/cones**: Flowers are small loose balls of white filaments in spring, interesting up close. Seed capsules follow and mature brown. **Native range**: Australia. **Adaptability**: Likes a hot climate and needs good drainage. May freeze at 17°F, zones 9 and 10. **Landscape use**: A smaller garden

tree with attractive foliage. Sometimes grown as a shrubby, cut-back perennial for its juvenile foliage for flower arrangements. **Street tree use**: Usually a bit too low-branched to recommend, but with pruning it can make a decent small street tree. **In the trade**: Sold as seed-grown.

Eucalyptus citriodora. See *Corymbia citriodora*

Eucalyptus dalrympleana
mountain gum, broadleaf kindlingbark

Broadleaf evergreen. A very tall tree with an upright-spreading form, usually with a clean single trunk, but sometimes low-branched or multi-stem, forming a broadly rounded crown. Fast-growing, moderately fine-textured, growing to over 100′ tall with a 50′ spread. Bark is smooth and white, darkening to cinnamon-orange each year, then exfoliating to white again, very attractive.

Foliage: Juvenile leaves are relatively large, bluish green and ovate, mature leaves are lanceolate, quite slender, up to 11″ long, blue-green. **Flowers/seeds/fruits/cones**: Small, white, little puffs of filaments, summer to fall; not especially showy in the landscape because they usually are at great height on mature trees. Small yellow-green capsules turn brown at maturity. **Native range**: Australia, Tasmania. **Adaptability**: One of the more cold hardy eucalypts, tolerant of varying soil moisture and acid and alkaline soils. May sustain damage at 12°F. Zones 8 to 10. **Landscape use**: A very large tree; give it room for its height, as it will develop a high canopy. The largest of the cold hardy eucalypts. The smooth white

Eucalyptus cinerea

Eucalyptus dalrympleana

Eucalyptus dalrympleana

Eucalyptus globulus

trunk is truly striking and can become its best feature, as fast growth will put foliage and flowers high overhead. **Street tree use**: Possible, but only if you have room for its size, and a planting strip wide enough to accommodate a very large trunk. **In the trade**: Sold as seed-grown.

Eucalyptus globulus
blue gum, Tasmanian bluegum

Broadleaf evergreen. Another very tall tree, upright in form with an oval canopy. Very fast-growing, medium texture, and reaching heights over 100′ with a spread of 40′. Bark exfoliates in brownish strips, revealing a pattern of orange-tan and shades of gray below.

Foliage: Juvenile foliage is ovate, bluish gray-green. Mature foliage is lanceolate, curving, and dark blue-green, up to 12″ in length. **Flowers/seeds/fruits/cones**: Flowers are white pom-poms of filaments in spring, showy up close but not as visible high in the canopy. Brown seed capsules look like

Eucalyptus globulus

little buttons (hence the epithet). **Native range**: Australia, Tasmania. **Adaptability**: Quite adaptable to hot areas, tolerates moisture and drought, not particular to soil pH. Zones 8 to 10. **Landscape use**: Widely planted in California in the late 1800s for windbreaks or timber, this practice was abandoned in the 1900s as lumber was poor quality, trees and shed leaves were found to be highly flammable, and some invasiveness has now been seen in the coastal strip. The species has given eucalyptus a bad name in the United States; the genus holds much better choices, which were not well known when these were widely planted. Now, landscape use is restricted to 'Compacta'. **Street tree use**: More likely roadside and freeway plantings, but 'Compacta' can be used if space allows for its large size. **In the trade**: Typically found only as 'Compacta', which is upright-growing with an oval canopy, somewhat smaller than the species, but don't be fooled by the cultivar name: it is still a big tree and can reach 70′ with a width of 30′.

Eucalyptus gunnii

Eucalyptus gunnii
cider gum

Broadleaf evergreen. A medium-sized tree by the standards of the genus, tall, upright oval to narrow oval. Moderately fine-textured, fast-growing to 60′ tall and 40′ wide. Bark exfoliates in gray-brown strips, revealing a pattern of tan, green, and gray.

Foliage: Juvenile leaves are broadly oval, and silvery blue-green. Mature foliage is long and narrow, lanceolate to 5″ in length, darker green to bluish green. **Flowers/seeds/fruits/cones**: White, frilled, in clusters, usually of 3, flowering summer to fall. Small green seed capsules follow. **Native range**: Tasmania. **Adaptability**: Best adapted to a hot climate, tolerates poor drainage better than most eucalypts, one of the most cold hardy. Successful in the Southeast, but occasional severe freezes can kill it to the ground. Trees

from the best seed sources may survive 5°F. Zones (7)8 to 9. **Landscape use**: One of the better choices for the garden, with good cold hardiness and tolerance of irrigated lawns and landscapes. Sometimes it is cut back yearly and maintained as a multi-stem for its outstanding juvenile foliage. **Street tree use**: Possible if lower limbs are pruned for clearance. **In the trade**: Sold as seed-grown.

Eucalyptus neglecta
omeo gum

Broadleaf evergreen. Broadly oval to round, moderately fine-textured, moderately fast-growing to 40′ by 40′. Bark is rough, gray and stringy on older trunks, exfoliating to reveal orange-brown, greenish, and gray.

Foliage: Juvenile leaves are large, rounded and blue-green with a purplish cast in cool weather; juvenile foliage persists into larger trees. Mature leaves are oblong-ovate, darker green. **Flowers/seeds/fruits/cones**: Small white flowers, like little puffs, in large clusters during summer. Green seed capsules follow, turning brown as they mature. **Native range**: Australia. **Adaptability**: Best in hot climates. Tolerant of wet soils, and one of the most tolerant eucalypts to temperature extremes, both hot and cold. Has at times withstood temperatures below 0°F. Zones 7 to 9. **Landscape use**: A medium-sized garden tree, spreading, bushy, and wide. A good screen. Appreciated for its long-lasting juvenile phase and often chosen for extreme cold hardiness among eucalypts. **Street tree use**: No, too wide and low-branched. **In the trade**: Sold as seed-grown.

Eucalyptus gunnii

Eucalyptus nicholii

willow-leaf peppermint, narrow-leaf black peppermint

Broadleaf evergreen. A small to medium-sized tree, small for a eucalypt, either single-trunked or multi-stem, with an upright-spreading habit and nodding branch tips, oval-shaped. Fine-textured, moderate growth rate to 30′ high and 20′ wide. Bark is grayish brown, fibrous, revealing orange-brown when it peels.

Foliage: Juvenile foliage is feathery, willow-like, linear to lanceolate, blue-gray on reddish stems. Mature foliage similarly shaped, larger and more substantial, to 5″ long, bluish gray to green. Leaves smell of peppermint, especially when crushed. **Flowers/seeds/fruits/cones**: Flowers small, white, in clusters, summer to fall. Urn-shaped green seed capsules turn brown when mature. **Native range**: Australia. **Adaptability**: Avoid wet sites, it needs good drainage. May freeze at 15°F or lower. Zones 8 to 10. **Landscape use**: One of the best small garden trees in the genus. Its growth rate is more manageable and its mature size a better fit for most residential lots, plus its upright form allows the space below the canopy to be used. One of the finest-textured eucalypts, its narrow leaf in the juvenile stage is unusual. The foliage and form combine to present a delicate and graceful image. **Street tree use**: Suitable as a smaller street tree if pruned to encourage the upright form. **In the trade**: Sold as seed-grown.

E

Eucalyptus nicholii

Eucalyptus nicholii

Eucalyptus parvula (E. parvifolia)
small-leaved gum

Broadleaf evergreen. A smaller tree, usually low-branched or multi-stem, spreading to a rounded shape, often flat-topped. Fine-textured, moderately fast-growing to 35′ by 35′. Bark is smooth, gray to gray-green and tan.

Foliage: Juvenile leaves are round to oval, small, and persist only while quite young, light bluish green. Mature leaves follow at an early age and are quite small, averaging just over 2″ long, blue-green. **Flowers/seeds/fruits/cones:** Small cream-colored puff-like flowers decorate shoots, summer to fall. The smaller size of the species and lower branching make the flowers more visible. Small green seed capsules ripen to brown. **Native range:** Australia. **Adaptability:** One of the more adaptable eucalypts, tolerant of wet and dry soils as well as colder weather than most, close to 0°F. Zones 7 to 9. **Landscape use:** A smaller, broad-spreading garden tree with a finer texture than most of the genus with quite fragrant foliage. Twigs have a reddish cast that contrasts nicely with the small leaves. The low-branched trunk can twist and curve artistically. **Street tree use:** No, too low and broad. **In the trade:** Sold as seed-grown.

Eucalyptus pauciflora subsp. *niphophila*

Eucalyptus pauciflora subsp. niphophila
snow gum

Broadleaf evergreen. A small to medium-sized tree, single-trunked or multi-stem, upright-spreading, often with a twisting or curving branching habit, especially if multi-stem, somewhat open in form. Medium fine texture, moderate growth rate, to 25′ height and 20′ spread. Bark is wonderful: greenish gray, tan, and white, exfoliating in patches to become smooth, light gray to nearly pure white in the sun.

Foliage: Juvenile leaves are ovate, bluish gray-green. Mature leaves are bluish gray to olive-green, lanceolate, rather thick, to 4″ long. **Flowers/seeds/fruits/cones:** Flowers are little white puffs of filaments held in larger clusters than most. Flowering is more visible because of the shorter stature of this tree. Seed is produced in the typical urn-shaped brown capsules of the genus. **Native range:** Australia, Tasmania. **Adaptability:** Probably the most cold hardy tree in the genus, reliable down to 0°F. Some individual trees have gone to much lower temperatures. This is a mountain tree, growing at the tree line in its native habitat and preferring a cooler climate than most eucalypts, with reasonable soil moisture. Zones 7 to 9. **Landscape use:** Appreciated for

Eucalyptus pauciflora subsp. *niphophila*

its small size, its outstanding bark, and its cold hardiness, which brings this eucalypt into the reach of more northern gardeners. A smaller garden tree with an informal appearance and a fairly open canopy that provides filtered shade. Eye-catching in any garden, but especially in a cooler climate, where a eucalypt is unexpected. **Street tree use**: Usually a little too low-branched and spreading for streets. **In the trade**: Sold as seed-grown.

Eucalyptus polyanthemos
silver dollar gum, red box

Broadleaf evergreen. A large tree, upright oval to broadly oval with a canopy that is fuller than most in the genus. Moderately fast-growing, medium texture, to 70′ tall and 40′ wide. Bark is mostly smooth, pale gray to warm brown, becoming rough and fibrous with age.

Foliage: Juvenile leaves are round, gray-green. Mature leaves are dark green and ovate, 2 to 4″ long, and hang from rather long petioles, dark bluish gray-green. **Flowers/seeds/fruits/cones**: Heavy flowering in spring, the creamy white flowers showy en masse. Seed capsules yellowish green, maturing more brownish. **Native range**: Australia. **Adaptability**: Definitely a tree for hotter climates, southern California to Arizona. Tolerates poor soils and drought, but needs good drainage. May freeze at 18°F. Zones 9 to 11. **Landscape use**: A large shade tree for roomy residential lots and commercial sites. **Street tree use**: One of the best eucalypts for the purpose, upright with clearance below. **In the trade**: Sold as seed-grown.

Eucommia ulmoides
hardy rubber tree

Deciduous. Upright-spreading to broadly spreading with a broad rounded crown, often growing wider than tall at maturity. Medium coarse in texture, moderately fast-growing to 45′ tall with a 50′ spread. Bark is gray-brown, ridged and furrowed.

E

Eucalyptus polyanthemos

Eucommia ulmoides

Foliage: Dark green, ovate to elliptical, a rather large leaf averaging 4 to 5″, with a handsome gloss. Fall color usually disappoints, yellowish green at best. **Flowers/seeds/fruits/cones**: Dioecious. Flowers are inconspicuous in the landscape; the males are bare greenish stamens and the female just a green pistil. **Native range**: Central China. **Adaptability**: Considered generally pest- and disease-free, it's also tolerant of a wide range of soils, including elevated pH. It can withstand some drought but is not for poorly drained sites. Zones 5 to 7(8). **Landscape use**: A handsome green shade tree. Its pest resistance is perhaps its best feature. Never has earned a strong following in city plantings or in the landscape trade, but is gaining more use as cities strive for diversity in their urban forest. No doubt the lack of any special ornamental display works against it. Development of a more upright cultivar with bright fall color would probably inspire greater use. **Street tree use**: Has been used successfully; needs a wide planting strip and pruning of lower branches for clearance. **In the trade**: Almost always sold as seed-grown. The lone cultivar of note is EMERALD POINTE, a narrow upright oval, nearly columnar, compact, and smaller-maturing selection of the species. Its form is quite different and appropriate for narrow street plantings. Foliage also differs from the species in that it is lighter green, more textured, nearly rugose, and more deeply serrate along the leaf margins. To 40′ with a 15′ spread.

Eucryphia ×nymansensis
Nyman eucryphia

Broadleaf evergreen. For the authors, the genus, with nine species and several hybrids, presents an identification nightmare: all have fragrant, predominantly white (rarely pink) flowers, opening from July to September; petals are 4-merous with a central brush-like mass of conspicuous stamens. *E. ×nymansensis* is a hybrid between two Chilean species, *E. cordifolia* (evergreen, simple leaf, tree to 70′) and *E. glutinosa* (deciduous or partially evergreen, compound leaf, 10 to 25′), and intermediate in characteristics with both simple and compound leaves (typically in 3s) persisting through winter. It makes a medium-sized upright tree, 20 to 30′ high. Growth is slow.

Foliage: The firm-textured leaves are in clusters toward the end of each shoot, lustrous dark green, 1½ to 2½″ long, 1 to 1½″ wide, with regularly serrated margins, either borne singly or compound. **Flowers/seeds/fruits/cones**: Honey-scented white flowers, 2 to 3″ wide, arrive in summer, opening over an extended period; petals are spreading, overlapping, with uneven margins; stamens are numerous with yellow anthers. Fruit is a woody capsule with persistent

Eucommia ulmoides

Eucryphia ×nymansensis

EMERALD POINTE

'Nymansay'

styles. **Native range**: Chile, *E. cordifolia* in temperate rainforests, *E. glutinosa* on rocky banks along rivers. **Adaptability**: Best adapted to coastal Pacific Northwest south to the San Francisco area, zones 8 to 10. Withstood 10°F without leaf damage. **Landscape use**: Beautiful specimen tree requiring exacting conditions. Cool, moist climates suit it best. Soils should be acid, well-drained, cool, and evenly moist. European literature noted it will succeed in chalk (high pH) soils and recommended that the roots be shaded from hot sun. In southwestern England, 50′ high trees are common. **Street tree use**: Have not seen it used thus but seems logical, as the form is appropriate. **In the trade**: Limited in the United States.

'Mount Usher'. Double and single flowers. It is closer to *E. cordifolia* in characteristics.

'Nymansay' ('Nymans A'). Small to medium-sized tree of dense columnar habit, the flowers 2″ wide and greater, open in August-September. Raised in the great Nymans Garden, Sussex, England, c.1914.

'Nymans Silver'. White-margined, green-centered leaves. Discovered as a branch sport of *E. ×nymansensis* at Nymans Garden, Sussex, in 2005.

Euonymus bungeanus
winterberry euonymus

Deciduous. Authors vacillate about usefulness because of scale susceptibility, but, in its finest hour, dangling with the yellowish white to pinkish capsular fruits, exposing pink to white seeds, it builds a case for second thoughts... Pretty habit, delicately rounded, clothed with slender, semi-pendulous, fine-textured branches. Nowhere common, but instantly recognizable because of its habit, fruit, and bark. Size 18 to 24′ high and wide, although authors observed a 50′ high specimen. Bark is unique, starting with wispy bright green first-year stems to the deeply ridged and furrowed, gray to black of mature trunks. The ridges are wide, flat, gray; the furrows deep, irregular, trending toward black. The most impressive representative of this characteristic resides in the Missouri Botanical Garden, St. Louis.

Foliage: Leaves are bright green, elliptic-ovate, to 4″ long with fine marginal teeth. They emerge early, often mature size by early April in zone 8! Fall color varies, yellow-green, soft lemon-yellow to pinkish red, at times quite showy. **Flowers/seeds/fruits/cones**: Flowers, yellowish green-white with purple anthers, 4-petaled, open in May, held in 1 to 2″ long cymes. The capsular, deeply 4-lobed, smooth fruit, typically pink (also yellowish white) matures in September-October, persisting after leaves have abscised. The seeds are covered with an orange aril, visible after the

Euonymus bungeanus

Euonymus bungeanus

capsule dehisces. **Native range**: Northern China, Manchuria. **Adaptability**: Zones (3)4 to 7(8), the range expanded based on North Dakota and Middle Georgia healthy trees. **Landscape use**: Pretty tree that is remarkably adaptable to extremes of cold, heat, drought, acid, and high pH soils. Requires full sun for maximum fruiting. Certainly, useful as a small specimen, in groupings, possibly large containers. The bark is sufficient justification to plant the species. **Street tree use**: Not recommended, too low spreading. **In the trade**: Several cultivars are described in the American and European literature. 'Pink Lady', introduced by the U.S. National Arboretum, has pink capsules, orange seeds, and yellow, bronze, and red fall color. PRAIRIE RADIANCE

E

Euonymus bungeanus

Euonymus europaeus

PRAIRIE RADIANCE

Euonymus europaeus

'Verona' develops a rounded crown, 20′ by 20′, with showy pink capsules that open to showcase the orange-red seeds. The high-quality rich dark green foliage develops intense pink to reddish fall color. We observed the cultivar in Minnesota, where the foliage was spotted and speckled yellow, a smattering of leaves glossy dark green. The most cold hardy (zone 3) of all winterberry clones tested in North Dakota.

Euonymus europaeus
European euonymus, common spindle-tree

Deciduous. What was stated for *E. bungeanus* could essentially be dittoed for this species. Again, when laden with the spider-on-a-thread, pink to red capsules, strewn among the dull dark green foliage, the gardener's heart rate increases. Forms an upright habit in youth, broadening with age, eventually rounded in outline. Usually small, 15 to 30′ high. Mature specimens are seldom encountered in the United States, although several magnificent old specimens are extant at the U.S. National Arboretum. Growth is slow. The first-year stems are smooth, green, tinged

Euonymus europaeus

with red, becoming gray-brown in the second year. Older trunks develop smooth gray-streaked patterns with darker rough-textured areas interspersed, becoming ridged and furrowed much akin to the bark of *E. bungeanus*. The hard wood was utilized for making spindles (hence one of the common names).

Foliage: Leaves are dark green, more prominently serrated than *E. bungeanus*, to 4″ long, ½ to 1¼″ wide, variable in fall color, from yellow-green to superb reddish purple. A tree on the University of Maine campus developed the most brilliant, fluorescent scarlet fall color. **Flowers/seeds/fruits/cones**: The yellowish green flowers are uneventful, opening in May after the leaves, each 4-petaled, ½″ wide, in 1 to 1½″ long, 3- to 5-flowered cymes. The capsule, 4-valved, to ¾″ wide, pink to red/scarlet, opens to expose the orange-ariled seeds. In zone 7, capsules have remained closed into late October, with seeds released by mid-November. Fruits, at their best, are alluring. **Native range**: Europe to western Asia. **Adaptability**: Zones 4 to 7, but best suited to colder climates. **Landscape use**: Excellent for fruit and fall color, in groupings, screens, borders. Adaptable like *E. bungeanus* and as the English references note, suitable for chalk (limestone) soils. Tolerates more shade than *E. bungeanus*. It is a common component of the famed English hedgerows, largely dispersed by birds. Scale is the limiting factor. **Street tree use**: No. **In the trade**: Cultivars, particularly in Europe, have been selected for foliage, fruit colors, and habit. 'Red Caps' was selected for the persistent bright red fruits by the University of Nebraska. 'Red Cascade' develops arching branches, rich scarlet autumn color, and prodigious quantities of rosy red fruit. Both are free-fruiting and have orange seeds.

Euscaphis japonica

sweetheart tree, Korean sweetheart tree

Deciduous. Monotypic genus. Accolades poured in before this tree was adequately vetted, and it has failed to make a commercial impact. However, in its finest dress, there are reasons to consider. An upright habit in youth opens to a rounded canopy, 15 to 25′ high and wide. Branching is rather stiff, coarse, with first-year stems quite chunky. Growth is slow. The bark, deep reddish purple, is striated with lighter colors, somewhat reminiscent of the snakebark maples. Bark becomes gray, lightly ridged and furrowed, the flat ridges darker than the furrows.

Foliage: Compound pinnate foliage is beautiful, leathery, lustrous dark green, finely serrated, with 7 to (9)11, to 4″ long leaflets. Authors have not observed sufficient trees to put an absolute imprint on fall color; to date, yellow-green to yellow and underwhelming. Literature cites fall color as mahogany-purple, which we have yet to experience.

Flowers/seeds/fruits/cones: The yellowish white, ¼″ wide flowers, borne in 4 to 12″ wide terminal panicles, open in May-June, later than the typical run of *Cercis* and *Cornus*. In zone 8, flowers were fully open in late April. The beauty resides in the rose to ruby-red, ½″ long, ¼″ wide pods, somewhat boat-shaped, three together, opening to expose the lustrous, steel-blue to black, plumpish, BB-shaped seeds. Fruits ripen in August-September-October and persist for several months. A fruit-laden tree is, indeed, a pretty picture. **Native range**: China, Korea, Japan. **Adaptability**: Northern limits are sketchy (zone 6), but has performed well in Nacogdoches, TX, zones 8 and 9. **Landscape use**: If the tree is properly sited, the benefits are manifest. Worthy choice for the adventuresome gardener and well sized for smaller properties. There's a 20′ high tree in Coach Dooley's Athens, GA, garden (zone 8) which no visitor has yet correctly identified. It performs best in moist, acid, well-drained soils in full sun. Authors observed good flowering and fruiting when sited in partial shade. Early promos praised its heat and drought tolerances, both compromised in zone 8. **Street tree use**: No. **In the trade**: Seed has a complex dormancy and is not readily germinated. No doubt improved cultivars will emerge as the tree becomes more widely grown.

E

Euscaphis japonica

Euscaphis japonica

F

Fagus grandifolia
American beech

Deciduous. A rather homogeneous genus of about 10 species, all with smooth, gray trunks. This, the only North American representative, oozes nobility. Through the years, American beech has been maligned as slow-growing, finicky, difficult to transplant, and slow to recover. Some element of truth to the initial slow rate of growth, but once established, it is off to the races. In our consulting work, we routinely recommend this species and have yet to lose a single tree. Trees planted 25 year ago are 40′ high. American beeches in forest habitats develop long, slender, silver-gray boles with an oval to rounded canopy. Open-grown trees branch low, with a short trunk and wide-spreading crown. We estimate 50 to 75′ in 50 years under landscape conditions. The thin, smooth-textured bark is light bluish gray to silver-gray on younger branches and large trunks. Indeed, in winter, the species is easily identified by this trait and the variably persistent (marcescent) foliage, often persisting until new flush of foliage emerges.

Foliage: Where to start? Tender silvery green, shimmering bright green leaves emerge from the bright brown bud scales in April (Georgia), May (Boston). Leaves mature to lustrous dark green, with 11 to 15 pairs of impressed veins, ending in coarse serrations, each to 5″ long, 2½″ wide. In autumn, color arrives late, in glorious yellows, bronzes, and golden browns, long effective. Foliage is freeze resistant, withstanding low 20s. Carried into winter, the leaves become light brown to ghostly gray, persisting into spring. **Flowers/seeds/fruits/cones**: Monoecious. Flowers arrive with the emerging leaves, silvery green, not showy, with male in globose heads; female in 2- to 4-flowered spikes. Fruit is a shiny brown, 3-winged nut, enclosed in a prickly, ¾″ high involucre. Fruits are often

Fagus grandifolia

Fagus grandifolia

devoid of sound seeds. **Native range**: Canadian Maritimes to Florida and Texas, in all manner of habitats. **Adaptability**: Authors have observed splendid specimens from Prince Edward Island, Canada, to Florida and Texas. Few native trees possess what we term "species ubiquity" (i.e., the ability to withstand extremes of climate and soil conditions). Such is the genetic propensity of *F. grandifolia*. Zones 4 to 9. **Landscape use**: Authors observed *F. grandifolia* utilized for street, park, campus, and large areas. Soils should be acid, well drained; however, in the Midwest, on mollisolic (high pH) soils, chlorosis is not evident. American beech is a

Fagus grandifolia

Fagus grandifolia

Fagus sylvatica
European beech

Deciduous. The European cousin of *F. grandifolia*, equally deserving of accolades but not as well adapted to heat, with zone 7 the southern limit for meaningful landscape success. Magnificent 100-year-old specimens are common in the Mid-Atlantic, Midwest, and New England. Habit is densely pyramidal, oval to rounded, branching to the ground. The winter silhouette is as beautiful as a tree in full leaf. There is much to love; little to dislike. European beech, like the American, requires ample real estate to spread its wings (read: branches). In the cooler areas, trees range from 50 to 70′ high, usually less in width. Growth is slow to moderate; faster in cooler climates. Bark is smooth, gray, usually darker than American beech; magnificent and bold-textured in all its permutations.

Foliage: The leaves have essentially entire margins and fewer veins (5 to 9) than American beech, otherwise similar

F

Fagus sylvatica

climax species, well adapted to full sun and shade. Mycorrhizal fungi are often correlated with successful transplanting and growth. Authors conducted a mini-experiment on newly planted seedlings by inoculating half with a slurry of soil collected under large native trees. The inoculated seedlings leafed out earlier (who knows why), but no growth differences were evident at the end of the season. Twenty of these seedlings in 3-gallon containers were planted in the Dirr garden in 2013. All survived with a few over 10′ high (2017). **Street tree use**: Yes. Our loving advice? Plant American beech. **In the trade**: The species (which shows surprisingly minimal natural variation in leaf and habit traits) is almost entirely sold seed-grown, and cultivars are rare. They include 'Cameron', a weeper, 'Diamond Bark' (just that), and 'Mr. Tee', a narrow upright form. A densely branched seedling selection with thick, dark green leaves has been sent to Schmidt for trialing.

Fagus sylvatica

Fagus sylvatica

'Aspleniifolia'

'Aspleniifolia'

in aesthetics, tender shimmering green, lustrous dark green at maturity, and golden copper/bronze in fall. Leaves are broad egg-shaped, to 4″ long, 2½″ wide, smaller than those of the American beech. They display excellent freeze tolerance into the low 20s and persist into winter, especially on young trees. **Flowers/seeds/fruits/cones**: Flowers are similar to those of *F. grandifolia*. Fruit is woody, pear-shaped, ¾ to 1″ long, with a 4-lobed involucre covered with bristles; otherwise similar. **Native range**: Europe, where it is found on calcareous soils. **Adaptability**: Based on performance in the United States, it is adaptable to acid, high pH (calcareous), well-drained soils in sun or shade. Zones 4 to 7. **Landscape use**: Remarkable noble tree, dignified, pedigreed, stately, and elegant; should be given ample room to maximize the genetic potential. It too is a climax species, meaning it will maintain its place in the forest, regenerate, and remain a permanent component. In Europe, seedlings are often used for hedging; they hold their leaves through winter as the juvenile state is continually maintained via pruning, creating continuous screening. The many cultivars permit creative uses owing to shape and size; upright-columnar types like 'Dawyck', 'Dawyck Gold', and 'Dawyck Purple' are superb choices where lateral space is restricted. The weeping forms develop into magnificent specimens. We do

not believe there is a "bad" beech cultivar. **Street tree use**: Suitable; remember that it is a big tree and its roots and trunk need room. **In the trade**: *F. sylvatica* displays phenomenal genetic plasticity, meaning variations in all manner of characteristics are common occurrences. The many cultivars hybridize between and among, resulting in rainbow foliage colors and mulligan-stew habits and sizes. Among the earliest recorded selections (1770) is 'Albovariegata' with

'Atropunicea'

'Dawyck Gold'

'Dawyck'

leaves margined and streaked with white. Some of the best cultivars offered in the North American trade follow.

'Aspleniifolia'. Delicately incised, fine-textured green leaves. Forms a densely branched oval-rounded habit, 60′ by 50′.

Atropurpurea Group. The umbrella term for seed-raised purple-leaf trees (e.g., 'Atropunicea', 'Cuprea'). Any purple-leaf seedling with normal, weeping, contorted, or fastigiate habit falls in this group.

'Aurea Pendula'. A weeping yellow-leaf form, quite worthy of specimen use.

'Dawyck', 'Dawyck Gold', and 'Dawyck Purple'. Fastigiate types with green, gold (yellow), and purple leaves, respectively. The latter two are narrower than the parent, 'Dawyck'. Trees have reached over 60′ in height in England. Chlorophyll counts, so the green 'Dawyck' rates the largest at 60′ by 10′; 'Dawyck Purple' and 'Dawyck Gold' are more likely to reach 40 to 50′ by 10′.

'Dawyck Purple'

'Purpurea Pendula'

'Pendula'

'Pendula'

'Pendula'. A magnificent green-leaf specimen tree with branches dipping, diving, arching, and cascading, reaching 50 to 60′ high, and often wider at maturity. Looking like a deep green waterfall, it is a favorite of the authors. Purple- and yellow-leaf weeping cultivars are extant.

'Purple Fountain'

'Purple Fountain'

'Purpurea Tricolor'

'Purpurea Tricolor'

'Purple Fountain'. More restrained habit than the green-leaf weeper, tending to send up a strong leader and weep rather narrowly, potentially to 30′ by 12 to 15′. A good weeper for narrow spots. The purple foliage color is diminished in the heat. 'Purpurea Pendula' is smaller, growing very slowly to 10′ with a broad, weeping, mushroom-shaped canopy.

'Purpurea Tricolor' ('Roseomarginata'). Slow-growing, oval-rounded form with leaves marked with rich pink, rose, white, and purple. Loses color in heat; ideally, site in some shade, even in cool climates. 'Tricolor' is a rarely found, slow-growing cultivar with a green center and white and pink margins; now often used as the common name for 'Purpurea Tricolor', but we miss the green version, which is a distinct cultivar.

'Red Obelisk'

'Riversii'

'Rohanii'

'Riversii'

'Red Obelisk'. Compact pyramidal-columnar habit with variably incised purple leaves similar to 'Rohanii'. Potential size is 40 to 50′ by 10 to 15′.

'Riversii'. Possibly the blackest deep purple emerging leaves, eventually purple-green. Similar to the species in habit, broadly oval, but slower growing, 50′ by 40′. The most common purple-leaf cultivar in commerce.

'Rohanii' ('Rohan Purple'). Slow-growing, estimating 30′ high, and more oval-rounded in outline, with brownish (bronze) purple leaves, the margins undulating and edged with round, shallow teeth. Dates from 1894. Various hybrids with 'Rohanii' include 'Rohan Gold' (yellow to green leaves), 'Rohan Obelisk' (narrow-upright, irregularly lobed red-purple leaves), and 'Rohan Trompenburg' (red-purple leaves, triangular teeth, upright habit).

'Spaethiana'. Along with 'Riversii', one of the most beautiful purple-leaf cultivars. 50′ by 40′.

f. *tortuosa*

'Zlatia'

f. *tortuosa* ('Tortuosa'). Scarcely qualifies for tree status, but a 20′ high, 30′ wide specimen is known. Branches are twisted, turned, and double-jointed, forming a mounded-spreading dome of green foliage. 'Tortuosa Purpurea' is a slower-growing, purple-leaf form.

'Zlatia'. A slow-growing selection with yellow new leaves, eventually green, and a species-like habit.

'Spaethiana'

Firmiana simplex
Chinese parasol tree

Deciduous. Authors occasionally receive queries about the unusual tree with gigantic leaves and frog-green branches and trunks. We question how this Asian species surfaces in places like Tuskegee, AL, Athens, GA, and Durham and Chapel Hill, NC. In Spartanburg, SC, it has regenerated to the point of invasiveness, and in Louisiana it has become major league pestiferous. So, the reader might ask, why discuss? It is a pretty tree, the polished, green bark alone sufficient reason to consider. If only sterile forms existed! Develops a rounded canopy, maturing 30 to 45′ high and wide. Literature cites trees to 60′ high. Stems are thumb-size in diameter, and the entire tree takes on the appearance of broom handles. Young trees may grow 6′ in a single season. Aggressive to a fault, so be cognizant. Bark on young trees is smooth, shiny gray-green to green; this signature trait is present on large trunks as well.

Foliage: The 3- to 5-lobed, rich green leaves, each to 8″ long and wider, are reminiscent of a maple on steroids. Fall color an attractive yellow; the degree of color development varies among seedling trees. **Flowers/seeds/fruits/cones**: The yellowish green flowers are borne in immense panicles, to 20″ long and wide in summer. Overall effect is somewhat diminished as color blends with foliage. Flowering is profuse, leading to numerous pea-sized fruits, attached to the edges of the dehiscent carpel wall. **Native range**: China, Taiwan, Japan; long cultivated in Japan and Taiwan. Also quite common in southern Europe and Mediterranean areas. **Adaptability**: Adapted to extremes of soil, except standing water, and tolerates full sun and heavy shade.

Firmiana simplex, CONTINUED

Zones 7 to 10. Trees grow in zone 6 but are injured in severe winters. **Landscape use**: Difficult to actually tout, knowing its invasive nature. Appears to be self-fertile, so a single tree produces many viable seeds. Authors observed the species seeding in and thriving under an oak-hickory canopy. **Street tree use**: Limited to none. **In the trade**: Seed-grown.

Firmiana simplex

Firmiana simplex

Frangula caroliniana (*Rhamnus caroliniana*)
Carolina buckthorn

Deciduous. A small tree, single-trunked and low-branched or multi-stem, sometimes shrubby. Upright-spreading then spreading wider with lax branches. Medium texture, slow-growing to 15′ height and spread. Bark is smooth, gray-brown, patterned with prominent raised lenticels when young, then gray with shallow fissures.

Foliage: Impressive foliage. Its leaves are elliptical, 2 to 6″ long, very dark green and glossy with 8 to 10 prominent, impressed, parallel veins. The veins give it a corrugated look and enhance the leaf's otherwise smooth texture and sheen. Fall color is usually an unimpressive yellow-green to fair yellow, but occasionally goes to orange. **Flowers/seeds/fruits/cones**: Flowers are inconspicuous, yellowish green, opening in spring. Fruit follows in summer, globose, ⅓″ wide, a striking bright red clustered against the dark green foliage, looking a bit like holly. The fruit holds a good bright red color through the late summer and early fall, eventually turning black when fully ripe. **Native range**: Maryland to Missouri and northern Florida to eastern Texas. **Adaptability**: Native to moist locations and likes such, but it is quite adaptable to most settings. Zones 5 to 9. **Landscape use**: A nice small tree or multi-stem plant, informal-looking in habit but quite elegant in foliage. Easily trained as a tree. Most often used in naturalized landscapes, but it also makes a fine garden-sized screen. **Street tree use**: No, too small and spreading. **In the trade**: Sold as seed-grown.

Frangula caroliniana

Frangula purshiana (*Rhamnus purshiana*)

cascara

Deciduous. A small tree with an irregularly upright-spreading form, usually single-trunked but sometimes multi-stem. Medium texture, moderately fast-growing to 30′ tall and 25′ wide. Bark is smooth, gray-brown with prominent lenticels when young, then darker gray with light gray patches, mostly smooth, with shallow fissures; it is extensively harvested, commercially, as a laxative.

Foliage: Dark green, elliptical, slightly glossy leaves are prominently veined, generally 4 to 6″ in length, and take on a yellow-orange hue in autumn. **Flowers/seeds/fruits/cones**: Flowers are inconspicuous, tiny and greenish in color, hidden in the foliage in spring. Globose fruit follows in summer, ¼″ wide, deep red at first, turning to purple-black as it ripens. **Native range**: British Columbia to western Montana and south to northern California, mostly coastal and in some cool mountain areas. **Adaptability**: Quite adaptable within its native range, liking moist acid soils but generally tolerant of any setting. Zones 6 to 8. **Landscape use**: An overlooked tree, one of the finest deciduous natives in its region, and more garden-sized than most. The smooth glossy foliage is rather elegant and sets it apart from other deciduous natives in the Pacific Northwest. Excellent in a naturalized landscape. **Street tree use**: Not a good choice because of its sometimes irregular form, but might be used in the event of a "native only" regulation, as the Pacific Northwest has very few deciduous natives from which to choose. **In the trade**: Uncommon, sold as seed-grown.

F

Frangula purshiana

Frangula purshiana

Franklinia alatamaha

franklinia, lost gordonia

Deciduous. A monotypic genus whose name honors Benjamin Franklin. The species—named (with a spelling variation) for the Altamaha River of Georgia, where it was originally discovered (c.1765)—was introduced into cultivation by John Bartram/William Bartram (1770/1778) and last seen in the wild in 1790. Refined, elegant small tree or large shrub, whose late-season Stewartia-like flowers are the seminal calling card that obsesses the true gardener. Trees develop an upright-spreading outline with branches often leafless in their lower extremities, creating an open, airy appearance, not unlike that of *Magnolia virginiana*. Most often develops a multi-stemmed shrub-type habit with maturity, becoming wider than high. 10 to 20(30)' is a reasonable height estimate. Growth is quite fast on young plants, slowing with age. The bark, an attribute seldom mentioned, is attractive—smooth, gray, divided by irregular fissures, with large trunks fluted (almost corrugated).

Foliage: Beautiful, shiny dark green leaves, to 6″ long, half as wide, serrate margin, turn brilliant orange-red in fall. Leaves hold late, display high freeze resistance, with colors persisting into mid-November in zone 6. **Flowers/seeds/fruits/cones**: The slightly cup-shaped flowers, pure white, with a center of yellow stamens, each 3 to 3½″ across, 5-petaled, fragrant, open in July; sporadically produced into August-September. In Oregon, flowering begins slightly later, and we were surprised to see flowers and bright red fall color occurring simultaneously. Flowers are produced on new shoots of the season, which means pruning could be accomplished in late winter–early spring without negatively impacting flowering. The capsule fruit, rounded, ¾″ wide, matures brown, splits at maturity into 10 segments. **Native range**: Once, the wilds of Georgia. Known only in cultivation with many theories surrounding its disappearance from the wild. **Adaptability**: Lovingly fickle and at times unforgiving of placement in the garden. Zones 5 to 8. **Landscape use**: Not amenable to everyday garden culture. Dirr has tried numerous times without success. However, beautiful plants have persisted and thrived at the Arnold Arboretum and Longwood Gardens. Never say never! Kudos

Franklinia alatamaha

Franklinia alatamaha

Franklinia alatamaha

to the North Carolina Arboretum for utilizing the species in its parking area, with a smattering of trees in reasonable condition; Asheville, NC, is a higher elevation (2,200'), which may account for success. Ideally, provide moist, acid, well-drained soils laden with organic matter, in full sun to partial shade. Avoid stress! A wilt (pathogen: *Phytophthora cinnamomi*) is an issue. Another thought is the genetic base (plasticity) is so narrow, with all trees in cultivation from Bartram's original collections, that inbreeding depression makes it unable to compete in stress-laden environments. **Street tree use**: No. **In the trade**: Sold as seed-grown. With it, Tom Ranney, North Carolina State University, created ×*Gordlinia grandiflora*, which see.

Fraxinus
ash

Any discussion of ash in North America now needs to begin with a preamble on the impact of emerald ash borer, an exotic invasive insect native to northeast Asia. It was first found in the Detroit region in 2002. Since that time, it has spread eastward to the Atlantic states, westward to Colorado, south to Georgia, and north into Quebec. It seems inevitable that the insect will continue to spread throughout temperate eastern North America, perhaps limited by cold in the far north. The openness of the Great Plains has slowed its spread west, as have the strong natural barriers of the Rocky Mountains and high desert of the West. The long-term fate of ash on the West Coast is uncertain.

Emerald ash borer larvae feed on the phloem and cambium of the tree's trunk. Borer attacks usually involve a great many larvae in a single tree. Trees are girdled, which kills them. There appears to be no natural resistance in North American native ash. Where the emerald ash borer has become established in North America, no living ash are left behind. The Asian species, *F. mandshurica* and *F. chinensis*, have demonstrated significant resistance but perhaps not enough to be certain of survival in the midst of a high population of borers.

Prior to emerald ash borer, *F. pennsylvanica* and *F. americana* were among the most successful and widely used shade and street trees in North America, especially in the upper Midwest. Their landscape use has completely stopped in that region. The planting of ash can no longer be recommended in eastern North America, with the possible exception of the cold Canadian Prairie, which may be beyond the tolerance of the insect.

Landscape planting of ash west of the Rocky Mountains may still be reasonable, as apart from the borer, ash are among the most problem-free and adaptable trees in this region.

Every tree species faces some potentially lethal insects and pathogens, so the risk to a newly planted ash in the West might not be any greater than the risks that face any other species. Given the multitude of challenges that face new street and landscape trees and its history of reliability, we still consider ash a viable option at the time of this writing. Urban trees don't live forever; an ash planted in the poor soil of a tree pit on a downtown street of a West Coast city may well live longer than a lot of other species. Use some caution, monitor the range of the insect, and always plant diversity.

Fraxinus americana
white ash

Deciduous. Upright and broadly pyramidal when young, becoming broadly oval and eventually rounded. Medium fast-growing to 60' by 60' or more but quite strong in branch structure. Medium coarse in texture. Bark is gray to gray-brown, smooth at first then rather neatly fissured into narrow ridges, becoming rougher with age, with ridges and furrows roughly diamond-shaped.

Foliage: Large pinnately compound leaves are opposite and dark green, smooth to rugose above and glaucous below. The full leaf can measure 7 to 15" long with 5 to 9 leaflets, usually 7. Leaflets are ovate, 2 to 6" long, with an entire margin or sometimes slightly serrate. Fall color is good and can be wonderful. Coloration often varies from the outer

F

Fraxinus americana

canopy to the inner, usually more reddish on the outside and yellowish inside, but it can also vary immensely on a single tree from year to year. Keeps things interesting in the fall. **Flowers/seeds/fruits/cones**: Dioecious. Flowers appear just before leaf emergence, ornamental value insignificant, the female panicles short, mostly exposed styles, the males even shorter, consisting of clusters of exposed stamens. Clusters of small samaras follow in summer and ripen to brown in fall. About 1 to 1½″ in length and quite light, they blow in the wind and present little mess. **Native range**: Nova Scotia to Minnesota and northern Florida to eastern Texas. **Adaptability**: Highly adaptable to a variety of climates, tolerant of a wide range of soil pH, preferring moist soil but tolerant of dry. Zones 4 to 9. **Landscape use**: Prior to the introduction of emerald ash borer, this was a go-to species over most of the United States. Easy to transplant, adaptable to a large variety of sites, with good landscape appearance and beautiful fall color, it was one of the most popular trees of the landscape trade. Where the borer is not present, it is still an outstanding park and shade tree. **Street tree use**: An excellent street tree with strong wood, provided low branches are pruned for clearance at a young age. **In the trade**: Occasionally sold as seed-grown, much more frequently as an improved cultivar. The list of these has shrunk considerably since the borer became part of the equation.

AUTUMN APPLAUSE 'Appldell'. A slower-growing form, more densely branched and upright oval, a little smaller and narrower than the other cultivars, to 40′ by 25′. Leaves are smaller than AUTUMN PURPLE and not as textured. Fall color is deep maroon-red to dark purple, coming on early, and leaves drop quickly after coloring. Male, seedless.

AUTUMN PURPLE 'Junginger'. By far the most popular cultivar, and rightly so. Foliage is dark green with an interesting rugose texture. The tree is fast-growing and broadly oval in form, eventually round, 60′ by 60′. Fall color always seems to be a wonderful kaleidoscope of colors, mixing yellows,

AUTUMN APPLAUSE

AUTUMN PURPLE

AUTUMN PURPLE

Fraxinus americana

orange, reds, and purple, and differing a little each year. We unconsciously hit the brakes when we see the first brilliant display of the season; fortunately, have not yet been rear-ended. Male, seedless.

NORTHERN BLAZE 'Jefnor'. An introduction from the Canadian Prairie, it alone carries a zone 3 rating. Rather upright and oval when young, it becomes broadly oval to round with age, 40 to 50′ tall and wide. Fall color is disappointing compared to other cultivars, yellowish to brownish red, but if you need zone 3 hardiness, it sure beats a dead tree. Male, seedless.

Fraxinus angustifolia

narrowleaf ash

Deciduous. Upright-spreading form develops a broadly oval to rounded canopy, slightly open. Fine-textured and fast-growing, to 50′ tall, 40′ wide. Bark is smooth, light gray on young trees, developing an irregular pattern of fissures and bumpy, slightly shaggy ridges in age.

Foliage: Leaves pinnately compound, 7 to 12″ long, opposite and medium green, usually 7 to 13 leaflets, finely serrate. Leaflets are distinctly narrow and lanceolate. Very fine-textured, almost lacy. Fall color is yellow to wine-red.

Flowers/seeds/fruits/cones: Andromonoecious, with a few male and mostly bisexual flowers, in simple racemes, males tightly clustered, females loosely clustered. Small, greenish, and not ornamentally significant. Samaras, 1 to 1½″ long, follow, ripening to brown in late summer. **Native range**: Spain, through southeastern Europe and into western Asia to Iran, often in moist bottomland soils. **Adaptability**: Tolerant of hot temperatures and low humidity. Tolerant of low or elevated pH soils. Zones 6 and 7 in the East, although the borer argues against its use there; better adapted on the West Coast, zones 6 to 9. **Landscape use**: Commonly used as a residential tree or grouped in commercial sites, especially in the West, where it tolerates the summer drought and low humidity. Valued for its very fine texture and light appearance in the landscape, as well as its fall color. **Street tree use**: An excellent large street tree. **In the trade**: Almost always appearing as 'Raywood' ('Flame'), an outstanding cultivar selected in Australia and now spread around the world. Fast-growing and more upright in form, it develops an oval to broadly oval, billowy canopy with ascending branches that eventually become somewhat vase-like in shape, providing natural clearance for street traffic below, 55′ tall and 30′ wide. The narrow leaflets provide filtered shade and break down quickly when they fall. Outstanding burgundy-red to maroon fall color. Sometimes listed as *F. oxycarpa*, which is now considered a subspecies of *F. angustifolia*.

'Raywood'

'Raywood'

Fraxinus excelsior

European ash

Deciduous. Broadly pyramidal when young, becoming broadly oval with age, medium fine texture, moderately fast-growing to 70′ tall, 60′ wide. Bark smooth and light greenish gray to gray on young trees, then darker gray, fissured and ridged with age.

Foliage: Leaves pinnately compound, 8 to 12″ long, opposite and dark green, with 7 to 11 rather narrow, lanceolate, noticeably serrate leaflets. Interestingly, winter buds are distinctly black. Yellow fall color. **Flowers/seeds/fruits/cones:** Polygamous, having a mix of male, female, and bisexual flowers on the same tree. Flowering in panicles before the leaves; stamens and stigmas are purplish and add a bit of early color. Clusters of 1½″ long samaras follow in summer and ripen to brown in fall. **Native range:** Europe, Ireland to southern Finland and Russia, northern Spain to the Caucasus. **Adaptability:** Formerly considered quite adaptable, tolerant of acid and high pH soil, it likes moist soil. But times have changed: in Europe, ash dieback (pathogen: *Hymenoscyphus fraxineus*) is taking its toll and reducing the use of this species, while in North America, lilac borer has always been a problem and now emerald ash borer makes the prognosis much worse. **Landscape use:** A large tree used in parks with smaller ornamental cultivars, but pest and disease problems make its future uncertain. **Street tree use:** Formerly good but no longer. **In the trade:** Available.

'Globosa'. Usually top grafted, it is very dense, compact, and moderately small, forming a perfectly symmetrical dark green ball, 20′ by 20′. Fall color is a fair yellow.

GOLDEN DESERT 'Aureafolia'. A smaller ash with bright golden yellow fall color and golden twig color, which is strikingly brilliant in the winter. Moderately slow-growing forming a round canopy, to 25′ by 25′, can become a little wider than tall. Successfully used on the West Coast, where it is still generally problem-free.

'Hessei'. A single-leafed ash. Rather than compound, it produces simple ovate leaves that are coarsely serrate and quite dark green. Fast-growing, pyramidal when young then broadly rounded, 50′ by 50′. 'Diversifolia' has a similar, simple leaf.

'Jaspidea'. Yellow-green spring foliage, upright-spreading tree with a broadly oval crown. Twigs are yellow but show some green lengthwise striping. Summer foliage turns light green, then develops yellow fall color. 35 to 40′ tall, 25 to 30′ wide.

Fraxinus excelsior

'Globosa'

Fraxinus excelsior

'Hessei'

GOLDEN DESERT

'Hessei'

GOLDEN DESERT

Fraxinus mandshurica
Manchurian ash

Deciduous. Upright oval, becoming broadly oval, strongly branched. Medium fine texture, moderate growth rate to 45′ by 35′ or more. Bark is smooth and gray when young, becoming fissured with age.

Foliage: Leaves pinnately compound, 8 to 14″ long, opposite, medium to dull dark green, with narrowly ovate leaflets having a lightly serrate margin. Yellow fall color. **Flowers/ seeds/fruits/cones**: Polygamo-dioecious. Flowers in short panicles before the leaves emerge, not showy. Samaras 1½″ long, ripening in the fall. **Native range**: Northeastern China, easternmost Russia, Hokkaido, Japan. **Adaptability**: Tolerant of varying pH as well as wet and dry soils. This species co-evolved with emerald ash borer and carries some resistance to it, although probably not enough to withstand an intense attack from a high population of insects. Very cold hardy, zones 3 to 6. **Landscape use**: Quite hardy and favored in communities near the Rocky Mountains, especially in Idaho, Montana, and British Columbia. Considering the isolation of these communities and the advantage of this species for the difficult climate where it is most often used, it seems a good choice, despite the possibility of emerald ash borer. The species carries the best possibility for breeding resistance to the borer. **Street tree use**: A good form for this purpose. **In the trade**: Sold as seed-grown, but more often as 'Mancana', a Canadian selection, cold hardy in Manitoba, with a very symmetrical upright oval shape, a little narrower than the species, with narrow, fine-textured leaflets and bright yellow fall color. 50′ by 35′.

'Mancana'

'Mancana'

Fraxinus nigra
black ash

Deciduous. A medium-sized tree with a slower growth rate than most ash species, it forms a somewhat open, oval to narrow oval crown. Medium fine texture, to 45′ by 25′. Bark is smooth and gray on young trees, becoming darker gray, rough, irregularly fissured, scaly, and flaky.

Foliage: Leaves pinnately compound, 8 to 14″ long, opposite, medium green, with narrowly ovate to lanceolate leaflets with acuminate tips and having a lightly serrate margin. Yellow fall color. **Flowers/seeds/fruits/cones**: Polygamous. Flowers small, in short, dense panicles just before leaf emergence, not ornamentally significant. **Native range**: Northeastern North America, Newfoundland to Manitoba, Virginia to Iowa. **Adaptability**: A wetland species in its native habitat, so it is happiest in moist soils and tolerant of both flooding and acid to high pH soils. Its native range coincides closely with that of the emerald ash borer infestation, so its existence is threatened. Zones 2 to 6. **Landscape use**: Has been used as a native landscape plant for wet soils, but plantings have nearly ceased because of the emerald ash borer. It may still have landscape use in colder areas of Canada once the borer's northern tolerance is known. **Street tree use**: A good form for the purpose, especially the cultivars. **In the trade**: Occasionally sold as seed-grown, mostly as cultivars.

'Fallgold'. A narrow pyramidal to narrow oval form with a good central leader and better density than the species, 40′ tall and 20′ wide. Neatly formed, dark green, lanceolate leaves and excellent bright golden yellow fall color. Extremely cold hardy, zone 3 and into the milder portion of zone 2 (2b).

'Fallgold'

'Northern Gem'. Dark green foliage, a broadly oval to rounded habit, and rather poor greenish yellow fall color, 40′ tall, 30′ wide. We prefer 'Northern Treasure'. A hybrid of *F. nigra* and *F. mandshurica*. Zone 3.

'Northern Treasure'. More upright and stronger growing than the similar 'Northern Gem', and with a better central leader. It makes an upright oval form, broader than 'Fallgold', growing to 50′ tall, 30′ wide. Dark green leaves are larger and bolder-looking than the species. Good bright yellow fall color. A hybrid of *F. nigra* and *F. mandshurica*. Zone 3.

Fraxinus ornus
flowering ash

Deciduous. Upright oval when young, becoming broadly rounded with age; individual seed-grown plants are variable in spread. Medium-textured, moderately slow growth rate, to 35′ with a 25′ spread. Bark smooth, gray-green on young trees, remaining smooth with age and darker gray.

Fraxinus ornus

Fraxinus ornus

Foliage: Leaves pinnately compound, 8 to 12″ long, opposite, 5 to 9 leaflets. Leaflets are ovate to elliptical, serrate, dark green to slightly bluish green, with a slightly satiny sheen. Fall colors are usually soft tints of yellow, sometimes infused with pinkish purple. **Flowers/seeds/fruits/cones:** Androdioecious. Unusual among ash in that it flowers on current year's shoot growth, in May and June. Showy panicles of white fringe-like flowers decorate the canopy, reminiscent of *Chionanthus*. Heavy seed set of samaras occur on bisexual trees; male trees are less common but are preferred because heavy seed production can be messy and stress the growth of the tree. **Native range:** Southeastern Europe, western Asia. **Adaptability:** Seems quite drought adaptable; native to the Mediterranean region and liking the similar climate of the North American West Coast. Grows in moderately acid to high pH soils. Limited by cold hardiness compared to other ash species, zones 6 to 8 on the West Coast, not recommended in the East. **Landscape use:** Popular on the West Coast and in Europe. A smaller garden tree, the flowers are a nice late-spring surprise, occurring when few other trees are in bloom. Flowering can be profuse. **Street tree use:** Cultivars can make good small street trees. **In the trade:** Sometimes sold as seed-grown, more often as cultivars.

'Meczek'. Dense compact form, broadly oval becoming globe-shaped with age, 15 to 20′ tall and wide. Very formal-looking. Typically grown in Europe as a top graft. If street use is intended, the graft must be high. Produces few seeds.

'Obelisk'. Narrowly upright and almost columnar when young, it widens to a tight oval, an excellent small street tree form, 30′ tall, 20′ wide. Produces considerable seed.

Fraxinus ornus

Fraxinus ornus

URBAN BOUQUET 'JFS-Coate'. An upright oval form that flowers heavily and spectacularly. Strong growing, male, seedless. A good street tree form, 35′ tall, 20′ wide. Fall color yellow with tints of purple.

Fraxinus pennsylvanica
green ash, red ash

Deciduous. A large shade tree, upright-spreading in habit with heavy ascending limbs, forming a broadly oval, somewhat open crown at maturity. Its many cultivars are usually tighter in form and more symmetrical. Medium texture, fast-growing to 60′ high with a 45′ spread. Bark is smooth and gray when young, then thicker, fissured into ridges, often developing diamond-shaped ridges and furrows with age.

Foliage: Leaves pinnately compound, 6 to 12″ long, opposite, medium to dark green with a smooth texture, 5 to 9 leaflets. Leaflets are ovate to long ovate with serrate or entire margins. Seedling leaves usually have a dull sheen, but many of the cultivars are glossy. Produces one of the clearest, brightest yellow fall colors, brilliant in northern climates. **Flowers/seeds/fruits/cones**: Dioecious. Dense panicles of small flowers before the leaves; no ornamental value. Yellow-green samaras follow, 1½″ long, turning light brown in the fall. **Native range**: Very broad, covering much of eastern North America, Nova Scotia to Alberta, south to Florida and Texas. **Adaptability**: "Adaptable" would have been a good name for this tree, as it's hard to find a place where it won't grow. Tolerates hot and cold, wet and dry, high pH or low, high humidity or dry winds. The nursery and landscape industry loved this tree because it was so easy to produce and successfully transplant. Of course the emerald ash borer has changed all that. Zones (2)3 to 9. **Landscape use**: So commonly planted as a street and shade tree that you would seemingly find it everywhere, especially in the colder and more difficult climate of the upper Midwest. Unfortunately,

Fraxinus pennsylvanica

Fraxinus pennsylvanica

Fraxinus pennsylvanica

CIMMARON

'Marshall's Seedless'

'Patmore'

it can now only be used where the borer is not present. **Street tree use**: Tough and excellent for the purpose, one of the most tolerant of the difficult urban tree pit environment, if borers not present. **In the trade**: The borer has cut demand for this tree by over 90%, so many cultivars have disappeared from the market. The best continue to be grown and are listed.

CIMMARON 'Cimmzam'. Strongly upright and slightly narrower than the species, this cultivar has excellent form as a street tree, 60' tall and 35' wide. Dark green summer foliage has a slight gloss and turns rusty orange in the fall, an unusual coloration for the species. Seedless.

'Marshall's Seedless' ('Marshall'). Old reliable, this cultivar has stood the test of time and is still popular. Before the introduction of 'Patmore', it was the most frequently planted ash. Large, fast-growing, upright-spreading with glossy foliage and bright yellow fall color, seedless. 60' tall, 40' wide.

'Patmore'. The most popular of the ash cultivars and the most cold hardy, quite adapted to the Northern Prairie, having been selected at the extreme northwestern edge of the species' range in Alberta. Its extreme cold hardiness may provide a refuge from the borer, as it is yet to be seen how far north the insect can survive. A beautiful tree, upright

oval with excellent density and symmetry, to 55' tall and 35' wide. Glossy dark green leaves turn bright yellow in the fall. Seedless. Hardy to zone 2.

PRAIRIE SPIRE 'Rugby'. One of the toughest cultivars, selected on the difficult plains of North Dakota. Quite upright, a dense oval, 50' tall and 25' wide. Its summer foliage is a rather dull medium green and fall color is yellow. Seedless.

'Patmore'

PRAIRIE SPIRE

'Summit'

'Summit'

'Summit'. Long used and still popular, it is quite upright when young and very symmetrical in habit, yet widens with age to become a broad oval to almost round, 45′ tall and 35 to 40′ wide. Good density with medium green, somewhat dull summer foliage but excellent bright yellow, early fall color. Seedless, with claims that it is a sterile female.

URBANITE

Fraxinus quadrangulata

Fraxinus quadrangulata

URBANITE 'Urbdell'. Broadly pyramidal to broadly oval, this tree becomes quite full. Foliage is glossy, leaflets broadly ovate with an entire margin. Deep bronze fall color. Introduced as seedless, but we have witnessed otherwise. Less cold hardy (zone 5), but better adapted to hot climates. 50′ tall, 40′ wide.

Fraxinus quadrangulata
blue ash

Deciduous. A large, upright-spreading tree with a slightly open crown, oval or narrow oval. Twigs have 4 prominent wings, set at 90° angles from each other (hence the epithet). Medium texture, moderately slow-growing, to 60′ high with a width of 35′. Bark becomes rough at an early age, gray, dividing into irregular flaky plates, shaggy; inner bark turns blue when exposed to air (hence the common name).

Foliage: Leaves pinnately compound, 8 to 14″ long, opposite, dark green, with a smooth to slightly textured surface and 7 to 11 leaflets. Leaflets long ovate to lanceolate and finely serrate. Yellow fall color. **Flowers/seeds/fruits/cones:** Flowers quite small and greenish, in loose panicles, before the leaves; no ornamental value. Greenish samaras follow, ripening to light brown in fall and sometimes persisting into winter. **Native range:** Southern Michigan and Illinois, south to Tennessee and Arkansas. **Adaptability:** Native habitat includes dry upland soils, often over limestone substrate. It will tolerate moist soils as well, but it does seem to prefer a higher pH. Zones 4 to 7. **Landscape use:** It is a great shade tree. **Street tree use:** Suitable in appropriate soils, where borer is not present. **In the trade:** Uncommon, sold as seed-grown. Difficult to propagate clonally, so the few cultivars that have been developed never gained traction.

Fraxinus uhdei

evergreen ash, shamel ash

Broadleaf evergreen. Upright-spreading, growing to an oval form, eventually broadening to round. Medium texture, fast-growing to 70′ tall, 60′ wide. Bark is smooth and gray when young and becomes finely fissured and ridged with age, gray-brown to gray.

Foliage: Leaves pinnately compound, 6 to 12″ long, opposite, smooth, glossy dark green, 5 to 9 leaflets. Leaflets are narrow, about 4″ long, lanceolate with a serrate margin. **Flowers/seeds/fruits/cones**: Dioecious. Dense panicles of small flowers before the leaves; not ornamental. Yellow-green samaras follow on female trees, ½ to 1½″ long. **Native range**: Mexico to Central America. **Adaptability**: May be semi-evergreen in cooler climates. Well adapted to the U.S. Southwest, and used in California, Arizona, and New Mexico. Zones 9 to 11. **Landscape use**: A popular shade tree, but losing favor because of overuse and large size. Good in parks and commercial sites but too large for most residential lots. **Street tree use**: Can serve, but it needs room for its roots, large trunk, and branch spread. **In the trade**: Sold as the species or (preferably) MAJESTIC BEAUTY 'Monus', which is upright-growing when young, eventually forming an oval to rounded canopy of glossy dark green foliage, 70′ tall, 60′ wide. Selected as a male, seedless.

Fraxinus uhdei

MAJESTIC BEAUTY

F

Fraxinus velutina

velvet ash, Arizona ash

Deciduous. Upright-growing when young, developing an upright oval canopy then widening with age and becoming more rounded, to 40′ tall, 30′ wide. Bark is smooth and gray when young, then becomes ridged and fissured, rough, gray, and a bit scaly.

Foliage: Leaves pinnately compound, 4 to 10″ long, opposite, lustrous, medium green with a smooth texture, 5 to 7 leaflets. Leaflets are ovate to long ovate with entire or lightly serrate margins. Yellow fall color. **Flowers/seeds/fruits/cones:** Dioecious. Dense panicles of small flowers before the leaves; not ornamental. Yellow-green samaras follow, 1 to 1½″ long, ripening light brown. **Native range:** U.S. Southwest and northern Mexico, restricted to riparian areas in this arid land. **Adaptability:** Very adaptable, it takes desert heat as well as cold nights. Stands up to wind, low humidity, and drought, although it does need some water. Zones 6 to 9. **Landscape use:** Widely used as a shade tree in residential areas as well as a street tree in central and southern California and east into Arizona and Texas. Its upright branch structure makes it well suited for yard use. If the emerald ash borer is kept out of this area, the tree will be a reliable choice. **Street tree use:** Upright-growing, moderate size, tough, it makes an excellent street tree when pruned up for clearance. **In the trade:** Available.

'Bonita'. A shorter and broader form, symmetrically rounded canopy, 35 to 40′ high and wide. A little short and wide for streets but a nice small shade tree. Bright yellow fall color. Male, seedless.

FAN-TEX 'Rio Grande'. Larger leaves, dark green, broadly oval to rounded symmetrical form, 40′ tall, 35 to 40′ wide. Yellow fall color. Male, seedless.

'Modesto'. Vigorous and upright-growing, developing a more oval canopy, to 50′ high, 35 to 40′ wide. Yellow fall color. Formerly very popular; anthracnose has become a significant problem in central California, and many cities have stopped planting. Male, seedless.

G

Ginkgo biloba

ginkgo, maidenhair tree

Deciduous gymnosperm. This is a living fossil, estimated at 190 to 220 million years of continuous reproduction and still going strong. Although restricted in its native China to a few small populations, in cultivation it is utilized world-wide. Extremely variable in habit and size but will reach 50 to 80′ in 100 years. Growth is slow, and young nursery-grown trees are often open and without character. Time rectifies all the juvenile shortcomings. Bark is attractive, gray-brown, ridged, with darker furrows. A 200-year-old ginkgo, less than 1¼ mile from the epicenter of the atomic bomb dropped on Hiroshima, survived and produced seeds; some resulting seedlings are planted at Batsford Arboretum, England. Ancient ginkgo trees have exposed roots near the trunk that look like chubby toes with corns.

Foliage: The bright green, fan-shaped, 3″ by 3″ leaves are unlike those of any other gymnosperm and perhaps the most useful identification characteristic; they are produced singly on current season's growth and in clusters of 3 to 5 on spurs from 2-year and older wood. Among the best trees for fall color, as the leaves glow yellow to gold, on occasion, after hard freezes, dropping at one time. Authors have observed this phenomenon; however, leaves abscise over an extended period from the majority of trees. **Flowers/seeds/fruits/cones**: Dioecious. Female ovules borne on a 2″ long stalk, males in 1″ long yellowish green catkins, just as leaves emerge. The actual reproductive structure is a naked seed with a fleshy outer covering; this fleshy part, with maturity, is notoriously stinky. Seeds are edible. **Native range**: China. **Adaptability**: Successfully cultivated from coast to coast, Minneapolis to St. Augustine. Well adapted to pH extremes.

Ginkgo biloba

Ginkgo biloba

Ginkgo biloba

Ginkgo biloba

Ginkgo biloba

'Autumn Gold'

'Autumn Gold'

Authors observed thriving trees in every imaginable soil except permanently wet. A report from Auburn University noted trees needed at least 600 chill hours for good bud-break; however, those receiving 1,100 hours showed the best growth. Doubtful whether the Florida tree ever experienced 600 hours of chilling. Zones 4 to 9. **Landscape use:** A magnificent noble tree for parks and any other large area, only becoming more beautiful and stately with age. For centuries it has been pollarded, pleached, and shaped, attesting to pruning tolerance. As a bonsai specimen it is superb. From gaunt, open, scraggly, to oval, rounded, wide-spreading, dense, to columnar-fastigiate, to small, dwarf, compact "brooms"—there is a ginkgo for every landscape niche. Prefers well-drained, moist soils for maximum growth and full sun. One of the few negatives is that only three caterpillar species use it as a food source, while 557 species feed on native oaks. Still, every neighborhood has room for at least one ginkgo. **Street tree use:** Suitable and common. The best landscape/urban cultivars are male, thereby avoiding the messy seeds. **In the trade:** Some major large tree types, all seedless males, are listed here. Sex expression is not 100% static, so if you are introducing a new cultivar, observe for a few years to be sure it is always male.

'Autumn Gold'. Symmetrical broad pyramidal crown, quite uniform in shape, broader with age. Pretty golden yellow fall color. 50′ by 30′. Selected in 1957 and still one of the most popular.

376

GOLDEN COLONNADE

GOLDEN COLONNADE

EMPEROR 'Woodstock'. Uniform oval crown, with central leader, relatively dense in habit, darker green leaves than typical, 50′ by 30 to 40′.

GOLDEN COLONNADE 'JFS-UGA2'. Upright oval habit, densely branched; branches at a 45° angle to central axis, medium green foliage, golden yellow fall color, 45′ by 20′.

'Golden Globe'. Broad rounded habit, pretty yellow fall color, 40 to 50′ high and wide, reportedly a faster-growing cultivar, produces a full crown at a young age.

GOLDSPIRE 'Blagon'. A tight, narrow, columnar-pyramidal selection, full to the ground, foliage remains quite dense. Touted as one of the best narrow forms. Introduced from France, 45′ by 10 to 15′.

'Magyar'. Pyramidal habit with symmetrical branching, 50′ by 25′, discovered in New Brunswick, NJ.

PRESIDENTIAL GOLD 'The President'. Upright oval-rectangular form, the parent tree 60′ by 40′. This cultivar fills in well and looks good at a young age, unlike many that are open for many years.

GOLDSPIRE

'Magyar'

PRESIDENTIAL GOLD

PRESIDENTIAL GOLD

PRESIDENTIAL GOLD

'Saratoga'

'Shangri-La'

PRINCETON SENTRY

PRINCETON SENTRY 'PNI 2720'. The standard for upright fastigiate, slightly tapered at the apex, fatter at base, 60' by 25'. Not always uniformly columnar-fastigiate.

'Samurai'. Broad pyramidal crown, 45' by 35', and listed as zone 3 hardy; introduced by Schichtel's Nursery, New York.

'Saratoga'. Akin to 'Autumn Glory' in habit with a distinct central leader; leaves narrow and semi-split, rich yellow fall color; smaller than most cultivars, 40' by 30'. After 'Autumn Gold' and 'Magyar', the most common shade tree type in commerce.

'Shangri-La'. Uniform compact crown with dense branching habit, excellent yellow fall color, 40' by 30'.

SKY TOWER 'JN9'. Dense, upright, slow-growing form, 15 to 20' high, 6 to 10' wide, from Garden Debut.

Gleditsia triacanthos

honeylocust

Deciduous. Upright-spreading, usually a little wide and open, with a gracefully curving and slightly irregular branching pattern, forming a broadly oval to rounded canopy. Fine-textured, fast-growing, to 50' high and 40' wide. Bark is brownish when young, then with maturity becomes gray and rough, broken by fissures into long, scaly, plate-like ridges running up and down the trunk. Seed-grown trunks may hold threatening, 3-pointed spines for years.

Foliage: Pinnately or bipinnately compound leaves depending on age and position on the tree, alternate, 6 to 10" long, with many tiny elliptical leaflets, each very finely (almost unnoticeably) crenate-serrulate, about 1" long and ⅜" wide. Bright and deep green in summer with excellent bright yellow fall color. **Flowers/seeds/fruits/cones**: Polygamo-dioecious, with perfect and single-sex flowers on the same tree. Flowers small, greenish and inconspicuous, emerging just after full leaf. Fruit a large, flattened, curving pod, reddish brown to black, usually 7 to 8" long, containing hard brownish black, ovoid seeds. Importantly for the landscape, some individual trees are completely dioecious, or nearly so, allowing selection of seedless cultivars. However, biology always carries a bag of tricks, and seedless cultivars occasionally revert, producing a few female flowers and surprising us with seed pods. Don't worry; they usually go back to being seedless the next year. **Native range**: Pennsylvania to Nebraska and south, from Alabama to Texas. **Adaptability**: Primarily a bottomland species (but also grows on upland soils) and so particularly well adapted to flooded soils; but surprisingly, it is also one of our most drought-tolerant landscape trees. This makes it perfectly adapted to the widely varying soil moisture of difficult urban sites. It is also well adapted to alkaline soils, as well as high salt levels. Compared to other species, it has high survival rates on highways with heavy use of de-icing salt. It's cold hardy, but it definitely likes summer heat. In the cool Pacific Northwest, it seems small and stunted compared to warmer parts of the country. Zones 4 to 9. **Landscape use**: A favored (not to say overused) landscape tree, especially in the Midwest and Northeast. But you can't argue with success, and success is what has made this species a landscape staple. And now, the fall of ash to the emerald ash borer has brought honeylocust forward again as one of the few trees that can stand up to the toughest urban environments. Valued for its ease of transplanting, its graceful shape, and its fine-textured foliage, which gives lightly filtered shade. It does have its share of insect and disease problems but remains a favored city tree for difficult soils in challenging climates. **Street tree use**: Excellent street tree; it is highly adaptable to the poor soils and moisture extremes of these sites, and its branching habit provides road clearance.

Gleditsia triacanthos

Gleditsia triacanthos

380

Gleditsia triacanthos

Gleditsia triacanthos

'Emerald Kascade'

HALKA

Always use the seedless, more upright cultivars. **In the trade**: Seedling trees produce thorns, so avoid. Occasionally you will see f. *inermis* ("thornless") in literature; this nomenclature is unnecessary for cultivars. All listed cultivars are thornless under normal growing conditions, and if carefully propagated, they remain that way. As with the aforementioned reversion of seedless cultivars, we have occasionally seen "thornless" cultivars produce thorns for a season, then resume unarmed growth the following season. Except where noted, the following are considered seedless.

'Emerald Kascade'. Neatly and distinctly weeping, dark green, but sometimes a little bare on top, to 15′ by 15′, depending on training. Made a brief splash when it hit the market, but it's easy to quickly think of a dozen much more ornamental weepers than a honeylocust.

HALKA 'Christie'. Rounded, full, and spreading broader than wide, this cultivar usually produces a crop of seed pods. Some landscape architects and designers favor the winter texture that the seed pods give; others dislike the mess. Great for broad roadside plantings or campuses, but messy on city streets. 45′ by 45′.

IMPERIAL

NORTHERN ACCLAIM

'Moraine'

IMPERIAL 'Impcole'. Presents a neat, formal, more managed appearance than most cultivars, forming a globe-shaped canopy with wider crotch angles. But on streets, it needs to be limbed a little higher if clearance is desired. 40′ tall, 35′ wide.

'Moraine'. The first patented honeylocust, ushering in the age of thornless and seedless honeylocusts for street plantings. Vase-shaped, with upward stretching and arching branches, it provides good clearance below, to 50′ tall and 30′ wide. The authors favor it, and nurseries should keep it in production.

NORTHERN ACCLAIM 'Harve'. The most cold hardy cultivar, it is upright and sturdy with a broadly oval to vase-shaped canopy, to 50′ tall, 35′ wide. Selected for the harsh North Dakota climate, but good anywhere in the northern half of the country, zone 3.

PERFECTION 'Wandell'. An upright-growing tree with a good branch structure, most similar to SKYLINE in form but a little broader and with less dominant central leader, 45′ tall and 35′ wide. Dark green foliage.

PERFECTION

'Ruby Lace'

'Shademaster'

'Shademaster'

G

'Ruby Lace'. Highly ornamental purple foliage, reddish purple in spring, when it is at its best, turning more bronze-green in summer. But it is hard to find a good mature tree; its trunk is weak and usually leans, and it usually spreads wider than tall. We have rarely seen a straight tree. Not for streets. 25′ tall, 25′ or more wide.

'Shademaster'. Selected as a possible replacement for the American elm, it is a good attempt at duplicating the elm's vase-shaped canopy. Fast-growing, and branches arch upward. It's no elm, but it does tend toward the classic vase shape and is an excellent street tree form, 50′ tall and 40′ wide. Quite popular, and increasingly favored for its demonstrated mite resistance.

383

SKYLINE

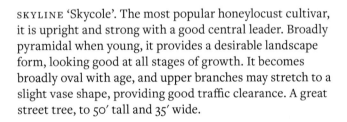

SKYLINE

STREETKEEPER

SKYLINE 'Skycole'. The most popular honeylocust cultivar, it is upright and strong with a good central leader. Broadly pyramidal when young, it provides a desirable landscape form, looking good at all stages of growth. It becomes broadly oval with age, and upper branches may stretch to a slight vase shape, providing good traffic clearance. A great street tree, to 50′ tall and 35′ wide.

SPECTRUM 'Speczam'. A yellow-leaf cultivar, similar in appearance to SUNBURST, which we prefer. Slightly better yellow color in late summer, but slower growing with a weaker trunk and branches that are more lax and spreading. Estimate 30 to 35′ tall and wide.

STREETKEEPER 'Draves'. Burst into popularity because it is the first and still the only honeylocust cultivar with a truly tall, narrow form suitable for narrow streets. The original tree was observed to be seedless for years, but in keeping with honeylocust flower trickery, it began producing seed pods soon after introduction. Still an excellent street form, but don't be surprised if you find pods. Very handsome dark green foliage. The narrowest honeylocust at 45′ tall and 20′ wide.

SUNBURST

'True Shade'

SUNSET GOLD

SUNBURST 'Suncole'. Long the standard yellow-leaf cultivar, and still our choice as the best, it provides bright yellow new growth in spring and early summer, fading to yellow-green by the end of summer. But in the heat of the Southeast, we see very little yellow, just green foliage. Good growth rate, although slightly slower than the green-leaf cultivars. Upright-spreading to rounded and arching, 40′ tall and wide.

SUNSET GOLD 'Sungolzam'. New growth starts with a slight orange tint, then is yellow, turning green in summer. Provides a nice flush of spring colors but does not hold bright yellow foliage into the summer as well as SUNBURST, with similar 40′ by 40′ size.

'True Shade'. Strong growing with upright-spreading form and strong crotch angles, it has lush dark green foliage and a very clean appearance. Becomes more vase-shaped with time, to 50′ by 35′.

×*Gordlinia grandiflora*

gordlinia

Broadleaf evergreen to semi-evergreen to deciduous, depending on cold. The genius and dedication of Tom Ranney, North Carolina State University, has fostered the breeding of many new, never-dreamt-of ornamental plants. But then, great plant breeders have the ability to see and seize the future. ×*Gordlinia grandiflora* is a *Franklinia alatamaha* and *Gordonia lasianthus* 'Variegata' hybrid. Seventy-five pollinated flowers resulted in nine seedlings, the rooted cuttings of which grew 25% faster than cuttings of either parent—hybrid vigor in action. Plants were 11½′ high after two growing seasons. Authors noted plants of the eventual release, 'Sweet Tea', in Delaware and Georgia, 10 to 15′ high, two-thirds as wide, with flowers present in September. Phytophthora root rot in poorly drained soils has wreaked destruction on *Franklinia* under cultivation. The thinking goes that ×*Gordlinia* might be more resistant. Bark is gray and smooth.

Foliage: Semi-evergreen in warm situations (zone 8), with a measure of foliage retained at end of shoots, elliptic, serrulate, entire toward base, 3 to 8″ long, 1 to 3″ wide, lustrous dark green, red to red-purple upon abscission, coloring from base to apex of shoot. **Flowers/seeds/fruits/cones**: Partially cupped to flattened, petals suborbicular, 3 to 4″ wide, opening in June, continuing into fall, on new growth of the season. Apparently sterile. **Native range**: Hybrid, known only in cultivation. **Adaptability**: Zones 6 to 9. **Landscape use**: A gee-whiz plant, and all who see covet. The best of the nine seedlings, 'Sweet Tea', has been freely (no patent) and widely shared. Stunning small tree when well grown and a perfect fit for the border, edge of woodland, perhaps even in a large container. We speculate that evenly moist, well-drained, acid soils, high in organic matter, in partial shade would prove ideal. On the flip side, nursery-grown Georgia trees in red, silty, clay loam soils under drip irrigation and in full sun were splendid. Certainly worth fishing for the best garden location to maximize return on Ranney's notable introduction. **Street tree use**: No. **In the trade**: 'Sweet Tea' is the plant just described. Cutting-grown.

'Sweet Tea'

'Sweet Tea'

'Sweet Tea'

Gymnocladus dioicus
Kentucky coffeetree

Deciduous. Give it time and you will be rewarded. Awkward and sparse when young, it soon fills in with wonderfully sturdy, upright arching branches and develops an oval crown. Bark is gray and quite rough, developing long scaly plates running up the trunk; the plates have characteristic upturned, curled edges. Medium texture in summer, but coarse and rugged in winter, accentuated by its bark. Moderately slow-growing to 60′ in height and 35′ in width.

Foliage: Lovely, lush and tropical in appearance. Bipinnately compound, alternate leaves reach 3′ in length. The leaflets are ovate, about 2″ long, green with a bluish tint. The rachis (leaf stalk) is so strong on these huge leaves that is it is often mistaken for a branch on young trees, surprising many when it falls off in autumn. Disadvantage: these are a little messy on the lawn. Fall color can be a good yellow. **Flowers/seeds/fruits/cones**: Dioecious or polygamo-dioecious, flowering late May to June, flowers small, white, fragrant, about ¾″, in panicles. Pretty up close, but usually not abundant enough to be very ornamental from a distance. Large light green seed pods follow, 5 to 10″ long and 1½″ wide, turning brownish black in autumn and eventually falling like old banana peels to the ground. **Native range**: New York to southern Minnesota and south to Tennessee to Oklahoma. **Adaptability**: Tough and adaptable, tolerating drought but also wet soils, liking limestone and happy in moderately acid to high pH soils. Zones 4 to 8. **Landscape use**: Like the ugly duckling that turns into the beautiful swan, this one-armed nursery broomstick slowly develops an elegant

Gymnocladus dioicus

Gymnocladus dioicus

Gymnocladus dioicus

Gymnocladus dioicus

G

387

Gymnocladus dioicus, CONTINUED

Gymnocladus dioicus

ESPRESSO

ESPRESSO

for parks, but messy over hardscape. The following seedless male cultivars are preferred. Note that we have seen trees that are male when young, but produce fruit with age, a trick that polygamo-dioecious trees can play on you.

DECAF 'McKBranched'. Branches better than seedling trees at a young age, producing a fuller canopy, with a finer-textured appearance. Carmel-colored new tip growth. 50′ tall, 40′ wide.

ESPRESSO 'Espresso-JFS'. The most popular cultivar, faster growing and providing a better branched canopy at an earlier age than the others. Particularly lush foliage. It grows upright to an oval form at a young age, then stretches into a broad vase shape. Excellent as a residential shade tree or a street tree that provides canopy cover, 55′ tall and 40′ wide. A favorite.

PRAIRIE TITAN 'J. C. McDaniel'. An upright-spreading form, it becomes broadly oval and develops a sturdy trunk with excellent architecture and a broad rounded crown, the widest of the cultivars at 50′ by 50′.

SKINNY LATTE 'Morton'. We are excited about this remarkably narrow cultivar, which originated at the Morton Arboretum in Illinois. Stiffly upright with main structural branches that ascend almost vertically, nearly columnar in form, just a bit wider on top than at the base. Valuable for narrow streets. To 50′ tall, only 15 to 20′ wide.

'Stately Manor'. Upright-growing with limbs ascending to form an oval canopy. It becomes a full-sized tree, but very slowly, the slowest of the listed cultivars, to 50′ by 35′. The original tree is beautiful, at the Minnesota Landscape Arboretum.

TRUE NORTH 'UMNSynergy' Upright habit with good branch architecture, its oval form is narrower than the species and well shaped for street use, 55′ by 35′. Dark green foliage, selected in Minnesota with proven zone 4 hardiness.

branch structure, becoming better each year to become one of the finest of the noble trees. A magnificent shade tree for large residences, parks, and campus use. To sit beneath one is a religious experience to a tree lover: the structure feels massive like an ancient cathedral, yet its foliage is as elegant as the stained-glass windows. We love this tree. **Street tree use**: Excellent street tree, with a growth habit that provides good clearance, and seedless cultivars that also give reliable shape. **In the trade**: Widely sold as seed-grown, but be aware that most of these will probably bear seed pods: fine

PRAIRIE TITAN

SKINNY LATTE

G

'Stately Manor'

TRUE NORTH

H

Halesia carolina

CRUSHED VELVET

Halesia carolina

Halesia carolina

Halesia carolina (H. *monticola,* H. *tetraptera*)

Carolina silverbell

Deciduous. A sensational native that is too frequently absent from American landscapes. At its best in April-May when the semi-pendulous, bell-shaped flowers appear on naked branches or as the leaves emerge. Greatly variable in habit, from a low-branched tree with a pyramidal to oval outline to rounded with several major trunks, 30 to 40′ high, 20 to 35′ wide under landscape conditions. However, authors have observed 60 to 70′ high specimens from the Midwest to East Coast, into the Southern Appalachians. Growth is moderate. Young stems, 2 years and older, develop a stringy, thread-like condition; mature bark is gray to brown to black, ridged and furrowed, the flattened ridges with scaly plates. Bark certainly adds seasonal beauty.

Foliage: Leaf buds are superposed, one above the other, at the nodes. Leaves 2 to 5″ long, a third to half as wide, with minute marginal serrations to almost entire, dark green, with at most a wisp of yellow in autumn. Somewhat difficult to identify in leaf; if leaf confounds, check stems for the stringy bark. **Flowers/seeds/fruits/cones:** Flowers are white (rarely pale rose), bell-shaped, shallowly 4-lobed (fused into a solid corolla), ½ to 1″ long, borne on 1″ long pedicels from year-old stems, in 2- to 5-flowered clusters, April-May. Flowering is often so profuse that as flowers abscise, they carpet the ground. From opening to abscission, they are effective for 10 to 14 days. The 4-winged, dry, ovoid drupe transitions from green to yellow to brown, often persisting into early winter. Each 1 to 1½″ long fruit contains 2 or 3 seeds. **Native range:** West Virginia to Florida to eastern Oklahoma, found (but not abundantly) as an

Halesia carolina

'Jersey Belle'

understory tree on the slopes of hills, ridges, and mountains, particularly along watercourses, in moist, acidic sandy soils, floodplains, streambanks, borders of swamps, and hammocks. **Adaptability**: Authors observed cultivated trees from Orono, ME, to Athens, GA. Zones 4 to 8. **Landscape use**: Every landscape would be well served by a silverbell. In our opinion, it perches just below *Cornus florida* and *Cercis canadensis* as a spring-flowering native tree. Safe to state that most people recognize the first two; few this Under cultivation, moist, acid, well-drained soils high in organic matter, sun to partial shade, are prerequisites. Chlorosis will develop in high pH soils. Utilize as a specimen, particularly as a woodland/understory element. Choose container-grown plants to mitigate root disturbance. Ideally, to showcase the flowers, place in front of large needle evergreens like hemlock or spruce. We have yet to experience the species in urban settings. **Street tree use**: No. **In the trade**: As well as the species, collector nursery offerings include 'Lady Catherine' (weeping) and several variegated foliage types with white to yellow patterns ('James Laubach' with gold and silver splashes on a green background is considered the best of these). Of the several pink-flowered selections, the most common are 'Arnold Pink' and 'Rosy Ridge'; both are tree forms in the 20 to 30' high range. Another with striking pink

flowers is 'Emily Marie', a compact small tree, 12 to 15' by 15 to 20'. Pink corolla color is most intense at cooler temperatures, severely diminished with heat.

CRUSHED VELVET 'JFS-PN2-Legacy'. Forms an oval habit, 20' by 15', with thick textured, pleated, dark blue-green leaves, and small white flowers. Perhaps useful under utility lines, in restricted planting spaces, or containers. It flowered in mid-April in the Dirr garden. Flowers are underwhelming.

'Jersey Belle'. Large white flowers in copious quantities on naked stems. Attractive yellow fall color and pretty bark add multi-season interest. Grows 25' by 20'. Princeton Nursery introduction.

'UConn Wedding Bells'. A small oval tree, 25' high, 20' wide, with prolific flowers that open more broadly than the species. It was discovered in Ohio, propagated via tissue culture, and introduced by Mark Brand, University of Connecticut.

Vestita Group. Encompasses variants that produce larger flowers, 1 to 1½" across, white to pink (e.g., 'Rosea'), with leaves pubescent below initially, glabrous at maturity.

'Jersey Belle'

'UConn Wedding Bells'

'Rosy Ridge'

Halesia diptera
two-winged silverbell

Deciduous. Less common in cultivation than *H. carolina*, but worth the effort to obtain as it is superior in several respects. Develops a low-branched, rounded canopy, 20 to 30′ high and wide. Authors observed both single- and multiple-trunked trees, the largest 40′ high. Growth is slow. Bark is similar to *H. carolina* but not as ridged and furrowed.

Foliage: Leaves are chunkier than *H. carolina*, at times approaching rounded, to 6″ long, 4″ wide, remotely serrated, dark green, yellow in autumn. The yellow fall color is more pronounced and consistent from year to year than that of *H. carolina*. **Flowers/seeds/fruits/cones**: White flowers, to 1½″ long (in Magniflora Group), are composed of 4 petals, cut to the base. Flowers are produced on ¾″ slender stalks in clusters along the naked branches of the previous season, opening mid-April in Athens, GA, the same time as *H. carolina*. The fruit is a drupe, 2-winged, flattened, to 2″ long, ¾″ wide, persisting into late fall/winter. Seeds are slow to germinate; the best approach is to sow, protect from marauders, and wait, usually 2 years. **Native range**: South Carolina to Florida and Texas, in moist soils (wooded floodplains, ravines, swamps, hammocks, and upland woods). **Adaptability**: It has prospered far removed from the native range, withstanding -25°F and flowering profusely. Zones 5 to 8. **Landscape use**: The species' virtues have been extolled, and for naturalized planting it has few equals. Ideally site in full sun to moderate shade, moist, acid, and well-drained soils. Like *H. carolina*, it is recalcitrant in transplanting and should be container-grown. **Street tree use**: No. **In the trade**: Available.

Magniflora Group (var. *magniflora*). The true Holy Grail and preferred over the species for larger flowers.

'Rosea'

'Rosea'

Halesia diptera

'Southern Snow'

Magniflora Group

Magniflora Group

'Southern Snow'

'PRN Snowstorm'. More upright in habit, 30′ by 25′, with larger flowers. It is considered zone 5 hardy. Introduced by Pleasant Run Nursery, New Jersey.

'Southern Snow'. Low-branched tree form with a central leader and prodigious flower production, introduced by Don Shadow. The original tree is 30′ high and spectacularly elegant.

'Yellow Leaf Selection'. An as-yet-unnamed yellow leaf form discovered by Phil Normandy, Brookside Gardens, Maryland. In June 2016 we bowed in admiration when viewing the tree, which was nestled in the woodland garden, growing in the understory of large tuliptrees, its leaves still a rich soft yellow. We hope to see it in commerce eventually.

Hamamelis

witch-hazel

Various species of *Hamamelis* will grow into shrubs, multi-stem trees, or small low-branched trees. We debated whether the genus really fit into a book written exclusively about trees, because so many are low and shrub-like, but the beauty and practicality of the more upright cultivars won out. They make wonderful small garden trees if pruned with a tree form in mind, particularly as they often develop vase shapes, which allows walking and gardening beneath as they gain size. We included the four species that can provide tree-size specimens with training and picked the best readily available cultivars. Trained as trees, they will be low-branched, or can be grown as a multi-stem trees. Reduce the number of stems and branches and prune to leave a vigorous upright growth to encourage height if a tree is desired. If you cut back the top, you will encourage low branching and a shrubby plant.

The species have many similarities, and because of this, most choices are best made at the cultivar level. All cultivars are propagated by grafting. The understock will produce suckers, which must be pruned off as cleanly as possible just below the ground where they emerge from the root: a shovel and pruners will do the work.

'Arnold Promise'

'Arnold Promise'

Hamamelis ×intermedia

hybrid witch-hazel

Deciduous. A large open shrub or small spreading tree. Usually multi-stem or low-branched as a tree form, vase-shaped to broadly vase-shaped. A large number of branches seem to grow at a 45° angle, but in opposite directions, crisscrossing in an artistic latticework pattern. Medium-textured in summer, fine-textured in winter, slow-growing, to 15′ tall with a 20′ spread.

Foliage: Leaves are broadly and irregularly elliptical to broadly obovate, always with a wavy margin, 2 to 4″ long, two-thirds as wide. Medium green with a dull surface. Yellow to reddish purple fall color. **Flowers/seeds/fruits/cones**: Flowers very early, January to March, depending on climate. Flower color is typically yellow for the species, extending to orange and red for selected cultivars. Flowers each have 4 strap-like petals, very thin and wavy, about ⅝″ long, up to 1″ on some of the best cultivars. Fruit, a small capsule, is not ornamental. **Native range**: Hybrid of Japanese (*H. japonica*) and Chinese (*H. mollis*) species. **Adaptability**: Likes a moist, well-drained, acid soil with organic matter, but reasonably tolerant. Keep out of wet clay. Will grow well in full sun or partial shade, but give it sun for the best flowering. Zones 5 to 8. **Landscape use**: Most of the hybrid cultivars are superior to the species for landscape use, and we generally recommend these. Breeders have developed a greater range of flower colors and have slightly increased the flower size. As they are at their best in winter, keep them close to your house where they are in sight from a window, as bloom time may be too cold to spend much time in the garden. Planted in the sun against a dark background, they almost glow when in bloom. Fall color can be almost as spectacular as the flowers. Great garden plants. **Street tree use**: No, too short, often too wide, needs better soil. **In the trade**: Available.

'Arnold Promise'. As this is written, 'Arnold Promise' glows bright yellow against the dark green of western hemlock in the Warren garden. A favorite cultivar because of its more upright vase-shaped habit, giving it more height and less spread, and making a good fit in the narrow border. Flowers are good size, bright yellow. Fall color yellow-orange. 20′ tall, 15′ wide.

'Diane'

'Jelena'

'Diane'

'Feuerzauber'

'Jelena'

'Diane'. Very good deep bronze-red flower color, and many consider it the best of the reds, but flowers are only of moderate size. It spreads slightly wider than tall, a bit too shrubby to make a good tree, but very popular. The fall color is as good as it gets and will rival any species, brilliant orange-red to true red, with leaves often accentuated by a thin yellow margin. 12′ tall, 15′ wide. Brown leaves sometimes hold in winter.

'Feuerzauber' ('Fire Charm'). One of the more impressive reds, a wonderful flower color, red with a magenta tint, maybe best described as plum-red. The large flowers glow even on a cloudy day, brighter than 'Diane'. 15′ by 15′.

'Jelena' ('Copper Beauty'). The best of the orange-flowered witch-hazels, its flowers glow bright coppery orange, impressive even from a distance. Flowers are distinctly

'Pallida'

'Primavera'

'Sunburst'

'Westerstede'

larger than those of most cultivars. A vigorous healthy plant, the upright vase-shaped habit is garden-friendly, and fall color is a very good bright orange to orange-red. An authors' favorite for both flower and multi-stem form. 15 to 20′ tall and wide.

'Pallida'. Soft yellow flowers evoke a gentle spring feeling. Excellent against a dark background. The flower is very large. The plant does hold more brown leaves in winter than some of the others. Spreading, 15′ by 15′.

'Primavera'. One of the best yellows, very bright, a medium-sized flower with a distinctly purple-red calyx. Upright vase-shaped plant. Fall color yellow to yellow-orange. 18′ by 15′.

'Sunburst'. Like the name says, this one is among the brightest of the yellows, an impressive lemon to golden yellow, and one of the largest flowers. Yellow fall color. A winner. Vase-shaped. 15′ by 15′.

'Westerstede'. A very bright yellow flower, abundant, but smaller than most. Vigorous with a good upright vase shape and yellow to orange-red fall color. 15′ by 15′.

Hamamelis japonica
Japanese witch-hazel

Deciduous. A large open shrub or small spreading tree. Usually multi-stem or quite low-branched as a tree form, vase-shaped to spreading and often flat-topped. Medium-textured in summer, fine-textured in winter, slow-growing, to 15′ tall with a 20′ spread.

Foliage: The leaves are broadly and irregularly elliptical to broadly obovate, always with a wavy margin, 2 to 4″ long, two-thirds as wide. Medium green with a dull surface. Yellow to reddish purple fall color. **Flowers/seeds/fruits/cones**: Flowers very early, January to March, depending on climate. Flowers are typically yellow, each with 4 strap-like petals, very thin and wavy, about ⅝″ long. Fruit, a small capsule, is not ornamental. **Native range**: Japan. **Adaptability**: Likes a moist, well-drained acid soil rich with organic matter, but reasonably tolerant. Will grow well in full sun or partial shade, but give it sun for the best flowering. Zones 5 to 8. **Landscape use**: See *H. ×intermedia*. Japanese witch-hazel tends to be a little more wide-spreading than some of the other species, more difficult to train to tree form. **Street tree use**: No, too short, often too wide, needs better soil. **In the trade**: 'Superba' has bright yellow petals, a little longer than the species, deep red calyx; wide-spreading with age, 12′ tall, 20′ wide. 'Zuccariniana' offers medium-sized butter-yellow flowers; upright when young, then spreading, 15′ tall, 20′ wide.

'Zuccariniana'

Hamamelis mollis
Chinese witch-hazel

Deciduous. A large shrub or small tree. Usually multi-stem or low-branched as a tree form, widely rounded to vase-shaped and spreading. Medium-textured in summer, fine-textured in winter, slow-growing, to 15′ tall with a 20′ spread, but usually smaller.

Foliage: The leaves are broadly and irregularly obovate, to almost irregularly rounded, always with a wavy margin, 3 to 6″ long, three-fourths as wide. Pubescent above and tomentose below, much more pubescent than the other species. Medium green with a dull surface. Yellow to orange-yellow fall color. **Flowers/seeds/fruits/cones**: Flowers early, February to March, depending on location. Flower is typically yellow with a reddish calyx cup and 4 very thin, wavy strap-like petals, each about ⅝″ long. Fruit, a small capsule, is not ornamental. **Native range**: Central China. **Adaptability**: A little more touchy than *H. ×intermedia*, with more susceptibility to spring frosts and summer heat; flower buds sometimes damaged in zone 5. Likes a moist, well-drained acid soil with organic matter. Will grow well in full sun or partial shade, but needs sun for the best flowering. Zones 5 to 8. **Landscape use**: See *H. ×intermedia*. Select by cultivar, as they vary. The best are quite bright and showy. As a species, it is the most fragrant. **Street tree use**: No, too short, often too wide, needs better soil. **In the trade**: Available.

'Boskoop'. One of the brightest yellows with a deep red calyx cup. Flowers are large and impressive. Quite fragrant. Yellow fall color. 15′ by 15′.

'Coombe Wood'. Bright golden yellow, very large flowers, and a lovely fragrance. Yellow fall color. 15′ by 15′.

'Early Bright'. Golden yellow flowers have just the slightest orange tint, giving them a warmer glow. 15′ by 15′.

Hamamelis mollis

H

'Boskoop'

'Coombe Wood'

Hamamelis mollis

Hamamelis mollis

Hamamelis virginiana

common witch-hazel

Deciduous. A multi-stemmed or low-branched small tree or large shrub, with upright-spreading and latticework-like branching and a broadly rounded crown. Medium texture in summer and fine texture in winter, medium slow growth rate, to 20′ by 20′.

Foliage: Medium green, broadly obovate to broadly elliptic, with a wavy leaf margin and a dull sheen, 3 to 6″ long, two-thirds as wide. Fall color is a rich yellow. **Flowers/seeds/fruits/cones**: Spidery 4-petaled flowers are similar to other species of the genus, but they open in the fall, the bloom generally coinciding with fall color. Unfortunately, the timing of the bloom reduces its effectiveness, as the flowers tend to be hidden. Nice fragrance. Fruit is a ½″ long, 2-valved capsule, not ornamental. **Native range**: Nova Scotia to Wisconsin and northern Florida to eastern Texas. **Adaptability**: Fairly adaptable; likes moist soils but is more tolerant of varied and difficult conditions and carries more cold hardiness than the Asian species. Zones 3 to 8(9). **Landscape use**: The form is usually a little more rounded than vase-shaped, so it tends to be wider at the base than the Asian species. Because of this, it appears a little more bulky and is less well suited to the small garden. It makes a great screen along large banks and is excellent for naturalistic commercial landscapes. **Street tree use**: No, too low and wide. **In the trade**: Usually sold as seed-grown. The cultivar 'Harvest Moon' is superior to the species; its prolific, fragrant lemon-yellow flowers are larger in size and appear later, so rather than being hidden in the fall foliage, the bloom is on bare branches and provides a much better display. Vase shape with a rounded crown, 20′ by 20′.

Hamamelis virginiana

Hamamelis virginiana

H

Heptacodium miconioides

seven-son flower

Deciduous. One of the latest-flowering small trees/large shrubs, introduced to the United States with great fanfare in 1980 by the Sino-American Botanical Expedition and promoted by the Arnold Arboretum. Habit is upright-spreading, multi-stemmed, but can be trained to a single stem, 15 to 25′ high. Bark exfoliates in strips, starting on 1″ stems, strikingly so on larger trunks, gray-brown and upon exfoliation revealing lighter gray to almost white inner bark.

Foliage: Soft yellow-green upon emergence; dark green at maturity, degrees of yellow in autumn with nothing memorable. Leaves emerge by late March; still present in late November, zone 8. Prettily textured/pleated leaf to 6″ long, with 3 impressed veins and an entire, wavy (undulating) margin. **Flowers/seeds/fruits/cones**: In August fragrant cream-white flowers open in 6″ long terminal panicles on the new growth of the season. Flowers open from the base to apex of the inflorescence and are effective for 4 to 6 weeks. The flowers are attractive to butterflies and hummingbirds, an important nectar source in late summer and fall. The authors believe the fruits (capsules) with the showy and long-lasting rose-purple sepals are more effective than the flowers, providing rich color for 2 to 3 weeks or longer in September, October, and later. **Native range**: China. Rare in its homeland; may no longer exist in the wild. **Adaptability**: Well adapted to any well-drained soil, preferably moist, acid. Authors noted healthy specimens in Chicago, IL (20′), Athens, GA (15′), Swarthmore, PA (18′), and Pownal, ME (15′), some in high pH (literally limestone-based) soils. Experiences slight tip dieback at -24°F, but since flowering occurs on new growth, the flowers and fruits will develop. Zones 5 to 8. **Landscape use**: Had become a landscape fixture in New England and the Midwest for its restrained size, fragrant summer flowers, and pretty rose-purple sepals. In recent years, a dieback, possibly canker related, has developed; it is not devastating as individual branches succumb, usually not the entire plant. Full sun facilitates maximum flowers; however, plants in partial shade (under *Pinus taeda*) in zone 8 performed well. The species is best used in the border or groupings. We advocate training as a single-stem small tree for use in restricted spaces. Again, precious few species offer as much late-season color. It's a cold hardy crapemyrtle alternative, but without the range of flower and bark colors. **Street tree use**: Possible if trained to a single trunk, but a little wide and floppy. It would fit under utility wires. **In the trade**: Available; variation in sepal coloration is evident in seedlings, from light to dark pink, rose, purple. It is surprising that a superior cultivar has yet to emerge.

Heptacodium miconioides

Heptacodium miconioides

Heptacodium miconioides

Hippophae rhamnoides
sea buckthorn

Deciduous. The species is touted for its orange fruit, which is put to many culinary uses and is an excellent source of folic and fatty acids, carotenoids, and vitamins A, C, and E. Now for the essence of its landscape worthiness...Develops small tree habit, spreading irregularly, loose and open, usually in the 10 to 20′ range, and prominently suckering, forming large colonies, 10 to 40′ wide. The stems are endowed with terminal and axillary spines, meaning—make sure you have a will before pruning.

Foliage: Leaves appear gray from a distance. Close inspection shows them to be dark green above, covered with silver-gray scales below, each linear in shape to 3″ long. They die off gray-green in fall. **Flowers/seeds/fruits/cones**: Dioecious. Flowers are yellowish, opening before or with the leaves in March-April; the males borne in short catkins, the female in short racemes. Pretty, bright orange fruits, globose to egg-shaped, ⅓″ long, ripen in September, persisting through April. The fruit is extremely acid and not palatable to birds. **Native range**: Europe, China, Himalayas. **Adaptability**: Zones 4 to 7. Described as hardy to -40°F. **Landscape use**: Restricted uses, primarily for fruit production but also for impossible infertile, sandy, acid soils as well as neutral to alkaline conditions in full sun. Displays high level of salinity tolerance. In Europe it is common in roadside plantings where maintenance is minimal. **Street tree use**: No. **In the trade**: Species is wind-pollinated and requires a male pollinator in proximity to guarantee fruit development. Many cultivars introduced from Russia are offered by specialty nurseries, One Green World (Northwoods), the most prominent. More common cultivars are 'Leikora' with profuse, large late-ripening fruits ('Pollmix' is a male pollinator for 'Leikora') and TITAN, whose abundant crops of large, bright orange berries can be used for juice and preserves.

Hippophae rhamnoides

Hippophae rhamnoides

Hovenia dulcis
Japanese raisintree

Deciduous. An attractive tree that may simply need a bit of promotion, as arboreta/botanical gardens are as yet its primary domain. Habit is upright oval in youth, almost vase-shaped to rounded at maturity. Matures at 30 to 40′ in height, most specimens toward the low end. Readily identified by the patterned bark, which is ridged and furrowed, with wide gray to brown flat ridges and shallow, narrow furrows.

Foliage: Leaves mature lustrous dark green, with, at best, a modicum of yellow in autumn. Individual leaves are sizable, 6 to 8″ long, with 3 prominent veins, and coarsely serrate margins. The pretty foliage remains pristine into autumn, absent pockmarks, holes, distortions. **Flowers/seeds/fruits/cones**: The fragrant, greenish white flowers, each only ⅓″ wide, are borne in many-flowered cymes, to 3″ wide, in summer (June-July). Flowers are not spectacular but are refreshingly pretty at a time when competition from other flowering trees is minimal. Fruit itself is a fleshy drupe, gray to brown. The reddish infructescence stalks are swollen, sweet, and edible, relished in Japan and China; we have tasted and found them to be palatable. **Native range**: China and Himalayas. **Adaptability**: Zones 5 to 7. Minus 10 to 15°F is the lowest range for successful cultivation. Widely cultivated in Japan and India. **Landscape use**: Authors observed beautiful specimens in Boston, St. Louis, and Washington, DC, and believe this species has been undervalued and underappreciated, deserving of a more prominent place in American landscapes. It dovetails with smaller landscapes, offering seasonal attributes, and has potential for urban landscapes. Our observations indicate it can be cultured in any soil except permanently wet. There are no Achilles' heels, no insect or disease issues. We have grown seedlings, some ascending 8′ in a single season. Unfortunately, in the Dirr garden, deer thought the foliage was cotton candy. Site in full sun, acid, well-drained, reasonably moist soil for maximum growth. **Street tree use**: Potential. **In the trade**: Sold as seed-grown.

Hovenia dulcis

Hovenia dulcis

I

Idesia polycarpa
Igiri tree

Deciduous. A monotypic genus and certainly a species that is not widely represented in cultivation. Habit is pyramidal in youth, rounded at maturity, potentially 40 to 60′ high and wide. Fast-growing; trees reached 35′ high in 16 years at the State Botanical Garden of Georgia in Athens. In winter, the bark is quite evident: smooth and grayish white; in zone 8, it simulates the effect of *Populus tremuloides* and the white-bark birches.

Foliage: Quite distinctive. The large, coarse-textured, to 10″ long leaves, deep green above, gray-green below, have crenate-serrate margins. The red petiole, to 6″ long, bears 1 to 3, raised concave glands, toward the middle. Fall color, yellow-green at best, has persisted into late November in zone 8. **Flowers/seeds/fruits/cones**: Dioecious. Nondescript, yellow-green, fragrant, apetalous flowers are borne in pendulous panicles, the male to 6″ long, the female to 8″ long, in June. It is doubtful if anyone recognizes the trees flowering, since the large leaves mask the effect. The great beauty resides in the pea-sized, rounded, cherry-red fruits borne on pendulous panicles, to 8″ long, and persisting into early winter in zone 8. To facilitate fruit set, male and female trees must be in proximity. Each fruit contains multiple seeds that are easily germinated. Authors have not observed the species becoming invasive, even though viable seed production is astronomical. We urge some caution here, as the species has characteristics that could make it invasive: heavy production of bird berries, quick germination, fast growth,

Idesia polycarpa

Idesia polycarpa

and some suckering. **Native range**: Japan, China. **Adaptability**: Zones 6 to 9. Interesting anecdote about hardiness: species exists as a dieback shrub in Boston; a 60′ tree at the Brooklyn Botanic Garden. Rapid growth and early fruiting (5-year-old trees) in Southeast reflect its adaptability to heat. In Oregon trials, it grew scary fast and flowered and fruited at a young age. **Landscape use**: Vigorous (almost to a fault), coarse in texture, and requires ample real estate, so is best utilized on parks, campuses, golf courses, estates. Authors envision groupings of 5 to 7 in an expanse of lawn or field. Site in full sun, provide acid to near-neutral, well-drained soil, reasonable moisture, and move out of the way. **Street tree use**: None yet, has potential if male clones appear. **In the trade**: Some availability as seed-grown. Seedlings will be either male or female, thus no guarantee of fruit. We suggest nursery selection and propagation of a male (seedless) cultivar until there is confidence that it will not become invasive.

Ilex
holly

Evergreen or deciduous. Hollies (400 species) occur worldwide, as small shrubs to large trees, in swamps to high mountains. Consistently dioecious. Flowers from the axils of the leaves; female flowers singly or in few-flowered clusters; males in greater numbers. The white to purple flowers are pollinated by bees; they open in March on certain Chinese species, as late as May on *I. opaca* in zone 8. White, yellow, orange, red, black fruits. Hybrids are rampant. Authors were once told by the *Ilex* breeders at the U.S. National Arboretum that any holly, evergreen or deciduous, will hybridize with another if they flower at the same time. The current discussion treats the most popular tree types, species and cultivars.

Hollies withstand extremes of climate, soil, sun, shade, and pruning. Please note the hardiness ranges ascribed to the tree hollies discussed herein. In most cases, soils should be acid, well-drained, and moist to maximize performance. Full sun increases fruit production; however, evergreen hollies display moderate shade tolerance while producing reasonable fruit loads. Hollies are best pruned during the dormant season. Authors observed 2′ wide 'Nellie R. Stevens' trunks chainsawed to within a foot of the ground regenerating new shoots. Hollies, especially the evergreen types, make magnificent specimen trees, either singly or in groupings. They serve as effective screens and function as superior hedges when properly pruned. Hollies are readily transplanted from containers or as balled-and-burlapped specimens. Evergreen hollies are remarkably successful in street and urban plantings.

Ilex aquifolium
English holly

Broadleaf evergreen. Forms a dense, pyramidal habit, loosening with age, reaching 30 to 50(80)′ high. Fruit is produced in great quantities, with the branches cherished for Christmas decorations.

Foliage: Leaves are lustrous dark green, almost black-green, and barbed-wire spiny, the serrations extending in multiple directions from the leaf margin. Size 1 to 4″ long, to 2½″ wide, the leaf margins becoming less spiny on mature trees and many of the cultivars. The emerging leaves and shoots are suffused with red-purple. Stems are reddish purple, a trait that is often manifest in the hybrids (e.g., *I. ×altaclerensis, I. ×meserveae, I. ×aquipernyi*). **Flowers/seeds/fruits/cones**: Flowers, 4-petaled, fragrant, dull white, occasionally pink-tinged, develop from the leaf axils in May. The bright red, ¼ to ⅜″ wide, rounded fruits mature in late summer–fall, persisting into winter. **Native range**: Europe, North Africa, western Asia. **Adaptability**: Adaptable to maritime and polluted conditions as well as high pH soils. Shade tolerance is legendary; authors observed it thriving in the understory of the New Forest, Hampshire, England. In the United States, the coastal Pacific Northwest into California and Cape Cod and Long Island offer favorable climates. In fact, in the Pacific Northwest, the climate is far too favorable. It has become one of the worst invasive plants and should not be planted. Its berries are widely dispersed by birds, and its shade tolerance allows it to persist and grow

Ilex aquifolium

'Argentea Marginata'

in mature forests. Warren fights new seedlings yearly in the shady woods behind his house. In the East, the species has been safe, so far. Zones 6 and 7 on the East Coast, to 10 on the West. **Landscape use:** English holly is the quintessential broadleaf evergreen in Europe; in its native continental climate, it grows in association with English oak and European beech, thriving in the shade and cultural competition. Has many of the same uses as the other hollies described herein. **Street tree use:** Spiny foliage would make it unpopular near sidewalks. **In the trade:** The numerous cultivars offer all manner of white, cream, and yellow leaf variegation patterns as well as yellow and the normal red fruit colors. 'Argentea Marginata' is a free-fruiting form with silver-margined leaves, the newly emerging leaves tinged pink. 'Aurea Marginata' with yellow-margined leaves produces a modicum of red fruit.

Ilex ×attenuata

Ilex ×attenuata
topal holly

Broadleaf evergreen. An important hybrid species, reflecting the parentage of *I. opaca* and *I. cassine* (Dahoon holly). The most significant advantage over *I. opaca* is the fast growth, estimating 2 to 3 times as fast. *I. cassine*, a 20 to 30′ high evergreen tree with shiny rich green leaves and red fruits, is strictly coastal in distribution, North Carolina to Florida to Texas, in moist to wet soils, including bald cypress ponds, swamps, marsh margins, and streambanks; it has never joined the ranks of the landscape species and cultivars, primarily because of lack of cold hardiness, light green foliage color, and often open, wispy growth habit. *I. ×attenuata* meshes the best qualities of *I. opaca* and *I. cassine* into fast-growing tree-statured selections, some 40 to 50′ high, with darker foliage and heavy fruit production. Bark is smooth, gray, beech-like on large trunks.

Foliage: Variable, elliptic, oblong-ovate to almost rounded, 1½ to 3″ long, with few to many spines along the margin, medium green to lustrous dark green; leaves of some cultivars entire or nearly so at maturity. **Flowers/seeds/fruits/cones:** White, 4-petaled, fragrant, borne in the leaf axils, April-May. The rounded, red, ¼″ wide drupes are often produced in supra-optimal quantities, persisting into and through winter. **Native range:** Hybrid. **Adaptability:** Zones 6 to 9. Leaves may be injured/killed in subzero temperatures, but stems and buds survive. Successfully cultivated from the Mid-Atlantic to the Southeast into Texas. **Landscape use:** *I. ×attenuata* is defined by its many cultivars, which have withstood the test of time and are in common use, as great specimens, groupings, screens, and hedges. The cultivars are often loose, open in youth, requiring some pruning to increase density. With age, either single or multi-trunked, they become quite graceful and elegant mid-sized trees. Soils should be moist, acid, and plants thrive in full sun to partial shade. Spittlebugs are a common insect, but little else appears bothersome. Fruits are abundant and foliage becomes yellow, as nitrogen moves from

405

'East Palatka'

'Savannah'

'Foster No. 2'

Ilex ×attenuata

'Foster No. 2'

foliage to developing fruits. An application of nitrogen (N) fertilizer when the green fruits are developing alleviates the issue. **Street tree use**: Suitable. **In the trade**: The best and most common tree types follow.

'East Palatka'. Shiny, dark green leaves, either entire or serrated toward the apex, airy, open habit in youth, ¼″ wide bright red fruits, eventually 30 to 40′ high. Vigorous grower.

'Foster No. 2' ('Fosteri'). One of a series developed in Alabama. This selection has narrow-oval, lustrous dark green leaves with 1 to 4 spreading spiny teeth on each margin. The bright red ¼″ wide fruits persist into winter. Habit is dense, conical-pyramidal, with mature trees opening a degree. Reaches 20 to 30(40)′ high, a quarter as wide.

'Savannah'. The largest and lightest green foliage of the cultivars listed here but produces the most abundant bright red fruits. Leaf margins are spiny from about the middle to apex. Habit is looser, more open, wider than previous two. Grows 25 to 30(40)′ high, a third as wide.

Ilex 'Emily Bruner'
Emily Bruner holly

Broadleaf evergreen. Emily and 'Nellie R. Stevens' are two of the most utilized hollies in zones 7 to 9 for specimen, screening, and hedging. Emily develops a broad-based, dense foliage, pyramidal outline, 20 to 30′ in height. At the Milliken Arboretum, Spartanburg, SC, trees are now over 40′ high. Emily is slightly more graceful than Nellie, the branches almost layered and semi-pendulous.

Foliage: Sparkling green upon emergence, leathery, lustrous dark green at maturity. Emily requires good fertility to maintain the dark green foliage coloration. Each leaf, to 3″ long, ovoid in outline, has irregular prominent teeth and impressed veins. In extremely cold winters, the deep green coloration is dampened/diminished. **Flowers/seeds/fruits/cones**: Flowers are fragrant, white, opening in March-April in zone 8. Fruit is a red drupe, to ⅓″ long, nested in leaf axils, persisting in good condition into winter. Fruit is, to degrees, hidden by the foliage. The color diminishes with age, becoming dull red. **Native range**: A hybrid between *I. cornuta* 'Burfordii' and *I. latifolia*. The two parental taxa are extremely heat and drought tolerant. **Adaptability**: Zones 7 to 9. **Landscape use**: Emily is destined for specimen use, in groupings, as a screen. She maintains a central leader and never grows old and scraggly. Could be pruned to a hedge, but why ruin her beauty? **Street tree use**: Certainly, if limbed up with a clear trunk, such use is possible. Passersby may take issue with leaves that poke them. **In the trade**: Available.

Ilex 'Emily Bruner'

Ilex latifolia
lusterleaf holly

Broadleaf evergreen. Superb large-leaf holly, deserving of significantly greater use in zones 7 and 8. It forms a broad, dense pyramid, literally impenetrable, and therefore a great screen/border plant. Typical landscape size is in the 20 to 25′ range. Authors observed 40′ specimens in South Carolina. In the wild, it is listed as reaching 60′ tall. Growth is slow.

Foliage: Leaves *Magnolia grandiflora*–like, to 8″ long, are thick, leathery, lustrous, dark black-green, and bullet- and insect-proof. The leaves are the largest of the commonly cultivated hollies. The leaf margin is adorned with evenly spaced, coarse teeth. **Flowers/seeds/fruits/cones**: The yellow-green, 4-petaled flowers occur in large bushy masses from the leaf axils. The dull red fruits, globose, ⅓″ wide, occur in dense axillary clusters and, like the flowers, completely encircle the stem. Fruits persist into winter, but the color is diminished. **Native range**: Southern Japan, China. **Adaptability**: Zones 7 to 9, perhaps 6, although less cold hardy than 'Nellie R. Stevens'; -3°F injured leaves but did not affect stems and buds. **Landscape use**: Absolutely first-class evergreen holly with possibly the most beautiful foliage of any. Authors' observations point to high shade tolerance as well as drought tolerance once established. Protect from excessive wind, especially in winter. Site on east/north side of home, near or under pines. A superb specimen, grouping, barrier, and screening plant. Quite difficult to prune because of the large leaves, which may brown on edges when severed. **Street tree use**: No. **In the trade**: Several cultivars, none common.

'Alva'. Cold-hardy selection from South Carolina with abundant, early-ripening red fruits and leaves slightly larger than the typical species; size approximates the species.

COOL FENCES 'ILDG'. Dense, pyramidal shape; leathery, coarse-textured, lustrous dark green leaves and red fruit; displays good shade and drought tolerance; ideal for screening, hedge, and specimen use; 20′ by 15′.

'Fusmu'. More compact, smaller leaves, red fruit. Dirr planted it, and 7 years on, without pruning, it was 14′ by 8′ and dense as concrete.

I. ×koehneana (Koehne holly). *I. latifolia* × *I. aquifolium*. Pyramidal habit, 20 to 30′ high, a third as wide, leaves generally quite spiny, lustrous dark green. Zone 7 hardy with leaf injury in zone 6. 'Agena' (female), 'San Jose' (female), 'Wirt L. Winn' (female), and 'Ajax' (male) are among the best.

Ilex latifolia

Ilex latifolia

'Wirt L. Winn'

'Fusmu'

'Wirt L. Winn'

COOL FENCES

Ilex 'Nellie R. Stevens'

Nellie R. Stevens holly

Broadleaf evergreen. Unequivocally the dominant evergreen tree holly for the Southeast. Categorized in the 15 to 25′ high range, but plants over 30′ are common. Habit is broadly pyramidal, dense, and full without pruning. Moderate growth rate.

Foliage: To 3″ long, lustrous dark green, veins impressed, bears 2 to 3 serrations (spines) per leaf margin, the entire leaf with slight twist. The leaf color is maintained in the winter months. **Flowers/seeds/fruits/cones**: The 4-petaled, white, fragrant, female flowers open in March-April and are effectively pollinated by male *I. cornuta* (Chinese holly). However, fruit will develop parthenocarpically (without) cross pollination. Fruit is bright red, to ⅓″ wide, rounded, and held in clusters in the leaf axils. Fruits are not as persistent as those of 'Emily Bruner'. **Native range**: *I. cornuta* × *I. aquifolium* hybrid that occurred in the early 20th century. **Adaptability**: Wildly reliable, thanks to the genes of the heat tolerant *I. cornuta*, it is successfully cultured from the Washington, DC, area to the Gulf Coast. Zones 6 to 9. **Landscape use**: Nellie is possibly overused but serves its purpose. Most gardeners, landscape designers, and architects want functionality and consistent great gobs of lustrous dark green. Nellie delivers. Commonly used for screening between properties, it withstands heavy pruning, allowing for an effective and aesthetic hedge. Grower friends and the authors hope for a comparable American holly, whose limiting factor is its slow growth; a quality 'Nellie R. Stevens' can be produced in half the time. **Street tree use**: Potential. **In the trade**: 'Golden Nellie' is a yellow-gold leaf selection from the University of Georgia campus; 25′ by 15′ in 30 years. Foliage emerges soft yellow, becomes golden, then gradually matures to green. Female and sets abundant red fruits that contrast vividly with the yellow-green mature foliage.

Ilex 'Nellie R. Stevens'

Ilex 'Nellie R. Stevens'

Ilex opaca
American holly

Broadleaf evergreen. The most common native evergreen tree holly in the United States and one of George Washington's prized trees, with several planted in 1785 extant. Often occurs in understory habitats, but the most noble specimens are located in full sun. Removed from competition, habit is densely pyramidal in youth with branches sweeping the ground; either pyramidal-conical at maturity to open, irregular, picturesque, with a central leader or with multiple leaders. Grows 40 to 50′ high with a variable spread; authors observed 50′ high trees that were as wide at the top as the bottom. The major commercial Achilles' heel is the painfully slow rate of growth, averaging 1′ per year. Bark is smooth, gray, similar to American beech bark. The wood is white and makes beautiful turned bowls.

Foliage: Varies from spiny to entire-margined, 2 to 3″ long, light to dark green, dull-surfaced to lustrous. **Flowers/ seeds/fruits/cones**: Flowers open late, typically May in zone 8. The 4-petaled, white flowers are ⅓″ in diameter and particularly attractive to bees. The dull red (to bright red), round fruit, ¼ to ⅓″ wide, ripens in fall (October), persisting into winter. Fruit effect is partially masked by the foliage; however, the combination of dark green and red is beautiful. To ensure fruit production, male and female trees should be in proximity. **Native range**: Cape Cod to Florida, west to Missouri, Oklahoma, Texas. Common throughout most of the range, often in the shade of hardwood forests, usually on hillsides, mixed with pines; in floodplains to upland sites. In the Congaree National Park, SC, trees are common in the floodplain, which is flooded up to 10 times a year. We have not observed the species in permanent standing water. **Adaptability**: Zones 5 to 9. In northern areas, winter wind and sun diminish foliage color. Authors observed complete leaf drop after -20°F with complete regrowth from overwintering buds the following spring-summer. **Landscape use**: Thrives with minimal inputs, just as the vast majority do in nature, serving as a specimen, in groupings, for screens and hedges. Seedlings are utilized for hedging with early to late leafing, green to bronze new growth, variable degrees of mature green, male and female, the whole a kaleidoscope. Prefers moderately moist, fertile, loose, acid, well-drained soil in full sun to partial shade. Leaf chlorosis may develop in higher pH soils. Leaf miner, scale, and spittlebugs are common insects. We encourage greater use of American holly, especially in northern areas where *I. aquifolium*, *I. ×attenuata*, Emily, Nellie, and others are not hardy. **Street tree use**: Potential.

Ilex opaca

411

Ilex opaca

In the trade: To our knowledge, controlled breeding has been minimal, with cultivars primarily selected from the wild. Gold/yellow-fruited selections include 'Canary', 'Goldie', 'Princeton Gold', the yellow coloration quite richly displayed against the dark green leaves; all are tree types, 20 to 30′ high. We recommend the following as well.

'Carolina No. 2'. One of the best, with beautiful leathery, spiny, lustrous dark green leaves and red fruits, eventually full, dense habit. Expect 30 to 40′ in height.

'Croonenburg'. Broad, oval-pyramidal form, leaves glossy, deep green with red fruits. Matures 30 to 40′ in height.

'Jersey Princess'. A superb red-fruited, densely branched selection, with lustrous midnight-green foliage. In Georgia trials, 'Jersey Princess' held the rich foliage and fruit color through winter. Slow-growing, 20 to 30′. From the breeding program of Elwin Orton, Rutgers University.

'Miss Helen'. Thick, dark green foliage and glossy, dark red fruit, forms a dense conical tree. Long considered one of the best cultivars.

'Satyr Hill'. Receives many accolades for its abundant, vivid red fruits, dark olive-green leaves, and broader, looser pyramidal habit. Grows to 30′ high.

'Carolina No. 2'

Ilex opaca

'Carolina No. 2'

'Jersey Princess'

'Jersey Princess'

J

Jacaranda mimosifolia

Jacaranda mimosifolia

Jacaranda mimosifolia
jacaranda

Deciduous to semi-evergreen. Upright-spreading, forming a wide, umbrella-like, broadly rounded crown, usually fairly open below. Sometimes grown multi-stem. Medium fine texture, moderately fast-growing to 35′ high and wide. Bark is light gray, smooth when young, then becoming finely fissured.

Foliage: Rather tropical-looking, bipinnately compound leaves resemble mimosa (hence the epithet). Leaves are very large, to 18″, but present a fine texture because the tiny elliptical leaflets are about ½″ long. The medium green foliage can be semi-evergreen in the warmest climates but is generally briefly deciduous in the U.S. Southwest. **Flowers/seeds/fruits/cones**: Flowers are lavender-blue, trumpet-shaped, each 2″ long, in 8″ clusters, and can completely clothe the tree. Flowering usually occurs in spring, following the brief deciduous period, before new foliage emerges, although trees occasionally flower in summer. **Native range**: Bolivia and Argentina. **Adaptability**: Definitely needs a warm climate. Mature trees can stand a brief mild freeze, but the flower buds may be lost. Zones 10 and 11. **Landscape use**: Used as a feature tree because of its spectacular flowering. The openness below its canopy also makes it a good shade tree. Be aware that the size of the flower clusters and leaves means that there will be some litter below the tree. **Street tree use**: The branches tend to arch upward, and with a little pruning for clearance, it can form a wide vase and make a good street tree. **In the trade**: Usually sold as the species, either seed- or cutting-grown.

Juglans nigra
black walnut

Deciduous. Beautiful large native tree, to 100′, forming an oval to rounded crown, often with immense spreading branches. Typical size is 50 to 75′ in height, with a comparable spread. Growth is fast in youth, slowing with age. Bark is rich dark brown to gray-black, divided by deep, narrow furrows into thick ridges, forming a roughly diamond-shaped pattern. The nuts are delicious and highly prized for baking, and the wood is utilized in all manner of ways, from furniture and gunstocks to turned bowls and veneers.

Foliage: Large, pinnately compound leaves, to 24″ long, are composed of up to 23 leaflets, the terminal one often missing, each 2 to 5″ long, ¾ to 2″ wide, dark green, and fragrant when bruised. Shape is ovate to oblong-lanceolate, oblique at base, evenly toothed. Fall color is green-yellow

Juglans nigra

Juglans nigra

to yellow and seldom overwhelming, as leaves often abscise early. **Flowers/seeds/fruits/cones**: Monoecious. Male flowers greenish in up to 3½″ long slender catkins on previous season's wood; female in axils of current season's shoot extensions, in May. Fruit is a rounded, light green, grainy-surfaced, glabrous, 1½ to 2″ wide nut; the sculpted wall (endocarp) blackish and thick. Fruits ripen in fall, abscising over a long period. Authors would collect green nuts, place on garage roof, allow the fleshy portion to rot, then extract the nut meats. Although it is far easier to purchase soft-shelled English walnuts, it's worth the effort to extract the meaty seeds of this species. The difference in taste is remarkable. **Native range**: Touches every state east of Mississippi, extending to New Mexico and Colorado. Often open-grown, but also in mixed deciduous woods. **Adaptability**: Authors recorded sizable trees from Prince Edward Island, Boston, Atlanta, to Minnesota, reflecting the species adaptability. Squirrels and other mammals "plant" the nuts everywhere digging is permitted, and like magic, a walnut emerges in out-of-the-way places. Zones 4 to 9. **Landscape use**: Certainly, an imposing tree, requiring ample real estate, both aerial and subterranean, to realize its genetic potential. For large (read immense) properties there is a place, but perhaps best observed and enjoyed from afar. Trees are messy, as leaves, rachises, fruits drop/abscise over an extended period. The fruit is particularly problematic; it presents a safety issue, stains concrete, and leaves a rock-solid mess. Juglone is contained in leaves and roots and may exert an allelopathic effect on surrounding vegetation (i.e., suppresses the growth of plants under or near the tree). With all the sidebars, one would question its use in contemporary landscapes, but certainly, if native/present on a property, then prize, cherish, and maintain with the knowledge that cleanup is necessary. It thrives in deep, moist, near-neutral soils and tolerates higher pH soils better than most trees. Growth is maximized in full sun. **Street tree use**: No, too messy and at risk: if you were a tree, you would tremble at the thought of a disease with a name like "thousand cankers disease," which is what black walnut now faces. A disease complex of the walnut twig borer and a fungus (*Geosmithia morbida*), it has emerged from the Southwest (where it may have been endemic to isolated *J. major*)

Juglans nigra

Juglans nigra

'Laciniata'

Juglans regia
English walnut, Persian walnut

Deciduous. The thin-shelled walnut of commerce, part and parcel of every Christmas nut assortment. With age, the habit is rounded, often spreading with an open crown, ultimately reaching 40 to 60′ in height with comparable or greater spread. Beautiful silver-gray bark, composed of large, wide, flat ridges, smaller darker furrows. For timber, the species is quite valuable, utilized for furniture, veneering, and gunstocks.

Foliage: Composed of 5 to 9(13), entire-margined, medium to dark green, elliptic to obovate to oblong-ovate leaflets, to 5″ long. Fall color is yellow-green to yellow. **Flowers/ seeds/fruits/cones**: Flowers similar to *J. nigra*. The nut, to 2″ wide, is covered by a smooth green, fleshy outer covering that abscises/opens to expose the thin-shelled endocarp (hard shell). The soft unripe fruits are made into pickles. **Native range**: Southeastern Europe to China and the Himalayas. **Adaptability**: Seldom encountered in the eastern United States but commercially farmed in California. Zone 5 depending on cultivar, to 9 and 10 on the West Coast. Leaves in the North are injured by early fall freezes. **Landscape use**: Adaptable and like *J. nigra* tolerates near-neutral soils. Deep, moist, loose soils in full sun are preferred. Primarily self-sterile, so must be out-crossed with another clone or seedling. Ideally, utilize in large areas where nuts do not present a litter issue. Pretty as a specimen tree, especially in a large expanse of grass. **Street tree use**: No. **In the trade**: 'Broadview' and 'Buccaneer' are self-fertile. 'Carpathian' and 'Hansen' were selected for colder climates, the former surviving -34°F. 'Laciniata' (a pretty dissected leaf selection with fine-textured leaflets), 'Pendula' (weeping), and 'Purpurea' (deep red-purple leaf) are occasionally available.

Juglans regia

to spread across the entire West, and has now been confirmed in several eastern states. **In the trade**: 'Sauber', with large nuts, has high-quality, light-colored kernels (seeds) that separate cleanly from the outer hull; 'Sparrow' bears nuts with exceptionally high total kernel percentage. These two cultivars are grafted, ensuring uniform performance. Beyond cultivars suitable for nut production, 'Laciniata', selected for its fine-textured dissected foliage, has merit for the collector who has *almost* everything.

Juglans regia

Juniperus chinensis

Juniperus chinensis
Chinese juniper

Evergreen conifer. Both the species and its tree-type cultivars are pyramidal-conical, densely needled and branched in youth; opening with maturity, more graceful and elegant. In the wild, trees exceed 60′ in height with trunk diameter to 4½′. Bark, seldom evident because of the evergreen foliage, is gray-brown to reddish brown, stringy, slightly ridged and furrowed.

Foliage: Needles are of two types, awl-shaped and scale-like. The awl-shaped, ⅓″ long, sharp-pointed needles range from green, blue-green, blue to yellow (gold), depending on the cultivar; this type of needle occurs on juvenile plants and those in heavy shade as well as some cultivars. Scale-like needles are appressed to the stem, one overlapping the next, the entire shoot not prickly. Under cold, windy conditions, needle color is often duller. **Flowers/seeds/fruits/cones**: Dioecious. Male flowers in small yellow-brown to orange-brown cones, the pollen shed in March-April. Female trees bear globose, ¼ to ⅓″ wide cones, initially waxy silvery blue, when ripe dark brown to brown-black. The waxy cones are eaten by birds, so stray seedlings may appear. Cones require 2 years to reach maturity. **Native range**: Southeastern Russia, Japan, Korea, Mongolia, China, and Taiwan, from sea level to 7,500′ elevation; this translates to significant differences in cold hardiness, depending on provenance. **Adaptability**: Without debate, an adaptable and tenacious needle evergreen, withstanding all manner of cultural and environmental extremes. It has

Juniperus chinensis

almost universal soil adaptability (except wet) as well as heat, drought, and cold tolerances. Zones 4 to 9, depending on cultivar. **Landscape use**: The species has been widely utilized for landscapes on a worldwide basis, offering via the many cultivars pancake ground cover to medium-sized trees. The tree-type cultivars make superb single specimens, groupings, screens, and, if necessary, tall hedges, producing 12 to 18″ of new growth per year and easily kept in bounds

'Hetzii Columnaris'

'Kaizuka'

'Kaizuka'

by sensible pruning. Soil tolerances are legendary, from acid to alkaline, dry to nutritionally impoverished. Plants are ideally transplanted from containers. Sun is a prerequisite. Junipers detest excess shade, becoming thin, open, and tatty therein. If tightly pruned into a shell of foliage, the interior will become totally brown. Prune only where needles are present, as bare branches and trunks, after pruning, do not produce new shoots. **Street tree use**: Acceptable. **In the trade**: Junipers in recent years have lost their allure, being replaced with spruce, fir, pine, holly, cryptomerias, Leyland cypress, and arborvitae. The species is now largely absent from commerce, but tree cultivars, such as 'Pyramidalis' (male), 'Robusta Green' (female), and 'Spartan', are available. Additional tree types follow.

'Hetzii Columnaris'. Bears awl- and scale-type, blue-green needles. It is a female and produces abundant waxy silver cones. Grows 20 to 25′ in 15 to 20 years and has performed admirably in the Southeast.

'Kaizuka' ('Torulosa'). An artistic form, branches slightly twisted, clothed with scale-like, soft-textured vivid green needles. Female, sets waxy silver cones. Extremely adaptable, growing from the Atlantic to Pacific coasts. Displays high salt tolerance. Grows 20 to 30′ high.

'Keteleeri'. A former staple in the Midwest with glossy light green foliage. Needles primarily scale-like. The cones, to ½″ wide, grayish green, borne on a recurved stalk. Grows 20′ high and greater.

STAR POWER 'JN Select Blue'. Believed to be a hybrid with *J. communis*. Upright-growing, dense and pyramidal with bluish foliage, it shows good resistance to winter burn in cold climates. Fast-growing, to at least 20′ by 10′.

'Trautman'. Very narrow, tightly pyramidal to the point of being almost columnar. Bluish green foliage, very hardy, zone 4, 20′ by 5′.

'Keteleeri'

STAR POWER

STAR POWER

'Trautman'

Juniperus scopulorum
Rocky Mountain juniper, Colorado redcedar

Evergreen conifer. Where adapted, the species and numerous cultivars are serviceable and beautiful pyramidal to pyramidal-oval trees, fully clothed with branches. Trees range from single to multiple trunks, the canopy opening with maturity, forming a round-topped outline, although the majority of trees authors witnessed were dense in old age. Landscape size 30 to 40′ high, to 15′ wide. Growth is slow to moderate. Many of the upright cultivars range from 15 to 25′ in height, usually quite narrow in width, especially in youth. Bark is brown to dark brown, maturing grayish brown, shredding and peeling in narrow strips or thin rectangular plates.

Juniperus scopulorum

Foliage: Needles variable in color, light green, gray-green, bluish green, blue to dark green, scale-like, tightly appressed to stem, generally soft to touch, prickly on juvenile plants and those grown in shade. **Flowers/seeds/fruits/cones**: Monoecious. Male flower with 6 stamens, compared to 10 to 12 of *J. virginiana*; the reader will chuckle, but the two species are difficult to separate. Female cone fleshy, globular, ¼ to ⅓″ wide, dark blue-black, but covered by a glaucous pale to bright blue wax, bearing 1 or 2, triangular, angled, grooved, reddish brown seeds, ripening in the second year. **Native range**: Rocky Mountains, central British Columbia, western North Dakota into Mexico. Open juniper, pine, oak woodlands, on dry, rocky ridges. **Adaptability**: Zones 4 to 7. Colder climates and drier conditions suit it best; excessive moisture promotes phomopsis, botryosphaeria, and seiridium needle blights and cankers. We have yet to witness a thriving *J. scopulorum* in the Southeast. **Landscape use**: Ideal for screening, hedging, and groupings, where adapted. Site in acid to high pH, well-drained soils in full sun. Best transplanted as container-grown material. In the Plains states, Midwest, and East, the blue-needle cultivars are cherished. **Street tree use**: Yes. **In the trade**: The range of *J. scopulorum* overlaps with the ranges of *J. horizontalis* and *J. virginiana*, resulting in hybrid swarms that serve as the main source for the many cultivars. The following street-tree types are in everyday commerce from coast to coast.

'Blue Arrow'. Similar to 'Skyrocket' with more intense blue needles, narrow-conical, 15 to 20′, 2 to 3′ wide, resembles 'Glauca' Italian cypress, but cold hardy.

'Blue Heaven'. Nifty narrow, pyramidal form, rich blue needles, female, 20′ in 15 to 20 years, more open than 'Blue Arrow'.

'Gray's Gleam'. Silver-gray needles on a pyramidal tree, male, 15 to 20′ by 5 to 7′.

'Moonglow'. Dense pyramidal-conical form with bluish gray-green needles, 20′ by 5′; most common cultivar grown by Oregon nurseries.

'Pathfinder'. Narrow pyramidal regular habit, bluish gray needles in flat sprays, 20′ by 6 to 8′ in 20 years.

SKY HIGH 'Bailigh'. A strongly columnar form with silver-blue needles, 12 to 15′ by 3 to 5′, seedling from North Dakota introduced by Bailey Nurseries.

'Skyrocket'. The narrowest columnar juniper, seldom more than 2′ wide, will grow 15′ high or more, needles primarily acicular (sharp-pointed) and bluish green. Serves as columnar Italian cypress look-alike in cold climates.

'Wichita Blue'. An old standard, pyramidal habit, bright blue needles, 20′ by 5 to 8′.

'Blue Arrow'

'Moonglow'

'Wichita Blue'

SKY HIGH

'Skyrocket'

Juniperus virginiana

eastern redcedar

Evergreen conifer. Infinite in shape, the habits vary from columnar totem poles, pyramidal-conical, to spreading canopies. Notable that the National Champion was 57′ high and 75′ wide. The norm is 30 to 50′ high, less in spread. In the Athens, GA, area, 60′ by 30′, softly pyramidal-oval trees are common. Growth is slow. Bark is a handsome gray (usual) to red-brown, exfoliating in strings and wide strips. Large trunks become fluted, and venerable old trunks are quite beautiful. Almost makes sense to limb up the lower branches on large trees. The wood is resistant to decay and is utilized for chests, cabinets, paneling, and wood bowls.

Foliage: Needles are similar in shape to those of *J. chinensis*, medium green, sage-green, to blue-green in summer, becoming brown-green, bronze-green, to yellow-green in winter. **Flowers/seeds/fruits/cones:** Typically dioecious. Male cones yellow-brown, small, abundant, releasing clouds of yellowish pollen in February-March; female up to ¼″ wide, brownish violet, silvery glaucous bloomy, ripening the first season. The cones are a valuable food resource for wildlife. **Native range:** From the Outer Banks of North Carolina, where salt and sand are the principal media, to the dry soils of the Plains states, it is at home. Found in well-drained, often impoverished soils in the open, on rock outcroppings. In the high pH soils and limestone outcroppings of Tennessee and Kentucky, it is a dominant species. **Adaptability:** Anywhere birds fly; they are the principle purveyors of the seeds, and it is normal to experience entire fence rows and areas under power lines with an endless seedling parade. The resiliency of the species is admirable for it can grow on a spot of land where nothing grew before. It blankets much of the United States from Maine to the Dakotas, south to Florida and Texas, a primary invader of pastures and fallow fields. Zones 3 to 9. **Landscape use:** Commonality incites contempt. However, the cultivars are worthy and satisfy many landscape expectations from screening, hedging, and groupings to single specimen use. One of the few needle evergreens that thrives on absolute neglect. Root systems are somewhat stringy, and containerized plants are preferred. The species serves as an alternate host for cedar apple, cedar quince, and cedar hawthorn rusts. **Street tree use:** Cultivars, when clear-trunked, are acceptable. **In the trade:** Many cultivars are known.

'Brodie'. Grass-green foliage and silver cones. Pretty pyramidal-columnar habit and grows 20 to 30′ high, 6 to 8′ wide. Female. Common in the Southeast, considered a var. *silicicola* (southern redcedar) selection.

Juniperus virginiana

Juniperus virginiana

Juniperus virginiana

EMERALD SENTINEL

'Burkii'

'Burkii'. A broad pyramid, 15 to 25′ high, two-thirds as wide, with bluish needles developing a purple cast in winter. Male.

'Canaertii'. Pyramidal outline, the dark green foliage tufted at the ends of the branches, 20 to 30′ high, slightly less in width. Produces quantities of small, grape-like, whitish blue, bloomy cones.

EMERALD SENTINEL 'Corcorcor'. Tight pyramidal-conical habit with dark green foliage. The foliage color is maintained in winter (zone 8). Among the fastest-growing *J. virginiana* types, averaging 2′ per year. Produces abundant blue-green cones. Listed in nursery trade at 15 to 20′ high, 6 to 8′ wide. Reached 30′ by 10′ in 15 years at the Milliken Arboretum, Spartanburg, SC.

PROVIDENCE 'JVBP3'. Dense, broad-based pyramidal form; root system and transplantability are superior to most cultivars of the species; 20′ by 10′.

TAPESTRY 'JVADR'. Very dense, upright pyramidal form; root system and transplantability are far superior to most cultivars of the species; 25′ by 15′.

PROVIDENCE

TAPESTRY

'Taylor'

'Taylor'

'Taylor'. Increasingly common, receiving plaudits for its narrow columnar form. It emulates the Italian cypress in habit but is more cold hardy. Summer needle color is sage-green turning off-green, bronze-green to brown in winter. Estimate 20 to 25′ high, 4′ wide. Female.

K

Kalopanax septemlobus (K. *pictus*)

castor-aralia

Deciduous. Monotypic genus. This species is a bold textural wonder with large leaves, immense inflorescences, and thickish, coarse stems armed with prominent (lethal), broad-based prickles, a good reason for any sensible nursery grower to leave it off the production list. Ultimate habit is broad-rounded. Large trees are impressive, particularly when the July-August flowers shroud the dark green canopy. Bark is black, deeply ridged and furrowed on large trunks.

Foliage: Like a sweetgum on steroids, 5- to 7-lobed, to 14″ wide, serrate, exceedingly lustrous dark green with potentially rich yellow fall color. Authors have never observed insects or diseases on the foliage. **Flowers/seeds/fruits/cones**: Flowers, white, are produced in spherical umbels 1″ across in large, to 24″ wide, flattish, terminal inflorescences in July-August. Precious few large, cold-hardy trees offer such a formidable flower extravaganza. Bees love the flowers. Fruit is a globose, ⅙″ wide, blackish drupe borne in massive quantities and harvested by the birds. **Native range**: Eastern Russia, China, Korean peninsula, and Japan. **Adaptability**: Since so few trees are planted in the United States, it is difficult to assess widespread adaptability. It is cited as being tolerant of alkaline soils and has a reputation for seeding in (invasiveness), which was an issue at the Arnold Arboretum. Authors were surprised by its hardiness, with fruiting specimens at the Universities of Wisconsin and Maine. Zones 4 to 7. **Landscape use**: Certainly, for the lone specimen tree that few will be able to identify, it might function. Trees

Kalopanax septemlobus

Kalopanax septemlobus

should be transplanted when young into a deep, moist, rich soil in full sun. Be careful around young trees, as even their branches are laden with the sharp prickles. Requires minimal care once established. **Street tree use**: No. **In the trade**: Sold as seed-grown, but very uncommon.

Keteleeria davidiana

David keteleeria

Evergreen conifer. A confusing genus, reduced from 14 species, with the "final" three, *K. davidiana*, *K. evelyniana*, and *K. fortunei*, now 20' high in the Savannah, GA, area. All develop fir-like needles and pyramidal habits in youth. *K. davidiana*, the most cold hardy and most common in cultivation, is detailed herein. It is pyramidal in youth, more open with maturity, typically 30 to 40' high, less in spread. A 35' high tree was recorded at the JC Raulston Arboretum, Raleigh, NC, and a tree exceeding 60' in height grew at Huntington Gardens, San Marino, CA. Growth has been slow in the Dirr garden, but the literature points to 2' per year over a 10-year period. Bark is gray-brown to grayish black, in flakes, elongated scales, and longitudinal furrows.

Foliage: Needles on adult trees are linear, flat, ½ to 1½" long, ⅛ to ¼" wide, shining bright to dark green, spirally arranged with leaf bases twisted and therefore appearing 2-ranked, entire, 2 pale green stomatal bands below, color persisting through winter, apex blunt and not sharp; young seedling trees bear sharp-pointed needles. For reference purposes, *K. evelyniana* has adult needles to 2" long, dull gray-green, 2 wide gray stomatal bands below on either side of the green midrib, stiffer and with a spiny apex; needles are not in the obvious 2-ranks and are curved, pointing upward toward the top of the shoot. **Flowers/seeds/fruits/cones**: Monoecious. Male yellow; female green-purplish to brown. Cones are erect, ripening the first year, pale brown, 3 to 8" long, 1½ to 2" wide, usually in the upper reaches of the tree, falling intact. **Native range**: China, Taiwan. Found in evergreen broadleaf forests. **Adaptability**: Zones 7 to 9, 10 on the West Coast. **Landscape use**: For Abies-deprived regions of the country (e.g., the Southeast, Southwest, and southern California), it makes a fine specimen conifer. The rich needle color is maintained through the seasons, and the large, cylindrical, rich green (before maturing) cones are

Keteleeria davidiana

beautiful. Apparently, an isolated tree will produce viable seed. Seedlings are slow out of the gate. Soils should be moist, acid, and well drained. Requires full sun, yet plants we observed in partial shade were healthy. As a group, the three species display high heat tolerance. **Street tree use**: Potential. **In the trade**: Scarce in commerce but worth the hunt. A contributing factor is slow seedling growth; the difficulty of rooting cuttings compounds the issue. Vegetative attempts to domesticate have been moderately successful.

Keteleeria davidiana

Koelreuteria bipinnata

Chinese flametree

Deciduous. Spectacular in late summer–early fall, when the vivid yellow flowers and soon-thereafter ripening pink capsules brighten a tired landscape. Young trees are similar to broomsticks, the canopy gradually broadening with age. Mature trees are 30 to 40' in height, about two-thirds that in spread. Bark is smooth, gray-brown. The Achilles' heel is the freedom with which it seeds. Authors were enamored of the

Koelreuteria bipinnata

Koelreuteria bipinnata

Koelreuteria bipinnata

pink to rose, 3-valved, papery capsules, each to 2″ long. For 4 to 6 weeks, even longer, the canopy luminesces yellow to pink. The capsules persist into winter, eventually losing the pink coloration. Seeds mature brown, every one viable, so be leery. If capsules are collected when pink and dried, the rose color is retained. **Native range**: China. **Adaptability**: Zones 6 to 8. If some stem tip injury occurs due to cold, plants will still flower, as flowers develop on current season's growth. **Landscape use**: Certainly a beautiful tree if only the seeds were not pestiferous. A prime candidate to breed for sterility. A well-nourished seedling will reach 6 to 8′ or more in a growing season, and 2-year-old seedlings produce flowers and fruits. **Street tree use**: Possibly, but messy. **In the trade**: Available. *K. elegans* (flamegold) is somewhat similar in flower and fruit, the habit more dense and rounded, 20 to 30′ high and wide. Taiwan, Fiji. Zones 9 to 10(11).

species in the past, but observing its fence-jumping ability has dampened enthusiasm.

Foliage: Bi- to tri-pinnately compound leaves, to 20″ and longer, lustrous dark green, arch gracefully and provide a tropical look. Each oval-oblong leaflet is 2 to 3″ long and without the lobing common to *K. paniculata*. **Flowers/seeds/fruits/cones**: Canary-yellow flowers in late summer, when precious few trees offer color, the inflorescences profusely borne, 12 to 24″ high to 18″ wide. Truly eye-catching, they open over a long period, then give way to the developing

Koelreuteria paniculata
goldenrain tree, pride of India

Deciduous. A spreading tree, usually low-branched and somewhat irregular in branching, it eventually develops a broadly rounded, symmetrical crown, with the mature canopy varying from globose to broad-spreading. Medium-textured in summer, more coarse in winter, with a moderate growth rate to 30′ tall, 35′ wide. Bark is thin and brownish when young, then gray-brown, ridged and furrowed.

Foliage: Large pinnately or bipinnately compound leaves are 6 to 18″ long, with leaflets 1 to 4″ long, irregularly lobed and incised. New growth emerges reddish, then unfolds to bright green, but is susceptible to spring freezes. Holds dark green summer color well in hot weather. Fall color is yellow to golden orange, sometimes good but often inconsistent. **Flowers/seeds/fruits/cones**: Individual flowers are small, about ½″ wide, but they are profuse and held in large panicles, over 12″ long and wide. Bright yellow, they occur in the heat of summer when little else is in bloom, from early June until late July, depending on location. The fruit is a 2″ long, papery seed capsule, greenish, maturing to light brown. They provide a second show of color in late summer; trees look as if they were decorated with tiny Chinese lanterns. **Native range**: China, Japan, Korea. **Adaptability**: Widely adaptable, taking heat, wind, drought and alkaline soils. Tolerates dry and poor soil but should have good drainage. Zones 5 to 8 in the East, and 9 in the coastal West. **Landscape use**: A bright spot in the summer landscape, it is particularly valuable for its uncommon flowering: few temperate trees produce bright yellow flowers, and few bloom in midsummer. Needs room in the landscape because of low branches and spreading form. Needs full sun to flower well. **Street tree use**: 'Fastigiata' is excellent, but other forms are too broad-spreading for most city applications, although they are well suited for roadside plantings and broad interchanges. **In the trade**: Widely sold as seed-grown. The cultivars are improvements, but they are difficult to propagate, so availability is often low.

'Coral Sun'. The spring color of shoots and foliage is a little otherworldly, shockingly beautiful when you first experience it. New shoot growth emerges coral-red, accompanied by unfolding orange-yellow leaves. As spring progresses, shoot color fades and the foliage becomes more yellow-green and then finally the typical green of the species. Fall leaves are yellow, held against the red rachis. 25′ by 25′.

'Fastigiata'. Strongly upright and extremely narrow, this plant is truly fastigiate in form. Expect a 25′ tall, 8′ wide column. Great for narrow garden spaces or tight street locations, for which it is well adapted; it can handle the reflected heat from concrete.

GOLDEN CANDLE 'Golcanzam'. Fastigiate form. In a side-by-side comparison with 'Fastigiata', we could not see a difference. Shy flowering.

'Rose Lantern'. A late-flowering selection with yellow flowers, produced from late August into September. Rose-pink to reddish seed pods are highly ornamental. Round in form, 30′ by 30′.

'September'. Late-flowering, from late August and into September. Differs from 'Rose Lantern' in that its seed pods do not turn red. Reproduces true-to-type from seed. Reportedly less hardy than other cultivars. 30′ by 30′.

Koelreuteria paniculata

Koelreuteria paniculata

'Rose Lantern'

'September'

'Coral Sun'

Koelreuteria paniculata

'Fastigiata'

K

SUMMERBURST

SUMMERBURST 'Sunleaf'. A nursery selection, chosen for its outstanding foliage, the deepest green and glossiest in the field during the heat of summer. Bright yellow flowers. Heat resistant, broadly rounded form, superior in appearance to seedling trees. 30′ by 30′.

L

Laburnum alpinum
Scotch laburnum, alpine goldenchain

Deciduous. Upright-spreading vase shape, sometimes wide-spreading but still upright, low-branched and often multi-stem. Medium texture, moderate growth rate, to 20′ tall and 25′ wide. Bark is smooth and green to olive-green when young, becoming olive-brown to grayish with age.

Foliage: Trifoliate, oval leaflets deep green above, light green below, nearly glabrous, 1½ to 3″ long. Stems are glabrous. Little fall color. **Flowers/seeds/fruits/cones**: Bright yellow pea-like flowers in long pendulous chains in May and June, to 1′ or more in length. Spectacular in flower. Seeds follow in flattened pods, ripening in the fall. Poisonous. **Native range**: South-central Europe. **Adaptability**: The most cold hardy *Laburnum* species. Otherwise similar to *L. ×watereri*. Zones 4 to 7, 8 in the West. **Landscape use**: Commonly found naturalized in Scotland and Ireland but rarely planted. Most landscape use is of the cultivar 'Pendulum', which is a charming little weeper for small garden spaces. **Street tree use**: Not recommended. **In the trade**: 'Pendulum', a small, tightly weeping ornamental, often top grafted, gains very little height except when it is staked. Otherwise it weeps gracefully to the ground. Leaves and flowers are somewhat diminutive compared to the species, but it's a cute plant and pretty in bloom. Very slow-growing, an old plant may reach 10′ tall and 5′ wide.

Laburnum alpinum

Laburnum alpinum

Laburnum anagyroides
common laburnum, goldenchain

Deciduous. Upright-spreading vase-shaped or widely vase-shaped, usually low-branched. Medium texture, moderate growth rate, to 30′ tall and 25′ wide. Bark is smooth and green to olive-green when young, staying smooth and becoming olive-brown to grayish with age.

Foliage: Trifoliate leaves, each leaflet elliptic to elliptic-ovate, medium green, 1 to 3″ long. Little fall color develops. Pubescent stems differentiate it from *L. alpinum*. **Flowers/seeds/fruits/cones:** Bright yellow pea-like flowers in 1′ long pendulous chains in May and June, finely pubescent. Spectacular in flower. Seeds follow in flattened, pubescent pods, ripening in the fall. Poisonous. **Native range:** Southern Europe. **Adaptability:** Similar to *L. ×watereri*. Zones 5 to 7, 8 on the West Coast. **Landscape use:** A small garden tree, now largely replaced by *L. ×watereri* 'Vossii'. **Street tree use:** Not recommended. **In the trade:** Sold as seed-grown, but mostly used as a rootstock for *Laburnum* cultivars. For 'Columnaris', see *L. ×watereri*.

Laburnum anagyroides

Laburnum ×watereri
hybrid goldenchain

Deciduous. A small, upright vase-shaped tree, usually stiffly branched, with some openness. Medium texture, moderate growth rate, to 25′ high and 20′ wide. Branches distinctly olive-green. Bark is smooth, green to olive-green on younger trees, becoming yellowish olive-brown to grayish with age.

Foliage: Trifoliate leaves, each leaflet 1¼ to 3″ long, elliptic with an acute tip, bright green. Little fall color develops. **Flowers/seeds/fruits/cones:** Spectacular in the flower. Bright yellow pea-like flowers cluster densely in pendulous chains (racemes) a foot or so in length, occasionally reaching 20″. Flowering is usually heavy, and the abundance of the flowers will color the entire tree until little green can be seen. Flowers in late spring after the tree has fully leafed out, May to June, depending on location. Quite fragrant. Seeds develop in flattened green pods that turn brown in the fall and split open to disperse seeds. All parts of the plant are poisonous, especially the seeds. **Native range:** A hybrid of *L. alpinum* and *L. anagyroides*, both European. **Adaptability:** A tree that likes a cool mild climate, well adapted to the maritime Pacific Northwest and western Europe. It needs well-drained soil. Zones 5 to 7, 8 in the West. **Landscape use:** Can be breathtakingly beautiful when it is in full bloom. But it doesn't have much to recommend it at other times of the year, and its highly poisonous seeds makes its use in areas where children are present a poor idea. Can be espaliered against walls and into arches. The root system seems to be rather weak, as almost all the larger trees we have seen growing in the winter-wet soils of the Pacific Northwest eventually take on a leaning posture. **Street tree use:** Not recommended due to soil conditions on streets, frequency of leaning, and poisonous seeds on public sidewalks. **In the trade:** Available.

'Columnaris' ('Sunspire'). Sometimes listed as *L. anagyroides*. Fortunately the plant is much more distinct than its name. Very tight, compact, upright form. Not really columnar, but a tight narrow oval form with ascending branches, to 16′ tall and 8′ wide. Short internodes make it dense. Bright yellow flowers are also in shorter chains, but so densely packed that the whole tree glows brilliant yellow in flower.

'Vossii'. By far the most popular cultivar of the genus. If you see a laburnum, this is probably it. Stiffly vase-shaped, but it appears much softer in form when in bloom because of the pendulous chains of flowers. Bright golden yellow in flower, the flower color seems to be slightly richer than its two parent species. Faster growing than either parent, 25′ tall and 20′ wide.

'Columnaris'

'Vossii'

'Vossii'

Lagerstroemia indica

common crapemyrtle

Deciduous. Extremely variable species that has given rise to every flower color but yellow and blue, while providing a range of growth habits from small shrubs to 40′ trees. From the authors' breeding experiences, a handful of seed leads to unfathomable variation. Unfortunately, this has promoted the introduction of untold cultivars, now over 1,000, with more in the wings. Although beautiful at their floral best, pure *L. indica* types are affected with mildew and cercospora, both diseases affecting leaf aesthetics and/ or retention. Growth habit is always multi-stemmed unless trained as a standard with a single stem. Inevitably, suckers (adventitious shoots) develop from bare trunks and should be removed. Growth is fast. Habit in the larger forms is always vase-shaped with slender shoots developing terminal flowers in the heat of summer. The smooth, sinewy bark runs a brief gamut from gray to brown. Exfoliating occurs in summer, with often shaggy sheets sloughing from the trunk.

Foliage: Leaves are 1 to 3″ long, elliptical to obovate, margins entire, apex pointed, emerging yellow-green, bronze, red-purple, maturing lustrous medium to dark green. Fall color is seldom considered an attribute but is often spectacular—yellow, orange, or red, often all colors interspersed—especially when fall is cool (but temperatures remain above 28°F). **Flowers/seeds/fruits/cones**: Rounded/spherical polished flower buds are attractive and open to 6-petaled, full flowers in 6 to 8″ long, 3 to 5″ wide panicles. Color range is enormous, white, lavender, purple, pink, and red, with shades in between. Additionally, the yellow stamens provide a pretty contrast to the petal colors. Fruit is a 6-valved dehiscent, ⅜ to ½″ wide, broad-rounded brown capsule containing numerous flattened winged brown seeds. Authors see no redeeming quality in the aging fruit. Ideally, plants can be tidied by removing the old fruit clusters, which otherwise persist through winter, often into the next flowering cycle. **Native range**: China, Korea. **Adaptability**: The greatest attribute of *L. indica* and kin, beyond floral propensity, is adaptability to almost any soil, except wet. Absolute cold hardiness ratings are nebulous, but (6)7 to 9 is reasonable. At the U.S. National Arboretum and University of Georgia, the search for a zone 5 common crapemyrtle was for naught. At -10°F some stem dieback will occur. Young foliage is quite susceptible to late spring frosts; below-freezing temperatures will injure the leaves. **Landscape use**: For summer flower effect, there are few equals. Since flowers are formed on new growth, color is nonstop through the growing season; as practiced in the Dirr garden (zone 8), spent flowers

Lagerstroemia indica

PINK VELOUR

PINK VELOUR

RED ROCKET

are removed, with a second, occasionally third, sequence of rebloom. Nor do flowers wilt in the searing heat. In 2016, Athens, GA, experienced 83 days of 90°F or greater; flowering was outstanding on specimens that never experienced any supplemental water. In warm-climate areas (middle to Deep South, Southwest, California), flowers are possible for 2 to 3 months. Plants require full sun to maximize flowering. Crapemyrtle transplants readily and once established is a lifer, adding year-round attributes to landscapes. Do not prune in late summer–early fall as this predisposes plants to early fall freeze damage. Aphids, Japanese beetles, ambrosia beetles, and a new scale are problematic. **Street tree use**: Many cities in the Southeast utilize *L. indica* and the hybrids for street tree plantings, which are more often successful than not. Forms with a clear single trunk as well as larger multi-stemmed cultivars are common along streets, walks, and in medians. **In the trade**: Carl Whitcomb, Lacebark Farms, Oklahoma, introduced many cultivars. Those listed here were derived from *L. indica*.

DOUBLE DYNAMITE 'Whit X'. A 2016 red-flowered, sterile introduction with wine-colored new growth. It flowered continuously for 100 days in Oklahoma. Estimated size is 8 to 10′, but it will probably grow larger.

DYNAMITE 'Whit II'. Crimson flower buds, cherry-red flowers, emerging crimson leaves, growing to 20′ high. Spectacular in flower. Susceptible to cercospora.

PINK VELOUR 'Whit III'. Bright pink flowers, burgundy-wine emerging foliage maturing purple-green to dark green, upright habit, 10 to 15′ high and half as wide.

RED ROCKET 'Whit IV'. A pretty selection with cherry-red flowers and dark green leaves, growing 15′ and higher. Observed slight mildew. Less susceptible to cercospora than DYNAMITE and superior to it in Georgia trials. From a distance difficult to discern from DYNAMITE.

Lagerstroemia speciosa
queen's crapemyrtle

Deciduous to semi-evergreen. A large tree to 75′ high, usually smaller under cultivation, 40 to 60′ by 30 to 40′. Habit is vase-shaped with a rounded canopy. Extremely fast growth; seedlings grew 8′ high in a single season in University of Georgia testing (and all were killed by cold the following winter). Bark is smooth, gray-brown, mottled and exfoliating.

Foliage: Leaves are 2 to 4″ long, dark green, becoming red in fall/winter. **Flowers/seeds/fruits/cones**: Flowers, light pink, saffron-pink to purple, are borne in 1′ long panicles, each flower up to 3″ wide. Flowering in Florida occurs in June and

July. Fruit is a rounded, ½″ wide, 6-valved capsule. **Native range**: China and southeast Asia. **Adaptability**: Adaptable species with tolerance to alkaline and acid soils as long as well drained. Best suited to zones 10 and 11, the warmer the better. **Landscape use**: Requires full sun. Reserved for South Florida, the Southwest, and southern California. Authors have observed in Orlando, FL, but plant was quite shrubby, possibly reflective of cold damage; leaves were still present when observed in December at H. P. Leu Gardens there. Excellent for urban areas, but seldom utilized except in warmer areas of the United States. **Street tree use**: Widely utilized where adapted. **In the trade**: Available.

Lagerstroemia subcostata var. *fauriei* (L. *fauriei*)
crapemyrtle

Deciduous. Relatively unknown Japanese tree species reaching 40 to 50′, usually low-branched with several large trunks, forming a cloud of foliage akin to an overloaded ice cream cone. Growth is fast. Bark is sensational, smooth, muscular, exfoliating, ranging in color from tawny cinnamon to rusted steel and deep Belgian dark chocolate; stems 2″ in diameter develop the rich coloration. This remarkable species was a major player in the late great Don Egolf's Indian series of crapemyrtle hybrids; Egolf combined it with *L. indica* and/or *L. limii* to produce a spectrum of flower colors, growth habits, and rich bark colors.

Foliage: The medium green, entire-margined leaves, 2 to 4″ long, turn shades of yellow in autumn, on occasion rivaling the color of birches. Leaves originate from stems in a slight arching, semi-pendulous orientation. **Flowers/seeds/fruits/cones**: Flowers are white, moderately fragrant, in 2 to 4″ upright panicles along the shoots. Flowers occur after the leaves have fully developed, typically before *L. indica* and the hybrids, in late May to early June in zone 8 Georgia. In cool-summer zone 8 Oregon, it takes until August or sometimes early September to accumulate enough heat for flowering. The effect is quite formidable, but there is typically no rebloom, as with *L. indica* and the hybrids. Fruits are 6-valved, rounded, dehiscent capsules containing numerous small winged seeds. Fruits persist on the plant through winter and are somewhat untidy. Considering the tremendous quantity of seeds produced by the genus in general, authors seldom witness stray, out-of-bounds runaways. **Native range**: Japan, where it occurs on slopes above watercourses. John Creech, U.S. National Arboretum, introduced the species to the United States in 1957. The mature specimens at the JC Raulston Arboretum are derived from this seed. **Adaptability**: If sufficiently hardened, estimate cold hardiness to -10°F. Zones 6 to 9. **Landscape use**: Transplanting has been something of an issue, and the superior flowering

Lagerstroemia subcostata var. *fauriei*

of the hybrids has simply overshadowed this taxon. Provide full sun, well-drained, preferably acid soils, and fertilize to stimulate shoot growth and thus large flowers. *L. subcostata* var. *fauriei* is more resistant to powdery mildew and cercospora leafspot; these advantages are ensconced in many of the hybrids. **Street tree use**: Authors speculated that the species and cultivars would become prominent urban street trees, but this has not occurred. **In the trade**: Several pure var. *fauriei* cultivars have been introduced, but they have been unable to compete with the hybrids.

'Fantasy'. A large tree, 30 to 40′ high, two-thirds as wide, typically low-branched, multi-trunked with sinewy, rust-red to cinnamon-brown exfoliating bark. Site with the expectation that it will consume a large expanse of the garden. Potential for street tree use. White flowers, yellow fall color.

HIGH COTTON 'Worthington's Upright'. Similar in many respects to 'Sarah's Favorite', this selection reaches 40′ by 25′. Flowers are white, bark is the beautiful exfoliating reddish brown typical of var. *fauriei* types.

'Kiowa'. One of Egolf's favorites, with attributes similar to 'Natchez' except with a much deeper rich brown bark. Difficult to produce from cuttings.

'Fantasy'

'Fantasy'

'Fantasy'

'Townhouse'

'Kiowa'

'Townhouse'

'Townhouse'. A slightly smaller, 20 to 30′ high version of 'Fantasy' with richer, deeper, dark rust-red to chocolate-brown bark. It is more wide-spreading than 'Fantasy'. Flowers are white.

'Woodlander's Chocolate'. Not well known, yet has the darkest chocolate bark, the outer lighter layers exfoliating in shaggy masses to expose the deep chocolate coloration. White flowers. Estimate 20 to 30′ in height.

Hybrids

The first wave of hybrids derived from *L. indica*, *L. limii*, and *L. subcostata* var. *fauriei* came from Don Egolf, in his pioneering work at the U.S. National Arboretum; his best tree types are listed here. Then, Cecil Pounders, Mississippi State University and USDA-ARS, orchestrated a transformational shift in *Lagerstroemia* traits with the development of DELTA JAZZ 'Chocolate Mocha'. The dark purple-maroon foliage displays greater resistance to mildew and cercospora diseases; the foliage and disease resistances are inheritable. Flowers are pink, usually not profuse. These characteristics encouraged breeders to venture forth, and the current introductions—all in series BLACK DIAMOND (9), 'Ebony' (5), DELTA (6), and BLACK MAGIC (5)—represent the tip of the iceberg. All have purple-maroon to dark chocolate-purple leaves, with flower colors of white, pink, lavender, purple, and red. Most are less than 10′ high, but upright, almost columnar MOONLIGHT MAGIC (white, 12′) and TWILIGHT MAGIC (rich pink, 16′) are easily fashioned into small trees. Larger tree types (20′ high and greater) like 'Muskogee' and 'Natchez' are effective for allées; we guarantee more are being bred as we write.

'Apalachee'. More upright, 15 to 20′ high, with light lavender flowers and gray-brown bark.

'Arapaho'. Grows 15 to 20′ high, produces red flowers with purple overtones, brown bark.

'Choctaw'. Bright pink, 20′.

'Miami'. Dark pink, 20′.

'Muskogee'. Along with 'Natchez', common in commerce. Produces lavender-pink flowers, light tan bark, growing 20′ and taller. Authors noted a 30′ by 30′ specimen at Norfolk Botanical Garden, foliage 100% intact, dark green, blemish-free in October. Often develops orange-red fall color.

'Natchez'. The best white-flowered cultivar, eventually 20 to 30′ high and wide, the bark cinnamon-brown. Lagerstroemias are rare in Oregon landscapes, but the Warren garden features a multi-stem 'Natchez' arching 30′ over the front of the house, chosen after testing numerous crapemyrtle

DELTA JAZZ

DELTA JAZZ

'Apalachee'

'Arapaho'

'Apalachee'

'Muskogee'

MOONLIGHT MAGIC

TWILIGHT MAGIC

cultivars for adaptability to the cool climate. Flowering is very late, but the mottled mosaic orange/tan/gray bark and the red fall color more than make up for this. A favorite.

'Sarah's Favorite'. Much like 'Natchez', possibly more cold hardy, with a longer flowering period. This was derived from Egolf's work and inadvertently named by a southern nursery; 20′ high and greater. Excellent red fall color on occasion.

'Sioux'. Beautiful rich pink flowers, lustrous leaves that emerge bronze in spring then turn dark green, on a 15′ high plant.

'Tuscarora'. Coral-pink flowers on 20′ high plant with light brown bark.

'Tuskegee'. Dark pink to near red, 20′ by 20′.

'Wichita'. Light magenta to lavender, 16 to 20′.

'Muskogee'

'Muskogee'

'Muskogee'

'Natchez'

'Natchez'

'Natchez'

'Natchez'

Larix decidua
European larch

Deciduous conifer. Pyramidal in form with a strong central trunk, the primary branches spreading horizontally and fine branches drooping. With age the crown becomes more rounded and the form more open. Fine-textured, fast-growing to 75′ high and 30′ wide. Bark is gray-brown, thin and scaly on younger trees, becoming ridged and fissured with age.

Foliage: Needles are bright, light green when they are fresh in spring, much softer appearing than those of evergreen conifers. Needles held singly on new growth, up to 1½″ long, needles on older growth in whorl-like clusters on spurs, usually slightly shorter. They become deep green by midsummer and turn yellow to golden amber in the fall before dropping. **Flowers/seeds/fruits/cones**: Monoecious. Immature female cones ½″ long, egg-shaped, reddish, developing into brown ovoid cones, to 1½″ long, at maturity. Male pollen cones are smaller, yellowish. Scales on mature cones are overlapping and not reflexed, differentiating it from *L. kaempferi*. Old female cones persist on the tree, looking a little scruffy on the bare winter branches. **Native range**: Central Europe. **Adaptability**: Likes a cool climate, tolerant of wet soils, but needs full sunshine. Zones 2 to 6. **Landscape use**: Suitable for parks or large properties. It can look stark when alone and bare in the winter, but planted in front of other large, dark conifers, its deciduous cycle of bright green spring needles and yellow fall colors contrasts beautifully. Most landscape use is of cultivars, specially selected for smaller size and less upright growth; these are much more suited to the residential garden. Larch casebearer is a serious imported pest; it feeds on the needles and can cause summer defoliation, leaving trees stressed. **Street tree use**: Not typically used but should be considered. Needs space on the street and moisture, so suitable locations would be limited. **In the trade**: Available.

Larix decidua

Larix decidua

Larix decidua

'Pendula'

'Varied Directions'

'Horstmann's Recurva'

'Horstmann's Recurva'. Fine-textured branches twist, curve, and turn in a fantastical manner, yet the central trunk grows vertically, producing a generally pyramidal form. The tree in winter form may be even more impressive than in summer foliage. Slower growing and smaller than the species, to 15′.

'Pendula'. Several weeping clones are sold under this name. Most are actually the *L. kaempferi* selection of the same name.

'Varied Directions'. Another weeping cultivar, more common, not quite so weeping. The trunk grows upward then bends to horizontal; branches spread stiffly outward, then weep downward, then the tips reflex outward: like the name says, varied directions. Size and form depend on training, 10′ tall and 20′ wide is typical. Sometimes listed as *L. ×eurolepis*.

Larix kaempferi

Japanese larch

Deciduous conifer. Pyramidal in form with a strong central trunk and radiating horizontal branches that sweep slightly upward, and fine secondary branching that tends to weep downward gracefully from the main structure. Becoming broader and more open with age. Fine-textured, fast-growing, to 75′ high, 40′ wide. Bark is gray-brown, thin and scaly on younger trees, developing platy ridges and fissures with age.

Foliage: Needles are bright, light green when they first appear in spring. Needles up to 1½″ long, held singly on new shoots, in whorl-like clusters on spurs on older growth. They become deep green in summer and turn golden to amber-orange in the fall. **Flowers/seeds/fruits/cones**: Monoecious. Pollen cones similar to *L. decidua*. Female cones also similar, but scales on cones are reflexed, curving outward and giving the cone a rosette appearance, probably the best characteristic to separate these two similar species. **Native range**: Japan. **Adaptability**: Prefers a cool climate, but will take a little more heat than *L. decidua* and *L. laricina*. Tolerant of wet soils, but needs full sunshine. Of the common larch species, it has the broadest adaptation to temperate climates and urban settings. Zones 4 to 7, 8 in the West. **Landscape use**: Uses similar to *L. decidua*. **Street tree use**: Needs a lot of space, but a street planting where the strip was wide enough would be beautiful. **In the trade**: Most available plants are smaller cultivars.

'Diana'. Truly elegant. When small, you would never think this cultivar would produce a straight trunk. The leader and branches all twist and curl like a corkscrew. But as it grows the trunk becomes straight and the form symmetrically pyramidal, with all fine branching tending to weep down gracefully, in curls. Grows slowly to 40′ tall, 15′ wide, taller and wider than the similarly contorted *L. decidua* 'Horstmann's Recurva'.

'Pendula'. A weeping form, generally growing as tall as it is staked, perhaps 10 to 15′, and then cascading directly to the ground and varying from a graceful cascade to a mop head, depending on pruning. Spend some time training it. The freshness of the spring foliage and the fall color create a very different effect than more common evergreen weeping conifers. This seems to be the common 'Pendula' in the trade.

Larix kaempferi

Larix kaempferi

'Diana'

Larix kaempferi

'Diana'

Larix laricina

eastern larch, tamarack

Deciduous conifer. Pyramidal in form, narrow when young, with a straight slender trunk and radiating branches. Small branches on older trees tend to droop. Mature trees become more open. Fine-textured, moderately fast-growing to 60' with a 20' spread. Bark is thin and smooth on younger trees, becoming reddish brown to gray and scaly with age.

Foliage: Needles ¾ to 1¼" long, held singly on new shoots, in whorl-like clusters on spurs of older growth. They are bright and fresh when they appear in spring but are more bluish green than those of other larches. Fall color is a clean bright golden yellow. **Flowers/seeds/fruits/cones**: Monoecious. Immature cones are small; females rosy and males yellowish. Mature female cones are ovoid, brown at maturity and less than 1" in length, considerably smaller than cones of *L. decidua* and *L. kaempferi*. **Native range**: Northern North America; Newfoundland, south to Pennsylvania and the Great Lakes and north to the Arctic Circle across most of Canada and central Alaska. **Adaptability**: Very cold hardy and needs a cool climate. Well adapted to wet, acid, boggy soils. Best used within its native range. Zones 2 to 5. **Landscape use**: A beautiful conifer for naturalizing, but respect its need for cool weather. Can be defoliated by larch casebearer. **Street tree use**: Not recommended. **In the trade**: Sold as seed-grown. The few named cultivars are dwarf, not tree types.

Larix laricina

Larix laricina

Laurus nobilis

true laurel, sweet bay

Broadleaf evergreen. Upright, dense, low-branched or sometimes multi-stemmed, broadly pyramidal to irregularly oval, although often seen sheared, hedged, or as a topiary in cultivation. Medium texture and rather slow-growing; garden plants may reach 20′ high and 15′ wide, although in an ideal climate the species can grow to 50′. Bark is smooth, light gray.

Foliage: Dark green, lustrous leaves, typically 3″ long, elliptic with an acute tip and a slightly wavy leaf margin. Highly aromatic; crush a leaf and the familiar smell will identify it. **Flowers/seeds/fruits/cones**: Dioecious. Fragrant cream-yellow flowers are borne in April, in axillary clusters. Although the flowers are small, the clusters contrast with the dark foliage and are more showy than their size would suggest. Dark purple to black, ½″ long fruits follow, ripening in autumn and holding into the winter on female trees. **Native range**: Scattered distribution in the Mediterranean region from Spain to Syria. **Adaptability**: Limited mostly by cold hardiness, although hardier individuals have been selected. Will grow in the South but happiest in warmer areas on the West Coast. Zones 8 to 11. **Landscape use**: A bushy garden tree, often sheared and frequently grown in containers as a topiary. The scent of this plant's foliage is a culinary experience; spaghetti sauce without bay leaves is just not spaghetti sauce. Often grown close to the kitchen for fresh use. **Street tree use**: No, too wide, slow, and dense. **In the trade**: Available.

'Angustifolia' (f. *angustifolia*). Narrow, willow-like foliage gives a finer-textured appearance; more symmetrical in form, 15′ tall, 10′ wide. Better cold hardiness than the type, can be used in zone 7.

'Aurea'. Bright yellow foliage, especially on the tips. Foliage color transitions to lime-green in the interior of the plant. 12′ tall, 15′ wide.

EMERALD WAVE 'Monem'. A narrow leaf form similar to 'Angustifolia' but with wavy leaf margins, giving it a more interesting texture. Upright, pyramidal, 15′ tall and 10′ wide.

'Saratoga'. Possible hybrid with *L. azorica*. Rounded shape. Leaves are larger, more oval than typical of the species. Vigorous, to 25′ tall and 20′ wide. Resistant to laurel psyllid but a little less cold hardy than others, consider it zone 9. Male, fruitless.

Laurus nobilis

Laurus nobilis

EMERALD WAVE

Libocedrus decurrens. See
Calocedrus decurrens

Ligustrum lucidum

waxleaf privet, glossy privet, Chinese privet

Broadleaf evergreen. Difficult for the authors to embrace this large, oafy species because of its highly invasive tendencies. Often found in old farmsteads in the Southeast, where trees 25′ high and greater are common. Habit is oval to rounded with a dense canopy. Growth rate is fast; seedlings reach 6 to 10′ in a growing season. Bark is gray-brown, relatively smooth with a fluted trunk.

Foliage: The leathery glossy dark green leaves with 6 to 8 vein pairs, 3 to 6″ long, 1 to 2½″ wide, are ovate (egg-shaped) with entire margins. Often confused with *L. japonicum* but differs in having translucent veins (vs. opaque in *L. japonicum*). **Flowers/seeds/fruits/cones**: In June-July the canopy is covered with cream-yellow flowers in 5 to 8″ high and wide panicles. Flowers remain effective for a month or longer and are followed by dull blue-black, ⅓ to ½″ long fruit. The fruits persist into winter and are widely dispersed by birds. Privet-like fragrance. **Native range**: Southern and eastern China. **Adaptability**: Remarkably (not to say dangerously) adaptable to hot, dry, wet, acid, alkaline, sun, and shade conditions. Zones 7 to 10. At -3°F in the Athens area, plants were severely injured or killed to the ground. Unfortunately, many resprouted from the base/roots, producing an impenetrable thicket of arrow-shaft stems. **Landscape use**: A suitable urban tree only if rendered sterile via modern breeding techniques. **Street tree use**: Utilized in

warm-climate countries. **In the trade**: Rarely available. Variegated cultivars are occasionally offered; even these will produce fruits and all will revert, so be vigilant about removing green shoots. 'Excelsum Superbum' and 'Excelsum Variegatum' offer creamy yellow- and white-margined leaves with green centers, respectively; they are slower growing than the species. 'Tricolor' has copper-pink young leaves with an irregular narrow border turning white with maturity; the emerging foliage is quite attractive; reportedly 35′ high.

'Excelsum Superbum'

'Tricolor'

Ligustrum lucidum

Ligustrum lucidum

Liquidambar acalycina
Chang sweetgum

Deciduous. The Sino-American Botanical Expedition of 1980 was responsible for the first arrivals of this species, which caused an initial stir with its rich reddish maroon new growth. Habit is similar to the native *L. styraciflua*, slightly more open, initially pyramidal, becoming oval-rounded. Growth is fast; authors have not observed weak branch structure.

Foliage: The 3-lobed leaves, 4 to 6″ wide, emerge red-maroon, mature dark green, turning degrees of burgundy in fall. In Georgia, leaves persist into December. Foliage is beautiful and does not suffer from leafspot that may occur on *L. styraciflua*. **Flowers/seeds/fruits/cones**: Monoecious. Male flowers in an upright panicle; females within a ¾″ rounded aggregate. Fruit is a soft bristly aggregate of capsules, typically 15 to 26 per. This is a reasonable separatory characteristic from *L. formosana*, which has 24 to 43 capsules per. **Native range**: China. **Adaptability**: The species exhibited good adaptability and was successfully grown at the Arnold Arboretum and in Athens, GA. Zones 6 and 7, but may perform well in zone 8. At -10°F plants were not injured. **Landscape use**: For the avid collector, it may prove worthy. As a park, golf course, arboretum specimen, there is merit. Grows best in acid, well-drained soils and is extremely heat and drought tolerant based on Georgia performance. **Street tree use**: Potential. **In the trade**: With so many cultivars of our native sweetgum in commerce, this species was not heavily promoted and is seldom available. The introduction from China by Canada's Piroche Plants was 'Burgundy Flush', so termed for the color of its emerging foliage. In all traits it paralleled the species description just given. Trees tested in Oregon showed occasional dieback from early fall freezes and no advantage over our native sweetgum.

Liquidambar acalycina

'Burgundy Flush'

'Burgundy Flush'

Liquidambar formosana
Formosan sweetgum

Deciduous. Beautiful tree in its finest incarnation, as it matures to a noble rounded specimen with large imposing branches. Growth is moderate to fast. In Georgia trials, the species reached 20′ by 14′ in 6 years; on the Georgia campus, a 50′ by 50′ specimen impresses. These two trees reflect the variability in fall color—the campus tree a beautiful yellow in late November into December; the trial tree bright orange-red to deep burgundy. Bark is gray-brown, ridged and furrowed. Worth noting that the species flowers 2 to 3 weeks ahead of *L. styraciflua*, so cross-pollination is impossible. No stray seedlings have ever occurred on either Georgia tree.

Foliage: Buds, to ⅝″ long, conical, are covered with silky brown hairs (those of *L. styraciflua* are green-brown-red and glabrous). Leafs out 2 to 3 weeks earlier than *L. styraciflua*. Leaves 3-lobed, finely serrate, to 5″ high, 6″ wide, emerge yellow-green to plum-purple (not unlike *L. acalycina*), mature lustrous dark green. Fall color varies, buttery yellow to burgundy; color is effective for 2 to 4 weeks. Resistant to early fall freezes, surviving at least 20°F, with a trickle of leaves persisting into mid-December. **Flowers/seeds/ fruits/cones**: Flowers and fruit are essentially the same as *L. acalycina*. Female flowers held upright in capsular globose heads, as if asking to be pollinated. The mature tree on the Georgia campus had no male flowers. Fruit is soft, bristly (not woody, spiny like *L. styraciflua*). **Native range**: Taiwan, China, Indochina. **Adaptability**: Zones 6 to 9. Authors observed large trees in Mobile, AL, area. **Landscape use**: Based on the limited number of specimens observed by authors, the species has much to offer, especially in warmer climates where noble deciduous trees with exceptional fall color are limited. The species is heat and drought tolerant, the latter fact more important in urban landscapes. In cooler Oregon trials, the species showed little fall color and held foliage too late, into December, and early snow load caused breakage. It's a warm-weather tree. **Street tree use**: Potential. **In the trade**: Seldom available. 'Afterglow' produces lavender-purple new growth and rose-red fall color. Monticola Group is the Chinese form with larger 3-lobed leaves, coloring well in autumn, and with greater cold hardiness.

Liquidambar formosana

Liquidambar formosana

Liquidambar formosana

Liquidambar styraciflua

American sweetgum

Deciduous. A large and impressive tree, neatly pyramidal when young with a strong, straight central leader and radiating branches, becoming more broadly oval with a rounded crown in age. Medium texture, fast-growing, to 60′ tall and 40′ wide. Bark starts developing as orange-brown corky wings on young stems; these develop into corky ridges and furrows at a young age, becoming a more typical gray, ridged and furrowed on older trees. Rough bark adds to winter appeal.

Foliage: Leaves 4 to 7″ long and wide, dark green, moderately glossy, finely serrate, palmate, generally with 5 pointed lobes. Some trees will carry small additional side lobes on the leaf, but most carry leaves that resemble a perfect 5-pointed star. Fall color is among the best, wonderfully variable among individual trees and from year to year. Colors range from yellow and orange through to red and dark purple, sometimes pure, at other times all mixed together on the same tree. **Flowers/seeds/fruits/cones**: Monoecious. Female flowers tiny, simple greenish ovaries with pistils clustered into ½″ dense globose heads; male flowers in dense upright panicles of stamens. Not showy. Fruit, a syncarp of capsules, develops over the summer and matures in fall into a spiny ball, about 1″ in diameter. The fruit is messy to say the least, and if you like to walk barefoot on your lawn, the nasty little balls will give you a good reason to curse. They drop over a period of time, so repeated cleanup is needed. **Native range**: Connecticut to southern Illinois and Florida to east Texas, with disjunct populations at higher elevations in Mexico and Central America. **Adaptability**: Adaptable, it likes moisture and can grow in swampy ground, but it also tolerates drier sites. Quick to regenerate, it colonizes fallow land quickly in a favored environment. Prefers acid soil, can become chlorotic at high pH. Given the broad native range, cold hardiness will vary by seed source and cultivar but is

Liquidambar styraciflua

Liquidambar styraciflua

Liquidambar styraciflua

Liquidambar styraciflua

Liquidambar styraciflua

'Cherokee'

generally considered zones 5 to 9. **Landscape use**: Valued for its impressive size, form, and fall color. It's a great park tree and a wonderful large residential shade tree, with considerable reservation due to the sharp fruit balls. Pay attention to cultivar selection, as individual seedling trees can vary from insignificant to fantastic in fall color, and fruit production can range from virtually seedless to heavy. Roots always seem to be shallow and large, so keep this fast-growing tree away from paved paths or other hard surfaces. Sweetgum is especially susceptible to early season snow and ice loads. It tends to hold foliage later than many deciduous trees, and southern selections planted in the North are especially likely to be surprised by early winter weather. Many times, we have seen late November or December snow and ice loads destroy trees that were still heavily clothed with leaves. Again, cultivar selection is the answer, as most selections drop leaves in a timely manner, unless indicated. **Street tree use**: Selected cultivars can be good street trees, and seed-grown trees can be used along roadsides, where predictability is less important. Roots are among the worst for lifting concrete, so wide planter strips are needed. **In the trade**: Seed-grown trees are widely sold, but we prefer cultivars, not least for their consistent fall color.

'Burgundy'. Named for its purple fall color, this broadly pyramidal selection was introduced in California and is a good choice there and in other southern locations. Late to defoliate; watch out in the North. 60′ tall, 40′ wide.

'Cherokee'. An Illinois selection, cold hardy to zone 5, its main claim to fame is low fruit production. Broader than most, a wide oval, can appear almost round, 50′ by 45′. Medium green foliage is less glossy. Not the most beautiful, but you get cold hardiness.

EMERALD SENTINEL 'Clydesform'. Compact, tightly pyramidal with great foliage, very dark green and quite glossy, presenting a near perfect, formal landscape appearance. Smaller than most, we estimate 35′ by 15′. Fruit production appears light. A favorite of ours, its narrow form makes it good in the city.

'Festival'. Pyramidal in form, somewhat narrow, 50′ by 20′, with dark green summer leaves and good orange to red fall color. A California selection, may hold foliage too late in the North.

EMERALD SENTINEL

'Festival'

EMERALD SENTINEL

GOLD DUST

GOLD DUST 'Goduzam'. A great name for a yellow variegated tree, but beyond the name, we can't distinguish it from 'Variegata'. 45′ by 30′.

'Golden Treasure'. Broad cream-yellow leaf margins, rather than the erratic splashes of 'Variegata'. Overall, it is much lighter in appearance, but we have seen some burning.

Slow-growing and barely rating tree size, perhaps 15′ tall and 10′ wide in 30 years.

HAPPIDAZE 'Hapdell'. A full-sized selection with fast growth, good nursery form, and very low fruit production at maturity. Handsome rich green summer foliage develops good maroon fall color. 60′ tall, 35′ wide.

'Golden Treasure'

'Moraine'

HAPPIDAZE

'Rotundiloba'

'Palo Alto'

'Silver King'

'Lane Roberts'. A British selection with broadly pyramidal form, it develops dark crimson fall color that impresses in bright sun but may look more purple-black on a cloudy day. 60′ tall, 35′ wide.

'Moraine'. Still the most reliably cold hardy of the cultivars. A little slower growing, it maintains a good pyramidal shape and develops reddish purple fall color, to 50′ tall, 25′ wide.

'Palo Alto'. Narrow pyramidal form with bright orange to red fall color, 50′ tall and 25′ wide. A California selection, good for more southern locations. Watch out for late leaf retention and snow load in the North.

'Rotundiloba'. An anomaly among sweetgum cultivars, it has broad rounded lobes rather than the normal acutely pointed ones. Highly glossy foliage is deep green and beautiful, but form is more rounded and open than most. Yellow fall color. Has the best reputation for seedlessness of the cultivars, but some fruits have been reported. A North Carolina selection, it holds its foliage very late in the season, and some plantings have been devastated by snow and ice breakage. We were initially excited, but now very cautious. 45′ tall, 25 to 30′ wide.

'Silver King'. Variegated white, green, and gray-green. Variegation is a bit unstable and mostly occurs as a thin margin. Quite a bit slower-growing than the species to 25′ tall and 15′ wide. We have seen some very pretty individual leaves when growing vigorously, but overall the foliage on the whole tree is usually more ho-hum, without the sparkle desired in a variegated cultivar.

455

'Silver King'

'Slender Silhouette'

'Slender Silhouette'

'Slender Silhouette'. This one gets a "wow." Truly columnar in form, it is a full-height tree, to 60′, but you can expect a width of only 8 to 10′ at maturity. Fastigiate growth is dense and holds tight to the trunk. Good deep green summer foliage; yellow-orange to red fall color. Individually, it is impressive as a landscape exclamation point, and if you plant a row, it makes a great screen. Can set abundant fruit; at least it drops close to the trunk.

'Variegata'

'Worplesdon'

'Variegata'

'Variegata'. Colorful throughout the spring, summer, and fall. Wonderful splashes of yellow and gold color the otherwise green foliage throughout the growing season, then the foliage turns to pink, orange, and red in the fall. Broadly pyramidal to oval in form, maturing slightly smaller than the species, 45′ tall and 30′ wide.

'Worplesdon'. A British cultivar, it performs and colors beautifully in the similar climate of the Pacific Northwest. Pyramidal to broadly pyramidal, it is strong growing to 60′ with a 40′ width. Easily identified by the foliage, the lobes tend to have a few smaller side lobes at the base, looking something like stubby thumbs. Orange-red and purplish mix of fall colors. The one drawback: it fruits very heavily, so use it where that won't be objectionable.

Liriodendron chinense
Chinese tuliptree

Deciduous. A large tree, upright and broadly oval in form. Very fast-growing, coarse in texture, to 70′ tall with a 40′ width. Bark is smooth and greenish brown when young, becoming gray to gray-brown and lightly ridged and furrowed.

Foliage: Big, bold leaves have 2 flaring lobes to each side like our native species, *L. tulipifera*, but the lobes are a little more deeply cut and leaves are significantly larger, sometimes to 12″ across. Foliage is medium green, usually a shade lighter than our native, but often carrying a maroon tint on the new growth. Fall color is yellowish, less impressive than *L. tulipifera*. **Flowers/seeds/fruits/cones**: Light yellow flowers appear with the foliage, 2″ high, with 6 petals surrounding many large, flaring, yellow stamens arranged around the central core-like receptacle of tightly packed pistils. Seeds are produced in a cone-like aggregate of samaras, which mature in fall and shed through the winter. **Native range**: China. **Adaptability**: Experience with this species in the United States has been limited. Seems well adapted to mild areas. Less cold hardy than *L. tulipifera*. Zones 6 to 9(10). **Landscape use**: A large but little-used shade tree. It satisfies the "different" but not the "better" criteria for use. Very similar to our native *L. tulipifera*. It was faster growing in Oregon trial, but slower in Georgia trial, when compared to our native, and its flowers lack the bright orange center of our native. It truly is a fine tree, but we fail to see an advantage over our native tuliptree, and we do have concern about potential weakness in structure. **Street tree use**: Could be tried, especially in the South, but needs lots of room. **In the trade**: Sold as seed-grown. Rare. 'Chapel Hill', a hybrid with *L. tulipifera*, reportedly flowers at an earlier age; uncommon.

Liriodendron chinense

Liriodendron tulipifera
tuliptree

Deciduous. Strongly upright with a sturdy trunk, forming an oval canopy; with age often clear-trunked below with a high canopy above. Medium coarse texture, moderately fast-growing to 70′ tall and 40′ wide; can grow very large, a 200′ specimen recorded. Bark on young trees is smooth and gray, developing a rather neatly formed network of furrows and rounded ridges with age, the furrows lighter gray than the ridges. Said to be the favorite tree of both George Washington and Thomas Jefferson; large trees planted in 1785 are extant at Mount Vernon.

Foliage: Large, medium to dark green leaves with 2 short, broad lobes flaring to each side, 4 to 8″ long and broad. Foliage turns bright yellow in autumn; often one of the best yellows of the fall color season. **Flowers/seeds/fruits/cones**: Bright yellow flowers appear in the foliage near the end of spring, 2 to 3″ in size, tinted with orange in the center. Very showy up close; too bad they are often so high above, where they are best appreciated from an upper-floor window.

Liriodendron tulipifera

Liriodendron tulipifera

Liriodendron tulipifera

Liriodendron tulipifera

Liriodendron tulipifera

'Ardis'

'Aureomarginatum'

EMERALD CITY left, seedling right

Six petals surround many large, flaring, yellow stamens arranged around the central core-like receptacle of tightly packed pistils. Seeds are produced in a cone-like aggregate of samaras, which mature in fall and shed through the winter. **Native range**: Eastern United States, from Massachusetts to Michigan, and Florida to Louisiana. **Adaptability**: Broadly adapted, but does not do well on dry sites; its big leaves require moisture. Nor does it tolerate soggy ground. Likes moist, reasonably well-drained soils; pH adaptable. Zones (4)5 to 9. **Landscape use**: A magnificent and noble shade tree. Give it room; the trunk can be heavy. Large residential lots, campuses, and parks are perfect places. It quickly makes size, yet has a moderate spread for its height and can easily be pruned up for clearance below. Known to be a favorite of aphids; the dripping honeydew can be a problem for the space below. Possible branch breakage is a concern. **Street tree use**: Look to more compact cultivars for streets. Not recommended over parking spaces because of honeydew. **In the trade**: Sold as seed-grown and increasingly as cultivars.

'Ardis'. Compact in every way; the height, trunk diameter, and leaf size are all about a quarter that of the species. Cute but not common, as its slow growth makes it impractical for most nurseries. Eventually to 20′ tall and 15′ wide, nicely shaped.

'Aureomarginatum'. Cream-yellow marginal variegation makes for beautiful foliage in spring. Very ornamental when young, but later in summer and especially later in life as the tree matures, the variegation becomes thin and less notable. 40′ by 20′.

EMERALD CITY 'JFS-Oz'. The most cold hardy cultivar and more suitable to city-sized landscapes, perhaps 20% more compact than seedling trees, with strong upright branching and desirable trunk stiffness, to 55′ tall and 25 to 30′ wide. Foliage is unusually dark green with an attractive gloss. EMERALD CITY is one of Warren's most popular introductions, surprising the authors by surviving cold Ontario and upper Midwest winters where adjacent seedling tuliptrees have died, yet performing beautifully in the heat of the South. Hardiness at least zone 4b.

'Fastigiatum'. A truly fastigiate form, fast-growing and staying columnar. It gets quite tall, like seedling tuliptree,

EMERALD CITY

'Fastigiatum'

EMERALD CITY

but stays more or less true to its narrow shape, 50′ tall and 15′ wide. A group makes a fine screen, and an individual is a definite accent. Often incorrectly sold under the invalid name 'Arnold'.

'Little Volunteer'. A cute little tree and wonderful for the smaller garden, it fits in spaces that a full-sized tuliptree would soon outgrow. Leaves are about a third the size of normal, and growth rate is a third to half as fast. A little faster growing than 'Ardis', thus more practical. Very uniform, pyramidal to upright oval form.

'Little Volunteer'

Lithocarpus henryi
Henry tanbark oak

Broadleaf evergreen. Certainly an unheralded and unknown genus in North American horticulture. Worldwide, more than 300 species are recognized, none native to our continent (the North American tanoak was recently reclassified as *Notholithocarpus*), all with evergreen leaves. Trees of this taxon are open in youth, rounded with maturity, 20 to 30′ high and wide. Growth is slow. Bark is gray-brown, smooth.

Foliage: At its darkest, quite attractive, shining pale green, 4 to 8″ long, 2″ wide, leathery, with an entire margin. Often turns off-yellow in winter, unfortunately. **Flowers/seeds/fruits/cones**: White flowers appear at the ends of shoots in February, in spikes 4 to 8″ long. Fruit is a globose brown acorn, borne on the spike like large beads on a string; acorns ¾″ wide, flattened at top, the cup shallow, thin, ⅛″ deep. **Native range**: China. **Adaptability**: Suited to Pacific Northwest into western British Columbia. Appears adaptable, and plants growing in clay to sand reflect this. Authors observed as far north as Boston, south to Savannah. A 25′ high specimen is extant at the U.S. National Arboretum. Zones 6 to 9. **Landscape use**: A well-grown tree is quite respectable. Given foliage discoloration in winter, a high needle evergreen canopy is warranted. **Street tree use**: No. **In the trade**: Minimally available. Difficult to propagate from cuttings; seed is the only realistic means.

Lithocarpus henryi

Luma apiculata (*Myrtus luma*)
Chilean myrtle

Broadleaf evergreen. A beautiful species, one of those a gardener covets but can seldom grow. References cite trees reaching 60′ in the wild. Under cultivation plants are more shrubby, with multiple stems that accentuate the pretty bark, the major highlight of the species. In Ireland, at Mount Usher, a remarkable 30′ specimen, with the luminescent orange, brown, and white-speckled bark, grew near the house; almost indescribable, but the photo herein does it justice. Growth is slow to medium.

Foliage: Leaves are small, ¾ to 1″ long, broad-ovate, entire; lustrous dark green and aromatic. Foliage maintains the dark green color through the seasons. **Flowers/seeds/fruits/cones**: The bowl-shaped, 4- to 5-petaled, ¾″ wide, white flowers open from midsummer into autumn. Stamens numerous with yellow anthers, forming a boss in the center of the flower. Fruits fleshy, globose, ⅜″ wide, dark purple. The purple fruits are produced in abundance, each ⅓″ wide, and edible. **Native range**: Chile and Argentina.

Adaptability: Adaptable, will grow in any well-drained soil in sun to partial shade, but reserved for the warmest areas, zones 10 and 11. Authors have never observed the species on the East Coast. **Landscape use**: It would make a refined single-stemmed accent tree, 20 to 25′, or multi-stemmed shrub. **Street tree use**: Potential. **In the trade**: Available but uncommon.

Luma apiculata

Luma apiculata

M

Maackia amurensis

Amur maackia

Deciduous. Upright and spreading stiffly to a vase shape with a rounded top, moderately compact. Fine-textured, rather slow-growing, to 25′ high and 25′ wide. Bark is olive-brown when young, becoming more coppery to brown, with curling exfoliation.

Foliage: Alternate and pinnately compound, leaves 8 to 11″ long with 7 to 11 ovate leaflets, each about 2″ long and ¾″ wide. Foliage often silvery gray pubescent and attractive when unfolding in spring, becoming dark green and glabrous in summer. Fall color is greenish yellow to a good yellow.
Flowers/seeds/fruits/cones: Fragrant white flowers, each about ½″ long, are held densely in erect panicles to 6″ long, making a nice display. It flowers when few others do, as the heat of summer comes on in late June to early July, depending on location. Seed pod slender, 1¼ to 2¾″ long, ⅜ to ½″ wide. **Native range**: Northeastern China, Korea, Manchuria.
Adaptability: A tough little cookie, this tree seems to prefer a cold and harsh environment over a mild one. Dry and cold suits it well, but give it full sun. Heat and soggy soils are not to its liking. Well adapted to poor soils, as it fixes its own nitrogen. Not pH sensitive. Zones (3)4 to 7. **Landscape use**: It has a great shape, which is so hard to find in small trees: the stiff upright vase form affords clearance below, making it useful as a small parking lot tree or along the border of

Maackia amurensis

a residence or business without crowding lawn or garden areas. Its fine texture and cold hardiness make it quite useful in many landscape situations. Summer flowers are a bonus we rarely see. Trunk canker has been a problem on newly transplanted trees. Once established, urban-tolerant, a great little low-maintenance tree for the North that should be used more. **Street tree use**: Its adaptability to poor soils and indifference to pH make it a good choice on streets, but it needs to be pruned up and planted in a wide enough strip for branches to clear traffic. **In the trade**: Available.

MAACNIFICENT 'JFS-Schichtel1'. The most consistent grower with the best form and fastest growth rate in nursery trials in Oregon. Symmetrical form, narrowest at the base and flaring up to the top, 30′ tall and 22′ wide. Silvery spring foliage is especially nice and then becomes dark green in summer.

'Starburst'

'Summertime'

MAACNIFICENT

Maackia amurensis

MAACNIFICENT

'Starburst'. A good grower, faster than the species, good density, with leaflets a little larger and more oval than typical, 25′ tall, 20′ wide.

'Summertime'. A proven Minnesota-hardy selection, symmetrical upright vase-shaped form, rounded on top, silvery in spring, summer leaves dark green, but slower growth. 25′ tall, 20′ wide.

M

Maackia chinensis (M. *hupehensis*)
Chinese maackia

Deciduous. Very similar to *M. amurensis*. Upright and stiffly spreading, rounded top, fine-textured, slow-growing, to 25′ high and wide. Bark is olive-brown when young, then brown, with curling exfoliation.

Foliage: Like *M. amurensis*, but usually 11 to 13 ovate leaflets, each 1½ to 2″ long and ¾″ wide. New spring shoots and leaves are quite silvery pubescent, more so than usually seen in *M. amurensis*. **Flowers/seeds/fruits/cones**: Flowers like *M. amurensis*, June to July, but seed pod differs, 1¾ to 3″ long, ¾ to 1″ wide. **Native range**: Central China. **Adaptability**: Similar to *M. amurensis*, less hardy and may be slightly more heat tolerant. Zones (4)5 to 7. **Landscape use**: Use as you would *M. amurensis*. The two species are very similar and hard to distinguish. Some information indicates they may be mixed in the United States, and seed sources are not reliable. **Street tree use**: Appropriate if pruned up for clearance. Tough and nitrogen-fixing. **In the trade**: Rarely sold, seed-grown. Included because future cultivars of this species may prove superior.

Maclura pomifera
Osage-orange

Deciduous. Broad, rounded, typically low-branched tree with sturdy and irregularly upward-spreading branches. Armed with stout, sharp thorns. Medium coarse in texture and fast-growing, maturing to 50′ by 50′. Bark is rough, with stringy to shaggy ridges, orange-brown to brown. Traditionally used for farm hedgerows and grown for its rot-resistant wood, used for fence posts.

Foliage: Dark green, quite glossy, oblong-ovate leaves average 4″ long with acuminate tips. Heat resistant, stays unusually dark and handsome in the heat of summer. In fall, it turns a respectable yellow. **Flowers/seeds/fruits/cones**: Dioecious. Flowers are rather inconspicuous in the foliage, borne in June. Up close, the female flowers are fascinating, in dense globose heads with hundreds of long, thread-like styles, looking a bit like some kind of a shaggy space alien; males are much more mundane, held in short, rounded greenish racemes. Fruit is a 4 to 6″ syncarp of drupes, yellow-green, heavy and dense. The fact that one female cultivar with 3-lb. fruit has been named 'Cannonball' suggests that sitting beneath the tree in the fall might be a poor idea. **Native range**: Arkansas, Oklahoma, Texas. **Adaptability**: Although it has a small native range, it is quite adaptable and has been used in farmsteads and landscapes over a much broader area. Drought tolerant, flood tolerant, pH adaptable; handles prairie heat and wind, and poor soils. Zones 4 to 9. **Landscape use**: Performs well in difficult urban sites. Plain and simple, one tough tree, increasingly appreciated for its lush foliage in the face of heat and drought. That said, transplanting is its weakness. It tends to be tap-rooted, and bare-root planting needs special care; balled-and-burlapped or container planting is easier, but still it needs early planting and first-season water. Development of seedless cultivars with fewer thorns has made its landscape use both practical and desirable. **Street tree use**: Certainly passes the "street tough" test. Tends to be low-branched; needs pruning and training for street clearance. Properly maintained, a very good candidate.

Maclura pomifera

Maclura pomifera

In the trade: Avoid seed-grown trees. Stay with the best cultivars, and use them in industrial sites, poor soils, difficult streets, and harsh climates to bring green back to our cities. Several have been introduced; we list the two male (fruitless) cultivars with the fewest thorns.

'White Shield'. Strongly upright-spreading, a bit wild and leggy when young. Its habit it more upright than 'Wichita', which makes it easier to raise as a street tree with clearance. Wonderfully dark green glossy foliage. Had the fewest thorns of any cultivar in Kansas testing; we have never seen any thorns develop on it. 35′ by 35′.

'Wichita'. Branches more fully and symmetrically than 'White Shield', but that also means it may take more pruning to create street tree clearance. Handsome green foliage. The runnerup in Kansas testing for thorns. We see some short thorns on young nursery trees; they seem to disappear with maturity. Side by side with 'White Shield', it is the better-looking form. 35′ tall, 30′ wide.

'White Shield'

'White Shield'

'Wichita'

M

Magnolia

magnolia

Deciduous and evergreen, *Magnolia* species are among the most cherished of landscape trees, with a superabundance of cultivars. Differentiating the truly great garden cultivars from the Mulligan stew is the challenge. Herein, we feature those prevalent in commerce/cultivation as well as several new introductions.

A major shifting of the tectonic taxonomic plates occurred when the former evergreen species of *Michelia* and *Manglietia* (and others) were merged into *Magnolia*. These genera are at best zones (6)7 to 10. Many of these species initiate flowers in December-January, continuing into May-June. They have been hybridized with the deciduous species to produce flowers with artistic flair. *Magnolia* breeding equates with the runaway freight train. Now that breeders realize the opportunities, the future is forever. For example, Dirr was given a plant that in every characteristic was similar to *M. grandiflora* except it was crossed with *M. sieboldii*. In the second year, it flowered with pristine white tepals, sweet fragrance, and pink stamens. Absolutely stunning! The given name is 'Exotic Star'. Who knew such a cross was possible?

Rather than reiterate details for successful culture and propagation of every species/cultivar discussed herein, a thoughtful management template is presented.

- Purchase plants with flower buds present and ideally on their own roots. Grafted plants are acceptable. Seedlings take many years to flower.
- Select later-flowering types where spring freezes are common. Magnolia tepals (petals and sepals are similar) are injured/killed at 28°F and below.
- Transplant container or balled-and-burlapped plants. Magnolia roots are coarse and lack root hairs (for water and nutrient absorption).
- Site in full sun for maximum flowers. Soil should be well drained, moist, and (in general) acid; chlorosis can occur in high pH soils. Root systems are shallow and are often partially visible above the soil surface.
- Prune after flowering, since the majority of species flower in spring. Flower buds on deciduous species are large and prominent. Learn to recognize the difference between floral and vegetative buds. In most areas of the United States, the flower buds for the next year are developed by June. Any later pruning reduces flower quantities the following spring.
- Promote germination by giving seeds (fleshy aril removed) a requisite 2 to 3 months of cold-moist stratification. Cultivars are rooted from cuttings and grafted.

Magnolia acuminata

cucumbertree magnolia

Deciduous. Qualifies as one of five eastern North American native magnolias. Magnificent, noble tree with massive trunk and branches, eventually forming a rounded to broad-rounded crown. In youth, the habit is distinctly conical-pyramidal. It is vigorous, and 10 to 15′ height increase is reasonable over a 4- to 6-year period. Mature size, 50 to 80′ high and wide. Bark is smooth gray-brown in youth, becoming ridged and furrowed with flat gray ridges and narrow vertical fissures; slight scaling-exfoliating on the flat ridges. The effect is dramatic on large trees, creating an imposing biological monolith.

Foliage: Variable in size, 4 to 10″ long, about half as wide, medium to dark green, entire, turning ash-brown, brown, to yellow-brown in autumn. As an aside, most deciduous *Magnolia* species exhibit similar fall coloration. **Flowers/seeds/fruits/cones:** Flowers are virtually forgotten and lost among the leaves because of the predominantly green (May-June) tepals and the late flowering, after the Asiatic species are reduced to memories. Each flower is 2½ to 3″

Magnolia acuminata

high, composed of 6 tepals, with colors ranging from green, blue-green, to greenish yellow. Many yellow-flowered magnolia hybrids have *M. acuminata* or subsp. *subcordata* in the parentage. Fruits are an aggregate of follicles, each follicle containing 1 or 2 seeds cloaked with a fleshy orange seed coat (aril). Fruits are initially green, turning pinkish red, the follicles splitting in October to reveal the seeds. Each 2 to 3″ long fruit is shaped (more or less) like a cucumber. Flowers are largely self-infertile so must be outcrossed for fruit production; however, self-fertile forms are in the trade. **Native range**: Ontario to Georgia, west to Illinois and Arkansas. **Adaptability**: Authors observed venerable specimens in the Midwest, Northeast, and along the Blue Ridge Parkway in the southern Appalachians. Has performed admirably in the cool, temperate climate of Europe. Adaptable to limestone (higher pH) soils. Does not adapt well to extremely dry conditions. Zones (3)4 to 8. **Landscape use**: Authors consider this one of the most beautiful deciduous magnolias and a terrific addition to large properties. Not suited to restricted planting spaces and urban environments. Provide moist, deep soils laden with organic matter, in full sun to partial shade. Will prosper with ideal cultural attention; languish without. **Street tree use**: Potential. **In the trade**: Not common, owing to lack of spectacular flowers. A few selections

of the true species are available, as are the more numerous yellow-flowered hybrids.

'Fertile Myrtle'. Produces abundant seed from its own pollen (self-fertile) and foreign pollen. Seedlings flower young, an obvious advantage in breeding; true *M. acuminata* but smaller and more upright, estimate 30 to 40′ high.

'Philo'. Selected by Joe McDaniel, University of Illinois, for the green flowers, which are covered with conspicuous waxy blue-white bloom, rendering flowers bluish in color. The original tree was discovered in Philo, IL. Similar to the species in size.

'Urbana'. Another self-fertile selection that was located a block from Dirr's Urbana, IL, home. It was named by McDaniel. Similar to the species in size.

Yellow flowers
Several of the best tree-type hybrids involving *M. acuminata* follow, the cream of European and American evaluations. The perfect yellow magnolia should flower freely and precociously, before the leaves appear yet late enough to escape frost.

M

Magnolia acuminata

'Butterflies'

'Butterflies'

'Gold Star'

'Elizabeth'

'Judy Zuk'

'Lois'

'Elizabeth'

'Lois'

'Anilou'. Deep yellow, 9 tepals, opening with the leaves; upright habit. *M. acuminata* × 'Elizabeth'.

'Butterbowl'. Soft yellow with a pink blush on outside of the tepals, opening before the leaves, smaller, to 2½′ high, with a sweet scent. 'Yellow Bird' × 'Sundance'.

'Butterflies'. Deep yellow flowers, 6 to 12 tepals, precocious, early and may be injured by frost, smaller spreading tree, 18 to 20′ high.

'Yellow Bird'

'Yellow Lantern'

'Petit Chicon'. Yellow flowers, similar to 'Elizabeth' but 6 to 10 days earlier, 30′ high.

'Yellow Bird'. Deep yellow flowers, small, upright tulip shape; open with and after leaves; neat round-canopied tree, resembling a crabapple; 40′ high, 30′ wide. *M. ×brooklynensis* 'Eva Maria' × *M. acuminata* var. *subcordata*.

'Yellow Lantern'. Lemon-cream flowers, large, elongated, tapering; stout, small upright tree, 16½′ high in 10 years; amenable to producing a single-trunked specimen. 'Miss Honeybee' × 'Big Pink'.

Magnolia campbellii
Campbell magnolia

Deciduous. This is a splendid, rounded, thick-canopied, strong-armed tree, fast-growing to 50 to 60′ high and wide, with potential to 80′. In youth, conical to pyramidal. Bark is smooth, gray on young trunks, developing large flat ridges with narrow vertical fissures. Trunks reach elephantine size, gray to gray-brown and quite impressive. The authors observed *M. campbellii* in the southwest of England and consider it and its cultivars the most spectacular of all magnolias. It is a humbling and inspirational experience to walk under these most noble magnolias in early spring, their pink flowers in full glory on bare branches. Emotion clouds judgment, for all who experience subsequently desire.

M

Foliage: Leaves, 6 to 10″ long, medium dark green, oval in outline, maturing after the flowers. No appreciable fall color. **Flowers/seeds/fruits/cones**: White flowers are apparently most typical of the species in the wild; literature reports seed-grown plants are usually pink, but also white and deep rose-purple. Their so-termed cup and saucer look is unique, with 12 to 15 tepals, the outer ("saucer") splaying, the inner ("cup") recurved. Flowers open before the leaves in February-March-April. Fruit is erect, elongated, pinkish red, to 8″ long. **Native range**: Himalayas from eastern Nepal to western Yunnan at elevations of 7,000 to 11,000′. **Adaptability**: Suited from British Columbia to San Francisco. Zones 8 and 9. English literature reported the deepest pigmented forms are the least cold hardy. **Landscape use**: Cherished specimen magnolia where it can be successfully cultured. Size restricts use to large properties. Maximum growth occurs in moist, acid, deep soils and where air temperature extremes are minimized. Be advised, seedlings may take 20 to 30 years to flower; grafted clones/cultivars flower sooner. **Street tree use**: No. **In the trade**: Numerous seedlings based on flower color have been introduced. Most of the early seed collection (1900s) found their way to England, specifically the gardens of Cornwall, although Kew and Sir Harold Hillier Gardens raised and named several selections.

'Elizabeth'. Cream-yellow, 40′ high after 22 years. *M. acuminata* × *M. denudata*.

'Gold Star'. Pale yellow (not gold) with 14 strap-shaped tepals, 4″ across, opening before the leaves; 20 to 30′ by 15 to 20′; cold hardiness of *M. stellata*. 'Miss Honeybee' × *M. stellata* 'Rubra'.

'Honey Flower'. Deep yellow, 2 to 3″ high, floriferous, before the leaves; regular, uniform crown, 25 to 35′ high. 'Miss Honeybee' × 'Elizabeth'.

'Judy Zuk'. Yellow to golden orange, 6 tepals, 5″ wide, held upright, fruity fragrance, 20′ by 18′. Name honors the late director of the Brooklyn Botanic Garden—one of the sweetest, kindest, and most noble of horticulturists.

'Lois'. Clear, unfading, primrose-yellow flowers with 9 tepals, 3 to 4″ long; 21′ high in 25 years from a rooted cutting; upright in youth, tight and dense, dark green foliage; oval to rounded and symmetrical with age. Tennessee growers like it best, as it resists frost cracking. 'Elizabeth' sibling × *M. acuminata*.

Magnolia campbellii

'Charles Rafill'

'Lanarth'

Magnolia campbellii

Alba Group. Includes the white-flowering selections 'Ethel Hillier' and 'Sir Harold Hillier'.

'Charles Rafill'. Deep rose-pink flower buds open rose-purple outside, with a pinkish purple marginal blush inside. A vigorous, early, and prolifically flowering form; raised at Kew in 1946. A hybrid between the species and var. *mollicomata,* the latter considered more cold hardy.

'Lanarth'. Spectacular, large, cyclamen-purple flowers with darker stamens. Raised from wild-collected seed at Lanarth in 1924.

Red flowers

Many red-purple hybrid magnolias have *M. campbellii* genes. Most were developed in New Zealand and are gradually entering U.S. commerce.

'Black Tulip'. Goblet-shaped, fragrant flowers composed of deep maroon tepals. Smaller-statured and slow-growing, proving worthy. 'Vulcan' seedling.

'Frank's Masterpiece'

'Genie'

'Vulcan'

BURGUNDY STAR 'JURmag4'. Later than 'Vulcan' with firm-textured, claret-red tepals borne on a distinctly upright tree. Three-fourths *M. liliiflora*, one-fourth 'Vulcan'.

'Felix Jury'. Red buds open rose-red, a consistent performer. 'Vulcan' parentage.

'Frank's Masterpiece'. A beauty, with 10 to 12″ wide, 8- to 9-tepaled, knockout reddish purple outer tepal color, light pink inner color with contrasting deep pink veins (striations). Flowers early, opening late March in the Dirr garden. Strong upright grower, 25 to 30′ high, 20 to 15′ wide. Even small plants, 6 to 8′ high, produce an abundance of flowers. In zone 8, the color is better than that of 'Vulcan'. Hybrid of *M. ×soulangeana* 'Deep Purple Dream' and 'Paul Cook'.

'Genie'. Bred by Vance Hooper in New Zealand, it produces small dark "red" (maroon to magenta) flowers as a compact, slow-growing plant, 13′ by 5 to 6′. Several more of Hooper's cultivars are already in Europe and, no doubt, will soon be in the United States.

'Ian's Red', 'Grant David', 'Ian's Giant Red', and 'Red Is Red', all from New Zealand and listed as red, require evaluation in the United States. Ian Baldick introduced two purple cultivars, 'Purple Sensation' and 'Ruth'.

'Margaret Helen'. Large reddish purple flowers; buds reminiscent of *M. liliiflora* 'Nigra'; and a long flowering season.

'Shirazz'. Purple-red flowers. *M. denudata* × 'Vulcan'.

'Strawberry Fields'. Strawberry-red flowers, the closest to red authors have observed. 'Spectrum' × 'Vulcan', so it has *M. sprengeri* genes in its makeup.

'Vulcan'. Early large, red, fragrant flowers, but performance (color intensity) is spotty, 15′ by 10′ in 10 years. Bred by Felix Jury, New Zealand, and utilized as a parent in many of the hybrids described here. *M. liliiflora* 'Nigra' × 'Lanarth'.

Magnolia denudata
Yulan magnolia

Deciduous. Distinctly upright pyramidal as a young tree, it broadens with maturity; eventually 20 to 30′ high and wide. Growth is slow; in zone 8, trees took 32 years to reach 25′ in height and width. Bark is relatively smooth, gray on large branches and trunks.

Foliage: Leaves 4 to 6″ long, 2 to 3″ wide, dark green in summer, holding green late or turning yellow-brown in autumn.
Flowers/seeds/fruits/cones: Cream-white to ivory flowers, each composed of 9 to 12 tepals, goblet-shaped initially, 6″ across when fully open, sweetly scented of lemon, borne on naked branches in (February) March-April, typically early March in zone 8. Flowers are, in a word, exquisite when unadulterated by cold and are borne in large quantities—the tree a drifting cloud of white. Fruit is an aggregate of follicles, cylindrical in outline, 4 to 6″ long, maturing green to rose to red with orange-red seeds on a white, silk-like

Magnolia denudata

Magnolia denudata

'Purpurascens'

'Purpurascens'

474

thread. Fruit is seldom produced. **Native range**: China, in moist woodlands of Anhui, Zhejiang, Jiangxi, and Hunan provinces. **Adaptability**: Authors observed specimens from Newburgh, ME, to Mobile, AL. A venerable tree at Longwood Gardens is extremely reproductive. Zones (4)5 to 8. **Landscape use**: At its best, a choice specimen for any open, sunny area; however, plants sited in partial shade, under pines for example, still produce respectable flowers. Worthy of a place in any residential, commercial, or recreational site. Authors witnessed it espaliered on homes in England. **Street tree use**: If trained to a central leader. **In the trade**: Unfortunately, not common in American commerce. Important species for breeding: with M. *liliiflora* spawned M. ×*soulangeana* and many of the yellow-flowered magnolias.

'Forrest's Pink'. Pretty pink flowers, darker at base, lighter at tips. Probably a hybrid, but most often listed here.

'Purpurascens' (var. *purpurascens*). Rose-red flowers, pink inside.

'Sawada' ('Sawada's Cream'). Perfectly formed, cream-white flowers on a more restrained plant; highly fertile and produces bright crimson fruit.

'Swarthmore Sentinel'. Cream to ivory flowers, with tinge of pink-purple at base; upright strict pyramidal growth habit, 40′ by 15′ after 20 years.

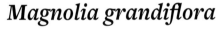

Magnolia grandiflora
southern magnolia

Broadleaf evergreen. Immense, coarse-textured pyramidal, oval-rounded, to broad-rounded tree. With few exceptions, habit is pyramidal, tightly branched, and uniform in youth, expanding in girth with age into mastodon-like behemoths; throughout the Southeast, trees to 80′ are common. The outer branches sweep the ground, often rooting in place and thus colonizing greater swaths of garden real estate. Fast-growing, easily 3′ or more per year. Bark is seldom noticed because of the cloaking foliage, but it's a pretty gray-brown, smooth to elephantine in texture, sometimes with scaly plates and strips.

Foliage: Leaves are like no other: striking, large, lustrous dark green, thickish, leathery, almost plastic; elliptical to obovate (fattest above the middle), 5 to 10″ long, half as wide. Although the tree stays evergreen, leaves abscise in spring and fall. They are slow to decompose and form a compost/ mulch pile under the parent tree. The dead leaves turn shiny brown and can be snapped like a thick potato chip. Walking through the brown leaves produces a snap-crackle-pop Rice Krispies symphony.

Magnolia grandiflora

Magnolia grandiflora

M

Magnolia grandiflora

'Bracken's Brown Beauty'

Magnolia grandiflora

'Claudia Wannamaker'

Flowers/seeds/fruits/cones: Spectacular flowers, cherished in gardens worldwide for their milk-white tepals and sweet fragrance, opening May-June and sporadically thereafter. Each is composed of 6 to 15, spoon to spatulate, concave tepals, maturing 8 to 12″ in diameter. Flowers are scattered throughout the canopy. The floral perfume fills the air, especially on warm evenings; it is one of nature's great gifts to gardeners. Fruit is typically 3 to 5″ long, about half as wide, rose to red with red seeds suspended from silky threads as individual follicles split in fall. Fruits, like leaves, create a litter problem. Authors simply rake fallen leaves and fruit carcasses under the branches. **Native range**: Found primarily in moist to wet areas, from North Carolina to Florida, Arkansas and Texas, often in shady habitats. **Adaptability**: Zones (6)7 to 9(10). Prized worldwide for its adaptability and beauty. Heat and drought tolerant once established. **Landscape use**: Utilized for gardens, large areas, screens, and hedges. The species, unless limbed up, retains branches and foliage to the ground, forming a midnight-green block of granite. Certainly it is not a choice for small properties, but cultivars 'Little Gem' and TEDDY BEAR will dovetail with restricted spaces. Growth and flowering are maximized in moist, deep, acid soils in full sun to moderate shade in warm climates.

Seedlings develop exuberantly in the shade of broadleaf trees and, in the Southeast, flower in 3 to 5 years. Transplanting can be tricky; container-grown trees are easy year-round, balled-and-burlapped best moved in August and into winter. Expect fast growth; a 1-gallon seedling in the former Dirr garden was 30′ in 13 years. Plants should be tip-pruned when young to develop fuller habits, but left to their DNA as they proceed to maturity. If properly pruned, a "normal" 80′ high cultivar can be aesthetically and functionally maintained at 10′. **Street tree use**: Potential, but give it a lot of room and prune low branches. Avoid in snowy areas because of heavy load on the evergreen foliage. European literature cites street use along the Riviera and Italy. **In the trade**: Numerous with the following commercial cultivars representing the diversity and adaptability (hardiness primarily) within the species.

'Bracken's Brown Beauty'. Lustrous dark green leaves, brown undersides, compact habit, cold hardy, 30 to 50′ by 15 to 30′. A 3-gallon plant grew 24′ high in 7 years in the new Dirr garden.

'Claudia Wannamaker'. Large pyramidal-oval form, 50′ and greater.

'Bracken's Brown Beauty'

'D. D. Blanchard'

'Edith Bogue'

M

'Claudia Wannamaker'

'D. D. Blanchard'. Polished black-green leaves, orange-brown undersides, 50′ and greater.

'Edith Bogue'. Lustrous dark leaves, cold hardy, more loose and open, 30 to 40′.

GREENBACK 'Mgtig'. Polished dark green leaves, foliage is convex, extremely thick and leathery, reflecting light like a chrome bumper on a Pinto, back of leaf without ferruginous pubescence, 30 to 50′ by 15 to 25′.

'Hasse'. Grand selection, upright pyramidal, dense, to 50′ by 15 to 20′; the best upright cultivar, holding tight columnar-pyramidal shape into old age. Slightly more difficult to transplant as large balled-and-burlapped material.

'Kay Parris'. Lustrous dark green leaves with brown undersides, restrained habit, repeat flower production, 20 to 30′ high.

'Hasse'

'Kay Parris'

'Little Gem'

TEDDY BEAR

'Kay Parris'

'Little Gem'

GREENBACK

'Victoria'

'Little Gem'. Wildly popular, smaller lustrous dark green leaves and continual flower production, still spitting flowers in October-November, 20 to 30′ by 10′, tends to open up with age unless pruned.

TEDDY BEAR 'Southern Charm'. Extremely dense compact pyramid with smaller lustrous dark green leaves, brown undersides; great option for a small garden or restricted planting space, 20′ by 10′.

'Victoria'. Popular in the Pacific Northwest for its cold hardiness and resistance to breakage from heavy snow loads. Glossy green leaves with rusty brown tomentum on undersides. 30 to 50′ by 15 to 30′. Develops a more open habit under southeastern conditions.

M

Magnolia insignis (*Manglietia insignis*)

red lotus tree

Broadleaf evergreen. Maintains a pyramidal-conical habit and central leader into maturity. Fast growth in youth, slowing later, reaching 100′ in the wild. Mature landscape size is 25 to 30′ high, 10 to 15′ wide. Bark is smooth, gray, largely hidden by the foliage.

Foliage: If it never flowered, the scintillating semi-tropical foliage elevates this species to first-class garden status for warmer areas. Leaves, narrow and willow-like, 4 to 8″ long, 2 to 3″ wide, lustrous dark green above, gray-green beneath, hold the rich color year-round. Developing leaves are shiny bronze. **Flowers/seeds/fruits/cones**: One of the most beautiful of all magnolia flowers, which is an elevated accolade. Pink, rose, to red on the outside of the 6 to 9 tepals, lighter inside, 3 to 4″ wide, fragrant, opening in May-June, sporadically over a long tenure, each lasting 2 to 3 days, even in the heat of the Southeast. Literature mentions flowers occurring in white. Flowers develop on 3- to 5-year-old seedlings; they are randomly produced throughout the canopy from buds formed the summer prior. Flower buds are 1″ long, with a bulbous middle, and borne at the end of the shoots. Do not prune except after flowering. In Georgia, flowers have opened in April, May, June, and September. Fruit is a small, ovoid-cylindric, knobby, aggregate of follicles, 2 to 4″ high and 1 to 1½″ wide, rose to red, seeds orange, maturing in late summer–early fall. **Native range**: Southern China across Yunnan and northern Vietnam, Myanmar, and northeast India to Nepal. **Adaptability**: Quite adaptable. To date, in Georgia evaluations, shows good sun tolerance (better than *M. maudiae* and *M. platypetala*), and no foliar insect or disease issues. A tree in the Dirr garden was magnificent after the hot and dry summer of 2016; in fact, the tree is planted on the ridge of an old cotton terrace. Who would have suspected such adaptability? Zones 7 to 9. Hybrids with *M. sieboldii* 'Colossus' should prove even hardier. **Landscape use**: Beautiful as a specimen or in groups. Maximum growth in moist, acid, organic-laden soils. **Street tree use**: Potential. **In the trade**: The species is being utilized for breeding, and the early hybrids show great promise for American gardens. 'Anita Figlar' flowers more profusely with 9 tepals, the inner 3 deep red on each side.

Magnolia insignis

Magnolia insignis

Magnolia insignis

Magnolia yuyuanensis

Magnolia maudiae

Magnolia yuyuanensis

Related species

Authors believe the evergreen magnolia species have much to offer warm temperate gardens. The species herein are reasonably common and have been proven in research trials and personal gardens. Their best garden days reside in the future.

M. doltsopa. Glossy dark green leaves, thickish, 3 to 7″ long, 1 to 3″ wide, fragrant, soft pale yellow to white, 3 to 4″ wide, 12- to 16-tepaled flowers in February-March, 20 to 40′ high and wide, branched to ground, zones 8 to 10 on the West Coast. China, Tibet, Himalayas. Spectacular in flower and observed only once at Caerhays Castle, Cornwall, England.

M. maudiae (smiling monkey forest tree). Similar to *M. platy-petala*, with larger, white, fragrant flowers, 5 to 6″ wide with 6 to 9 tepals. Its flower buds and young stems are not covered with brown hairs, otherwise it is a coin toss to differentiate the two. Expect 20′ high, 15′ wide; forms a small, dense, round-headed tree. Utilized as a street tree in Portland, OR.

M. yuyuanensis (*Manglietia yuyuanensis*; Chinese wood-lotus). Discovered in 1985 by a Chinese taxonomist. Taxonomy is confused, and the plant is occasionally misidentified. A tree prospered at the JC Raulston Arboretum, Raleigh, NC, and survived -3°F. Habit is pyramidal to 30′ high, 15′ wide. The lustrous dark green leaves are similar to *M. insignis* with keeled bottom. The slightly fragrant flowers are white, to 5″ wide, 9 tepals, with pretty dark red stamens in spring and pink-red fruits in fall. This grew for many years in the Georgia trials and flowered in September; typically flowers in spring into summer. China. Zones 7 to 10.

Magnolia kobus
Kobus magnolia

Deciduous. In youth, habit is conical-pyramidal, eventually spreading-rounded, 30 to 40(60)′ high. Young plants easily average 2′ per year over a 10-year period. Pretty, smooth gray bark, the color persisting on large trunks; in fact, because of light bark, large multi-stem specimens are reminiscent of a good white-bark birch, minus the borer maladies. An unheralded, underutilized species, but beautiful in its own skin and as the parent of *M. ×loebneri*. It serves as a universal understock for grafting other deciduous species.

Foliage: Emerging leaves bronze, maturing medium to dark green, obovate, 3 to 6(8)″ long, half as wide, turning yellow in fall. The foliage is clean into fall with no obvious insect or disease issues. **Flowers/seeds/fruits/cones**: Spectacular, unbelievable on mature specimens, to the degree swooning is induced. The fragrant, white flowers, 6 to 9 tepals, each with a faint purple line at the base, are 4″ wide, opening in March-April and persisting as leaves unfold. Flowers have opened in late January in zone 8 and unfortunately may be singed brown by frost. Fruit is pinkish, seeds bright red. **Native range**: Japan and South Korea. **Adaptability**: Adaptable to clay-based, rocky-sandy, acid, and limestone (high pH) soils, full sun to partial shade. Zones 4 to 8. Var. *borealis* from northern Japan carries a zone 3 designation. **Landscape use**: Terrifically slow to flower from seed, in Georgia taking 14 years; others reporting sparse flowering after 18 to 30 years. The negatives aside, when at its floriferous pinnacle in late winter–early spring, the effect is remarkably beautiful. Since most trees are seedling grown with no guarantee of reliable flower, utilize the species on campuses, golf courses, commercial grounds, cemeteries, and parks. Consider flowering a bonus as it develops into a beautiful specimen for future generations. **Street tree use**: Potential. **In the trade**: Certainly a recluse in the world of commercial magnolia species but worth the effort to secure; flowering plants reproduced via cuttings/grafts typically retain their propensity to flower earlier and regularly. A hybrid between this and *M. salicifolia*, *M. ×kewensis* 'Wada's Memory', makes a beautiful specimen plant, forming a narrow conical-pyramidal shape when young, broadening with age, 30 to 40′ by 20 to 30′. The white, fragrant, tulip-shaped, 6-tepaled flowers are 7″ across fully opened, each tepal spreading-arching at its tip.

Magnolia kobus

Magnolia kobus

Magnolia kobus

'Wada's Memory'

'Wada's Memory'

Magnolia ×loebneri
Loebner magnolia

Deciduous. One of the most beautiful and adaptable hybrid magnolias, a deliberate cross of *M. kobus* and *M. stellata* made by Max Loebner, Pillnitz, Germany, before World War I. Growth habit ranges from a bushy, twiggy small tree to broad-rounded, large-trunked trees, 20 to 30′ high and wide. Fast-growing, as much as 2′ per year under good conditions. Bark is similar to *M. kobus*, soft gray to gray-brown and a pleasing element in the winter landscape.

Foliage: Emerging leaves bronze, settling to dark green, elliptical to narrow obovate, 4 to 6″ long, 1 to 2″ wide. Leaves display excellent heat and drought tolerances, often turning yellow, bronze, or brown in autumn. Foliage is always clean, without blemishes, remaining so into late fall. **Flowers/seeds/fruits/cones**: Variable in tepal number, (9)12(15) into the 30s, each 2 to 3″ long, a quarter to a third or less as wide, slightly wider above the middle; buds pink, opening white, fragrant, February-March in South, April in North; subject to vagaries of weather. Display can be spectacular. **Native range**: Hybrid. **Adaptability**: Considered lime tolerant, so if soils are high pH, this and the many excellent cultivars are superb choices. Zones (4)5 to 8. **Landscape use**: Pretty winter-spring flowering magnolia for any open sunny location and certainly one of the best for the everyday gardener, prepared by its parents to face the vicissitudes of cold, heat, and drought, as well as acid and high pH soils.

M

Magnolia ×loebneri

483

'Ballerina'

'Ballerina'

'Leonard Messel'

'Leonard Messel'

'Merrill'

'Leonard Messel'

'Merrill'

M

Often shrub-like but can be grown as a small tree, single or multi-stemmed. Excellent choice for espaliers. Easy to root from cuttings and transplants without difficulty. **Street tree use**: If limbed up to produce a clear trunk. **In the trade**: Choice selections are available for small courtyard gardens to larger estates.

'Ballerina'. Approximately 30 white tepals, fragrant; 15 to 20′ high.

'Donna'. 12 or 13 white reflexed tepals, 6 to 7″ across; 15′ by 12′.

'Leonard Messel'. 12 to 15 purple-pink tepals on outside, white within, slightly crinkled-twisted, 4 to 6″ across; 15 to 20′ high; tepals are quite frost resistant.

'Merrill'. 15 white tepals, 3½″ across; 25 to 30′ high and wide; one of the best larger-growing forms; excellent dense habit and dark green foliage.

'Merrill'

'Merrill'

'Spring Snow'

SPRING WELCOME

'Spring Snow'. 15 white tepals; 25 to 30′ with a rounded outline.

SPRING WELCOME 'Ruth'. 11 to 15 pure white tepals coming from a lavender bud, 3 to 4½″ wide; it flowered heavily in our Oregon trials; dense oval habit, bred in North Dakota and cold hardy there.

'White Rose'. 22 white tepals, flowers 4 to 5″ wide; 20′ by 15′; no damage in zone 3 over an 18-year period.

'Wildcat'. 52 soft pink to white tepals, each flower 4 to 5″ across; 18′ by 8 to 12′.

Magnolia macrophylla
bigleaf magnolia

Deciduous. Rugged individualist in youth; branches stout, thick, and coarse. Growth is fast in youth, with just a few thick stems and an open, gaunt outline. Impressive at maturity, 30 to 40′ high and wide, cloaked with immense leaves, the largest of any eastern North American deciduous species, and a full canopy. National Champion is 70′ high, 56′ wide. Bark is smooth gray, like most magnolias.

Foliage: Leaves gargantuan, to 32″ long and 12″ wide, oblong-obovate, with auriculate (earlobe-shaped) leaf base; borne in pseudowhorls, appearing to originate from the same place on the stem. Leaves emerge in late spring. Fall color is yellow-bronze-brown, with leaves falling over several weeks, carpeting the ground like wind-disseminated grocery bags, their undersides a silver-gray. **Flowers/seeds/fruits/cones**: The cream-white, fragrant, solitary flowers, 6 to 9 tepals, inner 3 tepals stained purple at base, 8 to 10(14)″ across, open in May-June at the ends of the shoots, nestled in the foliage, often on the upper branches. Young trees are slow to flower. The aggregate of follicles is egg-shaped to rounded, pink to rose-tinted, 3″ long, slightly less in width, matures in September, the orange-red seeds suspended on silky strings. **Native range**: Sporadic distribution, typically in shady, moist woodlands from Ohio to Florida, west to Arkansas and Louisiana. It should be respected, cherished, and preserved in its native habitats. **Adaptability**: Zone 4 with tip damage; safest in 5 to 8. **Landscape use**: One of the most spectacular hardy specimen trees, especially in an open expanse of turf, where it can reach full potential. Serves admirably in parks, campuses, and large areas. A one-of-a-kind, easy-to-grow magnolia for the collector and as a conversation piece. Certainly not a tree for the typical residential landscape. Site in moist, deep, organic-laden, slightly acid to slightly higher pH soils for optimum growth. Suited to full sun and moderate shade. Avoid extremely

Magnolia macrophylla

subsp. *ashei*

Magnolia macrophylla

Magnolia macrophylla

subsp. *ashei*

windy locations. Does not respond well to pruning. **Street tree use**: No. **In the trade**: Sold as seed-grown. Minimal selection, and only a few cultivars extant.

subsp. *ashei*. Typically 10 to 20′ high, 10 to 15′ wide, although the National Champion (assuming correct identity) is over 50′ high. Authors have grown this with fond reverence because it fits the smaller garden and flowers early in youth (3- to 5-year-old seedlings, at only 30″ high). Flowers are fragrant, the tepals white, purple-stained at base, to 12″ wide in May-June (Athens). Considered zones 6 to 9, but completely hardy in Orono, ME (zone 5). Native to Florida panhandle, where it is endemic in eight counties along the Gulf Coast.

'Julian Hill'. Grows 40′ high, with pure white flowers; observed by authors in late June (Martha's Vineyard).

Magnolia platypetala
broadpetal lily-tree

Broadleaf evergreen. Develops a pyramidal-conical outline of loose-fitting branches. Growth is slow, reaching 20′ high and 15′ wide. In trials at the University of Georgia, seedlings grew quickly, but once planted in ground slowed significantly; the best seedling was 11′5″ by 7′7″ in 7 years. Bark is smooth and gray.

Foliage: Leaves are leathery, lustrous medium to dark green above, pale gray-green below, elliptical-ovate, tapering at their ends, entire, 2 to 5″ long, half as wide. The deep green foliage persists in shady environments. Sun exposure coupled with low temperatures causes degrees of discoloration, more yellow-green. **Flowers/seeds/fruits/cones**: Flowers are white, fragrant, 3 to 4″ in diameter, emerging from brownish pubescent buds in winter-spring. Tepal number varies, typically 8 or 9, with 15 present on the best seedlings. A plant may be completely covered in white, the leaves hidden among the floral display. Seedlings have flowered in September, November, December, January, and February in zone 8; Florida evaluations reported as many as 23 weeks of flowering. In the Dirr garden, depending on temperatures, tepals were at times injured, but the buds are numerous, opening over extended periods, ensuring some flowers. Fruit is sparsely produced. Follicles are individually and irregularly attached along the peduncle; seeds are orange and mature in July-August, the carpel wall (follicle) splitting to expose the orange aril. **Native range**: China. **Adaptability**: Zones 7 to 11. **Landscape use**: A wonderful addition to the list of winter-flowering trees. So out of synchronization with the typical deciduous magnolias that even neighbors inquire about identity. Based on authors' limited experience, a choice woodland, shade-tolerant species, but also capable of growing in full sun. Prefers a moist, acid, well-drained soil; the severe 2016 Georgia drought resulted in a few dead branches. Worth noting that cutting propagation is difficult and selected clones can be grafted. **Street tree use**: No. **In the trade**: Available. The 5- to 7-year wait for seedlings to flower is worth the investment. From Georgia seedlings, magnolia expert Richard Figlar selected 'Spring Bouquet', a more cold-hardy, prolifically flowering clone; striking in flower. 'Touch of Pink' has pink flowers.

Magnolia platypetala

Magnolia platypetala

Magnolia platypetala

Magnolia salicifolia

anise magnolia, willow-leafed magnolia

Deciduous. Slender, narrow, conical, pyramidal in youth, developing an irregular pyramidal-oblong crown at maturity. A moderate grower, 1 to 2′ per year, in youth, eventually 20 to 30(50)′ high, still taller than wide. The light silver-gray bark is beautiful and quite effective; outside of *M. zenii*, authors believe it is the most ornamental silver-gray bark of any magnolia. Often confused with *M. kobus*. A telltale identification characteristic: the slender, shiny brown-green stems, when bruised, emit a sweet lemon fragrance, approaching anise (hence one of the common names).

Foliage: The emerging leaves are tinted bronze-purple, maturing dull dark green, with yellow hues in autumn. Unique shape, tapered at the apex and base, 2 to 5″ long, to 2″ wide at maturity. **Flowers/seeds/fruits/cones**: Flowers pure white, fragrant, 6-tepaled, 3 to 4(6)″ wide, emerging from dark gray-brown (somewhat blackish) buds; the tepals may have a slight pink blush at their bases. Flowers early and sometimes spectacularly, February to March, before leaves, but more often than not, flowers are singed brown by cold weather. Fruits are rose-pink, 2 to 3″ long, with scarlet seeds. **Native range**: Grows naturally in rocky, granite soil at the side of forest streams in Honshu, Kyushu, and the Shikoku Islands, Japan. **Adaptability**: In Georgia, seedlings flowered after 5 to 6 years, opening in February, but their foliage was tattered by heat and drought. Best suited to northern climates. Zones (3)4 to 7. **Landscape use**: Authors have always admired this species and believe it is worthy of increased use. Wonderful choice in full sun, moist, acid, deep, organic soils. Utilize as a single specimen, in groupings, for parks, campuses, and commercial landscapes.

Magnolia salicifolia

'Iufer'

M

Magnolia salicifolia

Magnolia salicifolia

Street tree use: In our opinion, even if it never flowered, it still has merit, particularly as a street tree. **In the trade**: Except for larger flowers, the few selections offer little advantage over the species. 'Else Frye', 'Grape Expectations' (grape-scented flowers), 'Iufer' (white tepals, pink stamens), 'Jermyns', 'Miss Jack', and 'W. B. Clarke' are known.

Magnolia sieboldii
Siebold magnolia

Deciduous. A significant contributor to a new generation of hybrids. The species scarcely fits the tree designation, but it hybridizes with almost any magnolia, transmitting to its progeny its signature pinkish, rose-crimson to deep maroon-crimson stamen color, as well as later flowering. Most often a 10 to 15(20)′ large, loose, spreading shrub with an open, airy canopy. A 14-year-old plant was 20′ high and 21′ wide.

Foliage: Leaves are oblong to obovate-oblong with a pointed apex, 3 to 6″ long, 3 to 4″ wide, medium to dark green, grayish pubescent beneath, usually with 7 to 9 pairs of prominent veins. Fall color a greenish to decent yellow. **Flowers/ seeds/fruits/cones**: Buds are egg-shaped; white flowers nodding, cup- to saucer-shaped, 6 to 12 tepals, 3 to 4(5)″ wide, fragrant, opening May-June and sporadically thereafter. Authors observed flowers in late July in Minnesota. The flowers appear after the leaves, never in prodigious numbers; yet individually, with their cupped white tepals and richly pigmented stamens, they are elegantly appealing. A measure of flowers appears to form on new growth of the season; from a breeding viewpoint, this might result in the development of remontant or repeat-flowering magnolias. The carmine aggregate of follicles averages 2″ in length and houses the scarlet seeds. **Native range**: Extensive, including Manchuria, South Korea, southern China; Honshu, Shikoku, and Kyushu Islands, Japan. **Adaptability**: Hardier than the literatures states, and authors surmise the provenance of the seed has contributed to such assessments. We have observed flowering specimens at the Minnesota Landscape Arboretum. Not well adapted to the heat of the Southeast unless in a shady, moist soil environment. Zones 4 to 7. **Landscape use**: Worth considering for a moderately shady location in warmer climates; full sun in the North. Soils should be moist, acid, well drained, although the species performs well in higher pH situations. **Street tree use**: No. **In the trade**: Ethan Guthrie, curator at the Atlanta Botanical Garden, crossed *M. sieboldii* and *M. macrophylla* subsp. *ashei* to produce a compact, dense-foliaged, white-tepaled, pink-stamened hybrid of great beauty that flowers in April-May after leaves have developed. 'Colossus' × *M. insignis* resulted in semi-evergreen to deciduous, shiny dark green foliage, small tree stature (10′ in 5 years), and

Magnolia sieboldii

Magnolia sieboldii

spectacular, fragrant, 6- to 9-tepaled, richly saturated pure pink flowers with pink stamens; flowered from late April to late May in zone 8.

'Charles Coates'. Creamy white tepals, reddish anthers, fragrant. *M. sieboldii* × *M. tripetala*.

'Colossus'. 10 to 12(18) tepals. Overall, a more reliable performer than the species. Listed as a tetraploid or hexaploid, translating to larger flowers and foliage. For many years performed magnificently in the shade of lacebark elms in the Georgia trial garden, flowering in mid-May.

'Exotic Star'. Resembles *M. grandiflora* in foliage, producing 6 to 8″ wide, white, fragrant flowers with pink-rose stamens. Flowered in mid-May in zone 8. Zones 6 to 9. *M. grandiflora* × *M. sieboldii*.

'Colossus' × *M. insignis*

'Colossus' × *M. insignis*

M

Magnolia sieboldii

'Colossus'

Magnolia ×soulangeana

saucer magnolia

Deciduous. Wonderful species, a hybrid (*M. denudata* × *M. liliiflora*) by French soldier Étienne Soulange-Bodin, first flowered in 1826 and adorning gardens worldwide ever since, the standard by which all magnolias are judged. Size 20 to 30(40)′ high and wide. Plants are distinctly upright in youth; short trunked with wide-spreading branches at maturity. Growth is slow to medium; expect 10 to 15′ over an 8- to 10-year period. Bark is smooth, gray, and attractive, developing a degree of granulation, bumpiness with age. Sapsuckers (a type of woodpecker) are notorious for drilling concentric circles of holes in larger branches and the trunk, predisposing the tree to insects and disease.

Foliage: More akin to *M. denudata* than *M. liliiflora* in shape and size, 3 to 6″ long, half as wide, obovate to broad-oblong, and medium to dark green. Fall color, on occasion, is yellow-brown. **Flowers/seeds/fruits/cones**: This and *M. stellata* are the largest-selling magnolias in the United States because of outstanding floral display, which is predicated by bud development on young nursery plants. Authors observed consistent flower bud development from year to year, even when freezes decimate the flowers and young leaves. A few warm winter days trigger release from dormancy with brightly colored tepals peeking through the fuzzy buds. A spectacle when at its garden best, the entire tree aglow in white, pink, rose, burgundy, maroon, and combinations. Each fragrant flower is composed of 9 tepals, opening 5 to 10″ wide. Authors noted flowers in January in Florida; late February, early March in Georgia; late March in Oregon; April in Massachusetts. Fruit is an asymmetric, 3 to 4″ long, aggregate of follicles, maturing August-September, seldom in large quantities. **Native range**: A hybrid,

combining the best traits of the parents. **Adaptability**: Variable cold hardiness depending on the cultivar; trees are successful in small fenced gardens fronting Commonwealth Avenue in Boston to San Francisco; from Orono, ME, to Opelousas, LA. Zones 4 to 9. Evaluation notes and dates by Roger Luce (Newburgh, ME) pinpointed the most cold hardy selections; those noted flowered after exposure to -28°F. Most damaging are late winter temperature drops after unseasonably warm periods. A report from Arkansas noted plants in containers and landscapes were killed 30 to 80% by fluctuating high/low temperatures. **Landscape**

Magnolia ×soulangeana

Magnolia ×soulangeana

Magnolia ×soulangeana

'Alexandrina'

'Alexandrina'

use: Authors speculate *M. ×soulangeana* is the most popular magnolia on a worldwide basis, easy to propagate and grow and developing flower buds as young plants. If an Achilles' heel exists, it would be the early flowering—one day resplendent; the next after a 28°F freeze, brown mush. Provide full sun, well-drained acid to slightly neutral soils for maximum performance. Specimen use and groupings in expansive

'Amabilis'

'Brozzonii'

M

lawns are ideal. Minimize pruning as water sprouts (long shoot extensions) develop from branches/trunks, somewhat disfiguring the tree. It is quite pollutant tolerant, and venerable mature specimens are present in many urban centers. **Street tree use**: Certainly if trained to a single trunk. **In the trade**: Available. Plants are seldom labeled to the cultivar level; the few extant date from the 1800s and early 1900s, with minimal activity in the last 65 years.

'Alexandrina'. Dates from 1831 and several impostors (at least three) masquerade as the genuine article. The best bears tulip-shaped flowers, rose-purple outside, pure white inner, 8″ across. In the Dirr garden, reliably produced copious flower buds, never skimping, even when hammered by late winter/early spring freezes, the tree beat up heading into spring-summer; on 6 February 2017, the top of the plant was adorned with fully open deep vinous-purple flowers. More upright habit, 20 to 25′ high.

'Amabilis'. Cream-white, blushed pink, 20′, hardy in Maine.

'Brozzonii'. Flowers 2 weeks later than the standard, with 6 tepals, white inside and on tips, purplish rose at base with a pink bar on the outside, 10″ wide; vigorous; 20 to 30′ high and wide; hardy in Maine; originated in 1873.

'Lennei'

'Lennei Alba'

MERCURY

MERCURY

MERCURY

'Lennei'. Deep purplish magenta tepals (6), white on inside, goblet-shaped, fragrant, 15 to 20′ high and wide, c.1854.

'Lennei Alba'. A pure white form with 9 tepals, goblet-shaped, fragrant, 20′ by 15′, c.1905.

MERCURY 'NCMX1'. Upright pyramidal habit, quite dense, ideal for streets. Deep pink in bud, opens lavender-pink; flowers over a month later than typical species avoiding

'Rustica Rubra'

'Verbanica'

'Verbanica'

Magnolia sprengeri
Sprenger magnolia

Deciduous. Small to medium-sized tree, upright in youth, more upright oval as observed in English gardens, eventually rounded, 30 to 40′ high and wide. Growth is moderate. Bark on old branches and trunks is light gray, peeling in small flakes. Wonderful story surrounding the introduction of 'Diva', the rose-pink form, from seed collected by E. H. Wilson in 1900. Of eight plants raised from this seed, just one was rose-pink when it flowered in 1919. Considerable effort was expended since to catalog *M. sprengeri* in the wild; and in 2000, wild populations with deep rose-pink, white, and pale pink flowers were rediscovered in China.

Foliage: Pretty, obovate to lanceolate-elliptic leaves emerge bronze-purple, maturing dark green, glabrous to distinctly pubescent below, 4 to 7″ long, 2 to 4″ wide. **Flowers/seeds/fruits/cones**: Rose-pink, pink, or white flowers, stained purple at the base, typically 12 tepals, each 3 to 3½″ long, to 2″ wide, opening to 7″ wide saucers before the leaves. Fruit is slender, 3″ long. **Native range**: China. Common in moist woods and thickets at 3,300 to 5,700′. **Adaptability**: Appears to be better suited to culture on the West Coast, although Joe McDaniel, University of Illinois, flowered it in zone 5. Zones 6 to 9. **Landscape use**: Certainly a beautiful magnolia, the early flowers on naked branches a remarkable spectacle, but for the majority of North American gardens, not preferable to the best *M. ×soulangeana* cultivars or the 'Diva' hybrids 'Galaxy' and 'Spectrum'. For specimen use, parks, open areas, it is a worthwhile choice. Coach Dooley had a plant for 20 years before it flowered for the first time in 2017. Plant was growing in moderate shade, flowers borne in the upper reaches, pink and not overwhelming. **Street tree use**: No. **In the trade**: Cultivars, both selections and hybrids. *M. liliiflora* 'Nigra' × *M. sprengeri* 'Diva' resulted in 'Galaxy' and 'Spectrum' by the U.S. National Arboretum;

M

frost damage, up to 12″ across, fragrant; bred by Tom Ranney. On first seeing the original tree in summer, we were very impressed by its form and foliage quality.

'Rustica Rubra'. Rose-red, 9 tepals, inside white, rounded form, 20′ by 20′.

'Verbanica'. Always a favorite with later flowers, each pink-rose on the exterior, fading to white at the apex; lustrous dark green and disease-free foliage; 20 to 25′ high and wide; hardy in Maine.

Magnolia sprengeri

Magnolia sprengeri

'Galaxy'

'Galaxy'

'Galaxy'

'Copeland Court'. 12-tepaled flowers, 10″ wide, rose-purple outside, pale pink to white on the inside.

'Dark Diva'. A dark pink-flowered selection.

'Diva' (var. *diva*). Typically equated with the species, and the common representative of it in cultivation. Deep rose-pink tepal color, pale pink inside.

'Galaxy'. Upright in youth, the parent plant 25 to 30′ high and wide; in zone 8, at 10 years old, 20′ high and upright oval in habit. With pruning makes a good street tree, the red-purple, 12-tepaled, 6 to 10″ wide flowers opening spectacularly in March but subject to frost damage.

'Lanhydrock'. Cyclamen-purple flowers with 12 tepals.

'Spectrum'. Sister seedling to 'Galaxy', with deeper red-purple, 8- to 12-tepaled, 10 to 12″ wide flowers on a 25′ by 25′ framework. Distinctly pyramidal-oval in youth, spreading with age.

they are superior to 'Diva', with more intense flower color and easier to grow; however, the foliage, owing to *M. liliiflora* parentage, becomes tatty and weary in late summer–fall, especially in high heat and drought years. Authors witnessed original plants at the U.S. National Arboretum, and sizes presented are based on those experiences.

'Burncoose Purple'. Deep rose-purple flowers.

Magnolia stellata

star magnolia

Deciduous. Most often a large, densely twiggy shrub to refined small tree of oval to rounded outline, to 20′ in height. Growth rate is typically slow. Bark is smooth, gray, and attractive on mature plants. One of the best commercial magnolias because it floral presence in a nursery container, "wow in a bucket"; cultivars especially are extremely precocious, with even small container plants developing many flower buds.

Foliage: Distinct because of smaller size, 2 to 4″ long, half as wide, oval-elliptic, dark green, pristine into autumn when yellow to bronze hues develop. Foliage is frost resistant, persisting into late November in Georgia. **Flowers/seeds/ fruits/cones**: Numerous flower buds are formed along the previous year's stems and, depending on weather, are effective over an extended period, sometimes still present with the emerging leaves. Buds are typically pink, tepals opening light pink to pure white in February-March (Oregon), March (Georgia), and April (Chicago area). The fragrant flowers are composed of 1½ to 2(3)″ long, strap-shaped tepals, 12 to 18 in the species to over 50 in the cultivars, each flower opening flat, 3 to 5(6)″ across. The early flowers are at the mercy of cold and frequently singed (browned). Fruit is a reddish tinged, 2″ long, aggregate of follicles, usually with only a few developed orange-red seeds. **Native range**: Japan and apparently quite rare, found only in the mountains northeast of Nagoya. **Adaptability**: Safe to state that a cultivar exists for almost any garden, north to south, east to west. Zones 4 to 9. **Landscape use**: This is a choice small tree or large shrub for parks, residential landscapes, large containers; use singly and in groupings. The fluffy white, cloud-like floral display signals spring is close at hand. The species is adapted to sand, silt, clay soils, preferably on the acid side but near neutral will suffice. Full sun maximizes flower production yet in moderate shade, reasonable displays occur. A bonus is the pretty foliage, developing long-persistent yellow-bronze fall colors in mid to late November (Georgia). The silky flower buds resemble the catkins of pussy willows from leaf drop to flower bud expansion. An all-season magnolia, never disappointing, and always well groomed. **Street tree use**: Potential for taller-growing cultivars, but most are too low and wide. **In the trade**: A few selections are available in everyday commerce; we recommend 'Centennial', 'Centennial Blush', 'Royal Star', and 'Waterlily' for excellent small-tree performance.

Magnolia stellata

Magnolia stellata

M

Magnolia stellata

'Centennial'

'Centennial'

'Centennial Blush'

'Centennial Blush'

'Pink Stardust'

'Royal Star'

'Centennial'. Tree-like, 25 to 30′ high, narrow in youth, broadening with age; almost pure white flowers 5 to 6″ across, 28 to 33 tepals (41 on one occasion), fragrant, early, introduced in 1972 to celebrate the Arnold Arboretum's 100-year anniversary.

'Centennial Blush'. A seedling of 'Centennial' with 50 (66 on one occasion) tepals, rich pink in bud, white upon opening, vigorous grower, 20 to 25′, more upright in habit and better suited to small tree development. Bred at the University of Georgia. Sets flower buds at almost every node, making for a spectacular flowering display.

'Chrysanthemumiflora'. Beautiful pink-flowered, 40-tepaled selection, the tepals more frost resistant than 'Waterlily'; relatively compact, 15′ high and wide.

'Royal Star'

'Waterlily'

'Pink Stardust'. 40 to 50 rich pink tepals, lightening as they open, 4 to 5″ wide, on a 30′ high and wide tree. Vigorous grower, to 10′ by 8′ in 6 years in Georgia trials.

'Royal Star'. Flowers are produced in great quantities on a 15(20)′ high tree, year in, year out. Each fragrant flower, pink in bud, opening white with slight pink, is composed of 25 to 30 tepals. Selected in the 1950s and still among the best.

'Waterlily'. More than a single clone under the name, the best with 24 to 35 narrow tepals, rich pink in bud, pink to white when open, depending on heat. Upright in youth, eventually 15 to 20′ high and wide, and flowering in early March in Georgia.

Magnolia tripetala
umbrella magnolia

Deciduous. Rugged-individualist tree, the leaves borne in pseudowhorls near the ends of the branches, resembling an open umbrella in disposition (hence the common name). Habit is gaunt, open, stiff, and coarse-textured; to rounded at maturity with the large leaves shrouding the branches. Mature trees are more open, less dense in foliage canopy thickness than *M. macrophylla*. Growth is moderate with reasonable culture, to 30′ high. Bark is smooth and gray.

Foliage: Oblong-obovate, with a cuneate (wedge-shaped) leaf base, a feature separating it from *M. macrophylla* and its subsp. *ashei*, with auriculate bases. Leaves 10 to 24″ long, 6 to 10″ wide, dark green above, paler and pubescent below. Fall color is green, yellow, to brown, the large leaves forming a blanket on the ground. **Flowers/seeds/fruits/cones**: Flowers are creamy white, 6- to 9(12)-tepaled, 6 to 10″ wide, unpleasantly fragrant (turpentine-like), solitary, opening in May–early June, before *M. macrophylla*. Flower effect is muted, being obscured by the large leaves. Fruit is produced

M

Magnolia tripetala

Magnolia tripetala

Magnolia tripetala

in significant quantities, ripening in September-October. Each fruit is elongated, 4(5)″ long, cylindrical-cone-shaped, and pink to rose-red. The fruits are more showy than the flowers. The seeds are scarlet. **Native range**: Pennsylvania to Georgia, west to Mississippi and Arkansas, in deep, moist forests, often along streams and floodplains; authors observed large populations in such habitats in North Carolina and Maryland. **Adaptability**: More cold hardy than nativity suggests, with pristine trees at the Minnesota Landscape Arboretum. Zones (4)5 to 8. **Landscape use**: Size and texture point to use in shady, moist woodlands, forest edges, and open spaces in moist soil; however, authors observed splendid specimens in open, sunny, exposed locations on slopes and lawns. **Street tree use**: No. **In the trade**: 'Ginter Spicy White' produces ivory-white, 7″ wide, 12-tepaled, flat-faced, lemon-mint fragrant flowers in mid to late spring on a 25 to 50′ high, 20 to 40′ wide tree. Parentage includes *M. tripetala*, *M. sieboldii*, and *M. macrophylla* subsp. *ashei*.

Magnolia virginiana
sweetbay magnolia

Deciduous to evergreen. A multi-stemmed to single-trunked tree, soft pyramidal in youth, broad-oval at maturity, to 60′ high and greater (under cultivation, 30 to 50′ is reasonable); less in spread. Growth is moderate. Young stems are lustrous green. Bark is gray-brown.

Foliage: Leaves 3 to 8″ long, a third to half as wide, light to lustrous dark green, glaucuous (silvery) on the lower surface. Deciduous types develop yellow-green to yellow fall color. Certainly, a beautiful tree in summer when leaves are buffeted by the breezes, the silvery underside exposed. **Flowers/seeds/fruits/cones**: Flowers are creamy white, 9- to 12-tepaled, cupped when opening, eventually flattened, sweet lemon-scented, 2 to 3″ wide, more or less continuously produced on leafy shoots from April (Athens, GA) to September. Fruit is a knobby, rounded aggregate of follicles, 2″ long and wide, often dark red, the seeds lustrous cherry-red, ripening over a long period, from August into fall. **Native range**: Magnolia, MA, then to coastal North Carolina to Florida, west to Texas, inland to piedmont of Georgia, Tennessee, Oklahoma, and Arkansas, in swamps and extremely wet soil areas. Var. *australis* represents the southern evergreen population. **Adaptability**: Authors observed immense trees in the swamp of Weeks Bay Wildlife Reserve in Alabama. Adaptable to full sun and heavy shade in moist, acid, "normal" (not inundated) soils. Zones 5 to 9. **Landscape use**: Now accelerated, with the introduction of superior cultivars. Beautiful, graceful tree utilized for patios, specimens, and the best magnolia for sites with excess water, which is a liability for most species. Chlorosis occurs in high pH soils. Transplants readily and is gaining greater landscape

Magnolia virginiana

Magnolia virginiana

Magnolia virginiana

Magnolia virginiana

EMERALD TOWER

M

'Green Shadow'

acceptance as people learn the merits. Performance is almost guaranteed. Authors notice *Betula nigra* (river birch) in restricted growing space, often dropping leaves, where this would prove a better fit. **Street tree use**: Acceptable. **In the trade**: Under nursery production, the species is often grown multi-stemmed. Ask when purchasing a sweetbay about its foliar (deciduous vs. evergreen) proclivities.

EMERALD TOWER 'JN8'. Tight, upright, and more compact, maturing 20′ tall and 8′ wide. Glossy green foliage.

'Green Mile'. Develops a graceful pyramidal habit with single trunk, uniform branching and narrow, 5 to 6″ long, lustrous dark green leaves—arguably the most beautiful foliage of any clone. Selected in Tennessee, absolute cold hardiness is unknown. Best in zone 6.

'Green Shadow'. A cold hardy selection with a conical-oval habit, 30 to 40′ high, to 20′ wide. Leaves lustrous dark green, remained evergreen after -20°F. Named by Don Shadow, Tennessee.

'Henry Hicks'

KELTYK

'Mardi Gras'

'Henry Hicks'. Possibly the hardiest and most evergreen selection, with dark green foliage. Estimate 30 to 40′ high, 20 to 30′ wide. Develops a pyramidal-oval habit. Did not lose a leaf after -24°F exposure. One of the earliest evergreen selections, named for a Long Island nurseryman by John Wister, first director of Scott Arboretum.

KELTYK 'MVMTF'. An introduction from Moon's Tree Farm in Georgia with smaller, lustrous dark green evergreen foliage, abundant fragrant flowers, and refined billowy habit. Estimate 20 to 30′ high and wide.

'Mardi Gras' ('Mattie Mae Smith'). Variegated, irregularly yellow-margined and -streaked leaves with green centers. Quite effective color element at its best. Estimate 15 to 20′ high, 8 to 10′ wide. May suffer in cold winters. Best in zones 7 to 9.

MOONGLOW 'Jim Wilson'. Distinct upright habit, matures at 35 to 40′ by 15 to 18′. Dark green, semi-evergreen leaves with pronounced silver-blue undersides. Survived -28°F without damage. An outstanding selection.

'Northern Belle'. Darker green leaves than MOONGLOW and survived -35°F. Size is 25′ high, 8 to 10′ wide; somewhat narrow-fastigiate in outline.

MOONGLOW

MOONGLOW

KELTYK

'Santa Rosa'

'Santa Rosa'. A vigorous grower, easily 2′ per year, eventually 25′ by 20′, with larger evergreen leaves than others discussed herein. Originated in Florida, so best in zones (6)7 to 10.

'Satellite'. Reliably evergreen in zone 6, glossy dark green leaves, upright oval outline, 20′ by 15′.

Magnolia zenii

Zen magnolia

Deciduous. Extremely rare species, introduced into U.S. cultivation via the Sino-American Botanical Expedition in 1980 and first flowered in 1988 at the Arnold Arboretum. Resolutely pyramidal and quite fast in youth, becoming more open and growing more moderately with age. Expect 30 to 40′ by 15 to 25′ after 25 years. Young stem is dark purple-brown becoming silvery gray, with large trunks maintaining the color, reminiscent of American beech from a distance.

Foliage: Oblong to oblong-ovate, abruptly acuminate, emerging leaves bronze-purple, maturing medium to dark green, lighter below, margins entire, with 10 to 12 lateral veins on each side of midvein, 2½ to 6″ long, 1½ to 3″ wide. Fall color is yellow to yellow-brown. **Flowers/seeds/fruits/ cones**: Flower buds are silvery, silky pubescent and sparkle like diamonds during the fall and winter months. Flowers composed of 9 tepals, 3½ to 4½″ wide, opening in cup-like fashion, eventually the outer tepals splaying, color variable, often streaked purplish pink on outside, the interior white. Fragrance is possibly the sweetest of the deciduous magnolias. Fruit is a 2 to 3″ long, ½ to 1″ wide, cylindrical, aggregate of follicles, the seeds with a scarlet aril. The species is self-fertile, as a lone tree at the University of Georgia Horticulture Farm develops numerous fruits with viable seeds. **Native range**: Jiangsu, China, extremely rare endemic, said to be 18 trees extant on a single mountainside. **Adaptability**: Zones 5 to 8. A reference reported the species' flower buds are hardy to -28°F. **Landscape use**: A beautiful early-flowering magnolia that deserves greater appreciation and use. It is the earliest-flowering deciduous magnolia the authors have evaluated with a late January, early February peak in zone 8 (Athens, GA); in Boston, it flowers about 2 weeks before *M. denudata*, 3 weeks before *M. kobus* and *M. stellata*. Often a brief warm period triggers flower buds to open, and flowers may be injured by cold. Consistent,

'Pink Parchment'

'Pink Parchment'

Magnolia zenii

'Pink Parchment'

abundant flower buds are present every year; in over 20 years, authors have yet to note an off year. The remarkable attributes are the full sun, heat, and drought tolerances. For specimen use, in groupings, to soften huge walls of brick/concrete, this is a worthy choice. The summer foliage is clean and has yet to show drought/heat stress. **Street tree use**: Potential. **In the trade**: Available, particularly as 'Pink Parchment'. Hundreds of seedlings were germinated from the Arnold Arboretum tree in 1991, with 10 robust seedlings outplanted to the Horticulture Farm in 1993. In 2017, one remained, which earlier (2002) had been christened 'Pink Parchment'; 40′ high, 20′ wide, with 3 large basal trunks. Flowers fuchsia-pink, 9 tepals, to 5″ wide, wonderfully fragrant, eventually opening white on inside, lighter pink on outside; the cooler the temperatures, the more purplish pink the opening buds and outside of mature tepals. Listed as a hybrid by some authorities, but authors believe it is true *M. zenii*. DNA analysis will provide the absolute answer.

Malus
crabapple, apple

The genus *Malus* is of great importance, contributing the common domestic apple, usually classified as *M. domestica*, and grown worldwide. We will skip the fruit category in this treatment of landscape trees, concentrating on the ornamental crabapples instead. But the domestic apple can't be completely ignored in a discussion of crabapples, as a few of its genes have crept into the ornamentals. In fact, there is a fuzzy line between crabapples and domestic apples. Crabapple fruit is often more sour, but this is not always the case. Crabapple cultivars are edible and have been bred for eating, pickling, and cider production. Crabapples do encompass more species of *Malus* than those that contributed to the domestic apple. The International Crabapple Society simply defined crabapples as *Malus* with fruit that is less than 2″ in diameter; that's as good a definition as any.

Malus hybrid

The ornamental crabapples are a huge group, evolving over time, with new introductions almost yearly. Almost all crabapples in the nursery and landscape trade are now clonally produced cultivars. Most are hybrids of hybrids, and several generations removed from their original species. Only a minority of popular cultivars have documented origin. A few crabapples are sold under species names, but in fact, these are almost always unnamed selected clones of these species. Because of this, we will treat the individual species of *Malus* briefly, and instead concentrate our discussion on the plants as they actually appear in the nursery and landscape supply chain.

Any discussion of ornamental crabapples needs to include consideration of disease issues. Fifty years ago, ornamental crabapples were beautiful in flower: breeders had emphasized flower appearance above all. But they were highly susceptible to disease; most looked great in spring bloom, then horrible in midsummer leaf. Breeding work then turned to disease resistance. The most important diseases of crabapples are scab and fireblight; other major diseases include powdery mildew, rust, and frog-eye leafspot. Diseases are not static; they evolve. We have observed that scab-resistant crabs often do not stay resistant forever; a new cultivar may be resistant at the date of introduction but begin showing infection 20 years later. If you live where spring or summer rainfall is frequent or prolonged, scab will cause problems. If warm temperatures and high humidity or showers combine at flowering time, watch out for fireblight. Scab will not kill a tree, but fireblight can. All the listed cultivars have some degree of disease resistance. Knowing the climate and disease potential in your area will guide you to the best choices.

Over the years, more than 1,000 crabapple cultivars have been selected and named. Most are long forgotten, victims of the many diseases that challenge these trees or superseded by improved versions. But a surprising number continue to be actively produced and sold; we struggled to keep our list of recommendations under 70. To ease the confusion, we separated the cultivars into six groups by flower color, form, and fruit, corresponding to landscape needs: white, red, compact, weeping, columnar, and fruitless.

Species
The following *Malus* species were important in the development of modern crabapples.

M. angustifolia (southern crabapple). Native from southern New Jersey to Florida and west to Texas. Can form colonies from suckers. Described in the white-flowering group.

M. baccata (Siberian crabapple). A vigorous species with very early white flowers and ⅜″ wide yellow to bright red fruit. It has provided breeders with extreme cold hardiness, zone 2 for the species, and moderate scab resistance.

M

M. coronaria (sweet crabapple). Another North American native, New York to Illinois and North Carolina to Arkansas. Broad-spreading, open crown; single rose-pink flowers, zone 4 hardiness.

M. floribunda (Japanese flowering crabapple). Deep red buds open to pink-tinted flowers that fade to white when fully open, $\frac{3}{8}$″ wide yellow-orange fruit, zone 4 hardiness. A very nice unnamed clone of the species is widely sold as the cultivar 'Floribunda'.

M. hupehensis (tea crabapple). Native to China. Usually apomictic, coming true from seed, so little used in hybridization, although a few cultivars claim its heritage. Described in the white-flowering group.

M. ioensis (prairie crabapple). North American native, Wisconsin to southern Minnesota and Indiana to Arkansas, with scattered distribution south to Texas. Pink buds open light pink, then fade to white as flowers open. Foliage heavily pubescent on the underside. Fruit large at 1¼″ wide, yellow, softens early. Zone 4 hardiness. Contributed the cultivars 'Klehm's Improved Bechtel', 'Prairie Rose', and BRANDYWINE.

M. pumila var. *niedzwetzkyana* (Niedzwetzky apple). Native to central Asia. A taxonomic and nomenclatural enigma, you will find it listed under several different species names or even as a cultivar, but always with Niedzwetzky's name attached. This tree contributed the purple foliage color and the rosy magenta-pink flower color to the rosybloom crabs (or, more simply, the "reds"). Also contributed the genes for red flesh to orchard apple varieties.

M. sargentii (Sargent crabapple). Important as its own species. Native to Japan, it is the smallest of the species listed here and is usually sold as a clone under the species name. Small white flowers and small red fruits, zone 5 hardiness. Apomictic; we find it comes true from seed about 95% of the time, making seedling production viable but also offering breeding opportunity, hence several pink-flowered cultivars have been developed.

M. spectabilis (Chinese crabapple). Very large flowers, white with a pink tint, used in breeding for the flower size, zone 4 hardiness. Its older double cultivar 'Riversii' contributed the breeding of other double-flowering crabs.

M. toringo (*M. sieboldii*; Toringo crab). Native to Japan, China, and Korea. Cutleaf foliage, very small fruit, yellow to red, and good scab resistance make it valuable in breeding. Zone 4 hardiness. Closely related to *M. sargentii* and *M. zumi*.

M. tschonoskii. A unique, vigorous, upright crab with silvery white, pubescent new growth. It develops bright fall colors, but fruit and flowers disappoint. A clone sold under the

species name is described in the white-flowering group. Zone 5 hardiness. We have attempted to cross it with crab cultivars of finer flower and fruit, but the results unfortunately combine the worst elements of each parent; too bad, as the potential would seem to be great.

M. zumi. A Japanese taxon, recently split from *M. toringo* and elevated to specific status. Pubescent foliage, lightly lobed, with white flowers, yellow to red small fruit, zone 5 hardiness. Of importance for the popular cultivar 'Calocarpa', described in the white-flowering group.

Rootstock choices

Crabapples, like many other trees, can produce basal suckers that are a maintenance problem. Some nurseries produce crabs by rooting cuttings; these own-root crabapples produce suckers, but the suckers are genetically identical to the top. Own-root trees are less common than those grown on a rootstock. Some cultivars root easily while others do not. Root characteristics will vary by the cultivar and are not well known individually. Each is different, and anchorage and disease resistance characteristics are not well established. Any own-root suckers that develop may eventually develop into additional trunks. At present, we recommend own-root when multi-stem crabapple specimens are desired in the landscape, as rootstock suckers are hard to remove from multi-stem trees.

A few crabs are micropropagated via tissue culture; we have found these to have delayed flowering and sharp thorn-like spurs, a consequence of induced juvenility. We would avoid micropropagated crabs.

Most nurseries produce crabapples by grafting or budding onto a rootstock; in this case, the suckers come from the rootstock. Common rootstocks and our comments follow.

Domestic rootstock. This is the old standard, seedlings of domestic apples, long used, producing a vigorous, full-sized tree. Until 30 years ago, almost all crabapples were grown on domestic rootstock. It is deeply rooted, well anchored, inducing drought resistance in dry climates. Especially good in the cold dry Intermountain West. Its downfall? It is the heaviest suckering of all the rootstocks, which is especially problematic with more compact cultivars that cannot absorb its vigor.

Dwarfing rootstock. This offers the opportunity to turn 20 to 25′ crabapples cultivars into garden-sized trees of 8 to 15′, depending on the chosen rootstock. Malling 26 is a good choice for a dwarf tree, typically about 8′; Malling 106 makes a semi-dwarf around 15′.

Hardy crabapple rootstock. Seedlings of 'Dolgo' are usually used, although seedlings of other crabs are similar. These are very cold hardy and preferred in zone 4 and north, where prolonged frozen ground and lack of snow cover can sometimes damage roots. Nearly as vigorous as domestic rootstock, but produces fewer suckers.

RIGHTROOT and SPROUTFREE. Two trademarked rootstocks designed to reduce suckers. Both perform this task well, reducing suckers to a minimum, and are well adapted to a range of soil conditions. They produce full-sized trees that are perhaps 10% smaller than those grown on domestic rootstock, which is often an advantage in an urban landscape. RIGHTROOT has the additional advantage of being resistant to collar rot.

White flowers

Full-sized trees with white flowers, green foliage, generally upright-spreading, then rounded to slightly broad. Fruit varies from yellow to red.

'Adirondack'. Upright and narrow, like a stiff, inverted cone. Dense and slightly compact, slower growing than most, it spreads a bit with age but still presents an upright appearance. Flowers very heavily with pure white flowers. Persistent fruit is bright red, ½″ wide. Good disease resistance. One of our favorites. 18′ by 12′.

M. angustifolia. Flowers are pink to deep pink in bud, opening slightly pinkish then maturing white, fragrant, single, 1 to 1¼″ wide. Yellowish green fruit a little large for an ornamental, ¾ to 1″ wide. Growth habit is rounded to spreading, usually wider than tall, 20 to 25′ high and a little wider. Probably zones 6 to 9, depending on provenance. Unlike most hybrid crabs, it is well adapted to the heat of the Deep South and is sometimes used there as a native ornamental. Susceptible to cedar apple rust.

'Adirondack'

'Adirondack'

Malus angustifolia

Malus angustifolia

Malus baccata 'Jackii'

'Dolgo'

M. baccata 'Jackii'. This selection of the Siberian crab boasts zone 2 cold hardiness and is the first to burst into bloom in spring. White flowers are followed by glossy, dark green, scab-resistant foliage. Vigorous, growing to a symmetrically rounded shape and can reach 25′ by 30′, with ½″ deep red fruit in the fall.

'Dolgo'. A big tree, most often grown for its edible fruit. Growing as a broad upright oval, it can attain 30′ height with a spread to 25′. White flowers in spring, while fall brings tasty red oval fruit, 1½″ long. If you want an edible crabapple that doubles as an ornamental, this is the best choice. Maybe brew some hard cider!

'Donald Wyman'. One of the more reliable white-flowered crabs, with glossy green summer foliage and bright red, ⅜″ wide, persistent fruit in the fall. It has shown increasing scab susceptibility in recent years. The shape is rounded, then spreading wider than tall, 20′ by 25′.

'Donald Wyman'

'Donald Wyman'

'Floribunda'. Long a favorite of the landscape industry, this old cultivar has never gone out of style; it is still very good, especially beautiful in the spring, and a standard of comparison. Vigorous, but gracefully spreading with an artistic shape, it sports bright pink buds that open to white flowers in spring and yellow-red, ⅜″ wide fruit in fall. Good scab resistance. Performs well in the Southeast, zone 8, where few crabapples are happy. 20′ tall, 25 to 30′ wide.

GOLDEN RAINDROPS 'Schmidtcutleaf'. Fine-textured cutleaf foliage brings a whole new look to crabapples. Upright-spreading, with a bit of layering in its shape; the wonderfully clean, green foliage has the best scab resistance of all the cultivars but is susceptible to fireblight. A great tree for areas like the cool moist Pacific Northwest and our first choice there, where scab pressure is high but fireblight is rare. Star-shaped white flowers. Tiny golden fruit, ¼″ wide, gives it its name. 25′ tall, 20′ wide.

HARVEST GOLD 'Hargozam'. Upright oval in shape with nice dark green foliage that stays relatively clean. White flowers in spring, and ½″ wide golden yellow fruit in the fall. 22′ by 18′. Does well in the heat of the Southeast.

GOLDEN RAINDROPS

'Floribunda'

GOLDEN RAINDROPS

M

'Floribunda'

HARVEST GOLD

Malus hupehensis

'Mary Potter'

RED JEWEL

RED JEWEL

M. hupehensis. A broad-spreading, wide, vase-shaped tree, artistic in form and an old favorite of the authors. Deep pink buds open lightly tinted pink and fade to white when fully open, followed by ⅜″ wide dull reddish fruit, zone 5 hardiness.

'Mary Potter'. A slightly compact tree with a horizontal growth pattern, to 10′ tall and 18′ wide. Flowers are good-sized and come from bright reddish pink buds, opening with a pink tint, then white in full sun. Attractive fruit is ⅜″ in diameter, bright red. Good scab resistance and has succeeded in the Southeast. Much like the form of Sargent crab but one step larger in every regard.

RED JEWEL 'Jewelcole'. The most persistent fruit of any crabapple we have seen. In a mild climate, the bright red, glossy, ⅜″ wide fruit may last through winter and still be hanging as spring bloom begins. Flowers are white, fairly typical. Form is upright-spreading, 20′ tall and 15′ wide. The tree really comes into its own in the fall with its long-lasting, brightly colored fruit display. We have observed success in the Southeast.

'Satin Cloud'

'Snowdrift'

'Snowdrift'

STARLITE

M

'Satin Cloud'. Small, stiffly spreading tree, broadly rounded to wide-spreading. Moderately compact, to 10′ tall and 18′ wide. Spur-like growth is low, stiff, sharp, bushy, and awkward to prune: tough on the nursery grower but interesting in the landscape. Small leathery green leaves. Nice pure white bloom. Fruit is yellowish, ⅜″ wide.

'Snowdrift'. A longtime favorite among the white-flowering crabs and still popular. Reliable, noted for its very symmetrical, broadly rounded shape, rather formal, 20′ tall and wide. Fruit orange, ⅜″ wide.

STARLITE 'Jeflite'. Vigorous, broadly oval, becoming round in form, probably to 25′ tall and wide. Very early flowering. Flowers are white with narrow petals but look good en masse. Leaves are large, broadly oval, and have been scab-free. Fruit is rather sparse, ⅜″ wide, orange-red. Quite cold hardy, zone 2.

STARLITE

SUGAR TYME

SUGAR TYME

Malus tschonoskii

Malus tschonoskii

SUGAR TYME 'Sutyzam'. Upright-spreading becoming rounded, 20′ tall, 18′ wide. White flowers, a good display. The fruit is its best feature, bright red, ½″ wide, and quite persistent. It has been good in the hot Southeast.

M. tschonoskii. People would probably love this crab if they could pronounce its name (hint: ignore the "ts"). Because of high fireblight susceptibility, it is suited only to cool-spring climates like the Pacific Northwest. But it's highly resistant to scab, tightly upright oval in form, and has silvery foliage that sets it apart from all other crabapples. In many ways, it looks more like a silver-foliaged CHANTICLEER pear and in our opinion has better form and foliage. Dull greenish fruit, ¾″ wide. Wonderful fall color, usually a mix of oranges, reds, and purple tints. Makes a good street tree; we have seen it nicely used that way in Seattle and Portland. 30′ tall, 14′ wide.

M. zumi 'Calocarpa' (Zumi Calocarpa). Bright red in bud, it opens to clean white flowers. Foliage shows good disease resistance. Form is broadly rounded, spreading gracefully and broadly arching, 20′ tall and 25′ wide. Fruit, bright red, ⅜″ wide. Performs well with clean foliage in the Southeast. A reliable favorite in this category.

Red flowers

The rosybloom crabs. Full-sized with flower color some shade of magenta-red to pink. Foliage emerges reddish or purplish, then fades to a dull bronze or greenish in summer heat. Upright-spreading to rounded in form. Fruit is red to maroon.

'Adams'. Upright-spreading becoming rounded, but a bit open, to 20′ by 20′. Deep pink buds open to bright, light pink flowers. Foliage is green with a slight reddish bronze tint. Fruit is ⅜″ wide, red, persistent. Performs well in the Southeast.

BRANDYWINE 'Branzam'. Large, fully double, deep pink flowers are impressive, similar to 'Klehm's Improved Bechtel'. Foliage carries a bronze tint. Rounded, large tree, 20′ or more tall, 25′ wide. But fruit is 1¼″ in diameter and makes quite a mess, so use it only where that won't cause unhappiness. Susceptible to rust.

'Candymint'. A compact tree, but not a true dwarf, although a Sargent seedling. More rounded than Sargent, grows to a 14′ height and 18′ spread. Lovely flowers, light but bright

Malus zumi 'Calocarpa'

'Adams'

Malus zumi 'Calocarpa'

BRANDYWINE

'Candymint'

'Cardinal'

'Candymint'

'Cardinal'

pink with a red margin, emerge from bright reddish pink buds. One of the prettiest individual flowers of the crabs. Fruit, ⅜″ wide, red.

'Cardinal'. Purple-red, slightly glossy foliage holds its color well through the season, at least in cooler climates. Upright-spreading, becoming rounded to spreading in shape, 20′ tall, 25′ wide. It is a seedling of *M. hupehensis*, but its shape and leaf color indicate pollen came from elsewhere. Flowers are bright magenta-pink to reddish. Good scab resistance. Fruit purple-red to deep red, ½″ wide.

CENTURION 'Centzam'. Upright and oval in form but spreads with age to more broadly rounded, 20′ tall, 18′ wide. Foliage carries a purple-bronze tint in spring but becomes green in summer. Deep magenta-pink flowers are a bit dull by current standards. Fruit, ½″ wide, deep red.

GLADIATOR 'Durleo'. Upright, rather narrow when young but more oval with age, probably will reach 20′ tall with a 12 to 15′ spread. Magenta-pink flowers, purple-bronze foliage. Fruit is reddish purple, ⅜″ wide. Cold hardy, zone 2.

CENTURION

'Indian Magic'

'Indian Summer'

M

'Indian Summer'

GLADIATOR

'Indian Magic'. An upright-spreading tree with a spreading, arching top, 20′ by 20′. Magenta-pink flowers, and slightly bronze foliage that turns green in summer. Fruit is small, red, and distinctly ovoid in shape, a bit like an upside-down teardrop, ⅜″ long and quite pretty up close. Fruit colors early and stays effective for a long time. One of the best of the crabs in this color range.

'Indian Summer'. Broadly rounded in form and relatively vigorous, 20′ by 20′ or a little larger, with rosy magenta-pink flowers and bronze-green foliage. Deep red fruit in the fall, but a bit large at ⅝″ wide.

'Klehm's Improved Bechtel'. A cultivar of *M. ioensis*, it is spectacular in spring with its large, fully double, clean and pure pink flowers. Unfortunately, the foliage is rather susceptible to rust in moist climates, and the fruit is very large, greenish, 1⅛″ wide. It can develop good orange-red fall color. 20′ tall, 24′ wide.

'Morning Princess'. Slightly compact, it is suited to the smaller garden. Rounded, then spreading with drooping tips, to 15′ by 15′. Purple-bronze foliage, light pink flowers, ½″ wide purple fruit.

'Klehm's Improved Bechtel'

'Orange Crush'

'Klehm's Improved Bechtel'

PERFECT PURPLE

PINK PRINCESS

'Orange Crush'. One of the brightest flowers in the red group, they open with a deeper magenta-red than most and hold magenta-pink without completely fading. One of our favorites in flower and has shown good disease resistance. A slightly smaller tree, rounded to 15′ by 15′, with ⅜″ wide, medium red fruit.

PERFECT PURPLE. Upright-spreading with good symmetry, becoming quite round, 20′ by 20′. Noted for deep purple foliage that holds well in summer, probably the best foliage of the really dark purple crabs. Magenta-pink flowers, small purple-red fruit.

PINK PRINCESS 'Parrsi'. A hybrid of *M. sargentii*, it carries the horizontal-spreading form of the parent species yet combines it with magenta-pink flowers and purple-bronze-tinted foliage. A small spreading tree, but a little larger than Sargent, to 10′ high with a 15′ spread. Tiny fruit, ¼″ wide, red. Good disease resistance.

PINK SPARKLES 'Malusquest'. Upright oval to rounded in form, about 18′ by 20′. A cross of RED JEWEL and 'Prairifire', it bridges the gap between the rosyblooms and the white-flowered crabs. It has enough pink in the bloom to be included in this group, but it's unusual in that it has green foliage. Buds are bright pink, and flowers are soft pink. They

PINK SPARKLES

fade, but don't go completely to white. It presents a lovely and delicate, light pink impression. Fruit is ⅜″ wide, red.

'Pink Spires'. Quite upright and symmetrically oval when young, spreading to 20′ by 20′. This tree has largely fallen out of favor as its branches open up with age, and its foliage increasingly suffers from scab. Magenta-pink flowers, maroon ½″ wide fruit.

'Prairifire'. One of the most popular crabs ever introduced, it features extremely bright reddish to magenta-pink flowers, attractive purple-tinted foliage in spring, and glossy, deep red ⅜″ wide fruit. Form is rounded, then spreading slightly wider than tall, but form is often a little open, 20′ by 20′, then spreading to 25′. Disease resistance has been good, but scab is catching up with it. Still a reliable tree, beautiful in flower, and one of the best in this category. Has done well in the Dirr garden.

'Prairifire'

'Pink Spires'

'Prairifire'

'Purple Prince'

'Purple Prince'

'Profusion'

'Radiant'

'Robinson'

'Profusion'. Upright oval in form with a deep but slightly dull magenta-pink flower. Foliage emerges purple-tinted and soon becomes dull bronze. Fruit is maroon, ½″ wide, persistent. 20′ by 20′.

'Purple Prince'. Quite similar to 'Prairifire', but stronger growing and more upright, becoming a slightly taller tree.

Bright reddish magenta-pink flowers. Purple-tinted foliage becomes a nice summer bronze, and good ⅜″ wide maroon fruit. 25′ by 20′.

'Radiant'. Looked down upon because of its high scab susceptibility in most regions, but its cold hardiness, fireblight resistance, and beautiful flowers make it a favorite in the

'Red Barron'

ROYAL RAINDROPS

'Red Splendor'

drier climate of the Mountain States, where it performs very well. Rounded form, deep red buds open to rosy pink flowers. Fruit ½″ wide, red. 25′ by 20′.

'Red Barron'. Quite popular when first introduced because of its very narrow, vase-shaped form, but with time it was found to suffer from middle-age spread, to 25′ tall and spreading 18 to 20′ wide. We have observed quite a lot of scab lately. Purple-tinted foliage in spring, deep magenta-pink flower, and deep red ½″ wide fruit.

'Red Splendor'. Upright-spreading to broadly oval in form, 25 to 30′ tall and 20′ wide. Magenta-pink flowers, reddish purple spring foliage becomes bronze in summer. Fruit is ½″ wide, red, persistent.

REJOICE 'Rejzam'. A great-looking tree in the nursery row due to its symmetrical upright and slightly flaring form. But like many of the upright crabs, it does spread with age, so it's best considered broadly oval in the long term, 20′ tall

M

519

ROYAL RAINDROPS

'Royalty'

ROYAL RAINDROPS

SCARLET BRANDYWINE

SHOW TIME

SHOW TIME

'Thunderchild'

and 15′ wide. Magenta-pink flowers, bronze foliage, and ½″ wide maroon-red fruit.

'Robinson'. Fast-growing, vigorous, and easy to grow, so nursery growers like it, reaching 25′ by 25′. Rather typical magenta-pink flowers are not as bright as some, bronze foliage, and nice ⅜″ wide red fruit.

ROYAL RAINDROPS 'JFS-KW5'. The most popular crab on the market and for good reason. Upright-spreading and slightly arching on top, to 20′ by 20′. Bright magenta-pink flowers open with a reddish tint and age to a delicate pink. Foliage emerges reddish purple, and, unlike other crabs with similar foliage color, intensifies to deeper purple in late summer instead of fading to a dull bronze. Foliage is fine-textured and deeply cut with frilled margin. Develops nice orange fall color. Fruit is tiny, ¼″ wide, and bright red. Excellent disease resistance, but we have observed some scab recently. Good performance in the hot Southeast. A favorite of ours.

'Royalty'. For years, a favorite among the purple-leaf crabs because the darkness of its foliage holds well in summer. Unfortunately, it has little else going for it. Flowers are dark magenta-red, so dark that they blend into the emerging purple foliage and are hardly visible. Form tends to be open, 15′ by 15′, and fruit, at ⅝″ wide, is on the large side and is a dull maroon-red. Susceptible to scab.

RUBY DAYZE 'JFS KW139MX'. This entry into the crowded "red" crabapple field attempts to correct the group's shortcomings. It is more upright, with a tightly oval shape, allowing clearance to walk or garden below. It has the best scab resistance among the reds. Bright magenta flower in spring, purple-red foliage follows, becoming more bronze-purple in summer, followed by the tiniest red fruits we have seen in crabs, ¼″, thus not messy. To 22′ by 16′.

SCARLET BRANDYWINE 'Scbrazam'. Said to be an improved BRANDYWINE, with slightly deeper colored flowers, but we

VELVET PILLAR

prefer the original. We have seen slow and erratic growth and fruit over 1″ in diameter, despite claims that it is smaller. 15′ tall, 20′ wide.

SHOW TIME 'Shotizam'. Magenta-pink flowers are the show-off feature of this tree. Flowers are similar to those of 'Prairifire', but a little larger and possibly even brighter. Upright spreading in form becoming rounded, to 20′ tall and 22′ wide, with bronze summer foliage, fiery fall foliage, and ½″ wide red fruit.

'Thunderchild'. Deep purple foliage is among the darkest of the crabs. Unfortunately, leaves lack a surface sheen, so never really sparkle, and are susceptible to scab. Deep magenta flowers, ½″ wide purple-red fruit. 20′ by 20′.

VELVET PILLAR 'Velvetcole'. Introduced with the idea that its narrow, upright shape and purple-tinted foliage would make a good hedge, it has really become more popular as a single-trunk tree. Moderate scab observed. Magenta-pink flowers, somewhat dull purple foliage that soon turns bronze, and ⅜″ wide maroon fruit. 20′ by 15′.

CAMELOT

FIREBIRD

CORALBURST

FIREBIRD

CORALBURST

Compact habit

Slow-growing trees, maturing to half the normal size of a crabapple or smaller. These are often grown as top grafts on a standard to make a tree form; otherwise, low and rounded to spreading with no clearance. Mature height to 15′.

LANCELOT

LOLLIPOP

CAMELOT 'Camzam'. Broadly rounded, slightly open shape, to 10′ by 10′. Magenta-red buds open to nice bright pink flowers. Bronze foliage. Fruit ½″ wide, red.

CORALBURST 'Coralcole'. Slow-growing, compact, and semi-dwarf. Most often grown as a top graft. For the first 5 to 10 years in a landscape, it will seem like it will always be dwarf. But it keeps on growing, slowly, eventually becoming a 15′ wide ball. Red buds open to bright pink flowers. Flowers are usually single, sometimes semi-double. Foliage is dull, scab-susceptible, and rarely looks good in summer. Fruit can attain red color but is usually dull and scabby, ⅜″ wide.

FIREBIRD 'Select A'. A small tree, descending from *M. sargentii*, but growing larger than its parent. Consider it a compact tree rather than a dwarf, growing to an upright oval shape of 15′. Unlike *M. sargentii*, which is low and spreading with enough clearance for a rabbit to crawl under, you can walk under a mature FIREBIRD. White flowers in spring, bright red ⅜″ wide persistent fruit in the fall. Good disease resistance and good for small gardens, recommended.

LANCELOT 'Lanzam'. Rounded, dense and symmetrical, 10′ by 10′. Pink buds open to white flowers. Fruit is yellow, ⅜″ wide, not persistent.

LOLLIPOP 'Lollizam'. Well named, usually grown as a top graft, it truly looks like a lollipop when young. Slow-growing, compact and neatly rounded in shape, yet it will eventually become a 16′ ball. Typical white flowers and green foliage, followed by yellow ⅜″ wide fruit, recommended.

M. sargentii (Sargent). Dwarf, stiffly and artistically horizontal-spreading, low to the ground. Widely used due to its small size and excellent disease resistance. Dark green, lobed, small leaves give a fine-textured appearance. Sold under the species name but usually represented in the trade as a single, selected clone. Small flowers are bright white; fruit is ¼″ wide, red. Will grow to 8′ height with a 14′ spread. Performs well in the heat of Athens, GA, with clean foliage. A favorite of ours.

Malus sargentii

Malus sargentii 'Tina'

Malus sargentii 'Tina's Ruby'

SPARKLING SPRITE

SPARKLING SPRITE

M. sargentii 'Tina' (Sargent Tina). A dwarf, spreading tree, similar to Sargent but a bit smaller with a tendency to weep slightly, 6′ tall, 8′ wide when top grafted. Good disease resistance, but foliage lacks the sparkle of *M. sargentii*. Red buds open to small white flowers. Fruit, ¼″ wide, red.

M. sargentii 'Tina's Charm'. Faster growing than 'Tina', making a larger, bushier tree, 8′ by 8′ or more. Somewhat Sargent-like in form but more rounded. Small white flowers, orange-red fruit.

SPARKLING SPRITE

APRIL SHOWERS

M. sargentii 'Tina's Ruby'. A nice small, rounded to spreading tree, with ruby-red buds opening to pale pink flowers, which may fade to nearly white in the sun, 6′ by 8′. Bronze-red foliage is nice and bright in spring but disappoints in summer, due to what appears to be frog-eye leafspot.

SPARKLING SPRITE 'JFS-KW207'. Excellent disease resistance keeps its bright green leaves sparkling through the summer; the quality of the summer foliage really sets it apart. Slow-growing, tightly rounded in shape, and will stay small, eventually 10 to 12′ in height and spread. Red buds open to bright white flowers. Fall fruit is bright orange, ⅜″ wide, and persistent into winter. A winner, and our favorite among the top-grafted dwarf crabs.

Weeping habit
Relaxed form, finer-textured branches weeping to the ground. Trees may be white-flowered with green leaves or magenta-pink with red/bronze foliage. Fruit varies. Size varies by training, as height can be increased by staking or decreased by pruning to eliminate any leaders that develop; typical sizes are given.

APRIL SHOWERS 'Uebo'. A small weeping tree with slender branches, fine-textured, maturing a little smaller than most, probably to 10′ with an equal spread. White flowers and small red fruit.

'Louisa'

'Louisa'

'Luwick'

'Louisa'. Perhaps the best weeper we have seen to date, it is unusual in having true pink flowers combined with green foliage. Branches are slender, fine-textured, and weep gracefully to the ground, close to the trunk. Yellow fruit, ⅜″ wide, in the fall. The best disease resistance we have seen in a weeping crab. 10′ by 12′.

'Luwick'. We like this weeper almost as much as 'Louisa'. Branches are not quite as fine-textured, resulting in a somewhat wider, more mounded yet still weeping form. Buds are deep reddish pink, opening to white flowers. Fruit is one of the brightest among the weepers, red, ⅜″ wide. 10′ tall, 15′ wide.

MOLTEN LAVA 'Molazam'. A really nice-looking tree but a little hard to classify. Its form is somewhere between stiffly weeping and spreading. Looks like a slightly stiff weeper when young, eventually mounding into a broad-spreading tree with weeping tips, wider than others in this category, to 14′ by 20′. Foliage is resistant to scab, a nice clean green, flowers are white, and its bright red, ½″ wide fruit gives it its name. Top-rated in Ohio testing.

'Red Jade'. An older cultivar but still popular. White flowers, green foliage on delicately weeping branches, and bright red fruit, ½″ wide. Susceptible to scab; there are better choices in wet climates, but in dry, low-humidity areas, it's a favorite. 10′ tall, 15′ wide.

'Royal Beauty'. Probably the best of the red weepers, but that's not saying a lot, as this category really needs some improvement: none are fully resistant to scab. Breeders, there is an opportunity here. Nice graceful weeping form with fine-textured branches to the ground. Purple foliage holds its color well into the summer. Deep magenta flowers in spring; deep red, ⅜″ wide fruit in fall. 10′ by 10′.

'Red Jade'

RUBY TEARS 'Bailears'. Stiffly weeping, a little open and spreading, not as fine-textured and graceful as the similar 'Royal Beauty'. Bronze foliage is a bit dull, and we have observed scab. Magenta flowers; ⅜″ wide fruit is a nice red. 12′ by 15′.

M. sargentii 'Tina's Weeper'. Small, dainty, distinctly weeping, to 5′ by 6′ when top grafted, or creeps on the ground when cutting-grown and not staked. Flowers perhaps too small be very effective, white. Red fruit. Weaker and smaller than the slightly weeping 'Tina'.

MOLTEN LAVA

'Red Jade'

RUBY TEARS

'Royal Beauty'

Malus sargentii 'Tina's Weeper'

EMERALD SPIRE

IVORY SPEAR

Columnar habit

A newly emerging development in crabapples. We include only stiffly upright, truly columnar trees with forms that stay narrow, unlike earlier upright crabs that spread with age. Expect truly narrow trees with 20′ height and width of 8′ or less.

EMERALD SPIRE 'Jefgreen'. Densely upright and columnar in form with bronze-green foliage. Flowers are a very light magenta-pink. Red fruit is quite large, 1⅛″ wide, which can make it messy in the landscape. 20′ by 8′.

IVORY SPEAR 'JFS KW214MX'. Very tight and densely columnar, upright with stiffly ascending branches that maintain its narrow form. Spring brings reddish buds and clean white flowers. Bright green summer foliage is especially clean-looking, fireblight resistant and among the most scab resistant we have seen. Small fruit is of good ornamental size, ½″ wide, and very bright cherry-red. 18′ by 7′.

PURPLE SPIRE 'Jefspire'. Densely columnar habit and purple-bronze foliage make for impressive early summer form. Magenta-pink flowers in spring are a bit sparse. Fruit is purple but large, about 1″ wide, and can be messy. 20′ by 8′.

RASPBERRY SPEAR 'JFS KW213MX'. Very tight in form, stiffly upright and densely columnar, featuring magenta-pink flowers and clean dark purple foliage, bronzing in late summer and fall. Stiffness and shorter internodes mean it maintains its narrow form. Fruit is of good ornamental size, ½″ wide, purple-red ripening to bright red. Very good resistance to scab and fireblight. Handsome and recommended. 20′ by 8′.

IVORY SPEAR

IVORY SPEAR

RASPBERRY SPEAR

M

PURPLE SPIRE

RASPBERRY SPEAR

RASPBERRY SPEAR

MARILEE

'Prairie Rose'

'Spring Snow'

Fruitless

A high-demand category, as there are few fruitless (or nearly so) cultivars. Certain landscape sites, such as decks, patios, and sidewalks, demand neatness. In most situations, ornamental fruit is one of a crabapple's most beautiful features. But when cleanliness below the tree is paramount, you'll want fruitless. The cultivars listed are either completely fruitless or occasionally produce only a very few misshapen fruits, keeping hardscape below nice and clean. Full-sized, 20 to 25'.

MARILEE 'Jarmin'. Take a look at this crab as a possible street tree. It is strongly upright and quite narrow, a tight vase shape, 24' tall, 14' wide, and virtually fruitless. No mess on the sidewalk, no mess on the street. It is narrow enough to give clearance for traffic. Add in large fully double flowers from bright pink buds, and you have a cultivar that stands apart from the others. Light (but not bad) scab has been observed. Deserves both landscape and street tree use, our favorite in this category.

'Prairie Rose'. Large, true pink, fully double flowers adorn this plant in spring, looking much like 'Klehm's Improved Bechtel'. But this cultivar is completely fruitless, one of very few crabs that can make that claim. Rounded form. Some susceptibility to both scab and fireblight. 20' by 20'.

'Spring Snow'. Vigorous and upright oval in shape, becoming more rounded with age, 25' by 25'. Known for good cold hardiness. White flowers are fairly typical, as is the green foliage. Its one claim to fame is that it does not set fruit, and it has long been the tree of choice when fruitlessness is the prime criterion. Scab susceptibility is its downfall.

Melia azedarach
Chinaberry, bead tree

Deciduous. Those who know this species consider it pestiferous and invasive; especially in warmer climates, one can drive for miles and experience fencerows, fallow fields, and woodland edges overrun with it. Even when subzero temperatures kill trees to the ground, most resprout and flower in a few short years, producing seedy inoculum that initiates a new colonization process. So, you ask, why discuss? First as a warning, but also authors venture that if sterile selections were bred or genetically engineered, they would serve as excellent urban trees. Habit is rounded, 30 to 40' high and wide, with a full, fine-textured canopy. Growth is fast, weed-like in aggressiveness. Bark is gray-brown, ridged and furrowed.

Melia azedarach

Melia azedarach

'Jade Snowflake'

M

Foliage: Large, bipinnately compound leaf, 12 to 24(32)″ long, half as wide, composed of 1½ to 2″ long leaflets, each lustrous rich green, finely serrate, toothed and lobed. Leaves emerge later in spring than many deciduous species. Fall colors yellow-green; in perfect autumns, brilliant yellow-gold. **Flowers/seeds/fruits/cones:** Fragrant, ¾″ wide, lilac-lavender to violet flowers, borne in loose, fleecy 8 to 16″ long and wide panicles, open in May. Flowers occur on previous year's branches and are somewhat camouflaged by the foliage of the current season. Fruit, a rounded, ½″ wide, yellow to yellow-brown drupe with a hard, bony seed, ripens in September-October, persisting into winter and spring, apparently taken by wildlife, after other food sources are exhausted. Literature mentions fruit size to 2″ wide, although authors have yet to witness such magnitude. **Native range:** Northern India, central and western China. **Adaptability:** In a cultural sense, as intensely adaptable as *Ailanthus altissima*, but restricted to zones 7 to 10. Our observations point to insect and disease immunity; high heat and drought tolerances; adaptable to any soil but wet. **Landscape use:** Use should be tempered or forgotten until improvement is made. A sterile cultivar would prove a great polluted-urban-environment addition. Authors observed 30′ high trees without fruit and wondered if perhaps they were sterile. Work at the University of Georgia, Tifton, station has advanced selections of potentially sterile trees. Time is the arbiter, for sterility is a moving and unpredictable target. **Street tree use:** Utilized as such in Mediterranean countries. **In the trade:** In 'Jade Snowflake', leaves are speckled and splashed with white on the shiny green background; fast-growing, reaching 20 to 30′ high. 'Umbraculifera' (Texas umbrella-tree) assumes the shape of an inverted ice cream cone; reaches 20 to 25′ high, most often multi-trunked from base but could be trained to a single stem. Both cultivars reproduce true-to-type from seed.

Mespilus germanica

medlar tree

Deciduous. Little known, even less grown, small, round-headed to broad-canopied, low-branched tree; in fact, branches sweep downward, producing a semi-weeping effect. Size 15 to 20′ in height with an equal or greater spread. Originally cultivated by ancient Romans and Greeks; popular in the Victorian era in western Europe. A jelly made from the fruits may be likened to applesauce. On the many garden tours to Europe, beautiful specimens pop up, and we have yet to see a participant correctly identify.

Foliage: Leaves are dull dark green, pubescent on both sides, more prominently below, oblong-lanceolate, 2 to 5″ long, half as wide, minutely toothed, appearing sessile (short petiole). They are frost resistant, and their golden orange to red fall color persists. **Flowers/seeds/fruits/cones**: Flowers are white to blush-pink, 5-petaled, 1 to 1½″ wide, borne on short, leafy branches in May-June. Not overwhelming, but delicate and attractive on close inspection. The woolly pubescent sepals are triangular with a long narrow point that extends beyond the petals. The species is self-fertile, meaning a single tree will produce fruits. Fruit is hard as a rock and must be subjected to cold or stored cold to soften and ripen, a process called bletting. The fruit is a brown, apple- to pear-shaped, 1 to 1½″ wide pome, the 5 sepals still present. **Native range**: Europe to Iran. **Adaptability**: More cold hardy than recognized, potential to zone 4b, with 5 to 8 guaranteed. Authors observed fine specimens from Maine to Illinois. **Landscape use**: Although stigmatized as a fruit tree, it doubles as a pretty landscape tree, its interlacing branches creating a picturesque habit. Succeeds in full sun, well-drained, acid and neutral soils. Flowers develop from previous season's wood, so pruning anytime reduces flower and/or fruit potential. Our observations point to a trouble-free small tree for home garden use. Somewhat a mystery why this has not received more attention from horticulturists. **Street tree use**: No. **In the trade**: Surprising number of selections from specialist fruit nurseries, including 'Breda Giant' (large fruit, with sweet, flavorful, fine-textured flesh), 'Marron' (large, tasty, chestnut-colored fruit), and 'Royal' (sweet-tart, dark nut-brown fruit).

Mespilus germanica

Mespilus germanica

Mespilus germanica

Metasequoia glyptostroboides
dawn redwood

Deciduous conifer. It's big, fast, and tall. Narrowly pyramidal when young, always single-trunked, straight, and becoming slightly wider with age, but always pyramidal. Very fine-textured in foliage, but the winter appearance is coarser, and the trunk is definitely bold. Fast-growing to 80′ with a 25′ width. Time will tell; we will surely see much larger trees in favorable locations. Bark is red-brown when young, becoming more gray with a magenta-brown tint with age, in shaggy strips running up and down the fluted trunk.

Foliage: Needles are small and narrow, ½″ long and ¹⁄₁₆″ wide, resembling the foliage of *Sequoia sempervirens* but deciduous and therefore softer to the touch as well as softer in appearance. Needles are light green upon spring emergence, becoming darker green in summer. Leaf arrangement is opposite. Foliage turns a warm rusty orange in fall, never bright but always pleasant. **Flowers/seeds/fruits/cones**: Monoecious. Flowers insignificant. Cones are ovoid, brown, ¾″ long. **Native range**: When? This tree was first known as an "extinct" fossil, widespread in North American forests during the Mesozoic Era, before the surprising discovery of living trees in a limited area of central China, on wetter soils, in 1944. One of the most exciting plant discovery stories of all time. **Adaptability**: Despite its small native range, it has proven quite adaptable in North America and Europe, cold hardy, and not too picky about soils. We have seen it in standing water as well as very dry soils. It likes moisture, but it has proven to be tolerant of reasonably dry conditions as well. Zones 5 to 8. **Landscape use**: The authors love this tree. It's big. It's bold. It's massive yet delicate at the same time. Its muscular, fluted trunk is as strong as its foliage is soft. The trunk's straightness is absolutely linear, yet its branches sweep gracefully; it flares broadly at the base, and low branches emerge from mysteriously deep furrows in the lower trunk, such as might be portrayed in a dark and magical forest. The foliage renews each spring with the bright softness found only in a deciduous conifer. This tree is texture and form and size. It's different from the norm; use it for impact. **Street tree use**: Some cities are calling for the use of more conifers as street trees. Dawn redwood is a good candidate as its deciduous foliage allows light to penetrate during the darkness of winter. In siting, remember that it becomes large, and the base is buttressed. It needs the widest planting strips. **In the trade**: Mostly sold as seed-grown, and seed-grown trees are generally very nice. Most cultivars never gain traction; 'Goldrush', JADE PRINCE, and 'Miss Grace' are in the mainstream; the others rare.

Metasequoia glyptostroboides

Metasequoia glyptostroboides

M

Metasequoia glyptostroboides

Metasequoia glyptostroboides

Metasequoia glyptostroboides

AMBERGLOW

AMBERGLOW

AMBERGLOW 'Wah-08AG'. Yellow foliage with an orange tint in summer, pyramidal. A new introduction, listed as 15′ tall, 7 to 8′ wide, but we suspect it will, like other yellow forms, exceed this with time, probably 40′ by 20′.

'Goldrush'

JADE PRINCE

M

'Goldrush'

JADE PRINCE

'Golden Guusje' ('Kools Gold'). Yellow foliage. A newer introduction from Holland, with some claims of improvement over 'Goldrush'. We are waiting to see. 40′ tall, 20′ wide.

'Goldrush' ('Gold Rush', 'Ogon', 'Golden Oji'). Strikingly brilliant; wonderful when used against a dark green background. Foliage begins soft yellow in spring then becomes bright yellow. Authors have observed that in the Pacific Northwest, the yellow color brightens as the summer progresses, but in the South, it becomes more lime-green. Grows at half the rate of the species or less; we expect it to mature at about half the size. 40′ tall, 20′ wide.

'Jack Frost'. Green foliage is splashed white, more noticeably on new growth and on young trees, the effect lessening as the tree matures. 'White Spot', 'White Tips', 'Snow Flurry', and other similar white-splashed cultivars exist for the *Metasequoia* connoisseur. 60′ tall, 20′ wide.

JADE PRINCE 'JFS-PN3Legacy'. Outstanding lush foliage, cleaner and brighter green than the species, and the tree has better density in youth. Upright and pyramidal yet full in form. Superior appearance over typical seed-grown trees. Fast-growing and shapes up well in the nursery. Our favorite cultivar for a full-sized dawn redwood. 70 to 80′ tall, 20 to 25′ wide.

'Miss Grace'

'National'

'Urban Spire'

PALATIAL

SHAW'S LEGACY

'Waasland'

'Miss Grace'. Cute and little, gracefully weeping, a small tree that will take a long, long time to get to 15′ tall, 10′ wide.

'National'. Upright and a little narrower than typical of the species, probably 70′ by 30′. A U.S. National Arboretum selection, chosen for maintaining healthy foliage in the humidity of Washington, DC.

PALATIAL 'MG1042'. Upright pyramidal, dense, and appears a little tighter in form than the species, dark green in summer, orange-brown in fall. We estimate 60′ by 20′.

SHAW'S LEGACY 'Raven'. Propagated from an outstanding tree at the Missouri Botanical Garden, uniform and conical, a slightly broader pyramid. 70′ by 30′.

'Urban Spire'. Pyramidal, a little narrower than the species when young, but widening. Displays strongly upsweeping branches, which should allow more traffic clearance when pruned up, a good street choice. To 70′ by 25′.

'Waasland'. Distinctly narrow with tightly upright branching, not quite columnar but very narrowly pyramidal, much tighter than the species when young, but branches bend outward with time, making it wider, 80′ by 25′. Stiffer in look, not as graceful as other forms; the bark too has an unusual appearance, almost black.

Morus alba

white mulberry, common mulberry

Deciduous. Fast-growing. Beyond that, the form really depends on the cultivar. For the species, let's just say it's a weedy, unkempt, rounded tree, coarse in texture, to 40′ by 40′. Bark is orange-brown on young trunks, then gray-brown to gray, lightly ridged and fissured.

Foliage: Very dark green leaves are variable in shape, up to 7″ long by 6″ wide. Generally broadly ovate, they may be lobed or not, with lobes varying from one to many, shallow to deep. Leaves are coarsely serrate or dentate and prominently veined on the underside, typically glabrous except along veins. Leaves hold a good gloss, and from a distance the tree may appear to have the deepest green foliage in the landscape in the heat of summer. Yellow fall color. **Flowers/seeds/fruits/cones**: Polygamo-dioecious, but sometimes dioecious, allowing for fruitless selections. Flowers yellowish green, in spring, in pendulous catkins, not showy. Multiple fruits develop in summer, looking much like long blackberries, but vary in color: white, pink, red, or purple-black. Soft and messy, and birds spread the mess. The fruit is edible but bland; it looks much better than it tastes. **Native range**: China. **Adaptability**: Highly adaptable, it is naturalized widely throughout much of the world after being imported with the idea of farming silkworms. In some areas of North America it is considered invasive. Indifferent to soil pH, salt resistant. It takes the heat and drought of the semi-desert Southwest, where it is most popular. Zones 4 to 9. **Landscape use**: Because of both messiness and invasiveness, only male cultivars are recommended. Its value is its tolerance of the most adverse conditions. In more temperate climates, it has little to recommend it. It finds its place in hot, dry, and often high pH soils from Texas to California. A few cultivars, great improvements over the species, dominate use. Avoided in some communities because of allergenic pollen. **Street tree use**: Has a bad reputation for pavement damage, most are wide-spreading, usually not a good choice. **In the trade**: Avoid seed-grown trees and fruiting cultivars.

'Chaparral'. Weeping, mounding and ascending in a zig-zag pattern over time, with long lax branches weeping to the ground, 12′ tall, 16′ wide. Glossy dark green foliage, deeply lobed when young, ovate on more mature trees. Fruitless.

'Fruitless'. Fast-growing, rounded form. A good shade tree in climates where few will grow, 40′ by 40′. Commonly listed and sold as a cultivar name, but some authorities say it may be a synonym for 'Kingan' and 'Stribling'.

'Kingan'. Large, dark green, heart-shaped leaves on a rounded shade tree, 40′ by 40′. Fruitless.

Morus alba

Morus alba

'Pendula'. Weeping form, fairly common, fruits heavily so we recommend against it. We suggest 'Chaparral' instead. 12′ by 16′.

var. *tatarica* (Russian mulberry). Very cold hardy strain, grown from seed, with smaller leaves and fruit than species. Formerly common in windbreaks; now mostly used as rootstock. 40′ by 40′.

'Chaparral'

Morus nigra
black mulberry

Deciduous. Upright-spreading to wide-spreading habit, rounded on top, usually with a short, very stout trunk. Moderately coarse in texture, moderately fast-growing to 30′ tall and 35′ wide. Bark is gray-brown and lightly fissured on older trees, often gnarled. Historically cultivated for its fruit; George Washington grew it at Mount Vernon. Unlike the insipid fruit of white mulberry, the black mulberry is delicious.

Foliage: Variable shape, broadly ovate to broadly cordate with occasional irregular side lobes, dentate margin, prominently veined on underside, usually 4 to 7″ long and 2 to 5″ wide. Medium green. Pubescent (unlike *M. alba*): stiff hairs on upper leaf surface, softer and downy on the gray-green underside. Yellowish in the fall. **Flowers/seeds/fruits/ cones**: Monoecious or dioecious, and may change over time. Catkins short, green, pendulous, not showy. Blackberry-like clusters of multiple fruits follow, red when immature, black when ripe. **Native range**: Uncertain, long cultivated and escaped, but extinct in the wild. Believed to have originated in mountains of Iran and Iraq. **Adaptability**: Tough and adaptable, heat tolerant. Fortunately it does not have the invasive reputation of *M. alba*. Zones 5 to 9. **Landscape use**: Not common; most common in California. Usually planted for the fruit but does double duty as a landscape tree. The tasty fruit is messy if allowed to fall. **Street tree use**: Not recommended, too low and broad-spreading; fruit messy over sidewalks. **In the trade**: 'Black Beauty' has juicy, large, tasty fruit; makes a smaller, spreading tree, to 15′. 'Persian' also has large fruit but grows larger, to 20 to 25′. Both are self-fertile.

M

'Pendula'

Morus rubra

red mulberry

Deciduous. Upright-spreading, taller and more open than *M. alba*. Moderately coarse texture, moderately fast-growing to 50′ high, 45′ wide. Bark is gray-brown, with flattened ridges and shallow furrows.

Foliage: Ovate to broadly ovate, serrate, rough surfaced on top but soft pubescent below, 3 to 7″ long and 2 to 4″ wide. Leaves on slower-growing portions of the tree are usually without lobes, but those on vigorous shoots may have 1 to 5 irregular lobes and serrations that are coarser. Dark green, holding good color through the summer, then yellow in the fall. **Flowers/seeds/fruits/cones**: Usually dioecious, sometimes monoecious. Yellowish green, pendulous catkins, not showy. Blackberry-like clusters of multiple fruits, red to dark purple when ripe, edible and sweet. **Native range**: Eastern United States, from New York to southern Minnesota and Florida to east Texas. **Adaptability**: Climatically adaptable but likes rich, moist soil; not as drought tolerant as white and black mulberries. Zones 5 to 8. **Landscape use**: Has potential as a shade tree, although concern about bacterial disease needs investigation. As a U.S. native, there is no worry of invasiveness in the East. Selection of a male, fruitless tree with good form and foliage might add to our landscape diversity. **Street tree use**: Has potential as a large street tree, especially with selection for form. **In the trade**: Rarely seen; sold as seed-grown.

Morus rubra

Morus rubra

Morus rubra

N

showy, appearing with the leaves in spring; male in many flower clusters; female flowers solitary. Flowers provide early-season bee pasture. Fruit is a reddish purple to dark blue or purple, 1″ long, ellipsoidal drupe with thin flesh and an 8 to 10″ sharply ridged, stony endocarp (nutlet) that ripens in autumn. Fruit is borne singly on a slender stalk. **Native range**: Virginia to Florida, west to Illinois and Texas, following the watercourses inland. **Adaptability**: Zones 6 to 9. **Landscape use**: Has never been promoted to the gardening community, remaining the purview of foresters, but it is a terrific choice for planting in wet sites. May prove difficult to transplant large specimens, but small container-grown trees are acceptable. **Street tree use**: No. **In the trade**: Seedling material. The U.S. National Arboretum has bred several pretty hybrid progeny. The authors anticipate new *Nyssa* genetics will enrich our palette of noble trees.

Nyssa aquatica

Nyssa aquatica
water tupelo

Deciduous. Attractive U.S. native, hailing from floodplain forests, swamps, ponds, and lake margins, where it forms a narrow, open crown, eventually 50 to 80′ high. Adapts to drier soil situations, but growth is reduced. Bark is gray-brown to dark brown, ridged and furrowed with vertical fissures; ridges scaly to blocky, variable in shape. In wet areas, where trunk bases are inundated for long periods, the base becomes buttressed, much like *Taxodium distichum*. In South Carolina's Congaree National Park, where trees are flooded up to 10 times in a season and may exist year-round in standing water, the species is so common it forms solid stands with arrow-straight boles and swollen fluted bases. Walking among these magnificent trees left no doubt we made the best possible career choices. Quite a valuable timber tree but perhaps more worthy as a nectar and food source for an array of wildlife.

Foliage: Leaves 4 to 8(12)″ long, 2 to 4″ wide, oblong-ovate to elliptic, entire or angular toothed, dark green above, paler beneath, turning red to purple in fall. The lone tree on the Georgia campus developed pretty yellow fall color. Leaves are clustered at ends of current season's growth with bare stems beneath, resulting in a loose canopy. **Flowers/seeds/fruits/cones**: Effectively dioecious; however, perfect flowers also occur on single trees. The greenish flowers are not

Nyssa aquatica

Nyssa aquatica

Nyssa biflora (*N. sylvatica* var. *biflora*)
swamp tupelo

Deciduous. Another wallflower of the genus, underappreciated and worthy of bringing to the garden party. Under cultivation, the species has a fine-textured, soft-pyramidal habit in youth; developing a clear trunk and narrow crown at maturity; we estimate 40 to 50′ high, 30 to 40′ wide. Remarkable trees over 150′ are reported in the wild. Seedling growth is fast, 4 to 5′ in a single season. Bark is gray-brown, ridged and furrowed, the ridges exfoliating on old trunks. Fruits are palatable and relished by wildlife, especially ducks.

Foliage: Fine-textured, elliptical to narrowly obovate leaves, 3 to 6″ long, 1 to 2″ wide, are medium to dark green. Many lowland swamp trees do not develop great fall color; but surprisingly, seedlings of this species turn beautiful shades of orange, red, and purple. Obviously, an opportunity exists for selecting superior fall-coloring clones. **Flowers/seeds/fruits/cones**: Flowers are similar to *N. sylvatica*, green, except female occur in pairs (hence the epithet). Flowers

Nyssa biflora

Nyssa biflora

open with the developing foliage. Fruits are borne 1 to 2 per stalk, dark blue, ⅓ to ½″ long, the pulp thin, bitter, the stone prominently ribbed, ripening in October. **Native range**: Maryland to Florida, west to Arkansas and Texas, primarily coastal, but following watercourses inland as far north as Missouri and Illinois. Authors observed the species in the wild, where it inhabits swamps, bogs, bottomlands, pond and lake margins. **Adaptability**: Observation tells the authors the species is adapted to wet and dry conditions, full sun to partial shade, and acid soil. A lone seedling in the Dirr garden survived, in good condition, the debilitating summer of 2016 without supplemental water. Zones 6 to 9. **Landscape use**: Beautiful tree for large-area use in moist to wet soils. Observed trees prospering in containers at the University of North Carolina, Chapel Hill. Seedlings maintain a central leader, developing many fine-textured, thinnish branches compared to *N. sylvatica*. A large seedling population developed uniform fall colors, indicating strong genetic propensity. A surprising and pleasant result. Who knew? The seeds were collected in low, permanently wet areas along Mobile Bay, Fairhope, AL. Foliage will contract mycosphaerella leafspot, but not to the degree of *N. sylvatica*. **Street tree use**: With selection, would serve as a beautiful street element. **In the trade**: Seedling and small trees are sold. No effort yet expended to develop superior clones.

Nyssa ogeche
Ogeechee tupelo, Ogeechee-lime

Deciduous. Develops a dense, rounded canopy. Growth is slow, to 30 to 40′ high and wide. Bark is gray-brown, smooth on young branches, lightly ridged and furrowed later. Usually, there are several trunks, developing tapering bulbous bases. This species is the major source of tupelo honey; thousands of acres of it were planted in the Gulf Coast for bee pastures. Wildlife savor the fruits, the thick, juicy, extremely sour pulp of which can be made into jam and jelly.

Foliage: Leaves to 6″ long, occasionally more, half as wide, elliptic to obovate-oblong, lustrous dark green, pale gray-green below and often soft pubescent. Authors have yet to note fall color of consequence as leaves remain green into late fall (November) with a hint of yellow. Literature states red-purple fall color as a possibility. **Flowers/seeds/fruits/cones**: Dioecious; some flowers perfect. Flowers are green developing with foliage; scarcely noticeable. Fruit is unique among *Nyssa* species, ¾ to 1½″ long, ½ to ¾″ wide, ovate in outline, red blushed to bright red at maturity, often remaining attached after leaves fall. The stone has paper-thin wings that extend through the pulp almost to the outer skin. Fruits mature in fall. **Native range**: Restricted to South Carolina, Florida, and Georgia in swamps, borders of streams, lakes, and ponds. **Adaptability**: A swamp creature

Nyssa ogeche

Nyssa ogeche

Nyssa sinensis
Chinese tupelo

Deciduous. Received feverish attention when first introduced, but susceptibility to leafspot and canker significantly dampened enthusiasm. At its best a gracefully pyramidal tree with uniform branching habit. The few trees authors observed maintained this form at 30′. Estimate 30 to 50′ high, 20 to 30′ wide at maturity; moderate growth rate, 1 to 2′ per year. Bark is gray-brown, rough-textured, irregularly scaly.

Foliage: Leaves are thin, shiny to dull dark green, paler and lustrous below, narrowly oval, elliptic to oblong-lanceolate, 3 to 6″ long, a third as wide, tapering at both ends. New

Nyssa sinensis

with remarkable adaptability. Like *N. aquatica* and *N. biflora*, it resides in wet environments but is well adapted to drier soils. The tree in the Dirr garden displayed high heat and drought tolerance. Zones 6 to 9. **Landscape use**: Authors harbored high expectations for this species as a southeastern landscape tree because of its small size, soil tolerances, attractive foliage, Auburn University evaluated 200 tree taxa over 13 years, and this was rated in the top eight. But it requires fine-tuning to create an acceptable landscape version. Will this happen? Past efforts have yet to yield the desired results. Somewhat difficult to transplant, which limits field growing. An Achilles' heel is the willy-nilly development of shoots from roots; a lone tree in the Dirr garden exhibited this frustrating propensity. However, *N. ogeche*, even with the warts, is worth utilizing in native plantings. Foliage is not impacted by the leafspot that is so common on *N. sylvatica*. **Street tree use**: No, usually multi-trunked and so not well designed for this purpose. **In the trade**: Sold as small seedlings.

Nyssa sinensis

growth emerges bronze to plum-purple; in autumn, pretty hues of yellow and red. **Flowers/seeds/fruits/cones**: Dioecious. Greenish white flowers with the leaves in spring. Male is a ½″ wide rounded head at the end of a slender, hairy, 1 to 1½″ long stalk; females few on longer stalks. Fruit is a small, blue, oblong or obovoid drupe, ¼ to ½″ long. **Native range**: Vietnam, central China, in wet mixed forests along streams and valleys at 1,000 to 5,000′ elevation, according to Flora of China. **Adaptability**: Zones 6 to 9. Successfully grown at the Arnold Arboretum, Boston. **Landscape use**: In several years of testing in arboreta and research facilities, it has yet to receive first-class accolades. We tested it in Oregon and, ho hum, it's nice but why bother, as we prefer our native *N. sylvatica*. Difficult for authors to assess the future of the species. We know it is being utilized in breeding and have noted seedling populations. These trees are many years away from introduction. The habit is fine-textured, the branches not as rigid-stiff-coarse as *N. sylvatica*. As a park or residential element, it has inherent beauty. Requires moist, acid soil and full sun for maximum growth. The best tree we observed was situated in an expanse of turf on a dry slope. **Street tree use**: Potential. **In the trade**: Not common, tsunamied from commerce by a new wave of *N. sylvatica* cultivars. Until reliable clones or hybrids are introduced, *N. sinensis* is trapped in a biological cul-de-sac.

Nyssa sylvatica
black tupelo, black gum

Deciduous. Broadly pyramidal in youth, typically with horizontal branching from a central trunk, reminiscent of a young pin oak in winter profile, it becomes more rounded with age. Medium growth rate to 45′ high, 25′ wide, medium texture. Bark dark gray-brown to charcoal, roughly ridged and fissured, sometimes cross-checked into squiggly blocks.

Foliage: At best, the foliage is truly spectacular, both summer and autumn, but variation rules. Leaves are 3 to 6″ long, 1½ to 3″ wide, lustrous dark green and quite handsome, smooth on the surface and along the margin, generally elliptical, from slightly ovate to slightly obovate. Fall colors varies from lovely to breathtaking, from yellow-oranges to deep reds. **Flowers/seeds/fruits/cones**: Polygamo-dioecious. Tiny naked-looking flowers appear with the expanding leaves in spring, yellow-green to green and hard to see unless you look for them. Male flowers are yellow-green balls of stamens; females consist of little more than an ovary with an exposed pistil; nothing fancy, just the bare minimum for function. **Native range**: Most of eastern North America, from southern Maine to Michigan and Florida to east Texas, growing not only in swamps but in drier mesic woods to 5,000′ mountains in the southern Appalachians. **Adaptability**: Prefers deep acid soils and

Nyssa sylvatica

Nyssa sylvatica

moisture, but grows on dry ridges and quite tolerant of swamps. Avoid high pH soils. Otherwise, quite adaptable to varied conditions and urban soils. Does best in full sun but tolerates shade quite well. Zones (4)5 to 9. **Landscape use**: Difficult to transplant, but tough once established. A wonderful shade tree with a distinct form and foliage. The dark and glossy summer leaves give a quality appearance all

Nyssa sylvatica

Nyssa sylvatica

AFTERBURNER

AFTERBURNER

season then give way to some of the brightest fall colors in the landscape. Single specimens or groups jump out in the fall. Leafspot (pathogen: *Mycosphaerella nyssicola*) is a significant problem, marring the leaves with purple-black spots. It is most severe in the humid East. **Street tree use**: Cultivars with more upright branch patterns make fine street trees. Their moderate size and deep roots are compatible with hardscape. Avoid seedlings on streets as form is variable and lower branches may droop into traffic. **In the trade**: New cultivars highlight the best virtues of this tree, which is rapidly becoming a darling of the landscape.

AFTERBURNER 'David Odom'. Strongly upright, symmetrical, with a dominant central leader and upsweeping branches, excellent form, a little narrower than most, good for streets or where width is limited. Leafspot has been significant in humid Georgia, but foliage is clean in

'Autumn Cascades'

FIREMASTER

FIRESTARTER

low-humidity Oregon summers. Fall color comes on a week later than typical, starting burgundy-red, becoming bright red. Female. 45′ by 20′.

'Autumn Cascades'. A weeping form, with a central leader and lateral branches that begin horizontal, looking like it won't really be a weeper, then sway toward the ground. It tends to be irregular when young but gains a semi-respectable weeping shape with age, to 15 to 20′ tall and 12′ wide. Fall color is a mix of yellows and orange-red. Female.

FIREMASTER 'PRP1'. Pyramidal, upright, with a central leader, reddish spring new growth, dark green in summer, and good red in the fall. Female. 45′ tall, 25′ wide.

FIRESTARTER 'JFS-red'. An excellent pyramidal form with upsweeping branches and a good central leader, slightly narrower than the species, a good street tree form. It starts the fiery season of fall color by turning brilliant red a week before other cultivars. Its deep green summer foliage is just as appealing. Male, seedless. 40′ tall, 18′ wide.

FOREST FIRE 'TheJames'. Broadly pyramidal and fast-growing with moderately upsweeping branches, it

maintains a strong central leader. Summer foliage is hand-some glossy green with a red petiole, fall color is bright red. 45′ tall, 25′ wide.

FORUM 'NXSXF'. Quite formal form. Excellent upright growth habit, neat and symmetrical, broadly pyramidal. But lags behind the brightest cultivars in fall color, usually a nice yellow-orange. Female. 45′ tall, 25′ wide.

GREEN GABLE 'NSUHH'. Broadly pyramidal, symmetrical, full, with upsweeping branches. Foliage shines bright glossy green all summer. Named for its excellent summer appear-ance, but its bright red fall color is just as notable. Has shown some resistance to leafspot. Male, seedless. 50′ tall, 25 to 30′ wide.

GUM DROP 'JFS-PN Legacy1'. Slightly compact, dense, symmetrical and upright oval. Outstanding summer foliage, glossy and very deep green. Fall color is bright red. Male, seedless. 30′ tall, 20′ wide.

NORTHERN SPLENDOR. Broadly upright with dark green foli-age, turning bright red in fall. Selected in Michigan, it goes dormant early and claims zone 4, 45′ tall, 25 to 30′ wide.

FIRESTARTER

FORUM

FOREST FIRE

FORUM

GREEN GABLE

GUM DROP

'Sheri's Cloud'

GUM DROP

GREEN GABLE

RED SPLYNDOR

'Penwood Weeper'

'Penwood Weeper'

'Penwood Weeper'. A mature weeping habit, with glossy bright green summer foliage and yellow-orange fall color. Irregular and spreading when young, its central leader will gain height, and the tree eventually forms a rounded crown with branches weeping to the ground. Female. 35′ tall, 25′ wide.

RED RAGE 'Haymalred'. Outstanding summer foliage; the leaves are larger than most, deep green, and especially glossy. Form is a slightly loose, a more informal, broad pyramid, and fall colors are excellent, orange-red to bright red. Male, seedless. 45′ tall, 25′ wide.

RED SPLYNDOR 'NSMTF'. Pyramidal to oval, upright with central leader, red fall color. Female. 45′ tall, 25′ wide.

'Sheri's Cloud'. The best variegated selection we have seen. Leaves with cream-white margins and slightly grayish green interior. A large tree has a slightly ghostly appearance against a dark conifer background. Leaf margin turns pinkish orange in the fall. 30′ tall, 20′ wide.

RED RAGE

RED RAGE

TUPELO TOWER

WHITE CHAPEL

'Wildfire'

WHITE CHAPEL

'Zydeco Twist'

'Wildfire'

TUPELO TOWER 'WFH1'. Upright growth habit from a good central leader, it is one of the narrower cultivars with a form that's good for street use. Dark green summer foliage, orange fall color. Ohio provenance, probably more cold hardy than most. Female. 40′ by 20′.

WHITE CHAPEL 'Cherry Pie'. A loose, broader and more informal pyramidal shape with semi-spreading branches and a dominant central leader. Vigorous, bright green in summer with cherry-red fall color. 50′ tall, 30′ wide.

'Wildfire'. Stands out from the crowd early in the season, with bright red-tinted spring foliage. Leaves fade to green in summer then turn yellowish to red in the fall. Broadly pyramidal, fast-growing, with larger leaves and a little loose in form. Has shown some resistance to leafspot. Cold hardiness only to zone 6, apparently. Performs well in the Dirr garden. Male, seedless. 50′ tall, 25 to 30′ wide.

'Wisley Bonfire'. Pyramidal in form with a good central leader and horizontal branches, a form rather typical of the species. Bright fall colors range from yellow-orange to bright orange-red. 45′ tall, 25′ wide.

'Zydeco Twist'. Contorted trunk and branches twist and turn as they gain height. The form somewhat sprawling, needs staking to become a good tree. Of interest as a small tree for a collector; not sure a mature tree will shape up very well. Very bright glossy green summer foliage; orange-red in fall. Male. 20′ by 20′.

N

O

Olea europaea

Olea europaea
olive

Broadleaf evergreen. A picturesque small tree with sculptural habit, branches twisted, bent, curving, and arching in varied directions. Trees are rarely cleanly single-stemmed, more often low-branched or with multiple trunks, forming a billowy, irregular cloud of fine-textured leaves. Growth is slow, to 15 to 20(30)' high and wide. Bark is twisted, contorted, gnarled, creaky in the knees, gray-brown, ridged and furrowed. One of the earliest recorded cultivated fruits, dating to 2300 BC on Crete, olives remain an important commercial fruit crop, and olive oil a vital food product, especially in the Mediterranean region, where the species has been cultured for millennia. California has long been the center of production in the United States, but orchards are now established in the Southeast as well.

Foliage: Pretty, leathery, willow-like leaves are an elegant contrast to those of typical broadleaf evergreens. Each leaf is dark green to gray-green above, glaucous or silvery below, narrowly elliptic, to lanceolate, 2 to 3″ long, a third or less as wide. **Flowers/seeds/fruits/cones**: Small fragrant white flowers, ⅕″ wide, corolla and calyx 4-lobed, in axillary, 1 to 2″ long racemes, open in summer. Fruit is a drupe, the pit the endocarp, the fleshy outer portion edible; many shapes and sizes from oval to almost rounded, ½ to ¾″ long or more; green turning dark blue or black at maturity. Several different clones are usually necessary for effective pollination and fruit development. **Native range**: Suspected to be southwest Asia, with subspecies in China and Africa. **Adaptability**: Zones (8)9 to 10. 'Arbequina' was killed by 6°F in the Dirr garden. **Landscape use**: The species is a beautiful small specimen tree or container element. Trees long past their fruiting prime are often containerized and shipped to

'Swan Hill'

northern Europe for patio, container, and specimen use. In Charleston, SC, they are utilized for screening and hedging. Provide slightly moist, well-drained soils in full sun to partial shade. Several root diseases are problematic; drier,

Olea europaea

Osmanthus fragrans

'Swan Hill'

Osmanthus fragrans

more well-drained soils improve long-term survival. **Street tree use**: Acceptable where adapted, but fruits are messy. Ubiquitous in California on streets and in gardens, where it is perfectly adapted. **In the trade**: A visit to the olive station at more upscale grocers bears testimony to the many commercial cultivars. 'Arbequina', a self-fertile, early ripening, more cold hardy selection, is the most common one in U.S. commerce. 'Swan Hill' is a fruitless variety for ornamental or street use with no mess. Upright oval, the lack of fruit keeps it from spreading too wide. It has little or no pollen, appreciated by those with allergies.

Osmanthus fragrans
fragrant tea-olive

Broadleaf evergreen. Remarkably diverse species with hundreds of cultivars selected through the centuries by the Chinese. It makes a pretty, dense-foliaged, oval small tree, 20 to 30′ high, a third to half as wide. Growth is slow. Bark is smooth, gray, similar to *Ilex opaca*. Plants are often clothed to ground, so bark effect is minimized. The principal calling card is the sensuous floral fragrance, among the most refined of all woody plants, and the fact that some flowers

occur almost year-round only adds to the magic. Literature mentions the flowers are used to flavor teas and soups in China. Authors have yet to adjust their bean soup recipe.

Foliage: Two types; juvenile with oblong-lanceolate to elliptic, finely serrated leaves; mature are usually entire along the margins; both 2 to 4(5)″ long, maintaining dark green, lustrous color year-round; leaves thickish, leathery and wind-resistant. **Flowers/seeds/fruits/cones**: Dioecious. The small, ¼ to ½″ long, 4-petaled, white, fragrant flowers are borne in axillary clusters, never showy and at times lost among the foliage. Noticeable in the fall, but opening on warm days in winter into April-May. The fragrance "speaks" to passersby from great distances. Male flowers with 2 yellow stamens; female with a bowling-pin-shaped pistil in the center of the petals. In cultivation, most plants are male. Fruit is a broad, oval, olive-like drupe, ½ to ¾″ long, purple-black with waxy bloom coating. Fruit is camouflaged

553

'Aurantiacus'

Osmanthus yunnanensis

by the dense foliage and easy to miss unless at close range. **Native range**: China, Japan, in lowland evergreen forests. **Adaptability**: Negative temperatures (0 to -5°F) kill leaves and young stems. Maximum growth is realized in zones 7 to 10. At -3°F in Athens and north Georgia, many plants were killed to the ground. **Landscape use**: Outstanding small tree for sun and shade environments. Exceedingly drought and heat tolerant, requiring only well-drained, preferably acid soils. Prospers in the sandy soils of the Coastal Plain to the silty clays of the Piedmont of the Southeast as well as in California. Requires minimal maintenance and is resistant to insects and diseases. Excellent specimen, woodland, screen or hedging choice. **Street tree use**: Serviceable and brilliant choice. **In the trade**: Always offered multi-stemmed, as container- or field-grown. Few cultivars are available in the United States, but recent collection trips to China have added variegation, prolific flowering, and a range of flower colors. The following have been grown in Georgia by the authors and are highly prized.

'Aurantiacus' (var. *aurantiacus*). An anomaly, for the delicate fragrant bright orange flowers open at one time (rather than sporadically) in September-October. The foliage is extremely leathery, lustrous dark green, without the marginal serrations of the species, and each leaf has a slight twist to the long axis, another easy way to separate this

'Nanjing's Beauty'

from the type. Habit is distinctly upright oval, shaped like the nose-cone of a rocket. An added bonus is the increased cold hardiness, 1 or 2 zones greater than the species. Male. Estimate 20′ high at maturity.

'Nanjing's Beauty' ('Fudingzhou'). Supra-abundant, fragrant, cream to white flowers in October-November, sporadically thereafter. Slightly slower growing than the species, estimating 15′ at maturity. In fact, 'Aurantiacus' grew two times larger in side-by-side comparisons over a 10-year period at the University of Georgia Horticulture Farm.

O. *yunnanensis*, with sweetly scented, cream-white to pale yellow spring flowers, is one of several other potential tree species in the genus. Dark green, firm-textured leaves, 3 to 8″ long, carry up to 30 sharp teeth per margin, becoming entire at maturity. Authors noted 20 to 30′ trees in Europe. China. Zones 9 and 10, on the West Coast.

Ostrya virginiana
American hophornbeam, ironwood

Deciduous. Pyramidal when young, oval in the shade or becoming rounded or sometimes broadly rounded with age in the open. Upright-spreading branch structure. Shaggy gray-brown bark adds interest. Medium growth rate, medium texture. Height 40′, width 30′. Bark is gray-brown, in rough peeling strips running down the trunk, loose and curled at the ends.

Foliage: Medium to dark green foliage, 2 to 5″ long, half as wide, pubescent on the underside, ovate to elliptical with an acuminate tip, doubly serrate. Fall color is a decent yellow, invariably falling short of spectacular. Partially marcescent, often with some withered brown leaves hanging into winter. **Flowers/seeds/fruits/cones**: Monoecious. Flowers as the leaves emerge in spring. Male catkins, 1½″ long, held in groups of 3 at branch tips. Female catkins appear as chains of bracts with exposed reddish stigmas. Fruits, ⅓″ nutlets, develop inside a chain-like involucre of papery bracts that resemble hops and are rather ornamental in late summer and fall. The bracts have tiny sharp hairs that irritate the skin and punish the fingers of seed pickers, as both authors have found out. **Native range**: Eastern North America, from Nova Scotia to southern Manitoba and northern Florida to east Texas. Occupies drier soils and slopes, usually in the understory. **Adaptability**: Likes full sun but quite tolerant of shade. Reasonably tolerant of wet soil and has a broad pH range as well. Zones 4 to 9. **Landscape use**: Drought tolerant, low maintenance, but sensitive to transplanting, so plant early and keep watered during the first season. Tough once established. Not spectacular, but adds diversity to the urban forest and is especially valuable as a medium-sized shade tree that gives an informal and naturalized feel to a woodland garden. Both the name and the appearance of this species cause frequent confusion in the trade with American hornbeam, *Carpinus caroliniana*, but the pubescent foliage, forked leaf veins, and shaggy bark easily separate it.

Ostrya virginiana

Ostrya virginiana

Ostrya virginiana

O

AUTUMN TREASURE

AUTUMN TREASURE

Street tree use: Increasingly valued by city foresters for its moderate growth rate and low maintenance requirements. It is compatible with streets, urban soils, and narrow tree lawns. Seedlings are variable and may have low-hanging branches, so look to upright cultivars for reliable shape. Success on the streets means you will see more of this species. **In the trade**: Largely sold as seed-grown, but the first improved cultivars are hitting the market and providing more reliable form and performance. We hope to see more development in this species.

SUN BEAM

AUTUMN TREASURE 'JFS-KW5'. Upright, pyramidal, vigorous, with a good central leader and branch structure, it was selected with street tree use in mind, to 45′ tall and 25′ wide. Dark green in summer, brighter yellow in fall, and foliage that drops cleanly after autumn color fades.

SUN BEAM 'Camdale'. A cold hardy North Dakota selection (zone 3), slower growing, with a pyramidal to oval form to 35′ tall and 25′ wide. Develops yellowish fall color, then half the brown, marcescent leaves remain on the tree: interesting to some but objectionable to others.

Oxydendrum arboreum
sourwood

Deciduous. Erratically pyramidal to upright oval with a rounded top, often appearing layered, with gracefully drooping branch tips. It manages to gain height without much of a leader, artistically struggling upward. Always fine-textured and interesting in form. Slow-growing. We have seen 60′ trees in the woods of Georgia, but typical landscape size is smaller, 30′ tall with a 20′ spread in the warm, wet summers of the East. In the dry summers of the West, a 20′ height is a big tree. Bark is dark gray-brown, deeply furrowed and ridged, with ridges often cut horizontally into blocky chunks.

Foliage: Leaves long elliptical with an acuminate tip, margin finely serrulate to entire, slightly pubescent on veins, 3 to 8″ long, a little less than half as wide. Dark green and glossy in summer, then fall brings the potential for some of the brightest colors seen in the landscape. In Georgia, we see mixes of yellow, red, and maroon; in Oregon, the dry summer drought stress brings on reliable bright red. **Flowers/seeds/fruits/cones**: Long panicles of urn-shaped, ¼″ pendulous white flowers cover the tree at the beginning of summer, each panicle stretching 4 to 10″. The long-lasting flowers are pleasantly fragrant. With pollination, ⅓″ long capsules develop; from a landscape perspective they closely resemble

Oxydendrum arboreum

Oxydendrum arboreum

Oxydendrum arboreum

Oxydendrum arboreum

the flowers but with a yellowish tint, giving the impression the tree stays in bloom endlessly into the fall and winter. Capsules eventually brown and drop. **Native range**: Virginia to Kentucky and western Florida to Louisiana. **Adaptability**: Likes well-drained acid soils with adequate moisture, full sun to partial shade. Zones 5 to 9. **Landscape use**: A small ornamental tree for all seasons. The long-lasting flowers and look-alike immature fruits display all summer, then it only gets better. Like a drum roll, the fall color comes on slowly and intensifies, finally reaching a crescendo. Great

in naturalized settings or as single focal point. Slow growth demands patience in the North. It is difficult to transplant, containers are preferred. A favorite species of the authors. **Street tree use**: Forget it. Too slow and erratic, dislikes compaction. **In the trade**: Almost entirely sold as seed-grown, as cultivar propagation is difficult. Hard to grow well in the nursery because of slow growth and crookedness, but good plants are easy to sell. 'Chaemeleon' has excellent fall color, yellow-orange to purplish red; it is upright and straighter, more pyramidal in form, 20′ tall, 15′ wide.

P

Parrotia persica

Parrotia persica

Persian parrotia

Deciduous. Upright-spreading, artistically layered, usually low-branched and often multi-stemmed but may be pruned up into a clean-trunked tree form. Medium texture. Moderate growth rate to a height of 30′ with a spread of 25′, but variable; single-trunk trees tend to be narrower, multi-stem trees will spread wider and be broad-crowned. Bark smooth, exfoliating on older trees in mosaic patches of gray, gray-green, and orange-tan.

Foliage: Broadly oval to obovate, usually slightly asymmetric, wavy both between the veins and along the margin, becoming crenate toward the tip. Tip varies from rounded to acute. Leaf 2½ to 5″ long, 1 to 2½″ wide. Foliage moderately glossy, leaves always with slight waves and curls and held at slightly different angles; it projects a very textured appearance. Leaves usually tinged with purple along the margin in spring, becoming fully green in summer. Fall brings on wonderful hues of yellow and orange, and sometimes mixes of red and purple. **Flowers/seeds/fruits/cones**: Flowers late winter to very early spring; apetalous, tassel-like clusters of maroon-red stamens occur along the branches, bringing cheer to the cold dreary landscape. Fruit, a small fuzzy ⅜″ long capsule, contains ⅓″ long brown seeds. **Native range**: Iran, Caucasus. **Adaptability**: Likes a slightly acid, moist soil in a moderate climate, but quite adaptable and very drought tolerant. Will tolerate some alkalinity. Full sun for best fall color. Zones 4 to 8. **Landscape use**: Wonderful as a specimen, can be used in a naturalized setting or in a broad boarder. Upright cultivars fit more limited spaces. May seem shrub-like when young, but do keep in mind that it will grow considerably larger. It takes time for it to develop character. An all-season tree, valued for flowers, texture, spring

Parrotia persica

Parrotia persica

Parrotia persica

foliage, ornamental bark, and especially fall color. Rates as an authors' favorite. **Street tree use:** The upright cultivars are good choices, especially in a cooler, mild climate. Avoid seedling trees unless they have been raised to a large size and their form is evident, as seedlings are quite variable and often spreading. **In the trade:** Widely sold as seedlings, but newer cultivars are gaining popularity. Interestingly, most of the latter emphasize a narrow habit and make better tree form; for a broad multi-stem, choose a seedling.

'Biltmore'. The original tree, growing at the Biltmore Estate in North Carolina, is pushing the century mark. Multi-stemmed with a massive trunk and lovely exfoliating bark. Spreading branches form a rounded crown, 30′ by 30′.

CONTEMPLATION 'PPCM2'. Upright oval, dense, narrower than the species. Fall color is a mixture of yellow, orange, red, and purple; 20′ tall, 15′ wide.

GOLDEN BELLTOWER 'Chrishaven1'. Quite upright-growing, narrow oval form, half as wide as tall, a good street tree form, 25′ tall and 12 to 15′ wide. Fall color golden yellow to apricot-orange.

GOLDEN BELLTOWER

PERSIAN SPIRE

'Lamplighter'. Occasionally sold, a curiosity for the collector. Variegated foliage with cream-white margin, variable with much reversion, typically with as many green leaves as variegated. 12 to 15′ tall and wide.

'Pendula'. Weeping form, graceful. The true plant descends from an original at Kew and is slow-growing. Now mixed in the trade with a more horizontal form. True plants should show the weeping form while young. 10′ tall, 15′ wide.

PERSIAN SPIRE 'JLColumnar'. Compact, upright-growing, narrow oval form, to 20′ tall and 12′ wide. Leaves are considerably smaller than the species, giving this plant a finer-textured appearance. Foliage strongly purple-tinted in spring, green in summer, good yellow-orange and reddish purple mixed in fall.

RUBY VASE 'Inge'. Upright-growing, moderately narrow, with a vase-shaped form, to 28′ tall, 16′ wide. Suitable for street planting. New growth holds purple-red tints that remain on some leaves during summer. Nice yellow-orange fall colors, some purple tints.

STREETWISE 'PPS551'. Dense and upright-growing, narrower than the species, yellow-orange fall color; to 20′ tall and 10′ wide.

'Vanessa'. Upright-growing, moderately narrow, dense vase shape, to 28′ tall and 14′ wide. The first of the narrow cultivars to be introduced, so the ultimate shape is best known. Very good street tree form. Bright yellow-orange fall colors, sometimes mixed with red.

PERSIAN SPIRE

'Lamplighter'

RUBY VASE

STREETWISE

P

RUBY VASE

STREETWISE

'Vanessa'

'Vanessa'

Parrotia subaequalis

Chinese parrotia

Deciduous. Introduced c.1996. Forms a low-branched, densely branched, thickly foliated small tree, 20 to 30′ high, almost as wide. In the Dirr garden, growth is vigorous, 14′ high, 10′ wide in 5 years. Bark is smooth, shiny gray-grown, exfoliating with maturity, shedding jigsaw-puzzle pieces of outer black-brown bark, exposing greenish white inner bark.

Foliage: Ovate, flat dark green, 2 to 4″ long, two-thirds as wide, margins with variable mucronate (pin-point) serrations, holding late into November, extremely frost resistant. The brilliant red-maroon fall color initiates in late September, still vibrant in late November. **Flowers/seeds/fruits/cones**: Apetalous, yellow to maroon-red mass of 4 to 15 stamens with long anthers on naked stems in late winter. Fruit is a ⅜″ long, woody, 2-valved capsule that splits at maturation to expel 2 shiny brown oval seeds. **Native range**: Only five populations in eastern China, two each in Jiangsu and Zhejing provinces, one in Anhui, in mixed forests. **Adaptability**: Early evaluations are promising. Tolerates variations of soil, except wet. Full sun to woodsy shade with excellent fall color under both. Plants withstood -25 to -30°F with only tip injury in northern Ohio and prospered in the very hot and dry summer of 2016 in Athens, GA. **Landscape use**: Choice and rare specimen small tree or large shrub for any landscape opportunity. Who knew there was another *Parrotia* species? Quite a revelation and authors believe this will receive widespread acceptance as it becomes more available. Offers heat tolerance, consistent and long-persistent fall color, and greater cold hardiness than *P. persica*. It is also easier to root from cuttings than *P. persica*. Authors rate *P. subaequalis* among the best and most consistent small trees for exceptional fall color in the Southeast; this accolade has been echoed by plantsmen in the Northeast and Midwest. The 2016 fall was miserable for fall color expression, yet *P. subaequalis* proved outstanding. In Oregon, the species is slower growing, but color is consistently brilliant red, brighter than *P. persica*. **Street tree use**: Potential, but somewhat low-branched. An upright cultivar would make this use solid. **In the trade**: To date at least two accessions (clones) are in the United States. The plant in the Dirr garden came from China via Mikinori Ogisu to Ozzie Johnson in 2004. It is an outstanding clone and the one described herein.

Parrotia subaequalis

Parrotia subaequalis

P

563

Paulownia tomentosa

empress tree, royal paulownia

Deciduous. The common names do not always equate with biological reality. Certainly beautiful in flower; less so in fruit, which is the longer show. The habit is rounded, dense, with coarse, irregular branches. Usually 30 to 40′ high and wide, occasionally to 60′. Growth rate is excessive, with seedlings ascending 8 to 10′ in a single season. Bark is gray-brown, shallowly fissured even on large trunks. The wood is valuable and utilized for bowls, spoons, furniture, coffins, and crates.

Foliage: The blanket for all God's woodland creatures, when 12″ long and wide leaves are stitched into a quilt. Poetic hyperbole, actually realistic, considering actively growing shoots bear leaves to 2 to 3′ across. Dark green above, warm and furry pubescent beneath, with at best a hint of fall color that seldom inspires. Leaves emerge late, just after the flowers are fully expressed, abscising and covering the ground after a hard freeze. **Flowers/seeds/fruits/cones**: Flowers are spectacular, April-May, borne in 8 to 12″ long pyramidal panicles; each foxglove-shaped flower 2″ long, pale violet with darker spots and yellow spots inside, vanilla-scented, and effective for at least 2 weeks; on naked branches and lingering through leaf expression. Fruit is ragged, shaggy, rather ugly, and persistent, remaining on tree through winter into spring. Each a 2-valved, dirty brown, dehiscent capsule, 1 to 2″ long, housing thousands of seeds. Seeds germinate without pretreatment, leading to the species' invasiveness. **Native range**: China. **Adaptability**: Zones 6 to 9. Escaped from cultivation from New York to Georgia. Requires full sun and any spot of soil, acid or high pH, to gain a foothold. In the Southeast, it is common along highways, often growing from crevices in rocks. **Landscape use**: Limited as the tree is untidy, the flowers the only redeeming virtue. In Europe, trees are often pollarded and allowed to develop enormous leaves for textural effect in borders. Not to totally shortchange the species' usefulness, the grand allée at Longwood Gardens is spectacular in flower; Longwood removes the tired, unkempt fruit capsules to improve aesthetics. **Street tree use**: No. **In the trade**: Sold as seed-grown.

Paulownia tomentosa

Paulownia tomentosa

Persea borbonia
redbay

Broadleaf evergreen. Coastal Plain species, often exists as a large shrub of variable shape; tree forms develop a rounded outline. Growth is slow to medium. The National Champion is over 90′ high. Bark is gray-brown, shallowly ridged and furrowed, the ridges becoming scaly. Unfortunately, ambrosia beetle carries a fungus that is killing the species along the coast.

Foliage: Lustrous medium green, 2 to 6″ long, a third to half as wide, showing some discoloration in cold winters. **Flowers/seeds/fruits/cones**: Flowers, reminiscent of those of *Nyssa*, are creamy, not showy, borne in few-flowered cymes in June. Close inspection is required to acknowledge floral existence. Fruit is a ½″ long, dark blue to black, ovoid, drupe-like structure borne on a red pedicel, ripening in October and persisting into late fall. The species is self-fertile; a lone tree will fruit heavily. **Native range**: Coastal distribution from New Jersey to Florida and Texas, inhabiting dune areas, maritime woods, and well-drained sandy soils in shade and sun. **Adaptability**: Based on authors' observations in the wild, the species is salt tolerant. We observed trees in North Carolina in water habitats and Georgia, the largest 40′ high on Georgia's Jekyll Island. Zones (7)8 to 9. **Landscape use**: A 30′ high, 25′ wide multi-pronged specimen flowered and fruited with reckless abandon at the Arch, the historic entrance to the University of Georgia campus, and several pretty multi-stemmed specimens grow contentedly in the Piedmont of Georgia. Possibly useful for native plant restorations in sandy soils along the coast. **Street tree use**: No. **In the trade**: Limited availability, mostly from native plant nurseries.

Phellodendron amurense
Amur corktree

Nomenclatural note: *P. lavalleei* and *P. sachalinense* have been lumped into *P. amurense* by GRIN, therefore all *Phellodendron* cultivars are now included here.

Deciduous. Upright-spreading becoming broadly vase-shaped, rather open, with a rounded crown. Stout, heavy-appearing trunk and scaffold branches, often low-branched. Medium fast-growing to 40′ by 40′. Medium texture in summer; coarse texture in winter. Bark is dark gray, thickly ridged, corky.

Foliage: Pinnately compound leaves, 10 to 15″ long, with an odd leaflet count, 5 to 11. Each leaflet, held along a heavy rachis, ovate to broadly lanceolate, 2½ to 5″ long. Leaves dark green with a slight gloss, light green below, glabrous except for a few hairs along the center vein. Fall color pale to buttery yellow, can be outstanding. Early to defoliate. **Flowers/seeds/fruits/cones**: Dioecious. Flowers yellow-green, small, borne in 2 to 3½″ wide panicles in late spring, not showy. Fruit develops into ½″ wide rounded drupes, held in clusters, ripening to black in the fall. **Native range**: Northern China, Manchuria, Japan. **Adaptability**: Cold hardy, northern-adapted, likes moist, well-drained soil and full sun. We have seen beautiful specimens in various arboreta, but trees in city landscape settings often look stressed and

P

Persea borbonia

Phellodendron amurense

EYE STOPPER

'His Majesty'

'His Majesty'

Phellodendron amurense

have been less impressive. Zones 4 to 8. **Landscape use**: Use it as a large shade tree: its dimensions say medium-sized, but its low-branching habit and spread take up considerable room. Reportedly invasive along the Atlantic, so plant only male cultivars to avoid seeds. **Street tree use**: Try it with caution in northern sites with good soil condition. It has a reputation for urban tolerance, but we have yet to observe that. **In the trade**: Sold as male cultivars. Avoid seedlings, as female trees may become invasive.

EYE STOPPER 'Longenecker'. Rounded form, slightly smaller and broader than other cultivars, with the best fall color, such a bright yellow that it inspired the name, to 35′ by 35′. Formerly considered *P. lavalleei*. Male, seedless.

'His Majesty'. Upright, vase-shaped, taller and more arching, an excellent form, probably the best of the group, 45′ tall and 35′ wide. On visiting the original tree we were struck by its elm-like canopy. Minnesota origin, so quite cold hardy,

'Macho'

Phoenix canariensis

zone 3. Yellow in fall. Formerly considered *P. sachalinense* or a hybrid. Male, seedless.

'Macho'. Oops. Unfortunately named, "Macho" turns out to be a girl. Perhaps the clone is polygamo-dioecious and only partially female, but it has produced seeds in various locations. 40′ by 40′. Invasive concern because of seeds. Avoid.

SUPERFECTION 'Supzam'. Upright-spreading to 40′ by 40′, dark leathery leaves, male, seedless.

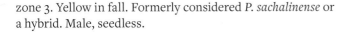

Phoenix canariensis
Canary Island date palm

Evergreen. We consider this majestic species the most elegant of the zone 8 and 9 tree palms. Habit is single-trunked, the crown rounded, arching and elegant. Grows 20 to 30′ or more high, 15′ or more wide. Slow-growing. The trunk is thick, gray-brown; diamond-shaped leaf bases mark the trunk, and old petiole bases persist below the crown; 2 to 3′ in diameter when mature.

Foliage: Arching compound pinnate leaf, 8 to 15′ long, with a central arching midrib to which are attached numerous lustrous dark green leaflets, each 12 to 18″ long, holding the color through the winter. Large sharp spine-like appendages at the base of each frond. **Flowers/seeds/fruits/cones**: Dioecious. Flowers cream-yellow, borne in a drooping, to 3′ long inflorescence, winter-spring. Fruit is a drupe, oblong-ellipsoidal, ¾″ long, orange-yellow, yellow-red, pale orange, held in large paniculate clusters, ripening in summer, edible. **Native range**: Canary Islands **Adaptability**: With warmer winters, has become more common along the Georgia coast through the entire Gulf Coast. Temperatures below 20°F injure the foliage but not the growing point (meristem); a 50 to 60′ high tree in Cairo, GA (zone 8), with all leaves killed, still developed new growth. Zones (8)9 to 11. **Landscape use**: The majority of tree-type palms are utilized as specimens, in large, closely-spaced massed groupings, and as lawn, park, and street trees. Palms create a tropical ambience, and as any snowbird knows, when palms appear in the landscape, warmer weather is close at hand. All palms function as great container elements for patios, pools, courtyards, and entrances. This species succeeds in urban situations where air pollution, compacted soils, and drought are the norm. The famous Palm Drive, leading to

P

the entrance of Stanford University, is lined with 166 Canary Island palms stretching for a mile, planted in 1893. The sight is incredible to a tree lover and worth the trip to see. Planted before the road was paved, the city has grown up around them, and they have proven their urban tolerance. Like all palms, easily transplanted. **Street tree use**: Suitable. **In the trade**: Sold as seed-grown.

Phoenix reclinata
Senegal date palm

Evergreen. Artistic species, forming a low-branched, multi-trunked habit, the main trunks wide-spreading and curving upward. It reaches 15 to 25(30)′ by 12 to 20′, wider at maturity. Trunk is brown, slender.

Foliage: Compound pinnate, with a central midrib and numerous green to yellow-green pinnate leaflets; each leaf ranging from 8 to 15′ long, 3′ wide, with vicious spines at the petiole base, relatively fine-textured. **Flowers/seeds/fruits/cones**: Dioecious. Flowers in 3′ long, branched inflorescences. Fruit is a drupe, oval-rounded, 1″ long, bright orange, somewhat edible. **Native range**: Semi-arid plains of Senegal. **Adaptability**: Successful from Orlando, FL, to Texas, Arizona, and California. Zones 10 and 11, warmest areas of zone 9. Leaf damage occurs below 28 to 30°F. **Landscape use**: Beautiful specimen palm, often more shrub-like in habit but still attaining tree proportions. Requires ample room to spread. Known to hybridize with other *Phoenix* species. Once established, drought and heat tolerant, as well as salt resistant. **Street tree use**: Limited. **In the trade**: Sold as seed-grown.

Photinia serratifolia (*P. serrulata*)
Taiwanese photinia, Chinese photinia

Broadleaf evergreen. Distinctly upright oval in youth, more wide-spreading with time, forming a rounded to broad-rounded crown. Typically 20 to 30′ high and wide, with an occasional 50′ specimen. Bold texture, moderate growth rate, 12 to 18″ per year. Bark is brownish black, exfoliating in large irregular strips, exposing lighter inner coloration. This handsome species has languished in the shadow of *P. ×fraseri* (redtip photinia), which produces brilliant red new shoots. Unfortunately, the latter is devastated by leafspot (pathogen: *Entomosporium maculatum*), which causes complete defoliation and eventually kills the plant. Enter *P. serratifolia*, which is totally resistant and occasionally produces reddish new growth. Red sells! So the ultimate goal is to develop a selection with red new growth.

This is an opportunity for enterprising young breeders to revisit this and the other 40 or so species in the genus; there is always a need for tree-statured broadleaf evergreens with cold, heat, drought, and disease resistances.

Foliage: Leaves lanceolate to oblong, thick-textured, 4 to 8″ long, a third to half as wide, finely serrate from base to apex, with an undulating surface. The petiole is often red, clothed with whitish pubescence when young. Juvenile leaves of seedlings are serrated and partially soft spiny-margined, looking nothing like the mature species leaf. Emerging leaves are apple-green to bronze to butterscotch, occasionally reddish purple, soon turning dark green; new shoots are often evident in February in zones 7 and 8. Dark green color

Photinia serratifolia

'Green Giant'

persists year-round; senescing leaves turn red. **Flowers/ seeds/fruits/cones**: Unfortunately malodorous like some of the hawthorns, buds tinged pink, open white, in terminal corymbose panicles, up to 7″ wide, in March-April. The 5-petaled, ⅜″ wide flowers contrast with newly emerging and mature dark green foliage, making quite the show. Fruit is a red, ¼″ wide globose pome, often produced in supra-optimal quantities. Fruits persist through winter, often present in spring. Birds disseminate the seeds and occasional seedlings pop up, particularly in woodland (shady) habitats. **Native range**: China. **Adaptability**: Will grow on an idle spot of ground where even crabgrass fails. Growth is fast with adequate moisture, drainage, acid to higher pH soil conditions (the latest edition of the *Hillier Manual* calls it "one of the most splendid lime-tolerant evergreens"); venerable, immense legacy specimens are common throughout the Southeast. Young leaves are remarkably frost tolerant. More cold hardy than *P. ×fraseri* and *P. glabra*. Zones 6 to 9. **Landscape use**: Full sun and dense shade are both ideal. In fact, on the north side of large buildings, plants are densely foliated. Should be considered for tall screens, groupings, single-specimen, and, yes, hedging use. Old leaves congregate under plants and are painfully slow to decompose. **Street tree use**: Easily fashioned into a small street tree by staking to a single leader. **In the trade**: 'Green Giant' is a beautiful selection from the University of Georgia campus; oval-rounded, more upright than typical, especially in youth, when it forms a broad column; extremely dense canopy; the young leaves apple-green; mature lustrous dark green; 30 to 45′ high, 20 to 30′ wide. Others have surfaced (CURLY FANTASY 'Kolcurl', 'Jenny', 'Marwood Hill'), most of European origin, none observed by the authors.

Photinia villosa
oriental photinia

Deciduous. Quite a variable species, with several varieties and a forma adding to the taxonomic stew and confusing identification. Although more often a large multi-stemmed shrub, it can be fashioned into a short-trunked, fine-textured small tree with a spreading canopy 10 to 15′ high. Growth is slow, perhaps moderate in youth. Bark is smooth, brown.

Foliage: Distinctly obovate to oblong-obovate, 1½ to 3½″ long, half as wide, apex drawn out into a long fine point, finely serrate, each serration gland-tipped, dark green above, villous (densely silky pubescent) below. Fall color yellow, orange, bronze to red; consistent, long persistent, typically into November. **Flowers/seeds/fruits/cones**: The white, ½″ wide flowers in 1 to 2″ wide corymbs appear in April (zone 8). Flowers are nestled among the leaves, their effect subdued. Fruit is beautiful, a glistening red, ⅓ to ½″

Photinia serratifolia

'Green Giant'

Photinia villosa

P

'Village Shade'

'Village Shade'

perfectly broad obovate, with 10 to 12 veins. Fall color a brilliant golden orange in the Dirr garden; described as making a tree, this single plant is distinctly shrubby. 'Village Shade', with vase-shaped outline, more tree-like stature, dark green foliage, heavier flower and fruit production, was introduced by the JC Raulston Arboretum.

Picea abies
Norway spruce

Evergreen conifer. A large tree, broadly pyramidal in form, with a strong central trunk and horizontal branches with upsweeping tips. Secondary branches weep down from the primaries. Medium texture, moderately fast-growing to 60′ or more tall and 30′ wide. A 226′ tall tree was recorded in Europe. Bark is thin and gray-brown on young trees, then thickening and developing irregular small surface plates.

long, ellipsoidal pome, maturing in October and persisting late unless consumed by the birds. **Native range**: Japan, Korea, and China, in forests, thickets, stream margins, slopes, roadsides, and waste areas. **Adaptability**: Successfully growing on the University of Maine campus (zone 4) and the Dirr garden (zone 8). Self-seeds. Authors had never considered the species invasive, but the literature and recent personal sightings of escaped plants in North Carolina, Maryland, and Delaware tell a different story. We often find escaped plants in dense forests and woodlands, less robust than in full sun, yet flowering and fruiting. Zones 4 to 7(8). **Landscape use**: Rare in cultivation. To be clear, the bright red fruits and consistent fall color, especially in combination, are highlights. The Achilles' heel is fireblight, a bacterial disease that can devastate trees. Authors are hesitant to recommend on a wholesale basis because of disease and invasive issues. As a small garden tree, the beauty perhaps outweighs the negatives. Prefers moist, acid, well-drained soil, full sun and moderate shade. Does not tolerate high pH soils. **Street tree use**: No. **In the trade**: Var. *laevis* is the common form in cultivation, the unfolding leaves margined with bronze, brilliant orange, and red in autumn. The defining distinction is the glabrous (or almost so) leaves,

Picea abies

Picea abies

'Acrocona'

'Aarburg'

Foliage: Very dark green, needles stiff, ½ to 1″ long, densely held along the orange-brown new growth branches. **Flowers/seeds/fruits/cones**: Monoecious. Male pollen cones are bright red-purple and ornamental in spring, ½ to 1″ long, ovoid. Female cones are greenish or red-tinted at first, growing to 4 to 6″ long and 1½ to 2″ wide, cylindrical, pendulous,

maturing to pale brown in one season and abscising intact. **Native range**: Northern Europe, east into Russia, and south at higher elevations to the Balkans. **Adaptability**: A very cold hardy and tough tree in the North, quite adaptable, needs a cool climate, in warmer regions it will suffer from the heat. Zones 3 to 7. **Landscape use**: The species makes a wonderful large screen or dark-foliaged backdrop for smaller, brighter-colored plants. The cultivars come in almost every size, shape, color, and form, making great specimens and focal points. **Street tree use**: Big, dark, and imposing—we would choose something else. **In the trade**: Sold as seed-grown, and especially as the many cultivars, most of which are dwarfs. The best of the tree-sized cultivars follow; all mature to a smaller size than the species.

'Aarburg'. Irregular and a bit fantastical in form, it is upright in overall habit with branches that spread slightly and erratically, then weep gracefully. If you want formal symmetry in your garden, forget it, but if you like the wild look, this is perfect. Faster growing, larger and more open than other weepers, probably will reach 25′ tall and 10′ or more in width.

'Acrocona'. Produces an unusually heavy crop of cones, which are bright reddish purple in spring and at first are held upright on branches, very ornamental. As the summer progresses, they enlarge, become pendulous, and turn tan. The weight of the cones makes this a broader-spreading, more irregular pyramid to 15′ high and wide.

'Clanbrassiliana Stricta'. A very dense compact pyramidal form, semi-dwarf, symmetrical, growing into a chubby, broader pyramid with age, about 15′ tall, 10′ wide.

'Cobra'. Looks like one, rising up from the ground with a long neck, arching its head, ready to strike. Often a little bare of foliage in the center, but if staked and trained high before it weeps, this will certainly get attention. Height depends on staking.

P

'Clanbrassiliana Stricta'

'Cupressina'

'Cobra'

'Pendula'

'Hillside Upright'

'Sherwood Compact'

'Cupressina'. Very strictly upright, dense, and tight in form, this is the skinniest cultivar. Produces a very narrow, cone-shaped tree to 20′ tall and 6′ wide. A perfect spire for narrow planting strips or used singly as a feature.

'Hillside Upright'. Narrowly pyramidal in form, but a little rugged and erratic, giving it a naturalistic appearance, looking a bit more like a beautiful wild plant collected off the hillside than a cookie-cutter form grown in a nursery. Very dark green needles. To 20′ tall, 8′ wide.

'Pendula'. A weeping form, needing staking. It will grow as tall as staked, vertically, angled, or horizontally, and its branches will weep to the ground. Included here because it is so dominant in the market; it only makes tree-sized proportions with a stake that is tall enough. 'Pendula' has been used as a collective name for all the numerous weeping forms of the species, resulting in a mixed bag in the trade.

'Sherwood Compact'. A very dense, compact pyramid. Intermediate in form between 'Cupressina' and 'Clanbrassiliana Stricta', to 15′ tall, 8′ wide.

Picea breweriana
Brewer weeping spruce

Evergreen conifer. Broadly pyramidal, with a straight central trunk, horizontal or slightly upsweeping primary branches and curtains of wonderfully long, pendulous branches hanging from the main structure. Fine-textured, moderately slow-growing to 40′ high, 20′ wide. Bark is thin, gray, and scaly.

Foliage: Needles medium green to slightly grayish green, 1″ long, a little less densely packed along the branches than many spruce, which combined with the form, gives the tree a looser, fluffier look than most spruce. **Flowers/ seeds/fruits/cones**: Monoecious. Immature cones are large and quite showy in spring and early summer: pendulous, purple, and cylindrical. They mature to reddish brown in one season, 3 to 6″ long and 1″ wide. **Native range**: Limited to a small area in the Klamath-Siskiyou Mountains at the Oregon-California border. **Adaptability**: A rather touchy tree needing regular water, but good drainage, and moderately cool temperatures. Zone 5 in the East, 5 to 7 in the cool-summer West. **Landscape use**: Striking in the landscape, but not easy to grow. Use it as a specimen for its structure and informality, highlighting the long pendulous branches, or as part of a mix in a native garden. **Street tree use**: No. **In the trade**: Not common. Usually sold as seed-grown.

Picea engelmannii
Engelmann spruce

Evergreen conifer. A narrow pyramidal form, spire-like, generally quite symmetrical and neat. Its narrow habit and short needles give it a fine-textured appearance. Grows at a moderate rate, to 60′ tall, 20′ wide in most landscape situations, although a 238′ tall tree has been recorded. Bark is relatively thin, gray-brown with a slight purplish tint, scaly, shedding small round flakes.

Picea breweriana

Picea engelmannii

Foliage: Needles rather short and stiff, ⅝ to 1″ long, 4-sided and prickly sharp, dark green to blue-green, densely packed on branches. **Flowers/seeds/fruits/cones:** Monoecious. Cones are pendulous and purple in spring, then mature 2 to 3″ long, ¾″ wide in fall, light brown. **Native range:** Mountains of western North America, from British Columbia to northern California and east to New Mexico. **Adaptability:** A fairly adaptable tree, used in the difficult climates of the Intermountain and Rocky Mountain West. It takes cold and moderate drought, but it is less adapted to heat and humidity. Zones 3 to 6, 7 in the West. **Landscape use:** Used as a lawn tree, grouped as a screen, in natural landscapes and in restoration. Eclipsed in landscape use by the more popular *P. pungens*, this is a finer-textured narrower tree, and some individuals can be quite blue. The authors think this tree has more potential for future selection. **Street tree use:** Its narrow form makes it a possibility in cooler climates where it's well adapted. **In the trade:** Available.

'Bush's Lace'. One of the most beautiful conifers we have seen, rivaling any Colorado blue spruce. An upright-growing trunk and pyramidal structure carries graceful and pendulous layers of fine branches covered with beautiful blue needles, draping toward the ground. 30′ tall, 15′ wide.

'Fritsche'. Strongly upright, broadly pyramidal with upsweeping main structural branches. Secondary branches gently hang from the main framework to 60′ tall, 20′ wide. Foliage is a soft grayish blue, subtly beautiful.

'Bush's Lace'

'Fritsche'

Picea glauca

white spruce

Evergreen conifer. Pyramidal in form, holding branches to the ground. Size and form vary over its extensive natural range from tall narrow forest trees over 100′ in the southern part of the range to shrubby dwarfs in the far north of the Arctic. Bark is grayish brown, thin and scaly, shedding small round flakes.

Foliage: Needles short, ½ to ¾″ long, 4-sided, pale gray-green to blue-green and glaucous (hence the epithet). Pungent odor when crushed; sometimes called skunk spruce. **Flowers/seeds/fruits/cones**: Monoecious. Cones are purplish then green when immature, maturing to pale brown in the fall, pendulous, 1 to 2½″ long, ½ to ¾″ wide. **Native range**: Widespread across northern North America, from the East Coast to Minnesota and north to Alaska. **Adaptability**: A cool-weather tree, native in the North and best adapted there. Likes moist soils with decent drainage. Avoid in hot humid areas. Zones 2 to 6. **Landscape use**: Seedling trees of the species are used in natural settings and occasional landscapes, but most landscape use consists of fine-textured, slow-growing cultivars under 20′. **Street tree use**: No. **In the trade**: Available.

'Conica' (dwarf Alberta spruce). Too small to meet the size criteria for our tree book, but too popular and well known not to mention. It's by far the most widely used cultivar of the species, a tiny dense tree, looking like a sheared pyramid, typically 6′ tall and 3′ wide, but with time can double in size. 'Blue Wonder' (blue foliage) 'Jean's Dilly' (more compact), and 'Rainbow's End' (yellow tip growth) are nice variations.

var. *densata* ('Densata'; Black Hills spruce). Slower growing, with a more compact form, and dense (hence the epithet). A broader pyramid than the species, 30′ tall, 20′ wide, with a bluish cast to the foliage.

'Montrose Spire'. Narrower form, very tight and with strongly upright branching, slightly gray-green needles, to 30′ tall, 10′ wide.

'North Star'. Selected for cold hardiness, it forms a classic pyramidal shape with very good density. Moderate growth rate and a reasonable size for a residential garden, to 15′ tall, 8′ wide, bluish gray-green foliage.

'Pendula'. Don't be fooled by the name. This is an extremely narrow, blue-green rocket launch of a tree with a trunk that is quite vertical; it gets its pendulous name from the short branches that hang down closely against the trunk, looking like they were weighed down by a heavy load of snow and

Picea glauca

Picea glauca

then got stuck in that position. Very striking and a beautiful focal point in a landscape, to 25′ tall and 6′ wide.

'Yukon Blue'. A dense and stiffly upright-growing pyramidal form, narrow and formal. Very nice blue-gray foliage, to 15′ tall and 8′ wide.

'Conica'

'North Star'

'Pendula'

P

Picea omorika

Serbian spruce

Evergreen conifer. Narrowly pyramidal with short branches that usually angle slightly upward, or may sweep down slightly and then up at the tips, forming a very tightly conical form. Medium fine texture, moderately slow-growing to 50′ tall and 15′ wide. Bark is scaly, flaking off in small plates, gray-brown to dark brown.

Foliage: Needles rather short, ½ to 1″ long, and flattened, not 4-sided like most spruce. Dark green above, with 2 silvery white stomatal bands below, giving needles a bicolor effect. Needles curve upward from below, and upper needles tend to orient toward the end of the branch. **Flowers/seeds/fruits/ cones**: Monoecious. Cones are oblong-ovoid, violet-purple when young, maturing to 1½ to 2½″ long, pendulous, cinnamon-brown. **Native range**: Serbia, Bosnia and Herzegovina, in limestone mountains. **Adaptability**: Very adaptable, probably the most widely adaptable spruce. Takes high pH but will also be happy on acid soil, even peat. Takes cold, takes the heat and humidity of the East and Midwest. Zones 4 to 7 in the East and at least 8 in the West. **Landscape use**: A great specimen, having a casual elegance, useful in formal

'Bruns'

Picea omorika

578

'Gotelli Weeping'

'Nana'

'Silberblau'

gardens or naturalistic alpine scenes. A favorite species of the authors. **Street tree use**: Narrow, tough, and reliable, a good choice where a conifer is desired. **In the trade**: Available, and lots of choices among the cultivars.

'Bruns'. Neat, narrow, formal form. Very nice blue-green foliage. Slightly compact, 30′ probable garden height, 15′ wide.

'Gotelli Weeping'. Upright with a straight trunk and central leader, but branches swoop downward with tips pointing back up. A little bit wild and irregular in habit, wider than other weepers, more informal in appearance, 25′ tall, 15′ wide.

'Nana'. Very compact and dense. It seems like a dwarf but don't be fooled, it keeps growing slowly but steadily into a very full, slightly squat pyramid, branching densely to the ground. Plan on 15′ tall, 12′ wide.

'Pendula'. Upright-growing, with a mostly straight trunk and leader, similar to the overall narrow outline of the species, except that the short branches droop, as if the tree has frequently held heavy snow. A little stiff when young, it becomes more graceful as it ages, to 30′ tall and 8′ wide. An authors' favorite, it brings a very alpine look to a warmer-weather garden.

P

'Pendula Bruns'

Picea omorika

'Pendula'

'Pendula Bruns'. Extremely narrow and upright but with curves, twists, and sometimes a slight lean as it ascends, becoming a living sculpture. A great feature plant. Short branches hang straight down, clothing the trunk so densely that it seems like a single continuous form, to 25′ tall and 4′ wide.

'Silberblau' ('Silverblue'). A full, upright pyramid, a little more dense and broad than the type, with needles that shine silvery blue on the outer growth and contrast against the darker interior foliage, a wonderful effect. A good choice for those wanting a blue spruce, but in a climate too warm for *P. pungens*, to 30′ tall, 15′ wide.

Picea orientalis

oriental spruce

Evergreen conifer. Neatly pyramidal, dense, symmetrical, and just a bit compact, forming a nearly perfect cone. Bark gray-brown, small peeling plates. Fine-textured, moderately slow-growing to 60′ tall and 20′ wide.

Foliage: You can't help but think those tiny little needles are so cute! Needles lustrous green-black, very short, almost stubby, the shortest in the genus, only ¼ to ½″ long, 4-sided, rounded at the tip rather than sharp like most spruce, densely covering the stems. **Flowers/seeds/fruits/cones**: Monoecious. The small bright red pollen cones are briefly ornamental on branch tips in spring, looking like little wild strawberries. Female cones become pendulous, cylindrical, red to purple when young, maturing in one season, 2 to 4″ long and ¾″ wide, brown. **Native range**: Caucasus region, Turkey. **Adaptability**: More widely adaptable than most spruce. It does likes cool climates but avoid cold dry winter winds. Reasonably tolerant of heat and does well in the humid Midwest and East. Zones 4 to 7. **Landscape use**: A great garden spruce, so dark and formal-looking. Reliable in its symmetry, wonderful in the texture of its perfectly formed, tiny needles. Good backdrop for brighter plants; witch-hazels flowering in late winter sun against it would be perfect. Use as a specimen or a large screen. **Street tree use**: Not the best choice among conifers unless the planting strip is wide, as it holds its branches to the base. **In the trade**: Commonly sold as the species. About the cultivars selected for yellow growth: yellow is nice, but for most uses, we prefer the darkness of the species.

'Aureospicata'. A broad pyramid, a little looser and wider in form than the species, with new growth that bursts out a light yellow-green, contrasting against the older foliage, then turns solid dark green by summer. Full-sized, 60′ tall and 20 to 25′ wide.

'Firefly'. Bright yellow needles, selected as a more compact seedling of 'Skylands'. A dense golden pyramid. First listed as a dwarf, but like a lot compact plants, give it time and it will grow, we think eventually 10 to 15′. A great garden-sized focal point.

P

Picea orientalis

'Aureospicata'

'Firefly'

'Nigra Compacta'

Picea orientalis

'Skylands'

'Nigra Compacta'. Slow-growing and very dense. Very dark green, short needles. A neat, chubby pyramid billed as compact, but it will eventually reach 15′ with a 12′ spread, full-looking, with solid foliage to the ground.

'Skylands'. A full-sized, narrow pyramidal form, a little less formal than the species, with bright yellow foliage year-round. It's big and bold, the center of attention in any landscape. 50′ tall, 20′ wide. Does well in the heat of zone 7 in the East.

'Skylands'

Picea pungens
Colorado blue spruce

Evergreen conifer. Pyramidal, dense, usually symmetrical when young but may become a little open with age, usually holds foliage to the ground. Medium-textured, moderate growth rate to 40′ tall, 20′ wide. Bark is thick for a spruce, gray to gray-brown, rough, fissured into flattened ridges.

Foliage: Gray-green to silvery blue, depending on seed source or cultivar; natural stands are mostly gray-green. Needles stiff, ¾ to 1¼″ long, 4-sided, sharp, densely held along the yellowish brown new growth twigs. **Flowers/seeds/fruits/cones**: Monoecious. Male pollen cones are red, borne at the terminal end of shoots in spring. Female cones are tinted purple-red at first, briefly held upright, then become pendulous and grow to 2 to 5″ long, 1 to 1¼″ wide, cylindrical, maturing to brown in one season. **Native range**: Rocky Mountains, at high elevations, Wyoming to New Mexico. **Adaptability**: Performs well in the difficult Intermountain West, as you might expect given its nativity. Tolerant of cold, drought, and wind. Accepts acid or high pH soils, but avoid saturated ground. Needs full sun. Best in cooler climates, suffers in the humid heat of the South. Zones 3 to 7, 9 on the West Coast. **Landscape use**: By far the most widely planted spruce in the United States, an outstanding specimen tree. Seed-grown trees vary in color and are good for natural settings. Many cultivars have been selected for density, which improves the appearance of dwarfs and semi-dwarfs; but in full-sized trees, too much density can cause branch crowding and structural problems, so we like the wider branch spacing of more open forms like 'Hoopsii'. May be subject to canker, aphids, spider mites, and

Picea pungens

'Avatar'

'Baby Blue'

'Baby Blueyes'

other pests and diseases. **Street tree use:** Generally no, too low-branched. **In the trade:** Usually sold as grafted cultivars. Some nurseries sell selected blue seed sources, which may be relatively consistent but don't equal the grafted cultivars.

'Avatar'. A bright blue pyramid, a little slower growing than most cultivars, with new growth that is especially soft blue in color, to 25′ tall, 15′ wide.

'Baby Blue'. Unique in being seed-derived, grown from a select seed orchard and producing surprisingly stable blue foliage at a lower cost. A full-sized tree, but as a seedling, there will be some variation in mature size and shape, 40′ tall, 20′ wide.

'Baby Blueyes' ('Baby Blue Eyes'). Slower growing, dense, but still upright pyramidal in form with a good central leader. Good blue color, 25′ tall, 15′ wide.

'Bakeri' ('Bacheri'). A dense full pyramid with good silvery blue foliage, to 30′ tall, 15′ wide.

'Bizon Blue'. One of the best for brilliant blue foliage, the needles retain their color well on the inside of the canopy as well as the outer portions. Slightly slower and denser than 'Hoopsii', 30′ tall, 15′ wide.

'Blue Diamond'. Broadly pyramidal, fairly dense, with very attractive silvery blue foliage. Slower growing than the species, probably maturing to 25′ tall and 15 to 20′ wide.

'Bakeri'

'Bonny Blue'

'Bizon Blue'

'Blue Select'. Good blue foliage, broad, full pyramidal form, 40′ tall, 20′ wide.

'Bonny Blue'. Bright blue needles are shorter than typical and held stiffly outward on the branch. Strongly upright, formally straight, but not overly dense, allowing it to show its handsome branch structure and form. 40′ tall, 20′ wide.

'Fat Albert'. A broad dense pyramid, maybe a little too dense, very full, with good bright blue color. Popular, widely grown because it fills in quickly in the nursery, but lacks character with age. 35′ by 25′.

'Fastigiata'. See 'Iseli Fastigiate'

'Gebelle's Golden Spring'. Wow. The spring color is a real surprise if you are expecting a "blue" spruce. New growth emerges bright yellow and contrasts with the dark green needles of the previous year. Very impressive for about a month in spring, fading to a disappointing yellow-green then eventually dull dark green for the rest of the year. For the collector who values the one-month color burst. 30′ tall, 20′ wide.

P

'Fat Albert'

'Hoopsii'

'Gebelle's Golden Spring'

'Hoopsii'

'Iseli Fastigiate'

'Koster'

'Hoopsii'. Long the standard of comparison among blue spruce. The intensity of the silvery blue foliage remans unsurpassed. Pyramidal, slightly broader, more open and a little more irregular than most, it presents a natural appearance. One of our favorites. 40′ tall, 20′ wide.

'Iseli Fastigiate' ('Fastigiata', 'Blue Totem'). Strongly and narrowly upright in form, this is the tightest of the cultivars. Looks impressive when young, but the density and narrow crotch angles work against it and cause structural problems as it ages. Moderately blue color, to 25′ tall and 10′ wide.

'Koster'. Perhaps the oldest cultivar (pre-1885) still commonly found on the market, it was originally a mixture of blue clones, then standardized. Pyramidal, moderately blue foliage, 40′ tall, 20′ wide.

P

'Montgomery'

'Pendula'

'The Blues'

'Sester Dwarf'

'Montgomery'. Small and very dense, it's bushy and wide when young but does develop a leader, eventually making a broad, dense pyramid, 10 to 15′ tall. Moderately blue color.

'Pendula'. A weeper with a tendency to produce a leader. With training it can grow straight up with downward-sweeping branches, forming a very narrow graceful pyramid; or it can be allowed to sprawl at any angle with a curtain of foliage. Variable in size to about 15′. 'The Blues', a branch sport, quite blue, slower growing and more pendulous.

'Sester Dwarf'. A small dense form, still very pyramidal and tree-like. Unlike 'Montgomery', it is conical rather than rounded when young, looking like a miniature version of a mature blue spruce. Good blue foliage, a very nice selection for a small garden, to 10 to 15′ tall and 8′ wide.

'Thomsen'

Picea sitchensis

'Thomsen'. An older cultivar (1928), still being grown for its thick, silvery blue needles, one of the best for color. Pyramidal, 40′ tall, 20′ wide.

Picea sitchensis

Sitka spruce

Evergreen conifer. Very large pyramidal tree with a stout trunk and buttressed base, very straight. Medium coarse texture, moderately fast-growing to 100′ tall, 30′ wide. Historic record tree was 314′. Bark is thin, dark grayish brown, flaking in scaly plates. An important timber tree; its strong yet lightweight wood was used by the Wright brothers and in World War I airplanes.

Foliage: Needles stiff, ¾ to 1″ long, 4-sided, sharp, dark green with 2 glaucous bands on the the underside lending a slight silvery blue tint, held on yellowish brown twigs.
Flowers/seeds/fruits/cones: Monoecious. Cones reddish

Picea sitchensis

P

green when immature, maturing to 2½ to 4″ long and 1″ wide by fall, cylindrical, pendulous, reddish brown drying to light brown. **Native range**: North America from Alaska to northern California, occupying a thin coastal strip, always within 50 miles of the ocean or its inlets. **Adaptability**: Needs a cool temperate climate, best within its native range. Tolerant of wet soils and moderate shade. Zones 6 to 8 on the West Coast near water. **Landscape use**: Used in native landscapes and restoration. Needs room, it gets big. **Street tree use**: No, too large. **In the trade**: Sold as seed-grown and, rarely, a few dwarf cultivars.

Picrasma quassioides
India quassiawood

Deciduous. A rare species, found primarily in arboreta and botanical gardens, but, based on outward appearance, worthy of greater use. The few trees authors observed were rounded in outline with uniform branching pattern. We

Picrasma quassioides

estimate average landscape dimensions 20 to 40′ high and wide. Growth is slow to moderate. Bark is gray-brown with shallow fissures and large flat ridges. All parts of the plant are bitter.

Foliage: In leaf, the tree is reminiscent of *Juglans nigra*, only smaller and nowhere near as messy; the terminal naked (no scale covering) buds are rich brown, pubescent, posturing like hands clasped in prayer. Leaves are compound pinnate, 10 to 14″ long, composed of 9 to 15 leaflets, each 2 to 4″ long, ovate to oblong-ovate with sharp serrations, lustrous dark green, turning orange-red in autumn, according to literature. We recorded yellow-green to yellow fall color (October, zone 6). **Flowers/seeds/fruits/cones**: Yellow-green, each ⅓″ wide, borne in 6 to 8″ long, almost as wide, loose corymbs in May-June. The red maturing to purple-black, obovoid to rounded, pea-sized berry ripens with the rose calyx still attached. **Native range**: Japan, Taiwan, China, Korean peninsula, India. **Adaptability**: Zones 6 and 7. Potential for increased hardiness from colder regions of the wide native range. **Landscape use**: Has potential for small properties, campuses. Succeeds in well-drained soil, acid to neutral, in full sun to part shade. European literature hails the species as trouble-free, and C. S. Sargent, noting its brilliant orange to red fall color, wrote that "few Japanese plants are as beautiful as this small tree." American literature is scant to nonexistent. **Street tree use**: Potential. **In the trade**: The shameful scarcity of plants in commerce provides opportunities for collection and evaluation.

Pinus albicaulis
whitebark pine

Evergreen conifer. Pyramidal, very slow-growing in a landscape, possibly to 30′, but in the wild, it is shaped by wind and storms and is usually smaller. Medium coarse texture. Bark is smooth and light gray to gray-brown, becoming roughened and patchy in age. The epithet means "white-stemmed"; dead trees at timberline elevation are often artistically snow- and wind-blasted, with the exposed wood bleached white in sun, and young trees definitely have light-colored trunks, but light silvery gray is as close to white as we have seen.

Foliage: Needles 5 per fascicle, margins entire, medium green, rather short and clustered around the branch, about 2″ long. **Flowers/seeds/fruits/cones**: Monoecious. Cones are 1½ to 3″ long, ovoid, short and squat, dark purple when immature, ripening brown. **Native range**: Grows at the highest elevations, at timberline, in the mountains of western North America, from British Columbia to California and Wyoming. **Adaptability**: Tolerates extreme cold and wind.

Pinus albicaulis

Pinus aristata

Pinus aristata

Susceptible to white pine blister rust, which can be a major problem. Zone 2 cold hardiness; with little landscape experience, we think it is probably adaptable up to zone 7 on the West Coast. **Landscape use**: Little used, but an intriguing plant with potential for use in high mountain communities in the West. Shape by pruning **Street tree use**: No. **In the trade**: Not common, seed-grown.

Pinus aristata / *Pinus longaeva*
Rocky Mountain bristlecone pine / Great Basin bristlecone pine

Nomenclatural note: These two closely related species were formerly considered one, then separated. As many cultivars were introduced before the taxonomic split, they are typically all listed under *P. aristata* in nursery catalogs, so we have combined descriptions, pointing out differences where they exist.

P

Evergreen conifer. Very broadly pyramidal to oval or even irregularly rounded with an upsweeping branch structure, variable, sometimes a bit confused-looking with crossing branches. Very slow-growing, possibly to 15′ tall and 10′ wide in a landscape. Medium texture. Bark is gray and smooth when young, eventually becoming irregularly fissured.

Foliage: Needles 5 per fascicle, short, dark bluish green, densely clustered around the branches. *P. aristata* needles are 1 to 1½″; *P. longaeva* needles are ¾ to 1″. In *P. aristata*, they are decorated with white flecks of resin, looking like snowflakes caught among the needles; *P. longaeva* lacks the white resin flecks. **Flowers/seeds/fruits/cones**: Monoecious. Cones purplish when immature and showing bristle-tipped scales, ripening in 2 years, 2 to 4″ long, elongated ovoid to cylindrical. **Native range**: *P. aristata* is native in the high mountains of Colorado, New Mexico, and Arizona; *P. longaeva* is found to the west, in the mountains from Utah to the Sierra Nevada of California.

'Formal Form'

'Horstmann'

'Joe's Bess'

Adaptability: Needs full sun and good drainage, very tolerant of poor, dry soils but not wet ones. Very useful in the cold dry climate of the Intermountain and Mountain West. Zones 3 to 7 in western states, less happy in the humidity of the East. **Landscape use**: Small bushy pines, valued for their outstanding foliage and suitability in dry mountain areas. Use as a focal point, especially the cultivars. **Street tree use**: No. **In the trade**: Sold occasionally as seed-grown; mainly as the cultivars.

'Blue Bear'. *P. longaeva*, selected for its bluish green needles. Very dense form, broadly pyramidal and full, 12′ tall, 10′ wide.

'Formal Form'. *P. longaeva* selection, upright-growing, narrower and more pyramidal, bluish green foliage. Symmetrical, formal in shape but open enough to be natural-looking. 15′ tall, 10′ wide.

'Horstmann'. Upright, symmetrically pyramidal, and somewhat dwarf but included here because of its wonderful white-flecked foliage, which marks it as *P. aristata*. 10′ tall, 8′ wide.

'Joe's Bess'. *P. longaeva* selection. Quite upright and pyramidal, a little smaller than 'Formal Form' but with more density, and ironically, a little more formal-looking. Symmetrical and nice. 10′ tall, 8′ wide.

Pinus ayacahuite

Mexican white pine

Evergreen conifer. The Southeast and warmer parts of the United States are in search of an alternative to the elegant *P. strobus*. To this end, *P. monticola*, *P. strobiformis*, *P. flexilis*, and *P. ayacahuite* (all soft-textured 5-needle pines) were trialed in Georgia, the latter surviving 20 years, reaching 20′ tall, with a full complement of blue-green needles; the others perishing. Habit on the lone Georgia tree was upright oval, more compact than described on native trees, the density due to slow growth. In the wild, plants reach 120 to 150′ tall; we estimate 30 to 50′ high with good cultural conditions. Bark is initially smooth, gray-green, developing scaly plates divided by shallow fissures on large trunks.

Foliage: Needles are 4 to 8″ long, $\frac{1}{25}$″ wide, thinnish, arching at their middle, finely serrated along the margins, persisting 2 to 3 years; their blue-green to gray-green color persists through winter. **Flowers/seeds/fruits/cones**: Female cones are initially green to blue-green, extremely resinous, pendulous, borne singly or in groups, 6 to 14″ long, 3 to 4″ wide, curved-cylindrical in shape. The lone Georgia tree formed numerous cones. **Native range**: Mexico and Central America, where it occurs at 8,000 to 10,000′ elevation in cloud forest environments. **Adaptability**: Zones 6 to 9(10). Successfully grown at Boston's Arnold Arboretum. **Landscape use**: Prefers atmospheric moisture, deep, moist, acid soils, and full sun. Certainly a beautiful specimen pine, and Georgia visitors often asked the identity of the lone tree. The species, which we envisioned as a substitute for white pine in hot climates, is closely related to *P. strobiformis* and has been hybridized with *P. strobus*, *P. flexilis*, and *P. wallichiana*. Many of the resulting hybrids have never been tested to any degree. Authors believe opportunities exist to ferret out several choice landscape pines. **Street tree use**: No. **In the trade**: Sold as seed-grown. *P. ×holfordiana* (*P. ayacahuite* × *P. wallichiana*) is a beautiful hybrid with soft-textured bluish needles.

Pinus ayacahuite

Pinus ayacahuite

P

Pinus banksiana

jack pine

Evergreen conifer. In youth, habit is open and straggly. Trees lack grace when mature, branches irregularly spreading and crooked in shape, reaching 35 to 50′ in height. Growth is slow. Bark is dark brown and scaly, flaky, becoming ridged and furrowed on large trunks, the ridges divided into irregular thick plates.

Foliage: Needles in fascicles of 2, each 1 to 2″ long, dark olive-green, flat on one side, convex on the other, slightly twisted, curved, the margin with minute teeth. Needles develop yellow-green color in winter and persist 2 to 4 years; nevertheless, the plant is often threadbare and open. **Flowers/seeds/fruits/cones**: Monoecious. Male cones clustered, ½″ long, yellow-brown; female greenish with 50 to 80 scales, ripening orange-brown, 1 to 3″ long, asymmetrical, ovoid-conical, curved at the tapered point, each scale armed with a small spine or unarmed; numerous cones remain closed on branches, turning gray to blackish (rather ugly) and releasing the winged seeds after fire; cones ripen (mature) in the second year and persist for many years. An ecological note: the seeds are important food sources for birds, specifically crossbills, whose bill tips are adapted for extracting seeds from the closed (unopened) cones. **Native range**: From near the Arctic Circle into New York, Minnesota, Wisconsin, and Michigan, on sandy, infertile soil. **Adaptability**: Somewhat of a pioneer species, establishing on dry, sandy, rocky, and acid soils, particularly in cold climates. It acts as a placeholder in the succession process, until other species become established. Authors observed trees on the Indiana University campus, Bloomington, growing in clay. In Canada, it is the most northerly pine, occasionally forming pure even-aged stands. Zones 2 to 6. **Landscape use**: In the grand parade of landscape pines, this ranks close to last. For use in cold climates and miserable, infertile, sandy, acid soils it has merit. Best use is as a pioneer species where few other pines will grow. On better soils it is naturally replaced by *P. strobus* and *P. resinosa*. **Street tree use**: No. **In the trade**: Primarily dwarf types derived from witch's brooms. 'Uncle Fogy' is a sprawling, weeping selection, yellow-green in winter and wild and woolly in habit, that can be grafted on a standard.

Pinus banksiana

'Uncle Fogy'

594

Pinus bungeana

lacebark pine

Evergreen conifer. Aristocratic species, with a tight pyramidal conical habit in youth, becoming more open and broad-spreading with maturity. Growth is slow. The trunk often divides near the base, and venerable specimens often have multiple trunks, the lower branches lost to time, showcasing the beautiful bark, the best of any *Pinus* species, exfoliating in jigsaw-puzzle pieces; the outer bark green to brown, exposing the cream to almost white, yellow, green, purple, and brown inner bark. Exfoliation occurs on 1½ to 2″ wide branches. Large trunks are often smooth and bone-white. In China it is revered, highly prized in temple and palace grounds as well as public areas; trees are 200 to 300 years old, some approximately 900 years; 80 to 100′ high specimens were recorded. The largest trees in the United States are typically found in botanical gardens and arboreta. Size 30 to 50′ high with a 20 to 35′ spread.

Foliage: Needles are held in fascicles of 3, each 2 to 4″ long, $\frac{1}{12}$″ wide, minutely toothed, lustrous rich to dark green, stiff, with a sharp pin-point apex. Needles persist 3 to 4(5) years, resulting in dense specimens. Needles hold bright green color in winter. **Flowers/seeds/fruits/cones**: Female cone is bright green initially, maturing yellowish brown, 2 to 3″ long, 2″ across, ovoid, releasing seeds at maturity, often remaining attached for several years before abscising; cone scales brown when dry, each with a flattened, decurved, stiff spine on its back at the end. **Native range**: Mountains of central China in moist, well-drained rocky soils, in association with *Caryopteris* species, *Cotinus coggygria*, and *Platycladus orientalis*. **Adaptability**: Zones 4 to 7, although the coldest reaches of zone 4 are tenuous. Plant was damaged in Maine. **Landscape use**: Utilize as a specimen, in groupings, at corners of buildings and against dark backgrounds to highlight the bark. The limbs are fairly brittle. No doubt the slow rate of growth frightens most nursery producers. Among the seedlings grown at the Morton Arboretum from wild-collected material in China (1990), the largest is 15′ high (2017) with 6 to 8″ the longest one-year shoot

Pinus bungeana

Pinus bungeana

P

extension; further, Morton reported, good drainage is essential for survival. In Georgia a 14-year-old plant was 9′ high and 5′ wide. Whatever the tariff, it is worth the expenditure. Well adapted to varied soils, including limestone, except wet; remarkably, a Georgia nursery grew splendid trees, albeit slowly (10′ in 10 years), in the reddest of red clay. Requires full sun for maximum growth. Has demonstrated high heat and drought tolerance in the Southeast. Collection trips to China describe the species growing on steep slopes and mountaintops under dry stressful conditions, which observations, when extrapolated, reflect performance in the Southeast. **Street tree use**: No. **In the trade**: Not common; growth is slow and patience is required. All listed are grafted, so availability is limited.

'Great Wall'. Accurately named by Don Shadow, Winchester, TN, including a nod to its Chinese heritage. Broad-columnar, thickly branched, 25′ specimens make a great wall if planted side by side.

'Rowe Arboretum' ('Compacta'?). Densely branched and compact. Grew 15′ in 20 years. Expect 20′ by 10′ in 25 years.

'Silver Ghost'. Pretty, early-developing white (silver-white) bark. Introduced by the Dawes Arboretum, Newark, OH.

Pinus canariensis
Canary Island pine

Evergreen conifer. Pyramidal in form and somewhat open in structure, this is a big tree, growing to 60 to 100′ tall with a spread of 35′ and a heavy trunk. The heaviness of the trunk, open branching, and long tufted needles give it a wonderfully coarse texture. Bark is thick, rough and furrowed, rusty brown.

'Great Wall'

Pinus canariensis

'Rowe Arboretum'

Foliage: Needles 3 per fascicle, margins finely toothed. Long, soft needles give trees a shaggy appearance; they droop gracefully from horizontal branches and hang from upward-oriented branch tips in umbrella-like skirts, 8 to 12″ long, bright green to medium dark green. **Flowers/seeds/fruits/cones**: Monoecious. In spring, light reddish brown pollen cones are held in large cylindrical clusters around branch tips, and as the new needles emerge above, they remind us of whimsical little pineapples. Female cones take 2 years to mature, 4 to 7″ long, 2″ across, elongated ovoid in shape, ripening in April, a rich lustrous brown. **Native range**: Canary Islands. **Adaptability**: This tree is all about heat and drought. Being superbly adapted to a dry Mediterranean climate, it is frequently used in central and southern California. It cannot tolerate a hard freeze. Zones 9 to 11. **Landscape use**: Very impressive in size, it's a big yard and park tree, radiating a rugged coarseness. Give it room. **Street tree use**: The trunk is too big for typical streets. Good for roadsides. **In the trade**: Sold as seed-grown.

![Pinus canariensis]

Pinus canariensis

Pinus cembra
Swiss stone pine, arolla pine

Evergreen conifer. Without question, one of the most beautiful of all pines because of the richly colored needles. Authors have photographed the species on Swiss mountainsides, where it had a broad, feathery, pyramidal habit, but most trees in U.S. cultivation are densely conical-pyramidal. Mature specimens are open, flat-topped and spreading, the branches semi-arching. Growth is slow, perhaps 25′ in 25 to 30 years. Estimate 30 to 40′ in height, 15 to 25′ width, potentially to 75′ high in nature. Bark is smooth, gray initially, gray-brown and scaly, flaking to expose reddish brown.

Foliage: Needles, fascicles of 5, densely set, creating a foxtail appearance, 2 to 3(5)″ long, $\frac{1}{12}$″ wide, margins finely serrate, dark green outside, bluish white inside, the overall effect from a distance blue-green, color holding in winter (perhaps slight diminution), persisting 4 to 5 years. **Flowers/seeds/fruits/cones**: Male cones, $\frac{1}{3}$ to $\frac{4}{5}$″

P

Pinus cembra

Pinus cembra

'Chalet'

long, red; female greenish violet/purple with about 50 scales when young. Female cones ripen to warm reddish brown, 2 to 3″ long, 2″ wide, ovoid, never opening; seeds are released through decomposition and birds. Scales without a prickled umbo. Described as not producing cones in its native stands until at least 50 years, eventually reaching 500 years and more (1,000 was cited). Countering this assertion, authors recorded mature cones on a 10-year-old tree in Minnesota. **Native range**: Alps and Carpathian Mountains of south-central Europe, from southeastern France to central Romania, where it forms pure stands or is mixed with other conifers, primarily larch. Grows at 5,000′ and above. **Adaptability**: Zones 4 to 7. In the cool summers of the Pacific West, it grows well into zone 8. Its montane, high-elevation nativity portends best success in colder regions; superb plants are thriving in St. Paul, MN (zone 4) and both Cincinnati and Philadelphia (zone 6). In the East, we have yet to witness a thriving specimen in

zone 7. The Gymnosperm Database lists hardiness to zone 1! **Landscape use**: For single specimen use, this species has minimal competition. All young landscape specimens are densely conical-pyramidal. For groupings, in borders, perhaps screening, it is architectural and aristocratic. It is worthy of greater use. **Street tree use**: Limited. **In the trade**: Available.

'Chalet'. Columnar with dark blue-green, dense needles, slow-growing, 5 to 10′ in 10 years.

PRAIRIE STATESMAN 'Herman'. Densely columnar with emerald-green needles clothing the stems. Zone (2)3 introduction from North Dakota State University; 30′ by 15′.

'Stricta' ('Columnaris'). The commonest form in commerce, more narrow and columnar than the species. The name may blanket more than one clone. 30′ by 15′.

PRAIRIE STATESMAN

'Chief Joseph'

Pinus contorta

lodgepole pine, shore pine

Evergreen conifer. This species consists of three distinct subspecies with surprising differences in growth forms and size. See the variety listings for descriptions. Bark is variable over its range, gray to brownish, fairly thin, lightly fissured, usually with flattened ridges.

Foliage: Needles 2 per fascicle, medium to dark green, twisted, margin finely serrated, 1 to 3″ long, persisting 3 to 8 years on the branches. **Flowers/seeds/fruits/cones:** Monoecious. Cones mature in 2 years, becoming broadly ovoid to nearly globose, 1 to 2½″ long. Brown. **Native range:** Var. *contorta* (shore pine) occurs along the Pacific coastal strip from northern California to Alaska; var. *murrayana* (Sierra lodgepole pine) in the Oregon Cascades and the Sierra Nevada range of California; var. *latifolia* (Rocky Mountain lodgepole pine) in the Rocky Mountains from the Yukon Territory to Colorado, the British Columbia coast range, and Washington Cascades. **Adaptability:** Obviously the species is highly adaptable, varying in its native habitat from zone 1 to zone 9, but individual seed sources are best used for similar climates. All need full sun but are tolerant of a variety

of soils, including very infertile ones. **Landscape use:** The short and twisted shore pine is used in coastal climates for a natural landscape appearance and also as a specimen, often pruned to accentuate its irregular shape; it can present a wonderful, windswept appearance. The two tall, narrow lodgepole pines are used for both natural landscapes and focal points; these tend to be tough trees, and you often see them in commercial landscapes that are intended to blend in with the local vegetation. **Street tree use:** Lodgepole pines are narrow and can be used if conifers are desired; shore pine is too spreading for most situations but is used on roadsides. **In the trade:** Sold as seed-grown, but pay attention to variety and seed source. Grafted cultivars also available.

'Chief Joseph'. Selected from var. *latifolia* for its yellow needles. Summer growth is yellow-green, and as fall approaches the entire tree turns bright yellow. All winter long, the tree glows, among the most brilliant yellows of the winter garden. Pyramidal in form and slower growing; we expect landscape size to be 10 to 15′ high. An authors' favorite and a featured plant in Warren's garden.

'Chief Joseph'

var. *contorta*

var. *latifolia*

var. *contorta*. The type is frequently shaped by the wind of the Pacific coastal strip into wonderfully artistic and contorted shapes (hence the epithet). Nursery-grown trees are more uniform, but the irregular spreading form persists, and with a little pruning they can duplicate the wild coastal appearance. To 20′ tall and wide.

var. *latifolia*. A complete contrast to var. *contorta* in form, growing straight as an arrow. It forms a narrow pyramidal shape and frequently grows over 50′ tall.

var. *murrayana*. Very straight and narrowly pyramidal, the tallest variety, 50 to 100′. For landscape purposes, it is very much like var. *latifolia*, although it's best to pay attention to seed source.

'Taylor's Sunburst'. Like 'Chief Joseph', this selection features yellow foliage, but the timing is different. The new growth candles emerge and unfold bright yellow in spring, contrasting against the older, dark green foliage. But the spring color is short-lived, as the new growth gradually changes to yellow-green as the summer season progresses, then somewhat dull green for the winter. Faster growing and makes a larger tree, 15 to 20′, pyramidal.

var. *murrayana*

'Taylor's Sunburst'

Pinus densiflora
Japanese red pine

Evergreen conifer. It starts its life in pyramidal form but soon becomes upright-spreading, irregularly branched, often multi-stem; at maturity broadly rounded to flat-topped and rather open below. Trunks are often artistically twisting. Moderately slow-growing, medium texture, to 50′ high, 40′ wide. Bark is orange to reddish brown, with peeling flattened scales, with age becoming more gray.

Foliage: Needles 2 per fascicle, margins finely toothed, a bright deep green, 3 to 5″ long, presenting a tufted appearance. Foliage may yellow in stressful climates in the winter. **Flowers/seeds/fruits/cones**: Monoecious. Cones ovoid, mature in fall, brown, and are small for a pine, 1½ to 2″ long. **Native range**: Japan, Korea, and northeastern China. **Adaptability**: Needs full sun and reasonable moisture, appreciates a temperate climate. Avoid windy, low humidity sites. Zones (4)5 to 7. **Landscape use**: Used as a featured specimen, usually singly. Its interesting form can be enhanced by a combination of artistic pruning and letting nature take its course. Opening up the lower portion of the tree displays the distinctive bark colors. It looks best with low twisted branches and multiple trunks, a wild windswept appearance. **Street tree use**: No, too wide and crooked. **In the trade**: Sold as seed-grown but mostly as smaller cultivars.

P

Pinus densiflora

'Burke's Red Variegated'

Pinus densiflora

'Golden Ghost'

'Burke's Red Variegated'. Similar to 'Oculus Draconis' with yellow-banded needles forming an "eye," but the banding pattern is brighter and more pronounced, and this cultivar is easier to grow, being more tolerant of adverse conditions. It's a smaller tree, a little open in form, to 15′ tall and wide.

'Golden Ghost'. Pale yellow variegated bands may extend over most of the length of the needles, giving the tree a light color. At different times of the summer it may appear ghostly pale or bright yellow. Appearance is soft and fluffy. Slower growing, probably to 15′ tall and wide.

'Oculus Draconis' (dragon's eye pine). The needles are variegated with 2 yellow bands, and when you look straight on at the shoot tip, they form yellow concentric circles, looking like a great eye. Viewed from a distance in summer, the tree comes off as yellow-tinted. 20′ tall, 25′ wide.

'Oculus Draconis'

'Umbraculifera' ('Tanyosho'). Grows with multiple trunks from near the ground, flaring up and then angling outward, leading to a flat-topped canopy. Typically sheared in the nursery and sometimes pruned to pom-poms, it looks much better after it gains height and is allowed to develop a more natural appearance, with multiple flat layers of foliage, its reddish bark exposed below. Grows to 15′ tall and 20′ wide. Not to be confused with 'Umbraculifera Compacta', which grows only to about 6′.

Pinus flexilis

limber pine

Evergreen conifer. Pyramidal in form, usually a little uneven, becoming more rounded on top with maturity, 40′ tall and 25′ wide. Medium texture, slow-growing. Bark is smooth when young, light gray or greenish gray, becoming gray-brown, fissured into rough, flattened plates, horizontally checked.

Foliage: Needles 5 per fascicle, margins entire, very dark green to bluish green, 2½ to 3½″ long, persisting up to 6 years and held rather densely along the branches. White stomatal bands can give the tree a bright sheen. **Flowers/seeds/fruits/cones**: Cones are an elongated ovoid shape, 3 to 6″ long and 1½ to 2″ wide before opening and taking 2 years to mature. Green when immature, brown when ripe. **Native range**: Rocky Mountains from British Columbia to New Mexico, and west at higher mountain elevations through the Great Basin into California. **Adaptability**: Very adaptable, grows on some of the toughest mountain sites, very exposed, windy, and usually on seasonally dry soils. It has proven to be one of the most adaptable to landscape

'Oculus Draconis'

'Umbraculifera'

Pinus flexilis

P

603

Pinus flexilis

'Extra Blue'

'Vanderwolf's Pyramid'

'Vanderwolf's Pyramid'

use at the lower elevations of the Midwest, where its pH tolerance helps, as well as to the Northeast and Mid-Atlantic states. Full sun. Zones 4 to 7. **Landscape use:** A fine specimen or can be grouped as an informal screen. The bluish tint of the most popular selections is among the best of the pines. **Street tree use:** If a conifer is wanted on the street, 'Vanderwolf's Pyramid' could be considered. **In the trade:** Sold occasionally as seed-grown, mostly as the cultivars.

'Extra Blue'. Well named, it boasts more intensely blue needles than 'Vanderwolf's Pyramid', really beautiful, and a more irregular, tufted appearance on a frame that's a little shorter and broader, 25′ tall and 20′ wide.

'Vanderwolf's Pyramid'. One of the best known and most widely planted of all conifer cultivars, which speaks to its beauty and landscape success. Dense narrow pyramidal form, slightly upsweeping branches, and bright bluish green foliage appears crisp and clean. Landscape size 25 to 30′ tall, 15′ wide.

Pinus halepensis

Aleppo pine

Evergreen conifer. Large and spreading, it begins with a pyramidal form but soon the heavy structural branches spread and ascend, and it develops an irregular, broadly rounded to flat-topped, open canopy. Medium coarse texture, moderately fast-growing to 60′ high, 40′ wide. Bark is thick, deeply furrowed, orange-brown to charcoal-gray.

Foliage: Needles 2 per fascicle (sometimes 3), light green, 2 to 4½″ long. Foliage presents a soft appearance. **Flowers/ seeds/fruits/cones**: Monoecious. Cones are narrow conical, 2 to 5″ long by 1″ in diameter, then open to ovoid, 2 to 3″ wide, orange-brown. **Native range**: Lower altitudes surrounding the Mediterranean Sea. **Adaptability**: Full sun. Very drought tolerant. Likes a Mediterranean climate and is widely planted in coastal California and the Southwest. Tolerant of high pH. Zones 8 to 10. **Landscape use**: This is a large and spreading pine, often with heavy low branches, so give it room. Its irregular shape gives it a rugged look. Used in commercial sites and parks; residential use would require a very large yard. **Street tree use**: Occasionally used. Rather crooked-growing but does develop an overhead canopy, so clearance is possible. Trunk needs room. **In the trade**: Sold as seed-grown.

Pinus halepensis

Pinus halepensis

P

Pinus heldreichii (P. leucodermis)
Bosnian pine

Evergreen conifer. Pyramidal to broadly pyramidal, erect, usually dense and symmetrical. Moderately slow-growing, medium texture, 50′ or more tall, 15 to 20′ wide. Bark is thick, gray, fissured into irregular small blocks.

Foliage: Needles 2 per fascicle, lustrous dark green year-round, 2 to 4″ long, stiff and sharp. **Flowers/seeds/fruits/cones**: Cones are conical to elongated ovoid, 2 to 3½″ long, 1″ wide, dark bluish purple when immature, then opening wider and ovoid, light brown. **Native range**: Higher elevations of the Balkan Peninsula and southern Italy. **Adaptability**: Very tolerant of both heat and cold, poor soil, and drought. Salt tolerant as well. Zones 5 to 8. **Landscape use**: Dominated by much smaller, finer-textured cultivars that retain the species' formal, perfect look. A reliable landscape plant. Symmetrical form combined with outstanding foliage quality make this a great accent plant, and its dense foliage and fairly narrow shape mean it works well in groups as a large screen. A favorite species of the authors. **Street tree use**: Broadest at the base, not a good choice for traditional street use, but larger seedling trees are suitable for roadsides because of salt tolerance. **In the trade**: Available.

'Compact Gem'. A dense, compact, and moderately narrow little pyramid, very slow-growing to 10 to 15′.

'Emerald Arrow'. Narrow, very tight and upright, smaller and more compact than the species but reaching a tree-sized height, to 20′ tall and 8 to 10′ wide. Its slender form makes it a good fit in a small garden.

'Indigo Eyes'. Named for the young cones, which are cobalt-blue on the branch tips in spring, later turning brown. A broad pyramid, 20′ tall, 15′ wide.

'Mint Truffle'. Compact and dense, it grows slowly to a broad pyramid to ovoid shape, 15′ tall, 12′ wide, holding its high-quality foliage with full form to the ground.

'Satellit' ('Satellite'). Quite upright and narrow, its foliage is a little more open than other cultivars, but fills in with age, 20′ high and 10′ wide.

Pinus heldreichii

Pinus heldreichii

'Indigo Eyes'

'Compact Gem'

'Emerald Arrow'

'Mint Truffle'

'Satellit'

Pinus jeffreyi

Jeffrey pine

Evergreen conifer. A very large, tall tree with a stout, straight trunk and an open, pyramidal form. Coarse in texture, moderately fast-growing, will reach at least 100′ tall and 30′ wide; the record tree in nature is 300′. Bark reddish brown, thick, deeply furrowed.

Foliage: Needles 3 per fascicle, usually slightly twisted, margin finely serrulate, dark green to bluish gray-green, very long, 6 to 10″, matching the scale of the tree. The needles persist for 5 to 8 years. **Flowers/seeds/fruits/cones**: Cones are very large, 5 to 12″ long, ovoid, becoming broadly ovoid when open and orange-brown in color with thick scales that end with a sharp barb. **Native range**: Southwest Oregon through California into northern Baja, restricted to the mountains. Grows at higher elevations than ponderosa pine. **Adaptability**: A tree of hot summers and cold winters, it can take temperature extremes. It's quite tolerant of drought and poor soils. Zones 5 to 7. **Landscape use**: Mostly used in natural landscapes in mountain communities and for restoration. **Street tree use**: No, too large. **In the trade**: Sold as seed-grown. 'Joppi', a very small selection, is a broadly rounded compact pyramid. The needles are full-sized and look disproportionately large on this plant, almost like they were glued onto a little tree. A formal fluffy ball, slow-growing to 10 to 15′ tall and wide. An interesting appearance.

Pinus jeffreyi

'Joppi'

Pinus koraiensis
Korean pine

Evergreen conifer. Elegant, feathery pine with a loose, graceful habit, more open than *P. cembra*, and with a slightly faster growth rate. Authors have misidentified these two species on several occasions; the best way to separate them is by cones, twice as large on *P. koraiensis*, and the thicker needles, toothed to the apex. Growth is described as painfully slow for the first 5 years. Expect 30 to 40′ in height, less in width, on mature landscape specimens. Trees grow to over 100′ high in the wild. Bark is smooth, gray-brown initially, becoming darker, scaly, shallowly ridged and furrowed with maturity. The Korean population has been depleted by excessive timbering.

Foliage: Needles borne in fascicles of 5, 2 to 5″ long, dark green on outside, grayish on inner, overall effect is blue-green, margins more coarsely toothed than most pines, serrations extending the entire length, persisting 2 to 3 years, arching gracefully at their extremities. **Flowers/seeds/fruits/cones**: Monoecious. Male flowers ½ to ⅕″ long, red; young female cones green to purple with approximately 90 scales. Mature cones cylindrical-conical, 3½ to 6″ long, 2 to 2½″ wide, ripening reddish brown, the scales diamond-shaped with a small, triangular umbo; cones abscise the year after maturing, releasing the seeds. **Native range**: Mountains of Honshu, Japan; Korea eastward to Amur River region of eastern Russia and northeastern China. **Adaptability:** Adaptable to well-drained, acid, clay-based soils. Zones 3 to 6 in the East, to 8 in the cool-summer Pacific Northwest. Several conifer authorities suggest it could grow well in zones 6 and 7 and cite a thriving 'Morris Blue' in Milledgeville, GA, and a healthy 12-year-old tree in the Cox Arboretum, north of Atlanta. Authors observed 40′ specimens in Illinois, Ohio, and Kentucky. Plants with Amur River region provenance are exceptionally cold hardy. **Landscape use**: No quibbling with the landscape potential for this species, but it is reserved for colder climates. Utilize as a specimen, groupings, and screens. **Street tree use**: No. **In the trade**: Available.

'Glauca'. May be an umbrella category for all blue-needled selections; trees so labeled sport gracefully long, soft-textured blue-green to blue needles.

'Morris Blue'. Develops a more pyramidal habit, the branches clothed with silver-blue needles with a wonderfully tousled texture. Potential to 40′ high. Originated at the Morris Arboretum.

'Oculus Draconis'. Yellow banding on the needles create a "dragon's eye" effect when viewed straight on, although not as obvious as the similarly banded cultivar of *P. densiflora*. Overall tree has a slightly yellowish green color.

Pinus koraiensis

Pinus koraiensis

P

'Morris Blue'

'Morris Blue'

'Oculus Draconis'

Pinus leucodermis. See P. heldreichii

Pinus longaeva. See P. aristata

Pinus monophylla
single-leaf pinyon pine

Evergreen conifer. Easy to identify, it's the only single-needled pine. Pyramidal in youth, it broadens to become rounded and more open with upsweeping branches, spreading on top with age. A smaller pine, to about 25′ tall, 15 to 20′ wide. Medium texture, slow-growing and long-lived. The bark is thick, scaly, and brownish to gray. One of the pinyon pines; the seeds (pine nuts) were an important food source for Native Americans of the Southwest.

Foliage: Really quite attractive. Needles held singly, green with a bluish gray tint, 1 to 2″ long, persisting up to 6 years. Because needles are held singly, they appear less dense and more evenly spaced along the branch; young branches look a bit like big green bottlebrushes, but we mean that as a compliment. **Flowers/seeds/fruits/cones**: Cones are ovoid, 1½ to 2½″ long, becoming more globose upon opening, light brown. The seeds are edible and delicious. **Native range**: Dry mountains of the Great Basin, from the dry side of California's central Sierras to Utah and south into Baja and Arizona. **Adaptability**: Very drought tolerant, growing on hot slopes in the arid West, and tolerant of higher pH and cold dry winds. Full sun. Limited landscape experience, but we expect adaptability to zones 4 to 8 in the West.

Pinus monophylla

Pinus monophylla

Pinus nigra

Landscape use: Highly unusual appearance because of its single needles, which give it a very different texture. This beautiful little tree is a great choice for the native landscape or for xeriscaping in the West. We like it and think it should be used more. **Street tree use**: It could be appropriate in form with time, but so slow-growing the street would probably be widened before it creates a canopy. **In the trade**: Sold as seed-grown.

Pinus nigra
Austrian pine

Evergreen conifer. Broadly pyramidal, full, and dense when young. With age becoming broader on top, even irregularly flat-topped, while the sturdy lower branches and trunk become more open and bare. Medium fast-growing to 60′ high, 35′ wide. Medium coarse texture. Bark is rough, furrowed, gray with patches of yellowish brown to rusty brown.

Foliage: Needles 2 per fascicle, stiff, sharp-pointed, margin finely toothed, very dark green, almost appearing blackish

green en masse on the tree, 3 to 6″ long. Young branches are densely clothed in needles, which usually persist for 4 years and hold into the interior. **Flowers/seeds/fruits/cones**: Monoecious. Cones take 1½ years to mature, reaching an ovoid shape, brownish, 2 to 3″ long; seeds are dispersed in fall. **Native range**: Southern Europe and Turkey, in mountains and at higher elevations. **Adaptability**: A very tough adaptable tree, one of the most urban-tolerant pines. It can take a wide variety of soils, from wet to dry, and a broad range of pH. Holds up in wind and drought. Zones 3 to 7, 8 in the cool-summer West. **Landscape use**: Widely used as a landscape conifer, especially on commercial sites because of its toughness. Inexpensive and reliable, new residential developments often see it as a builder's grade landscape tree, often planted on sites too small to accommodate its eventual size. It is a beautiful tree, one that becomes more interesting in form with age, but it needs room. Its cold hardiness and wind resistance make it a popular landscape tree in the Mountain West. Quite susceptible to pine wilt disease, which limits its use in the Midwest and East. **Street tree use**: Wide at the base when young, it's not shaped for traditional street use, but it's good for roadsides and interchanges where room allows and a conifer is desired. **In the trade**: Widely available.

Pinus nigra

'Arnold Sentinel'

'Oregon Green'

'Arnold Sentinel'. Very dense, narrow, stiffly and tightly upright, columnar when young, it maintains a very narrow pyramidal form with age, to 30′ tall and 10′ wide.

'Oregon Green'. Needles brighter green and shorter than the species, and spring new-growth candles are nearly white against the older foliage. Needles also curve closely around the branches, giving a more open and textured feel. 40′ tall, 25′ wide.

Pinus palustris

Pinus palustris
longleaf pine

Evergreen conifer. A wonderful species, long-associated with wiregrass (*Aristida stricta*). Discrete growth habits are evident in youth and maturity; the former (the grass stage) a single-stem sapling with long needles producing a drooping mane; the latter a grand tree with a central trunk, oval to rounded outline, and spreading, curved branches. The grass stage lasts 3 to 4 years. Growth is slow, particularly in the early years. Growth accelerates later, with 40 to 60′ high trees the landscape norm, potentially to 100′. Bark is orange-brown to reddish brown, thick, with irregular flaking (scaling) ridges, divided by broad dark gray furrows. The timber is highly prized, and throughout the Coastal Plain, giant native stands of it, once totalling more than 60 million acres, have been decimated by timber harvesting, development, and lack of fires, which had served to reduce/eliminate competing grasses and woody vegetation. The endangered red-cockaded woodpecker breeds only in mature longleaf pine stands.

Foliage: Needles in 3s, occasionally 2s, to 18″ long in the grass stage; in the adult stage, 6 to 12″ long, dark green to shiny yellow-green, straight or slightly twisted, finely serrate, persisting 2 years. **Flowers/seeds/fruits/cones**: Monoecious. Male cones 1 to 2(3)″ long, purple; female green with 40 to 100 scales. Mature female cones are ovoid-oblong, ripening dull brown, opening to release seeds, and abscising in winter, 6 to 8(10)″ long, to 5″ wide at base. **Native range**: Southeastern Virginia to central Florida to southeastern Texas on the Coastal Plain, where it develops pure stands (or is mixed with oaks) on flat sandy soils and slight slopes. **Adaptability**: Native soils are sandy, nutrient-deficient, and dry. Large trees are evident along the coast in exposed maritime locations. Zones 7 to 10. **Landscape use**: The species is ideal for native situations, and thousands of acres of it are being enthusiastically replanted. Prefers deep, sandy, dry soils, but also grows in seasonally flooded flats. Trees successfully grown on the University of Georgia campus are now 30′ high (20 years old), growing in red clay. **Street tree use**: No. **In the trade**: Seedlings are available.

P

Pinus palustris

Pinus parviflora
Japanese white pine

Evergreen conifer. From an identification viewpoint, this is one of the easiest to spot: it usually carries copious cones in youth, unlike any other cultivated pine species. In youth, the habit is dense, conical to pyramidal, developing wide-spreading branches, flat-topped head, and sculptural, picturesque character with age. Growth is slow. Although described as a 75 to 100′ tall tree in nature, most plants in cultivation are less than 30′, often as wide as high, with the spreading branches upturned at their tips. Bark is dark gray to brown, becoming scaly, eventually narrowly ridged and furrowed.

Foliage: Needles in fascicles of 5, densely clustered, slightly twisted, forming brush-like tufts at the end of the branches, 1 to 2½(3)″ long, $\frac{1}{25}$″ wide, blue-green, margins finely serrated; color persisting through winter, typically abscising in the third year. **Flowers/seeds/fruits/cones**: Male cones, ¼″ long, clustered, reddish brown; female green with 30 to 80 scales. Mature female cone is pretty blue-green, waxy, resinous when young, transitioning to yellowish brown, reddish brown, and dark brown, cylindrical to oblong-ovoid, closer to egg-shaped, 1½ to 4″ long, almost as wide, most often borne in whorls of 3 to 4, remaining 6 to 7 years. **Native range**: Extensive, and at minimum five varieties are cataloged, each with a different provenance. Found in Japan, Korea, Taiwan, southern China, and northern Vietnam on mountaintops and hilltops. **Adaptability**: Zones 4 to 7, 8 in the West. Successful in Orono, ME, and Edmonton, AB. **Landscape use**: Graceful, small conifer, choice specimen, accent plant, at its ornamental best in an open expanse of lawn, well adapted to any well-drained, acid soil in full sun. It is seldom utilized in zone 7 landscapes; however, moving north, authors recorded outstanding specimens in Maine and Minnesota. **Street tree use**: No. **In the trade**: Available.

Pinus parviflora

'Bergman'

Pinus parviflora

'Aoi'

'Glauca'

'Glauca'

'Glauca Brevifolia'

'Aoi'. Short, blunt needles emerge green, then become blue on the underside. Dense conical form, a little irregular and sculpted, it becomes brighter blue as the summer progresses. Attractive small cones. To 25′ by 10′.

'Bergman'. Smaller and more compact, dense, with curved and twisted blue-green needles, a broad pyramid to 15′ by 10′.

'Blue Wave'. Upright with short, blue-green needles on twisted branches; 15 to 20′ by 8 to 10′.

'Gimborn's Ideal'. Pyramidal to columnar habit, the blue-green needles on short branches create a tufted appearance; 15 to 20′ high, 6 to 8′ wide.

'Glauca' (Glauca Group). Home to what qualifies as the small to medium-sized tree with spreading habit and rather dark blue-green, twisted needles. This appears to be the common form in U.S. cultivation. The largest specimen authors recorded was 30′ high at Heritage Gardens, Sandwich, MA.

'Glauca Brevifolia'. Bears shorter, slightly twisted needles that engulf the stems; develops an open, pyramidal outline, 15 to 20′ high, 10 to 15′ wide; requires candle pruning in spring to create a denser specimen.

'Tempelhof'. A vigorous selection, glaucous blue needles; narrow upright in youth, dense pyramidal at maturity. 30 to 40′ high.

P

Pinus pinea

stone pine, Italian stone pine

Evergreen conifer. Rounded when young, developing many upright-spreading structural branches and forming a broadly rounded to flat-topped canopy high above the sturdy trunk. The canopy is mushroom-like at first, more umbrella-like at maturity, staying quite open below. Medium growth rate, medium texture, growing to 50′ tall and wide. Bark is orange-brown to reddish brown with gray patches and scaly plates divided by fissures. The cones are often collected as the source of delicious edible pine nuts.

Foliage: Needles 2 per fascicle, margin minutely toothed, bright medium green, 4 to 8″ long. Juvenile foliage is very different, the needles are single and much shorter, about 1″. The foliage matures to the adult type between 5 and 10 years of age. **Flowers/seeds/fruits/cones**: Cones are broadly ovoid, 3 to 6″ long, and take 3 years to mature, chestnut-brown. The seeds (pine nuts) are large, to ⅞″ long. **Native range**: Mediterranean region, from the Canary Islands and Spain to Turkey. **Adaptability**: Well adapted to dry sandy soils and drought. It likes a Mediterranean climate and is popular in California. Zones 8 to 10. **Landscape use**: This tree has a great look for the beach, and it's well adapted to the soils often found there. Broad-spreading and rather large for most residential lots, but its canopy is high at maturity and it is quite open below, so space around the base is usable. **Street tree use**: Its umbrella-like habit can make a great street tree at maturity, and it lines many streets in and around Rome. But when young, it is broad at the height of traffic, which needs consideration in planning, purchasing, and pruning. **In the trade**: Sold as seed-grown.

Pinus pinea

Pinus pinea

Pinus ponderosa

ponderosa pine

Evergreen conifer. A very large, tall tree with a strong, straight trunk and narrowly pyramidal form, with stouter branches becoming more open with age. Coarse in texture, moderately fast-growing, will reach at least 100′ tall and 30′ wide; record tree 268′; pioneer logging records say some reached 300′. Bark is brown to charcoal on young trees, becoming thick and furrowed with long plates and taking on a beautiful color with age, yellow-orange to orange-brown. In many ways, the symbol of the old West, and a very important timber tree; foresters call the big ones "yellow bellies."

Pinus ponderosa

Foliage: Needles 3 per fascicle, ridged, curved, minutely toothed, dark green, 5 to 9″ long, usually held 3 years. **Flowers/seeds/fruits/cones**: Cones 3 to 6″ long, ovoid, thick scales have an outward prickle tip, brown. **Native range**: Western North America, from the western Plains states to the Pacific, with extensions into British Columbia and northern Mexico. Five regional subspecies are recognized. **Adaptability**: Takes heat and drought, high and low pH. Its extensive natural range indicates it is broadly adapted, but each subspecies has its niche. It's good to go with a reasonably local seed source. In Oregon, west-side native ponderosa will take wet soil, while east-side sources are adapted to heat and drier soils and air. Zones 3 to 8 in the West, probably 3 to 6 in the East. **Landscape use**: Widely used in natural landscapes, either as preserved trees as development encroaches, or as intentional plantings. It's used to maintain a sense of place in the interior West, and it is certainly the most majestic, noble tree of the region. If you live within its native range, have room, and want to look like you belong, this is the tree. **Street tree use**: Too big to be a traditional city street tree, but it lines roads in many areas. **In the trade**: Sold as seed-grown.

Pinus ponderosa

Pinus radiata
Monterey pine

Evergreen conifer. Forms a dome-shaped canopy with large upward-spreading branches, clothed with needles at the tips. Landscape size 40 to 60′ high, less in width, with mature trees 100′ and greater. Where adapted, growth is exceptionally fast, 4 to 5′ per year; report from England noted an 18-year-old tree was 52′ high and a 28-year-old tree was 79′ high. Bark is dark gray-brown, irregular ridges, divided by deep reddish brown fissures. Mature trunks are striking. A tremendously important timber species in Australia, New Zealand, Chile, South Africa, and Spain; in certain areas, it is invasive.

Foliage: Needles in fascicles of 2 or 3, occasionally 5, each 3 to 6(8)″ long, firm, slightly twisted, margin minutely toothed, bright green to dark yellow-green, persisting 3 to 4 years. **Flowers/seeds/fruits/cones**: Male cones, $\frac{2}{5}$ to $\frac{1}{5}$″ long, yellow-brown; female green with 90 to 180 scales. Mature female cones are obliquely conical, 3 to 6(8)″ long, 2 to 3″ wide at base, pale reddish brown at maturity, typically remaining closed and persisting. **Native range**: Now rare (limited), near the coast from California to Mexico. **Adaptability**: Reserved for the maritime (salt-laden), mild environment of the California coast. Authors have yet to witness in the East. Zones 8 to 10. **Landscape use**: Strictly a specimen for large areas or use in the forest industry. Reminiscent of a green Charles Atlas, with bulging branches

Pinus radiata

P

tufted at their ends with clusters of needles; authors noted 80′ by 60′ trees in Ireland and, initially, had no idea of their identity. Growth is fast in any well-drained soil. **Street tree use**: No. **In the trade**: Literature reports natural variation in populations, and considerable propagation research has been devoted to developing superior clones by rooting cuttings. Seedlings are available, but there is a paucity of ornamental introductions. Aurea Group includes the yellow-needle variants.

Pinus resinosa
red pine, Norway pine

Evergreen conifer. Heavily branched and needled in youth, soft pyramidal in outline. Old trees develop a symmetrical oval crown with tufted needles. We estimate 40 to 60′ high, less in width under cultivation; trees in the wild have exceeded 100′ in height. Bark is orange-red, scaly and flaking on young trees, eventually developing large, flat, reddish brown, scaly ridges. At one time, one of the most important timber species. One common name is derived from the reddish bark, the other from the Norwegians who logged it.

Foliage: This 2-needle pine is confused with *P. nigra* except needles snap in red pine; simply bend in Austrian pine.

Pinus resinosa

Needles are 5 to 6″ long, densely arranged, slender, the margins finely and regularly toothed, lustrous medium to dark green, persisting 3 to 4 years. **Flowers/seeds/fruits/cones**: Male cones, ½″ long, purple; female green with 50 to 80 scales. Female cones are oval-conical (egg-shaped), 1½ to 3″ long, about as wide, shiny light brown to reddish brown; maturing to release the seeds, then abscising. **Native range**: Eastern Canadian provinces, including Newfoundland and Nova Scotia, to Manitoba; Massachusetts, Minnesota, Illinois, and the Appalachians to West Virginia. It forms pure stands or grows mixed with oaks, aspens, and other pines on dry, sandy soils. **Adaptability**: Possibly second only to *P. banksiana* in cold hardiness among North American species and has withstood winter lows greater than −40°F. Zones 2 to 5. We do not remember a red pine growing anywhere south of zone 6. **Landscape use**: Certainly picturesque at maturity, and young trees develop a full, soft-textured, graceful canopy of delicate needles. Like *P. banksiana*, it is ideal for infertile, acid, sandy, rocky soils but is less likely to invade clear-cut land. In cold-climate gardens, it functions in groupings, screenings, and as a backdrop for herbaceous and shrub borders. In the southern part of its range and where utilized as an ornamental, it is quite susceptible to the European pine shoot moth. **Street tree use**: No. **In the trade**: Seedlings.

Pinus rigida
pitch pine

Evergreen conifer. Irregularly pyramidal in youth, often open, branches spreading, originating from a central trunk, oval-rounded crown at maturity. Estimate 40 to 60′ high, 30 to 50′ wide. Varies from gnarly krummholz specimens in windswept maritime conditions on Cape Cod to 100′ trees in Georgia. Growth is moderate under good cultural conditions; slow in sandy, rocky habitats. Bark is gray-brown to red-brown with elongated scaly ridges divided by shallow furrows.

Pinus rigida

Foliage: Needles in fascicles of 3, rigid, slightly curved and twisted, ending in a sharp point, finely serrated, 3 to 5″ long, pale to dark green, persisting 2 to 3 years. **Flowers/seeds/fruits/cones**: Monoecious. Male flowers ¾ to 1½″ long, soft yellowish brown; female green with 90 to 140 scales. Seed cones in whorls of 3 to 5, prolific, ovoid-conical, 2 to 3″ long, 1 to 1½″ wide, light brown to orange-brown, opening on the tree to disperse seeds, some cones remain closed, persisting 2 years or more, prominent sharp prickle on back of scales. **Native range**: Extended higgledy-piggledy range in eastern North America, from Canada to Florida with disjunct and continuous populations. **Adaptability**: Another adaptable species like *P. banksiana*, its greatest attribute. It has the ability to survive in pure sands, rocky crevices, and seasonally flooded, lowland ponds; on Cape Cod it grew around the edges of the Atlantic white cedar swamp. Zones 4 to 7; warmer considering the Florida habitat. **Landscape use**: This is a difficult sell when competing with the graceful, artistic 5-needle *Pinus* species; however, for "impossible" infertile, sandy soils and maritime environments, there is justification for use. In Maine, authors hiked through pure stands growing on Isle au Haut, an island of rock. It is one of few pines that produces adventitious shoots from trunks, cut stumps, or when injured by fire. Reasonably easy to identify, for tufts of needles develop on large trunks. It may produce up to 3 whorls of branches in a single season. **Street tree use**: No. **In the trade**: 'Sherman Eddy' is a 15′ high form with pom-pom tufts of needles. The closely related *P. serotina* (pond pine), with needles typically twice as long, is found in poorly drained, wet habitats. Hybrids combine the hardiness of *P. rigida* with the faster growth and timber quality of *P. taeda*.

'Sherman Eddy'

Pinus rigida

Pinus strobiformis

southwestern white pine

Evergreen conifer. Pyramidal form, tall, straight, and slender. Medium texture, moderate growth rate to 50′ tall and 20′ wide. Bark is dark gray-brown, rough and furrowed.

Pinus strobiformis

Pinus strobiformis

Foliage: Needles 5 per fascicle, margin finely serrate, dark blue-green, 2 to 4″ long. **Flowers/seeds/fruits/cones**: Cones are 4 to 10″ long and 1½ to 2″ wide before opening, cylindrical in shape and usually slightly curved, with thick scales, maturing in 2 years, light brown. **Native range**: High elevations in the mountains of Arizona and New Mexico, south into Mexico. **Adaptability**: Needs full sun. Despite its restricted native habitat, it is widely adapted to landscape situations, taking heat and cold. Zones 4 to 8. **Landscape use**: Used in natural landscapes in the Southwest as well as in ornamental plantings over a much broader area, valued for its handsome foliage and narrow pyramidal shape. Moderate in size compared to many western pines, making it more suitable for residential planting. **Street tree use**: Its narrow form and trunk size make it appropriate if a conifer is desired. **In the trade**: Sold as seed-grown.

Pinus strobus

eastern white pine

Evergreen conifer. One of the tallest trees, broadleaf or evergreen, in eastern North America, and no pine is more easily identifiable simply based on habit: graceful and broadly pyramidal in youth; open, flat-topped, with horizontally stratified branches, carrying plume-like tufts of needles at maturity. We estimate "normal" landscape dimension, 50 to 80′ high, 20 to 40′ wide; the National Champion is 132′ high, 72′ wide. Growth is fast, 2 to 3′ per year. Bark is smooth, grayish green in youth; dark gray-brown on large trunks, often furrowed longitudinally into broad, irregular, thick ridges. Important timber species, but doubtful that there are any virgin forest populations remaining. England harvested the tallest trees for ship masts in our country's early history.

Foliage: Needles are borne in fascicles of 5, thin, soft, pliable, arching, finely serrated, green to bluish green, the inner surfaces gray to white, 2 to 4(5)″ long, persisting into fall of the second year, then abscising. **Flowers/seeds/fruits/cones**: Male cones are ½″ long, clustered, yellowish brown; female purple-tinged green with 100 scales. Seed cone cylindrical with slight curve, 3 to 7(8)″ long, 1½″ wide, ripening light brown and spotted with white resin, opening in second year when seeds are dispersed. Cones develop on young trees so regeneration is amazingly reliable; white pine seedlings are as common as grass in abandoned fields, roadsides, and burned-over land. **Native range**: Eastern North America, Canada south to north Georgia and Alabama. **Adaptability**: Cold-climate tree. Zones 3 to 7, 8 in the Pacific West. In Atlanta-Athens (zone 8), there are splendid trees; however, some die for no obvious reason (although root rot has been mentioned). **Landscape use**: We are confident there is a variant for any size garden, assuming

Pinus strobus

climatic conditions are suitable. Where adapted, a choice specimen, grouping, screen, and hedge. The latter appears counterintuitive because of the immense size, but seedling hedges were maintained at prescribed heights simply by pruning the new growth (candles) each spring. This also produces increased vegetative buds behind the cut, resulting in a thicker hedge. Well-drained, acid soils, and full sun are ideal. Authors noted chlorosis (yellow needles) on landscape trees in high pH situations. The species is susceptible to white pine blister rust, which may kill trees, and white pine weevil, which kills the leader, thus deforming trees. Authors have not observed either pest in recent travels. A final thought relative to size as historical anecdotes cite trees over 250′ high with 12′ diameter trunks. Authors suggest that hybrids with other white pines (see *P. ayacahuite*) would demonstrate greater heat tolerance and unique ornamental traits. The literature reported successful hybrids with most 5-needle species. **Street tree use**: Possible for the upright cultivars. **In the trade**: Many selections, including several for yellow and blue needles.

Pinus strobus

'Angel Falls'

'Fastigiata'

'Fastigiata'

'Angel Falls'. A pretty weeper with graceful descending branches, clothed with blue-green needles; size listed as 40′ by 30′, although staking is necessary to develop height.

'Contorta' ('Torulosa'). An odd duck, requiring an open mind from the gardener as the twisted needles and branches form an open, irregular pyramid; 25′ high, 6 to 10′ wide. Authors observed trees larger than this.

'Fastigiata'. Narrow columnar in youth, more open and elegantly pyramidal with age as branches ascend at a 45° angle; at landscape maturity, 50 to 70′ high, 20 to 25′ wide.

'Glauca'. Logically interpreted as an umbrella term for bluer needle types; those so labeled are large trees; a specimen in the Arnold Arboretum was 60′ by 60′.

'Louie'. Yellow to yellow-green needles that do not discolor in full sun. Very tight, conical form. Grows 20′ by 8′.

'Pendula'. Pendulous branches, cascading, diving, arching, eventually forming a large tangle of curious configuration. 'Niagara Falls' and 'Stony Brook' belong here.

'Stowe Pillar'. Narrow and columnar when young, similar to 'Fastigiata' but tighter in form, with darker, more blue-green needles, quite handsome. Probably stays a little narrower than 'Fastigiata', but time will tell.

'Winter Gold'. Slow-growing; tree-type habit, needles become bright yellow in winter.

'Pendula'

'Louie'

'Stowe Pillar'

P

Pinus sylvestris

Scotch pine

Evergreen conifer. Certainly, a most beautiful conifer at its genetic best, with many variations in hardiness, needle color, and growth characteristics over its extended geographical range. In the United States, the bluish needle type is common and forms an irregular pyramid with short spreading branches; with age picturesque, wide-spreading, flat- or round-topped, umbrella-shaped. Growth is quite slow in the Southeast; moderate in colder climates. Expect 30 to 60′ high, 30 to 40′ wide; authors spotted open-growth native trees in Scotland, and all were taller than wide, with long straight trunks and cloud-like assemblages of lateral branches and needles. Bark is grayish to reddish brown on large trunks, fissured into irregular, longitudinal, scaly plates; in the upper branches, orangish to orange-brown, peeling in paper flakes. Of what he called the Highland pine, Wordsworth wrote, "I prefer [it] to all other trees except the oak, taking into consideration its beauty in winter, and by moonlight, and in the evening."

Foliage: Needles in fascicles of 2, rather stiff and flattened, twisted; margins minutely serrate; blue-green but variable from lightest to dark green; 1 to 3(4)″ long, persisting 2 to 4 years. **Flowers/seeds/fruits/cones**: Monoecious. Male cones quite small, ⅛ to ½″ long, pink to yellow; female green with 70 to 100 scales. Seed cones ovoid-conical, 1½ to 3″ long, lustrous or dull yellowish brown, reddish brown to grayish brown; opening on the tree, dispersing the seeds; back of cone scale with a blunt point. **Native range**: Spain and northern Europe to Siberia and Mongolia. The most widely distributed pine species and, among conifers, second only to *Juniperus communis*. **Adaptability**: Zones 2 to 7, 8 in cool maritime climates of the Pacific West and Europe. **Landscape use**: This species, once the dominant Christmas tree in northern states, is now superseded by *Abies fraseri* and other firs. Utilize for screens, windbreaks, and possibly specimens. Full sun and acid, well-drained soil are requisites for best growth, although it has performed well

Pinus sylvestris

'Gold Coin'

Pinus sylvestris

Fastigiata Group

in the high pH soils of the Midwest. In the wild, it is found in numerous soils and climates, rendering specifics super-fluous. Subject to nematodes, diplodia tip blight, and pine wilt in the Midwest, so much so that the Morton Arboretum considers it unsuitable for contemporary landscapes there. **Street tree use**: No. **In the trade**: Seed purveyors offer as many as 11 provenances. Only a few tree types are available.

Aurea Group. Includes yellow-needled types, small or large. 'Gold Coin' bears thick, light green needles that become intense yellow with the first freezes of autumn, color per-sisting into spring. Habit is upright, broad-conical, develop-ing into a small tree.

Fastigiata Group (sentinel pine). Narrow columnar form with blue-green needles, branches are subject to bending and breaking in snow and ice; somewhat sparse in needles, bare branches evident, to 25′ high.

'Watereri'. Often considered a dwarf conifer forming a densely pyramidal to broad, flat-topped crown of pretty steel-blue needles; however, the original plant reached 25′ high and 35 to 40′ wide, and a 30′ wide specimen was recorded at the Hillier Arboretum, England. Logically, train to a standard and then allow to spread its wings.

Pinus taeda
loblolly pine

Evergreen conifer. A primary invader of roadsides, fal-low fields, any open ground, it thrives where few woody coniferous species could gain a foothold. In youth, the habit is broad pyramidal, loose and open to quite dense. Mature trees develop an oval-rounded crown, secondary branches almost perpendicular to the main trunk. One of the fastest-growing southern pines, easily 2 to 3′ per year in youth; 40 to 60′ high and greater at maturity. Bark is

P

'Watereri'

Pinus taeda

Pinus taeda

Pinus taeda

gray-brown to red-brown, with rounded ridges and deep furrows, fragmented into elongated scaly plates. This is the dominant species lining the fairways at the Augusta National Golf Club, home of the Masters, and the most important timber tree among the southern pines (the others being *P. elliottii*, *P. palustris*, and *P. rigida*).

Foliage: Needles are held in fascicles of 3, occasionally 2, slender, twisted, margins finely serrated, dark yellowish green (variably yellow-green to shiny dark green), 6 to 10″ long, ⅟₂₅ to ⅟₁₂″ wide, persisting to the end of the second growing season, then abscising. **Flowers/seeds/fruits/cones**: Monoecious. Male cones ½″ long, clustered, yellow-brown; female green with 120 to 160 scales. Seed cone is ovoid-cylindrical, buff-rust brown, yellow-brown, each scale with a stout, sharp recurved prickle, 2 to 4(5)″ long, opening on tree to release the seeds; often remaining 3 to 4 years before falling. There is not a single season when cones universally fall. Daily cone pickup goes hand-in-hand with owning a loblolly. Young trees 4 to 7 years old may produce heavy cone loads. **Native range**: Coastal Plain and Piedmont from New Jersey to Florida, into Texas and Arkansas, where it forms pure stands or mixed associations with hardwoods in old fields to swamp margins. **Adaptability**: Will grow anywhere, displaying a tenacious and unflinching adaptability to the vagaries of soil and moisture. Originally growing under moist, lowland conditions, it has colonized great upland acreage. In Georgia, it is one of the primary invaders of any type of real estate, including one's backyard. Zones 7 to 10. **Landscape use**: A great choice for quick screens and backgrounds, and in the lower Southeast, the species of choice for groupings. Planted together, trees develop long slender boles, the lower branches shedding. Seven-year-old trees are 20′ high in the Dirr garden; when limbed up, they provide light shade for hydrangeas, rhododendrons, and Japanese maples, among others. Heat stress is reduced, while growth and flower bud set are maximized on the understory plants. Shoot tip moth, rust, and bark beetle are worrisome for foresters, but gardeners typically do not need to be concerned about them. **Street tree use**: No. **In the trade**: JC Raulston Dwarf (NCSU Dwarf Group) loblollies originated from witch's broom seed collected in Washington, DC. The seedlings have compact crowns and are now 25 to 30′ high. They must be propagated by grafting. The original trees are extant at the JC Raulston Arboretum, Raleigh, NC.

Pinus thunbergii

Japanese black pine

Evergreen conifer. Broadly pyramidal when young, developing a layered appearance and often becoming artistically irregular. Landscape size of 40′ high and wide is typical, but it can grow quite large and is often kept smaller by pruning, frequently to develop an Asian garden look. Bark is gray on young trees; thick, black, and plated on the mature trunk.

Foliage: Needles 2 per fascicle, dark green, stiff, crowded and twisted, sharp-pointed, margins finely toothed, 2½ to 4½″ long. Needles persist 3 to 5 years. **Flowers/seeds/fruits/cones**: Cones 2 to 3″ long, 1½ to 2″ broad, narrow ovoid opening to broad ovoid, brown. Mature in 2 years. **Native range**: Coastal Japan and Korea. **Adaptability**: Resistant to salt, as its native habitat suggests. Zones 6 to 9. **Landscape use**: Used as a focal point and very important in traditional Japanese gardens. Often pruned like a giant bonsai and used near the ocean coasts this way. Quite susceptible to pine wilt disease, which limits its use in the Midwest and East. **Street tree use**: No, too wide-spreading and irregular. **In the trade**: Available.

MAJESTIC BEAUTY 'Monina'. Slightly more compact than the species but with similar form, 30′ by 30′. Rich dark green foliage color holds up well.

'Thunderhead'. In winter, the new growth buds are bright white and contrast with the high-quality dark green foliage. A compact form, growing as a broad irregularly upright pyramid to 15′ tall and wide.

Pinus thunbergii

'Thunderhead'

Pinus thunbergii

Pinus virginiana
Virginia pine, scrub pine

Evergreen conifer. The word "scrub" fits its unruly aspect, i.e., scruffy, unkempt, and coarse, in mid to old age distinctly so, with numerous ragtag branches. Habit is broad pyramidal, becoming flat-topped, the branches springing irregularly from the trunk. Growth is fast. Expect 15 to 40′ high in the landscape; authors recorded 60′ tall specimens in several arboreta. Bark is scaly on young and old trunks, platy, grayish brown, divided into irregular, narrow blocks/strips, divided by shallow furrows. The species trends toward yellow-green, especially under colder temperatures. Nevertheless, an entire Christmas tree industry was centered on this species in the Southeast; to effectively market the tree, largely choose and cut, involved dyeing them green.

Foliage: Needles in fascicles of 2, twisted, spreading, stout, apex sharp-pointed, margins minutely serrated, yellow-green to dark green, 1½ to 3″ long, persisting 3 to 4 years. Young shoots covered with pale purplish bloom (wax), distinguishing it from other pines with short needles in pairs. **Flowers/seeds/fruits/cones**: Monoecious. Male ½″ long, yellow-brown; female green with 50 to 120 scales. Seed cone is oblong-conical, symmetrical, 1½ to 2½″ long, 1 to 1½″ wide, reddish brown, either opening on the tree or remaining closed for years, backside of cone scale with a sharp prickle; cones are persistent and rather unsightly, turning dark brown, almost black, with age. **Native range**: Long Island, through Appalachians, western Tennessee to Florida. Common in Kentucky, where pure stands grow from the limestone rocks. **Adaptability**: Tenacious, growing in dry hillsides, sandy rocky abandoned fields, fire-prone sites and other spots where few plants survive. In Georgia, Christmas tree production was in heavy, acid, silty-clay loam soils. Zones 4 to 8. **Landscape use**: Limited for both gardens and commercial landscapes, as there are superior species. **Street tree use**: No. **In the trade**: Available.

'Ancient Wonder'. Perfectly describes an irregular, broad-spreading form, estimated age of more than 150 years, with a sculpted, windswept habit; found by Tom Cox, Cox Arboretum, Canton, GA. Low-slung branches and similarity in overall habit to *Cupressus macrocarpa*. Landscape estimate 20′ high and wide.

'Wate's Golden'. Needles turn yellow-gold with cold weather, remaining colorful into spring. Reasonable growth rate; authors recorded a 25′ high tree, still rather open and straggly. It might be eye-opening to grow seedlings from this, as some may be true to the parent (i.e., yellow).

Pinus virginiana

'Wate's Golden'

Pinus wallichiana

Himalayan pine

Evergreen conifer. Broadly pyramidal in form and quite full in appearance, with branches that sweep out and gently upward. Moderately fine-textured, moderately slow-growing, reaching 40 to 50′ high and 35′ wide. Bark is gray-brown, with shallow fissures and roughened plates.

Foliage: Needles 5 per fascicle, slender, margin minutely toothed, gray-green to bluish green, 5 to 8″ long, persisting for 3 to 4 years. On new growth, the needles are held more upright; on older growth, they are soft, relaxed, and drooping. **Flowers/seeds/fruits/cones**: Monoecious. Cones 6 to 10″ long, 2″ broad, cylindrical, slightly curved. Violet-green at first, maturing in 2 years to light brown. **Native range**: Eastern Afghanistan to southwest China. **Adaptability**: Appreciates a temperate climate or a protected location. Winter wind can burn the foliage. Zones 5 to 7, 8 in the West. **Landscape use**: Usually used as a specimen, to highlight its classy and distinct appearance. Although upright, the tree has the air of a graceful weeper, thanks to its long, drooping needles. It is wide growing and holds branches to near the ground, so it needs room. **Street tree use**: No, too wide at traffic height. **In the trade**: Mostly sold as seed-grown.

'Prairie Giant'. A broadly pyramidal form with blue-gray needles. Notable for its proven cold hardiness in the upper Midwest, definitely zone 5 and probably safe in zone 4. Considered a hybrid with *P. strobus* and listed as *P. ×schwerinii*. 50′ tall and 40′ wide. *P. ×schwerinii* may have potential in the South.

'Zebrina'. Variegated form, with several yellow bands across each needle. This is wide tree, more broadly oval than pyramidal, and more open than the species, 30′ tall and 25′ wide. It is a very soft-appearing plant, combining the weeping needle effect with an overall creamy yellow to yellow-green color.

Pinus wallichiana

Pinus wallichiana

'Zebrina'

P

'Prairie Giant'

Pistacia chinensis
Chinese pistache

Deciduous. Upright-spreading with a rounded crown, often spreading a bit wider than tall with age. Medium growth rate to 30′ by 30′, medium fine texture in summer, a little more coarse when dormant. Bark is dark brownish gray, scaly. The species has a reputation of being deer resistant.

Foliage: Pinnately compound, usually 10 or 12 leaflets on a slender curved rachis. Leaflets lanceolate with a slightly acuminate tip, each leaflet 2 to 4″ long and ¾″ wide, margin entire, glabrous. Dark green, slightly glossy, handsome summer foliage. In autumn, the tree fires up, turning yellow, orange, orange-red, or bright red. **Flowers/seeds/fruits/cones**: Dioecious. Male flowers in dense panicles, green with red stamens. Female flowers green, in loose panicles, 7 to 9″ long. Flowers just before leaves emerge in spring, but not showy. Fruit follows in clusters of rounded ¼″ drupes, ripening to blue, each containing a single seed. **Native range**: China, Taiwan, Philippines. **Adaptability**: A tree for warm climates. It likes heat, even needs it. It appreciates moderate moisture but withstands drought and tolerates high pH. It grows well in the humid South, the stressful Southern Plains, and the dry Southwest. Needs full sun; avoid soggy

'Zebrina'

Pistacia chinensis

Pistacia chinensis

Pistacia chinensis

WESTERN SON

'Pearl Street'

soils. Zones 6 to 9, 10 in the West. **Landscape use**: Use for its small size and the effect of its lacy foliage. The narrow leaflets dance nicely in the winds of summer. Fall colors can be among the brightest of all trees and are especially appreciated in southern climes, where brilliant fall color is a rarity. Potentially invasive, so plant male cultivars. **Street tree use**: A bit low-branched, but it can be pruned up for use as a street tree on a wider tree lawn. It can definitely handle urban soil, tree pits, and heat reflected off the pavement. **In the trade**: Sold as seed-grown, but we recommend the following seedless male cultivars, to eliminate the risk of invasiveness.

'Keith Davey'. Upright, slightly compact, developing a rounded crown. Selected for bright fall color, and it delivers: bright orange-red to true red, one of the most reliable. The favorite cultivar in California. 25′ by 25′.

'Pearl Street'. Taller, more upright than the species, with a crown suitable for street use with traffic clearance. We tested it in Oregon and found it was 2 weeks later to defoliate; plants eventually died in an early freeze. Should be tried in the South. 30′ tall, 20′ wide.

'Sarah's Radiance'. Upright-spreading form, rounded, with intense red to purple-red fall color. Claims zone 5 hardiness; if true, this is the most cold hardy selection. 30′ by 30′.

WESTERN SON 'Pair's Choice'. Robust, thick-trunked, more vigorous and upright with sturdy branching and less likelihood of low-hanging branches, making it a good choice for streets. Fall color orange to orange-red. 30′ by 25′.

Platanus ×acerifolia

London planetree

Deciduous. Very large, upright then spreading, with a heavy trunk and branch structure, pyramidal when young then becoming very broadly oval. Fast-growing, coarse in texture, to 80′ high, 70′ wide, even larger in favorable settings where trunks can become massive, so do think about your sidewalk. Bark exfoliates attractively in patches, creating a mosaic of cream, gray, green, and brown.

Foliage: Palmate, maple-like, 5 to 8″ long and 6 to 10″ wide, with 5 major lobes, the lobes usually toothed, points acute, medium green on top, lighter green below, finely pubescent on the underside. If you work in a production nursery and you spend time in the thick of the foliage, you know that the little hairs on the leaves make your eyes water and your nose sneeze and drip, but this is not a problem in casual encounters in the landscape. **Flowers/seeds/fruits/cones**: Monoecious. Flowers in spring as the leaves emerge, not showy. Both male and female flower appear in globose

Platanus ×acerifolia

Platanus ×acerifolia

Platanus ×acerifolia

'Bloodgood'

'Bloodgood'

clusters of exposed stamens and pistils, respectively. Fruit ripens in fall as 1″ wide balls of seeds (multiple achenes), usually held in pairs on a stalk. **Native range**: A hybrid of *P. occidentalis* from eastern North America and *P. orientalis* from southeastern Europe and western Asia. **Adaptability**: Very adaptable and easily transplanted. A truly urban tree. The hybridization occurred naturally in England in the 1600s, and the tree became a dominant member of the early industrial urban forest in London, earning a reputation (and its common name) for resisting air pollution. Anthracnose is the most common problem. The authors studied various cultivars in similar plantings in Oregon and South Carolina and found opposite results for anthracnose susceptibility; it's unresolved whether this is climate effect or the genetics of the disease. Zones 5 to 9. **Landscape use**: A wonderful tree where space allows. Think big. Great for parks, campuses, roadside plantings, parking lots and plaza shade, and large residences. The mosaic of bark patterns makes it one of the most beautiful trees in winter. It does have one of the fastest-expanding trunk diameters of temperate deciduous trees, so keep that in mind as you site it. **Street tree use**: Give it root space, crown space, and allow for a potential 5′

trunk diameter, and it makes one of the best large canopy street trees. If space is insufficient, plant something smaller. **In the trade**: Sold exclusively as the cultivars.

'Alphen's Globe'. A compact form, forming a globose head, to 20′ by 20′. Usually top grafted on a high stem for pedestrian clearance. Selected in Europe, where urban trees are often carefully maintained. Given the vigor of the species, we doubt it will stay truly small without regular pruning.

'Bloodgood'. The longtime U.S. standard among planetrees because of its anthracnose resistance in the northern and western United States, although curiously susceptible in the South. Still highly valued, as it has stood the test of time. Graceful form for such a large tree and has very nice mottled bark. 70′ tall and 50′ wide.

'Columbia'. The large leaves are more deeply divided and toothed, a little closer in appearance to *P. orientalis*, although it is truly a hybrid. Better adapted to the heat of the South and does well, but rates only zone 6 hardiness in the North, where it suffers anthracnose. 70′ tall and 50′ wide.

'Columbia'

EXCLAMATION!

EXCLAMATION!

EXCLAMATION! 'Morton Circle'. Recently hybridized at the Morton Arboretum, this cultivar is rapidly becoming a favorite. Straight-growing and symmetrical with good density and a narrower pyramidal habit. Spring pubescence adds a slight silver-gray sheen to the green foliage. It has shown good anthracnose resistance and cold hardiness. Our current favorite. 60′ tall and 35′ wide.

'Huissen'. An excellent Dutch selection, named for the village where it was found. Strong and fast-growing, very straight, slightly narrower than most with good branch arrangement. Attractive, light-colored exfoliating bark. 70′ tall and 50′ wide.

'Liberty'. Introduced by the U.S. National Arboretum along with 'Columbia', it has proven to be the better plant in the North, more cold hardy and with better anthracnose resistance there. Rivals 'Bloodgood' in quality and appearance. 70′ tall and 50′ wide.

METROSHADE 'Metzam'. Fast-growing with dark green foliage and broadly pyramidal, 70′ by 50′, but we have observed more anthracnose than seen on 'Bloodgood', EXCLAMATION!, and 'Liberty'.

MONUMENTAL 'Morton Naper'. Broadly pyramidal with a dominant central stem and leader, nicely subordinate branching at uniform 45 to 60° angles, and a dense canopy. Branches and young trunk are light gray and bright in winter. Nursery growth is strong and straight. Good anthracnose resistance. Original tree is now 47′ tall, we estimate mature size to be 70′ tall, 50′ wide.

'Huissen'

'Liberty'

MONUMENTAL

'Liberty'

P

'Pyramidalis'

'Suttneri'

'Tremonia'

'Pyramidalis'. Good straight trunk and somewhat narrower form. Large dark green leaves with a slight gloss. Bark exfoliates less; appears darker than others. The authors have observed that this cultivar has an unusually heavy seed set of larger-than-typical seed balls, which discourages its use. 70′ tall, 40′ wide.

'Suttneri'. Leaves variegated cream, yellow, and green in an irregular splash-like pattern, but the variegation can be subtle and is often hardly noticeable. And with a little age, the foliage will be high overhead, where the leaves simply appear green. The cultivar's most outstanding feature is its exfoliating bark, which peels to almost pure white, developing at an early age and persisting. Grow it for its trunk. 60′ tall, 45′ wide.

'Tremonia'. Narrow form, similar to 'Pyramidalis', but it too suffers from heavy seed ball formation at an early age. Attractive exfoliating bark, light gray to light green when exposed, lighter in color than most. 70′ tall, 40′ wide.

'Yarwood'. Large blocky leaves with shallow sinuses, seed balls held singly, and light-colored trunk suggest it's closer to *P. occidentalis*. Selected in California for mildew resistance. In Oregon, it was the cultivar most susceptible to anthracnose, while in South Carolina, it succumbed to bacterial leaf scorch and is no longer planted. 60′ tall, 50′ wide.

'Yarwood'

Platanus occidentalis
American planetree, sycamore, button-ball tree

Deciduous. An iconic species, one of the most beautiful of all North American hardwood species, patently identifiable by its cream-white bark in the upper reaches of the trunk and branches. In youth, pyramidal, quite dense; eventually round-headed, massive, with immense secondary branches in muscular repose. Growth is remarkably fast in youth; slowing with age but still formidable, easily 75 to 100′ high and wide, the huge trunks occasionally hollow. Bark is beautiful, scaly, gray-brown, to red-brown initially, flaking and exfoliating in jigsaw-puzzle pieces; the inner bark cream-white; without equivocation the most aesthetic bark on any North American species, including the white-bark birches. The wood is used for furniture, particleboard, pulpwood, and butcher blocks, the latter because of its resistance to splitting. Trees may live 250 to 400 years. Be respectful of this biological treasure...preserve, protect, and love. *Platanus* species are a food source for 45 caterpillar species.

Platanus occidentalis

'Yarwood'

P

637

Platanus occidentalis

Foliage: Large leaves, with 3 to 5 lobes, shallowly lobed, sometimes deeply so, remotely and prominently toothed along the margin, 4 to 9″ long and often wider, with a cordate to truncate base, young leaves emerge gray- to silver-green, thick with short hairs (floccose-tomentose), maturing medium to dark green, at best papery yellow-brown in autumn. **Flowers/seeds/fruits/cones**: Monoecious. Tiny flowers, not particularly noticeable, in dense pendulous heads with the leaves in spring (April). The female inflorescence develops into a 1 to 1½″ wide, rounded, multiple fruit of achenes; fruits typically one per 2 to 4″ peduncle, maturing in October and persisting in various disintegrated states into the next spring. **Native range**: Every state east of the Mississippi as well as Iowa, Montana, Arkansas, Louisiana, Nebraska, Kansas, Oklahoma, and Texas, chiefly in moist to wet lowland areas, along streams and rivers, in floodplains. **Adaptability**: A primary invader of open sites, such as fallow fields, roadsides, and embankments. Zones 4 to 9. **Landscape use**: Too enormous for average landscape use. A single mature tree would umbrella the average residential lot. A case can be made for selecting a smaller-statured version, about a third the size of the species. Will drop interior leaves in response to extreme drought. Qualifies as a somewhat messy lawn tree, for leaves, small twigs, fruits, and bark detritus require large dust pans. Any deep, moist, preferably acid soil and full sun facilitate maximum growth; however, stray seedlings show up on drier, virtually barren soil; testimonial to its tenacity. Anthracnose, in wet springs, can kill emerging foliage and twigs, leaving the tree bare until late spring; the result is witch's brooming, with many short small twiggy growths. Other maladies occur; bacterial leaf scorch (pathogen: *Xylella fastidiosa*) is a serious disease of *Platanus* in the Southeast (which is why *P. ×acerifolia*, with degrees of anthracnose resistance at least, is prevalent in the nursery industry). **Street tree use**: No. **In the trade**: 'Howard' has bright yellow new growth that fades to green in summer heat. SILVERWOOD 'Grenickel', a Greenleaf Nursery introduction, maintains its pretty white bark to the very base of the trunk at maturity; size approximates the species.

Platanus orientalis

oriental planetree

Deciduous. Large, rounded to broadly rounded tree with a stout structure, pyramidal when young, becoming rounded with age. Moderately fast-growing, coarse in texture, to 70′ high and wide, larger on favorable sites. Bark exfoliates attractively in patches, dark gray with light green, tan, and creamy gray.

Foliage: Palmate, 4 to 8″ long, 5 to 9″ wide, with somewhat finger-like lobes, lobes more slender and deeply cut than on *P. ×acerifolia*, with or without points on the lobes. Medium green, pubescent in spring, the hairs irritating to the eyes and nose, becoming more glabrous as the season progresses. **Flowers/seeds/fruits/cones**: Monoecious. Flowers in spring as the leaves emerge, not showy. Both male and female flowers appear in globose clusters of exposed stamens and pistils, respectively. Fruits more heavily than *P. ×acerifolia*, ripening in fall as 1¼″ wide balls of seeds (multiple achenes), with 2 to 6 per stalk. **Native range**: Southeastern Europe, Asia Minor. **Adaptability**: As you might suspect from the native range, this tree likes drier climates. We have found it to be more susceptible to anthracnose and cankers than *P. ×acerifolia*. Zones 7 and 8. **Landscape use**: A large tree with a broad canopy. **Street tree use**: 'Digitata' has good form for such use. **In the trade**: Not common, sold as seed-grown. 'Digitata' is the only cultivar we consider worth listing, although it underwhelmed in Georgia trials. In trials in Oregon, it grew more slowly than *P. ×acerifolia* and its pyramidal form and appearance were nice, but it seemed to want a warmer climate. Interesting leaves with narrow finger-like pointed lobes, smaller, more delicate-looking, and slower than the species, to 45′ tall, 35′ wide. An elegant plant, worth trying in the right climate as a fine-textured alternative to the species, but otherwise we prefer the cultivars of *P. ×acerifolia*.

'Digitata'

'Digitata'

Platanus orientalis

P

Platanus racemosa
California sycamore

Deciduous. Tall, slender, open branching and irregularly twisting in form, often multi-stem in nature. Most landscape plantings seek to recreate the natural look. Fast-growing to 70′ tall and 35′ wide, depending on form. Coarse-textured, but in graceful way. Bark is exfoliating, with a mosaic pattern of light gray, gray-green, and tan, and a very light-colored appearance overall.

Foliage: Palmate, 3- to 5-lobed, trident to star-shaped, lobes are deeply cut with no side teeth or minor lobes. Leaves 5 to 9″ long, 5 to 10″ wide. Densely pubescent in spring but becoming nearly glabrous on top in summer, maintaining pubescence below. In fall, it may go greenish to tan-brown from drought or develop a nice golden yellow, depending on the weather. **Flowers/seeds/fruits/cones**: Monoecious. Flowers in spring as the leaves emerge, not showy, globose clusters of exposed stamens or pistils. Fruit 1″ wide seed balls (multiple achenes) are bristled, typically sessile along the stalk. **Native range**: California and northern Baja, along canyon creeks and waterways. **Adaptability**: Its native habitat is the dry-summer climate of California; it takes the high heat and low humidity but does need soil moisture. In Oregon trials, we found the frequent spring rains brought on severe anthracnose. Anthracnose is also common in California, but the weather there quickly turns dry and the tree recovers. Consider it a tree well adapted to its native habitat and use it there, in the dry Southwest. Will need irrigation in most California landscapes. Zones 7 to 10. **Landscape use**: Use it to create a naturalistic effect and informal feeling. Multi-stem forms are often preferred. Also used for restoration. Much more slender-trunked than *P. ×acerifolia*. **Street tree use**: No, a little too unwieldy in form. **In the trade**: Sold as seed-grown.

Platanus wrightii
Arizona sycamore

Deciduous. Upright-spreading, broadly oval, irregular and open with a sturdy trunk. Moderate growth rate, to 50′ tall and 40′ wide. Coarse-textured. Bark is exfoliating, light-colored, creamy tan to grayish white.

Foliage: Palmate, usually 5-lobed, 4 to 10″ long and wide, very similar to *P. racemosa* but a little more deeply cut, two-thirds of the way, and less pubescent, becoming glabrous. Golden tan fall color. **Flowers/seeds/fruits/cones**:

Platanus wrightii

Platanus wrightii

Similar to *P. racemosa* but seed balls (multiple achenes) smooth and usually each held on a short stalk. **Native range**: Arizona, western New Mexico, northern Mexico, restricted to growing near watercourses. **Adaptability**: Heat tolerant, full sun, but definitely needs irrigation in arid Southwest landscape settings. **Landscape use**: A nice shade tree within its native range; also used for restoration along creeks. Similar to the closely related *P. racemosa*, but for landscape purposes, the Arizona sycamore is more of a sturdy upright tree and less sinuous in form. **Street tree use**: A bit irregular in form, but well-pruned trees could serve if irrigated and given plenty of root and trunk space. **In the trade**: Sold as seed-grown.

Platycladus orientalis (*Thuja orientalis*)
oriental arborvitae

Evergreen conifer. Monotypic genus. The true species is somewhat open pyramidal in outline. Growth is slow, 30 to 40′ high, 10 to 15′ wide. Bark is gray, stringy, peeling, shallowly ridged and furrowed, seldom visible, as branches clothe the trunk.

Foliage: Needles soft-textured, ½″ long, closely pressed to stem, green on both surfaces, forming fan-shaped sprays borne in vertical planes; not aromatic when bruised; becoming yellow-bronze-brown in cold weather. **Flowers/seeds/fruits/cones**: Monoecious. Male cones $\frac{1}{12}$″ long, yellowish. Fruiting cones are roundish egg-shaped, scales (6) are fleshy, waxy (bloomy) glaucous green to blue-green, eventually reddish brown, ¾″ long, the tip of each scale with a reflexed horn-like projection, seeds BB-like, brown, rounded, and germinate without pretreatment. **Native range**: Korea, Manchuria, China, eastern Russia, at 150 to 11,000′ elevation in varied habitats. **Adaptability**: Considered by some authorities to be the most widely adapted of all conifers in cultivation. Authors recorded plants from Stonington, ME, to Key West, FL. Displays significant heat and drought tolerance; 100-year-plus plants in Oconee Hill Cemetery, Athens, GA, zone 8, persisted in the throes of debilitating drought and record heat. Zones 5 to 11. **Landscape use**: Serviceable needle evergreen for any well-drained, acid to neutral soil in full sun. Withstands pruning to the degree of *T. occidentalis*. Although slightly more deer resistant than *T. occidentalis*, it is still browsed to unacceptable degrees. The many garden selections are almost always smaller, conical-pyramidal, densely branched, 20′ high at best. Cemeteries, campuses, older neighborhoods hold the greatest concentration of cultivars, typically the

Platycladus orientalis

'Van Hoey Smith'

P

old 'Aurea Nana', functioning as screens, hedges, accents, or specimen. Authors noticed reference to cercosporidium needle blight affecting older plantings. **Street tree use**: No. **In the trade**: The numerous cultivars with screaming variation in degrees of yellow can induce landscape heartburn. Authors germinated over 200 seedlings from a *P. orientalis* "yellow cultivar"; the 100 or so that produced yellow needles were reduced to one selection with yellow summer needles, orange in winter. It was eventually scrapped: the solution to color pollution is to pitch. 'Aurea Nana' ('Berckman's Golden') is the old (c.1868 by Fruitlands Nursery) yellow-foliaged standard; 15 to 20′ by 10 to 12′. 'Van Hoey Smith' offers yellow-orange sprays speckled with green and white. Foliage is spectacular, but growth is loose, open, the vertical orientation still evident, to 15′ tall. Deer have made Swiss cheese of this in the Dirr garden.

'Aurea Nana'

Podocarpus macrophyllus
Chinese podocarpus, bigleaf podocarp, southern yew

Broadleaf evergreen. A large genus, second only to *Pinus* among coniferous genera, with 82 species, most distributed in the southern hemisphere in warm temperate and tropical environments and seldom grown in American gardens. This is the hardiest tree species. Habit is upright, conical to pyramidal, almost cylindrical as authors observed, supposedly becoming irregularly dome-shaped, more open, with numerous slender, horizontal to upswept branches. Growth is slow, to 20 to 30(50)′ tall, half as wide. Bark is initially gray-brown, smooth, becoming scaly and shallowly furrowed with age.

Foliage: Needles variable, shiny dark green to yellow- and blue-green, flattened and strap-like with a triangular apex, somewhat leathery, 3 to 5(7)″ long, ¼ to ½″ wide, radiating around the stem. Needles persist 2 to 3 years. **Flowers/seeds/fruits/cones**: Dioecious. Although lumped with conifers, the reproductive structure is a fleshy, naked, red to dark purple seed, covered with a waxy bloom, ¼ to ¾″ long, ⅓ to 1″ wide, the seed attached to an outer fleshy covering (aril). **Native range**: Japan, China, South Korea, growing in the understory of warm temperate evergreen forests and in disturbed habitats. **Adaptability**: The only *Podocarpus* species of ornamental significance for zone 7 to 10 gardens. **Landscape use**: A beautiful evergreen suitable for specimen use, screens, groupings, and hedges. Displays modicum of salt tolerance as well as deer resistance. Scale will occasionally infest the foliage. Any well-drained, acid soil, in sun (some winter discoloration) or shade is acceptable. The species (just described) is best suited to lower Gulf Coast and West Coast; var. *maki* is the common form in cultivation in the Southeast. Plants can be fashioned (shaped) into forever hedges and espaliered; both are common in Charleston, SC, for such purposes. A particularly cold hardy selection found in Edgefield, SC, has prospered in the hottest summers without irrigation for nearly two decades in University of Georgia trials; a remarkable performance, considering cultural conditions are diametrically opposed to the species' native evergreen forest habitats. **Street tree use**: Potential for the species. **In the trade**: Recent collecting expeditions to Japan yielded several striking foliage selections. The enthusiasm for color in all landscape plants has the industry seeking more such variants.

'Aureus' with yellow-margined/striped leaves and 'Argenteus' marked with white were introduced in 1861.

Podocarpus macrophyllus

EMERALD FLAME ('Royal Flush'). Bright pink young needles eventually maturing to green; each subsequent flush during the growing season retains the pink characteristics.

LEMON SPARKLER ('Golden Crown', 'Gold Crown', 'Chollipo'). Cream-yellow new growth, maturing green.

var. *maki*. More cold hardy than the species (true zone 7) with shorter needles, ½ to 2¾″ long, ¼ to ⅜″ wide, spirally arranged on the stem, creating a bottlebrush effect; needles are leathery, lustrous, waxy, dark green above, glaucous (grayish) below. Estimate 15 to 20′ high, less in spread. The Edgefield selection equates with these characteristics but is looser, with an upright branching habit.

'Variegata'. Pretty cream-white new growth, eventually green; the contrast between the cream and green is striking. ROMAN CANDLE ('Miu') is a commercial rename.

Poliothrysis sinensis
Chinese pearltree

Deciduous. Monotypic genus. A latecomer to Western gardens, even in England, where it received an RHS Award of Garden Merit in 1960; reintroduced to the Arnold Arboretum via seeds from Shanghai Botanical Garden in 1981. The authors originally pegged it as 15 to 20(25)′ high and wide, but subsequent sightings at the Arnold Arboretum and U.S. National Arboretum support 40 to 50(60)′ high at maturity, with 30 to 40′ high trees maintaining a full, dense complement of branches and foliage. Young seedlings are exceptionally fast, reaching 6 to 8′ in a season (Athens); often, fast-growing species are weak-wooded, but this species has been rock-solid to date. Bark is gray-brown with horizontal lenticels, becoming ridged and furrowed, ridges somewhat bumpy-blocky, fissures relatively shallow on young trees; on large trunks, bark is gray and deeply furrowed.

Foliage: Large, coarse, bronze to reddish green on emergence, becoming shiny dark green, broad-ovate, 3 to 6″ long, three-fourths as wide, with 3 prominent veins and a pubescent red petiole, to 2″ long; fall color may be warm yellow, deep purple-bronze to yellow-burgundy in October-November. **Flowers/seeds/fruits/cones**: Fragrant, cream to cream-yellow, ⅓″ wide flowers in 6 to 8(10)″ long, fleecy, terminal panicles in July; flowers are quite spectacular against the dark leaves. Fruit is a 3(4)-valved dehiscent, ½ to ¾″ long ovoid capsule, lime-green, maturing brown, long persistent, shedding winged seeds in autumn; capsules dehisce (open) at apex and base. Seeds germinate like grass and are produced in supernumerary quantities, which

Poliothrysis sinensis

Poliothrysis sinensis

Poliothrysis sinensis

makes us concerned about potential invasiveness. **Native range**: China. **Adaptability**: From Boston to Georgia on well-drained, acid soils, it has prospered. Zones (5)6 to 8. **Landscape use**: Summer-flowering trees, especially with blockbuster exploding-fireworks floral displays, are rare. Authors observed trees under severe drought that showed no ill effects. Certainly a useful park and urban tree based on tenacity but has yet to develop much of a footprint. We may be missing some buried Achilles' heel, but foliage, flowers, and heat and drought tolerances strongly suggest that untapped potential may be residing in the DNA. Smaller stature, improved fall color, and sterility (no viable seeds) would be a positive first step. **Street tree use**: Potential. **In the trade**: Sold as seed-grown, limited availability. Authors grew large seedling populations with little difference in characteristics.

Populus alba
white poplar

Deciduous. Large, upright-spreading or wider-spreading tree, usually low-branched, somewhat open, medium coarse texture, fast-growing, to 70′ by 70′. Bark is smooth and gray-green on young trees, developing unusual diamond-shaped marks as the trunk expands, then becoming dark and furrowed with age.

Foliage: Irregularly palmate, with 3 to 5 lobes and a sinuate to toothed margin, broadly ovate to roughly triangular in overall shape, 2 to 5″ long and slightly less in width. Dark green on upper surface, tomentose and silvery white beneath. **Flowers/seeds/fruits/cones**: Dioecious. Reddish male catkins 2 to 3″ long; green female catkins 3 to 4″. Flowers in spring just before the leaves emerge. Seeds develop quickly in spring, cottony, and blow in the wind. **Native range**: Europe through central Asia. **Adaptability**: Easy to grow, tolerant of flooding. Fast-growing but susceptible to many insects and diseases. Zones 3 to 9. **Landscape use**: Often seen around old farmsteads but now rarely planted because of pest problems, suckering, and brittleness. The narrow cultivars are used for fast-growing windbreaks, but otherwise it's hard to find a good reason to recommend it. **Street tree use**: There are better choices. Brittleness is a concern. **In the trade**: 'Pyramidalis' (Bolleana poplar) is columnar when young, becoming narrowly oval, can broaden to a moderately narrow pyramid. 'Raket' is a little broader than 'Pyramidalis', very upright, narrow, becoming pyramidal with age; nice yellow fall color.

Populus alba

Populus alba

'Pyramidalis'

'Pyramidalis'

P

Populus angustifolia
narrowleaf cottonwood

Deciduous. Upright pyramidal, finely branched, rather slender. Suckering, usually found in thickets. Fine-textured, moderately fast-growing, to 50′ high and 25′ wide. Bark is very attractive, light gray and smooth when young, then furrowed and gray-brown.

Foliage: Leaves lanceolate, glossy dark green above, lighter green below, serrulate, narrow and willow-like, 2 to 5″ long, ½ to 1″ wide. Yellow fall color. **Flowers/seeds/fruits/cones**: Dioecious. Flowers before leaves emerge, males reddish, females greenish, elongating with seed capsules, which release cottony seeds. **Native range**: Scattered distribution through the Rockies from southern Alberta to northern Mexico, growing in the mountains along streambanks. **Adaptability**: It needs moisture and likes full sun and dry air. Well adapted to Rocky Mountain landscapes, but foliar diseases cause problems in areas with humidity. We tried in Oregon, but the wet weather made for serious leaf disease. Zones 3 to 6. **Landscape use**: Unusually fine-textured for a cottonwood. Tall, slender, light and airy. A good native landscape tree in the Rockies and adjacent areas. We were impressed seeing it in landscapes and native groves in the Rockies and think the species deserves exploration in dry-air climates beyond its range. A bit like quaking aspen, it gives an informal and natural feel. **Street tree use**: Sometimes used in mountain towns where native trees are best adapted. Short life and suckers are problems. **In the trade**: Sold as seed- or cutting-grown.

Populus ×canadensis
Carolina poplar, Canadian poplar

Deciduous. A group of hybrid cultivars (*P. deltoides* × *P. nigra*).

'Nor'easter'. Upright when young becoming a good oval form. Yellow fall color. Nebraska bred, zone 3. Seedless.

'Prairie Sky'. Tall, columnar when young becoming a moderately narrow oval. Resistant to septoria canker and rust. Extremely vigorous. Yellow fall color. A cross using the columnar *P. nigra* 'Afghanica'. Manitoba bred, definitely cold hardy, zone 3. Seedless.

'Robusta'. An older cultivar, originated in France around 1895. Upright when young becoming oval, a bit open. Handsome foliage, bronze when young becoming glossy green. Yellow fall color. Zone 4. Seedless.

'Nor'easter'

Populus ×*canescens* 'Tower'

Tower poplar

Deciduous. A hybrid (*P. alba* × *P. tremula* 'Erecta'). Tall, columnar, staying narrow, dark green leaves with silvery white tomentose undersides, to 50′ tall and 14′ wide. Its rather triangular foliage resembles *P. alba*, while the narrow form comes from 'Erecta', but 'Tower' is slightly looser in form and grows a little wider. Foliage usually clean and disease-free. Zone 2.

Populus ×canescens 'Tower'

Populus deltoides

eastern cottonwood

Deciduous. Large and upright-growing, with an open pyramidal habit in youth becoming an irregular broad vase with age. Trunk and major branches can be massive. Very fast-growing, medium coarse texture. Reaches 100′ high and 75′ wide. Young trunks are smooth and yellowish green to gray-green, soon becoming deeply furrowed and ridged, heavily so on older trees; bark on mature trees is gray.

Foliage: Leaves deltoid to deltoid-ovate, 2 to 5″ long and wide, finely serrate margin. Lustrous medium green above, lighter green below. A good yellow fall color can develop. **Flowers/seeds/fruits/cones**: Dioecious. Flowers early in spring before the leaves. Male catkins reddish purple, 3 to 4″ long; female catkins greenish, 3 to 5″ long. Cottony seeds, released June-July, float in the wind. **Native range**: Massachusetts to southern Alberta and Georgia to Texas. **Adaptability**: Very vigorous, easy to grow, likes moisture but

Populus deltoides

P

Populus deltoides

'Jeronimus'

'Siouxland'

subsp. *wislizeni*

'Siouxland'

NORTHERN ESTEEM

tolerates drought and a wide range of pH. Adapted to the rigors of the Plains states. Zones 3 to 9. **Landscape use**: Valued as a tough and fast-growing shade tree in the difficult climate of the Northern Plains and drier areas of the West. Its fast growth can make it weedy. Like other members of the genus, it has more than its share of pests and diseases, as well as weak wood. Use it where you can't grow more noble trees. **Street tree use**: Not recommended due to size and breakage. **In the trade**: Available.

'Jeronimus'. Popular in Colorado and adjacent High Plains and mountain areas, it is well adapted to the rigorous, cold, dry climate. Locally considered a cultivar of *P. sargentii*, which GRIN now includes under *P. deltoides* subsp. *monilifera*. Uniform in growth habit, it is pyramidal when young with a straight leader, then spreads to broadly oval. Thick, silvery gray, rough bark in age, to 60′ tall, 40′ wide. Seedless.

subsp. *monilifera* (*P. sargentii*; plains cottonwood). A tough, cold hardy tree, native from the Canadian Prairie, across most of the northern states and south to Texas. Broad-spreading, it can reach 100′ in height. Fast-growing, thick gray trunk.

NORTHERN ESTEEM 'Schreiner'. Selected in North Dakota for solid zone 3 performance. Glossy, dark green foliage and improved resistance to diseases and insects. Broadly oval to rounded.

'Purple Tower'. Spring foliage emerges purple and purple-red color holds through spring, becoming more bronze in summer. Upright, narrow oval.

'Siouxland'. Very vigorous, upright-growing becoming oval to broadly oval, reaches 75′ tall with a width of 35′. Nice yellow fall color. Has shown moderate rust resistance. In drier air, it has had among the cleanest foliage in the genus, but we saw it defoliated in Cincinnati. Makes a large shade tree quickly in difficult environments. The most popular cultivar, well proven, reliable, and widely used. Seedless.

'Sparks'. Upright and narrow, has a reputation for longer life than most. Seedless.

subsp. *wislizeni* (Rio Grande cottonwood). Native to the river valleys of northern Mexico to southern Colorado and sometimes elevated to species status. Needs water, but is otherwise well adapted to the temperature extremes of the interior Southwest and used in landscapes there, including 'Fiesta Gold', a fall color selection.

P

Populus fremontii

Fremont cottonwood, western cottonwood

Deciduous. Large sturdy tree with a heavy trunk, upright when young then open and spreading, becoming wide and rounded on top, a bit vase-shaped. Coarse-textured, fast-growing to 60′ high and wide. Bark is gray-brown, smooth when young, becoming deeply furrowed, rugged-looking.

Foliage: Medium green, slightly lustrous, deltoid to cordate, lightly crenate to dentate margin, the teeth rounded, tip acuminate, 1 to 3″ long and wide. Fall color yellow to yellow-orange. **Flowers/seeds/fruits/cones**: Dioecious. Flowers in spring as foliage emerges, male catkins reddish, females yellowish green, 2 to 4″ long. Seeds cottony, dispersed in late spring. **Native range**: U.S. Southwest, California to Colorado, northern Mexico and west Texas. **Adaptability**: Its natural habitat is the streambanks and wetland edges of the arid Southwest. Needs soil moisture, but foliage is well adapted to heat. Hot, dry air with plentiful water in the root zone makes it happy. Zones 5 to 10. **Landscape use**: Good for restoration or at the back of large lots bordering on water. A quick-growing shade tree, but thirsty in a land of limited water. Grow it on the riparian sites where it belongs. **Street tree use**: Not a good choice—heavy limbs, breakage concerns, needs regular water. **In the trade**: Usually grown from cuttings, but sold as the species. Ask for male trees, which are seedless ("cottonless").

Populus fremontii

Populus fremontii

Populus grandidentata

bigtooth aspen

Deciduous. Fast-growing, tall, pyramidal when young becoming oval, open and irregular. Texture medium coarse, to 70′ high, 35′ wide. Bark is smooth, attractive gray when young becoming more mundane brownish gray with age. Grown for its pulp. Closely related to the Eurasian *P. tremula* and sometimes classified as a subspecies.

Foliage: Leaves medium green above, silvery to gray-green and pubescent below, becoming more glabrous as the season progresses, 3 to 4″ long and wide. Broadly ovate and distinctly toothed (hence the common name). Yellow fall color, sometimes bright to golden with a hint of orange. **Flowers/seeds/fruits/cones**: Dioecious. Flowers in early spring before the leaves. Catkins 2 to 4″ long. Cottony seeds dispersed in late spring to early summer. **Native range**: Nova Scotia to southeastern Manitoba and North Carolina to Iowa. **Adaptability**: Grows on wet or dry soils, full sun. Zones 3 to 5(6). **Landscape use**: There are better choices. A quick-growing primary succession species, useful for native restoration, short-lived, suckering. **Street tree use**: Not recommended. **In the trade**: Seed-grown.

Populus grandidentata

Populus grandidentata

Populus 'Highland'

Highland poplar

Deciduous. A hybrid (*P. acuminata* × *P. sargentii*). Adapted to the Mountain States and High Plains and used in that region. It grows quickly but matures smaller than many poplars, to about 50′ with a 30′ spread. Upright; dark green foliage, yellow in fall. Like most poplars, it is susceptible to leaf diseases in areas of high humidity and greater rainfall. Male, seedless. Zones 3 to 7.

Populus nigra

black poplar

Deciduous. Upright when young, becoming open and broadly spreading, but commercial cultivars are all columnar; see cultivars for size. Fast-growing, medium texture. Bark is smooth and gray when young, becoming dark gray to black (hence the epithet), fissured and roughly ridged.

Foliage: Leaves deltoid, dark green, 2 to 4″ long and wide, with an acuminate tip and serrate margin. Moderately glossy dark green. Yellow fall color. **Flowers/seeds/fruits/cones**: Dioecious. Flowers in early spring before the leaves. Catkins 1 to 4″ long, males are reddish, females green. Cottony seeds follow and blow in the wind. **Native range**: Europe to western Asia, now rare because of extensive development in its native floodplain habitat. **Adaptability**: Takes wet soil, some drought, wind, and cold. But needs dry air to stay healthy, and in most climates it is short-lived. In North America, it does best in the dry air of the interior

Populus 'Highland'

'Italica'

West. Zones 3 to 9. **Landscape use**: Its narrow cultivars are used for windbreaks. **Street tree use**: Not recommended. **In the trade**: Represented only by its narrow cultivars.

'Afghanica' (Theves poplar). Tall, narrow, columnar. Similar to 'Italica', but slightly shorter, to 60' by 15'. Very nice glossy green foliage. It has a reputation for better canker and foliage disease resistance; consider the resistance improved but still incomplete. Lighter-colored bark. Female, produces seed.

'Italica' (Lombardy poplar). Narrow, fastigiate form to 100' tall and 10 to 15' wide. Common as old windbreak rows on farms of the West. Most trees we see are skeleton-like or only half alive. May stay healthy and be reasonably long-lived in dry, low-humidity climates, especially in the interior West, but suffers disease and canker in wet and humid areas; use only where known to do well. Male, seedless.

'Afghanica'

Populus tremula
European aspen

Deciduous. Moderately fast-growing, upright when young, becoming oval, open and irregular. Texture medium when young, coarse when mature, to 70' high, 35' wide. Bark is gray-green and smooth when young, then developing large dark lenticels, becoming fissured and darker with age.

Foliage: Bronze-tinted in spring becoming slightly gray-green, 1 to 3" long and wide. Broadly ovate to round, distinctly toothed, although juvenile leaves on seedlings and suckers are larger, more deltoid, and serrate. Flattened petiole causes leaves to tremble in wind. Fair yellow fall color. **Flowers/seeds/fruits/cones**: Dioecious. Male catkins greenish brown, 2 to 4" long, females green, 1 to 2" long. Seeds cottony, dispersed in summer. **Native range**: Widely distributed throughout Europe and northern Asia, from Iceland to Kamchatka and south into colder areas of central China. **Adaptability**: Likes cool climates; in the southern

'Erecta'

P

'Erecta'

part of its range it is restricted to mountains. **Landscape use**: Only the cultivar is common: the handsome 'Erecta' suckers, even at a surprising distance from the trunk. It is sometimes bothered by rust but seems more resistant at lower elevations than quaking aspen. Use it as a strikingly tall focal point or as a screen. **Street tree use**: 'Erecta' is a good columnar form, but its suckers require maintenance. **In the trade**: 'Erecta' (Swedish columnar aspen) is tall and narrow, with tightly fastigiate branches, to 50′ by 10′. Dark, slightly grayish green foliage rustles in the breeze. Fair yellowish orange fall color. Foliage generally more disease-free than most *Populus* species, but we have observed leafspot in Illinois. Attractive gray bark. Columnar shape is among the tightest of trees, and we consider it one of the best narrow trees for cold climates. Best in zones 3 to 5 in the East, and up to 8 in the drier summers of the West. Male, seedless.

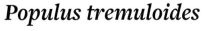

Populus tremuloides
quaking aspen

Deciduous. Upright-growing, slender, loosely and narrowly pyramidal to moderately narrow oval and often artistically irregular and a bit open. Moderate growth rate, to 40′ by 15′, wider if multi-stem. May form clumps from root suckers. Medium fine texture. Bark smooth, grayish to greenish to brilliant white, beautiful. The silvery trunks of aspen have been the subject of so many artistic photographs that they almost become cliché. As tree lovers, we never get tired of seeing them, whether in photos or—even better—in person. Interestingly, quaking aspen in nature are almost always found in clonal colonies, spreading vegetatively from root suckers from an original seed-derived tree, probably long past, and persisting successionally, as genetically identical individuals for many generations, often for centuries.

Populus tremuloides

Populus tremuloides

654

Populus tremuloides

Populus tremuloides

Foliage: Leaves very broadly ovate to orbicular with a short acuminate tip, 1½ to 3″ long and wide, finely serrate. Medium green to slightly bluish green, dull satiny to slightly lustrous, glabrous. Petiole flattened, allowing leaves to tremble in the breeze. Fall color yellow, often brilliantly so, occasionally orange-tinged. **Flowers/seeds/fruits/cones**: Dioecious. Catkins are fuzzy, 1 to 3″ long, males silvery red and females silvery green and lengthen to 4″ as seed develops in capsules. Tiny cottony seeds blow in the wind. **Native range**: Northern North America, from eastern Canada to Alaska, south to Pennsylvania and Iowa, with populations scattered throughout the mountains of the West, especially the Rockies, and with a few high-elevation populations in Mexico. The most widely distributed tree in North America but restricted to cooler locations and grows only at high elevations at lower latitudes. **Adaptability**: Likes cooler summer weather, as its native habitat indicates. It needs regular soil moisture and may grow in nearly saturated conditions. Often found on rocky sites in the mountains, but subsurface moisture is always there. Insect and disease problems abound and become more serious when cool-loving aspen are planted in urban heat islands. Zones 1 to 6, and to 8 in the cool coastal West. **Landscape use**: Very popular, especially when grown as clumps. Used for an informal, natural appearance. Best when used in settings similar to its native habitat: think cool and moist soil, but humidity and wet leaves can bring on foliage diseases. A favorite in the mountain towns of the West. In some of these towns, frost can occur at any month of the summer, and this is one tree that can take it. Light and airy in appearance, its silvery stems can be as important to a landscape as its foliage. **Street tree use**: In warmer climates it can be short-lived, and there are better choices. Sometimes used in the mountains, but it will need maintenance for suckering. **In the trade**: Widely sold as seed-grown, but its huge range suggests regional cultivars should be selected. The authors believe that many cultivars listed here are spontaneous hybrids with *P. tremula* 'Erecta', which disperses its pollen in the wind and is commonly grown in the same nursery and landscape settings as quaking aspen. The hybrids all have dentate-crenate leaf margins and narrow, tightly upright form, both characteristics of *P. tremula* 'Erecta'. These hybrids all seem to have improved resistance to the foliage diseases common to quaking aspen.

'Bethel Spire'. Upright oval form, 40′ by 15′. Not commonly grown. Weak grower with severe leafspot in Oregon trials. A true quaking aspen.

DANCING FLAME 'KMN01'. Bronze-red new growth, dark green in summer, orange fall color. Upright narrow oval form, 40′ by 12′. Improved resistance to foliage disease, appears to be a hybrid with *P. tremula* 'Erecta'.

P

DANCING FLAME

PRAIRIE GOLD

FOREST SILVER

MOUNTAIN SENTINEL

MOUNTAIN SENTINEL

FOREST SILVER 'Drifest'. Upright, narrow pyramidal to almost columnar. Dark green foliage turns yellow-orange in fall. Nice silvery trunk. Improved foliage disease resistance. Probably a hybrid with *P. tremula* 'Erecta', but a little looser in habit and more oval in form, to 40' tall, 12' wide.

MOUNTAIN SENTINEL 'JFS-Column'. Narrow, columnar with fastigiate growth to 35' tall, 8' wide. Similar to *P. tremula* 'Erecta' in form and probably a hybrid with it, but foliage is more similar to a quaking aspen. Improved foliage disease resistance. Lovely golden yellow fall color and nice silvery gray trunk.

PRAIRIE GOLD 'Ne Arb'. A true quaking aspen from an isolated native prairie stand in Nebraska. More tolerant of the warmer weather and summer humidity in the Midwest, but more susceptible to foliage disease in Oregon's wet springs when compared to typical seedlings. Recommended for the Midwest and Plains. Yellow fall color. Upright oval, 40' by 15'.

'Prairie Skyrise'. Columnar form, tightly fastigiate, and densely branched, 40' tall, 12' wide. Probably a hybrid with *P. tremula* 'Erecta' but differs in having bright green spring foliage. Golden yellow fall color.

SUMMER SHIMMER 'Select Klaus'. Selected in Minnesota for its large, clean leaf and vigorous growth, to 40' tall, 20' wide.

Prunus campanulata
Formosan cherry, bell-flowered cherry

Deciduous. Upright-spreading small tree, delicate and fine-textured, open below, rounded on top. Moderate growth rate, 25' high, 20' wide. Smooth, gray, with prominent lenticels when young, then irregularly roughened and darker gray with age.

Prunus campanulata

Prunus campanulata

Prunus campanulata

P

'Abigail Adams'

'Dream Catcher'

'First Lady'

Foliage: Dark green, slightly lustrous, ovate, oval, or slightly obovate, with an acuminate tip, finely serrate. Leaves 2½ to 4½″ long, half as wide. Fall color yellow-bronze to orange-red. **Flowers/seeds/fruits/cones**: Very early flowering, right after or overlapping with witch-hazel. Flowers small, ¾″ wide, fuchsia-pink, bell-shaped, delicate and prolific. After petal fall, the calyx holds on the tree, deeper magenta-red, and gives a brief second show of color. Fruit a ½″ wide ovoid drupe, red, ripening to maroon. **Native range**: Taiwan, southern China, Ryukyu Islands. **Adaptability**: Likes a warm climate, the best-adapted cherry for the South. All cherries like good drainage, but this one seems more tolerant of soil wetness than most. Reports of invasiveness in New Zealand. Zone ratings vary, listed individually for the cultivars; for the species zones 7 to 9, 10 in the West. **Landscape use**: Site it where you will see it in early spring, before other plants have leafed out. It's small, graceful, and understated for 11 months of the year, but when it is in bloom, it really stands out with intense color. Own-root (cutting-grown) plants are preferred; they grow quickly and are beautiful but are not long-lived. Trees are often defoliated by late summer in the warm, humid Southeast. **Street tree use**: Upright enough if good soil conditions are present and the climate is favorable. **In the trade**: Generally sold as cultivars, most of which are hybrids with other species, but grouped here because of affinity.

'Abigail Adams'. A true *P. campanulata* with flowers fully double, very deep pink, close to magenta-pink, hanging in clusters. Released from the U.S. National Arboretum primarily for breeding, but the tree may be suitable for landscape use in warm climates. 25′ tall and wide. Very early flowering, zones 8 and 9.

'Dream Catcher'. Upright-growing and oval to vase-shaped, this seedling of 'Okame' is slightly narrower with a flaring top and flowers about a week later. 25′ tall, 12 to 15′ wide. Single, medium pink flowers. Early bloom, but after the species. Dark green summer foliage turns yellow-orange in the fall. Zones 6 to 8.

'Felix Jury'. A true *P. campanulata*. Deep fuchsia-pink single flowers, bright yellow stamens, upright growth, very early flowering. 25′ tall, 20′ wide.

FIRST BLUSH 'JFS-KW14'. A breakthrough in this group, the first hybrid with large, fully double flowers. Bright pink blossoms are considerably larger than the similarly colored single-flowered forms. Quite upright in habit, it is narrow enough for street use, growing to 25′ tall, 12 to 15′ wide. Early bloom, but after the species. Zones 5 to 8.

FIRST BLUSH

'Okame'

FIRST BLUSH

'Okame'

'First Lady'. A hybrid of 'Okame' and *P. campanulata*. Very upright at first, narrower than 'Okame', growing to an upright oval, slightly open shape, 30′ by 15′. Flowers are single, very deep magenta-pink, probably the deepest color of the hybrids. Early bloom, with 'Okame', but after the species. Zones 6 to 8(9).

'Okame'. The best-known cultivar, a hybrid of *P. incisa* and *P. campanulata*. It grows as an upright oval, then widens to a broadly oval canopy to 25′ tall and 20′ wide. Floriferous, fine-textured, with lovely small, pink, single flowers. Trees look like soft clouds of pink. Early bloom, but after the species. Pretty, good for maybe 20 years. Zone 5.

P

Prunus caroliniana

Carolina cherrylaurel

Broadleaf evergreen. Terribly weedy native species, transported by birds to every nook and cranny of the countryside; one of those volunteer trees that pops up in the flower bed, shrub border, and fencerow, and requires dynamite to extricate. Most often a large multiple-trunked shrub but does form a pleasing round-topped tree at maturity, 20 to 30(40)′ high, almost as wide. Young trees are typically pyramidal to pyramidal-oval, broadening with age. Bark is smooth, dark gray to almost black, broken into thin squarish plates on large trunks by vertical and longitudinal fissures. Leaves, stems, and seeds are poisonous, producing hydrocyanic acid when wilted or eaten.

Foliage: Shiny dark green in summer, slight discoloration in winter, each leaf 2 to 3(4)″ long, 1 to 1½″ wide, oblong to oblong-elliptic, usually with a few spiny teeth toward the sharp apex or entire; seedlings show more pronounced serrations. New spring leaves often bronze-green, losing color quickly. **Flowers/seeds/fruits/cones**: White, almond-scented, each ¼ to ⅓″ across, held in 1½ to 3″ long, ¾ to 1″ wide racemes in March-April. Somewhat masked by the foliage, but still virtuous on account of earliness. An out-of-control biological machine, churning out more fruits than birds can possibly harvest; top-shaped drupe, dull black, ½″ wide, ripening in October, persisting into winter and often until flowering the following spring, astringent, sour mealy flesh and, at times, the last resort for the fowl. **Native range**: Coastal plain, Virginia to Florida to Texas; inhabiting open woods, maritime forests, vacant lots, fencerows, and abandoned fields; often forming dense, impenetrable thickets. **Adaptability**: Zones 7 to 10. **Landscape use**:

You might think, given the previous text, all hope appears lost. However, the species is native and tenacious, so where screening, wildlife habitat, or just having green is important, then why not? Foliage and flowers, at their best, are attractive. Foliage is dense, so the species serves as an effective screen in sun or shade. Greatest foliar density occurs in full sun but will tolerate moderate shade. Easily pruned into any shape and excellent for topiary. The leaves may develop shot

Prunus caroliniana

Prunus caroliniana

Prunus caroliniana

Prunus caroliniana

BRIGHT 'N TIGHT

hole (pathogen: *Wilsonomyces carpophilus*), rather unsightly purple to reddish lesions that also affect the cultivars described here. The species, albeit a native, is one of the most aggressive plants on the planet. Many native plants are significantly more aggressive than many nasty exotics. Black cherry, American sweetgum, common persimmon, black locust, tuliptree, red maple, et al., can invade fallow real estate faster than many immigrant plants. Does this make them "evil"? We think not! We suggest landscape use within its native range. John Ruter, University of Georgia, is breeding for sterility and colored foliage. **Street tree use:** The restrained cultivars are possibilities. **In the trade:** Available.

BRIGHT 'N TIGHT 'Compacta' ('Monus'). A tightly branched, conical-pyramidal form with smaller leaves than the species and superior to it for screening, hedging, and barriers. We estimate 15 to 20′ high plants in 20 years.

CENTRE COURT 'GRECCT'. A dense, pyramidal selection with glossy dark green leaves. Very much like BRIGHT 'N TIGHT in habit, only larger, 30′ by 15′. Garden Debut introduction, Greenleaf Nursery, Oklahoma.

Prunus cerasifera

cherry plum, purple-leaf plum

Deciduous. Moderately fast-growing, upright-spreading, then broadening with a rounded top. Medium texture, 15 to 30′ tall and wide, depending on cultivar. Bark is dark gray-brown, rough, with shallow fissures.

Foliage: The species is green-leafed, but all cultivars have been selected for foliage of some shade of purple, red, or bronze-green. Leaves generally elliptic, varying from slightly ovate to obovate with an acute or acuminate tip, serrate, 1½ to 3″ long, one-half to two-thirds as wide. **Flowers/ seeds/fruits/cones:** Flowers very early in spring, ¾ to 1″ in diameter, white in the species, but most cultivars have been selected for pink flowers. Fruit an edible drupe, a 1″ wide plum, ripening in summer, red to purplish. **Native range:** Balkans to western Asia. **Adaptability:** Easy to grow, adaptable to a variety of soils, not especially pH sensitive, but not considered a long-lived tree, subject to a number of disease and insect problems. Think in terms of bright landscape colors for 15 to 30 years. Shorter-lived in the East; better adapted in the West, where disease and insect problems are less intense. Zones (4)5 to 8. **Landscape use:** In Oregon, the flowering plums scream "spring" like nothing else. Witch-hazel and a few magnolias may precede, giving encouragement that winter is waning, but the sheer abundance of the plum's pink bloom and the suddenness of the appearance shouts out to all. Often maligned as overused, too often used as a cheap "builder's grade" tree in new developments, these are nevertheless functional trees, if you want summer purple, and it's hard to argue with the brightness they bring in spring. They hold up much better in winter storms than Callery pear, and they are more tolerant of wet feet than most cherries. **Street tree use:** Generally not a good choice, too low and spreading for clearance. 'Thundercloud' and 'Krauter Vesuvius' are upright and large enough to be pruned up successfully if the tree lawn is wide and some maintenance done. **In the trade:** Only cultivars are sold.

'Atropurpurea' ('Pissardii'). An older (1880) selection, often referred to but rarely seen. Of importance as a parent to many of the newer purple-leaf varieties. Purple foliage, pink single flowers, upright rounded.

P. ×blireana. A hybrid between 'Atropurpurea' and a double-flowering *P. mume*. Combines purple foliage with large,

'Atropurpurea'

×blireana

CRIMSON POINTE

CRIMSON POINTE

very double flowers, a beautiful true pink, lovely in bloom. Rounded to wide-spreading form, 15′ tall, 20′ wide. Foliage goes bronze in summer, not holding color as well as the best purple-leaf plums. Suffers severe brown rot in wet springs of the Northwest. A little less cold hardy than others, questionable in zone 5.

CRIMSON POINTE 'Cripoizam'. Strongly upright, almost columnar when young then widening to a V shape, but we have seen it spread broadly open within a few years from the weight of 1″ fruit on its branches, disappointing. Probably wider than advertised, don't expect it to stay columnar, we estimate 20′ tall, 12 to 15′ wide. Foliage purplish green, flowers white.

'Hollywood'. A combined ornamental and fruit tree. Choose it for the fruit if you want it; otherwise, messy. Foliage purplish green, flowers break pink, soon fade to white, but its fruit is its claim to fame: high-quality, 2″ wide red fruits with reddish flesh, tasty. 25′ tall, 20′ wide. Not to be confused with 'Spencer Hollywood', a rare dwarf clone with similar fruit.

'Krauter Vesuvius'. Dark purple foliage, bright true pink flowers. Large upright then broadly oval to rounded form, 30′ tall, 25′ wide. Flowers peak a couple days later than 'Thundercloud', otherwise hard to tell them apart. In nursery production, we noticed wind breakage to young branches, while 'Thundercloud' did not suffer. Favored in hotter climates, especially popular in California.

MT. ST. HELENS 'Frankthrees'. A sport of 'Newport', selected for increased vigor and brighter foliage color. Leaves just slightly larger, a bit more red in spring, and tree grows slightly faster. Preferred, but the difference becomes minor with time. Rounded, 20′ by 20′.

662

MT. ST. HELENS

MT. ST. HELENS

'Krauter Vesuvius'

'Purple Pony'

'Newport'

'Thundercloud'

'Thundercloud'

'Thundercloud'

'Newport'. An old standard but still popular. Introduced in Minnesota and quite cold hardy, solid zone 4. Foliage red-purple becoming purple-bronze, not as deeply colored as 'Thundercloud'. Flowers small, light pink. To 20′ by 20′, rounded.

'Purple Pony'. Dark purple foliage, smaller leaves, single pink flowers. Finer texture, slightly slower growing, smaller, maturing to about 15′ by 15′.

'Thundercloud'. Excellent dark purple foliage, holding its color even in summer; bright true pink flowers. Flowers appear just slightly brighter and cleaner en masse than 'Krauter Vesuvius', which is otherwise almost identical. Large for a plum, upright then broadly oval form. In Oregon, it is generally the longest-lived and healthiest of the cultivars. The most popular and our favorite among the purple-leaf plums. To 30′ high, 25′ wide.

Prunus incisa

Fuji cherry

Deciduous. A small bushy tree, finely branched, upright at first, soon spreading with a broadly rounded top. Fine-textured, slow-growing to 15′ tall and wide. Bark is smooth, reddish brown with prominent lenticels when young, then rougher and gray-brown.

Foliage: Leaves are delicate, dainty-looking, quite a bit smaller than most cherries, green, elliptical with an acuminate tip, doubly serrate, 1 to 2″ long, two-thirds as wide. **Flowers/seeds/fruits/cones**: Flowers are small, white or pale pink, bell-shaped, to 1″ wide; one of the first cherries to flower in spring, very early, January to February in Georgia. Fruit, purple-black drupes, ⅓″. **Native range**: Japan. **Adaptability**: It is happy in a temperate climate, both in the East and the West, but suffers from climatic extremes. Needs full sun. It's less hardy than some flowering cherries, best considered zones 6 and 7, although some cultivars are cold hardy in zone 5. **Landscape use**: The species is almost always represented by cultivars, and some of the cultivars have hybrid parentage. Decisions on use should be based on the cultivar. **Street tree use**: No, too small and wide-spreading. **In the trade**: Available.

FRILLY FROCK / LEMON SPLASH 'FPMSPL'. Holds British / U.S. trademarks. Weeping form with variegated foliage, green leaves with a yellowish cream margin. Early white spring flowers have a slight pink tint. Hard pruning after flowering encourages variegated foliage display. Fall brings tints of orange, orange-red, and purple-red. A sport of 'Snow Showers'. Small, dainty, fine-textured, 10′ tall and wide.

'Hilling's Weeping'. Hybrid, a British introduction from around 1964. Small delicate weeper with white flowers, opening bell-shaped, then wider. It looks much the same as 'Snow Showers' and SNOW FOUNTAINS. If identical, 'Hilling's Weeping' was the original. However, the catchy "snow" names sell better. To 12′ tall, 10′ wide.

'Kojo-no-mai'. Can be grown as a shrub but usually seen as a top graft on a clean 3 to 6′ trunk; it will grow to about 8′ with a 6′ spread when top grafted. Very diminutive and cute, upright-spreading with twisting branches, very small leaves, and tiny bell-shaped spring flowers that are white with a slight pink tint. Good resistance to brown rot blossom blight.

LITTLE TWIST 'CarltonLT'. Dwarf, twisting, very similar to 'Kojo-no-mai', we have not seen a difference.

Prunus incisa

'Kojo-no-mai'

Prunus incisa

LITTLE TWIST

PINK CASCADE

FRILLY FROCK / LEMON SPLASH

PINK CASCADE

SNOW FOUNTAINS

SNOW FOUNTAINS

'Snow Goose'

'Pendula'. Weeping form, white flowers develop a deep pink center as they age. Appears a little stiffer than other weepers presented here, arching wider than SNOW FOUNTAINS, 'Snow Showers', 'Hilling's Weeping'. 12′ tall, 15′ wide.

PINK CASCADE 'NCPH1'. A hybrid (SNOW FOUNTAINS × 'First Lady'). Similar to SNOW FOUNTAINS in its delicately weeping habit but much more colorful in spring, when it wows us with beautiful soft pink single flowers. Susceptible to brown rot blossom blight in the wet springs of the Pacific Northwest. Grows to 12′ by 12′, but could be trained to other shapes and dimensions. Very early bloom, a few days earlier than SNOW FOUNTAINS. A great improvement and a real favorite of the authors.

SNOW FOUNTAINS 'Snofozam'. Small weeper, widely grown in the United States. Graceful, delicately branched, growing in a mounded form with branches quickly arching and weeping onto the ground. Mature size of 12′ by 10′ if not shaped by pruning. The tree may be raised higher with a stake and then allowed to weep, or trained low and horizontally. Flowers are white, opening bell-shaped, then wider. Early bloom.

Susceptible to brown rot blossom blight in the Pacific Northwest. Fall color is orange-bronze. Believed to be a hybrid.

'Snow Goose'. A hybrid of *P. speciosa* and *P. incisa*. It is much bolder in appearance than others in this group, having both larger leaves and stouter branching. Very upright, dense, almost columnar when young, becoming broader and much more rounded with age, to 25′ tall and 20′ wide. Foliage is bright grass-green and flowers are single, large, and pure white.

'Snow Showers'. Small weeping hybrid, grown in Britain. Considered a synonym for 'Hilling's Weeping' by some and looks much the same as SNOW FOUNTAINS. 12′ tall, 10′ wide.

'Umineko'. Very similar to 'Snow Goose', a hybrid of the same parentage, but slightly more upright, with a slight red tint to the new growth and foliage that is not as bright green. Single white flowers, large. Very stiffly upright, almost columnar at first, widening to a V shape, then more broadly oval. Shape is appropriate for street use, 25′ tall, 16′ wide.

P

667

Prunus laurocerasus

cherry laurel, English laurel

Broadleaf evergreen. Usually grown as a large shrub, often pruned into a hedge, but if left free-form, it will make a tree, 25′ high and wide. Trees usually low-branched or multi-stem, upright, then broadly spreading. Moderate growth rate, dense, and trees are medium coarse in texture. Bark smooth, gray-green to gray-brown when young, becoming gray with age.

Foliage: Dark green, thick and glossy, oblong, margin slightly serrate to entire, with a small acuminate tip, 2 to 10″ long, about a third as wide. **Flowers/seeds/fruits/cones**: White flowers in spring, fragrant, perhaps overly so, in spike-like racemes up to 5″ long, held nicely out from the foliage. Fruit a ⅓ to ½″ long drupe, red at first, ripening blue-black. **Native range**: Southeastern Europe, Asia Minor. **Adaptability**: Likes a temperate climate, well adapted to the Pacific Northwest, the Mid-Atlantic, and less extreme areas of the South. Needs decent drainage. Likes full sun in the Northwest, partial shade in the hotter South. Zones (6)7 to 9. **Landscape use**: So monotonous, so overused and boring when used as a sheared hedge; but, we will admit, very functional as a bright green screen. Allow it to grow freely and clean off the lower trunk, and you create a tree of considerable interest. As a tree form, the evergreen foliage casts a heavy dark shade, so prune up the trunks and branches to allow in light. Bacterial and fungal diseases are fairly common and cause shot hole symptoms in the foliage. **Street tree use**: No, too wide-spreading. **In the trade**: Most cultivars are shrubs selected for compact growth. For tree form, we suggest the following large cultivars.

'Caucasica'. Long narrow leaves, improved disease resistance. Vigorous, more stiffly upright, can be raised into a tree form, 20′ tall, 15′ wide. 'Caucasica Nana' is a slightly compact version.

'Magnoliifolia'. Very large, broad, magnolia-like leaves, lustrous and dark green. Vigorous, can be trained up into a tree, but branches have a more relaxed habit with arching tips, 15′ tall, 20′ wide.

'Magnoliifolia'

Prunus laurocerasus

'Magnoliifolia'

Prunus lusitanica

Portuguese laurel

Broadleaf evergreen. Usually a large, bushy, dense shrub but can grow into a tree if trained or given time. Trees are dense, rounded, usually low-branched or multi-stem. Grows 15 to 20′ tall and wide, potentially larger. Medium texture, moderately slow-growing.

Foliage: Long ovate, serrate with an acuminate tip, leaves 2½ to 5″ long, a third to half as wide. The petiole and young stems are purplish red, which lends a faint purple tint to the overall appearance. **Flowers/seeds/fruits/cones**: Fragrant white flowers in spring, in many-flowered, rather lax racemes up to 10″ long, held nicely out from the foliage. Fruit a ⅓″ long drupe, red at first, turning blue-black. **Native range**: Spain, Portugal, southwest France, Morocco. **Adaptability**: Likes a warm Mediterranean climate, does well on the West Coast to the point of being somewhat invasive in the Pacific Northwest, where it should be avoided. Also successful in the South. More tolerant of heat and drought than *P. laurocerasus*, sun or shade is fine. Zones 7 to 9. **Landscape use**: Very handsome foliage on a small dense tree, either sheared or free form. Foliage is slightly glossy with a crisp, neatly formed look and the red petioles add to the appearance. Resistance to leafspot is better than cherry laurel. **Street tree use**: Not often used, but pruned up and trained, it can make a good low-maintenance street tree. Just keep in mind that it is evergreen; winter darkness and snow loading are concerns. **In the trade**: Available.

'Angustifolia'. Longer, narrower leaves than the species, dense, pyramidal to oval to 15′ tall, 12′ wide. Deep red petioles and stems.

'Myrtifolia'. Leaves are shorter, ovate, and densely spaced on a more compact plant. A little slower growing but will attain tree size, 15′ tall, 12′ wide.

'Variegata'. Cream variegation on the leaf margin, a bit irregular but a nice contrast to the dark leaf center. Variegation looks best when not sheared. Mostly used as a shrub but can make a small tree, to 15′ by 15′.

Prunus lusitanica

'Variegata'

Prunus lusitanica

P

Prunus maackii

Amur chokecherry

Deciduous. Upright-spreading branches create an oval head, which broadens to become quite round with age. Medium texture and medium growth rate, to 30′ tall and wide. The bark is smooth and shiny on younger trees, golden orange to reddish brown, with horizontal lenticels, becoming darker red-brown and exfoliating as it ages.

Foliage: Leaves are medium green, long ovate with an acuminate tip, 2 to 4″ long, half as wide; surface is dull but textured. Yellow fall color. **Flowers/seeds/fruits/cones**: Small white flowers in May after the foliage has expanded, clustered in tight 2 to 3″ long racemes. Pendulous clusters of fruit follow, ¼″ wide drupes, red at first, ripening to purple-black in late summer. **Native range**: Korea, Manchuria. **Adaptability**: A choice tree for cold climates. It does not like heat or wet soils. Wet soils can lead to root rot diseases. Use it in the North on soils with good drainage. Zones 3 to 6. **Landscape use**: A great ornamental tree, at its best when the bark can be highlighted in the landscape; for maximum impact, give it full exposure to the east and west, so that the low angle of the sun at sunrise and sunset will hit the trunk and light up the bark's colors. It is effective as a multi-stem, low- or high-branched tree. **Street tree use**: Can work in the right place but requires structural and maintenance pruning for clearance. Be careful about drainage and avoid street runoff and compacted wet soil. **In the trade**: Available.

'Amber Beauty'. A vigorous grower, upright pyramidal at first, becoming rounded like the species, 30′ tall and 25′ wide. A good choice if street use is intended. Selected for an especially nice glossy golden orange bark, more yellowish, lighter and brighter than most.

GOLDSPUR 'Jefspur'. Compact, tight growth habit is dense, tidy, and symmetrical. It's upright when young, then becomes oval, but matures smaller than seedling trees; we estimate 18′ tall and 12′ wide. Golden orange bark. Selected in Manitoba, appears to be hardy to zone 2.

KLONDIKE 'Jefdike'. A seedling of GOLDSPUR, but not compact, reaching the full size of the species. Excellent orange-red bark and upright-spreading to rounded form. Has shown resistance to black knot disease. We expect mature size of 25′ tall, 20′ wide. Zone 2.

Prunus maackii

KLONDIKE

Prunus maackii

Prunus maackii

GOLDSPUR

GOLDSPUR

KLONDIKE

Prunus maackii

P

Prunus mume

Japanese apricot

Deciduous. Somewhat fickle and usually not long-lived but remarkably beautiful in flower. The species, a small round-headed tree with supple green branches, varies greatly in size, 15 to 20(25)′ high and wide, and has produced many different growth forms, from fastigiate to corkscrew to weeping. Growth is fast with long shoots that develop next season's flower buds in summer and fall. The species has been cultivated for some 1,600 years in China; it was introduced to Japan, where it has been one of the most popular garden trees for centuries.

Foliage: Ovate to broadly ovate, with a crooked acuminate (long extended) apex, cuneate base, finely and sharply serrate, rich to dark green, 2 to 4″ long, 1 to 2″ wide; fall color is yellow-green to yellow. Leaves often appear droopy, as if water-stressed, but are in a normal repose. This species has always proven difficult for Dirr to identify in leaf. **Flowers/seeds/fruits/cones**: Self-fertile fragrant flowers, 5-petaled, single and double, white, pink, rose, and red, open on naked stems, primarily in January to March but as early as late December in Athens. Each flower 1″ wide, resembling a tiny bauble before full expression, produced singly or in pairs, opening from base of previous season's growth toward apex; flowers are also produced on short spur growths along the inner stems and branches. Fruit is a hard, globose, yellow, 1 to 1½″ wide drupe, the fleshy portion largely inedible but sometimes canned or pickled in salt (the latter termed Japanese pickled plum, umeboshi). Authors observed hundreds of the pretty yellow fruits scattered on the ground under the branches in June-July. Obviously, Americans know nothing about pickling. **Native range**: China, Korean peninsula, in forests, forested slopes, streamsides, at elevations to 10,000′. **Adaptability**: Flowers are frost and freeze tolerant, but fully open flowers may be injured around 25°F. Zones 6 to 10. **Landscape use**: For small gardens, parks, campuses, commercial grounds, it is a welcome addition. A well-drained, moderately fertile, acid soil in full sun maximizes flowering. Trees under pine shade produce a respectable show. Suffers brown rot blossom blight in the wet springs of the Pacific Northwest. The winter–early spring flowering window makes it a rarity among flowering trees; in fact, authors were stumped trying to name flowering trees that fill this time period. Witch-hazels might qualify but usually exist as shrubs. Prune after flowering to induce the long supple shoots that bear next year's flowers, or remove selected

Prunus mume

branches to tidy and shape. Also, removing half the branches every year guarantees a measure of flowers. Our advice is to leave the tree alone. **Street tree use**: Too low-branched and wide-spreading for most situations. **In the trade**: Not exactly an everyday item. The gardener may have to treasure hunt, but the better cultivars are out there.

'Alba Plena'. Double white flowers; 20′ high and wide.

'Bridal Veil'. Fragrant double flowers, pale pink opening white, on arching branches; estimate 25′ high and wide, Camellia Forest Nursery introduction.

'Dawn'. Large, ruffled, double pink flowers, performs well in the Southeast. It is a later-flowering cultivar; 20′ high and wide.

'Fragrant Snow'. Large, semi-double, fragrant flowers on a vigorous plant; estimate 25′ high and wide.

'Hokkai-bungo'. Fragrant pink-red flowers followed by abundant apricot-sized, light green fruit; 25′ high and wide.

'Kanko Bai'. Fuchsia-red flowers, red-tinted foliage, orange-red fruit; 15′ high and wide.

'Kobai'. Not the most vigorous grower but produces semi-double red flowers; 15′ high and wide.

'Matsurabara Red'. Double red flowers; as observed by authors, closer to rose-red on a 20′ high tree.

'Dawn'

'Kobai'

Prunus mume

'Dawn'

'Matsurabara Red'

P

'Nicholas'. Soft pink, semi-double flowers and 25′ by 25′ size.

'Peggy Clarke'. Pretty, double, deep rose flowers with long stamens and a red calyx (sepals); relatively common in Georgia, with flowering recorded in late December and early February; 15′ high and wide.

'Rosemary Clarke'. Large, fragrant, double white flowers with red calyces, early flowering; 15′ high and wide.

'W. B. Clarke'. Double pink flowers on a gracefully weeping tree, also develops respectable yellow fall color; 10 to 15′ high and wide.

'Yuh-Hwa'. Semi-double pink flowers with lighter pink edge; size is 20′ high and 20′ wide.

'W. B. Clarke'

'W. B. Clarke'

Prunus padus
European birdcherry, Mayday tree

Deciduous. Upright and pyramidal when young, rather fast-growing, soon spreading to become fully round. Usually low-branched, medium texture, to 30′ tall and wide. Bark smooth with prominent lenticels when young, then slightly roughened, purplish brown to gray-brown. The fruit makes it a bird lovers' tree.

Foliage: Medium green, obovate to elliptic with an acuminate tip, 2½ to 5″ long, half as wide, dull surface, finely serrate margin. One of the first trees to leaf out in spring. Unimpressive yellowish fall color. **Flowers/seeds/fruits/cones**: Small white flowers tightly held in drooping 3 to 6″ long spike-like racemes, fragrant. It blooms early, with the new foliage. Fruits, ¼″ wide drupes, purplish black, in clusters in summer. **Native range**: Eurasia; very wide distribution from Ireland to Kamchatka. **Adaptability**: Cool-weather adapted and favored in northern landscapes. Tolerant of wet soils. Quite susceptible to black knot, which limits its use in some areas. Very cold hardy, zones 3 to 6. **Landscape use**: Deserves more attention in the United

Prunus padus

States. Its soft green new leaves are one of the first signs of spring, and when it blooms, the bees are even happier than you. Best adapted and most used in the cold and stark climates of the Mountain States and Northern Plains, where the spring show is truly appreciated, and popular in Canada and northern Europe. It is similar to *P. virginiana* but has a reputation for producing fewer suckers. **Street tree use**: Rather low-branched and wide, but more upright cultivars are appropriate. **In the trade**: Available.

'Albertii'. An improved form for street use. Upright when young, a little narrower and more oval than the species, 30′ tall and 18′ wide. Green foliage.

'Colorata'. Soft pink flowers are lovely in spring, reddish purple new shoots, leaves purplish bronze becoming green above and purplish below. Matures slightly smaller than the species at 20′ by 20′.

Prunus padus

Prunus padus

MERLOT 'Drietree'. Good for streets. Vigorous and upright-growing when young, it matures to an upright oval form, 30′ tall, 18′ wide. Foliage emerges green but turns dark purple in summer, like *P. virginiana* 'Canada Red'.

'Nana'. Small, compact, dense, and globe-shaped. Grows to about half the size of the species, to 15′ tall and 12′ wide. Flowers and leaves are also a bit smaller, green foliage.

'Pandora'. Provides more clearance than other cultivars, thus making it a choice for streets. Pale pink flowers, bronze foliage in spring becomes green in summer, quite upright when young becoming vase-shaped, 25′ tall and 20′ wide.

MERLOT

SUMMER GLOW

P

675

'Watereri'

SUMMER GLOW 'DTR 117'. Has the lax racemes of the species. Leafs out green but foliage turns deep purple in summer, similar to *P. virginiana* 'Canada Red'.

'Sweetheart'. Pink blooms in spring, reddish tint to new growth, similar to 'Colorata'. 25′ tall and 20′ wide.

'Watereri'. Quite impressive in flower with the longest racemes, up to 8″, heavily displayed and covering the foliage. Green foliage, vigorous, 30′ tall and 25′ wide.

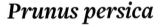

Prunus persica
common peach, flowering peach

Deciduous. Develops a broad-spreading, rounded canopy, 15 to 25′ high, as wide or greater. Growth is quite fast in early stages; slowing with maturity. Bark light brown with horizontal lenticels. Peaches should be considered short-lived trees, recognized primarily for their delicious fruits. Their commercial culture is fraught with nagging issues, including pests and diseases, insufficient chilling hours, and late freezes; the cultivars that have been introduced as ornamentals were often offshoots from fruit improvement programs. Through all the adversity, few fruits can compete with a sweet, juicy, succulent, perfectly textured ripe peach. In Georgia, many pits have been pitched from speeding autos; the trees have escaped, forming interstate orchards along roadsides and in abandoned fields, always dressed in floral pink.

Foliage: Somewhat semi-pendulous posturing, appearing in need of water; elliptic-lanceolate, broadest at or slightly above the middle, long acuminate, finely serrate, lustrous dark green, 3 to 6″ long, ¾ to 1½″ wide; abscising green or with yellow hues in autumn. **Flowers/seeds/fruits/cones:** Typically degrees of pink, 5-petaled, 1 to 1½″ wide, solitary

Prunus persica

Prunus persica

or paired, opening on naked stems of the previous year's growth in March-April. A well-maintained peach orchard in spring flower is a splendid experience; the ornamental flowering peaches, especially the doubles, are spectacular. Nothing prettier than a tree laden with the 3″ wide, almost rounded, yellow to reddish pubescent drupes; available cultivars ripen early, midseason, and late, June to August. **Native range:** Open to question, but China is most often cited as the home base. **Adaptability:** More cold hardy than credited, with commercial orchards in Maine. Peaches require a certain number of chill hours (32 to 45°F) to flower uniformly. Breeding has developed low-chill peaches that are adapted to North Florida. Zones 5 to 9. **Landscape**

'Alboplena'

'Corinthian Mauve'

'Corinthian Pink'

'Corinthian Mauve'

use: Homeowners should be leery about attempting to produce healthy fruit crops (see the aforementioned nagging issues), but for ornamental use in smaller gardens, there is a selection to fit every nook and cranny. Many double-flowered types do not produce fruit; for this reason, as well as for their spectacular floral display, they are preferable. Acid, well-drained, moist soils and full sun is required for maximum flower production. Extremely susceptible

to peach leaf curl in the wet-spring Pacific Northwest, but resistant varieties such as 'Frost' are available locally. **Street tree use**: No. **In the trade**: Hundreds, perhaps thousands worldwide, primarily fruiting types. We list only cultivars developed as ornamentals.

'Alba', 'Alboplena', and 'Alboplena Pendula' are single white, double white, and double white weeping, respectively. 'Alboplena' grew 20′ high with 2 to 2½″ wide pure white flowers on the University of Georgia campus, occasionally producing fruit whose seeds came true-to-type.

Corinthian series. These columnar cultivars created quite a stir when first introduced, but have not shown high

P

677

'Corinthian Pink'

'Corinthian Rose'

landscape tenacity. Mauve, pink, rose, and white, all doubles, are part of the series. Quite pretty and effective for restricted spaces, when at their best. Susceptible to the same maladies as the fruiting peach. Branches may splay (open) with time, negating columnar designation.

'Foliis Rubris' ('Royal Red Leaf'). Reddish purple young leaves, deepening to maroon, becoming bronze-green-purple. Flowers are single, deep pink, and the fruit is edible. There are other purple-leaf selections with dwarf, columnar, and weeping habits.

'Helen Borchers'. A vigorous form with 1½" wide, semi-double, rose-pink flowers.

'Peppermint Stick'. Unique with white, red, and red-and-white striped/streaked, large, double flowers on the same tree. Quite vigorous, to 20 to 25′ high.

Prunus sargentii
Sargent cherry

Deciduous. Upright-spreading, with a stout trunk and strong structural branches that ascend and spread somewhat, producing a broadly vase-shaped canopy. Medium texture, moderately fast-growing, to 35′ high and 30′ wide. Bark is moderately shiny, reddish brown to purple-brown with prominent horizontal lenticels, staying smooth and attractive for many years before roughening a bit with age.

Foliage: New growth emerges with a reddish bronze tint, quickly turning dark green, darker than most cherries. Leaves broadly ovate to broadly obovate with an acuminate tip, serrate margin, textured surface, usually with purple-red petioles, 2½ to 5″ long and two-thirds as wide. Probably the best cherry for fall color, bright orange to red to reddish purple. **Flowers/seeds/fruits/cones**: Flowers in early spring just as leaves begin to push, generally light pink but varying from almost white to bright pink. Single, 1 to 1½″ across, in clusters of 2 to 6. Fruit, ⅓″ long drupes, reddish at first, mature to purple-black in early summer. Fruit is usually sparingly produced, so little mess. **Native range**: Japan. **Adaptability**: It has a reputation for being the longest-lived and toughest of the Japanese cherries; certainly it grows to the largest size and is the most cold hardy among them. Like most cherries, it does not like wet feet, but Sargent seems more tolerant of that situation than most cherries. It does best in moderate to cool climates and suffers from heat in the Deep South. Zones 4 to 7. **Landscape use**: A great multi-season ornamental. Beautiful with its burst of spring flowers, handsome as its dark green foliage holds well through the summer, and attention-getting in the fall with its intense show of colors. Its upward- and outward-oriented branches allow more clearance underneath for use of the garden space below. **Street tree use**: Although cherries are not the best for tolerance of compacted urban soils, Sargent is probably the best of the lot for street use, especially the narrow cultivars. With good soil, use it in favorable climates. **In the trade**: Available.

'Accolade'. A hybrid of *P. sargentii* and *P. subhirtella*. Semi-double flowers are large and impressive, true pink. The cross gains it beauty in bloom but loses ground in disease resistance. Open spreading form, shorter and wider than Sargent, but not as long-lived, 25′ by 25′.

'Columnaris'. A longtime favorite, named at Arnold Arboretum in 1939. Narrow upright V shape, spreading slightly to a narrow vase to 35′ tall and 10 to 15′ wide. Grows to the full height of the species but only half or less as wide, allowing clearance below and use close to tall buildings. Dark green foliage, light pink flowers, orange-red to purple fall color.

PINK FLAIR 'JFS-KW58'. Impressive selection raised from seed originating at the northernmost range of the species in Japan. It has been cold hardy in North Dakota and may rate zone 3. Form is a narrow vase, not quite as narrow as 'Columnaris' but more compact, maturing at 25′ tall and 15′ wide. Flowers are larger and brighter pink, and it leafs out 2 weeks later than normal, avoiding frost and allowing for a more foliage-free floral display. Foliage has been unusually disease-free and has held up in the heat of South Carolina; bright orange-red fall color. An authors' favorite.

'Rancho'. Narrow form, very similar to 'Columnaris'. Authors have compared adjacent trial plots and observed that foliage is duller green in summer with a bit less fall color. 30′ tall and 15′ wide. We prefer 'Columnaris', but the difference is small.

'Spire'. A hybrid of *P. sargentii*, with the cross variously ascribed to *P. incisa* or *P. ×yedoensis*. In any case, we don't think this is an improvement, as it shows increased foliage disease. Narrow, upright V shape a little wider than 'Columnaris', flowers lighter pink, closer to white, but we will credit it for having nice orange-red fall color. 30′ tall, 15′ wide.

SPRING WONDER 'Hokkaido Normandale'. Selected from a seed source in Hokkaido, the northernmost of Japan's islands, it has proven cold hardiness in zone 4. Wide vase shape similar to the species, good medium pink flowers, 25′ tall, 20 to 25′ wide.

'Tiltstone Hellfire'. A cross between 'Rancho' and 'Spire', with pinkish white flowers and known for its bright fall colors, 25′ tall, 20′ wide.

Prunus sargentii

Prunus sargentii

Prunus sargentii

P

'Columnaris'

'Accolade'

'Columnaris'

PINK FLAIR

'Accolade'

PINK FLAIR

'Rancho'

PINK FLAIR

'Spire'

'Spire'

Prunus serotina

black cherry

Deciduous. A pretty, graceful pyramidal tree in youth becoming oval-crowned with looser arching branches, semi-pendulous, reaching 50 to 60′ high, occasionally over 100′, less in spread. Growth is fast, the root system tenacious, resisting attempts to extricate by mere mortals. Tractors are required. Bark is shiny, smooth, brown with horizontal lenticels; grayish black to black and scaly on larger trunks. One of the easiest trees to identify in forest habitats because of the mature bark. Tremendously important timber/lumber species, the wood prized for all manner of uses, including furniture, veneer, cabinets, paneling, musical instruments, and wood turning; but in garden situations exceptionally weedy and pestiferous. In the Dirr garden, there are more stray black cherry seedlings than any other broadleaf species. Prussic acid is present in the leaves, stems, and seeds; bruised/broken/scratched stems smell like almonds and taste bitter; listed as toxic to livestock. From a wildlife perspective, however, it is second only to *Quercus*, oaks, for the number of caterpillar species that feed on its foliage, and the fruits provide sustenance to more than 40 bird species and many mammals. This poses a conundrum, as do the saplings stay or go? An ethical and environmental dilemma to be sure.

Foliage: Leaves are sparkling shiny soft green, maturing lustrous dark green, ovate to lance-oblong, serrate with small sharp incurved teeth, 2 to 5″ long, 1 to 1¾″ wide. Leaves emerge as early as late March in zone 8. **Flowers/seeds/fruits/cones**: Flowers are white, slightly fragrant, 5-petaled, ⅓″ wide, borne in 4 to 6″ long, ¾″ wide racemes from the axils of the shoots in April-May, after the leaves have reached full size. Profuse, but somewhat dampened by foliage. The ⅓″ wide, rounded, fleshy drupe, shiny green to red, finally black, ripens in summer–early fall. Quantities are prodigious; the bittersweet flesh is utilized for wine and jelly. Authors have yet to sample either. **Native range**: Canada, Maine to Florida, west to Minnesota, New Mexico, Arizona, Mexico into Central America, abundant everywhere except where permanently wet; in the southern

Prunus serotina

Prunus serotina

Prunus serotina

Appalachians, it occurs in lowland and upland woods and along streams to 5,000′. **Adaptability:** To not have encountered a black cherry means you never left the house. Zones 3 to 9. **Landscape use:** For large-area use, wildlife habitats, and timber orchards, it is valuable. Grows best in deep, moist, acid soils in full sun to partial shade. A partial list of habitats where it succeeds includes pastures, fencerows, old fields, forests, any fallow ground. We suggest gardeners appreciate the species for its contributions to wildlife and the timber industry. **Street tree use:** No. **In the trade:** Cutleaf ('Aspleniifolia') and a weeping ('Pendula') forms are mentioned in English literature. 'Spring Sparkle' is decidedly more weeping with lustrous deep green leaves that turn yellow and wine-red in October; the original tree was 26′ high and 22′ wide when 35 years old.

Prunus serrula

paperbark cherry, Tibetan cherry, birchbark cherry

Deciduous. Upright vase-shaped, narrower than most cherries, moderately slow-growing. Fine-textured, to 30′ high and 20′ wide. The high-gloss bark resembles the finest varnished mahogany on a classic wooden yacht, wonderful coppery brown to purple-brown. A striking pattern of horizontal lenticels adds to the effect. Papery strips will periodically peel on older trees. Bark doesn't get any better than this!

Foliage: Darker green than most cherries, but the narrowness of the leaves gives the tree an open feeling. Leaves lanceolate with an acuminate tip, 2 to 4″ long and ½ to 1¼″ wide. Margin finely serrate. **Flowers/seeds/fruits/cones:** White flowers in spring, ¾″ wide, in small clusters, not as impressive as most cherries. Fruit ⅓″ long drupe, reddish. **Native range:** Western China. **Adaptability:** If only it were more adaptable. Likes the cool mild climates of the Pacific Northwest and northern California, Britain, northern Europe. Zones 6 to 7, 8 in the West. **Landscape use:** Grow it for its bark. Period. Better in winter than in summer. Avoid soggy soil. And plant it where the bark can be viewed up close. Fortunately, its growth habit is quite upright and it is typically low-branched, so the bark is usually well displayed. **Street tree use:** No, too touchy for the street. **In the trade:** Usually sold as unnamed grafted clones selected for the bark, sometimes seed-grown.

P

Prunus serrula

Prunus serrula

Prunus serrulata
Japanese flowering cherry

Nomenclatural note: Some disagreement regarding *P. serrulata* and *P. lannesiana*. It has been proposed that these and others be lumped under the classification Sato-zakura Group, the village cherries. We choose to follow the traditionally accepted *P. serrulata* as having wider landscape acceptance, not as a stance on nomenclature.

Deciduous. Most trees are of medium texture with medium growth rate, 25 to 30′ height and spread, but varies greatly by cultivar; see individual listings. Bark too varies but generally is coppery brown to purplish brown, smooth and slightly shiny with prominent lenticels when young, then developing vertical fissures and becoming rougher and more gray as the trunk expands.

Foliage: Dark green, 2 to 5″ long, about half as wide, ovate to ovate-lanceolate with acuminate tip, serrate margin. Fall colors yellow to yellow-orange. **Flowers/seeds/fruits/cones**: Flowers highly ornamental, many double; they are described by cultivar. Fruit a ¼″ purple-black drupe; some cultivars are seedless. **Native range**: Japan, China, Korea. **Adaptability**: Prefers all things moderate: temperature, moisture, exposure, soil. Happiest in the climates of the Pacific Northwest and the Mid-Atlantic, Britain and western Europe, but used successfully over a much wider range. Quite sensitive to wet soils; please provide good drainage. Zones (5)6 to 8 for most cultivars. **Landscape use**: Widely loved and widely used. It's hard to imagine a more beautiful tree in spring bloom. The multitude of cultivars provide shapes suitable for almost every landscape concept: specimens, features, backgrounds, screens, patios. High-quality foliage, but diseases and insects can be significant in some areas. Japanese beetles find them tasty. In the Pacific Northwest, blossom brown rot is a serious early season disease; 'Kanzan', 'Royal Burgundy', 'Shirofugen', 'Shirotae', and 'Taihaku' have shown the most, although incomplete, resistance. **Street tree use**: Used in favorable climates, although certainly not the toughest trees for difficult sites. Choose narrow upright cultivars. **In the trade**: Choose own-root plants, grown from cuttings, whenever they can be obtained. They avoid possible swelling at the graft union and have wider soil tolerance and a longer life.

'Amanogawa'. Narrowest of the cultivars, with strongly fastigiate, near vertical branching that forms a dense columnar shape. Flowers double white, with a nice light pink tint. Form may open a bit with age, to 20′ high, 6 to 8′ wide.

'Hokusai'. Strong growing, upright, then spreading with age, becoming broadly vase-shaped to 25′ high and 35′ wide.

'Amanogawa'

Flowers are large, double, light pink with an apricot tint, new growth bronze.

'Horinji'. Semi-double flowers are delicate pale pink on an upright-growing tree, 22′ high, 18′ wide. Form and appearance are similar to 'Kanzan', but with a softer-colored, understated bloom. A favorite.

'Ichiyo'. Double pale pink flowers. Although it grows upright at first, its more slender branches spread more than ascend, creating a wide, rounded crown, 20′ tall, 30′ wide.

'Kanzan' ('Kwanzan', 'Sekiyama'). The standard of comparison, and for good reason. Its beauty, form, and vigor make it an obvious choice and, therefore, quite common. Flowers

'Amanogawa'

'Ichiyo'

'Hokusai'

'Horinji'

'Kanzan'

are large, very double, and bright pure pink. Form is a stiff upright vase, especially when young, allowing clearance below. With age, it spreads, but clearance is easy to maintain, to 30′ high, 25′ wide. Foliage is dark green with a bronze-red tint in spring. Generally seedless. Better disease resistance than most in this group. One of the later cherries to bloom.

P

'Kanzan'

'Kiku-shidare-zakura'

'Kiku-shidare-zakura'

'Pink Perfection'

'Royal Burgundy'

'Royal Burgundy'

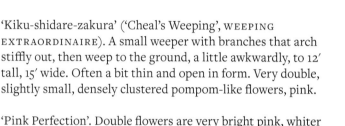

'Shirofugen'

'Kiku-shidare-zakura' ('Cheal's Weeping', WEEPING EXTRAORDINAIRE). A small weeper with branches that arch stiffly out, then weep to the ground, a little awkwardly, to 12′ tall, 15′ wide. Often a bit thin and open in form. Very double, slightly small, densely clustered pompom-like flowers, pink.

'Pink Perfection'. Double flowers are very bright pink, whiter toward the center, crowded with petals, heavy flowering. Upright-spreading to a broad vase shape with a broadly rounded top, to 25′ by 25′.

'Royal Burgundy'. Originated as a nursery-discovered vegetative sport of 'Kanzan', doubles up on the purple pigments while suppressing the green. The resulting foliage is purple all season, especially the new growth, which is glossy deep purple. Similarly, the large double flowers are identical to 'Kanzan' in size and form, but deeper in color, a strong magenta-pink. Upright-spreading, slightly less vigorous than 'Kanzan' due to decreased chlorophyll function, to 20′ tall and wide. The purple pigments are most striking when the tree is young. As it ages, its colors are less strong; it looks much more like 'Kanzan'. Late bloom.

'Shirofugen'. Widely spreading, with strong bronze foliage as it leafs out in spring. Bold in form, wider than tall, it tends to spread stiffly with a flat-topped appearance, 18′ tall, 30′ wide. Flowers are very similar to 'Shogetsu' being fully double and white, but with a deeper magenta-pink tint. As the flowers age, they darken nearly as pink as 'Kanzan'. Late blooming.

'Shirotae' ('Mount Fuji'). Vigorous and wide-spreading, with arching branches that stretch out with graceful, almost sinuous form, to 18′ high and 35′ wide. Flowers are very large white semi-doubles. Midseason bloom. A great tree if you have room for its wide-spreading, low canopy. We have seen it nicely sited on an unevenly rolling slope, where it seems to hug the ground.

P

'Shirofugen'

'Shirotae'

'Shirotae'

'Shogetsu'

'Taihaku'

'Shogetsu' ('Shimidsu'). Spreads with arching branches, becoming wider than tall, with a mounded, umbrella-like appearance, like a big white mushroom when in bloom, 18′ tall, 25′ wide. Flowers are large, fully double, delicate white with a pink tint, emerging against green foliage. Mid-season bloom.

'Sunset Boulevard'. Strongly upright, forming a narrow vase shape to 25′ high and 14′ wide with a form appropriate for street clearance. Single white flowers have a slight pink tint.

'Taihaku' (great white cherry). Large, pure white single blooms reach 2½″ in diameter. Vigorous, stout-trunked, upright-spreading then stiffly wide-spreading, with large (to 8″) leaves, dark green, 18′ high, 25′ wide.

'Ukon'. Very unusual yellow-green flowers are large and double. The flower color sounds odd but looks surprisingly good and is a real attention-getter. Upright, with a vase shape similar to 'Kanzan', 25′ tall, 20′ wide. Worth looking for if you want something unusual in the spring.

'Ukon'

Prunus subhirtella

higan cherry, spring cherry

Nomenclatural note: Now often listed as *P. pendula*, but we consider the nomenclature unresolved.

Deciduous. Form varies from upright to weeping, moderately fast-growing. Vigorous, but with slender branching. Fine texture. Size varies with cultivar. Bark is gray-brown with prominent horizontal lenticels, becoming fissured and rougher with age. Often top grafted in nursery production, and if so you are usually looking at a *P. avium* trunk, smoother and more reddish brown.

Foliage: Dark green, moderately lustrous, long ovate to oblong-ovate with an acuminate tip, serrate margin, 1½ to 4″ long, half as wide. Fall color yellowish to yellow-orange. **Flowers/seeds/fruits/cones**: Typically single flowers but double cultivars exist, white to pink, small, about ¾ to 1″ wide. Fruit purple-black, ⅓″ long drupes in summer. **Native range**: Japan. **Adaptability**: Similar to *P. serrulata* in liking mild climates, but a little more vigorous, more cold hardy, adaptable, and long-lived. But it is quite susceptible to blossom brown rot in the wet springs of the Pacific Northwest, more so than *P. serrulata*. Zones 5 to 8. **Landscape use**: Valued for the impact of very early spring flowers combined with refined, fine-textured form. The weepers make wonderful specimens; upright forms are often high grafted for use in plazas or patios or to line driveways. **Street tree use**: No, too wide-spreading. **In the trade**: Available.

‘Accolade’. See *P. sargentii*

‘Autumnalis’. Semi-double, very pale pink flowers become white and appear sporadically in November and December in mild climates, followed by a full bloom in very early spring. A mild spell in winter can pop out some flowers. Upright-spreading to wide-spreading shape, 25′ by 25′.

‘Autumnalis Rosea’. Fall- and spring-flowering, like ‘Autumnalis’, but with more color. Deep pinkish red buds opening to light pink flowers that still fade but never to fully white. Foliage is deeper green. The dominant clone in U.S. production. Sometimes confused with ‘Autumnalis’. 25′ by 25′.

‘Fukubana’. A smaller, more fine-textured tree, dense and a bit shrubby, usually top grafted, growing to 20′ by 20′. Flowers very heavily, semi-double, pink. Less vigorous, seems more delicate in both appearance and survival.

‘Hally Jolivette’. A hybrid. Small, very fine-textured and twiggy, dense, delicate, usually top grafted, but sometimes grown own-root. Flowers small, double, opening white then aging to very pale pink with a magenta-red center.

‘Autumnalis’

‘Autumnalis Rosea’

Moderately slow-growing, typically 12 to 15′ tall and wide, mature height being partly based on graft height, but we have seen trees to 20′ tall.

P

'Hally Jolivette'

'Hally Jolivette'

'Pendula'

'Pendula'

'Pendula'. A larger, wonderfully weeping tree. It ascends with weeping layer stacked upon weeping layer, to 20′ high and 30′ wide, potentially taller. A few very similar weeping clones are sold under this name, so consider it a group name for single-flowered weepers. The weeping habit will be maintained in a good percentage of seedlings, and seed-grown weepers have been sold in the past under this name. Single pink flowers, with clones varying from pale pink to bright pink.

'Pendula Plena Rosea' ('Yae-shidare-higan'). Called "Double Sub" or "Weeping Double Sub" in the U.S. trade. Weeping form, graceful, much like 'Pendula', but with smaller double pink flowers. Blooms a little later, opening deep pink, a delicate pink when fully expanded. Slightly slower growing than 'Pendula', to 18′ tall, 25′ wide. WEEPING PINK INFUSION 'Wepinzam' was examined side by side; we could not see a difference.

'Pendula Plena Rosea'

'Pendula'

'Whitcomb'

'Pendula Plena Rosea'

PINK SNOW SHOWERS

'Pendula Rubra'. A weeping clone selected from 'Pendula' for bright, deeper pink flowers, 20′ high and 30′ wide.

PINK SNOW SHOWERS 'Pisnshzam'. Selected from 'Pendula' for bright, clean pink flowers and slightly larger and lustrous, brighter green leaves that seem to show better disease resistance. An improved and reliable weeping form, to 20′ tall, 30′ wide.

'Whitcomb'. This is the first of the spring-flowering higan cherries (excluding the two fall-flowering 'Autumnalis' clones) to bloom. It bursts forth quite intensely, heavily flowering and making a strong spring statement with a bright, deep pink bloom. Very welcome after winter. Upright-spreading, 25′ high, 30′ wide.

P

Prunus virginiana

chokecherry

Deciduous. Small, bushy tree, either single-trunked or suckering into a multi-stem or clump. Oval, becoming irregularly rounded. Fast-growing, medium texture, to 25′ tall, 20′ wide. Bark is gray-brown with noticeable lenticels, smooth in youth, becoming roughened to slightly scaly. The "cherries," reminiscent of miniature clusters of grapes, are sometimes used in cooking and jams, proving what a little sugar can do.

Foliage: Medium green with a light luster, broadly ovate with a blunt acuminate tip, leaves 2 to 4″ long, two-thirds as wide, finely serrate margin. Not noted for fall color, but we have seen good oranges in some years. **Flowers/seeds/fruits/cones**: Flowers in spring, small and white, each about ½″ wide, but densely clustered into 3 to 6″ long spike-like cylindrical racemes. Fragrant. Fruits ⅓″ wide drupes, red at first then deep purple, and pucker-me-up astringent. **Native range**: Widespread. Coast to coast across the continent in the northern United States and southern Canada. **Adaptability**: Likes a cooler climate, as its nativity indicates. Tolerant of low and high pH, salt, wet soils, and some drought. Popular in the Mountain States because it takes early and late frosts. Zones 3 to 6, 7 on the cool-summer West Coast. **Landscape use**: The green-leaf species is mostly used in native landscapes, screens, and restoration, probably more often as multi-stem than tree form. The purple-leaf cultivars are widely used as ornamentals, usually tree form, and mostly valued for the impact of their deeply colored summer foliage. Suckering is a maintenance problem, so consider using the purple-leaf cultivars in multi-stem form as well. **Street tree use**: Not the best choice, but sometimes used. Plan on maintenance for suckers. **In the trade**: Sold as seed-grown. The most popular landscape cultivars were selected for purple foliage.

‘Canada Red’. Foliage emerges green in spring and then transforms, as if by magic, to deep purple by early summer. The purple is held for the rest of the season, becoming brighter and closer to red in fall. Broadly oval, 20 to 25′ tall, 20′ wide.

‘Canada Red Improved’ and ‘Canada Red Select’ (‘Schubert Select’). Similar nursery sports of ‘Canada Red’, with leaf color identical to ‘Canada Red’ but chosen for their faster growth, straighter trunks, and more upright form; we prefer both of these over the original when grown as tree form because of their greater vigor, 30′ tall, 20′ wide. For a smaller multi-stem plant, we would stick with the original ‘Canada Red’.

‘Schubert’. The original purple-leaf selection, foliage emerges green and turns red in May to June. Largely replaced by ‘Canada Red’ and its improved sports. 20′ by 20′.

‘Canada Red’

Prunus virginiana

SUCKER PUNCH 'P002S'. A purple-leaf cultivar selected for reduced suckering and claiming to be sucker-free. We hope so, as that would be a big improvement, but time will tell. Purple foliage doesn't seem as bright as 'Canada Red'. It is slower growing, so we expect a slightly smaller mature size, 15 to 20′.

'Schubert'

'Canada Red Improved'

'Canada Red Improved'

SUCKER PUNCH

Prunus virginiana

Prunus ×yedoensis

Yoshino cherry

Deciduous. Upright-spreading, then more broadly spreading, developing a broadly rounded top, eventually as wide or wider than tall. Moderate growth rate, medium fine texture, 25′ tall and 30′ wide. Bark is smooth, gray to gray-brown with a slight purple tint and prominent horizontal lenticels, eventually showing some fissuring and roughening.

Foliage: Bright lustrous green, ovate to elliptic to slightly obovate leaves, with an acuminate tip and a very neatly and finely serrate to doubly serrate margin. Foliage is extremely handsome and develops a good yellow fall color. **Flowers/seeds/fruits/cones**: Pure white single flowers are 1 to 1½″ in diameter with broad rounded petals, appearing early in spring before the leaves. When flowers first open, the anthers give a slight yellow coloring to the flower center, but after the pollen sheds, the center takes on a magenta-pink color and the flower an overall pink tint. Fruit, ⅓″ wide drupes, are red at first, ripening to purple-black by midsummer. **Native range**: A hybrid originating in Japan. Parentage uncertain. **Adaptability**: Like the *P. serrulata* cultivar group, it likes moderate conditions and needs decent drainage. Our experience is that it may be a little more forgiving of marginal sites and is a bit longer-lived. Performs better in the South than most cherries. Zones 5 to 8. **Landscape use**: A small to medium-sized garden ornamental, used as a single specimen, in borders or by a patio, and beautiful in groups in larger landscape settings. Spreading, but with a little pruning you can maintain clearance underneath. A frequently used ornamental in commercial landscapes. This is the cherry of the famous Tidal Basin planting in Washington, DC, its spectacle of bloom attracting thousands of visitors every spring. **Street tree use**: Too low and spreading for most situations, but possible with pruning and enough setback to allow for traffic below. **In the trade**:

Own-root (cutting-grown) plants are recommended, as the root system performs better than grafted rootstocks in warm, wet soils.

'Akebono'. An excellent cultivar, differing from 'Yoshino' by a lovely pink tint in the buds and flowers, and leaves with a wavy margin. It is upright at first, then more horizontal, developing a slightly layered form that adds to its textural appeal, 20′ tall, 25′ wide. It has shown increased resistance to blossom brown rot. An authors' favorite.

'Helen Taft'. A hybrid, the seed parent a 'Yoshino' from the 1912 Tidal Basin trees, the pollen from *P. campanulata*. Flowers resemble 'Yoshino' in size and form but pick up the lovely pink color of the pollen parent, probably the pinkest in this group. Yellow to red fall color, zone 6 rating.

'Pink Shell'. A spreading form, a little less vigorous than 'Yoshino' and more lax. Flower buds are bright pink and open light pink, cup-shaped, hanging down from branches; fully open flowers are white, with the slightest pink tint remaining.

'Akebono'

'Akebono'

'Yoshino'

'Shidare Yoshino'. A small percentage of seedlings of 'Yoshino' grow with a weeping ("shidare") form. Several clones have been sold under this designation; depending on supplier, you will see variation. Smaller trees, weeping a little stiffly, with white flowers, 10 to 15′ size range. We think other cherry species have more graceful weeping forms. 'Ivensii' is a named, stiffly weeping clone.

'Yoshino'. 'Somei-yoshino' is probably the correct cultivar name, but it is almost always listed with only the hybrid species name, simply as *P. ×yedoensis*. The tree is clonal, thus a cultivar, and always called by its common name Yoshino, hence we use 'Yoshino' as the cultivar designation. Genetic testing has shown that current nursery production at Schmidt nursery in Oregon is identical to the clone planted in the Tidal Basin, beginning in 1912. The description under the species applies to this cultivar. All other listed cultivars were derived from it. Plain and simple, a horticultural winner that has stood the test of time. White-flowered, upright-spreading, 25′ by 30′.

'Shidare Yoshino'

'Yoshino'

Pseudocydonia sinensis
Chinese quince

Deciduous. A monotypic genus related to and sometimes included in *Cydonia* or *Chaenomeles* (as *C. sinensis*). In its best persona, a 20′ high tree, potentially taller, and usually less in spread. Growth is slow; specimens in Athens took 55 years to reach 30′. Often low-branched or multi-trunked, but readily trained to a single stem (standard), with an oval-rounded, dense canopy. The chief ornamental asset is the beautiful bark, which flakes to an irregular schizophrenic mosaic of gray, green, orange, and brown. Exfoliation initiates on 2 to 3″ wide branches. Larger trunks are fluted, resembling corduroy, only gently wavy. Fruit, though cannonball firm, is utilized for jelly.

Foliage: Pretty, lustrous dark green leaves emerge early (March) and persist late in fall, turning yellow, orange, and red; all colors occasionally intermingled on a single tree. Each leaf ovate-oval to obovate, 2½ to 4½″ long, 1½ to 2½″ wide, leathery, with gland-tipped serrations. **Flowers/seeds/fruits/cones**: Self-fertile flowers, 5-petaled, primarily pink, also deep rose, 1 to 1½″ wide, on year-old shoots or on short spurs with the leaves in April-May. Delicately attractive on close inspection, but not on a par with flowering crabapples and cherries; from a distance they are lost among the foliage. Fruit is a biological hand grenade and almost as dangerous; smooth citron-yellow skin, fattened egg-shape, 5 to 7″ long, two-thirds as wide, aromatic when ripening in October-November and falling over an extended period. A 3-year-old tree produced fruits. **Native range**: China.

Pseudocydonia sinensis

Adaptability: Demonstrates high heat and drought tolerances, and leaves are quite frost-resistant to about 28°F. Zones (5)6 to 8. **Landscape use**: Lovely garden tree for moist, well-drained, acid soils in full sun. Authors experienced trees in moderate shade that were healthy and relatively dense. Utilize as a specimen, accent, or in groupings. In the Coker Arboretum, University of North Carolina, Chapel Hill, a group of three low-branched, 30′ by 25′ specimens would inspire gardeners to plant. Foliage is pest-free, the only liability being fireblight susceptibility. We noted remarkable bonsai specimens, crafted in single-stemmed and multi-stemmed habits. **Street tree use**: No, we suspect, for liability from falling fruit would not be covered by Lloyd's of London. English literature mentions its being common on the Italian Riviera. Without the fruits, it would prove a pretty presence along streets. **In the trade**: Available. No cultivars exist to authors' knowledge. Could the species be hybridized with flowering-quince, *Chaenomeles speciosa*, to develop improved flower size and colors?

Pseudocydonia sinensis

Pseudocydonia sinensis

Pseudolarix amabilis
golden larch

Deciduous conifer. What a beauty. Certainly requires space, as the species is reported to reach 100 to 130′ in height with 2 to 3′ trunk diameter, and old trees in the Northwest, Northeast, and Mid-Atlantic states are now 50 to 60′ high, resembling *Cedrus libani* in outline. Young trees are pyramidal, often irregular (but easily coiffured by pruning), becoming rounded with wide-spreading horizontal, stratified branches. Moderate to fast growth rate; a 20-year-old tree is 20′ high and almost as wide in Georgia trials, but

Pseudolarix amabilis

John Ruter and Tom Cox reported a 22′ high tree in 10 years in Tifton, GA. Bark is grayish brown to brown on larger branches and trunks, shallowly and irregularly furrowed with broad ridges transversely cut to form a brick and block-like pattern.

Foliage: Needles are soft, flat, light/bright green above, gray/blue-green below, 1½ to 2½″ long, to ⅙″ wide, singly and spirally arranged on first-year shoots; radiating cluster (15 to 30 needles per) on short spur-like branches; needles turn magnificent golden, aging to golden brown in autumn. Often green, gold, and brown needles are present at the same time. In a humble way, reminiscent of *Ginkgo biloba* for reliability and consistency of fall coloration. **Flowers/seeds/fruits/cones**: Monoecious. Pollen cones ⅕ to ⅖″ long, yellowish green, clustered at the end of short, spur-like branchlets. Seed cones are pretty, glaucous, bloomy, lime-green to golden to reddish brown, each 2 to 3″ long, 1½ to 2″ wide, resembling an artichoke in shape, ripening the first season and shattering at maturity. Cones are often formed in great quantities and are nestled in the delicate foliage. This is a conifer where the cones are as attractive, perhaps more so, than many fruiting trees. **Native range**: Eastern and central China, growing with deciduous hardwoods and other conifers in moist, mixed forests of acidic reaction; so widely planted, its original "home" is not absolutely clear. **Adaptability**: Although now restricted to China, fossil records substantiate its presence in eastern Asia and western North America, spreading throughout boreal North America. Zones 5 to 8. **Landscape use**: A beautiful specimen conifer, more stately and noble with maturity. Requires moist, acid, well-drained soils and full sun, but eminently successful in less-than-perfect soil and climatic conditions in Raleigh, NC, Athens, GA, and Tifton, GA. The tree at the University of Georgia Horticulture Farm has received no supplemental irrigation over the past decade; even in the very hot and dry summer of 2016, this established specimen did not burn or prematurely lose needles, and it developed excellent, long-persistent, golden yellow fall color in late October, November. Grows beautifully in the Pacific Northwest. For fertile/viable seed, the story goes, outcrossing must occur, as the species is self-infertile; however, Missouri Botanical Garden, St. Louis, raised many seedlings from its singular tree, and an isolated tree in Italy produced numerous seedlings under its boughs. **Street tree use**: Potential, the deciduous conifers offer interest and diversity as well as appropriate forms for street use. **In the trade**: Limitedly available as seed-grown, but worthy of pursuit.

Pseudolarix amabilis

Pseudolarix amabilis

Pseudolarix amabilis

P

Pseudotsuga menziesii

Douglas fir

Evergreen conifer. The coastal type is the dominant tree in Pacific Northwest forests west of the Cascades, where it can easily exceed 100'. A height of over 100' with a 30' width is a reasonable landscape size to plan on in the West, half that height in the East. The historic record tree from logging stretched an amazing 415', topping the redwoods. Fast-growing, with a straight trunk, often clear-stemmed to a great height, narrowly pyramidal with branches that radiate out and sweep gracefully down; medium texture. The thick roughly furrowed brown bark provides fire resistance in its native habitat.

Foliage: Narrow needles, 1 to 1½" long, arranged completely around the twigs, soft to the touch despite their pointed appearance. Coastal trees typically have bright green to dark green needles; east of the Cascade Mountains and into the Rockies the foliage appears more blue-green. **Flowers/seeds/fruits/cones**: Monoecious. Cones pendulous, long ovoid, pointed at the bottom, green when young ripening to brown, with distinct 3-pointed, protruding bracts, 3 to 4" long and 1 to 1½" in diameter. Cones mature in one season and are persistent, releasing seed in fall, winter, and spring as their scales gradually spread open. Cones eventually fall intact. **Native range**: The type, var. *menziesii*, grows along the Pacific coastal strip from British Columbia to northern California; the interior Douglas fir, var. *glauca*, grows in the Rockies from central British Columbia to New Mexico. **Adaptability**: Likes acid well-drained soil with adequate moisture in spring and summer, and a cooler climate. Zones 4 to 6 in the East, and up to zone 9 along the cool-summer Pacific coast. **Landscape use**: A great and noble landscape tree, rugged in its trunk and delicate in its fine-textured foliage. Tall and spire-like, but with graceful and airy branch spacing. Use singly or in groups, but this is a big tree, so be sure you have room. Strong wood, long-lived. In the Pacific Northwest, most landscape trees are retained native stands, including a cherished cluster of 150' trees preserved on Warren's property. The interior form, var. *glauca*, is the best choice for landscape use in the Midwest. **Street tree use**: Works well if a conifer is wanted in a wide median or broad roadside planting, but not where road salts are used. **In the trade**: The type, var. *menziesii*, is mostly sold as seed-grown, although its varietal designation is rarely used in commerce. Local seed sources are best in the native range. The cultivars are grafted.

'Blue'. Wonderful blue needles; you might at first think you are looking at a Colorado blue spruce. Softer foliage and appearance, more relaxed but still a full pyramidal shape. Like var. *glauca*, it matures smaller than the coastal form, but it's still is a big conifer, estimate 40 to 50' tall, 15 to 20' wide.

'Emerald Twister'. A contorted form with twisting branches. It looks positively painful when young, but it does grow into a more normal pyramidal form and becomes more attractive as it ages, like a naturalistic, windblown tree in the wild, to 20' tall, 12' wide.

Pseudotsuga menziesii

Pseudotsuga menziesii

'Fastigiata'

Pseudotsuga menziesii

'Emerald Twister'

'Blue'

P

var. *glauca*

'Graceful Grace'

'Pendula'

'Waggin Tails'

'Fastigiata'. Tall, densely branched, narrowly pyramidal, as if it has been neatly sheared, skinny and conical, to 40′ tall, 10 to 15′ wide. More than one clone has carried this name, but the one in current commerce has bluish green needles.

var. *glauca*. Interior and Rocky Mountain form, seed-grown, with blue-green foliage, shorter and more full and dense than the coastal form. Landscape size is about half to two-thirds that of the coastal variety, but this still means a tree of 40 to 80′, depending on location. A good choice in the Midwest or East.

'Graceful Grace'. A selected weeper, with needles tinted blue-green, more densely clustered along the branches than in 'Pendula' forms. The leader ascends and may be trained upward or to the side, creating a weeper of desired height, up to 25′. Develops a few strongly irregular side branches, then all the finer branches weep down. Beautiful and unique, no two are alike.

GREEN CANYON 'Winterscape'. Selected from var. *glauca* in North Dakota for extreme cold hardiness and greener foliage than usually seen in the Rocky Mountain form. Densely pyramidal to 40′ tall and 20′ wide in the cold Midwest, and rated zone 3.

'Pendula'. More than one weeping form has been sold under this name. The dominant clone is ascending with curves and leans, reaching significant height, with irregular weeping branches hanging from the main stem. Will reach at least 30′, not a small tree. 'Glauca Pendula' is a bluish needle weeping form.

'Waggin Tails'. Aptly named, the trunk and branches twist and turn like the wagging tail of a dog. Upright, irregularly pyramidal, much slower growing than the species and more of a garden-sized tree, maybe to 20′ with a 10′ width, an artistic contorted form. Good foliage color and density. We like the tree as well as its name.

Ptelea trifoliata
hop-tree, wafer-ash, stinking-ash

Deciduous. A North American native that labors in near obscurity. Habit is low-branched with a bushy, rounded crown; grows slowly to 15 to 25′ high and 10 to 15′ wide. Plants may sucker, forming colonies, but two trees in the Dirr garden show no propensity to do so. Bark is smooth, dark gray, with warty protuberances. The species serves as a food source for six caterpillar species. Its bitter fruit is used as a substitute for hops in brewing beer (hence hop-tree).

Foliage: Composed of 3 leaflets (hence the epithet), each lanceolate-ovate to elliptic-oblong, entire or with fine serrations, lustrous dark green, 2½ to 5″ long, half as wide, middle leaflet the largest, pungent when crushed; a member of the citrus family, Rutaceae, and with a fruity fragrance, the leaf blade is dotted with visible oil glands; fall color yellow-green, on occasion pretty yellow. **Flowers/seeds/fruits/cones**: Flowers somewhat hidden by the leaves, greenish, unisexual, each ⅓ to ½″ wide, borne in

Ptelea trifoliata

'Aurea'

P

2 to 3″ wide terminal clusters on short lateral branches, May-June. Flowers emit a stinky, off-odor (they are pollinated by carrion flies). Fruit is a compressed, broad-winged, quasi-rounded, ¾″ wide, indehiscent, brown samara, the bulging center containing the single to multiple seeds; matures in fall, persisting into early winter. **Native range**: Extensive, Canada to Florida, west to Minnesota, Wisconsin into Utah, Colorado, Arkansas, California, into Mexico. Most often in rocky, well-drained understories, stream terraces, and lowlands. **Adaptability**: Widely adaptable, virtually unassailable, and extremely cold hardy and heat tolerant. So why is it absent in American gardens? Quite remarkable, when one thinks about the citrus family and lack of hardiness, that *P. trifoliata* is the northernmost New World representative (zone 3). Authors observed many seedlings in the woods in the Minneapolis–St. Paul area. Zones 3 to 9. **Landscape use**: Rather undistinguished and undistinguishable (the majority of gardeners could not identify it if it were labeled), but useful and effective as an understory, woods-edge, grouping, and wildlife addition. Requires only well-drained, acid soil in sun or moderate shade. Once established, displays excellent heat and drought tolerance. We have read many descriptions of floral "fragrance"; perhaps the kindest was "slight lemon-like, unpleasant musky odor." **Street tree use**: Limited. **In the trade**: Specialist nurseries offer 'Aurea', a pretty yellow-leaf form raised in Germany in late 1800s. The emerging leaves are pure birch-fall-color yellow, becoming green in warm weather. Color persists better in zones 3 to 5. When seed-grown, a measure of the seedlings come true-to-type with yellow foliage. For gardeners who prefer just a spring hint of yellow foliage, this is the ticket; a small plant in the Dirr garden elicits the typical "What is it? Where do I buy it?" 'Glauca' has blue-green leaves and is a pleasant contrast to the shiny green of the species.

Ptelea trifoliata

Pterocarya fraxinifolia
Caucasian wingnut

Deciduous. Appropriately named: the fruit wings do resemble the wings of a metal nut. The species and its handful of Asian relatives develop into medium to large, rounded, broad-spreading trees of great beauty. Size under cultivation 30 to 50(60)′ high and wide, with potential to 100′ and greater; the largest trees the authors recorded were in Canada and England, the Canadian specimen 70′ by 70′, at Vineland Station, ON. Fast-growing, especially in moist, acid, loamy soil. Rough-textured bark, irregularly ridged and deeply furrowed, ridges somewhat rounded, rough and fissured, gray-brown, ruggedly attractive on large trees.

Pterocarya fraxinifolia

Foliage: Majestic foliage, compound pinnate, with 7 to 25(27) sessile leaflets, the leaf to 18″ long, each leaflet 3 to 5″ long, a third as wide, ovate-oblong, sharply serrate, shiny-glistening dark green; leaflets are borne on a central axis (rachis) that is unwinged, a fact that separates it from *P. stenoptera*. Leaves die off green to yellow-green. **Flowers/ seeds/fruits/cones**: Monoecious. Male flowers in greenish cylindrical catkins (spikes) to 5″ long on old wood or at base of spring shoots; female on the terminals of new shoots to 20″ long in May-June. The naked buds (no scale covering) are shaped like small leaves, covered with brownish hairs, an easy identification character. Fruit is a winged nut(let), ¾″ wide, green, maturing brown in September-October and persisting on the 12 to 20″ long, pendulous spike. Each fruit is sessile on a long, pendent peduncle. Wings of fruits are spreading and more rounded than those of *P. stenoptera*. No other hardy tree has such a reproductive structure. **Native range**: Caucasus to northern Iran, where it inhabits moist places. **Adaptability**: Best adapted to planting along streams, rivers, and lakes; the Dutch report it tolerates prolonged flooding. Many reports in the English literature of trees dropping their leaves during extended droughts.

Species has demonstrated above average heat and drought tolerances in Athens, GA. Zones 5 to 8. **Landscape use**: Authors have pondered the lack of landscape presence in the United States. From Chicago to Boston to Louisville to Raleigh to Athens, we recorded trees, and all were in good health. Specimen use on large properties suits it well. The root systems of all pterocaryas are aggressive; trees are planted along watercourses to stabilize the soil and prevent erosion. **Street tree use**: Potential, but seeds a bit messy. The species serves as such in Portland, with trees now 45′ by 35′. **In the trade**: Uncommon, sold as seed-grown.

Pterocarya stenoptera
Chinese wingnut

Deciduous. Forms a large, broad-rounded outline, 40 to 60′ high and wide. Growth is fast; reports noted 20′ in 5 years. At Georgia Southern University, Savannah, a 12-year-old tree was 55′ high, still holding yellow-green leaves in December. Bark is similar to *P. fraxinifolia*, gray, ruggedly ridged and furrowed, in places blocky, scaly, formidable.

Foliage: Leaves are compound pinnate (odd pinnate), each 10 to 16″ long, composed of 11 to 21(25) leaflets, each 2 to 5″ long to 2″ wide, oblong to narrow-oval, finely and uniformly serrate, lustrous dark green; leaf rachis is winged; fall color at best yellow-green. **Flowers/seeds/fruits/cones**: Similar to *P. fraxinifolia*, except female spikes shorter, to 8″ long, and the wings of fruits are narrow and erect. **Native range**: Alpine forested areas on mountain slopes and riverbanks in eastern and central China, from near sea level to 5,000′. **Adaptability**: Often listed as the hardiest of the genus: the Morton Arboretum has no *P. fraxinifolia* in the collections, but seven accessions of *P. stenoptera*; the lowest temperatures there would be in the -15 to -20°F range. Zones 5 to 8, 9 on the West Coast. A large tree is growing in Jacksonville,

P

Pterocarya fraxinifolia

'Fernleaf'

Pterocarya stenoptera

Pterostyrax hispida

FL, zone 9. **Landscape use:** Utilized as a shade tree in China. Many trees labeled as *P. fraxinifolia* turn out, when carefully examined, to be *P. stenoptera*; they are that similar in landscape reality. Said to be more prone to suckering than *P. fraxinifolia*. Used as a rootstock for walnuts because of its high resistance to phytophthora. **Street tree use:** It develops a shallow, aggressive root system, so use is reserved for large expanses of soil, away from sidewalks. **In the trade:** 'Fernleaf' ('Fern Leaf') has feathery, fern-like, deeply cut and incised leaflets. The single tree we observed, in North Carolina, was beautiful; unfortunately, an early April freeze killed it. Originated in England in the 1980s in a batch of *P. stenoptera* seedlings.

Pterostyrax hispida
fragrant epaulette-tree

Deciduous. Pretty flowering species, typically 20 to 30(50)′ high with a similar or greater spread. Habit is somewhat loose and open in youth; developing an open rounded crown of slender spreading branches. Growth is fast in youth, 12 to 14′ in 7 to 8 years. Bark is gray-brown, ridged and furrowed.

Foliage: Leaves large, coarse-textured, oval to oblong-ovate, 3 to 7½″ long, 1½ to 4″ wide, bristle-toothed, bright green, turning yellow-green in fall. **Flowers/seeds/fruits/cones:** Fragrant white flowers, corolla 5-lobed, divided almost to base, held in fine-textured, 5 to 10″ long, 2 to 3″ wide, pendulous pubescent panicles on ends of short, lateral branches, May-June, after the leaves mature. The effect is striking and extends the small-tree flowering season. Nothing to shake the timbers, but fruit is a curious, ½″ long, cylindrical to spindle-shaped, 10-ribbed, densely bristly, dry drupe, maturing in fall and persisting into winter. **Native range:**

Pterostyrax corymbosa

Japan, China. **Adaptability:** Zones (4)5 to 8. Uncommon in the zone 7 and 8 gardens of the Southeast. **Landscape use:** Potential for residential properties, parks, and campuses. The authors have recorded the species primarily in arboreta and botanical gardens. Requirements are few, simply moist, acid, well-drained soil and full sun for maximum growth and flower. Trees in partial shade appear thrifty; small trees will often flower. **Street tree use**: Limited. **In the trade**: Rare. Authors envision a pink-flowered selection as a worthwhile goal; in our experience, embedded in the DNA of many white-flowered species is the pink gene, simply waiting to be expressed. *P. corymbosa* (little epaulette-tree) is even rarer but worth considering. Leaves are smaller to 4½" long, thicker, more substantial, *Hydrangea macrophylla*–like, with bristle-tipped serrations pointing out from the margin. The fragrant white flowers occur in corymbose panicles, 2 to 5" long, in June; fruits are ovoid, ½" long, prominently 5-winged, densely tomentose drupes. One reference lists size in the 30 to 40' range. We witnessed a 40' high specimen but estimate it will be smaller under cultivation. Japan, China. Zones 5 to 7.

Pyrus calleryana
Callery pear

Deciduous. Moderately fast-growing, upright, dense with many crossing limbs, co-dominant leaders common, pyramidal becoming broadly oval. Moderately coarse in texture, 40' high and 30' wide. Note that seed-grown trees are quite thorny as a juvenile characteristic, but the cultivars are thornless. Bark is smooth, thin, and gray-green with noticeable lenticels when young, soon becoming gray to charcoal-gray and rough, lined with vertical fissures.

Foliage: Glossy dark green, broadly ovate, 1½ to 3½" long, two-thirds to three-fourths as wide, acuminate tip, margin finely crenate-serrulate. Fall color yellow-orange to purple-red. **Flowers/seeds/fruits/cones**: One of the first trees to flower, very early in spring, but unfortunately malodorous. White, ½ to ¾" wide, clustered in corymbs, anthers are bright purple and make the flowers attractive up close. Fruit develops through the summer, globose to ovoid, ⅓ to ½"

Pterostyrax hispida

Pterostyrax corymbosa

Pyrus calleryana

P

Pyrus calleryana

'Aristocrat'

Pyrus calleryana

'Aristocrat'

wide and russet brown when ripe in the fall. **Native range**: China, Korea. **Adaptability**: Very adaptable, which is both its main virtue and its downfall, as it is invasive in the Mid-Atlantic, central, and southeastern United States (but a new, nearly fruitless, triploid introduction from NCSU may help solve this problem). Driving interstate highways along the East Coast in early spring shows the extent of its invasion, as the open fields are white with the flowers of Callery pears. The species is tolerant of both drought and soggy soils, high and low pH, and compaction. This is one tough city tree. It's no surprise that the 9/11 "Survivor Tree" turned out to be a Callery pear (CHANTICLEER). Blasted and broken down to an 8′ main trunk, burned and buried deeply in the rubble, it was the last living thing uncovered at Ground Zero. Hauled away to a park department nursery site, it recovered fully and was replanted as part of the memorial. It has now regrown to 30′. Zones 5 to 9. **Landscape use**: Needs full sun but otherwise an easy tree to please, which has made it very popular with the landscape trade, a nursery and landscape contractor's joy. Easy to grow, relatively inexpensive to buy, it lives on almost any site and looks great through the guarantee period. Used (overused) everywhere. Very prominent in commercial plantings. Young trees have handsome form; the problems start developing 5 to 10 years later. As the tree ages, it invariably becomes dense and forms crowded, narrow crotches; its brittle wood breaks, resulting in multiple leaders and more narrow crotch angles, which leads to additional storm breakage. If you want a great-looking tree for 5 years, plant a Callery pear; if you want a great-looking tree for 50 years, plant an oak. **Street tree use**: Widely used as a small to medium-sized street tree. CHANTICLEER is the only cultivar we can recommend strongly, with 'Aristocrat' as a possible second where a broader form is desired. They survive well on the street, but some breakage is inevitable. **In the trade**: Omnipresent.

'Aristocrat'. Pyramidal to broadly pyramidal in form, this cultivar is less dense than most, which is a good thing, to 40′ tall and 28′ wide. It tends to grow with a central leader and horizontally radiating branches, thereby having fewer narrow crotch angles and thus less breakage. We say less, not none, as it still a Callery pear. Moderate fireblight resistance.

'Autumn Blaze'. A little smaller than typical, dense, bushy, confused branching, broadly rounded to 25′ by 25′, can become wider than tall. It shows some of the best fall colors in the group: oranges, reds, and purple-reds. It may produce a few thorns. The most cold hardy cultivar, zone 4.

'Bradford'. Friends don't let friends plant 'Bradford'. Please don't plant. Pyramidal when young but becomes densely rounded with age with multiple leaders, growing to 35′ tall and 30′ wide. Breakage and splitting is legendary. Why is it still grown? Give it credit for beautiful dark green foliage. A great tree if you only need it for 10 years and then want firewood.

'Autumn Blaze'

'Bradford'

P

'Bradford'

'Bradford'

'Capital'

'Capital'

CHANTICLEER

CHANTICLEER

'Capital'. The only word of advice we have about planting this? Don't. It doesn't deliver what it promises. Introduced as a narrow columnar selection, which is true for the first 5 years or so, when it looks very good. But soon the tree opens up; the long ascending branches splay widely outward, and the tree often leans to the side, many trees ending up at a 45° angle. Add to this the worst susceptibility to fireblight of the pears. By 10 to 15 years of age it's a very wide, open, irregular, leaning vase shape, 25′ by 20′.

CHANTICLEER 'Glen's Form' ('Cleveland Select', 'Stonehill'). Finally, we get to a really good selection of the species. Upright and distinctly narrow pyramidal when young, becoming narrow oval, to 40′ tall and 15′ wide. It's usually the longest-lasting, best-formed cultivar, but eventually even its canopy begins to open up, and you will see some breakage. If most Callery pear cultivars look good for 10 years, you can count on CHANTICLEER for 20. Widely used as a street tree, and a good one because it is so tolerant of urban soils and conditions. Just don't expect it to live as long as an oak. Handsome dark green glossy foliage and very good orange-red to purple-red fall color. Unfortunately, it has recently been attacked by a new strain of powdery mildew that disfigures spring foliage; curiously, the strain does not (yet) affect other cultivars. Cold hardy and fireblight resistant. This is as good as it gets in a troubled species.

CHASTITY 'NCPX2'. A very exciting new introduction, bringing near seedlessness to this cultivar group. An induced triploid of hybrid parentage, now named *P. ×triploida*, fertility has been reduced by 99.14%; in short, hardly any viable seeds. Curiously, fruit is reduced by only 93%, but most fruit that do form have no viable seeds. Moderate growth rate, upright pyramidal to oval in form, floriferous, with good structure. Foliage dark green, slightly glossy in spring and summer, becoming a bit dull before showing nice yellow to red-purple fall color. This cultivar should replace others where invasiveness is a concern. Highly resistant

CHANTICLEER

CHASTITY

JACK

to fireblight. From the breeding program of Tom Ranney, NCSU. To 30′ tall, 25′ wide.

'Fauriei'. We list this because of the confusion it has caused. This is a true cultivar of *P. calleryana*, a large upright pyramidal tree, 35′ tall, 25′ wide. The species *P. fauriei* is totally different, a small rather dwarf shrubby tree.

JACK 'Jaczam'. An unusually formal-looking pear, semi-dwarf, dense, and tightly conical, eventually becoming broadly oval. It really stands out in a landscape. Grows slowly to 16′ tall and 10′ wide. A very useful little tree, slow enough and small enough to make breakage less of a concern.

JAVELIN 'NCPX1'. A hybrid of CHANTICLEER and *P. pyrifolia* 'Ohara Beni'. The narrowest of the pears, columnar to narrow pyramidal form, 35′ tall, 10′ wide. Slower growing than other cultivars. It's only half *P. calleryana*, so we are hopeful it will not develop the problems typical of the species. Purple new growth, bronze-green summer foliage. Attractive red flower buds, and flowers open with a very slight pink tint. Fruit larger than other cultivars, about ¾″ wide. Fireblight resistant.

LIL JILL 'Liljilzam'. A sister of JACK, it's similarly slow-growing and semi-dwarf, but round in shape and more open in habit, to 15′ by 15′. We think JACK is the better-looking plant.

NEW BRADFORD 'Holmford'. Pyramidal in form when young, becoming dense and broadly oval, 35′ tall and 25′ wide. Billed as an improved 'Bradford', which wouldn't take much. At a young age it does look good, but its density indicates structural problems. Our observation of heavy breakage following a recent ice storm confirmed our suspicion, as it was the most severely damaged tree we saw.

P

JAVELIN

JAVELIN

CHANTICLEER

NEW BRADFORD

'Redspire'

'Redspire'

'Redspire'. Another pyramidal form, very nice in the nursery, with bright green glossy leaves and yellow to orange-red fall color. It becomes a broad pyramid as it ages, and its canopy does open up some, 35′ tall and 20′ wide. Susceptible to fireblight. Usually a fine-looking tree in the landscape for 10 to 20 years.

'Trinity'. A broadly pyramidal form that becomes more oval to rounded with time, it does seem to have improved branch spacing, 30′ tall, 20 to 25′ wide. We like its form, but time will tell about breakage. Reported to have lighter fruit load than most Callery pears, and trees we observed had few fruits. Orange-red fall color. Good cold hardiness.

'Trinity'

'Whitehouse'

'Trinity'

'Whitehouse'. Upright pyramidal form, reminiscent of
CHANTICLEER, relatively narrow, 35′ tall, 15 to 20′ wide.
Unfortunately the foliage is of much poorer quality and
seems always to be accompanied by leafspot. Largely abandoned by the nursery trade, and rightly so.

P

Pyrus fauriei

Korean pear

Deciduous. Small shrubby tree, branching is low, dense, and confused. Slow-growing, fine-textured, growing to a height of 10′ and a spread of 15′. Bark is gray-brown, rough and fissured.

Foliage: Leaves dark green, ovate with a short acuminate tip, finely serrate, usually 1 to 2½″ long. Bright yellow-orange to red in fall. **Flowers/seeds/fruits/cones**: White flowers, similar to *P. calleryana* but smaller, fruits ½″ wide, dark brown becoming almost black. **Native range**: Korea. **Adaptability**: Northern-adapted, quite cold hardy, zones 4 to 8. **Landscape use**: Can be used as a low, dense screen. The cultivars are a little larger, mostly used in the North for their cold hardiness, valued as small ornamental garden trees. **Street tree use**: No. Too small and bushy. **In the trade**: Rare as seed-grown, more often as cultivars.

KOREAN SUN 'Westwood'. A vigorous faster-growing selection of true *P. fauriei*. Small and spreading, densely branched, less bushy; makes a larger tree to 12′ tall, 18′ wide, and can be pruned up for some clearance. Excellent fall color, one of the best of the pears for brightness, orange-red to bright red.

'Silver Ball'. A hybrid of uncertain parentage, possibly *P. fauriei* × *P. betulifolia*, included here for lack of a better place. Semi-dwarf, dense rounded pyramid, it is globe-shaped at first but with time gains some height, possibly to 15′ tall, 12′ wide. Very cute with tiny silvery tomentose foliage, very fine-textured and quite different. Small white flowers, ⅜″ wide fruit. Fireblight resistant and hardy to zone 4. Usually top grafted, appropriate for small spaces. Nice yellow-orange fall color.

KOREAN SUN

'Silver Ball'

Pyrus fauriei

Pyrus kawakamii

evergreen pear

Semi-evergreen to deciduous. Closely related to (or sometimes included in) *P. calleryana*. Upright-spreading, rounded, 25′ by 25′. Bark is very rough, gray to charcoal-gray, first fissured and then horizontally cracked into plates, later forming thick, rough ridges.

Pyrus kawakamii

Foliage: Similar to *P. calleryana*, except leaves thicker, darker green, and usually only briefly deciduous. Red fall color. **Flowers/seeds/fruits/cones**: See *P. calleryana*, very similar, flowers slightly larger. **Native range**: Taiwan. **Adaptability**: Tender, likes a warm climate, avoid hard freezes. Zones 8 to 10. **Landscape use**: We see this tree in central and southern California, where it is valued for its bright white spring bloom and red fall color (in a climate where fall color is rare). Quite popular but its use is decreasing, as it is highly susceptible to fireblight. **Street tree use**: Not a good choice, wide-spreading, low-hanging branches. **In the trade**: Sold under the species name, but available trees are usually an unnamed clone.

Pyrus salicifolia

willowleaf pear

Deciduous. Upright-spreading, irregularly rounded and a bit open. Produces some thorns. Moderate growth rate, fine-textured, to 25′ high and wide. Bark is rough, gray, with fissures and ridges that crack horizontally.

Pyrus kawakamii

Pyrus salicifolia

P

'Pendula'

SILVER FROST

Foliage: Leaves very willow-like, narrow lanceolate, 1½ to 3½″ long, ⅜ to ¾″ wide, entire, new growth covered with bright silvery gray pubescence through the spring months, becoming a little less pubescent and more gray-green in summer. Little fall color. **Flowers/seeds/fruits/cones:** Flowers white, ¾″ wide, in small corymbs, opening with the emerging foliage, which is similarly colored, diminishing the flowering effect. Fruit is pear-shaped, green, about 1¼″ long, not ornamental and large enough to be messy. **Native range:** Southeastern Europe, western Asia. **Adaptability:** Tolerant of drought and a variety of soils and pH. Most successful in areas with cool spring weather, as the plant is highly susceptible to fireblight, and warm moist springs favor the disease. Zones 4 to 7. **Landscape use:** Only the weeping cultivar is used, often as a specimen for its unusual form, texture, and foliage color. A very different-looking tree that commands attention. Either you like it or you don't. **Street tree use:** No. **In the trade:** 'Pendula' always looks like it's having a wild and windblown, silvery, mop-headed bad hair day. But in a strange way, it's rather attractive. Yes, really. It can be grown as a rank weeper, growing up and irregularly outward, then weeping to the ground, or it can be formally trained into a variety of topiary shapes. Even a little pruning can civilize it. Spring foliage very silvery. Size 18′ by 18′, depends greatly on training and pruning. SILVER FROST 'Silfrozam', also weeping, is at least similar; we have not seen a difference; same size estimate.

Pyrus ussuriensis
Ussurian pear

Deciduous. A sturdy, upright-oriented tree, broadly pyramidal when young, becoming broadly oval and then nearly round, sometimes broader than tall. Symmetrical, with a full and neatly formed canopy. Medium growth rate and medium texture, to 40′ tall and wide. Bark is gray with vertical fissures and flattened ridges that crack horizontally.

Foliage: Dark green, ovate to broadly ovate with an acuminate tip, sharply serrate. Leaves 2 to 4″ long, two-thirds to three-fourths as wide, slightly lustrous. Fall color yellow-orange to red. **Flowers/seeds/fruits/cones:** Flowers light pink in bud, opening white, 1″ wide, in clusters just before the leaves and giving a beautiful white display. Green fruit follows, round, 1 to 1½″ in diameter, ripening to yellowish tan in the fall. **Native range:** Northeast Asia. **Adaptability:** Well adapted to cold climates, it has found its place in the Northern Plains of the United States and Canada; not for the South. Tolerant of a variety of soils and pH. Shows good resistance to fireblight. Zones 3 to 6, 7 in the West. **Landscape use:** A reliable ornamental flowering pear for the North. Flower display is among the best of the pears, as is its fall color. It has better density and symmetry than

MOUNTAIN FROST

MOUNTAIN FROST

PRAIRIE GEM

PRAIRIE GEM

other species, giving a formal rounded appearance. It grows more slowly and has better structure and strength than *P. calleryana*, thus we have less concern about breakage. Its only negative feature is its large fruit, which can be messy; however, fruiting is usually light, as it needs pollination by another variety. **Street tree use**: Adaptable, but too broad for most locations. Could be used in a wide tree lawn or with pruning for clearance. **In the trade**: MOUNTAIN FROST 'Bailfrost' is the narrower cultivar and better street tree, more upright-growing, developing a well-formed, broadly pyramidal to upright oval canopy, to 30′ tall and 20′ wide; fruit ¾″ wide. PRAIRIE GEM 'MorDak' is upright, dense, compact, becomes round, to 25′ tall and wide; good branch structure, golden orange to orange-red fall color. Fruit is round and a little more than 1″ in diameter.

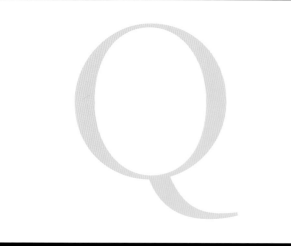

Quercus

oak

What's not to love? The genus offers approximately 530 species of deciduous and evergreen trees, a few shrubby, with wide distribution in the northern hemisphere, from cold temperate to tropical areas. Oaks are adaptable to extremes of soil and climate, growing in habitats from river bottoms to upland soils to mountaintops in the southern Appalachians. In North America, which is particularly blessed with noble species, diversity increases as you move south, with Mexico having nearly twice as many species as the United States (about 160 vs. 90). In the West, Washington state has only one native oak species. Moving south, a couple more species are picked up in southern Oregon, and then California has more than 20, many in the coastal canyons. In the dry interior Southwest, oak species become plentiful in the mid-elevation mountain habitats and are mostly evergreen or briefly drought deciduous. In Mexico, oak species are common in both montane and tropical forests.There is an oak for almost any landscape opportunity; where space allows, there are countless options, and for restricted spaces, upright, columnar, fastigiate cultivars are available. Species specificity dictates maximum performance, so select the best-adapted species or cultivar for a given site/outcome. For example, *Q. alba* is an upland species suited to well-drained soils; *Q. michauxii* grows naturally in floodplains inundated as many as 10 times per year.

Why elaborate on oaks?

- They are essential components in forest ecosystems.
- They are often climax species, meaning they are the end-points in forest succession, continually reproducing and maintaining their presence. When a seedling is pulled/removed, a carrot-like initial taproot foreshadows an oak's ability to compete and survive.
- Their timber/lumber is utilized for all manner of construction, furniture, turned bowls, barrels, even planters. Your bourbon is aged in white oak (*Q. alba*) barrels.
- They are, collectively, the most noble of all shade trees, long-lived (centuries old), largely pest-free, and worthy of every citizen's effort to plant, prize, protect, and cherish for future generations.

What characteristics constitute an oak?

- Alternately arranged leaves and buds.
- Leaves: entire, lobed (rounded or bristle-tipped), deciduous, semi-evergreen to evergreen. Difficult to fathom, but 557 species of caterpillars count on oak leaves as a food source.
- Buds: clustered at the terminals, usually 2 to 5, each covered with overlapping scales, pointed to rounded, ¼ to ½″ long, gray, gray-brown, brown, chestnut-brown, reddish brown; glabrous or pubescent.
- Variable in the aforementioned leaf and bud traits, as oaks hybridize freely, producing many intermediate possibilities.
- Hybridization occurs only with species in the white or red groups, never between.
- Plants are monoecious, with male flowers yellowish, in pendulous/drooping catkins of varying lengths before or with the emerging leaves in spring; females single, paired, or clustered, sessile or on a stalk of various lengths, when mature, nestled in the axils of the emerging shoots.
- Fruit is classified as an acorn, consisting of a cap/cup, covering the top or most of the brown (variable shades) nuts. A nut is defined as a bony, hard-coated, one-seeded fruit; think hickory, walnut, and pecan when imagining a true nut. Acorns mature in autumn, abscise, and cover the ground. They are essential food sources for all manner of wildlife, from our feathered friends to the black bear, and have provided sustenance to humans.
- Acorns mature the first year on species in the white oak group; second year in the red oak group. White oak group acorns may be collected and sown as soon as mature; shoots and roots develop 3 to 4 weeks after sowing in a warm greenhouse. Red oak group acorns require cold-moist stratification, so sow outside in beds or containers in the fall and protect from rascally varmints; germination occurs in spring. Authors have grown thousands of seedlings through their careers and are still doing so.
- Transplanting difficulty has long been associated with oaks. Modern nursery production techniques (including air pruning young seedlings, and root pruning larger liners and field-grown finished trees) alleviate the issue. Clonal oaks are usually budded/grafted on seedling understock. Several nurseries are competently rooting cultivar oaks from cuttings, so there is no opportunity for incompatibility of scion and rootstock. Successful rooting is now possible for selections in some species from both

the red oak and white oak groups; in fact, these own-root trees are successfully transplanted year-round except when soft growth is present, about 6 weeks in spring.

Quercus acutissima
sawtooth oak

Deciduous. In youth, pyramidal to broad pyramidal, often densely branched; at maturity rounded to broad-rounded with low-slung, wide-spreading branches. What appears to be a compact tree in youth will eat expanses of real estate with age. Mature size 40 to 60′ high and as wide or greater; in England, at Hillier, a tree reached 72′ high. Oaks, in general, have a reputation for slow growth; however, sawtooth oaks direct-seeded into Mississippi floodplain grew 28 to 34′ high in 14 years. Bark is ash-brown, deeply ridged and furrowed, developing a cork-like (*Q. suber*) texture on old trunks. The early acorns serve as a food source for wildlife, especially wild turkeys, for which the open-pollinated 'Gobbler' was introduced.

Foliage: An anomaly among commonly planted oaks, in that the leaf resembles a chestnut (*Castanea*), with prominent bristle-tipped serrations, each leaf obovate to oblong to narrowly oval, with 12 to 16 parallel veins, 3½ to 7½″ long, 1 to 2¼″ wide. Leaves emerge brilliant to golden yellow in early spring before settling to lustrous dark green, remaining pristine until clear yellow to toasty yellow-brown hues develop in late fall. A smattering of leaves is retained into winter. **Flowers/seeds/fruits/cones**: Monoecious. Catkins quite attractive, slender, golden, 3 to 4″ long, with the emerging leaves in April. The acorn is Halloweeny, the nut covered about two-thirds its length by cap (involucre) composed of elongated, spreading and recurving scales, resembling a bad hair day. Entire acorn 1″ long, nuts ¾″ long, shiny rich brown, maturing and falling earlier than most oaks, often by late September in Athens, GA; often abundant and almost covering the ground beneath the tree. **Native range**: Extensive, including Japan, China, Korea, Thailand. **Adaptability**: Trees thrived at the Morton Arboretum (Lisle, IL) and at UMass Amherst, where old trees survived -15 to -25°F. Zones 5 to 9. **Landscape use**: A beautifully structured tree for use in parks, campuses, golf courses, commercial grounds, and other large areas. The seasonal foliage transformations are beautiful, and, although many people do not appreciate the marcescent foliage, a wise professor extolled the sound (symphony) of the rustling leaves in the winter months. However, all is not coming up roses for this oak. It's increasingly reported as invasive in the woodlands of eastern states, surprisingly widely scattered from Georgia to Wisconsin. With so many native oaks from which to choose, we urge caution. Species is easily grown, requiring well-drained, acid soils. Once established it is drought tolerant. Chlorosis occurs in high pH soils. **Street tree use**: No. **In the trade**: Sold as seed-grown.

Quercus acutissima

Quercus acutissima

Quercus acutissima

Q

719

Quercus agrifolia
coast live oak

Broadleaf evergreen. Young trees rounded when open-grown, somewhat loosely branched, typically without a central leader, and open; with maturity forming a wide-spreading dome of arching branches. Authors have seen artistically contorted hill-huggers in the California canyons; the National Champion there measures 60′ high with a crown spread of 110′. Landscape expectations approximate 40 to 70′ high and wide. Growth is moderate. Bark is dark gray, smooth or furrowed, the flat ridges with transverse cuts, creating irregular cracks and fissures.

Foliage: Beautiful glossy, holly-like foliage, oval to roundish, hard/thick-textured, lustrous dark green, margin with slender, spiny teeth, 1 to 2″ long, ¾ to 1½″ wide, paler beneath with tufts of hairs in the vein axils. Old leaves are shed in spring as new leaves emerge. **Flowers/seeds/fruits/cones**: Monoecious. Catkins clustered with the emerging leaves. Acorns cone-shaped, 1 to 3″ long, widest at base, tapering to a point, the cap covering about a third of the brown nut, borne solitary or in pairs, sessile on the stem; ripening the first year. **Native range**: Central and southern California, occurring as far south as the Baja of Mexico, the foundation for the coastal California hardwood forests and common on the hills in open grasslands; most of its distribution within 60 miles of the ocean. **Adaptability**: Naturally occurs in a Mediterranean climate with mild, wet winters and hot, dry summers. Zones 8 to 10. Cold hardy to about 15°F. **Landscape use**: Choice and majestic oak for California landscapes, where it is an essential native and landscape species, protected by tree ordinances; longevity is projected at 150 years and greater. Requires full sun and well-drained, acid to near-neutral soils. It is moderately salt tolerant. California literature emphasizes that established specimens should

Quercus agrifolia

Quercus agrifolia

Quercus agrifolia

not be irrigated (via lawns), but newly planted and irrigated trees can remain under irrigation. Once established, however, the species is drought resistant. **Street tree use:** Sometimes used, but low spreading branches are a problem. **In the trade:** Sold as seed-grown.

Quercus alba
white oak

Deciduous. Perhaps the most noble of all North American oaks, but we ask the reader to opine on their favorite(s). Pyramidal in youth; often dense and foliage-rich; oval-rounded to broad-rounded with massive spreading branches at maturity. Mature size, 40 to 80′ high and wide. Slow out of the gate, then more vigorous with age. Bark is ash-gray to brownish, divided into small vertically arranged blocks and scales, flaking on their surfaces; on occasion irregularly plated to deeply fissured, with narrow ridges; sometimes with rather smooth, gray areas on large trunks. Authors have observed many permutations, including bark loose at the edges, not unlike a planetree. Every third-grader should be able to identify a large specimen by bark alone. White oak barrels are utilized for whisky/bourbon/scotch and beer (yes, bourbon-flavored beer) and recycled for planters. The lumber is prized for furniture, flooring, interior finishing, boat building, baskets, and wood turning. Every civic group, tree commission, and breathing citizen should plant a white oak; it will serve and inspire future generations as well as provide sustenance for wildlife.

Foliage: Inspiring and foreshadowing the greatness of the species; soft fuzzy gray to pinkish when unfolding, dark blue-green to dark green in summer; yellow, russet-red to red in fall, some trees dropping the bulk of their leaves in late fall; others with persistent brown leaves into and through winter; retention is most pronounced on young trees (juvenile condition). Leaves obovate to oblong-obovate, 5 to 9(11) rounded lobes, sinuses deeply cut to midrib, 4 to 8½″ long, half as wide, the leaf base cuneate (wedge-shaped). **Flowers/seeds/fruits/cones:** Monoecious. Yellowish catkins, 2 to 3″ long. Acorns have a cap covering less than a third of the nut, sessile or short-stalked, ¾ to 1″ long, nut deep Hershey's Kisses chocolate-brown; maturing in one season, often in abundance with the radicle emerging from the nuts as they rest in place after abscising.

Quercus alba

Quercus alba

Quercus alba

Q

Quercus alba

Native range: Eastern Canada and in all states east of the Mississippi; also Iowa, Montana, Arkansas, Louisiana, Kansas, Oklahoma, Texas. Usually in well-drained soils, upland or lowland, in pure stands or mixed with other species, from near sea level to 6,000′ elevation. **Adaptability**: As common in waste areas as in gardens. Zones 3 to 9. **Landscape use**: Superb large shade tree, where space allows. Mature size frightens most gardeners. Reserve for expansive area use. Smaller bare-root, containerized, and balled-and-burlapped trees are establishable. Once the root system is grounded, then it's off to the races. Longwood Gardens lost an American elm allée and replaced it, in part, with *Q. alba*; authors witnessed, and considering the trees are seed-grown, their uniformity is spot-on. Every autumn, we collect white (many other species) acorns, plant in 3-gallon containers, bark medium, 5 to 10 nuts per, covered 1″, then protect from wildlife with a screen; germination ensues in fall-spring and by the following fall, seedlings are 3′ high. They are divided and separated in winter, transplanted singly to 3-gallon containers, with 4 to 6′ high, often branched trees the second season, ready for gifting or outplanting. **Street tree use**: Worthy and wonderful, but cities are rightfully cautious because of issues with establishment. **In the trade**: Sold as seed-grown. Transplanting difficulty has limited wholesale nursery acceptance. Many attempts to select and, more challenging, to propagate, a superior clone. The reader might ask what constitutes a superior clone. Criteria follow: uniform habit, dense canopy, dark blue-green leaves, red fall color, clean leaf drop, and ease of propagation and transplanting.

Quercus bicolor
swamp white oak

Deciduous. Authors have always embraced this species, and we confidently state that one criterion, ease of transplanting, elevates it over the equally superb *Q. alba*. Habit is pyramidal in youth, more open than young *Q. alba*. Mature trees are magnificent, rounded to broad-rounded, with massive spreading secondary branches. Growth is moderate with adequate water and fertilizer, slowing in old age. Mature size 50 to 60′ high and wide. Bark on young trees (3 to 5″ in diameter), flaking, curling, in thickish papery pieces, gray-brown to darker brown; on large trunks rugged, with deep longitudinal furrows and elongated flat, scaly ridges. Bark is coarser than that of *Q. alba*.

Foliage: Young leaves are lettuce-green to bronze-green, maturing dark green, often lustrous, grayish and pubescent beneath; oblong-obovate to obovate, somewhat bass-fiddle-shaped, with 6 to 8(10) pairs of coarse, obtuse, marginal teeth, or occasionally lobed halfway to midrib, 3 to 7″ long, 1 to 4″ wide. Fall color is yellow-bronze to russet-red; leaves will persist into winter. **Flowers/seeds/fruits/cones**: Monoecious. Yellowish catkins with the emerging leaves. The acorn is 1″ long, usually paired on a 1 to 3″ long, slender peduncle (stalk), the thick cap fringed at edges, covers a third to half of the shining light brown nut. **Native range**: Maine to North Carolina, west to Minnesota and Montana, principally in swamps, bottomlands, floodplains, and stream margins. **Adaptability**: Somewhat

Quercus bicolor

Quercus bicolor

Quercus bicolor

Quercus bicolor

shade tolerant, competing in the understory until achieving climax status. Zones 4 to 8. **Landscape use**: Ten years past, at least in the Southeast, *Q. bicolor* was largely absent from landscapes. It is now common and gaining ground. Cultural requirements include moist, acid soils and full sun. Chlorosis may occur in high pH soils; in Salt Lake City (pH 7.5), trees ranged from deep dark green to yellow. Once established, tolerates heavy clay-based soils and displays excellent heat and drought tolerance. A new shopping center in Athens utilized the species in parking islands; even in the hot and dry summer of 2016, trees did not flinch. It is a superb choice for large areas and features as the principal species in the 9/11 memorial landscape in New York City. **Street tree use**: Superb. Allow room. **In the trade**: Available, both the species and its selections; new hybrids with *Q. bicolor* genes are also presented herein.

AMERICAN DREAM 'JFS-KW12'. Warren selected this J. Frank Schmidt & Son nursery introduction. Vigorous, upright-growing becoming broadly pyramidal and eventually more oval. Strong central leader, good branch structure and density. Broad deep green glossy leaves, anthracnose and mildew resistant; improved, brighter yellow fall color, defoliates gradually. Superb performance in the heat and drought of zone 8, 50 to 60′ tall and 40′ wide.

BEACON 'Bonnie and Mike'. A Dirr selection, discovered with his wife, Bonnie. Strongly upright and tightly columnar in form, this is the narrowest true *Q. bicolor* we have seen. Clean green summer foliage, then golden yellow fall color turning amber-brown and slowly defoliating, 40 to 50′ tall and 15′ wide.

Quercus bicolor

AMERICAN DREAM

AMERICAN DREAM

AMERICAN DREAM

BEACON

BEACON

SUN BREAKER

Q. ×schuettei. Hybrid (*Q. macrocarpa × Q. bicolor*). Utilized in the upper Midwest for its increased tolerance of high pH soils, owing to the Q. *macrocarpa* parent. Seedlings will be variable in foliage/habit, but should maintain the pH tolerance. The authors have observed large specimen trees, 60′ by 60′.

SUN BREAKER 'Green Nova'. Vigorous, upright, broadly pyramidal and then becoming rounded. Leaves are especially large, dark green, and lustrous. Amber-yellow fall color, then it defoliates cleanly, 50 to 60′ tall and 40′ wide.

Q

SUN BREAKER

Quercus cerris

turkey oak

Deciduous. Beautiful, massively rugged, thoroughly imposing specimen oak as observed in England, where it has escaped from cultivation (invasive). It develops a conical-oblong crown in youth; haystack-shaped to rounded to shapely, uniform, broad-rounded crown at maturity. We project 40 to 60′ high, as wide or wider. Considered the fastest-growing oak in the British Isles; at Knightshayes Garden, Somerset, England, massive trees (128′ high) reside contently in a large park-like field. Bark is dark gray-brown to black; furrows reddish brown, ridges irregular in length, often divided into blocks.

Foliage: Pretty dark lustrous green leaves, dull green below, persist into fall, dying off green to yellow-brown. Each 2½ to 5″ long, 1 to 3″ wide, margins with 5 to 7 triangular lobes or coarse teeth; 7 to 10 vein pairs in the Laciniata Group with narrow, spreading, mucronate (sharply pointed) lobes, the sinuses cut almost to the midrib. **Flowers/seeds/fruits/ cones**: The acorns, 1″ long, covered half their length by a fimbriated cap, the scales reflexed and resembling Medusa's snake-do; generally sessile, 1 to 4 together, ripening the second season. **Native range**: Southern Europe, southwestern Asia. **Adaptability**: European literature touts its adaptability to chalky (limestone, high pH) and maritime conditions. Uncommon in the United States but worth consideration where adapted. Zones 5 to 7. **Landscape use**: Beautiful contributor to parks, campuses, golf courses, and commercial landscapes. We noted noble behemoths in Newport, RI, and New Haven, CT, and superb specimens at the Morris Arboretum, Chestnut Hill, PA, and Spring Grove Cemetery, Cincinnati, OH. Based on the few trees authors recorded, well-drained, acid soil and full sun are sufficient. **Street tree use**: Potential. **In the trade**: Available. The uncommon 'Argenteovariegata' offers leaves with broad creamy white margins and a dark green center; a rounded tree, growing more slowly than the species. 'Wageningen' is a hybrid of *Q. cerris* with *Q. suber* (classified as *Q. ×hispanica*). Grown in Europe, it is evergreen near the Mediterranean and semi-evergreen farther north; cold hardy to zone 7. Rounded form; thick glossy leaves.

Quercus cerris

'Argenteovariegata'

Quercus cerris

726

Quercus coccinea

scarlet oak

Deciduous. One of the prettiest native species in the red oak group. Pyramidal in youth, becoming open with large upright-spreading branches, maturing 70′ high and 40 to 50′ wide. Grows over 100′ high in the wild; the National Champion is 128′ by 122′. Has the potential for 1½ to 2′ of growth over 10 to 20 years; in Kansas trials, growth rate averaged 13″ per year over a 10-year period. Bark is dark gray to brown, narrowly fissured into scaly ridges and narrow plates; bark does not stand out like that of mature *Q. rubra*. Sometimes confused with the latter, as well as *Q. palustris* and *Q. shumardii*. Authors often find themselves asking the question, "Is that scarlet oak?" Hint: three characteristics to assess. 1) Are the sinuses C-shaped? 2) Are the ovoid-globose buds covered by reddish brown hairs above the middle? 3) Is the acorn as wide as high, with concentric grooves/stippling at the nipple end? Have at it!

Foliage: Lustrous dark green when mature, lighter lustrous green below, variable in fall from scarlet to red-purple, one of the latest oaks to develop fall color before the snow flies; at its best provides the brightest fall color of the red oak group, but fall color is inconsistent from tree to tree. Each leaf ovate or oval, (5)7 to 9 lobes, sinuses C-shaped, 3 to 6″ long, 2½ to 4½″ wide. Leaves often persist into winter, seldom dropping cleanly. **Flowers/seeds/fruits/cones**: Monoecious. Catkins 2 to 3″ long, yellow-tinged. The acorn cap is unique, being turban-shaped, covering a third to half of the nut; acorns are ½ to 1″ high and wide, solitary or paired, 2 years to mature; nuts shiny brown, recognizable by concentric rings or stipules at apex. **Native range**: Found in every state east of Mississippi, except Florida, also Missouri and Arkansas; restricted to drier upland soils, often on ridges and mountaintops to 5,000′ elevation. On Rabun Bald, Georgia's second-highest mountain at 4,696′, it dominates at the summit, forming a krummholz thicket. Not as prevalent in the wild as, for example, *Q. alba*; authors note trees on sporadic basis but always in well-drained soils, often infertile, sandy, rocky. **Adaptability**: Zones 4 to 9.

Quercus coccinea

Quercus coccinea

Quercus coccinea

Q

Quercus coccinea

Quercus ellipsoidalis

Quercus ellipsoidalis

Landscape use: Mature trees are inspiring and deserving of ample real estate to fully exploit their genetic potential. Provide sandy, rocky, even clay-based soils as long as well drained with an acid reaction. Established trees are tenacious, displaying high heat and drought tolerances. Does not develop chlorosis to the degree of *Q. palustris*. Hybridizes with *Q. rubra* (*Q. ×benderi*) and other red oak species, so apply the characteristics enumerated herein to properly identify the trees. **Street tree use**: Suitable. **In the trade**: Sold as seed-grown. Fall color can be reliable from a good seed source.

Quercus ellipsoidalis
northern pin oak

Deciduous. In overall shape, it is reminiscent of a chubby *Q. palustris*. Authors walked among native stands in Minnesota and observed more irregular rounded habit and horizontal branching compared to pin oak; however, leaves, buds, and acorns are reminiscent of *Q. palustris*, so identification is not automatic. Young trees as described, are more open. Mature landscape size is in the 50 to 60′ height range, perhaps slightly less in width. Growth is fast, and young trees are densely branched and foliated.

Foliage: Silky tomentose when emerging, lustrous dark green later, variable russet-red to red fall color; obovate, 5 to 7 lobes, 2½ to 6″ long, 2 to 4½″ wide, leaves persisting into late fall, sinuses C-shaped like scarlet oak. **Flowers/seeds/fruits/cones**: Monoecious. Catkins 2 to 3″ long, yellowish. The acorn is ellipsoidal to subglobose; cap covers a third to half of the nut; ½ to ¾″ long; nut brownish with blackish striations; takes 2 years to mature. **Native range**: Limited; Canada, middle and western parts of Great Lakes region, Michigan, Wisconsin, Illinois, Indiana, Minnesota, with disjunct populations in Ohio, Missouri, and Arkansas. USDA describes the wild habitat as xeric (dry), growing on sandy plains, sandstone hills, and acid, sandy soils. This is counter to what authors noted in Minnesota. **Adaptability**: With a higher pH tolerance and a northern Midwestern–southern Canada range, this is a better fit than *Q. palustris* where chlorosis is an issue. Large trees at the Morton Arboretum and Chicago Botanic Garden attest to its adaptability to clay soils and high pH. Zones 4 to 6. **Landscape use**: An excellent candidate for use in high pH, limestone soils. Certainly a worthy species, but seldom known and grown beyond the native range. Recommended for parks, campuses, commercial landscapes, golf courses, and specimen use. **Street

MAJESTIC SKIES

Quercus falcata

tree use: Well suited, more pH tolerant than pin oak, with branches that are less drooping. **In the trade**: A good species from seed, with a couple of available cultivars. Bailey Nurseries, St. Paul, MN, was the first to domesticate the species with the introduction of MAJESTIC SKIES 'Bailskies', which is pyramidal when young, becoming broadly oval; summer foliage glossy green, fall color a good deep red to maroon, then leaves brown and hold on the tree, much like scarlet oak; 60′ tall and 45′ wide. 'Hemelrijk' has reliable deep red fall color.

Quercus falcata
southern red oak

Deciduous. Where few oaks can grab a toehold, where soil conditions are miserable, *Q. falcata* is an option, with the genes to achieve nobility. Young trees pyramidal; massive and broad rounded at maturity. Fast-growing to 70 to 80′ high and wide. Bark is dark brown to black with narrow fissures and flat ridges.

Foliage: Obovate to ovate, with a curved (falcate) midrib; leaf base rounded, different from most common red oak species; lustrous dark green above, russet-red in fall at best, never pure red; holding late; undersides covered with short grayish pubescence; 3- to 9-lobed, 5 to 9(12)″ long, 4 to 5″ wide; leaves slightly drooping in summer almost as if drought stressed. **Flowers/seeds/fruits/cones**: Monoecious. Yellow-green catkins. Acorns are subglobose, shallow cap covering a third to half of the ½″ long nut, alternating light and dark brown striations from base to apex; mature in 2 years. **Native range**: Long Island to Florida, west to Illinois, Missouri, Arkansas, Oklahoma, and Texas, in sandy, loamy or clay soils, alone or in mixed hardwood forests. In the Southeast, it is a common upland species, colonizing the drier, poorer, acid soils of the Piedmont; venerable specimens frequent open fields, woodland edges, and forests. **Adaptability**: Seedlings will sprout on barren soil in sun or shade. Zones (6)7 to 9. **Landscape use**: The tremendous soil adaptability, including clay, is a major asset. Certainly for use in restoration, wildlife habitats, impoverished soils, it has merit. Mature trees are impressive and worth preserving. Bartlett Tree Experts mentioned that root disturbance during construction can be lethal. Authors know this to be

Q

729

Quercus falcata

Quercus falcata

var. *pagodifolia*

true through their consulting experiences. Once planted or inherited, be gentle around the roots. **Street tree use**: Limited. **In the trade**: The inherent tenacity warrants the introduction of superior selections. Leaves alone are bewildering in their shapes, sizes, and the number of lobes. The 3-lobed types are fine-textured. Start with superior summer and fall foliage. The challenge has been issued.

var. *pagodifolia* (*Q. pagoda*; cherrybark oak). Inhabits better-drained bottomland and river sides, developing a long central bole and oval crown, reaching 80 to 100′. Trees may grow 30′ in 10 years. The lustrous dark green leaves are 5- to 7-lobed with a central midvein. Fall color is yellow-brown to russet. Leaves persist into winter. Magnificent 100′ trees grow in Georgia's Oconee River floodplain. Southeastern United States. Zones 7 to 9.

'QXMTF'. A *Q. falcata* × *Q. shumardii* hybrid with dense pyramidal habit, shiny foliage, and consistent orange fall color.

Quercus frainetto
Hungarian oak

Deciduous. Fair to characterize as a magnificent, immense tree with wide-spreading branches and thick canopy at maturity. Open-grown trees in English gardens are reminiscent of the great *Q. alba*. Size 60 to 80′ high and wide. Bark is gray-brown, lightly ridged and furrowed.

Foliage: Obovate, extremely dark and lustrous green, thickish, gray-green below, yellow-brown in autumn, 6 to 10 lobes, often deeply cut (one-half to three-fourths) toward the midvein, the leaf base with a pair of short auricles, 6 to 8″ long, 3 to 4½″ wide. **Flowers/seeds/fruits/cones**: Monoecious. Catkins greenish yellow, 1 to 3″ long. Acorns are ½ to 1¼″ long, 2 to 4 together, almost sessile, cap encloses half the brown nut; ripening the first year. **Native range**:

Quercus frainetto

Southern Italy, Balkans, Romania, Hungary. **Adaptability**: Its native range hints at its adaptability and tolerance of summer dry soils. European literature states it is adaptable to all soil types, including chalk (limestone). Relatively unknown in the United States but gaining popularity on the West Coast due to its adaptability to a Mediterranean climate. Zones 5 to 7. **Landscape use**: Foliage holds up well in the hot summer and low humidity of the West. Authors attest to its majesty in European gardens. **Street tree use**: Suitable, and increasingly put to this use in the West. **In the trade**: Available.

FOREST GREEN 'Schmidt'. Stronger growing and more upright than the species, with a dominant central leader and developing a pyramidal to moderately narrow oval form, ideal for street use. Foliage is glossy and an especially rich dark green, shows improved mildew resistance and is noted for drought resistance. Fall color yellow-amber, then defoliating cleanly. 60′ tall and 30′ wide.

'Trump'. Upright-growing, but short and stocky in the nursery, becoming a broader oval as it matures, dark green leaves, yellow-amber fall color. 60′ tall and 50′ wide.

Quercus garryana
Oregon white oak, Garry oak

Deciduous. A large and iconic white oak, the only oak native to the Pacific Northwest. Upright oval in form, it spreads to be rounded when grown in the open, or more vase-shaped when crowded. Slow-growing but long-lived, mature trees reach 75′ tall and 50′ or more wide. Bark is dark charcoal-gray, fissured and checked. Remaining stands are highly valued in areas of intense farming and development. The grandfather-sized trees that dot the older farmsteads of the Willamette Valley are often remnants from pioneer days. Natural reproduction seems poor as we rarely find new seedlings growing, even though acorn crops may be heavy. The historic fire cycle probably played a part in its reproduction.

Foliage: Leaves are very dark green, thick, leathery, and durable in the intense summer sun and low humidity of their native habitat. Leaves obovate with rounded lobes, sinuses usually cut about halfway to the midrib, 2 to 5″ long, half as wide. Fall color is yellow-brown at best. **Flowers/seeds/fruits/cones**: Monoecious. Catkins 1½ to 3½″ long, yellowish. The light brown acorn is ovoid, 1 to 1¼″ long, ¾″ wide, cup scaly and shallow, covering a third of the nut.

Q

FOREST GREEN

Quercus garryana

Quercus garryana

Quercus garryana

Native range: Very southern British Columbia to central California, with disjunct population in the foothills of the southern Sierras, growing in oak savannas, in stands in wet lowlands and on drier hillsides, both shallow-soiled and rocky. **Adaptability:** The tree is uniquely adapted to winter-saturated lowland soils with periodic standing water that alternate with clay-cracking summer drought; a second-favored habitat is droughty hillsides. Adapted to the Mediterranean climate of the U.S. West. Zones 6 to 9. **Landscape use:** Its native habitat indicates it would be a tough urban tree in poor-quality soils, and it is. Also planted for restoration. Don't expect a canopy cover until your children grow old. Once established, avoid root disturbance. **Street tree use:** Sometimes used, although form is quite variable; increasingly planted along roadsides. **In the trade:** Sold as seed-grown.

Quercus glauca
Japanese evergreen oak

Broadleaf evergreen. Habit is upright oval on young trees, with maturity rounded to broad-rounded. In fact, a giant mushroom-shaped specimen, 30′ by 40′, grew in Brookgreen Gardens, Murrells Inlet, SC; this is the largest authors observed. Growth is slow. Bark is smooth, gray, similar to American beech; sapsuckers may drill concentric rings of holes around the trunk, predisposing the tree to insects and disease.

Foliage: Thick, leathery, lustrous dark green leaves hold their color throughout the seasons. Though alternate, leaves are closely set at the end of the stem, appearing whorled; leaves are bronze to purple-green at emergence, obovate-oblong, entire toward base, strongly serrate in upper portion of margins, gray-green below, with 8 to 12 prominent vein pairs, 2½ to 5½″ long, 1 to 2½″ wide. **Flowers/seeds/fruits/cones:** Monoecious. Catkins yellow-green; acorns occur in 3s to singly, oval-oblong, brownish black, ¾″ long, the cap with 6 to 7 raised concentric rings covering a third of the nut; ripen in one year. **Native range:** Japan, Taiwan, China, Himalayas. **Adaptability:** Although less cold-hardy than *Q. myrsinifolia*, it is still a useful tree for the coastal Carolinas to Florida, Texas, California, to mild areas of the Pacific Northwest. Thirty some years ago, in severe cold (-3 to -9°F in the Athens-Atlanta areas), the species was killed to the ground; a notable specimen at the University of Georgia Botanical Garden resprouted, now with 11 trunks and 30′ high and wide. Zones 7 to 9. **Landscape use:** Certainly a beautiful and underutilized species in warmer, more

Quercus glauca

Quercus glauca

moderate climates. Makes an effective specimen, grouping, and screening element. The emerging foliage is quite colorful, contrasting explosively with the mature green leaves. Any well-drained soil supports good health. Full sun to moderate shade are ideal. Rare in cultivation, but worthy of the pursuit. Most often offered as a smaller container-grown plant. **Street tree use**: Doubtful and would provide a haven for roosting birds. **In the trade**: Sold as seedlings.

Quercus hemisphaerica

laurel oak

Semi-evergreen, tardily deciduous. Distinctly pyramidal in youth; oval-rounded at maturity, densely branched and foliated. Growth rate is fast; size 40 to 60′ high, 30 to 40′ wide. Trees are known to 100′ high and wide. Often considered less desirable than Q. *phellos*, but a well-grown tree has great presence. On the University of Georgia campus, over a 30-year period, trees reached 60′ high and 40′ wide. Certainly no shrinking violet. Bark is gray-brown, shallowly ridged and furrowed, surface rough-textured.

Foliage: Lanceolate, elliptic to oblanceolate, new growth soft lettuce-green, early leafing, maturing lustrous dark green, persisting into spring, dropping most as the new foliage emerges, shiny green on lower surface, margins with a bump, bulge, or with a few shallow lobes or teeth, especially on young trees; 1½ to 4″ long, ½ to 1¼″ wide. **Flowers/seeds/fruits/cones**: Monoecious. Catkins yellowish, 2″ long. The acorn is subglobose to ovoid, cup covering about a quarter of the sessile, ½″ long, brown nut. **Native range**: North Carolina to Florida, west to Arkansas and Texas. Found principally in dry sandy soils, dunes, sandhills, streambanks, and mixed woods. **Adaptability**: Zones 6 to 9.

Quercus hemisphaerica

Q

Quercus hemisphaerica

Quercus hemisphaerica

AVALYN

Landscape use: It has the ability to succeed on a range of soils with excellent growth return for minimum inputs. Useful for parks because of uniform habit, clean foliage, and rapid growth. **Street tree use**: Suitable and has served as such in the Piedmont and Coastal Plain of the Southeast; in Athens, GA, birds commandeered them for roosts because of the protective winter foliage retention. **In the trade**: The species' acceptability could be improved with superior clones. One such, AVALYN 'QHMTF', is broadly pyramidal, becoming more oval with age. Lustrous dark green foliage, nearly evergreen in the South with orangish color before defoliating; 50′ by 40′.

Quercus imbricaria

shingle oak

Deciduous. Pyramidal to upright oval in youth; haystack-shaped to broad-rounded at maturity, often with drooping lower branches—authors observed every habit permutation imaginable, except fastigiate. Reaches 50 to 60′ high, as wide or wider, on occasion over 100′ tall. Growth rate is moderate, but reasonable moisture and nutrition accelerate the process. Exceptionally fast growth rate at Milliken Arboretum, Spartanburg, SC, with a single tree reaching 30′ in 15 years. Bark is gray-brown, eventually with broad, low ridges separated by shallow furrows. The common name derives from the use of the wood for shingles.

Foliage: Oblong-ovate, lanceolate, reddish bronze when first unfurling, lustrous dark green, pubescent and pale green or slightly brownish below, then yellow-brown to russet-red hues in fall, dark brown and persisting in winter; entire margin revolute (curved under at edges), with a single bristle tip at apex, 2½ to 6″ long, 1 to 3″ wide, widest near or at middle. The bristle-tipped apex signifies this is a member of the red oak group. **Flowers/seeds/fruits/cones**: Monoecious. Yellow catkins. Acorns are subglobose, solitary, the thin bowl-shaped cup enclosing a third to half of the brown nut, ⅝″ long, nearly as wide, ripening the second year. **Native range**: Pennsylvania to Alabama, west to Iowa, Kansas, and Texas. Quite common in the Midwest, blanketing Illinois, Indiana, Ohio. Literature describes native habitat as rich soils along streams, rich hillsides, dry uplands, with intolerance toward shade. **Adaptability**: Under cultivation authors recorded massive trees in Cincinnati clay that in drought years contracts to form puzzle pieces. This empirical observation points to an adaptable species. Zones 4 to 8. **Landscape use**: Develops into an imposing specimen tree, as on the Vanderbilt University campus, Nashville. Obvious in the winter landscape: for gardeners, the interminable period for complete leaf abscission drives the perfectionist crazy; others love the windblown leaves and rustling music. Useful for boulevard, campus, and large areas. **Street tree use**: Suitable, but foliage persists. **In the trade**: Sold as seed-grown.

Quercus imbricaria

Quercus imbricaria

Quercus imbricaria

Q

Quercus lobata

Quercus lobata

valley oak

Deciduous. Handsome, massive, upright-spreading, quasi-weeping twisted branches form a rounded to broad-rounded crown. In youth the habit is pyramidal-oval, somewhat open and in no manner reflective of the mature greatness. Mature size 50 to 70′ high and wide; the literature describes trees 100 to 150′ high, with 8 to 10′ diameter trunks on deep, moist loam in some of the California valleys. Considered moderate to fast-growing; 2 to 3′ per year are reported. Bark is gray to gray-brown, distinctly blocky, similar to *Diospyros virginiana*. The acorns are an important food source for deer, California ground squirrel, and many birds.

Foliage: Oval to obovate, rounded or blunt at apex, tapered at base, 4 or 5 rounded lobes on each side, sinuses cut more than halfway to midrib, medium to dark green, dull beneath, the margin edged with fine hairs, 1½ to 3″ long, ⅝ to 1¾″ wide, in fall, muted yellow-gold, orange-bronze. **Flowers/seeds/fruits/cones**: The acorn slenderly conical, pointed, 1 to 2″ long, usually solitary, the cup covering a quarter of the shiny light brown nut. **Native range**: California endemic. Grows both in valleys and on slopes and savannas where climate is hot and dry. **Adaptability**: Like many

Quercus lobata

of the endemic, California-centric oaks, suited only to the Mediterranean climate (cold, moist winters; warm, dry summers). Zones 7 to 10. **Landscape use**: Noble oak for West Coast conditions, growing rapidly in rich, moist soil and full sun. Prized for urban and park plantings. **Street tree use**: Deserves consideration, but large trunk and broad spread demand space. **In the trade**: Sold as seed-grown.

Quercus lobata

Quercus lyrata
overcup oak

Deciduous. Scarcely known in commerce until the late 1990s, when nurseries discovered its many virtues including fast growth, relatively uniform habit from seed, ease of transplanting, adaptability, and pretty foliage, the latter, on occasion, allowing for confusion with Q. *alba*. In youth the habit is pyramidal-oval, oval-rounded, to rounded, to broadly so at maturity. The branches are upswept. Growth is fast. We estimate 40 to 60′ high, as wide or wider at landscape maturity, but trees have surpassed 100′ in the wild. Bark is gray to brownish gray, similar to Q. *alba*, perhaps not as scaly-flaky. Appropriate common name, as the acorn cap covers most of the chubby nut.

Foliage: Obovate-oblong, bronze-green when unfolding, maturing lustrous dark green, undersides green to gray (densely hairy), rich yellow-bronze to tannin-brown in fall, 6 to 8″ long, 1½ to 3(5)″ wide, with 3 to 5(9) pairs of obtuse lobes, the widest two directly opposite, forming right angles with the midvein. **Flowers/seeds/fruits/cones**: Monoecious. Catkins 4 to 6″ long, yellowish. Acorns are subglobose to rounded, cup covers three-fourths of the dark brown nut, ¾ to 1″ high and wide, mature in one year, often the nut is only visible through a small opening in the cup. **Native range**: New Jersey to Florida, following the rivers in Ohio, Indiana, Illinois, Missouri, to Oklahoma and Texas. Always in low wet soils, bottomlands, along streams. **Adaptability**: Native habitat notwithstanding, phenomenally heat and drought tolerant, once established. Mature, majestic trees on the University of Georgia and University of North Carolina campuses and Mt. Airy Arboretum, Cincinnati, OH, attest to longevity and adaptability. Zones 5 to 9. **Landscape use**: Fascinating species, an awesome work of biology and art that has broadened the palette of commercial oaks for streets, parking lots, and large-area use. Possibly no single feature has elevated its status, rather the sum of many

Quercus lyrata

Q

Quercus lyrata

Quercus lyrata

ENDURANCE

GREEN SPRING

HIGHBEAM

useful parts. It is one of the most drought-tolerant oaks, prospering without flinching on dry slopes and tree lawns. **Street tree use**: Superb. Limbing up for vehicular clearance is largely unnecessary. **In the trade**: Several nurseries and universities are developing superior clones.

Q. ×*comptoniae* (Compton oak). Hybrid, the result of a cross between Q. *lyrata* and another member of the white oak group, Q. *virginiana*, an evergreen species. Trees are intermediate with semi-evergreen foliage.

ENDURANCE

MARQUEE

MARQUEE

HIGHBEAM 'QLFTB'. Superior rootability from cuttings. Uniform habit with upswept branches, yellow-orange-red fall color. Fast-growing and approaches the species in size. Plantings in Oklahoma City had 7½″ trunk diameter in 2010; 4 years later 12″ wide. In downtown Raleigh, NC, 5″ wide in 2007; 12½″ 8 years later. 55′ tall, 45′ wide.

MARQUEE 'Hopeulikit'. Leaves more lustrous dark green than typical overcup seedlings and occasionally develops reasonable red to red-purple fall color; tree develops an upswept pyramidal habit that makes it suitable for street tree use, 55′ by 45′.

RESILIENCE 'QLRS10'. Oval-rounded habit, lustrous dark green leathery leaves, yellow and burnt-orange fall color, uniform leaf drop, gray-brown winter branches and trunk are scaly-textured, very tolerant of heavy low-oxygen wet urban soils, but adaptable to dryer conditions; 50′ by 40′.

STREAMLINE 'QLR552'. More oval-upright in outline than RESILIENCE; orange-burgundy fall color; clean and uniform leaf drop; 50′ by 30′.

Q. ×tottentii. Hybrid (Q. lyrata × Q. michauxii). Vigorous, broad pyramidal, fast-growing.

ENDURANCE 'QCE295'. First clonal Compton oak available on its own roots; pyramidal in youth, more open and wide-spreading at maturity; glossy dark green summer foliage; no fall color of consequence with approximately 20% foliage retention through winter; promises to have a great future as an urban tree; 60′ by 40′.

GREEN SPRING 'Dahlonega'. Leafs out several weeks earlier than most overcup oaks and develops orange-red fall color; pyramidal habit when young, wider at maturity, 50′ by 45′.

RESILIENCE

STREAMLINE

STREAMLINE

Quercus macrocarpa
bur oak, mossy-cup oak

Deciduous. Another noble member of the oak family. Time is its greatest ally: as a young plant it is stiff, coarse, open, and a tad scraggly; at maturity, rounded to broad-rounded with bold rough/coarse-textured secondary branches. No shrinking violet, for trees range from 70 to 80′ high, potentially wider. National Champion measured 90′ by 130′. Growth is slow. Bark is dark gray to gray-brown, extremely rough-textured, deeply ridged and furrowed, young branches develop corky extensions and protuberances. We have always admired the phrase "an open-grown tree of the prairie," which perfectly describes the isolated trees of the Midwest, growing on sacred islands in soybean and corn fields, spared the fate of the John Deere by appreciative landowners.

Foliage: Obovate to oblong-obovate, bass-fiddle-shaped, lustrous dark green above, grayish beneath, with yellow-brown fall color; 7 to 10 pairs of lobes, the terminal lobe consisting of half the leaf; quite variable, the middle deeply cut almost to midrib, 4 to 10(12)″ long, half as wide. **Flowers/seeds/fruits/cones:** Monoecious. Catkins 2 to 3″ long, yellowish green. Acorns are broad-ovoid, the largest of the eastern

Quercus macrocarpa

Quercus macrocarpa

North American species, the cap covering half or more of the brown nut, the margin conspicuously fringed, ¾ to 1½(2)″ long; acorn size and degree of fringing are greatly variable over the native range. **Native range**: Sizable; Nova Scotia to Pennsylvania, Alabama, west to Wyoming and southeast Montana to Texas. Found in bottomlands, dry slopes, and uplands, especially in limestone soils. **Adaptability**: One of the best choices for high pH (limestone) soils. Zones 3 to 8. **Landscape use**: Principal uses are for specimen and shade, where space is adequate. Has a reputation for being somewhat difficult to transplant and may require a few years to establish. **Street tree use**: Acorn size is a concern, some like golf balls, but URBAN PINNACLE is appropriate because of form and small acorns. **In the trade**: Available but has yet to approach *Q. lyrata* and *Q. bicolor* as a commercial force. Hybrids with the latter and *Q. alba* show promise.

COBBLESTONE 'JFS-KW14'. A big bold traditional bur oak form, celebrating its coarse texture and deeply furrowed, corky bark. Selected for the most impressive bark at a young age, along with clean, deep green foliage that resists mildew and anthracnose. Broadly oval in form becoming more rounded, to 70′ tall and 60′ wide.

Q

Quercus macrocarpa

URBAN PINNACLE

COBBLESTONE

URBAN PINNACLE

JORDAN STREET 'Atwood'. Impressive toughness. Introduced as a hybrid with Q. *alba*, but leaf resembles a true bur, which we think it is. Broadly pyramidal when young, then upright-spreading, developing a very broadly oval form with a rounded crown. Original tree 90′ tall, 75′ wide.

URBAN PINNACLE 'JFS-KW3'. Selected as a street-tree-appropriate bur oak with manners for big city life. Very upright and narrower than the species, it maintains a pyramidal growth habit. The acorns are very small, about ½″, and not threatening when they fall. Foliage is especially clean, dark green, glossy, and resists mildew and anthracnose. 65′ tall, 35′ wide.

Quercus michauxii

swamp chestnut oak

Deciduous. Another majestic member of the white oak community, distinctly pyramidal-oval in youth, broadening with age, forming a massive trunk and secondary branches. We estimate 60 to 70′ high and wide at maturity. Trees in the wild were documented at 140′ in height. At Milliken Arboretum, Spartanburg, SC, this grew the second-fastest out

of 15 oak species over a 25-year period and 40% faster than Q. *montana*, with which it is often confused. Bark on small diameter trunks is exceedingly scaly, platy, exfoliating; eventually gray to gray-brown, variably (lightly) fissured with scaly ridges. Acorns are consumed by mammals and birds, including deer, turkey, squirrels, and woodpeckers. They are also eaten by cows.

Foliage: Obovate, widest above the middle, light green upon emergence, lustrous dark green, lower surface grayish

Quercus michauxii

Quercus michauxii

Q

Quercus michauxii

pubescent, then yellow-bronze to russet-red in autumn, late to color, with brown leaves often persisting into winter; 9 to 14 deeply impressed parallel veins extend from the midrib to margin, ending in large rounded teeth, 4 to 8(11)″ long, about half as wide, leathery textured. **Flowers/seeds/fruits/cones**: Monoecious. Catkins 2 to 4″ long, yellow. Acorns are ovoid, the sessile to short-stalked cap enclosing a third to half of the dark brown nut, 1 to 1½″ long, sweet-tasting, ripening the first year. **Native range**: New Jersey to Florida, west to Indiana, Illinois, Missouri, Oklahoma, and Texas. Always in moist areas, river bottoms, swamp edges, and ravines. **Adaptability**: Observational data suggest excellent adaptability to many soil conditions, preferably acid. A denizen of moist to periodically wet habitats and therefore an excellent option for wet soil areas; authors observed mammoth trees in Alabama and South Carolina prospering in association with other species ecologically adapted to wet soils, including *Magnolia grandiflora*, *M. virginiana*, and *Viburnum nudum*. In South Carolina's Congaree National Park, trees 100′ high, with 3 to 4′ diameter trunks, grow in the floodplain, often inundated as many as 10 times per year. The authors were able to touch these marvelous specimens and bow in humble admiration. Yet the species also performs

well in better-drained soils and tolerates dry conditions. Young (15-year-old) trees on the Georgia campus sited on a 45° dry slope reached 20 to 30′ in height, were pyramidal in habit, densely branched and foliaged. The species is more cold hardy than the native range reflects, with a 40′ high specimen in the Morton Arboretum. Zones 5 to 9. **Landscape use**: Beautiful foliage, habit, and bark should foster greater landscape use. Once seen, difficult not to admire for its stature and majesty. We suggest *Q. michauxii* for use in wetland restoration situations, as shade and specimen trees. **Street tree use**: Suitable. **In the trade**: Sold as seed-grown. This is another species that is ripe for clonal selections.

Quercus montana (*Q. prinus*)

chestnut oak, basket oak

Deciduous. Pyramidal, oval to rounded in youth; rounded with upright-spreading branches at maturity. Growth is relatively fast, 12 to 15′ over 7 to 10 years. Bark is gray-brown to gray-black, somewhat cork-like in texture, irregularly and deeply ridged and furrowed on mature trees. Acorns are an important food source for wildlife from the gray squirrel to the black bear.

Quercus montana

Foliage: Obovate to oblong-obovate, lustrous dark yellowish green in summer, midrib pronounced yellow, lower surface green to grayish, orange-yellow to yellow-brown in fall, russet-red fall color on occasion, 10 to 14 pairs of parallel veins running from midrib to margin ending in obtusish, often mucronate teeth, 4 to 6(12)″ long, 1½ to 4″ wide,

Quercus montana

Quercus montana

similar to the foliage of *Q. michauxii*. **Flowers/seeds/fruits/cones:** Monoecious. Catkins 2 to 4″ long, yellowish. Acorns are ovoid, cup enclosing a third to half of the rich dark brown nut, 1 to 1¼″ long, ¾″ wide. **Native range:** Maine to Ontario to Georgia, Alabama, Mississippi, Louisiana, growing on poor, dry, rocky, upland soils, always well drained, in association with scarlet and black oaks. Common in the southern Appalachians to 5,000′, abundant along the Blue Ridge Parkway in North Carolina and Virginia, poking its leafy branches from the sides of the mountains. **Adaptability:** Zones 4 to 8. **Landscape use:** Somewhat difficult to portray this species as anything but a wonderful native for restoration and large-area use, especially in dry, rocky, sandy soils. Witnessing the species clinging to mountainside boulders affirms its tenacity. Easy to transplant. Auburn University's 13-year trial of shade trees showed it to be a superior species. **Street tree use:** Potential. **In the trade:** Uncommon, seed-grown.

Quercus muehlenbergii
chinquapin oak

Deciduous. Another majestic species, and, per usual, the authors query why it is not more common. Pyramidal to oval when young, rounded to broad-rounded at maturity. We estimate 40 to 50′ high and wide under landscape conditions; however, the largest trees observed were consistently 60 to 70′ high and wider. Bark is ash-gray, gray-brown, scaly and flaky, ridged and furrowed, becoming somewhat blocky on large trunks.

Quercus muehlenbergii

Q

745

Foliage: Oblong, oblong-lanceolate, oblong-ovate, soft green when unfolding, lustrous dark green, then yellow to orangish brown in fall; 8 to 13 pairs of parallel veins, ending in acute, often incurved marginal teeth, 4 to 7″ long, a third to half as wide, midrib and petioles yellow (distinct feature). **Flowers/seeds/fruits/cones**: Monoecious. Catkins 2 to 3″ long, yellowish. Acorns are globose-ovoid to ovoid, cap encasing half the brown nut, ¾ to 1″ long, ripening the first year. **Native range**: Ontario, Maine, Vermont to Virginia, west to Minnesota, Nebraska, Texas, and Mexico. Found on dry, sandy, rocky, clay soils of wooded slopes, most frequent in limestone areas and high pH soils. **Adaptability**: Its extensive range reflects climatic and soil adaptability.

Tremendously well-adapted to limestone (high pH) soils, where it reaches maximum genetic potential and in which authors have witnessed magnificent specimens. Great trees occur in the Midwest. Beautiful specimens in Spring Grove and Cave Hill cemeteries, Cincinnati and Louisville, respectively, with trunks 3′ in diameter. Zones (4)5 to 7(8). **Landscape use**: An unheralded and for many unidentifiable oak, confused with *Q. montana* and *Q. michauxii*. Leaf diseases, especially anthracnose, cause problems in humid nursery production, but open-grown trees with air circulation are usually clean. For specimen and large-area use, it is meritorious. In Georgia trials, it maintained pristine green foliage into October. **Street tree use**: Potential. **In the trade**: Sold as seed-grown. Worth the effort to locate, purchase, plant, and nurture to its fullest genetic potential.

Quercus myrsinifolia
Chinese evergreen oak

Broadleaf evergreen. Develops into a densely branched and foliaged, oval-rounded tree, typically 20 to 30′ high. Authors recorded specimens to 50′ high in Savannah, GA, and Washington, DC. Growth is slow. Bark is smooth even on large trunks, gray, beech-like. Sapsuckers drill concentric circles of holes around the trunk, predisposing the tree to insects and disease.

Foliage: Ovate to elliptic, emerging foliage stunning bronze-purple, maturing medium green to olive-green, glaucous green beneath, often becoming sickly yellow-green in winter, especially in open, sunny, windswept areas; 10 to 16 vein pairs, each leaf 2½ to 4″ long, ¾ to 1½″ wide, serrated from near base to apex; foliage emerges later than *Q. glauca*, thus avoiding spring freezes/frosts. **Flowers/seeds/fruits/cones**: Monoecious. Catkins 1 to 2″ long, yellow-green. Acorns are oval-oblong, cap covering a third to half of the brownish black nut, 2 to 4 together, ½ to 1″ long, cap with 3

Quercus muehlenbergii

Quercus muehlenbergii

Quercus myrsinifolia

Quercus myrsinifolia

to 6 (7 to 9) concentric rings. **Native range**: Eastern Asia, Japan, Taiwan through China and the Himalayas. **Adaptability**: The most cold hardy of the Asian evergreen oaks: when -3°F killed the others (*Q. acuta*, *Q. glauca*, *Q. salicina*) to the ground, *Q. myrsinifolia* was unscathed. Zones (6)7 to 9. **Landscape use**: At its best a pretty evergreen tree, reserved for warmer climates, where it has been utilized for lawn and park plantings. In fact, mature 40′ trees pop up in Savannah in residential areas; the question arises, who was growing them 40 to 50 years past? Species tolerates sand- and clay-based soils as long as well drained in full sun to partial shade. Transplanting larger balled-and-burlapped material has been difficult, so container-grown trees are preferable. **Street tree use**: Suitable and used as such. **In the trade**: Sold as seed-grown.

Quercus nigra
water oak

Tardily deciduous. Irregular conical-pyramidal in youth; rounded, densely branched at maturity. Branches develop numerous short shoots, creating a prickly, pseudo-spiny condition that makes pruning and limb removal a combative exercise. The wood is extremely hard, and the sharpened chainsaw has to fight its way through large branches/trunks. Fast-growing and tenacious to a fault, and although criticized as a short-lived tree, giant specimens abound. Expect 50 to 80′ high and wide at maturity with a percentage of branches dying, breaking, and littering. Bark is gray-brown, lightly fissured, nothing to inspire. In the Southeast, the species has weed-like proclivities, showing up like an uninvited, unwanted houseguest, seeding into flower beds, fencerows, vegetable gardens, and waste areas.

Q

Quercus myrsinifolia

Quercus nigra

Quercus nigra

Quercus nigra

Foliage: Variable, lobed in the seedling stage, obovate to spatulate, entire to 3-lobed at apex at maturity, bronze-green when emerging, lustrous dark green, then holding late (December) with hints of yellow-green, 1½ to 4″ long, ½ to 2″ wide. **Flowers/seeds/fruits/cones**: Monoecious. Catkins 2 to 3″ long, yellowish. Acorns are subglobose, the cap covering a quarter to a third of the nut, alternating vertical striations of brown and black, ½″ long and wide, produced in raindrop quantities, carpeting the ground like marbles in fall. **Native range**: Found in bottomlands to upland soils from New Jersey to Florida, west to southeast Missouri and eastern Oklahoma. **Adaptability**: Adaptable to poorly drained soils, but common in drier upland situations. Zones 6 to 9. **Landscape use**: Serves as a quick fix on worn-out, impoverished soils. Quite agonizing for the authors to recommend the species for urban and suburban landscapes. The best description authors noted in literature referenced it as a rapidly growing tree, frequently planted (by nature) for shade, but of low quality because of the susceptibility of older trees to rot. **Street tree use**: Usable. It's everywhere along streets in the Southeast, but there are better choices. **In the trade**: Seldom offered, for the reasons enumerated.

Quercus nuttallii (Q. *texana*)
Nuttall oak

Nomenclatural note: Q. *texana* is the correct name, and no doubt this recent change will be gradually accepted; however, we continue to list under Q. *nuttallii*, the name that is universally used in the industry.

Deciduous. A beautiful tree, pyramidal in youth, oval-rounded in middle age, more open at maturity. Size 40 to 60′ high and wide. Growth is fast. Bark is gray-brown, lightly ridged and furrowed, with age dark and with scaly ridges.

Foliage: Obovate, maturing lustrous dark green; yellow-orange and red in fall; 5- to 9-lobed, sinuses rounded, lobes narrow, 4 to 9″ long, 2 to 5″ wide. Some trees develop reddish to ruby-red-purple new growth; most do not: in Oregon, authors recorded a lone colored seedling in a population of 6,000. The cooler the spring weather, the

Quercus nuttallii

Quercus nuttallii

Quercus nuttallii

Quercus nuttallii

Has gained popularity for campuses, commercial grounds, and residences. No species is perfect, and bacterial leaf scorch (pathogen: *Xylella fastidiosa*) has raised its ugly head on occasion; this is most insidious during extended hot, dry weather. **Street tree use**: Yes, commonly utilized for the purpose. **In the trade**: Once growers tested seedlings, it became obvious there was a future in clonal selection. The development of own-root (cutting) propagation propelled cultivar selection and the perpetuation of uniform traits. Those described herein are possibly the tip of the introduction iceberg. In particular, we speculate the possibility of a leaf type that develops red-purple spring growth and maintains the color throughout the growing season.

ARCADE 'QNSTG'. Upright branching habit, consistent red foliage with each flush, yellow-orange to orange-red fall color, to 60′ tall, 40′ wide

BIG BOY 'QNJB'. Pyramidal habit in youth, new growth pure green, intense red fall color, 50′ by 50′, named for Glenn "Big Boy" Simmons of Natchez, MS.

BREEZEWAY 'Ochlocknee'. Upright pyramidal habit with upswept branches, foliage is lustrous dark green; fall color is subdued yellow, burnt-orange to dark red; 60′ by 40′.

CHARISMA 'MonPowe'. Chocolate-colored new growth, maturing to green. 60′ tall.

ESPLANADE 'QNSTC'. Fast-growing with slight upright habit, upswept branching, pleasing pyramidal-oval habit in youth, dense canopy, and the best red fall color of the Nuttall cultivars. 60′ tall and 40′ wide.

HIGHPOINT 'QNFTA'. Dense habit, consistent yellow-orange-red fall color, and ease of cutting propagation. Extremely fast growth in Chapel Hill, NC, Athens, GA, Nashville and Chattanooga, TN, with caliper diameter doubling and tripling in 7 to 12 years; 50′ tall, 40′ wide.

more prolonged the reds and purples, if present. **Flowers/seeds/fruits/cones**: Monoecious. Catkins 2 to 3″ long, yellowish. Acorns are ovoid-oblong, cap covers a third to half of the brown nut, ¾ to 1¼″ long, with brownish vertical striations; cap is hemispherical. **Native range**: Western Alabama to east Texas and Oklahoma, north to southeastern Missouri and southern Illinois. Common in floodplains, bottomlands, and river terraces. **Adaptability**: Zones 6 to 9. **Landscape use**: The species wallowed in obscurity until nurseries realized its aesthetic merits and ease of culture/transplanting; advantages over *Q. shumardii*, according to producers in the South, include faster growth, quickness to caliper, maintenance of a central leader, pH adaptability (wider range), tolerance of wet soils, ease of early summer digging, and development of a fuller head at an early age.

BIG BOY

BREEZEWAY

HIGHPOINT

BREEZEWAY

RUBY SPRING

SANGRIA

ICON

ICON 'QNI374'. Pyramidal in youth; oval-rounded in maturity; uniform-dense branching structure; lustrous dark green foliage; yellow fall color; 50′ by 40′.

'New Madrid'. A northern-hardy selection with deep purple spring foliage, glossy green in summer, bright crimson in late fall, to 50′ tall, 40′ wide.

RUBY SPRING 'Betterred'. Red-purple new growth, dark glossy green at maturity, summer growth flushes are red, yellow-bronze-gold fall color, 50′ by 50′, authors consider this selection of the species a breakthrough.

SANGRIA 'QNSTD'. Dense canopy, rounded habit, deep red new growth, dark green summer foliage, yellow-orange to orange-red fall color, to 60′ tall and 40′ wide.

SOLSHINE 'QNSR'. A strong grower with lustrous dark green leaves, yellow-orange fall color, 50′ by 50′.

TYTLEST 'QNMTF'. Red new growth, maturing to lustrous dark green, to 50′ tall, 40′ wide.

RUBY SPRING

TYTLEST

SANGRIA

Quercus palustris
pin oak

Deciduous. Formerly the dominant landscape oak species in the East, Midwest, and Upper South because of uniform pyramidal habit and ease of transplanting. The upper branches ascend, middle spread, and lower descend, creating the most recognized branching pattern among oaks. With maturation, trees develop large spreading branches, scarcely reflective of the midlife outline; in fact, this and *Q. coccinea* are easy to misidentify in the geriatric stage of life. Growth is fast, with 60 to 70′ high, 25 to 40′ wide a reasonable landscape estimate. Authors noted trees 80′ high and greater. Bark is gray-brown, smooth, shiny, green when young, eventually with shallow furrows and flat ridges; only larger trees with wide furrows.

Foliage: Elliptic or elliptic-oblong, obovate, emerging green, maturing lustrous dark green, glossy green below with brown tufts of hairs in the vein axils, coloring russet-red

Quercus palustris

Quercus palustris

Quercus palustris

Quercus palustris

Q

'Crownright'

GREEN PILLAR

EPIC

GREEN PILLAR

to red in fall, persisting into and through winter on young trees, this trait diminishing as trees mature; 5- to 7-lobed (most often 5); 3 to 6″ long, 2 to 4″ wide. **Flowers/seeds/fruits/cones**: Monoecious. Long yellow catkins. Acorns are solitary or clustered, nearly hemispherical, cap covers a quarter to a third of the striated brown nut, ½″ high, ½ to ⅗″ wide, mature second year. **Native range**: Massachusetts to Delaware, into Wisconsin and Arkansas. Found in soils subject to flooding and poorly drained upland soils. **Adaptability**: Large, mature trees on the University of Georgia campus, far removed from the native range, attest to its heat and drought tolerances. Tolerance of moist, wet soils is another plus. Zones 4 to 8. **Landscape use**: The species has stood the test of time and is still commonly planted. Its unique cookie-cutter habit is especially evident in young trees. Major park, campus, and shade tree. Soils must be acid, for chlorosis (yellowing) is an issue; in high pH environments, trees may become Big Bird yellow with time. The species has lost landscape traction due to the increased production of *Q. alba*, *Q. bicolor*, *Q. macrocarpa*, *Q. robur* 'Fastigiata', and their hybrids: white oak group cultivars are more reliable when grafted than the red oak group. **Street tree use**: Used, but downsweeping branches and pH sensitivity make it second choice to other oaks. **In the trade**: Mostly sold as seed-grown, which we prefer.

'Crownright'. More upright habit, the secondary branches at a 30 to 60° angle to the central leader, to 60′ tall, 35′ wide. Suffered incompatibility in the landscape.

EPIC 'QREP20'. Distinctly upright oval, dense branching, relatively fast growth rate, clean leaf drop in fall, consistent red-burgundy fall color; considered a hybrid by the introducer, Select Trees, Athens, GA; selected for rootability; 60′ by 30′.

GREEN PILLAR 'Pringreen'. Very narrow, with a fastigiate growth habit and a columnar form. Glossy green leaves turn rusty orange to deep red fall. Eventually 50′ tall, 15′ wide.

PACIFIC BRILLIANCE 'PWJR08'. Fast-growing, with a strong central leader and excellent pyramidal form. Very glossy dark green leaves, truncated leaf base, and upright branch angles indicate this is probably a hybrid with *Q. coccinea*. Very handsome red fall color. 60′ tall, 35′ wide.

PROMENADE 'QS20'. Upright dense branching pattern, considerably more upright habit than seedling-grown trees, consistent yellow-orange fall color. 60 to 70′ by 25 to 30′.

'Sovereign'. The lower branches do not sweep the ground and are positioned at 90 to 45° angles to central leader. 60′ tall, 35′ wide.

STREETWISE 'QRSW18'. Distinctly oval-rounded in outline, dense canopy, clean leaf drop in fall; consistent red-burgundy fall color; considered a hybrid by the introducer, Select Trees, Athens, GA; selected for rootability; 60′ by 40′.

Q

GREEN PILLAR

PACIFIC BRILLIANCE

PROMENADE

STREETWISE

'Sovereign'

Quercus phellos

willow oak

Deciduous. Pyramidal in youth; oval-rounded to broad rounded and massive with maturity. Assume 40 to 60′ high, 30 to 40′ wide or wider at maturity. Trees over 100′ high and wide are known. Plan for 2′ of linear growth per year over a 10- to 20-year period. Bark is gray-brown, lightly ridged and furrowed; on old trunks fluted with a rough, pebbly surface. Just as *Q. palustris* and *Q. rubra* of the red oak group dominate northern landscapes, this dominates the Southeast, valued for its fine texture, ease of transplanting, and full canopy, even in youth.

Foliage: Narrow, elliptical or lance-shaped, willow-like (hence the common name), bright green in spring, dark green in summer, yellow, bronze-yellow to bronze-orange in fall, 2 to 5½″ long, ½ to 1″ wide, green on the lower surface; leaves emerge as early as mid-March in zone 8. **Flowers/seeds/fruits/cones**: Monoecious. Catkins 2 to 3″ long, yellowish. Acorns are solitary or paired, subglobose, cap covering a quarter (rarely half) of the pubescent, striated brown/black, ½″ high and wide nut, matures in second year. **Native range**: New York to Florida, west to Missouri and Texas. Common in bottomlands, floodplains and adjacent slopes, and rich uplands to 3,300′ elevation. **Adaptability**: Based on the great performance in miserable environments, the species can survive almost anywhere. Zones 6 to 9. **Landscape use**: A great, aesthetic, functional, and time-tested oak that is possibly overplanted in the Southeast, but, to date, has weathered the host of insects and diseases that negatively impact the genus. Urban areas, campuses, parks can always entertain a willow oak. Ease of transplanting adds to its usefulness. Soils should be well-drained, moist, and acid. **Street tree use**: Appropriate and recommended, but give it room to spread with age. Especially along streets, willow oaks are too often planted on close spacings. Authors recommend 30′ distance, for in 15 years branches will be touching. **In the trade**: Much like Q. *nuttallii*, cultivars were selected for improved habit, summer foliage, and fall color.

Quercus phellos

Quercus phellos

Quercus phellos

Q

Quercus phellos

Quercus phellos

ASCENDOR

ABUNDANCE 'QPAB64'. Dense form with fine texture, naturally developed central leader, uniform distribution of secondary branches; dark green foliage, yellow fall color; 60′ by 40′.

ASCENDOR 'QPSTJ'. Dense canopy, dominant central leader with upswept branches, yellow fall color, relatively fast growth rate. Leaves are narrower than the typical species. 50′ tall, 25 to 30′ wide.

KINGPIN

WYNSTAR

WYNSTAR

HIGHTOWER

FORTITUDE 'QPFT06'. Dense form with fine texture, naturally developed central leader, uniform distribution of secondary branches; dark green foliage, yellow fall color; 60' by 40'.

HIGHTOWER 'QPSTA'. Lustrous dark green foliage, mite resistance, pyramidal habit, central leader, and fast growth have proven outstanding. Trunk diameter doubled in 6 years in street plantings in Chattanooga, TN. Mature size, 55' by 35'.

KINGPIN 'Greenenvy'. Pyramidal when young, upright oval with age, foliage lustrous dark green (proclaimed darker green than any other willow oak), with yellow fall color, estimated to 60' by 45'.

SHIRAZ 'QPSTB'. A dominant central leader, dense canopy, consistent deep red fall color, to 60' by 40'.

UPPERTON 'RT3'. Upright pyramidal with dense branching, dark green foliage, longer leaves than the species, 60' by 35'.

WYNSTAR 'QPMTF'. Uniform habit, dense green leaves, russet-orange fall color, improved spider mite resistance, 60' by 50'.

Q

Quercus prinus. See Q. montana

Quercus robur
English oak

Deciduous. The grand old patriarch of the English countryside, pyramidal to rounded in youth, broad-rounded at maturity, with ancient, creaky secondary branches and a short trunk. In the United States, 40 to 60′ high, and wider, is a reasonable estimate of size at landscape maturity. Large trees occur from coast to coast, with the National Champion 93′ by 89′ in Ada, ID. Growth is slow; a Kansas study recorded 1′4″ per year over a 10-year period. Bark on old trees is "ruggedly handsome," gray-black to black, deeply ridged and furrowed, the ridged, blocky texture like an alligator's hide; authors observed many permutations. A Kew Gardens report calls the species the "unrivaled king of the forest in Britain[,] synonymous with strength, size, and longevity." There (and in continental Europe) it is revered for home building and historically was utilized in ship building.

Foliage: Obovate to obovate-oblong, light green upon emergence, then dark, almost blue-green, lower gray-green, and green to yellow-brown in autumn; 3 to 7 smallish rounded lobes, the leaf base earlobe-shaped (auriculate), 2 to 5″ long, ¾ to 2½″ wide, leaf of thickish, firm texture. Leaves persist late into fall. **Flowers/seeds/fruits/cones**: Monoecious. Catkins 2 to 3″ long, yellowish. Acorns are narrow elongated-conical (bullet-shaped), cap encloses a third to half of the shiny brown nut, 1″ long, one or several on a slender, pendulous, 2 to 5″ long peduncle, mature the first year. **Native range**: Western two-thirds of Turkey, North Africa, the Caucasus, and Europe. **Adaptability**: It is pH tolerant, with an adaptability to both acid and alkaline soil conditions that is unusual among oaks. Performs magnificently on limestone soils. Authors observed many Fastigiata Group types in the low rainfall, high pH soils of Utah and specifically Salt Lake City. Zones 4 to 8. **Landscape use**: The species has been long cultivated in the United States, yet is nowhere common, except as represented by the Fastigiata Group. Splendid tree in its finest embodiment, but not as suitable as the native U.S. species for general use. Foliage is susceptible to powdery mildew and leafspot(s), which disfigure the trees. The many upright-columnar hybrids are useful where lateral space is limited. **Street tree use**: Yes. The narrow columnar hybrids are especially appropriate. **In the trade**: In Europe, through the centuries, numerous Q. robur selections with weeping and columnar habits and variegated, narrow, unlobed, cutleaf, and crinkled leaves were introduced. Most are being replaced with better-performing hybrids. Wind pollination can make for interesting mixes! We group these Q. robur hybrids here for convenience. Hybrids with Q. alba are Q. ×bimundorum. Hybrids with Q. macrocarpa are Q. ×macdanielii. Hybrids of Q. robur f. fastigiata and Q. bicolor are Q. ×warei.

Quercus robur

Quercus robur

Quercus robur

'Chimney Fire'

CRIMSON SPIRE 'Crimschmidt'. Narrow columnar form, fastigiate and good density. Foliage green, with a slight bluish tint. Good powdery mildew resistance. Strong growth. Hardy and reliable in the tough climate of the Plains and Mountain States. Very popular. Red fall color, then holds brown leaves into winter. *Q. ×bimundorum*. 45′ tall, 15′ wide.

'Fastigiata'. Usually listed as a cultivar, but more properly forma *fastigiata* or Fastigiata Group. A lofty tree, found throughout the United States. Comes partially true from seed, so many different trees, both seed-grown and selected grafted plants, have been sold under this name. Columnar form when young but usually opening up with time. The mature form is a mixed bag at best; you are better off with one of the named columnar cultivars with a known growth habit. 45′ tall, 20 to 25′ wide.

FOREST KNIGHT 'Tabor'. Broadly oval, full form, with a sturdy upsweeping branch structure. Dark green, glossy foliage shows good mildew resistance. Yellow-orange fall color with hints of red. *Q. ×bimundorum*. 50′ tall, 40′ wide.

'Birthday Candle'. Narrow columnar form, fastigiate and tight, with dark green foliage, reddish fall color. *Q. ×warei*. 45′ by 18′.

'Chimney Fire'. Narrow columnar form, fastigiate growth habit. In spring, the attractive new growth is tinted red; leaves can turn a good red in fall. *Q. ×warei*, but in looking at the leaf shape and fall color, we suspect *Q. alba* is part of the parentage. 50′ by 18′.

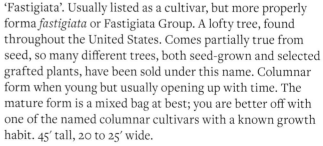

CRIMSON SPIRE

'Fastigiata'

CRIMSON SPIRE

FOREST KNIGHT

FOREST KNIGHT

HERITAGE

HERITAGE

HERITAGE 'Clemons'. Broadly pyramidal form with good symmetry and a rounded top. A nice street tree form. Very attractive clean, dark green, glossy foliage. We have seen a little mildew, but never serious; seems to have moderate resistance. Golden yellow fall color. *Q. macrocarpa* parent gives it cold hardiness, zone 4. *Q. ×macdanielii*. 50′ tall, 40′ wide.

KINDRED SPIRIT 'Nadler'. Narrow columnar form, fastigiate and dense. Good mildew resistance. A sister seedling of REGAL PRINCE, its foliage is less glossy but is a good dark green, has a slightly tighter growth habit, and grows a bit more slowly, staying smaller and narrower. Yellowish fall color. *Q. ×warei*. 40′ tall, 10′ wide.

'Koster'. Narrow fastigiate form. An older selection that has been popular in Europe. In our Oregon trials, it was superior to seedling 'Fastigiata', but its form was slightly loose and opened up more than we expected. 45′ tall, 20′ wide.

PRAIRIE STATURE 'Midwest'. A broadly pyramidal form, becoming more rounded with age. Strong structure. Leaf shape similar to white oak. Yellow-orange to red fall color, then holds brown leaves into winter. Good mildew resistance. *Q. alba* parent gives it additional cold hardiness, to zone 3. *Q. ×bimundorum*. 50′ tall, 45′ wide.

Q

KINDRED SPIRIT

REGAL PRINCE

PRAIRIE STATURE

REGAL PRINCE

REGAL PRINCE 'Long'. Narrow columnar form when young with a fastigiate growth habit, it widens and opens a bit with age, becoming more of a narrow oval. In Oregon, we have seen it fall completely open, a product of the weight of fast growth. In the Midwest and East, growth rate is slower, and it tends to maintain a narrower form. Glossy dark green foliage is especially nice. Good powdery mildew resistance. Very popular and widely planted. *Q. ×warei*. 45′ by 18′.

ROSEHILL 'Asjes'. Upright and narrow with a fastigiate habit when young, but it broadens with age to a more oval form. We have seen the head spread wide open; falling out of favor because of this. *Q. ×warei*. 45′ tall, 20 to 25′ wide.

SKINNY GENES 'JFS-KW2QX'. Narrowest of the narrow. Columnar form and fastigiate habit with branches ascending very close to the trunk. Especially dark green foliage is

ROSEHILL

SKINNY GENES

SKYMASTER

SKINNY GENES

SKYROCKET

STREETSPIRE

SKYROCKET on right, Fastigiata Group on left

impressive all summer. Good powdery mildew resistance. Yellow fall color, then leaves hold amber-brown and drop gradually in late fall. *Q. ×bimundorum.* 45′ tall, 10′ wide.

SKYMASTER 'Pyramich'. A strong-growing pyramidal form with a dominant central leader and good branch angles. A true English oak with improved cold hardiness and structure, making a nice large street tree form. 50′ tall, 30′ wide.

SKYROCKET 'Fastigiata'. Narrow columnar form, fastigiate growth habit. Twenty years ago, we thought this was the best columnar English oak. Still the best columnar form of true English oak, but we think it's been surpassed by the hybrid cultivars. Yellow fall color, then holds brown leaves into winter. 50′ tall, 20′ wide.

STREETSPIRE 'JFS-KW1QX'. Columnar and narrow when young, it features shorter and sturdier branches with better branch angles, rather than gaining its narrowness with long ascending branches. Its ultimate form is more of a narrow oval, but the canopy is less likely to fall open. Best powdery mildew resistance. Handsome summer foliage, reddish fall

STREETSPIRE

TRIPLE CROWN

WALKENBACH

color, then leaves drop cleanly, which is unusual in this group. Excellent street tree when pruned up. *Q. ×btmundorum*. 45′ tall, 16′ wide.

TRIPLE CROWN 'Taylor'. Broadly oval form, becomes full and quite round. Dark green glossy foliage. We have observed powdery mildew on it. Reported to be resistant to oak gall in the Midwest. Yellowish fall color. Believed to be a three-way hybrid (*Q. robur*, *Q. macrocarpa*, and *Q. muehlenbergii*). 50′ tall and wide.

WALKENBACH 'Adeline'. Narrow columnar form, one of the best. This cultivar looks much like the popular REGAL PRINCE, but branches are a little shorter and stiffer, so it may hold its narrow form better. Foliage is dark green and glossy. We have observed slight powdery mildew, but the resistance rates good. Yellow-orange fall color. Zone 4. *Q. ×warei*. 45′ tall and 15′ wide.

Quercus rubra

red oak

Deciduous. Possibly the most important member of the red oak group, with a dominant presence in North American forest communities. Habit is rounded in youth and in old age. Growth is fast, averaging 2′ per year over a 10-year period, to 60 to 75′ high and wide at maturity. Bark is smooth, greenish brown on young trunks; brown to almost black; wide, flat, gray ridges, separated by shallow fissures; often deeply ridged and furrowed on old trees.

Foliage: Oval to obovate, emerging pinkish to dusty red-bronze, covered with pubescence, maturing lustrous dark green, yellow-brown to russet-red to bright red in fall; 7- to 11-lobed, sinuses shallow, 4½ to 8½″ long, 4 to 6″ wide. **Flowers/seeds/fruits/cones**: Monoecious. Catkins 2 to 3″ long, yellowish green. Acorns are solitary or paired, subglobose, cap covering a fifth to a fourth of the gray-brown nut, ¾ to 1¼″ long, maturing the second season. **Native range**: Nova Scotia to Georgia, west to Minnesota and Oklahoma. The species grows on the shoreline along the Maine Coast to over 5,000′ elevation in the Southern Appalachians. **Adaptability**: Adaptable to extremes of soil, except wet. Soil tolerances include sandy, gravelly, rocky to deep, more fertile soils on slopes and ravines. Displays a modicum of salt tolerance (aerial) based on the vigorous healthy trees in

coastal Atlantic habitats. Certainly best adapted to northern areas, but occurs in the wild around Athens (zone 8) with 70′ high trees on well-drained slopes in the University's Botanical Garden. Zones 4 to 7(8); solid in zone 8 in the Pacific West, usable in zone 9 in cool-summer coastal areas. **Landscape use**: Throughout New England and the Midwest, it is one of the primary red oak group landscape trees, in recent years having supplanted Q. *palustris*. At its best, a magnificent and cherished oak, possibly the best of the red oaks for parks, campuses, and residential properties. Relatively easy to transplant and adaptable, criteria that constitute a reliable specimen shade tree. Requires full sun

Quercus rubra

Quercus rubra

Quercus rubra

768

and acid soil as chlorosis may occur in high pH situations. **Street tree use**: Yes, a ubiquitous presence along streets, including remarkably resilient old specimens along US 1 and the Arborway in the Boston area, which although bumped, bruised, and growing in minimalist soil, are still impressive and beautiful. **In the trade**: Sold as seed-grown, which we recommend in this species. Several cultivars have arisen in Europe. The most common, 'Aurea', with bright yellow young leaves, later yellow-green maturing to green, has reached 60′ in England; we observed the tree at Hillier as the leaves were first unfolding. Quite spectacular.

Quercus rubra

Quercus rubra

Quercus rysophylla
Mexican loquat-leaved oak

Evergreen to deciduous, depending on cold. In the 1980s, several Mexican oak species were newly promoted as landscape options, especially in hot, dry, alkaline soil regions. David Creech, Stephen F. Austin State University, Nacogdoches, TX, evaluated the lot, with this the major-league star. The species grows to over 80′ in the wild. Authors observed a magnificent, 35′ high, pyramidal-oval specimen at Hillier Arboretum; 17 years later, the tree had reached 65′. Creech reported a 28-year-old tree was over 60′ high with an almost perfect oval-rounded silhouette. Bark is grayish black, lightly ridged and furrowed, somewhat blocky with age.

Foliage: Leathery, thick-textured, bullate, lustrous dark green, the lobes with bristle tips above the middle, elliptical to obovate-lanceolate, undulating margins, 2 to 8″ long, a third as wide, glabrous below with tufts of hairs in vein axils; emerging leaves salmon to bronze, older leaves shed in late winter–spring. **Flowers/seeds/fruits/cones**: Acorn ½″ long, brown, pointed, the cup covers a third to half of

Quercus rysophylla

Q

Quercus rysophylla

the nut. **Native range**: Mexico (Nuevo Leon, Tamaulipas, San Luis Potosi), in mountains at mid to lower elevations. Occurs in humid canyons and on north-facing slopes in oak-pine woods. **Adaptability**: The species was not injured at 0°F, and Creech reports it "never blinked" in the heat and drought of 2010 and 2011, when summer temperatures topped 106°F. In a wide-ranging, intensely documented treatment of the species, Allen Coombes mentioned its use from North Carolina and Texas to California and Oregon. Zones 8 to 10. **Landscape use**: Beautiful oak with spectacular foliage, particularly when the new growth contrasts with the old. In *New Trees* (2009), John Grimshaw wrote of it, "If only one 'new tree' were to be grown, this should perhaps be it." For maximum expression of genetic potential, site in well-drained, acid to higher pH soil, in full sun. Utilize for lawn, park, and campus plantings. A lone tree in the State Botanical Garden of Georgia is the worse for wear, semi-evergreen to deciduous, misshapen, and in no way capable of competing with native southeastern oak species. **Street tree use**: Yes. **In the trade**: Available but may not always be true-to-type from seed, as it hybridizes with many red oak group species. One such hybrid, 'Maya', has deep bronze-red emerging foliage, maturing to green.

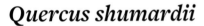

Quercus shumardii

Shumard oak, swamp red oak

Deciduous. Authors consider this one of the unsung heroes of the red oak group, rivaling *Q. palustris* and *Q. rubra* in aesthetic traits and cultural adaptability. Young trees, 8 to 10 years old, are densely branched and foliated, with an upright branching structure, pyramidal in outline, becoming more spreading, eventually 40 to 60′ high and wide. Moderate to fast growth rate; Dirr was stopped by police for collecting acorns under a magnificent specimen in a Home Depot parking lot, and a resultant seedling planted out to the garden was 10′ high in 3 years. Bark is gray-brown, slightly ridged and furrowed.

Foliage: Obovate to elliptic, lustrous dark green, yellow, bronze, russet-red to red in fall; foliage is retained into winter on young trees, with some seedlings still green in early December in zone 8; 7 to 9 lobes with sinuses narrow and deeply cut to midrib; 4 to 6(8)″ long, 3 to 4″ wide. **Flowers/seeds/fruits/cones**: Monoecious. Catkins greenish yellow. Acorns are ovoid, cap covering a quarter of the striated brown/black nut, ¾ to 1½″ long. **Native range**: Eastern North America; isolated populations in Michigan and Ontario and then continuously from Indiana and Ohio south to Florida and west to Texas. **Adaptability**: Adapted to both bottomland and upland soils. Studies have emphasized its superior growth in pH 7.8 to 8.0 alluvial soils. Zones 5 to 9. **Landscape use**: Shumard oak should play a major role in landscaping, with its inherent soil adaptability, relative ease

Quercus shumardii

Quercus shumardii

of transplanting, and neat, tidy, full habit as a young tree. The lower branches are horizontal to ascending (upswept), thus requiring minimal limbing up when used along streets, in parks, and anywhere machinery is prevalent, while pin oak, with its descending lower branches, is, at times, a maintenance headache. Unlike *Q. palustris* and *Q. rubra*, authors have yet to observe chlorotic foliage, although it is reported in the literature. In Auburn University's 13-year shade tree evaluations, the species proved superior. It varies considerably over its extensive native range, north to south and east to west; provenance is important in performance. **Street tree use**: Yes. Excellent form and adaptability for the purpose. **In the trade**: Generally sold as seed-grown. In recent years, several own-root cultivars were introduced, providing uniform habit and consistent fall color; the three listed here are of U.S. Southeast provenance.

Quercus shumardii

Quercus stellata

Quercus shumardii

Quercus stellata

MADISON 'ACNRT1'. More fastigiate to narrow oval, dark green foliage, tight branching, dense canopy, 60' by 20'.

PANACHE 'QSFTC'. A possible hybrid. Upright, with upsweeping branching forming a broadly pyramidal form, becoming broadly oval. Good density. Glossy dark green leaves turn red in fall. 60' tall, 50' wide.

PROMINENCE 'QSSTH'. A possible hybrid, resembles both Shumard and Nuttall oak. Fast growth, upright, dense, with branches neatly ascending at 45° angles, tightly pyramidal, becoming more broadly pyramidal. Good red fall color. 65' tall, 45' wide.

Quercus stellata

post oak

Deciduous. An open-grown tree develops a rounded to broad-rounded outline; spectacular, isolated trees are found in places only a runaway squirrel would have traveled, the foliage so dense, the artistic muscular branches are camouflaged. Often listed as moderate in size, 40 to 50' high and wide; however 60 to 70' high trees are common in the Southeast, with the National Champion over 100' high. We have observed trees of every shape and size, some upright-spreading with twisted, gnarled secondary branches. Slow to moderate growth rate. Young stems covered with gray-brown tomentose pubescence; the gray-brown to ash-gray trunks, from a distance, easily confused with *Q. alba*, but with narrower and flatter ridges, narrower furrows, and outer bark not as scaly, exfoliating; with extreme age becoming more deeply ridged and furrowed.

Foliage: Arguably the most beautiful mature foliage of the oaks; thick, leathery-textured, polished dark green above, grayish to brownish beneath; obovate, 2 to 3 broad, obtuse lobe pairs, the middle pair much larger; the outline cruciform, 4 to 8" long, 3 to 4" wide; fall color yellowish to golden brown. **Flowers/seeds/fruits/cones**: Monoecious. Catkins yellow-green, 2 to 4" long. Acorns are sessile, brown, ¾ to 1" long, a third to half of the nut covered by the top-shaped cap, the scales of which are slightly longer and

Q

Quercus stellata

Quercus suber

Quercus suber

looser than those of white oak; mature in one year. **Native range**: Massachusetts to Florida, west to Iowa and Texas, growing in sandy, rocky soils to heavy clays. **Adaptability**: Remarkably adaptable to extremes of soil, except permanently wet. In fact, on the Georgia campus, many specimen trees grow on dry slopes and have endured great droughts and prolonged heat. Authors recorded trees from Martha's Vineyard to the prairies of Oklahoma, and many locations in between, all prospering under uniquely different cultural conditions. Zones 5 to 9. **Landscape use**: Although seldom utilized in contemporary landscapes, this beautiful native oak is worthy of consideration, and authors believe it has suitable attributes to create a meaningful landscape footprint. Certainly a single specimen is a powerful force of nature; however, groupings and mini-groves become potent representatives of this unsung species. Ideally transplant container-grown and balled-and-burlapped trees to full sun locations. **Street tree use**: Not common, but perhaps worth considering. **In the trade**: Sold as seed-grown.

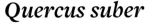

Quercus suber

cork oak

Broadleaf evergreen. Besides being the source of wine corks, the species doubles as a handsome shade tree, 40 to 60′ high and wide, of moderate growth, and a source of sustenance for all manner of wildlife. Bark is gray-brown, thick, spongy. Quite amazing that trees over 250 years old are still being harvested of their bark (cork). The harvest begins when trees are around 25 years old and continues thereafter every 10 to 12 years. The cork is derived from cambium, which arises in the phloem tissue; the bark is stripped, leaving a covering to protect the cambium and allow for regrowth. Cork has been harvested for thousands of years. The Romans utilized it for buoys, for fishing nets, and for making sandals; it is also used for shoe insoles, gaskets, washers, fishing rod grips, bulletin boards, and insulation. Portugal is the major cork producer, providing 50% of the world's supply.

Foliage: Oval, ovate to oblong, 1 to 2½″ long, ⅝ to 1½″ wide, spiny toothed on the margins, except near base, the margins often curved downward, glossy dark green, lower surface

Quercus suber

Quercus velutina

clothed with minute gray tomentose pubescence, leaves persist through the second year. **Flowers/seeds/fruits/ cones**: Acorn, 1″ long, brown, covered by a deep cap fringed with elongated scales. **Native range**: Western Mediterranean basin in the coastal regions of Europe and Africa, including Algeria, France, Italy, Morocco, Portugal, Spain, Tunisia, and the islands of Corsica, Sardinia, and Sicily, growing in association with the evergreen *Q. ilex* (holm oak), stone and maritime pines, wild olive trees, and in open grasslands. **Adaptability**: Superbly adapted to California, where it is mainly found in the United States. Zones 8 to 10. **Landscape use**: Worthy shade tree for Mediterranean climates as it grows best in areas with cold, moist winters and hot summers. Requires well-drained, acid soils and full sun. Excellent for campuses and parks. **Street tree use**: Yes, where space allows for its fairly wide spread. **In the trade**: Several hybrids make beautiful, imposing trees. *Q. ×hispanica* (*Q. cerris* × *Q. suber*) is a wide-spreading, semi-evergreen oak to 100′, with corrugated bark similar to *Q. cerris*. Leaves 2 to 5″ long, 1 to 2″ wide, glossy green, lower covered with close pubescence, oval to ovate, 7 to 9 parallel veins running to margins and forming the tips of triangular sharp teeth. Hybrid was first raised c.1763. It produces viable acorns, and many seedlings were raised and named, including the exceptional 'Lucombeana' (Lucombe oak).

Quercus texana. See Q. *nuttallii*

Quercus velutina
black oak

Deciduous. An open-grown black oak is a splendid experience. Irregular pyramidal in youth; broad-rounded with wide-spreading branches at maturity. Mature height 50 to 60′ with spread variable, usually wider than tall. Growth is moderate. Young stems are quite pubescent, eventually glabrous, reddish brown or reddish; mature bark gray-black with a blocky, alligator-hide texture. The bumpy bark separates it from other members of the red/black group. Acorns are an important food source for wildlife.

Quercus velutina

Quercus velutina

Quercus velutina

Foliage: Leaves can be mistaken for *Q. rubra*, but the 5-sided, woolly pale yellowish gray, ¼ to ½″ long buds are golden for corroboration. Emerging leaves tinted orange, copper, red, maturing to lustrous dark green; oblong-ovate to obovate, 7 to 9 lobes, 4 to 10″ long, 2 to 6″ wide; turning yellow, tawny brown, orange to red-brown in autumn. Authors observed considerable variation in fall color; leaves hold into late fall. **Flowers/seeds/fruits/cones**: Monoecious. Catkins yellow-green. Acorns are ovoid to hemispherical, red-brown, often with striate markings, ½ to ¾″ long, the cap covering a third to half of the nut; mature the second year. **Native range**: Every state east of the Mississippi, feathering into Nebraska, Oklahoma, Arkansas, and Texas, often on infertile, dry, sandy to clay soils. In Georgia, for example, it occurs in drier upland soils in association with *Q. falcata* and *Q. nigra*. **Adaptability**: Evidence points to soil adaptability, with tolerances of both drier soils and higher pH conditions. Zones 3 to 9. **Landscape use**: Nowhere common in contemporary landscapes but a serviceable and utilitarian species. Authors have encountered it throughout eastern North America, primarily in nature, but occasionally on campuses and in parks. In our travels, when identifying oaks, this is the last species to enter the conversation.

Literature usually indicates it is difficult to transplant, but with good nursery culture, it's probably on par with *Q. rubra*. Considered easier to transplant than *Q. macrocarpa* or *Q. alba*. **Street tree use**: Not the first choice among the oaks. **In the trade**: In recent years, the species' cultural attributes have caused nursery producers to become more accepting. Seedling trees are available.

Quercus virginiana
live oak

Broadleaf evergreen. Often open, sparsely branched and rounded in youth; improves with age, forming a broad-spreading, dome-shaped outline; eventually massive, 40 to 80′ high, 60 to 100′ wide, and may live 500 years and more. Growth is moderate, 1 to 2′ per year. Bark is dark, almost black, with checkered, blocky, raised squares in the mold of an alligator hide; massive trunks and low-slung branches are beautiful. This is the State Tree of Georgia; magnificent specimens shade the squares of Savannah, and at the Augusta National Golf Club, iconic trees grow to the right of hole 18 and near the club house. But in general, inland trees do not approach the majesty of the coastal inhabitants, with their picturesque horizontal and arching branches.

Foliage: Elliptic-obovate, often spiny margined on seedling trees, similar to holly foliage, spring growth bright olive-green, maturing lustrous dark green, grayish undersides, leathery, margins recurved/revolute, old leaves abscising in spring with emergence of new foliage; 1½ to 3(5)″ long, ½ to 1(1½)″ wide. **Flowers/seeds/fruits/cones**: Monoecious. Catkins 2″ long, yellowish green. Acorns are ellipsoidal, cap covers a quarter to half of the dark shiny brown to black nut, ¾ to 1″ long, produced 1 to 5 on the long stalk (peduncle), maturing in the first season. **Native range**: Coastal Southeast from Virginia to Florida, west to Texas, Oklahoma, and Mexico. Coastal plain in dry sandy soils, occasionally moist habitats. Found facing the Atlantic and Gulf, often sculpted by the maritime (salt) exposure. **Adaptability**: Trees in Atlanta and Athens survived cold winters (-3 to -9°F) with various degrees of leaf burn/drop. Stems were not injured. Zones 7 to 10. **Landscape use**: Signature tree of the coastal Southeast, dominating parks, neighborhoods, golf courses, and campuses. It is commonly used for streetscapes with the understanding that pruning is part of the long-term care proposition. The species grows in sand, clay, and salt-laden environments in full sun, although trees are moderately shade tolerant. It is a climax species and continues to reproduce and form pure stands. Nurseries have mentioned that transplanting success varies from 80 to 90%; many produce container-grown material, thus facilitating transplanting success. **Street tree use**: Yes, but give it plenty of space for its trunk and spread. **In the trade**: Research in the 1980s

Quercus virginiana

Quercus virginiana

Quercus virginiana

Quercus virginiana

with cutting propagation paved the way for own-root, superior cultivars.

BOARDWALK 'FBQV22'. Pyramidal habit with a dominant central leader, upswept branches, and narrow, lustrous dark green leaves. The parent tree was 25′ by 21′ with a 12″ caliper in 12 years.

'Cannon-Sharp'. Dominant central leader with secondary branches borne at a 60° angle to vertical; leaves are attractive glossy dark green.

CATHEDRAL 'SDLN'. Dark green leaves, central leader with side-angle branches, resulting in a dense habit. 60′ tall, 65′ wide.

'Empire'. Faster growing than some of the patented and named cultivars. It is produced by seed.

HIGHRISE 'QVTIA'. Pyramidal-columnar in youth, becoming more oval-rounded with age. Projected to be smaller than the species at 40′ tall, 30′ wide, but might exceed this.

MILLENNIUM 'CLTFZ'. Rounded habit with central leader and strong secondary branches; leaves are larger than typical, lustrous dark green, tree was 29′ high and wide with a 13″ caliper at 13 years of age.

PARK SIDE 'FBQV1'. Broad pyramidal habit, becoming more oval-rounded with age; branch angles 70°; 13-year-old tree was 25′ high, 18′ wide, with an 11″ caliper.

'Southern Shade'. Seed-produced cultivar with a short, broad trunk, long horizontal branches, and broad-spreading, dense crown.

Q

R

Rhamnus purshiana. See *Frangula purshiana*

Rhodoleia henryi

Henry's rose tree

Broadleaf evergreen. One of the tenets of this book is to introduce the reader to new species and cultivars. The word "new" is best translated as new to everyday cultivation. This and the similar *R. championii* are members of the witch-hazel family, Hamamelidaceae. The description herein references *R. henryi*. It grows 15 to 30′ high, two-thirds as wide, and produces multiple 4 to 5′ growth flushes, according to Ted Stephens, Nurseries Caroliniana, North Augusta, SC. The bark is smooth, gray.

Foliage: Borne in pseudo-whorls at the end of the shoots, elliptic-oval, tapered at ends, thick-textured, entire, 3 to 6″ by 1 to 2″, lustrous medium to dark green, glaucous below, holding as long as 5 years. **Flowers/seeds/fruits/cones**: Rose-pink to red, 2 to 3″ across, borne in the leaf axils in late winter–spring, reminiscent of semi-pendulous feather dusters. Flowers are stunning and bear no resemblance to most members of the Hamamelidaceae. **Native range**: China, growing on mountains to 8,500′ elevation. **Adaptability**: The better-known *R. championii* has been injured or killed in zone 8, whereas *R. henryi* is unfazed: Stephens notes the flowers were uninjured after 19°F. At the University of Georgia Horticulture Farm, a lone plant, sited in full sun, has never experienced foliar injury. Quite remarkable. Plants do not read books, so they know more than the authors.

Zones 7 to 9, 10 on the West Coast. **Landscape use**: A rare broadleaf evergreen with floral elegance seldom available in anything except rhododendrons. Specimen and accent use in the garden are primary targets. Consider integrating in a woodland garden under high broadleaf shade/pine trees. Provide well-drained, acid soil. Other attributes are no pest issues and resistance to deer browsing. Propagation difficulties have limited nursery production; however, the clone Stephens named 'Scarlet Bells' has proven easier to root, and he now has four clones, ranging from pink to red with upright to spreading growth habits. The species would make a great breeding partner for *Distylium*, *Loropetalum*, *Sycopsis*, *Parrotia*, and other genera in the Hamamelidaceae. Authors became excited researching *Rhodoleia* and recently found a nursery that offered seeds. We look forward to the future. **Street tree use**: No, at least at present. **In the trade**: Limited. 'Scarlet Bells' is available.

'Scarlet Bells'

Rhus typhina

staghorn sumac

Deciduous. Upright, widely branched, open in form, a small shrubby tree, suckering and forming colonies. It can be maintained to a single trunk by controlling the suckers, or it can be allowed to spread into a bushy grove. Branches velvety pubescent and spreading at wide angles, reminiscent of deer antlers in velvet (hence the common name). Texture is medium in summer, coarse in winter. Moderately slow-growing. Size is typically 10 to 20′ tall and wide, depending on maintenance. Bark is gray-brown, smooth except for bumpy lenticels when young, becoming slightly roughened with age.

Foliage: Pinnately compound, leaves 1 to 2′ long with 13 to 27 lanceolate leaflets, serrate with acuminate tips, 2 to 5″ long and a quarter as wide. Medium green, slightly lustrous, turning orange-red to bright red in the fall. **Flowers/seeds/**

fruits/cones: Dioecious. Tiny light yellowish green flowers form dense panicles in early summer, the male heads a little looser than the females. The infructescence is much flashier, forming bright crimson-red, narrow, fuzzy conical heads, 4 to 8″ long, highly ornamental and holding into the winter on bare branches. **Native range:** U.S. Northeast and adjacent southern Canada, from Nova Scotia to Minnesota and south to north Georgia. **Adaptability:** A tough little tree, widely adaptable, takes poor soil, drought, extreme heat and cold. Zones 4 to 8. **Landscape use:** A very effective landscape plant, most commonly used as a spreading large shrub along a border; with pruning, it becomes a multi-stem small tree. It can fill an area well. Fine-textured foliage feels a little tropical; winter branching form is distinctive and especially interesting when holding the red seed heads. The only drawback is its suckering nature if you want to keep it confined. **Street tree use:** Not recommended. **In the trade:** Seed-grown plants grow a little taller than the cultivars.

'Laciniata'. Female. Wonderful lacy foliage, deeply cut-leaf, dark green in summer and turning brilliant shades of orange-red in fall. It produces a nice ornamental load of crimson seed heads and carries the striking staghorn winter silhouette. A bit smaller than the species at 10 to 15′. 'Dissecta', also with cutleaf foliage, is very similar.

TIGER EYES 'Bailtiger'. Cutleaf new growth emerges chartreuse-green and brightens to yellow in summer, becoming more golden as the season progresses, finally orange-red in fall. Colors are better in cool climates. Really too small to be called a tree, but included here because of its incredible foliage, bushy, to 10′ at most. Red seed heads sparsely produced.

Rhus typhina

'Laciniata'

TIGER EYES

R

777

Robinia pseudoacacia
black locust

Deciduous. A large upright tree, oval at first then becoming more open and irregularly vase-shaped. Branches armed with nasty sharp spines. Suckering from the roots. Medium texture in summer, coarse in winter, fast-growing to 60′ tall and 30′ wide. Bark dark brown to gray-black, furrowed. Invasive in the West, far outside its native range, and spreads aggressively in the East.

Foliage: Pinnately compound, leaves 8 to 14″ long with 7 to 19 leaflets. Leaflets elliptical, 1 to 1½″ long, margin entire, dark green to slightly blue-green. Yellow fall color, probably brighter in the West than the East. **Flowers/seeds/fruits/cones**: Fragrant white flowers in dense racemes 4 to 8″ long, flowering in late spring with the foliage. Fruit is a flat pea-like pod, 2 to 4″ long, brownish black when ripe in the fall, with 6 to 10 flattened seeds. **Native range**: Eastern United States, Pennsylvania to Missouri and Georgia to Oklahoma. **Adaptability**: A very tough and adaptable plant, nitrogen-fixing and growing on poor, rather wet as well as very dry soils, pH tolerant. Zones 4 to 8, 9 in the West. **Landscape use**: A tough tree for tough sites. More appreciated in Europe than in its native country, where the destructive locust borer can make its lifespan uncertain. Locust leaf miner can turn foliage brown in summer. **Street tree use**: The growth habit is good for this purpose, and the tree is adapted to harsh conditions, but pay attention to the local prevalence of the locust borer. Use spineless or nearly spineless cultivars that are listed as having good street potential, as brittleness is a problem in some, especially the more ornamental hybrids. **In the trade**: Sold as cultivars, several of which are hybrids, some of uncertain parentage. Here we list hybrid cultivars (crosses with *R. viscosa* are *R. ×ambigua*; crosses with *R. hispida* are *R. ×slavinii* and *R. ×margaretta*) along with true *P. pseudoacacia* selections.

'Bessoniana'. Compact and upright oval with a slower growth rate and a mature size about two-thirds of the species, broadening on top with age, 40′ tall and 25′ wide. It features branches that are almost totally free of spines. It flowers sparsely, therefore produces little seed. Good structure. This is our choice for street use, and we think it should be considered more often.

'Casque Rouge' ('Pink Cascade'). Hybrid (*R. ×margaretta*). Flowers deep magenta-pink to rose, approaching the color of 'Purple Robe'. Spines small. 35′ tall, 30′ wide.

CHICAGO BLUES 'Benjamin'. Selected in Chicago with street tree use in mind, it has blue-green foliage, darker than typical. 50′ tall, 35′ wide.

'Decaisneana'. Hybrid (*R. ×ambigua*). Flowers soft pink with a slight magenta tint. 45′ tall, 25′ wide.

Robinia pseudoacacia

Robinia pseudoacacia

'Bessoniana'

Robinia pseudoacacia

Robinia pseudoacacia

'Casque Rouge'

'Frisia'

'Idahoensis'

'Frisia'

'Purple Robe'

TWISTY BABY

'Pyramidalis'

'Purple Robe'

'Frisia'. Bright yellow foliage on an upright tree, growing to nearly the size and form of the species. Leaves go green in the heat of Southeast summers, but in the Pacific Northwest, their color seems to intensify in late summer, becoming golden in the fall, perhaps the brightest yellow large tree there. 40 to 50′ tall, 25′ wide.

'Hillieri'. Hybrid (*R. ×slavinii*). Flowers very light pink to almost white but with a purple tint and calyx. In trials in Oregon we noted some browning of foliage and early leaf drop, and we favored the other cultivars. 25′ tall, 20′ wide.

'Idahoensis' ('Idaho'). Hybrid (probably *R. ×ambigua*). Flowers deep magenta-pink, slightly lighter in color than 'Purple Robe' and grows a bit slower, to 30′ tall and 20′ wide. New growth with bristly hairs. Popular in the dry Intermountain area.

'Purple Robe'. Flowers in large clusters, a wonderful soft violet, the deepest color of all the cultivars. New growth emerges in spring with a reddish purple tint and soon goes slightly bronze-green. The flower color certainly points to a hybrid background, but parentage is uncertain. Matures a little smaller than *R. pseudoacacia*, probably to 45′ tall and 25′ wide.

'Pyramidalis' ('Fastigiata'). Very narrow, fastigiate in habit, forming a narrow oval to nearly columnar form, 40′ tall, 15′ wide.

TWISTY BABY 'Lace Lady'. Slow-growing and semi-dwarf, with a highly contorted growth habit, it's at its best as a low-branched or multi-stem tree highlighting its irregular structure. Branches twist their way upward to form a low overhead canopy, about 20′ tall and wide.

'Umbraculifera'

'Umbraculifera'

'Umbraculifera' ('Globe'; globe locust). Almost perfectly round-headed, it earns its common name. Always produced by top grafting on a straight trunk, to 15′ by 15′. Formal and symmetrical; however, its branch structure is brittle. Sometimes improperly labeled 'Inermis'.

S

Sabal palmetto

Sabal palmetto
cabbage palm

Evergreen. Develops a dense crown, the lower leaves gently arching. Usually reaches 30 to 40′ high, 15′ wide, known to 60′ in the wild. Growth is slow to moderate. Bark is gray-brown, leaf base cleanly abscising or with a few persisting below the crown; trunk consistent diameter from base to apex.

Foliage: Costapalmate, fan-shaped, somewhere between pinnate and palmate, to 6′ long, 3′ wide, divided a third of the way to the base with many fibrous, thread-like pieces peeling along the tips and margins; gray-green to green. **Flowers/seeds/fruits/cones**: Cream-white, fragrant, in large panicles, extending beyond the leaves, summer, attractive to bees. Fruit is a drupe, rounded, ⅓″ wide, black, containing a single seed; ripens in late summer. **Native range**: Southeast corner of North Carolina to Florida, west to Texas, usually growing on hammocks, dunes, flatwoods, and brackish areas, in sun and shade. In the coastal marshes, it is everywhere in evidence, a lone sentinel to dense, close-knit colonies. Not known to occur over 75 miles from the coast. **Adaptability**: Literature states that the foliage is reasonably tolerant of salt spray, but the species is intolerant of salt in the root zone. Considering it grows in/near brackish water, this soil salt intolerance is questionable. Zones 8 to 11. Planted in zone 7 with increasing frequency. **Landscape use**: Certainly the most common and reliable tree palm for use along the coast in its native range and possibly the best tree palm for general landscape use. Every new commercial enterprise along the Southeast's coast has this in the parking lot islands or in an open area. Stalwartly windfirm—still standing in Charleston, SC, after Hurricane Hugo. Uses equate with

P. canariensis, except this species is more available, less expensive, and easier to transplant and grow. A newly planted *S. palmetto* appears dead, with a few upper leaves remaining, often the trunk staked/propped. Root systems are corn-like, close to the trunk, not spreading like deciduous trees. Similar to installing a fence post, i.e., dig a hole and insert. The University of Florida has thoroughly researched the species, and a visit to their website will fill in any gaps. **Street tree use**: Yes, but fruit is messy when planted along pedestrian sidewalks and vehicular ways. **In the trade**: Sold as seed-grown.

Salix
willow

A large and complex genus of 250 to 500 species, depending on the authority. *Salix* is almost entirely native to the northern hemisphere, with the majority of species being northern in distribution and ranging to the extreme Arctic. The species are dioecious and are both insect- and wind-pollinated. Hybridization occurs frequently, and many taxonomic questions exist. Over the years, the nomenclature of the genus has been a little like musical chairs, with species and cultivars frequently moving and then settling briefly into a new name. Because of this, some cultivars are well known in the nursery and landscape trade by names that differ from the latest proposed by the scientific community. We followed Yulia Kuzovkina's 2015 *Checklist* of cultivars.

In this treatment, we will describe the *Salix* species briefly, as it is rare that plants are used ornamentally based on the species. Cultivars completely dominate the trade, as they are very easily propagated by cuttings. We have grouped all the cultivars together for description and comparison; some are probably hybrids of unknown origin.

Willows are wet-soil tolerant but brittle and susceptible to fungal and bacterial leaf disease. Good for parks and large estates and campuses, the weeping cultivars are classic when placed near water. None should be used as street trees. The smaller cultivars make good garden ornamentals.

Species
S. alba (white willow). A large tree, 50 to 100′ tall. Native from western Europe through central Asia. Many cultivars traditionally designated as selections of this species are now considered hybrids or have been assigned elsewhere.

S. babylonica. Traditionally considered a weeping willow, but the most recent nomenclature includes the upright-growing trees formerly listed as *S. matsudana*, now as *S. babylonica* var. *pekinensis*.

S. caprea (goat willow). A smaller tree, somewhat shrubby, usually growing to 15 to 25′. Ornamentally, it features large catkins, 2″ long, with males being bright yellow in spring. Before expanding, the catkins are soft silvery gray and fuzzy, like pussy willows. Native from western Europe into central Asia.

S. ×fragilis (crack willow). A hybrid of *S. alba* and *S. euxina*, grows to 50′. It gets its name from the brittleness of its twigs. Native from western Europe into central Asia.

S. integra. A large shrub, native to China, Japan, Korea, and far eastern Russia.

S. ×pendulina. A hybrid, believed to involve *S. alba*, *S. babylonica*, and *S. ×fragilis*. Grows to 50′.

S. pentandra (laurel willow). Extremely glossy foliage. A small tree or large shrub, native to northern Europe and western Asia.

S. ×salamonii. Hybrid of *S. alba* and *S. babylonica*; includes the former *S. ×sepulcralis*. Medium to large trees.

Cultivars
As a group, consider all willows fast-growing, water-loving, and susceptible to a variety of leafspots and blights. They do best with moisture in the soil but not in the air. The healthiest willows seem to be near water in dry climates. They have their place but may look best at a distance. Some of the most important tree cultivars of *Salix* follow. Some *Salix* hybrids have no species name; cultivars of unknown parentage are simply listed by cultivar name (e.g., 'Flame').

Salix alba

Salix pentandra

S

Salix pentandra

'Britzensis'

'Babylon'

'Babylon'. This is the classic weeping willow of old, originating in China and introduced into Europe in the late 1600s. Well known from history but rare in the present day and infrequently grown. Very gracefully weeping with new branches greenish in summer and reddish brown in winter, hanging to the ground, to 40′ tall and wide. If you see yellow twigs on a weeping willow, it's a different cultivar. Better adapted to warmer climates, zones 6 to 9. *S. babylonica*.

'Blanda' (Wisconsin weeping willow). Vigorous, growing to 40′ high and 50′ wide. Broadly rounded, it weeps, but a little stiffly, not as graceful and pendulous to the ground as 'Babylon' and 'Chrysocoma'. It gets its Wisconsin name because it is cold hardy to zone 4. Foliage somewhat glossy, dark green. *S. ×pendulina*.

'Britzensis'. Strong-growing and upright-spreading, broadly oval to rounded form. It will make a medium-sized tree, 35′ by 30′, but it is often cut back to encourage vigorous new growth, which is brightly colored, from golden yellow at the base to coral-red at the tips. Looks its best in winter. *S. ×fragilis*.

'Chrysocoma' ('Tristis'; golden weeping willow). Listed by most U.S. nurseries as *S. alba* 'Tristis', but 'Chrysocoma' is the proper name. Call it what you will, this is by far the most popular and widely planted weeping willow. Fast-growing, making a large weeping tree to at least 40′ high and 50 to 60′ wide. Gracefully weeping, fine branchlets hang straight to the ground. Yellow fall color. Zones 4 to 8. *S. ×salamonii*.

'Crispa'. More of a curiosity than a beauty, this is a large weeping form with leaves that twist and curl upon themselves. A good choice if you want your neighbors to say, "What's wrong with your tree?" 30′ by 30′. *S. babylonica*.

'Curly Locks'. Sort of upright, and sort of weeping, a little crazy, with branches twisting and curling in every direction.

'Crispa'

'Curly Locks'

'Chrysocoma'

'Chrysocoma'

Imagine having a bad hair day then sticking your finger in a light socket. Attention-getting and attractive in an odd way. 8′ tall, 10′ wide. *S. caprea*.

'Fan Giant'. A large weeping willow reportedly more resistant to borers and twig blight. We haven't seen it and would like reliable confirmation of resistance. 40′ tall, 60′ wide. *S. ×pendulina*.

'Flame'. A small oval tree, usually multi-stem, with very bright red-orange new growth, looking its best in winter, grows to 15 to 20′ unless cut back to encourage the very colorful new growth.

S

'Flamingo'

'Hakuro-Nishiki'

'Golden Curls'

'Pendula'

'Pendula'

'Prairie Cascade'

'Flamingo'. A sport of 'Hakuro-Nishiki' and very similar to it, also top grafted, which is the only way it makes tree proportions. It is claimed to be more upright in growth, but we see it as spreading and shrub-like, like the original. Variegated green and white foliage does seem to be just a bit more colorful in early spring than 'Hakuro Nishiki', the new growth a slightly deeper pink, but as the plant ages in the landscape, we see little difference. Functionally, they are interchangeable.

'Golden Curls'. Upright-spreading, rounded, and slightly weeping from the lower branches. Smaller branches are golden, twisting and contorted. The tree looks best in the winter. Despite its shrub-like looks when small, it will grow large, to 35′ by 25′.

'Hakuro-Nishiki'. Really a shrub, it makes a small tree only when it is top grafted, a common production technique, growing to 10′ tall and 15′ wide, very broadly rounded. Wonderful variegated foliage, new growth comes out mottled pink and white then becomes green and white with age.

'Pendula' ('Kilmarnock'). A small weeping tree, it grows as tall as it is staked and then weeps to the ground, and gains height only by slowly twisting its way upward. Typical size, 8′ tall and 10′ wide, but depends on training. A graceful weeper for small gardens, with pussywillow-type catkins that open large and yellow with pollen, a male. *S. caprea*.

'Prairie Cascade'. A weeping hybrid, selected for cold hardiness in Manitoba. It has unusually glossy dark green foliage. Stiffly weeping, not as graceful as 'Chrysocoma', but with similar golden twig color and greater cold hardiness. 30′ tall, 40′ wide. Zones 3 to 6.

PRAIRIE REFLECTION 'Silver Lake'. Upright-growing to a broadly rounded form, 35′ tall, it has extremely glossy, very dark green foliage and resists chlorosis in higher pH soils. Selected for cold hardiness in North Dakota, zones 3 to 6. *S. pentandra*.

SCARLET CURLS 'Scarcuzam'. Usually grown multi-stem or low-branched, its form is broadly upright-spreading, with semi-weeping finer branches. It features twisting and contorted growth, with bark that is yellow on larger branches, scarlet on the newest growth. Irregular growing but could reach 20′, often pruned lower to encourage new stems.

'Snake'. Vigorous upright oval form with highly contorted branching. It is very similar to 'Torulosa', perhaps more vigorous and taller. A fast-growing feature plant, 35′ tall and 25′ wide. *S. babylonica*.

S

'Prairie Cascade'

'Snake'

PRAIRIE REFLECTION

SCARLET CURLS

'Snake'

'Torulosa'

'Vitellina'

'Umbraculifera'

'Torulosa' (corkscrew willow). Well known, with a good common name, as branches twist upward in a contorted manner and then weep slightly from their tips. Commonly grows 30′ tall, 25′ wide. *S. babylonica*.

'Umbraculifera' ('Navajo'). Widely planted in the arid Southwest, where it is called 'Globe Navajo' willow. Drought tolerant and broadly rounded, to 50′ tall and 60′ wide. Zones 5 to 9. *S. babylonica*.

'Vitellina'. A large tree, growing to 60′ with a broadly rounded form. Featuring bright yellow to golden orange stems that are best in winter, it is often grown as a cutback shrub. The golden stem color is seductive in young nursery stock, but it will disappoint as a big old tree. *S. alba*.

'Weeping Sally'. A small weeping female clone of *S. caprea*, otherwise similar to 'Pendula', which we prefer. 8′ tall, 10′ wide.

S

Sapindus saponaria var. *drummondii* (*S. drummondii*)

western soapberry

Deciduous. Low-branched, small to medium-sized tree with spreading-arching branches, developing an oval-rounded to broad-rounded outline. We estimate normal landscape dimensions at 25 to 30′ high and wide, although trees over 50′ are known. Growth is fast, and 3- to 4-year-old seedlings produce flowers. Bark is shallowly furrowed, ridges platy, scaly, upon shedding exposing a patchwork of gray-brown and orange-brown to red-brown. Soap was made from the fleshy portion of the fruits (hence the epithets).

Foliage: Evenly compound pinnate, 10 to 15″ long, with 8 to 18 leaflets, each obliquely lanceolate, sickle-shaped, entire, 1½ to 3½(5)″ long, ½ to 1″ wide, lustrous medium to rich green. Fall color, yellow to deep golden yellow, is consistently outstanding in zone 8. **Flowers/seeds/fruits/cones**: Yellowish white, each ⅕″ wide, borne in 6 to 10″ long, loose terminal panicles, May-June; effect is minimized against the foliage. Fruit is a yellow-orange, subglobose, ½″ wide drupe, matures in October, persisting through winter, the flesh often turning black; flesh is translucent initially, the black seed visible. Fruits are toxic, inedible, and produced in supraoptimal quantities; stray seedlings are common. **Native range**: Missouri, Kansas, New Mexico, Arizona, Arkansas, Colorado, Texas, Oklahoma, Louisiana, and Mexico. Occurs on upland limestone soils, fields, wood edges, fencerows, along watercourses. **Adaptability**: Widely adapted to extremes of soils, including acid and alkaline reactions. Authors noted native populations in western Oklahoma growing in miserably infertile, high pH, dry soils. Zones 6 to 9. **Landscape use**: Not common or esteemed in the pantheon of trees: we have yet to hear a tree lecture that even mentioned this taxon. But for residential properties, parks, campuses, and golf courses, it is worthy of trial for its heat and drought tolerances, disease- and insect-resistant summer foliage, and oft-spectacular golden yellow fall color. Requires full sun and well-drained conditions. The species supposedly produces unisexual (either male or female) flowers; since the lone tree in Athens, a large 35′ by 45′ specimen, produces quantities of fruit with fertile seeds, authors believe unisexual male

Sapindus saponaria var. *drummondii*

Sapindus saponaria var. *drummondii*

Sapindus saponaria var. *drummondii*

and female flowers occur in the same inflorescence. Seeds germinate readily when cleaned of outer flesh and provided 45 to 60 days cold-moist stratification. **Street tree use**: Potential. Utilized as such in Wichita, KS. **In the trade**: Sold as seed-grown. We believe that with breeding/selection, the species is well suited for the urban environment. A nonaggressive male selection is a necessary goal.

Sassafras albidum
common sassafras

Deciduous. An absolutely gorgeous tree, characteristically irregular in branching structure, sometimes pyramidal in youth, then all hell breaks loose with stout, contorted branches spreading to form a flat-topped, irregular, oblong-rounded head at maturity. Translation: every tree is iconoclastic, no two exactly alike. Size approximates 30 to 60′ in height, 25 to 40′ in spread, on occasion developing a skirt of suckering shoots. Growth is fast in youth.

Beautiful bark deserves but is seldom afforded accolades; cinnamon-brown, mahogany-brown, to reddish brown, deeply ridged and furrowed, the wide flat corky ridges with horizontal cracks. All parts of the plant are spicy aromatic when bruised/scratched.

Foliage: Unique, ovate, 3-lobed, left-hand mitten, and right-hand mitten, all mixed or on occasion only the ovate form; 3 to 7″ long, 2 to 4″ wide, bright to medium green, glaucous (gray) below, entire; fall color brilliant yellow, orange, red, scarlet, and purple. **Flowers/seeds/fruits/cones**: Dioecious (usually). Yellow, slightly fragrant, in 1 to 2″ long terminal racemes, April, before the leaves; readily apparent in fencerows, along roadsides, the naked yellow-green to red-green stems hold the flowers aloft like Olympic torches. Fruits are dark blue, ½″ long, ovoid drupes, borne on a long scarlet pedicel (stalk) in September and feasted upon by birds. Fruits are produced only on female plants; usually not in great quantities. **Native range**: Maine to Ontario and Michigan, south to Florida, to Kansas, Oklahoma, and Texas. Common in open woods, fencerows, and fallow fields. **Adaptability**: Zones 4 to 9.

Sassafras albidum

S

Sassafras albidum

Sassafras albidum

Landscape use: A beauty, found everywhere in the wild, seldom (ever) in cultivated landscapes; if present do not remove, simply prize, preserve, and cherish. In brief, a "stinker" to transplant. In consulting work, we specified *S. albidum*, located a few nursery-grown trees, installed on the site, and all died to the ground. Abundant shoots (suckers) regenerated from the roots; however, a tree was the goal, not a thicket. And so the story goes with sassafras...Young container-grown trees offer the best transplanting success. Sassafras is best served by well-drained, acid soils in full sun to partial shade; chlorosis may occur in high pH situations. Along with *Nyssa sylvatica* and *Oxydendrum arboreum*, it is a superb native species for reliably spectacular fall color displays. Use in native restorations, wood edges, for wildlife plantings, and open areas where room to spread is ample. **Street tree use**: No. **In the trade**: Uncommon, but available seed-grown. The reader will never find it offered at the local garden center; native plant nurseries are the best hope.

Sciadopitys verticillata
umbrella pine

Evergreen conifer. Pyramidal, often tightly so when young, becoming a broader and looser pyramid with age. Slow-growing, medium coarse in texture, growing to 30′ tall and 15 to 20′ wide. Bark is thin, orangish to reddish brown, fissured and peeling in long stringy strips.

Foliage: Needles 2 to 5″ long, ⅛″ broad, in whorls of 20 to 30 at ends of the branches and at nodes, slightly curved like the ribs of an umbrella. Shorter, scale-like needles are held along the shoots. Color varies from slightly yellowish green to dark green. **Flowers/seeds/fruits/cones**: Monoecious. Cones are held more or less upright, oval to broadly ovate, 2 to 4″ long and 1 to 2″ wide, greenish at first and taking 2 years to mature, dark brown. **Native range**: Southern Japan. **Adaptability**: The only species in the genus, and the only

Sciadopitys verticillata

Sciadopitys verticillata

'Sternschnuppe'

'Gruene Kugel'

'Wintergreen'

'Joe Kozey'

genus in the Sciadopityaceae, hanging on against the forces of extinction since the age of the dinosaurs. As a relict species native to only a small area, you can guess it's not the most adaptable tree. But few pests know how to attack it, and it does well in a temperate landscape, given rich, well-drained acid soil. Full sun is preferred but light shade is tolerated. Zones 5 to 7, 8 in the cool-summer West. **Landscape use**: A great accent plant, with a distinctive prehistoric look in keeping with its ancient lineage. Much coarser in texture than true pines. Popular in the Northeast, where it does well. Usually used as a single specimen but also nice in groupings. **Street tree use**: Not recommended. **In the trade**: Available.

S

'Gruene Kugel'. A smaller, slow-growing cultivar, stays tight and compact, 8′ tall, 4′ wide. Glossy green foliage holds well. Slightly rounded when young, becoming densely pyramidal as it gains height.

'Joe Kozey'. The narrowest cultivar, tall and straight, forming a very narrow pyramidal shape and approaching the full height of the species, 25′ high, 6 to 8′ wide. Dark green foliage, a great exclamation point of a landscape specimen.

'Wintergreen'

Sequoia sempervirens

'Sternschnuppe' ('Green Star'). A straight-growing pyramidal form, its needles are thick and twice as wide as the species, creating a very coarse-textured appearance. 25' high, 10' wide.

'Wintergreen'. Pyramidal form selected for glossy foliage and dark green color that holds up through the winter. A favorite. 25' tall, 12' wide.

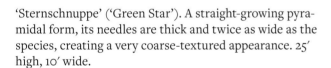

Sequoia sempervirens
redwood, coast redwood

Evergreen conifer. The world's tallest tree, a fast-growing narrow pyramid. Call it medium-textured as a compromise: its needles are very fine, but its rugged bark and great size would be called coarse. Landscape size depends on conditions; expect a 50' tree on the East Coast, 100 to 150' on the West Coast. In their native habitat, redwoods can live over 1,000 years, and a few over 2,000 years have been recorded. Current champion for height is 349'; taller records have succumbed to wind, and historic trees are believed to have topped 400'. The bark is beautiful, becoming very thick, deeply furrowed and ridged, a warm reddish brown, fibrous.

Foliage: Needles small, ⅜ to ⅞" long, narrow, dark green above, light green below, with 2 pale stomatal bands on the underside. Needles are held flat along the branches. **Flowers/seeds/fruits/cones:** Monoecious. Pollen cones are tiny, at the tips of branches. Female cones ¾ to 1¼" long and two-thirds as wide, broadly ovoid, brown, ripening in one season and releasing ⅛" long seeds that blow in the wind. **Native range:** The Pacific coastal fog belt from central California to southern Oregon. **Adaptability:** Needs rich soil with good drainage. Prefers a cool climate with high humidity. Tolerates shade but grows best in full sun. Zones 7 to 9 on the West Coast, and certainly best in the coastal belt. Zones 7 to 8(9) in the East, but trees will not be as happy. Performs well in the mild, ocean-influenced climates of the British Isles and northern Europe. **Landscape use:** Planted with awe and an appreciation of nature by those who want to celebrate the tallest living thing on earth. A specimen to talk about, but also a magnificent and noble tree to grace your garden. As its top climbs too high to see, you gain appreciation for

Sequoia sempervirens

'Aptos Blue'

Sequoia sempervirens

its sinewy-fibrous, rough, reddish bark. A grove is a beautiful site, both in its natural state and in a landscape. We have fond memories, long ago, of hiking into the canyon of Redwood Creek and seeing the grove that then held world's tallest tree. To a tree lover, it is an awe-inspiring place. In fact, we can't imagine anyone who would not be inspired by that grove with its incredible size and sense of timelessness. Farther south, we loved seeing the way the buildings of the University of California at Santa Cruz are nestled and hidden in coastal valley folds of a wonderful redwood forest, truly an incredible natural landscape setting, a sight to see. **Street tree use**: Too big, but consider roadside use in wind-protected coastal areas. **In the trade**: Available. All cultivars can exceed 100′ in the coastal climate of the West, maybe half that height in the East.

'Aptos Blue'. Tight pyramid, very dark green foliage with a slight blue tint, form quite dense, branches horizontal, slightly upsweeping, more formal, a winner.

S

'Filoli'

'Soquel'

'Soquel'

'Filoli'. The bluest cultivar we list. Handsome blue-gray needles stand out from the normal green of the type. Pyramidal form is a bit wider and more open than others. Better blue color than 'Aptos Blue', but the form is not as neat and dense.

'Santa Cruz'. Soft-colored, medium green foliage, branching less dense, more open, smaller branches droop, a more relaxed appearance both in color and form.

'Soquel'. Green foliage carries a blue tint on the underside, shorter needles, fine texture, a slightly fuller pyramid with branching horizontal to a bit upward-oriented.

Sequoiadendron giganteum

giant sequoia

Evergreen conifer. Tightly pyramidal when young with branches to the ground; it grows for years in this form, and most garden specimens maintain a formal pyramidal shape within the life of the landscape, tapering slightly toward a narrow, spire-like crown. But giant sequoias are among the world's oldest living organisms, to 3,500 years old, and with great age, the lower trunk becomes bare and the upper canopy is more rounded and open. Trunks become very large at an early age, with a buttressed base, then just plain massive. Fast-growing, with coarse texture, to at least 100′ in the landscape with a 40′ spread. The current record tree is 274′ tall with a 27′ trunk diameter. Bark is very thick, fibrous-spongy, furrowed, reddish brown on young trees and then more orange-brown with great age.

Foliage: Needles are short, ⅛ to ½″ long, dark bluish green, awl-shaped, closely pressed against the shoots and with flaring tips, persisting 3 to 4 years. **Flowers/seeds/ fruits/cones**: Monoecious. Pollen cones and female cones form at branch tips. Female cones take 2 years to mature, reaching 1½ to 3″ long and 1¼ to 2″ wide, broadly ovoid in shape, green when immature then turning brown. In an unusual reproductive strategy, cones are held on the tree for 8 to 12 years and may release seed intermittently when conditions cause the cones to dry and scales to separate. **Native range**: Restricted to a small range on the west slope of the central Sierra Nevada in California between 4,500 and 8,000′ elevation. **Adaptability**: The sole living species in the genus, but the fossil record shows that its ancestors were once widespread across North America and Eurasia, hinting at its greater adaptability. Despite its limited natural range, it's quite successful in landscapes in the western and eastern United States as well as in Europe. It can be difficult to transplant, and it does need good drainage. Zones 6 to 8 on the West Coast; not as happy in the East. **Landscape use**: Use it in a large landscape, when you want to make a big statement, singly as a large feature or in groves. It will become the center of attention. Be sure to give its trunk room, as not only does it gain thickness quickly, its

S

Sequoiadendron giganteum

Sequoiadendron giganteum

797

Sequoiadendron giganteum

'Barabit's Requiem'

roots flare at the base; we measured a 5′ trunk diameter on a 35-year-old tree at the Schmidt Arboretum in Oregon. **Street tree use**: No, too big. **In the trade**: Available.

'Barabit's Requiem'. A narrow weeping pyramid form, slightly loose and open, from a single, upright trunk. The trunk is relatively straight-growing, and branches weep down and sway slightly outward; reaches 30′ high and 12′ wide. Compared to the much more common 'Pendulum', this is a less interesting, more traditional form.

'Glaucum'. The foliage is quite blue, and the tree is a little narrower than the species, with more upright branching, and a bit slower growing, to 50′ by 30′.

'Greenpeace'. Foliage is very bright, more intensely green than species. It is a dense and compact form, almost rounded when young then becoming a broad, chubby pyramid, 15′ by 15′. We suspect it will continue growing beyond that with the age potential of the species. Gains height at about half the rate of the species.

'Hazel Smith'. A very broadly pyramidal form, full and developing a somewhat rounded rather than spire-like crown, 50′ by 30′. Foliage tinted blue, good cold hardiness.

'Pendulum'. Like something straight out of Dr. Seuss, it wiggles its way upward, occasionally throwing odd branches at unusual points along the trunk, all of which droop with slender pendulous growth. Each tree is a one-of-a-kind sculpture, a living and growing piece of artwork. Fortunately, much more garden-sized than the type, to 25′ tall and 10′ wide. Try planting three as a group and see what evolves. The authors love this tree.

'Von Martin'. A dwarf form, but everything is relative. It grows at about a quarter the rate of the species, making a very dense compact pyramid, 18′ tall and 12′ wide. Use it in a smaller garden, but keep in mind that even the dwarf form of one of the world's most massive trees is hardly a dwarf.

'Greenpeace'

'Pendulum'

'Glaucum'

'Hazel Smith'

'Von Martin'

Sinojackia rehderiana
jacktree

Deciduous. We believe this rarity could be a sleeping giant, waiting for superior selections to advance its use. Habit is loose and open, branches bereft of any regularity. Trees in shade are more open; those in sun compact and shrub-like. Growth is slow to moderate, potentially 15 to 20(30)′ high. Bark is like other members of the Styracaceae, young branches relatively smooth, with peeling stringy bark fragments.

Foliage: Ovate to elliptic-obovate, 1 to 4″ long, two-thirds as wide, entire or with minute serrations, thick-textured, lustrous dark green, yellow-bronze fall color. In zone 8, leaves emerge early, often in March, and are injured by spring frosts. **Flowers/seeds/fruits/cones**: Delicate, shaped like spiders on a dangling thread, white, 1″ across, 5- to 7-petaled, borne on 3- to 5-flowered cyme at the ends of lateral shoots along the stem; flowers open before or with developing leaves, in mid-April (Athens), mid-May (Boston). Fruit is a curious, woody drupe, shaped like an upside-down acorn; shiny brown, ¾″ long, ½″ wide. **Native range**: Eastern China. **Adaptability**: The numerical base line for realistic assessment is unknown because of insufficient plants to evaluate; however, from Boston to Athens, trees have performed admirably. In fact, a plant in the Dirr garden maintained pristine, leathery dark green foliage into November before turning yellow-bronze. No insects, no diseases, no leaf scorch in the hot and dry summer of 2016. But a plant in our Oregon trial appeared stressed and stunted out at about 6′. We speculate it wanted more humidity than Oregon's summer dry air gives. Zones 6 to 8. **Landscape use**: Authors

Sinojackia rehderiana

Sinojackia rehderiana

'La Grima'

'La Grima'

have grown to love this species and envision many uses in contemporary landscapes. Based on its heat, drought, and soil tolerances (as long as well-drained), as well as adaptability to full sun and partial shade, it would succeed in urban environments. Cuttings are easy to root, and container production suits it well. Any gardener would be delighted with jacktree. It is a great conversation piece and stump-the-visitor option. **Street tree use**: No, too small. **In the trade**: Uncommon. 'La Grima' is a broad fastigiate form with the attributes of the species; 'Linda Carol' is a stiff, semi-arching selection.

Sinowilsonia henryi
Henry Wilson tree

Deciduous. Like *Sinojackia*, this monotypic genus is a curiosity and collector's rarity, offering historical links to the great Ernest Henry Wilson, perhaps the greatest of the plant hunters. A specimen at Planting Fields, Long Island, NY, was 30 to 40′ high, rounded in outline, multi-trunked, and loaded with fruit. Seedling growth is fast, but growth slows over time. Bark is gray, relatively smooth. We doubt whether many gardeners and nursery professionals would recognize this species as a member of the Hamamelidaceae; its leaves, flowers, and fruits bear no family resemblance.

Foliage: Broad ovate to obovate, margins with bristle-like serrations, 4 to 6″ long, 4″ wide, medium to dark green above, covered with stellate pubescence below, greenish yellow in fall. Leaves emerge late, and by mid-April in Athens stems were still bare. **Flowers/seeds/fruits/cones**: Monoecious. Greenish, male in 1½ to 2″ long pendent catkins; female in ½ to 1½″ long racemes, April-May, lengthening to 6″ in fruit. Fruit is ovoid, 2-valved, ¾″ long, woody, dehiscent capsule, containing 2 jet black seeds. Fresh seed germinated without pretreatment. **Native range**: Central and western China, collected along a stream in mesic, mixed deciduous forest in rocky soil at 4,300′. **Adaptability**: In the United States, besides the Planting Fields specimen, the species was recorded by the authors at the Brooklyn Botanic Garden, the Cox Arboretum, Canton, GA, the Hoyt Arboretum, Portland, OR, and the Morton Arboretum, Lisle, IL. Numerous seedlings were grown in Georgia, including several plants in the Dirr garden; became obvious quickly that heat, drought, and canker are limiting factors in zone 8. Appears more at home in cooler climates; both the Long Island and Oregon trees were quite vigorous. Zones (5)6 to 7. **Landscape use**: Authors categorize this as a BIO plant, Botanical Interest Only, and have satisfied their curiosity in zone 8 from collecting seed, germinating same, and planting in the garden, only to experience broken dreams. **Street tree use**: No. **In the trade**: Rare.

Sinowilsonia henryi

Sinowilsonia henryi

Sophora japonica. See *Styphnolobium japonicum*

S

Sophora secundiflora. See *Dermatophyllum secundiflorum*

Sorbus alnifolia
Korean mountain ash

Deciduous. Upright oval in form, becoming broadly oval, egg-shaped to round and quite symmetrical. Medium texture, moderate growth rate, to 40′ tall, 30′ wide. Bark is dark gray with diamond-shaped lenticels when young, becoming smooth gray and eventually lightly fissured.

Foliage: Leaves simple, broadly ovate to elliptic with a short acuminate tip, serrate, alder-like (hence the epithet). Foliage is medium to dark green with little luster, usually slightly pubescent on the underside. Fall color can be wonderful, yellow to glowing golden orange. **Flowers/seeds/fruits/cones**: Flowers white, ½″ wide, in 3″ wide corymbs in May. Fruit is small for a mountain ash, about ⅜″ wide, and goes through a series of colors in the fall as it ripens from pink to orange-red to red. **Native range**: Central China to Korea and Japan. **Adaptability**: Like other mountain ash, it likes cool conditions. Borers can be a problem in hotter climates, but the species may be a little more resistant than others in the genus. Although not immune, we have observed this *Sorbus* species to be more fireblight resistant than others. Zones 4 to 6 in the East, to 8 in the maritime Pacific Northwest. In any of the warmer zones, proximity to cool ocean air in summer is important. **Landscape use**: Our favorite mountain ash. If all you know of the genus is the common *S. aucuparia* and its compound leaves, the simple leaves of this species will leave you guessing as to its identity. A more delicate and finer-textured plant than the simple-leafed European *S. aria*. Use as a specimen in a garden for its symmetry, summer texture, and beautiful colors in the fall. Both the fruit and the fall color develop slowly over a long period of time and encompass a range of different but complementary colors. Many years it appears to glow in the autumn. We think this species deserves more attention. **Street tree use**: Not a good choice, intolerant of urban stresses and too wide near the ground. **In the trade**: Sold as the species, either seed-grown or unnamed grafted clones.

Sorbus alnifolia

Sorbus alnifolia

Sorbus americana
American mountain ash

Deciduous. A small tree, variable, shrubby to upright with a rounded top. The texture is fine in summer but medium coarse in winter. Slow-growing to 20 to 25′ high and 20′ wide. Bark is gray and smooth when young, roughening as it ages.

Foliage: Pinnately compound, 6 to 12″ long, with 9 to 17 leaflets, dark green, slightly glossy. Leaflets are lanceolate, sharply serrate, 2 to 3″ long, slender, about a third to half as wide. Fall color can be very nice, yellow-orange to reddish purple. **Flowers/seeds/fruits/cones**: Flowers white, ⅜″ wide, in dense, many-flowered 3 to 6″ wide corymbs. Fruit, ¼″ wide, round, ripens in late summer, bright orange-red to red. **Native range**: Cool areas of northeastern North America, higher elevations in the Appalachians and north through New England, Newfoundland to northern Minnesota. **Adaptability**: Limited geographic adaptability. Needs a cool climate, reasonable moisture, and well-drained soil. Quite susceptible to fireblight and borers in warmer climates. Useful in its native range and in the cool maritime Pacific Northwest. Zones 3 and 4 inland, to 6 or 7 where coastal weather keeps summers cool. **Landscape use**: Where adapted, it is a wonderful small-tree addition, and quite ornamental when in fruit. **Street tree use**: Only as the cultivar in a low-stress climate. **In the trade**: Uncommon, usually represented by the single cultivar. RED CASCADE 'Dwarfcrown' is a beautiful tree, tightly pyramidal and appropriate for small spaces because of its narrowness. Glossy foliage is dark green with a bright red rachis and petiole. Very neatly formed leaflets, long and narrow, wonderful texture. Bright orange fruit display and yellow-orange fall color. One of prettiest little arboreal pyramids you'll see; too bad its adaptability is limited to cool-summer climates. 20′ tall, 10′ wide.

Sorbus americana

RED CASCADE

RED CASCADE

S

Sorbus aria
whitebeam

Deciduous. Upright and broadly pyramidal when young, usually dense, becoming very broadly oval with age. Medium in texture, moderately fast-growing, to 40′ tall and 30′ wide. Bark is smooth and gray-green with prominent horizontal lenticels when young, then gray and a little rougher.

Foliage: Silvery white in spring (hence the common name), the color provided by very heavy pubescence. In summer the leaves become dark green on top but stay light below. Leaves simple rather than compound, 3 to 5½″ long, two-thirds as wide, serrate, broadly elliptical with an acute tip. Fall color is minor, a fair yellow in a good year. **Flowers/seeds/fruits/cones**: Flowers white, ½″ wide, in 2 to 3″ wide dense, many-flowered corymbs in May, malodorous. Fruit ½″ wide, orange-red to bright red, ovoid to round, ripening in fall. **Native range**: Europe, Ireland to the Black Sea and south to the tip of North Africa. **Adaptability**: Like most *Sorbus* species, it prefers a cooler climate and moist but well-drained soils. Although its native range includes warm southern areas, it occurs there at higher altitudes. Adaptable to higher pH soils. Highly susceptible to fireblight. Zone 5 in the East, but up to 8 in the coastal, cool-summer parts of the West. **Landscape use**: Striking foliage, silvery white and ghostly in spring against a dark background. The corrugated leaves provide great texture and become more contrasty in summer when the upper surface turns dark green. Fall fruit display is excellent. A useful garden tree in the Pacific Northwest and Canada in areas cool enough to escape fireblight; rather popular in Britain and northern Europe. **Street tree use**: Not recommended because of fruit load except on a wide, grassy tree lawn. **In the trade**: Available in Europe, uncommon in the United States.

Sorbus aria

Sorbus aria

Sorbus aria

'Lutescens'

'Lutescens'. The name means "becoming yellow," but that's quite a stretch. The spring foliage is cream-white and does have a slightly warm cast that you might call yellowish if the light was right. Broadly oval, 40′ by 25′, a good form, orange-red fruit.

'Magnifica'. Upright and somewhat narrow when young, dense and with good symmetry, it spreads out to a broader oval with age, 40′ tall, 20′ wide. Fruits to ⅝″ wide, bright red.

Sorbus aucuparia

Sorbus aucuparia
European mountain ash

Deciduous. Quite upright, symmetrical, and neatly oval in youth, but spreading to a broad oval or rounded form with age. The branches tend to flare outward and even hang under the fruit load. The texture is medium fine but more coarse in winter, with a medium growth rate, to 35′ high and 25′ wide. Bark is smooth, greenish gray when young, then orange-brown in strong sun to gray-brown, becoming a little rougher with age.

Foliage: Pinnately compound, 5 to 9″ long, with 5 to 15 leaflets, dark green, dull surface. Leaflets are oblong to lanceolate, serrate, ¾ to 2″ long. Fall color yellow-orange to orange-red, nice but not exhilarating. **Flowers/seeds/fruits/cones**: Flowers white, ½″ wide, in dense, many-flowered corymbs in May, malodorous. Fruit, ¼ to ⅜″ wide, round, ripens in late summer, orange to orange-red. **Native range**: Europe. **Adaptability**: Likes a cool climate, reasonable moisture, and well-drained soil. In warmer climates, stress brings on borers. Reports regarding fireblight are mixed; we consider it quite susceptible. Best used in cool northern areas, where these problems are unlikely. Quite cold hardy, content only in zones 3 and 4 inland in the East, but can be used up to zone 8 if ocean air keeps summers cool, as in the Pacific Northwest. **Landscape use**: Often used as a residential tree, and great for attracting wildlife, as birds love the tiny fruit. The form is neat and tidy when young, but it needs room; the branches will splay outward with the weight of the fruit. **Street tree use**: Not recommended, but the narrower cultivars may be appropriate in the most favorable climates; avoid stress and keep the fruit load in mind. **In the trade**: Available.

Sorbus aucuparia

'Aspleniifolia'. Cutleaf foliage. Leaflets deeply serrate at the tip, then progressively more deeply cut, sometimes to the midrib at the base. Very lacy, fine-textured appearance. Broadly oval and a little open in form. Orange-red fruit.

CARDINAL ROYAL 'Michred'. Upright-growing, narrow, good structural form and stiffness, it holds its shape well even with a fruit load, possible for street use, 35′ tall and 20′

CARDINAL ROYAL

S

CARDINAL ROYAL

'Rossica'

Sorbus ×hybrida / Sorbus ×thuringiaca

hybrid mountain ash / oakleaf mountain ash

Nomenclatural note: *Sorbus* can reproduce apomictically (without pollination), forming virtually identical seedlings. When two *Sorbus* species hybridize, the resulting cross will sometimes reproduce apomictically, giving rise to a group of similar plants that are called a microspecies by some botanists and a nomenclaturally confusing mess by the rest of us. *S. ×hybrida* is said to be a hybrid of *S. aucuparia* and either *S. obtusifolia* or *S. rupicola*, but these latter two "species" may simply be varieties or forms of *S. aria*. *S. ×thuringiaca* is a hybrid of *S. aucuparia* and *S. aria*. For practical purposes, these two hybrid species look almost identical, and their cultivars may be listed incorrectly. The take-home message? Ignore the species designation and pay attention to the cultivar.

Deciduous. Upright oval to broadly oval, neatly formed when young and opening slightly with age. Medium texture, grows at a moderate rate to 35′ tall and 25′ wide. Bark is smooth, gray-green to gray-brown when young, then gray and a little roughened.

Sorbus ×thuringiaca

wide. Foliage is deeply colored, almost blue-green. Fruit is small and more highly colored, bright red. Our favorite of the cultivars.

'Rossica'. A sturdy upright grower, a little slower growing and stiffly branched, oval, 30′ tall, 18′ wide. Fruit ⅜″ wide, orange-red. Has a solid reputation for cold hardiness in zone 3.

'Sheerwater Seedling'. Stiffly upright-growing, forming a neat, oval crown. Popular and used as a street tree in Britain, good orange-red fruit.

Foliage: Leaves are very unusual, varying from simple at the tip to compound at the base. The distal portion of the leaf is simple with lobes that become progressively more deeply incised toward the stem. The basal portion of the leaf is usually cut completely to the midrib, forming a compound leaf base. The underside of the leaf is pubescent. **Flowers/seeds/fruits/cones**: Flowers white, ½″ wide, in dense corymbs 2 to 5″ across. Fruit is ½″ wide, round to slightly obovoid, orange-red to bright red. **Native range**: Scandinavia. **Adaptability**: All mountain ash are pH adaptable and need cooler climates and moist soil, but with good drainage. Susceptible to fireblight, which is most prevalent in warmer climates. Best in cool parts of the Pacific Northwest and Canada. Zones 3 to 7(8) in cool parts of the West, but only zones 3 and 4 in the humid, hot-summer East. **Landscape use**: Usually seen as a garden ornamental, valued for its spring flower display, its unusual foliage and texture, and its bright fall fruits. **Street tree use**: Not recommended because of low-hanging branches and fruit drop. **In the trade**: Available.

‘Fastigiata’. Upright, tightly oval, uniform shape. Nice orange fall color, to 35′. In side-by-side testing in Oregon, 3-year-old nursery trees had orange-brown trunks, while trunks of ‘Quercifolia’ were blackish brown; otherwise, the trees were virtually indistinguishable. Listed as *S. ×thuringiaca*.

‘Gibbsii’. Broader oval, more rounded form, shorter at maturity, to 20′. Listed as *S. ×hybrida*.

‘Quercifolia’ (‘Oakleaf’). Upright oval, good density, symmetrical, very similar to ‘Fastigiata’. Good orange fall color, to 30′ tall and 20′ wide. Usually listed as *S. ×hybrida*, but we have seen it under both hybrid names.

‘Gibbsii’

‘Quercifolia’

Sorbus ×thuringiaca   ‘Quercifolia’

S

Stewartia malacodendron

silky stewartia

Deciduous. Primarily a large multi-stemmed shrub; occasionally low-branched pyramidal to wide-spreading tree, 15′ high and as wide or wider; a wonderful wild-collected seedling population of 15 to 20′ high, 20 to 25′ wide trees grows at Mt. Cuba, Greenville, DE. Growth is slow. Bark is gray-brown, largely smooth, with thin vertical fissures. When stewartia is mentioned, exfoliating, multi-colored bark comes to mind; this, *S. ovata*, and *S. rostrata* do not produce the showy exfoliating bark.

Foliage: Ovate to obovate, elliptic-oblong, with fine serrations, 2 to 4″ long, dark green, pubescent beneath, no appreciable fall color. **Flowers/seeds/fruits/cones**: The floral beauty is unmatched. Flowers, pristine white, 2½ to 3(4)″ wide, on short pedicels (stalks), 5-petaled, petals often stained and streaked merlot at the base with a boss of purple-filamented, blue-anthered stamens, appear singly from the leaf axils in May (Athens), June (Asheville, NC). Petals wavy and cut at their ends. Fruits are egg-shaped

Stewartia malacodendron

Stewartia malacodendron

to rounded, woody, 5-valved, ½″ wide, dehiscent, brown, short-pointed capsules containing wingless lustrous brown seeds. **Native range**: Virginia to Florida, west to Arkansas, Louisiana, and Texas. Found on rich wooded bluffs, ravine slopes and creek banks, and sandy soils, usually in the shade of broadleaf trees, often in association with common witch-hazel. **Adaptability**: Root rot in the heavy, wet soils of the Georgia Piedmont is an issue. More cold hardy than credited, with a tree surviving -17°F. Zones 6 to 9. **Landscape use**: Superb specimen plant as well as useful in the border, wildflower garden, and understory plantings. Every cultural specification recommends partial shade and moist, well-drained, acid soils, but we noted trees in full-sun situations. Perfect plant along a creek or stream in partial shade. If only...it was easy for nurseries to grow and gardeners to keep alive, but alas, such is not the situation. Worth procuring, absolutely, and Dirr has tried for more than 70 garden years, with yet another small container specimen ready for installation. Why drive yourself to tears? **Street tree use**: No. **In the trade**: Uncommon. All stewartias are beautiful but difficult to propagate.

Stewartia monadelpha

tall stewartia

Deciduous. One of the fastest-growing stewartias, 12 to 18″ of growth per year in youth, slowing with age. Young plants are pyramidal-conical in outline, low-branched, often with multiple stems. Under cultivation, expect 20 to 30′ in height, similar spread; at Callaway Gardens (Pine Mountain, GA), 30- to 40-year-old trees sited in pine shade are 25′ high and have developed wide-spreading horizontal to upright-spreading branches. Literature cites trees in the wild reaching 75 to 80′ high. Bark is flaky-scaly on 1 to 2″ wide branches, extending to large-diameter trunks, cinnamon-brown to red-brown. Magnificent large-trunked specimens with flaky, exfoliating, cinnamon-colored bark occur in English gardens; in the United States, the Arnold Arboretum, Heritage Gardens (Sandwich, MA), and U.S. National Arboretum house eye-worthy plants.

Foliage: Elliptic to oblong-elliptic, finely serrate, 1½ to 3″ long, to 1½″ wide, dark green, often lustrous, gray-green below, on occasion developing deep red-maroon fall color; foliage holds into December (zone 8) and is frost resistant to about 28°F. **Flowers/seeds/fruits/cones**: The flowers and fruits are the smallest of the *Stewartia* species. Flowers 1 to 1½″ wide, 5-petaled, cupped, white with yellow stamens, opening over a 4-week period in June-July; subtended by 2 large, leafy, green bracts, the entire floral cup abscising intact. Fruit is a woody, brown, 5-valved, ½″ long, sharply beaked, dehiscent capsule with appressed pubescence; capsules persist into winter, still holding a measure of the shiny

Stewartia monadelpha

Stewartia monadelpha

Stewartia monadelpha

Stewartia monadelpha

brown seeds. **Native range**: Japan, South Korea, Jeju Island. **Adaptability**: Our experience with the genus suggests this is the easiest-to-grow species in the Southeast. In the Pacific Northwest, *S. pseudocamellia* is the favored species, but *S. monadelpha* grows as well. Zones (5)6 to 8. **Landscape use**: All stewartias are aristocratic trees; however, this species, with its ease of culture, might be the first option. As a small understory tree, it offers four-season beauty. It could be integrated into woodland plantings with spring ephemerals like trillium, phlox, and foamflower. For single specimen, accent, and shrub border use, it is superb. Ideally, soils should be rich in organic matter, moist, acid, and well drained. Full sun is acceptable, but partial shade suits it best. Stewartias are not easy to propagate by vegetative methods, i.e., cuttings, budding, and grafting. Even seed presents challenges; however, *S. monadelpha* germinated in high percentages after 3 months warm, 3 months cold stratification. Seedlings are growing around the Callaway Gardens plants. **Street tree use**: No. **In the trade**: Available.

S

Stewartia pseudocamellia

Japanese stewartia

Deciduous. The time-honored, most beloved and sought-after *Stewartia* species. Pyramidal-conical in youth, opening with age, but always taller than wide. Size 20 to 40′ in height under cultivation, to 60′ in the wild. In the United States, authors have yet to experience anything approaching 40′, with the exception of several specimens at Heritage Gardens (Sandwich, MA). The tendency is to develop multiple trunks with low-slung lateral branches; the magnificent bark is better displayed in such forms than in a single-trunked tree. Growth is inherently slow. Bark is richly colored and patterned, multi-hued, gray, orange, brown, red-brown, exfoliating in various puzzle-piece sheets; exquisite and unrivaled in the sphere of ornamental-barked trees and shrubs. Trunks develop a sinuous, muscular texture with age not unlike that of *Carpinus caroliniana*. A caveat: the former *S. koreana* has been taxonomically merged with *S. pseudocamellia* and descriptions herein mesh traits of both.

Foliage: Elliptic-ovate to obovate, 2 to 3½″ long, thick-ish, with fine serrations, medium to dark green, turning yellow, red, purple in fall (October-November), often all colors interspersed. We have not witnessed serious insect or disease issues with the foliage of this or any *Stewartia* species. **Flowers/seeds/fruits/cones**: 2 to 3(4)″ wide, cup-shaped to flattened (a koreana trait), white, 5-petaled, stamens with white filaments and orange (yellow) anthers, June-July. Floral cup falling intact. Fruit a broad-ovoid, 5-valved, dehiscent, ¾ to 1″ long, beaked (sharp-pointed), pubescent capsule, with shiny brown seeds; fruits persist into winter. **Native range**: Japan, Korea, growing in open to dense forests to 5,000′ elevation. **Adaptability**: Well adapted and happy in the maritime Pacific Northwest, preferring partial shade but also succeeding in full sun. Authors experienced thriving plants on both coasts and in middle America, where soil conditions allow. Significant cold hardiness (St. Paul, MN) and heat tolerance (Atlanta, GA). Zones (4)5 to 7(8). **Landscape use**: Certainly the most spectacular of all the stewartias and a terrific specimen, accent, woodland-understory addition; group in 3s, 5s, 7s for major effects. In the Southeast, trees are ideally sited

Stewartia pseudocamellia

Stewartia pseudocamellia

in partial shade. Soils should be moist, acid, well drained, and rich with organic matter. Flowering is excellent even under shade, and authors noted beautiful specimens and flower production under the shade of lofty *Liriodendron tulipifera* at Brookside Gardens, Wheaton, MD, and under *Tsuga canadensis* at Heritage Gardens. The merging of *S. koreana* into *S. pseudocamellia* is logical since absolute identification/separation is nearly impossible. Taxonomists created the Koreana Group, which umbrellas the forms with wider-spreading, more or less flat-faced petals, darker bark, and bright autumn color. Regardless of affinity, all are outstanding garden plants with proven performance and reliability. **Street tree use**: No. **In the trade**: Usually sold as the species, as cultivar propagation is difficult. Somewhat messy as to exact parentage; many are hybrids.

'Ballet'. 3½ to 4″ wide flowers, glossy dark green leaves, 46′ high, 33′ wide, with 12″ trunk diameter in 2008; the branches arch gracefully (hence the name). A Polly Hill Arboretum introduction, from open-pollinated seed from the Arnold Arboretum in 1966.

'Harold Hillier'. Reliable autumn color.

S. ×henryae (*S. monadelpha* × *S. pseudocamellia*). More prevalent in arboreta and botanical gardens than acknowledged. Foliage, flowers, and bark are intermediate, the flowers 2″ wide, white with yellow stamens; bark scaly, flaky, cinnamon-brown, with the large lightning-bolt patches of *S. pseudocamellia*.

'Milk and Honey'. Distinct strong-growing upright form with abundant, 3 to 4″ wide, flat-faced, ruffled white flowers, reddish brown bark; autumn color is orange-red; 40′ high, 30′ wide in 42 years. Introduced by the Polly Hill Arboretum, West Tisbury, MA.

'Mint Frills'. White petals blushed with pale green; original tree is 40′ by 29′; Polly Hill Arboretum introduction.

'Pilar Bella'. Narrow, upright form from Crispin Silva, Molalla, OR.

'Scarlet Sentinel'. Dense upright habit, grew 30′ high, 16′ wide in 18 years. White flowers and red-pink stamens; gray-brown bark exfoliates in thin strips; fruits form but soon abort. Chance seedling (*S. ovata* var. *grandiflora* × *S. pseudocamellia*) from the Arnold Arboretum.

Stewartia pseudocamellia

Stewartia pseudocamellia

'Pilar Bella'

S

'Scarlet Sentinel'

Stewartia sinensis

Stewartia sinensis

Chinese stewartia

Deciduous. Beautiful, graceful species, delicately branched and round-headed. A 50′ high specimen with 30″ trunk diameter was noted in China, but expect 15 to 25′ in height and width under garden culture. Growth is typically slow, like all stewartias; an 8″ seedling took 15 years to reach 15.4′ high and 13.5′ wide. On the other hand, authors recorded 2′ of height increase on containerized plants in a single season. Bark is spectacular, arguably the most beautiful of all species. From our experience, every tree is different and typecasting bark coloration is nonsensical—but here goes. On young branches and trunks, it exfoliates in irregular tan, amber, and brown wax-paper-like sheets and fissures, exposing a sandstone to deeper, close to purple-brown, smooth underbark. Large trunks are "as smooth as alabaster and the colour of weathered sandstone," according to an English reference.

Stewartia sinensis

Stewartia sinensis

Foliage: Leaves are elliptic-obovate to oblong-elliptical, medium green above, bright green below, remotely serrate, 1½ to 4″ long, ⅝ to 1¾″ wide, emerging leaves tinged red, quite pubescent, both features disappearing quickly; fall color yellow to subdued red to orange-red. **Flowers/seeds/ fruits/cones**: Not as large as *S. pseudocamellia*, 1½ to 2(2½)″ wide, composed of 5 white petals and light lemon-yellow filaments in the center, fragrant, open in June, continuing into July. Does not overwhelm from a distance, but pretty on close inspection. Fruit is a woody, ovoid to globose, 5-angled and -beaked, ¾″ wide dehiscent capsule, ripening in October and persisting into winter. **Native range**: Moderate elevations in the mountainous regions of east-central China. **Adaptability**: Successful on both coasts and the upper South. Zones 5 to 7. **Landscape use**: Too often relegated to an arboretum or botanical garden, this species is worthy of greater use in American gardens. What else can we deliver in the way of accolades? As with other *Stewartia* species, moist, acid, well-drained soil and full sun to partial shade are ideal. Provide supplemental water in drought periods; leaves will develop brown (necrotic) margins if water-stressed. Strictly a garden tree where cultural conditions are managed. This and other stewartias are not troubled by insects. Specimen, accent, or perhaps even groupings where the bark in all its exfoliating and color manifestations could be expressed. Worth dreaming about. **Street tree use**: No. **In the trade**: Seed-grown, not common.

Styphnolobium japonicum (*Sophora japonica*)
Japanese pagodatree

Deciduous. Develops and maintains an upright-spreading branching habit from youth until old age, with main structural branches stretching high above. Form is usually oval with trees taller than wide, although some are more

Styphnolobium japonicum

Styphnolobium japonicum

rounded. Moderately fast-growing, medium fine texture, reaching 60′ high and 40′ wide. Bark is very soft and green for many years. Older trees grow slowly, with much tougher, gray-brown, ridged and furrowed bark.

Foliage: Pinnately compound leaves, 6 to 10″ long, with 7 to 17 leaflets. Leaflets oval with an acute tip, 1 to 2″ long, half as wide, entire, dark green and slightly glossy. Fall color is yellowish but rarely impressive. **Flowers/seeds/fruits/cones**: One of the best summer flower displays among temperate trees. Flowers creamy white, in large panicles to 12″ long and lightly fragrant. Flowering can be heavy and turn the entire canopy white. **Native range**: China, Korea. **Adaptability**: Difficult to establish, but once established in a favorable climate, it can be relatively problem-free and long-lasting. Needs good drainage and is drought tolerant. In the United States, it performs best in the Northeast and Mid-Atlantic.

S

'Gold Standard'

MILLSTONE

'Pendula'

It is problematic when young, as its bark scratches easily, and scratched bark or frozen tips quickly lead to destructive fungal cankers. Many nurseries have stopped producing the species because of this; however, the tree becomes reliable with age. Zones 5 to 7. **Landscape use**: A large tree, quite tolerant of city conditions, it makes a park or residential shade tree that is valued for its summer flowering. Its upright-spreading branch structure is easily pruned for clearance, rendering the area below usable. **Street tree use**: Very good in favorable climates once established, but remember that the green bark of young trees is susceptible to cankering. **In the trade**: Available.

'Gold Standard'. Golden yellow new growth branches, showiest on young trees in the winter. Color fades to a more traditional gray-brown after a couple seasons' growth. New foliage is yellow-green. Rounded form, probably to 30'.

MILLSTONE 'Halka'. Upright oval in form, more compact and narrower than 'Regent', and with the best canker resistance we have seen. Slightly finer texture. Probably the best choice for street use. 45' tall, 35' wide.

'Pendula'. A beautiful, mounded, weeping form rarely seen in the United States, and only a little more common in Europe, to 20' by 20'. In this species, the form causes us to worry about breakage. Rarely flowers. Comes partially true-to-type from seed.

'Regent'. The most popular variety, very fast-growing, upright oval to rounded in form, 55' by 45', with especially handsome, glossy dark green foliage. We have observed that its rapid growth makes it more canker-prone at a young age.

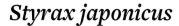

'Regent'

Styrax japonicus

Styrax japonicus
Japanese snowbell

Deciduous. Beautiful, dainty, elegant tree, valued for its dense oval to rounded form, 20 to 30′ high and wide. Growth is slow to moderate, and newly planted trees respond (1 to 2′ per year) to good husbandry. Bark is gray-brown, smooth, sinewy, developing irregular, orangish brown, interlacing fissures; it's eye-catching and a great identification feature.

Foliage: Ovate to elliptic-oblong, 1 to 3½″ long, ½ to 1½″ wide, remotely toothed or entire, medium to dark green leaves. Foliage may appear later than many trees in spring; authors suspect this is partially mediated by lack of sufficient chill hours, particularly in the Southeast. But leaves hold late, sometimes turning a good yellow but more often remaining green, dying off same, with a hint of yellow or ruined by a freeze. A 30′ high, 35′ wide, broad rounded specimen was in full green leaf at Norfolk Botanical Garden in

Styrax japonicus

late October. Foliage is resistant to pests and diseases and highly heat and drought tolerant; authors were surprised to find no foliar damage in the recent severe drought years in the Southeast. **Flowers/seeds/fruits/cones**: Fragrant white flowers, yellow-stamened, 5-lobed, bell-shaped, ¾″ high and wide, each on a pendulous, 1½″ long pedicel (stalk), from short lateral shoots, each with 3 to 6 flowers, April-May, after leaves develop and visible on the underside of the branches. Fruits are ovoid, dry drupes, gray, ½″ long, lost among the foliage and often produced in prodigious quantities; outer covering dries, splits, and releases hard-coated, shiny brown seed. **Native range**: Wide distribution in China, Korea, Japan, Philippines, and Taiwan. **Adaptability**: Zones 5 to 8. Significant variation in cold hardiness; Korean collections by the U.S. National Arboretum are possibly the hardiest. **Landscape use**: One of the prettiest small flowering trees, it has received increased attention from growers and gardeners for its ease of transplanting; and with the infusion of cold- and heat-tolerant cultivars, there is even more to love, a selection to grace any garden. For maximum growth, provide moist, acid, well-drained soil abundantly endowed with organic matter. Site in full sun to partial shade, ideally where the flowers will be viewed from below. Once established, trees prove tenacious and durable; heritage specimens are extant in arboreta and college campuses, with a 100-plus-year-old tree at the Arnold Arboretum, a 60-year-old at University of Massachusetts, and a 40-year-old at Milliken Arboretum in Spartanburg, SC. A troubling insect, ambrosia beetle, has injured and killed trees. During spring freezes, the cambium may be damaged, resulting in latent injury; seedling trees and some cultivars may break bud erratically because of this. Despite these issues, the majority of trees survive and prosper. **Street tree use**: Potential; use narrower upright varieties. **In the trade**: Seed-grown trees are variable and performance is spotty. Cultivars are strongly recommended and increasingly available; most emerged in the last 20 years. Exciting breeding work portends a purple-leaf weeper.

'Carillon'

'Carillon'. White-flowered, stiff, weeping form with tortuous, decurved branches, growing 8 to 12′ high. Ideally, top work on the species understock to produce a small tree, or stake and train.

'Emerald Pagoda' ('Sohuksan'). Magnificent, vase-shaped (young) to oval-rounded (mature) selection, with larger, leathery, lustrous dark green, heat- and drought-tolerant foliage, flowers to 1″ long, smooth gray bark, and 20 to 30′ height. Flowers develop on 2- to 3-year-old seedlings. We observed magnificent specimens in Georgia and North Carolina, yet the industry has difficulties producing this cultivar. Late winter–early spring freezes when the sap is moving appear to injure the cambium with sporadic late leafing and branch dieback resulting. A J. C. Raulston introduction from Korea.

'Evening Light'

'Evening Light'. A sought-after selection for small gardens. Dense upright oval habit and purple-maroon emerging leaves, becoming maroon-green and holding color into fall in zone 8; white flowers with contrasting maroon calyx (sepals). During a 2016 tour with over 300 people visiting the Dirr garden, this was one of the most asked-about plants.

'Fragrant Fountain'. More graceful tree form than 'Carillon', with slender arching secondary shoots and finer-textured, lustrous dark green foliage, estimate 12′ by 8′.

'Fragrant Fountain'

'Emerald Pagoda'

'Evening Light'

'Fragrant Fountain'

S

'Frosted Emerald'

MARLEY'S PINK

MARLEY'S PINK

'Frosted Emerald'. Pretty white-margined, green-centered leaves; not vigorous but certainly eye-catching, no doubt best suited to partial shade.

MARLEY'S PINK 'JL Weeping'. Pink-flowered weeper with lustrous dark green foliage; this is a particularly vigorous selection; excellent performance in Dirr garden; requires

staking to develop a leader, then secondary branches rise and arch gracefully on their own; estimate 10 to 15′ high. Pink has not faded in the heat of zone 8. Our Oregon trials showed it is the best pink weeper yet, in both vigor and flower color.

'Pink Chimes'. 15′ high and wide in University of Georgia trials, produces large quantities of pink flowers in late April–early May; lustrous dark green foliage; has weathered terrible heat and drought with pristine foliage into November. Oregon trials found it to be less vigorous and less reliable than most white-flowered forms, pink flowers pale in sun.

PRYSTINE SPIRE 'MTFSJ'. Strongly upright, almost columnar when young with ascending branches, becoming narrow oval, the tightest cultivar of the species. Dark green, lustrous, leathery foliage. Heavy flowering, white. Heat tolerance in zone 8, reaching 20 to 25′ tall, 8′ wide.

SNOW CHARM 'JFS-E'. Vigorous, healthy, upright-spreading, growing to a broadly oval form, 25′ tall, 20′ wide. White flowers are broader-spreading than typical, leaves are darker green and a bit larger. Best yellow fall color of the cultivars. Selected for reliable spring bud break without the regrowth failure that often occurs in *Styrax*. An authors' favorite.

'Pink Chimes'

SNOW CHARM

SNOWCONE

SNOW CHARM

SNOW CHARM

SNOWCONE 'JFS-D'. Narrower than the species and finer-textured, with smaller and more abundant leaves. Flowers are equally abundant; perhaps the most prolific flowering we have seen among the cultivars. Form is extremely neat, a near perfect cone, estimate 25′ by 15′. If pruned up, it can make a small street tree for narrow tree lawns. Like SNOW CHARM, it was selected for reliable spring bud break without the regrowth failure that plagues *Styrax*.

S

SNOWCONE

'Spring Showers'

'Spring Showers'. Selected by the U.S. National Arboretum for late bud break, 2 to 3 weeks later than typical, avoiding spring frosts. Upright oval to rounded form, good growth, but fairly average medium green summer foliage. A superb performer for over 10 years in Georgia trials.

Styrax obassia
fragrant snowbell

Deciduous. Big brother to the smaller, more restrained, finer-textured *S. japonicus* and a beautiful flowering tree in its own right, pyramidal-oval in youth, more open and rounded with age, with sturdy ascending branches and a robust persona. Size 20 to 30′ high and wide, but 50′ trees are known. Growth is fast in youth, slowing with age. Bark is gray to gray-brown, smooth, marked with thin, shallow, orangish brown vertical fissures. On 2- to 3-year-old stems, the bark exfoliates in papery sheets and flakes.

Styrax obassia

Foliage: Suborbicular to broad-ovate, sometimes tri-cuspidate (3-lobed) at apex, finely and remotely toothed above the middle, 3 to 8″ long, two-thirds as wide, medium green, slightly dull, thickish pubescence below, on occasion beautiful golden yellow fall color. Leaves emerge early, often in early April in Athens, and a late frost kills leaves and emerging flowers with full foliation by June. **Flowers/seeds/fruits/cones**: Develop with the emerging leaves; fully expressed when leaves are full size; each white, fragrant, bell-shaped, 1″ long, borne in 4 to 8(10)″ long gracefully arching panicles in April-May; flowers peek out from the foliage, opening from base to apex, the peduncle turning slightly upward toward the apex. Fruit is similar to *S. japonicus*, a ¾″ long, ovoid, dry, pubescent gray drupe. **Native range**: Japan, Manchuria, Korea. **Adaptability**: More consistently cold hardy than *S. japonicus*, tolerating -25°F. Zones 5 to 8. **Landscape use**: Authors believe the species deserves greater use in American gardens. Seedling populations flowered in 3 years, but even if trees never flowered, garden use would be justified, as the smooth trunk and inherent twists, turns, and sinuations of the branches add great architectural winter beauty. Like *S. japonicus*, the species is well suited for specimen use, parks, and campuses. A Great Plant Pick by Seattle's Elisabeth C. Miller Botanical Garden. Provide moist, well-drained, acid soils laden with organic matter, in full sun to partial shade. **Street tree use**: Potential. **In the trade**: All plants are seed-grown; variation is a given. No cultivars are known.

Syringa reticulata
Japanese tree lilac

Deciduous. Stiffly upright-spreading, forming a broad inverted cone to oval shape. Medium texture, medium slow-growing, to 25′ tall and 20′ wide. Bark is cherry-like, attractive, slightly reddish brown to grayish, with prominent horizontal lenticels.

Foliage: Leaves simple, ovate to broadly ovate with an acute to acuminate tip, margin entire, dark green, 2 to 5½″ long and two-thirds as wide. The leaf surface is slightly reticulate, sheen slightly satiny. Fall color is dull yellow-green to a nice yellow. **Flowers/seeds/fruits/cones**: Flowers tiny, each about ¼″ wide, with 4 petals, but in dense, upright panicles 8 to 12″ long and almost as wide, creamy white to pure

Styrax obassia

Styrax obassia

Syringa reticulata

S

Syringa reticulata

IVORY PILLAR

'Golden Eclipse'

'Ivory Silk'

SNOWDANCE

white. Flowers in June at a welcome time, although some don't like the privet-like scent, very showy. Seed capsules, ¾″ long, brown, clustered in fall, not ornamental. **Native range**: Northern Japan. **Adaptability**: Likes a cooler climate with distinct seasonal change; well adapted to the upper Midwest's warm summers and cold winters. Does well in the North and the Northeast but does not like the continuous heat of the South. Successful in the Pacific Northwest but probably better east of the Cascades with drier air and more sun, which it needs. pH adaptable. Quite cold hardy, zones 3 to 7. **Landscape use**: A great little garden tree, flowering in summer, after the abundance of the spring blooming season has passed. Upright branching leaves good clearance below, providing useable space right up to the trunk and making it suitable for smaller gardens. Very few small flowering trees are upright enough to allow such use below the canopy. **Street tree use**: Excellent for the purpose, especially the cultivars noted as being more upright and narrow in form. **In the trade**: Available.

'Golden Eclipse'. Variegated, the leaf center dark green and the broad margin progressing from a hardly discernible light green in spring to glowing bright yellow in summer. Quite pretty on the right day, but we have found the yellow portion can burn and some leaves appear almost completely green. Cream-white flowers, oval form, 18′ tall, 15′ wide.

IVORY PILLAR 'Willamette'. Upright and narrow, a bit tighter than 'Ivory Silk', to 25′ tall and 15′ wide. Cream-white flowers. A good street tree form.

'Ivory Silk'. By far the most commonly planted cultivar, and it would be hard to argue that it is not the best. A nice upright form, tightly oval to flaring a bit on top to an inverted cone, 25′ tall, 15′ wide, with good clearance below, excellent for streets and gardens. Ivory-white flowers. Reliable, well proven, and still our favorite.

SNOWCAP 'Elliott'. Slower growing, more compact than the type, to 18′ by 18′. Cream-white flowers, good for a small garden.

SNOWDANCE 'Bailnce'. Selected for early and heavy flowering, cream-white flowers. Despite prolific bloom, it sets a low fruit load. Spreads as wide as tall or a little more, about 20′ by 20′. Use as a garden ornamental where its low width and spread are desired, not for streets.

'Summer Storm'. Selected for its fast vigorous growth and uniform size in production. Upright and broadly pyramidal to oval in shape, 25′ tall, 15′ wide. Cream-white flowers.

'Ivory Silk'

Syringa reticulata subsp. *pekinensis* (*S. pekinensis*)

Peking lilac

Deciduous. Upright-spreading to broadly spreading, usually low-branched or multi-stem, loose and informal. Moderately fine-textured, medium growth rate, to 20′ tall and wide. Bark brown with prominent horizontal lenticels, exfoliating. It can be outstanding, peeling in paper-thin, curled layers and hanging from the trunk, orange-brown at its best, but it can also be rather plain on some seed-grown trees.

Foliage: Leaves simple, ovate to long ovate with an acute or acuminate tip, margin entire, dark green, 2 to 4″ long and 1 to 2″ wide. Leaf surface varies from satiny to glossy. Fall color is usually yellowish, not especially bright. **Flowers/ seeds/fruits/cones**: Very small creamy white to pure white flowers held in dense panicles, 6 to 12″ long and almost as wide. Flowers in June when few other trees are blooming, fragrant and quite showy. Seed capsules are held in clusters in the fall, brown and not ornamental. **Native range**: Northern China. **Adaptability**: Likes a continental climate, cold winters and hot summers; well adapted to the upper Midwest. Needs well-drained soil but is tolerant of a wide range of pH. More heat tolerant than *S. reticulata*. Good cold hardiness, zones 3 to 7. **Landscape use**: A great small flowering tree. Use it for its summer bloom and fragrance. Multi-stem and low-branched trees look great when pruned up to expose the bark. As such, a four-season ornamental, fit for a fine garden. **Street tree use**: A little low and spreading for the purpose, but the more upright cultivars can work with pruning. **In the trade**: Available. Some cultivars have been selected for bark characteristics.

BEIJING GOLD 'Zhang Zhiming'. Selected for its creamy yellow flowers, quite different from the other cultivars. The leaves are longer and more slender, quite glossy. Cinnamon-brown bark is average for the species. 20′ by 20′.

GREAT WALL

BEIJING GOLD

Syringa reticulata subsp. *pekinensis*

Syringa reticulata subsp. *pekinensis*

SUMMER CHARM

CHINA SNOW

CHINA SNOW 'Morton'. Selected for its wonderful exfoliating bark, amber to orange-brown, which glows when highlighted by the sun. White flowers. Finer-textured appearance, with small dark green leaves. The authors love this tree as a multi-stem to show off the bark; we think it is the best choice for that characteristic. 20′ by 20′.

COPPER CURLS 'SunDak'. Selected and named for its brown, curling, exfoliating bark in North Dakota, where its cold hardiness was well proven. White flowers. A little slower growing than the aforementioned cultivars. 20′ by 20′.

GREAT WALL 'WFH2'. Symmetrically branched, upright, and a narrow oval in shape, this cultivar has an outstanding and easily maintained form, compared to the loose and broad-spreading form of the subspecies. The best choice for street use. Nice exfoliating bark. Handsome glossy green foliage turns yellow in the fall. 25′ tall, 18′ wide.

SUMMER CHARM 'DTR 124'. The first subsp. *pekinensis* selection, very tight and compact in form, with elegant dark green foliage. Gray-brown bark has little character. Slower growing and maturing to a smaller size, with a more neatly rounded shape, 15′ tall and wide. White flowers.

S

T

Taiwania cryptomerioides
Taiwan redwood, coffin tree

Evergreen conifer. Monotypic genus. A rare but elegant sharp-needled conifer, maintaining a central leader with horizontal-arching secondary branches from which tertiary shoots emanate, suspended like curtains. When well grown, it is one of the most beautiful of all needle evergreens, somewhat reminiscent of *Picea breweriana* in habit. Ultimate North American landscape size is unknown, with 30 to 40′ in height after 20 years a reality in Vancouver, BC, and a 40′ high plant in Portland, OR, at Elk Rock Garden. In the Southeast (Norfolk, VA; Savannah, GA; Atlanta, GA) the largest observed was 30′ high. Why list the varied sizes? Because in the wild, the species ascends 200′ and greater. Bark has flat gray-grown ridges and reddish brown furrows, with age fibrous, stringy, peeling in strips; seldom visible because lower branches persist and shroud the trunk. The rot-resistant wood was used for coffins (hence coffin tree).

Foliage: Needles straight or sickle-shaped, diamond-shaped in cross section, pointing toward end of shoot, stout, extremely sharp-pointed, ⅓ to ¾″ long, spirally arranged and fully encircling the stem; green, blue-green, sides of needles with waxy white bands; needles may discolor in cold, windy sites and full-sun exposure, turning bronze-brown. **Flowers/seeds/fruits/cones**: Monoecious. Cones are cylindrical, egg-shaped, ½ to 1″ long, half as wide, slow to develop; the 20-year-old British Columbia trees did not produce cones. **Native range**: *Taiwania cryptomerioides* now includes *T. flousiana*, so the extended range is China, Myanmar, Vietnam, and Taiwan. **Adaptability**: Choice specimens are scattered across the continent from Virginia to Florida to Cascadia. Zones 7 to 9, 10 on the West Coast.

Taiwania cryptomerioides

Taiwania cryptomerioides

Landscape use: Probably resides in the domain of the collector. Is there a reason the species is not widely planted for specimen use or in groupings? Availability is probably the limiting factor, and few gardeners know of its existence. Makes a striking specimen as a young plant, with its wide-spreading lower branches literally sweeping the lawn. Soils should be moist, well drained, with an acid reaction. A suitable environment offers full sun to partial shade and shelter from severe winds. Seeds germinate without pretreatment but perished after transplanting in Georgia work. Assuming cuttings could be rooted, authors speculate they must be taken from vertical shoots to avoid plagiotropism, a condition where lateral shoots grow horizontally as shrubs, vertical shoots as trees (orthotropism). Pest- and disease-free, it is one of those plant-and-enjoy species. Elegant to view; lethal to touch (extremely prickly). **Street tree use**: Probably not. **In the trade**: Uncommon.

Tamarix ramosissima

Tamarix chinensis / Tamarix ramosissima

Chinese tamarisk / salt cedar

Nomenclatural note: These two species, considered synonymous by some, are very difficult to separate. *T. chinensis* flowers on last year's growth; *T. ramosissima* on current season's. They may be confused in the trade. Descriptions and comments apply to both.

Deciduous. Loose, open, upright large shrub or low-branched tree, wild in form. Foliage and flowers are very fine-textured, but the winter form is coarse. Fast-growing to 15′ tall and wide. Bark is reddish brown and smooth at first, then gray-brown; fissured and rough at an early age, becoming ridged and scaly.

Foliage: Bright green to gray-green scaly leaves, each ⅛″ long, appressed to the stems, juniper-like. Yellow fall color. **Flowers/seeds/fruits/cones**: Attractive flowers in early summer, which is when the plant has some redeeming value. Flowers held in dense racemes, 1 to 3″ long, bright pink, along long flowering shoots, giving an arching or fountain-like effect as they bend the tip growth. Seeds

tiny, less than ¹⁄₁₆″ long, with tufts of hair that make them wind-borne, up to 500,000 produced per plant. **Native range**: Eurasia, usually on saline soils. **Adaptability**: Grows in hot, dry, adverse environments. Adapted to salinity and desert conditions. Zones 3 to 8. **Landscape use**: We have to admit it is quite pretty in flower. And we have to admit it is tough and will grow where little else will. But therein lies the problem: this is one of the most aggressively invasive plants, especially so along the ecologically sensitive watercourses of the desert West. There, they disrupt the environment by withdrawing scarce groundwater and depositing salt-laden foliage on the soil surface, making soils more saline and inhibiting other plants, to their advantage. Highly salt tolerant, and invasive in many other areas on dry sandy and gravelly soils. Our advice is simple: don't plant it. There are plenty of other choices. **Street tree use**: Not recommended. **In the trade**: Several cultivars, none seedless, so we don't recommend.

Tamarix ramosissima

Taxodium distichum

common baldcypress

Deciduous conifer. Another superb native species and one of the great landscape trees, providing beauty, reliability, adaptability, and permanence. Invariably pyramidal-conical in youth, widening with age, yet still maintaining a full canopy. Another version occurs with trees developing a flat-topped head of irregular wide-spreading branches and tall central trunk. Authors observed both growth forms in the wild and under cultivation. Landscape size approximates 50 to 70′ in height, 20 to 30′ wide, to 80 to 100′ in the wild. Quite a track star, averaging 2′ or more per year. A Wichita, KS, study reported more than 2½′ per year over a 9-year period. Bark is reddish brown, grayish brown, fibrous, stringy, sloughing in strips, strongly buttressed and fluted

Taxodium distichum

Taxodium distichum

Taxodium distichum

at base (especially in wet soils, swamps). A baldcypress swamp is a never-to-be-forgotten experience, the gigantic buttressed clear trunks ascending and narrowing to a flat-topped, spreading canopy 90′ above the ground. Congaree National Park, SC, is home to a remarkable old-growth baldcypress forest.

Foliage: Needles are arranged spirally around the stem but disposed in a 2-ranked, flattened position, each linear-lanceolate, ⅓ to ¾″ long, 1/16 to 1/12″ wide, bright yellow-green when emerging, soft sage-green in summer, rich pumpkin to russet-orange to brown in autumn, persisting into November-December. **Flowers/seeds/fruits/cones**: Monoecious. Male in pendulous, 4 to 5″ long panicles, March-April; female cones subglobose with spirally arranged peltate scales. Cones are globular or ovoid, short-stalked, 1 to 1½″ wide, green to purple, resinous when young, brown at maturity, ripening the first year. **Native range**: Delaware, Virginia, to Florida; west to Oklahoma and Texas, north along rivers to southeast Missouri, Illinois, and Indiana. Always in or near water, forming pure

Taxodium distichum

Taxodium distichum

Taxodium distichum

stands, swamps, floodplains, riverbanks, even brackish water. **Adaptability**: Extraordinarily well adapted to drier, urban soils and colder climates. Authors remember the giant baldcypress along the Riverwalk in San Antonio; as street trees in Augusta, GA; and 60 to 70′ specimens on the University of Illinois campus, Champaign-Urbana. Any soil,

except high pH, is suitable. Have observed trees growing in sand along the shoreline of Mobile Bay, AL, and in a swamp at Dawes Arboretum, Newark, OH. The message of this travelogue...adaptability as far north as Minneapolis–St. Paul. Zones (4)5 to 11. **Landscape use**: Uses are infinite and controlled by the vision of the designer, from street/avenue/ boulevard tree to rain garden/wetland mitigation option. Hails from swamps, but, in brief, once established, it does not require consistent moisture in the root zone. In fact, the "cypress knees" develop from the roots of trees in evenly moist to wet situations. The knees are an obstacle course for mowers and other landscaping equipment. Mites may attack trees in hot, dry weather and diminish foliage color, but do not otherwise cause damage. **Street tree use**: Excellent. **In the trade**: The many cultivars offer consistency of habit from upright pyramidal (SHAWNEE BRAVE) to weeping ('Cascade Falls', 'Falling Waters') to a thickish telephone pole eventually with 45° angle branches ('Peve Minaret'). We owe a debt of gratitude to Earl Cully, Heritage Trees, Jacksonville, IL, who understood the inherent greatness of *T. distichum* and var. *imbricarium*. DEBONAIR, 'Prairie Sentinel', and SHAWNEE BRAVE were among the first introductions and have inspired others to introduce superior clones.

T

AUTUMN GOLD

'Cascade Falls'

'Cascade Falls'

'Cascade Falls'

DEBONAIR

'Falling Waters'

AUTUMN GOLD 'Sofine'. Soft-textured, compact pyramidal form with strong central leader, dense branches, sage-green needles, and rusty orange fall color. Southern nurseries report it to be a good grower, 60′ by 30′.

'Cascade Falls'. Wild, sprawling, arching, weeping form. Can be trained to a neat weeping form, or branches can be allowed to build into an octopus-like habit 20′ and greater; fast-growing and benefits from staking to develop a leader/trunk; discovered in Auckland, New Zealand, and introduced to the United States by Stanley and Sons Nursery, Boring, OR.

DEBONAIR 'Morris'. Fine-textured, pyramidal selection, more open and feathery than 'Prairie Sentinel', medium green needles turn bronze in autumn, evaluated for 37 years before introduction, during which time it withstood -28°F. Estimated size of 40 to 50′ by 12 to 20′. A var. *imbricarium* form.

'Falling Waters' ('Falling Water'). Another weeper, with secondary branches cascading-pendulous, but it must be trained (staked) to develop a central leader. Minor

'Falling Waters'

T

differences between this and 'Cascade Falls' based on side-by-side comparisons in Oregon and Georgia; both pendulous, but 'Falling Waters' slightly stiffer, with reflexed tips.

'Fox Red'. More loose, open in habit with bright green needles, turning orange-red, estimate 60′ high and 15′ wide. A var. *imbricarium* form.

GREENFEATHER 'Carolyn Malone'. Fast-growing, uniform, upright-narrow selection with soft, feathery, bright green needles, orange-brown fall color, 50′ high, 20′ wide, a var. *imbricarium* form. Introduced by John Malone and named for his wife.

GREEN WHISPER 'JFS-SGPN'. Pyramidal habit; very lush-looking, foliage reminiscent of fluffy bright green feathers, needles don't go off-color in midsummer; rusty orange fall color; 55′ by 30′.

var. *imbricarium* (pond cypress). This has been through the taxonomic ringer as two separate taxa, *T. ascendens* and *T. distichum* var. *nutans*. This latest varietal designation is largely because of hybridization and intergradation with

T. distichum. A major if inconsistent difference is the slender needle- to awl-shaped leaves, which are appressed to the stem, juniper-like, rather than spreading as in *T. distichum*. The prominently ridged and furrowed bark is thicker than on *T. distichum*, and trees are more compact (narrow, ascending branches), reaching 70 to 80′ high, 15 to 20′ wide, potential to 100′. Occurs naturally in shallow ponds and wetlands from Virginia to Louisiana, rarely at elevations above 100′, zones 5 to 11. Authors boated through immense var. *imbricarium* in Georgia's Okefenokee Swamp, where *Pieris phillyreifolia* grows inside the dead bark, sending lateral branches out from the trunks.

LINDSEY'S SKYWARD 'Skyward'. Upright-columnar, the branches ascending tightly to form a symmetrical column, green needles, rusty orange fall color, listed as 25′ by 10′, but probably larger; parent plant was listed at 23′ by 6′ after 20 years.

var. *mexicanum* (*T. mucronatum*; Mexican baldcypress). The National Tree of Mexico, cultivated in warm-temperate climates like southeastern Australia and coastal California; reserved for zones 8 to 10(11). A bushy, rounded tree with graceful drooping semi-evergreen to evergreen needles, possibly better adapted to high pH alkaline soils. The famous specimen in Oaxaca was 117′ high and 145′ wide;

GREENFEATHER

GREEN WHISPER

GREEN WHISPER

var. *imbricarium*

a tree in Cameron County, TX, was 68′ high, 99′ wide. A tree at the JC Raulston Arboretum, Raleigh, NC, still held green needles in mid-December; however, cold damage was evident, possibly related to an early fall freeze. Native from southern Texas through Mexico to Guatemala on wet soils, primarily in the highlands. Hybrids between this and *T. distichum* continue to be developed in China; one such, 'Nanjing Beauty', was brought to the United States by David Creech, whose *Taxodium* collection at Stephen F. Austin State University, Nacogdoches, TX, is the most comprehensive in the country.

'Peve Minaret'. Initially a telephone pole with soft green needles, opening with age, and much larger than the original literature (10′) with 25′ high trees in cultivation. Authors noted significant spider mite damage on this cultivar.

'Prairie Sentinel'. The narrowest form, tight-columnar in youth, a degree chunkier and more open with age, soft green needles, orange-brown fall color; 50 to 60′ high, 10 to 15′ wide; beautiful in large groupings or as an accent tree; a serviceable street tree where lateral space is restricted. A selection of var. *imbricarium*.

SHAWNEE BRAVE 'Michelson'. Tight pyramidal outline, maintaining this shape into maturity, tremendous for streets or boulevards; fast-growing; parent tree was 75′ high, 25′ wide, from Johnson County, IL. Probably the most uniform habit of all the introductions, as large trees look like little trees...only taller. Good cold hardiness in the North.

var. *mexicanum*

'Nanjing Beauty'

T

'Peve Minaret'

LINDSEY'S SKYWARD

'Prairie Sentinel'

SHAWNEE BRAVE

var. *imbricarium*

'Prairie Sentinel'

SHAWNEE BRAVE

Taxus baccata

English yew, common yew

Evergreen conifer. Throughout the British Isles, this somber yew graces churchyards, manor houses, estates, gardens, and parks as a one-of-a-kind tree. Habit varies from broad-rounded to broadly spreading, with large fluted, thick trunks. Size 30 to 60′ high, 15 to 25′ wide, often wider at maturity. Trees 85′ high with 8′ trunk diameter are known. In Scotland, at Dundonnell House, a 300-year-old tree is still in remarkable condition. Growth is slow in youth and slower toward maturity. Bark is reddish brown, thin, scaly, flaky, fibrous to corky, peeling to reveal purple-red areas; eventually fluted on old trunks yet maintaining the sloughing scales and flakes. The elastic wood was prized for longbows and the bent parts of Windsor chairs.

Foliage: Needles are spirally arranged around the stem, more or less 2-ranked on horizontal shoots or on shade-grown plants, slightly sickle-shaped, ½ to 1″ long, ¹⁄₁₆ to ¼″ wide, convex, with fine-pointed apex, shiny black-green above, paler and yellowish green below. Extremely susceptible to deer browsing and yet can be toxic to cows if ingested. **Flowers/seeds/fruits/cones**: Usually dioecious. Male globose, stalked, from leaf axils on previous year's growth, each with 6 to 14 stamens, releasing clouds of pollen in March-April; female solitary, green in leaf axils. Fruit is actually a rounded, globose, naked seed covered by a fleshy red aril, ¼ to ⅜″ long and wide; ripening in summer-fall; seeds are poisonous; the red aril is not; ripen the first year. **Native range**: Most of Europe, North Africa, Turkey, Caucasus to the southern shore of the Caspian Sea. Grows in deciduous or mixed forests, near streams, or on moist slopes with limestone soils. **Adaptability**: At home on pure chalk (sea shells, limestone) soils as well as acid soils as long as well drained: heavy, wet, waterlogged soils are anathema. Zones (5)6 to 7, 8 to 9 on the West Coast; suited to most of zones 7 and 8 only at higher elevations.

Landscape use: Cherished and utilized for centuries as a landscape plant, particularly hedges, screens, specimens, and topiary. Amenable to severe pruning; even large trunks cut to almost ground level regenerate new shoots. Authors have reservations about the species' suitability for general landscape use as a tree, but for a hedge, it is a perfect choice since it has no fear of pruning shears. In the United States, the most common manifestations of the species are low-growing, bushy, shrubby cultivars, useful for foundations, groupings, and masses, especially in shady environments; in fact, *Cephalotaxus*, *Taxus*, *Tsuga*, *Torreya*, and *Podocarpus* are the best shade-tolerant needle evergreens. **Street tree use**: No. **In the trade**: 'Fastigiata' (Irish yew) is a broad-columnar, fastigiate form with rigid upright branches, shining blackish green needles, 15 to 30′ high, 4 to 8′ wide; male and female selections are in cultivation;

Taxus baccata

Taxus baccata

Taxus baccata

as a young specimen it is quite narrow, belying its eventual broad stature; common in English churchyards and formal gardens. Fastigiata Aurea Group produces deep yellow new growth; color diminishes with maturation and heat.

Taxus brevifolia
Pacific yew

Evergreen conifer. Conical to dome-shaped, becoming more open and irregular with age. Majority of references list size as 50 to 80′, but authors estimate a third that large under cultivation; the largest reported U.S. specimen was 54′ high, 30′ wide. Growth is slow. For a time, the thin, scaly reddish brown bark was stripped/exploited by pharmaceutical companies for the extraction of a cytotoxic alkaloid marketed as Taxol, a drug utilized in the treatment of several cancers; it's now known the compound (taxine) can be extracted from the needles of several *Taxus* species and cultivars. The tough durable wood was used for fence posts, canoe paddles, bows, and tools.

Fastigiata Aurea Group

'Fastigiata'

Taxus brevifolia

T

837

Foliage: Needles, linear, ½ to 1″ long, ⅟₂₅ to ⅛″ wide (shorter than *T. baccata*; hence the epithet), dark green above, grayish green below, with a fine-pointed tip, arranged in opposite horizontal rows, persisting 4 to 5 years. **Flowers/seeds/ fruits/cones**: Dioecious. Pollen cones only ⅛ to ¼″ long. Reproductive structures are naked seeds, flattened, conspicuous within the bright red or orange-red aril, ¼ to ⅓″ long. **Native range**: Southern Alaska to northern California, southeast to British Columbia and northern Idaho. Grows in the understory of moist stream/riverside forests and canyons. **Adaptability**: Zones 6 to 9 on the West Coast. **Landscape use**: Useful in native plant restoration projects and in shady environments. Nowhere common, even in its native habitat. This is a perfect example of a North American native that has never been domesticated via cultivar selection; our *T. canadensis* and *T. floridana* suffer the same fate, while *T. baccata* (European) and *T. cuspidata* (Asiatic) are everywhere. **Street tree use**: No. **In the trade**: Rare.

Tetradium daniellii

Tetradium daniellii (*Euodia daniellii*)
beebee tree, evodia

Deciduous. Consistently uniform, rounded to broad-rounded, dome-shaped, with somewhat layered branches supported by a stout trunk. Size varies from 25 to 30(50)′ high, as wide or wider. Growth is extremely fast as a seedling, slowing with age. Bark is gray, smooth, similar to beech bark. Serves as a nectar source for bees, whose activity is at a fever pitch during this species' summer bloom period, at a time when few trees are flowering.

Foliage: Compound pinnate, 9 to 15″ long, composed of (5)7 to 11, ovate to oblong-ovate, 2 to 3″ long leaflets, finely serrate, lustrous dark green, with no appreciable fall color. **Flowers/seeds/fruits/cones**: Small, white, with yellow anthers, pungently scented, borne in 4 to 6″ wide, broad, flat-topped corymbs on current season's growth in summer (July, zone 6). Fruits are pretty, red to black dehiscent capsules, with 4 or 5 carpels (segments) splitting from the top to expose shiny brownish black seeds. The fruits, like the flowers, are quite showy and are prominently displayed, as they occur at the ends of the shoots in late summer–fall. **Native range**: Northern China, Korea. **Adaptability**: Grows in any well-drained soil, acid to neutral, in full sun. Displays significant drought tolerance when established. The majority of trees observed by the authors were in good to great condition, seemingly fending for themselves, as maintenance was in absentia. Zones 5 to 8. Reports of cold damage are conflicting, yet specimens grow in Lisle, IL, and Orono, ME, which coincide with zones 4 and 5. **Landscape use**: An enigma, somewhat of an orphan among the flowering trees, largely shunned in commerce, yet surfacing in

Tetradium daniellii

arboreta, botanic gardens, and campuses. No one person or nursery has taken the biological ball and tried to score a touchdown. Authors recorded sufficient first-class specimens to realize the species' value; habit, flowers, fruit, and bark, at their best, constitute a worthy landscape entity.

Tetradium daniellii

Would function as a pretty lawn, street, park, and campus tree. We have heard the knock about short-lived (15 to 40 years), but a 50-year-old tree in the Arnold Arboretum defies this contention. Seed requires no pretreatment and can be sown immediately after collection with high germination ensuing. **Street tree use**: Potential. **In the trade**: Sold as seed-grown. To our knowledge, no cultivars have been selected. As the fruit is "bird berry" size, we would like to see a sterile cultivar to avoid any potential for invasiveness.

Thuja occidentalis
eastern arborvitae

Evergreen conifer. Quite attractive needle evergreen, with a dense-foliaged, columnar-pyramidal to broad pyramidal habit, often multi-trunked, 40 to 60′ high, 10 to 20′ wide in the wild; 20 to 30′ high under cultivation. The soft-textured foliage is naturally retained at ground level, creating the prototypical Christmas tree shape. Growth is slow. Bark is gray, gray-brown to reddish brown, primarily gray-brown in native stands, fibrous, stringy, and peeling. The rot-resistant wood is utilized for fence posts, Adirondack chairs, raised garden boxes (sides), canoe frames.

Foliage: Scale-like needles, $\frac{1}{12}$″ long, overlapping in horizontal, laterally compressed sprays, bright green above, paler below, often discoloring yellow-green-brown in cold windy locations, emitting a tansy-like (fruity) fragrance when bruised. **Flowers/seeds/fruits/cones**: Monoecious. Cones not showy, males reddish, early spring. Fruiting cones are oblong, $\frac{1}{2}$″ long, composed of 8 to 10 scales, green, maturing yellow, eventually brown, shedding the small $\frac{1}{8}$″ long winged sides at maturity, often persisting into winter; maturing in a single season. **Native range**: Nova Scotia to Manitoba, south to Virginia, North Carolina, Tennessee, and Illinois. **Adaptability**: Fascinatingly broad, from

Thuja occidentalis

swamps to dry cliff faces, often on calcareous soils. Authors have experienced the species in the wild from Canada south to Virginia, where it grows in deep ravines/gorges in the limestone soils of the Natural Bridge. In Maine, on Cadillac Mountain, it emerges from cracks, crevices, between boulders and in Orono on hummocks in sphagnum (acid) bogs. In landscape reality, it will grow under almost any conditions. Zones 3 to 8. **Landscape use**: Possibly the most important native needle conifer in general landscape use, owing to the infinite variation of habits and foliage colors. For nurseries, it is easy to produce; for gardeners, relatively maintenance independent. We have developed admiration for this "street fighter" evergreen, which is utilized for numerous landscape applications. The dwarf types reside in rock gardens, dwarf conifer, and foundation plantings; the tree types for hedges, privacy screens, groupings, color (yellow needles), and accents/specimens. Amenable to butcher-shop pruning practices, including eccentric topiary. Soils of most persuasions are acceptable; in the wild it grows in high pH soils. Once established it is quite drought

T

Thuja occidentalis

'Degroot's Spire'

Thuja occidentalis

tolerant. Bagworms and leaf miners occasionally munch on foliage. Deer browsing is a major debilitating factor on plants used for hedging, screening, and barriers. Mites appear in hot, dry weather. Trees are long-lived, approaching 1,000 or more years. **Street tree use**: Yes. **In the trade**: Several choice cultivars retain measures of green needles in winter.

'American Pillar'. A sport of 'Wintergreen', 20 to 30′ by 3 to 5′, hardy to -40°F.

'Brabant'. Spire-like habit, medium green needles, more resistant to winter discoloration, 12 to 15′ high.

'Brandon'. Soft green foliage, persisting bright green year-round, forms a narrow cone, 12 to 15′ high, 6 to 8′ wide. Zones 3 and 4.

'Emerald'

'Jantar'

'Nigra'

'Emerald'

'Degroot's Spire'. Narrow columnar form, somewhat twisted rich green sprays, bronzes in cold, 15 to 20′ by 3 to 5′.

'Emerald' ('Smaragd'). The most commonly grown compact narrow pyramidal-columnar cultivar; lustrous emerald-green foliage does not discolor to the degree of some forms, still some discoloration; with time 20′ by 3 to 5′, usually smaller; the standard hedging/screening arborvitae.

'Jantar'. A yellow-gold needle version of 'Emerald'; listed as 20 to 25′ by 3 to 4′.

'Nigra'. Broad pyramidal form, foliage sprays loosely arranged, dark green, persisting (not perfectly) through winter, 20 to 30′ high, 10 to 15′ wide, one of the best for cold climates; North Dakota State University rated it as one of the best for zones 3 and 4.

NORDIC SPIRE 'Rebild'. Pyramidal, loose and informal, slightly weeping green branchlets, 25 to 30′ by 20 to 25′.

NORTH POLE 'Art Boe'. Naturally symmetrical columnar selection of 'Wintergreen', resistant to windburn, 12 to 15′ by 5 to 7′.

'Pyramidalis'. Narrow pyramidal-columnar, quite formal in outline with bright green foliage; susceptible to winter discoloration, 20 to 30′ by 5 to 8′; North Dakota State University lists it as hardy as 'Brandon'.

T

'Rushmore'

'Wintergreen'

'Techny'

'Rushmore'. Narrow columnar form, dark green foliage, good resistance to wind and cold discoloration, 12 to 25′ by 3 to 6′.

'Skybound'. Superior for foliage color and resistance to winter burn.

'Sunkist'. Broad pyramidal habit, the new growth chartreuse, maturing gold, contrasting with green inner needles; 10 to 15′ by 6 to 8′.

'Techny' ('Mission'). An old standard in the vein of 'Nigra'; dense broad-based pyramidal form with excellent dark green foliage year-round; 10 to 15(25)′ by 6 to 8′.

'Wintergreen' ('Hetz Wintergreen'). Columnar-pyramidal selection retaining reasonable green foliage in winter; 20 to 30′ by 5 to 10′; faster growing than most *T. occidentalis* cultivars.

Thuja orientalis. See *Platycladus orientalis*

Thuja plicata

western red cedar, giant arborvitae

Evergreen conifer. Large and stately, broadly pyramidal with graceful downward-arcing limbs from a strong central trunk, flaring and buttressed at the base. Medium texture, medium growth rate to 70′ high and 25′ wide. Record trees in the wild have exceeded 200′. Bark is red-brown on young and middle-aged trees, reddish gray with age, always fibrous and stringy, relatively thin for such a large tree.

Foliage: Tiny, medium to dark green scale-like leaves are tightly appressed to the shoots, ¼″ or less in length, held as drooping sprays of foliage, more lustrous than *T. occidentalis*. Color generally holds well in winter; some seed sources and cultivars bronze slightly. **Flowers/seeds/fruits/cones**: Monoecious. Pollen cones ⅛″ long, borne at branch tips. Female cones ellipsoid, ½″ long, maturing light brown in the fall, scales flaring widely to release seeds. **Native range**: Mostly coastal, from southeastern Alaska to northern California, with a separate inland distribution in the valleys of the western Rocky Mountains from central British Columbia to

Thuja plicata

Thuja plicata

Thuja plicata

T

843

Idaho and Montana. **Adaptability**: In the wild, it is mostly restricted to moist bottomlands by fire and competition. But this is a highly adaptable tree with seed sources ranging from normally frost-free valleys of northern California to the extreme cold of the British Columbia Rockies. It has performed well in the upper Midwest, the Northeast, Mid-Atlantic, the upper South, and in Europe. Selection from the extreme northern part of its range could extend landscape adaptability. Prefers moist acid soils. Zones 5 to 7, 8 in the West. **Landscape use**: An elegant and noble large conifer, at home in both formal and informal gardens. Use as a single specimen or in groves; the narrow forms as a large screen. A prime choice within its natural range for native landscaping. Most major cities in the Pacific Northwest are in lowlands, where this tree once flourished. Foliage is deer resistant. **Street tree use**: The narrow forms are occasionally used on streets within its native range where planter width allows. **In the trade**: Sold as seed-grown for restoration, more commonly as the cultivars.

'Atrovirens'. Glossy dark green foliage, a neat clean narrow pyramid with slightly upsweeping branches and good density. Some winter foliage bronzing in the South. 50′ tall, 20′ wide.

'Excelsa'. Compact, narrow, and dense but maintains the graceful character of the species, good when used for screens. Some winter bronzing. 40′ tall, 15′ wide.

'Fastigiata'. A very narrow form, selected and named in France in 1867. The name is often misapplied to 'Hogan' or other narrow forms now in commerce. 60′ tall, 15′ wide.

'Golden Spire' ('Daniellow'). New growth bright golden yellow with a hint of orange. Color holds well in winter. Older, inner foliage more greenish. Pyramidal, slightly slower growing than the species. 35′ tall, 15′ wide.

'Green Giant' ('Gigantoides'). Believed to be a hybrid with *T. standishii*. Fast-growing, making a big wide pyramid. Popular in the Midwest, and extremely popular in the South, where it shows better heat tolerance than other cultivars. It's bright green in summer but shows some winter bronzing. 70′ by 25′.

'Hogan'. A curious native stand in Gresham, OR, now protected, holds hundreds of very narrow, dense, nearly columnar trees. Warren lives nearby. Walked the trail on a snowy December morning and observed how the branches get shorter and the trees more spire-like over a mile-long stretch to the center of the stand. We muse on the wonders of evolution and speculate these unusually narrow forms may have been selected by the very frequent ice storms that occur here, at the west end of the Columbia River Gorge. These trees breed true from seed picked from within the stand. Second-generation seed may lose this character, so

'Atrovirens'

'Green Giant'

'Hogan'

'Virescens'

'Green Giant'

'Hogan'

'Zebrina'

T

look for cutting-grown or grafted specimens. Very tight, with short upsweeping branches, dark green foliage, usually holding good green winter color. A Warren favorite. 60′ tall, 15′ wide.

SPRING GROVE 'Grovepli'. A very narrow pyramidal form with good density and dark green foliage, maintaining its color in the winter. Proven zone 5 hardiness in the Midwest. 50′ tall, 15′ wide.

'Virescens'. Very dense upward-oriented branching. It gives up some of the grace of the species as a trade-off for its tight form. Holds deep green foliage all winter. Suggested for a tall dense hedge. 40′ tall, 15′ wide.

VIRGINIAN 'BFC68'. Listed by introducer as 14.5′ by 6.5′, a sport of 'Green Giant', narrower, shorter. The patent document indicates slower, denser, more compact pyramidal growth. We think 30′ tall and 15′ wide is more realistic.

'Zebrina'. From a distance, it's a golden-foliaged broad pyramid, but the foliage sprays are in fact zebra-striped, alternating bright yellow and green. Graceful in form, bright in foliage, and curiously interesting up close. The color holds true in a northern garden, but in Georgia trials, foliage was green. 40′ tall, 25′ wide.

'Zebrina Extra Gold'. A brighter yellow form of 'Zebrina', selected as a sport. A little brighter when young, but little difference with age. Like 'Zebrina', green foliage in Georgia. 40′ tall, 25′ wide.

Tilia americana
American linden, basswood

Nomenclatural note: *T. heterophylla*, formerly considered a separate, more southern species, is now included here, reduced to var. *heterophylla*.

Deciduous. A tall tree, pyramidal and upright-growing when young, becoming rounded on top and more open with age. Medium coarse to coarse in texture, moderately fast-growing, 70′ tall and 40′ wide. Bark is charcoal-gray and neatly lined and fissured; it is thin when young and sometimes damaged by winter sunscald.

'Zebrina'

Tilia americana

Tilia americana

Tilia americana

Tilia americana

Foliage: Leaves large, 4 to 8″ long and almost as wide, cordate with a base that is somewhat oblique, tip acuminate, margin serrate, medium green. Fall color is usually a good yellow. **Flowers/seeds/fruits/cones**: Pale yellow flowers, ½″ wide, held in 5- to 10-flowered pendulous cymes hanging from a 3 to 4″ spatulate bract, typically opening in June. Fruit a nutlet, ⅜″ long, ovoid. **Native range**: Maine to eastern North Dakota and south to Florida and Alabama, with the southern third of the distribution being var. *heterophlylla*. **Adaptability**: Adaptable to various soils and pH levels. Cold hardy and good in the Midwest and Northeast. Zones 3 to 8(9). **Landscape use**: A large shade tree for lawns and parks or use in native landscapes. **Street tree use**: The species is large, but cultivars are straight and several are narrow, with good shape. Reflection from concrete can often cause sunscald in the species, but 'Redmond' is quite tough, a long-proven street tree. **In the trade**: Available.

AMERICAN SENTRY 'McKSentry'. Straight, upright, well-formed narrow pyramidal canopy. Considerably narrower than the species, to 60′ tall, 25′ wide.

'Boulevard'. Tall, narrow, and very straight-growing, ascending branches, to 60′ and spreading to only about 25′.

'Continental Appeal'. A selection of var. *heterophylla*, and as such probably a little more southern-adapted, although origin is Illinois. Huge leaves to 10″ long in the nursery,

T

'Boulevard'

'Continental Appeal'

'Continental Appeal'

medium green on top and silvery on the underside, very straight-growing, strongly upright and narrow, 60′ tall, spreading to only 25 to 30′.

FRONTYARD 'Bailyard'. A broader pyramidal form with a rounded top and good symmetry, selected with the appearance of a classic front-yard shade tree in mind, 60′ tall, 40′ wide.

LEGEND 'DTR 123'. A neat and distinct broad pyramid. The parent tree, at 55 years, was 55′ tall, 36′ wide. Foliage bright green, crisply serrate, good yellow fall color.

'Redmond'. Probable hybrid origin; certainly it fits with *T. americana* and usually considered to be a cross with *T. ×euchlora*, but we're not so sure. Something makes this cultivar much more urban-tolerant than typical *T. americana*. A little shorter, denser, and more compact than the species or

FRONTYARD

LEGEND

'Redmond'

'Redmond'

other cultivars listed here, it forms a very neat pyramid to 40′ tall and 20′ wide. Well shaped and long proven in years of urban use, and reliable as a street tree choice.

TRUE NORTH 'Duros'. Upright with a strong leader and moderately narrow pyramidal form. Yellow fall color. Selected on the Canadian prairie, proven hardiness to at least zone 3. 50′ by 20′.

T

Tilia cordata
littleleaf linden

Deciduous. Distinctly pyramidal when young becoming broadly pyramidal and with a somewhat rounded top in age, with a strong central leader and mostly upward-angled branches. Medium texture, moderate growth rate, to 55′ tall and 35′ wide. Bark is gray-brown, smooth when young, becoming lightly fissured, then ridged and furrowed. Bees love linden flowers, so avoid if you are allergic.

Foliage: Leaves smaller than most other lindens (hence the common name), 1½ to 3½″ long and almost as wide. Dark green and satiny above, lighter below, glabrous except in the vein axils, cordate with an acuminate tip, coarsely serrate. Very nice bright yellow fall color. **Flowers/seeds/ fruits/cones**: Pale yellow, ½″ wide, in pendulous cymes of 5 to 7 flowers, hanging from a 1½ to 3½″ long spatulate bract. Bloom is typically late June to early July in most northern locations, fragrant. Fruit a nutlet, ¼″, round to ovoid. **Native range**: Europe, northern Spain to southern Norway and east into Russia. **Adaptability**: Very adaptable in cooler climates, it grows well in acid soils or on high pH. It likes a well-drained soil but is quite tolerant of heavy clay. One of the most adaptable trees to varied urban soil conditions. Widely planted in cities because of its tolerances. Suffers in the heat and grows more slowly in the South. Zones 3 to 7. **Landscape use**: A highly reliable shade tree and a staple of landscaping in the Midwest, Northeast, and Mid-Atlantic states, especially since emerald ash borer removed the once dominant *Fraxinus* genus from the tree palette. Used in every imaginable situation, from residential shade tree to parks to commercial-site screens on difficult soils. Quite susceptible to Japanese beetles and aphids with accompanying sooty mold. Cultivars abound and dominate planting, making near perfect pyramidal shapes possible. **Street tree use**: Quintessential street tree, at least in the northern United States. Several ideal shapes are available among the cultivars, the size is right, and adaptability is street tough. We still prefer oaks for their longevity, but lindens rate high in practicality. **In the trade**: Available.

'Akira Gold'. Yellow foliage looks bright in spring, soon lime-green and then just green. Impressive at first, then disappoints. Loose pyramidal form to 30′ tall, 20′ wide. From Akira Shibamichi and may be the same as patented 'Shibamichi Gold'.

'Böhlje'. Slower growing, pyramidal when young, it becomes a broader and looser pyramid with age, more rounded on top and a little less formal-looking, 45′ tall, 35′ wide.

Tilia cordata

Tilia cordata

CORINTHIAN 'Corzam'. The narrowest cultivar in the group, it also features the smallest leaves, somewhat darker and blue-green, very attractive. It forms a neat and narrow pyramidal shape, but watch for narrow crotch angles and prune out at an early age. Grows to full height of 50′ but only 15 to 20′ wide.

'Glenleven'. The fastest-growing of the cultivars, it makes the tallest tree, still pyramidal but with a looser, more rounded top, relaxed and natural-looking, to 55′ by 30′. A hybrid (*T. ×flavescens*) with *T. americana*. Larger leaves than true *T. cordata*.

'Golden Cascade'. A broader and shorter, more rounded form, as wide as tall, 30 to 35′. Branches with somewhat weeping tips. Leaves smaller than typical with golden yellow fall color, excellent cold hardiness, zone 3.

GREENSPIRE 'PNI 6025'. By far the dominant cultivar and for good reasons. If a contest were held for the tree with the ideal pyramidal shape, this would be the winner. A tight narrow pyramid, with good density and near perfect symmetry, it maintains this shape to an older age than other cultivars, eventually becoming a neat but broader pyramid, 45′ tall, 30′ wide. Clean handsome dark green foliage and good yellow fall color. Performs well in zones 4 to 8. A longtime winner.

'Akira Gold'

Tilia cordata

CORINTHIAN

T

CORINTHIAN

GREENSPIRE

'Glenleven'

'Harvest Gold'

'Golden Cascade'

'Harvest Gold'

GREENSPIRE

'Harvest Gold'. Nicely shaped pyramidal form becomes a broader and looser pyramid with age, 45′ tall, 30′ wide. Foliage is darker green with more gloss than straight *T. cordata*, and fall color tends to be a brighter golden yellow, perhaps the best of the group in this regard. A hybrid with *T. mongolica* (and sometimes listed under that species), but its form, size, and appearance are closer to *T. cordata*. A favorite of ours, should be used more. Does well in Southeast, zone 8. Very cold hardy, zone 3.

NORLIN 'Ronald'. Vigorous; fastest-growing *T. cordata* in our Oregon testing, makes a broad pyramid but with a looser habit than most cultivars. Dull green foliage. Very cold hardy, zone 3.

'Rancho'. Pyramidal when young, loosening and broadening slightly with age, a little slower growing and not as tightly pyramidal as GREENSPIRE. 40′ tall, 30′ wide.

SHAMROCK 'Baileyi'. A good broadly pyramidal form, eventually rounding on top, looser than GREENSPIRE, one of the faster growers, good summer green in color. 45′ tall, 30′ wide.

SUMMER SPRITE 'Halka'. Small, very tight and dense with a compact habit, slow-growing, broadly pyramidal and rounded on top, to 20′ tall and wide. Does well in the South.

T

'Rancho'

SHAMROCK

SUMMER SPRITE

SUMMER SPRITE

Tilia ×euchlora (T. ×*europaea* 'Euchlora')
Crimean linden

Deciduous. Broadly and loosely pyramidal, somewhat rounded on top. Medium texture, medium growth rate, to 50′ tall and 35′ wide. The dark gray bark becomes fissured with age.

Foliage: Here is where the tree really stands out from *T. cordata*. Foliage is both very glossy and very bright green, and the margin is neatly serrate like a fine-toothed saw. Leaves 2 to 4″ long and wide, cordate with a slightly oblique base and a short acuminate tip. Fall color yellow. **Flowers/seeds/ fruits/cones**: Greenish yellow, ½″ wide, in pendulous cymes of 3 to 7 flowers, hanging from a spatulate bract. Bloom is typically in late June, heavy and fragrant. Fruit a nutlet, ⅜″ long. **Native range**: A hybrid of *T. dasystyla* (native from Crimea to Iran) and *T. cordata* (native to Europe and western Asia). **Adaptability**: Zones 5 to 7. **Landscape use**: A good shade tree, lower branches spread wide, flowers heavily, quite pleasant to walk under. Reportedly less prone

Tilia ×euchlora

to aphids than other lindens. Tends to be a slightly shorter, broader form than most *T. cordata*. The glossy foliage seems perfectly formed. New growth of branches in winter is red-brown on the sunny side and at the tips, transitioning to yellow-green at the base, providing some winter brightness. **Street tree use**: Useful as an avenue tree and favored because of its reputation of fewer aphids, but needs pruning for clearance as it tends to be low-branched. **In the trade**: Listed as *T. ×euchlora* in the United States, and as *T. ×europaea* 'Euchlora' in Europe, probably the same plant. In the United States, it is represented by a single clone.

Tilia ×europaea
European linden, common lime

Deciduous. Large tree with a broadly pyramidal to broadly oval habit, usually widest at the base. Medium texture, moderately fast growth rate. The trunk is heavy, often with large burrs and suckers at the base. The largest of the *Tilia*

Tilia ×euchlora

Tilia ×europaea

Tilia ×europaea

Tilia ×europaea

'Pallida Typ Lappen'

species, 80′ tall and 50′ wide is typical, but many exceed 100′ and the record is 151′. Bark is smooth and gray-green when young, then gray, ridged and fissured.

Foliage: Dark green, cordate with an acuminate tip, serrate to coarsely serrate, the base unequally cordate, slightly pubescent below, 2½ to 5½″ in length and width. Twigs and buds greenish when first formed and in the shade, but they become deep reddish to red-brown in full sun. **Flowers/ seeds/fruits/cones**: Pale yellow, ½″ wide, in pendulous cymes of 4 to 10 fragrant flowers, hanging from a spatulate bract. Bloom is typically in early June. Fruit a nutlet, ⅜″ long. **Native range**: A natural hybrid of *T. cordata* (native to Europe and western Asia) and *T. platyphyllos* (native to western and central Europe). **Adaptability**: Recognized as a good urban-tolerant tree. Zones 4 to 7. **Landscape use**: A very large tree, widely used in Europe, historically, for parks, large estates, and avenues where space allows, sometimes formally pleached or maintained as a hedge of great proportion. Rarely seen in the United States outside of arboreta, perhaps because of its large potential size and the popularity of other *Tilia* species. Basal suckering is a maintenance issue and detracts from appearance. Susceptible to aphids. **Street tree use**: Yes, but needs a lot of space, trunk can be very large, suckering is a problem. **In the trade**: The dominant clone is 'Pallida', a Dutch distribution of 1945 but historically a clonal group going back to at least 1796. Upright and neatly pyramidal when young, it becomes broadly pyramidal and more rounded on top with age. Dark green foliage with a light yellowish green underside; twigs and buds reddish brown in winter. This is the tree planted on Berlin's historic cultural boulevard, Unter den Linden. 'Pallida Typ Lappen', a selected clone from Berlin, perhaps part of the old original Pallida group, is strong growing, with a dominant central leader, upward-angled branches and pyramidal to broadly pyramidal form. Both are quite large, 80′ tall, 50′ wide.

Tilia mongolica
Mongolian linden

Deciduous. A smaller linden with a loose, rounded shape and branch tips that droop or weep slightly; a relaxed but sometimes slightly wild look. Semi-weeping lower branches put the wonderful leaves, which are the tree's highlight, in view. Fine-textured, slower growing, to 30′ tall and 20′ wide. Bark is smooth and gray-green when young, then dark gray, fissured.

Tilia mongolica

Tilia mongolica

Foliage: Glossy dark green, smaller than most lindens, 1½ to 3(4)″ long and wide, deltoid, but irregularly so, with deeply cut coarse serrations, like jagged teeth with an occasional lobe that looks like a sharp fang on the side. Tip acuminate, longer and more pointed than other lindens. Fall color yellow to golden, often quite bright. **Flowers/seeds/fruits/cones**: Pale yellow, ½″ wide, in pendulous cymes of 6 to 15 flowers, hanging from a 1½ to 2½″ long spatulate bract. Blooms in early summer, fragrant. Fruit small, rounded nutlet. **Native range**: China, Mongolia. **Adaptability**: Soil adaptable, will tolerate elevated pH, but may prefer acid. Quite cold hardy. Zones 3 to 6. **Landscape use**: Use in cooler climates for its unusual foliage and texture. An intriguing small tree, but not yet ready for prime time. Has a reputation for aphid resistance. **Street tree use**: Has potential, but it's a little wide and seed-grown trees are inconsistent. **In the trade**: Uncommon, sold as seed-grown. There is one hybrid (see 'Harvest Gold' under *T. cordata*), but cultivars are lacking. We need breeders to come up with a good selection with reliable form and density.

Tilia petiolaris. See *T. tomentosa*

Tilia platyphyllos
bigleaf linden, large-leaved lime

Deciduous. A large upright tree with strong ascending structure, forming a broad pyramid with a rounded top. Moderately coarse texture, medium growth rate, to 80′ tall, 60′ wide. Bark gray, finely fissured and ridged.

Foliage: True to its name, its leaves are larger than *T. cordata*, 2½ to 5″ long, but they are smaller than *T. americana*, dark green above, lighter green below and slightly

T

Tilia platyphyllos

'Örebro'

Tilia platyphyllos

'Laciniata'

pubescent, cordate, usually with an oblique leaf base and an acuminate tip, serrate margin. Twigs and buds reddish brown in the sun and in winter. Fall color yellow. **Flowers/seeds/fruits/cones**: Pale yellow, ½″ wide, in pendulous cymes of 3 to 5 flowers, hanging from a 1½ to 2½″ long spatulate bract. One of the earliest lindens to bloom, usually early June, fragrant. Fruit ⅜″ long, ovoid nutlet. **Native range**: Western and central Europe. **Adaptability**: Long planted in Europe, showing its urban adaptability, but rarely used in the United States, where cultivars of *T. cordata* are preferred. Tolerant of higher pH soils. Zones 4 to 6, 7 in the West. **Landscape use**: A large tree often used in parks; it is also suitable as a shade tree for a large residence. **Street tree use**: Good for the purpose, especially 'Delft' and 'Örebro'. **In the trade**: Available in Europe, uncommon in the United States.

'Delft'. Pyramidal upright shape, symmetrical, becoming broadly pyramidal, 60′ tall, 40′ wide. New stems green, not reddish. Said to be less susceptible to aphids.

'Laciniata'. The leaves are slender, curiously lobed, deeply cut, with a little twist. We would call it misshapen, but the tree apparently has some popularity. Broadly pyramidal but smaller than the species, to 45′ by 30′.

'Örebro'. Narrowly pyramidal and stiffly upright, eventually widening slightly to a more oval form, an excellent shape for streets. Its slower growth produces a smaller mature size, 45′ tall, 25′ wide.

'Rubra'. Selected for its bright reddish shoots and buds, most intensely colored in winter. It is a large upright tree, growing to the full size of the species, 50′ tall, 30′ wide. Hard pruning produces vigorous new growth that best shows off the stem color.

Tilia tomentosa

silver linden, silver lime

Deciduous. Upright and pyramidal with a good central leader when young, becoming broadly pyramidal to broadly oval with age. Medium texture, moderately fast-growing, to 70′ tall and 45′ wide. Bark smooth and gray at first, then gray-brown, ridged and furrowed. The flowers are highly attractive to bees, but something about the flowers is either narcotic or toxic to certain bee species. Honeybees are apparently unaffected, but certain species of bumblebees are often found lying on the ground in an apparent state of stupor. Many eventually stir and fly away, but some may not. Puzzling, and a tree you don't want to walk under barefoot while it's in flower. A study of the effect of this species and its various cultivars on bumblebees is needed to guide planting to avoid harming pollinators.

Foliage: Outstanding foliage. New growth emerges silvery pubescent, then leaves become dark green and dull satiny above, remaining silvery white pubescent beneath. Leaves 2 to 5½″ long and wide, cordate with an oblique base, serrate, with a short acuminate tip. Yellow fall color. **Flowers/seeds/fruits/cones**: Pale yellow, ½″ wide, in pendulous cymes of 4 to 10 flowers, hanging from a 1½ to 2½″ long spatulate, gray-green, pubescent bract. Bloom is usually the latest of the cultivated lindens, typically at the beginning of July, fragrant. Fruit a nutlet, ¼″ long, round to ovoid. **Native range**: Southeastern Europe. **Adaptability**: More tolerant of heat and drought than other lindens and will take a higher pH, as well as acid soil. Quite urban-tolerant. Zones 5 to 8. **Landscape use**: Our favorite linden. Its foliage provides wonderful contrast, dark green but showing its silvery underside with the slightest breeze. Its use has increased greatly in recent years, partly because it is much more resistant to Japanese beetle than other lindens. Compared to the more popular *T. cordata*, it is a broader-spreading, bulkier-looking tree. It makes a large residential shade tree, but be aware of bees on the ground and in the flowers if you are allergic. **Street tree use**: An excellent street tree, but large and broad, so it needs room. Its tomentose foliage gives it aphid resistance, which is nice on the streets; other lindens often drip sticky aphid honeydew. **In the trade**: Available. It lacks the truly narrow pyramidal cultivars that have made *T. cordata* so popular on narrower streets.

'Brabant'. Leaves dark green, silvery below. New growth cool silver-toned. Straight, more compact and densely pyramidal at first, maturing broadly pyramidal to broadly oval, 65′ tall and 40′ wide.

Tilia tomentosa

Tilia tomentosa

T

GREEN MOUNTAIN

GREEN MOUNTAIN

GREEN MOUNTAIN 'PNI 6051'. Deepest green leaves, but still bright silvery on the underside. Foliage provides the most beautiful contrast of the cultivars. Strongly upright, very straight, slightly narrower, symmetrical with a good branch structure, an excellent street tree form, 65′ tall, 40′ wide. The form and foliage combine to make it our first choice among the cultivars.

'Petiolaris'. Listed as a species (*T. petiolaris*), but really a selection, we believe, of *T. tomentosa*. Upright-growing, ascending to the full height of the species, but with fine pendulous branch tips, making a very large tree that seems to weep from high above, like a giant fountain, to 70′ tall and 60′ wide. Excellent for parks and estates, but not a form for streets.

SATIN SHADOW 'Sashazam'. Silvery new growth is soft and slightly warmer in tone, with just a hint of yellow. Vigorous, growing to a broad pyramid, more spreading branches, 65′ by 40′.

'Silver Lining'. Pyramidal, a little narrower than the species, dark green above and silvery below, a good street tree form, 65′ tall and 35′ wide.

'Petiolaris'

'Sterling'

'Sterling'

'Sterling'. Probably the best-known cultivar, as it has been on the U.S. market the longest. Forms a broad-shouldered pyramid to broadly oval shape, 65′ tall and 45′ wide, foliage quite silvery in spring and holding a light silvery green color longer into summer.

Toona sinensis
Chinese toon

Deciduous. A tree of some worth yet nowhere common in horticulture. Almost shagbark hickory–like in character. At Monticello, there is a splendid 70 to 80′ high specimen; expect 30 to 40′ under "normal" cultivation, less in spread. It will sucker and form colonies, similar to *Ailanthus*, and, in fact, resembles the latter in foliage characteristics. Growth is wicked fast, especially shoots that develop from roots. Bark is gray-brown, in long, loose, peeling strips, minimally reminiscent of *Carya ovata*. Known in China as the tree vegetable, the young leaves contain 9.4% protein, vitamins C, A, B, and B2, and aromatic compounds. Obviously this culinary use has not caught on in the United States.

Foliage: Pinnately compound, 10 to 20″ long, composed of 10 to 22 short-stalked leaflets, each oblong to lance-oblong, 2 to 6″ long, unequal base on each side of midvein; entire or remotely toothed, bronze-purple when emerging, dark

Toona sinensis

T

861

Toona sinensis

'Flamingo'

needed. **Street tree use**: Potential. **In the trade**: 'Flamingo' is worth considering for its knockout spring foliage, leaves emerging hot flamingo (neon) pink, becoming cream, and maturing green. Possibly should be coppiced to produce long shoot extensions each spring.

Torreya californica
California nutmeg

Evergreen conifer. Forms a broad, loose pyramid with lax branches and a rounded top. Typically grows in the shade, which can result in an open canopy. Medium fine texture, slow-growing; 30′ high and 20′ wide is a reasonable garden estimate, although the current record tree in the wild is 105′. Bark is yellowish brown to reddish brown when young, becoming more gray and finely fissured with fine scaly ridges.

Foliage: Dark green needles, twisted at the base to lie flattened along both sides the branch, 1¼ to 2″ long and ¹⁄₁₆″ wide, very sharp-pointed, which is probably why the foliage

green at maturity, yellow in autumn at Blithewold, Bristol, RI; when bruised or crushed, with an onion odor. **Flowers/seeds/fruits/cones**: White, small, campanulate, ⅕″ high, "fragrant" (actually malodorous), borne in 12″ long terminal panicles in June. Fruit is a capsule, shaped like a rose, 1″ high and wide, containing winged seeds; noted fruit on a tree growing outside the U.S. Capitol. **Native range**: Northern and western China. **Adaptability**: Tremendous cultural and environmental adaptability. Our limited observations point to great adaptability to different soils, pH 5.5 to 8, as long as well drained, and a requirement for full sun. Zones 5 to 7(8). A small grove of shoots has persisted in Athens, GA, for over 40 years but is not happy. **Landscape use**: The species has languished in obscurity since its 1862 introduction; however, with devastating pandemics like emerald ash borer and the demise of *Fraxinus* in cities, town, neighborhoods, parks, and the wild, there is an opening, certainly not wholesale, for such a species. We safely postulate that the average citizen does not know the difference between an ash and a toon. No insect or disease problems have surfaced. In trials in Oregon, the species grew so fast it scared us; we cut it down. It may be better suited to a less favorable climate where growth is more restrained. More regional trials are

Torreya californica

is deer resistant. **Flowers/seeds/fruits/cones**: Dioecious. Male cones are globose, ¼″ long, pale greenish, held along the underside of the branch. Female cones are tiny at first but develop ovoid, green, fleshy fruits, 1 to 1½″ long, with a single nut-like seed, held singly or in a small group, maturing in 18 months. The fruits resemble a nutmeg, although the plants are not related. **Native range**: California, in the canyons of hilly areas, central coast and Sierra foothills. **Adaptability**: Likes full or partial shade, some humidity, and moist soil with good drainage. As you can imagine from its restricted range, it is not a widely adapted plant. Needs a mild climate. Zones 7 to 9. **Landscape use**: For a shaded woodland garden or natural landscape, providing interesting texture and an exotic feel in a native plant. **Street tree use**: No. **In the trade**: Sold as seed-grown.

Torreya taxifolia

Torreya taxifolia

stinking cedar, Florida nutmeg

Evergreen conifer. Broadly pyramidal, loose in form. Medium fine texture, slow-growing, 25′ high and 15′ wide. Bark is slightly orange-brown to darker gray-brown; ridged and furrowed pattern can resemble braided bread, peels in strips.

Foliage: Dark green needles are reminiscent of *Taxus* (hence the epithet). Needles twisted at the base, flattened along both sides the branch, 1 to 1¾″ long and 1/16 to ⅛″ wide. Needles persist for 3 to 4 years, are very sharp-pointed, and release a pungent odor when crushed. **Flowers/seeds/fruits/cones**: Dioecious. Male cones are globose, ¼″ long, pale greenish, lining the underside of the branch. Female cones are tiny at first but develop ovoid, green, fleshy fruits, 1 to 1½″ long, with a single nut-like seed, maturing in 2 years. The fruits resemble a nutmeg, unrelated. **Native range**: Formerly included southern Georgia but now restricted to shady river ravines in a small area of northern Florida. **Adaptability**: Struggling to survive in the wild, suffering from fungal infection and poor reproduction. Needs moisture and drainage. Native to a shaded habitat but grows well in full sun. Zones 6 to 8. **Landscape use**: Most garden use is by those with interest in preserving this endangered species. Certainly a plant with an interesting story, providing a different landscape texture and giving bragging rights to those who grow it. **Street tree use**: No. **In the trade**: Sold as seed-grown, quite uncommon.

Torreya taxifolia

T

Trachycarpus fortunei

Chusan palm, Chinese windmill palm

Evergreen. Without equivocation, the most cold hardy tree-type palm. Crown is ovoid-globular, leaves borne in horizontal and upswept positions. Size approximates 15 to 20′ in height, about 6 to 10′ across. A 40′ high plant was witnessed in England; a 30′ specimen grew in Athens, GA, but was cut down. Growth is slow; a plant in the Dirr garden took 7 years to reach 4′, and a Florida reference reported 12′ of growth in 10 years. The trunk is smaller at base, widening toward middle-top; 1′ in diameter, covered with shaggy gray to brown stringy fibers.

Foliage: Palmate, rounded, 2 to 3′ wide, cut almost to base with 40 to 50 incisions, light to dark green, grayish green below, the flattened petiole 1½ to 2(3)′ long, with fine teeth along both edges; leaf forms V-shaped trough, bifurcate leaf tip. **Flowers/seeds/fruits/cones**: Dioecious, sometimes bisexual. Yellow flowers, borne in large, 2 to 3′ long panicles

Trachycarpus fortunei

in spring. Fruit is an oblong to rounded drupe, ½″ wide, black (blue) and covered with a white bloom (wax). Fruited abundantly in the palm collection at the University of Georgia Horticulture Farm. **Native range**: China, Taiwan, Zhoushan Island. **Adaptability**: Adaptable to sun and shade. Zones 7 to 9, 6 with protection (partial shade, for example); in the Dirr garden, it is growing under oaks. Displays wind, drought, and salt tolerances. Survives 0°F without foliar injury; no damage at 6°F in Dirr garden. **Landscape use**: This easy-to-grow palm requires nothing more than a hole in well-drained soil to succeed. Choice one-of-a-kind biological conversation piece for the garden, especially attractive in containers and mixed annual/perennial plantings. One of the best palms for debilitating shade. The species has become a common fixture in the 21st-century garden. Possibly the easiest palm for home gardeners. Lower leaves become tatty and should be removed. **Street tree use**: Potential. **In the trade**: Sold as seed-grown.

Trachycarpus fortunei

Trochodendron aralioides

wheel tree

Broadleaf evergreen. Monotypic genus. Single-stemmed or as a multi-stemmed large shrub, this rare species develops artistic horizontally tiered branches, forming a pyramidal to broad pyramidal outline. Reaches 60′ high in the wild; grows slowly to 10 to 20(30)′ high, half as wide under cultivation. Bark is green on small stems and larger trunks, aromatic when bruised. Quite attractive.

Foliage: Although alternate, they appear whorled, clustered at the end of the stem, rhombic-ovate to elliptic-lanceolate, 3 to 6″ long, half as wide, leathery, serrate toward the apical end, bright apple- to lustrous dark green, paler below. **Flowers/seeds/fruits/cones**: Certainly unique but somewhat modest, lost among the leaves; bright yellow-green, 2 to 3″ long racemes in April-May; each flower with a spoke-like arrangement of 40 to 70 stamens, each ¼″ long, inserted on a broad disk. Fruit is a follicle, ¾″ wide, splitting at maturity, green to yellow-brown. **Native range:** Mountain forests in Japan, Taiwan, and Korea. **Adaptability:** Equally at home on both coasts. Difficult to assess adaptability, but zones 6 to 8 are logical based on where plants have been successful.

Landscape use: Occasionally surfaces at public gardens like Longwood in Pennsylvania, its pretty evergreen leaves and green stems brightening the winter landscape. Wherever we noted healthy specimens, they grew in shady, protected environments in moist, acid, well-drained soils high in organic matter. Ideally protect from winter sun (southern and western) and desiccating/discoloring winds. A Great Plant Pick by the Elisabeth C. Miller Botanical Garden, Seattle, and a choice option for the woodland, rhododendron/azalea, and wildflower garden. Always a conversation piece because of the vivid foliage and tiered branch disposition, similar to *Sassafras albidum* and *Cornus alternifolia*. **Street tree use:** Limited. **In the trade:** Available but not common.

Tsuga canadensis
Canadian hemlock, eastern hemlock

Evergreen conifer. Elegant, fine-textured, soft-needled, gracefully pyramidal. Under landscape conditions, grows 40 to 70′ high, 25 to 35′ wide, with the National Champion

Trochodendron aralioides

Tsuga canadensis

159′ by 45′. Expect 25 to 50′ height increase in 15 to 30 years. Bark is reddish brown, somewhat scaly on smaller trunks, eventually deeply furrowed with wide flat ridges. Seeds provide sustenance for birds and rodents. Trees provide cooling shade along mountain streams where trout are prevalent. Unfortunately, many old growth trees have been killed by the hemlock woolly adelgid, the insect painfully evident as white encrustations on the undersides of the needles. Most of the devastation has taken place in the Southeast—ghost-like, gray trunks visible on the slopes a telltale sign of it. North Carolina's Joyce Kilmer Memorial Forest was once the domain of Canadian hemlocks that touched the sky; in 2016, only a few small seedlings were evident. Enough to bring tears to the eyes of the authors. In the Northeast (Massachusetts and north), trees have not been as severely impacted.

Foliage: Needles 2-ranked, spreading around stem, linear, flattened, soft to touch, ½ to ¾″ long, 1/12 to ⅛″ wide, minutely toothed, lustrous dark green above, 2 whitish stomatal bands below, maintaining the rich dark green in winter. **Flowers/seeds/fruits/cones**: Monoecious. Male light yellow, female pale green. Cones are ovoid, stalked, pendulous at maturity, ½ to 1″ long, green to brown at maturity, persisting into winter and later; maturing the first season. **Native range**: Canada to the mountains of South Carolina, Georgia, and Alabama, west to Minnesota, typically in moist forests, moist slopes, rocky ridges, ravines, and stream valleys, from 5,700′ elevation in Appalachians to sea level in northeastern Canada. In Georgia, driving north from Athens, the species becomes evident on slopes at about 1,500′. **Adaptability**: Plants in the wild literally grow in rocky, low-fertility soils on the sides of mountains, so there is inherent toughness. Does not tolerate excessive heat and drought, yet in zone 8 (Athens), a respectable specimen occasionally surfaces, posing the question of luck or genetically based increased heat tolerance. Zones 3 to 7(8). **Landscape use**: Superior and refined needle evergreen functioning as a specimen, in groupings, for screens, and for hedging, particularly in shady environments. Withstands pruning to the nth degree; hedges can be maintained at a prescribed height indefinitely. Container-grown and balled-and-burlapped plants transplant without difficulty. Provide moist, acid, well-drained soils in sun or shade. Avoid extremely open, windswept locations, as needles will discolor. Hemlock cultivars are primarily grafted and rooted via cuttings; some of the more compact ones are well suited to contemporary landscapes. **Street tree use**: Not a good choice, too easily stressed. **In the trade**: Plant people have been collecting variants from the wild and in cultivation for hundreds of years. Only a precious few are available, predominantly compact, slow-growing, and spreading forms. The USDA-ARS and U.S. National Arboretum are breeding adelgid-resistant hybrids; we have observed these resistant trees at Beltsville, MD, and are excited about their eventual introduction.

'Albospica'. Pure white new shoots, the needles eventually becoming dark green; requires shade as new growth will scorch; pyramidal habit; 10 to 15′ by 6 to 8′. Pretty small tree, providing color seldom available from a shade-tolerant conifer.

GOLDEN DUCHESS 'MonKinn' and GOLDEN DUKE 'Monjers' are recent yellow-gold needle selections; the latter is said to have improved sun tolerance, turning yellow-orange in winter. Young plants simulate tree-like habit, but growth will be painfully slow.

'New Gold'. Bright yellow-gold new growth, maturing green; similar in habit and size to the species. Authors doubt the similar-size-to-the-species tagline. Majority of the colored needle forms are slower growing due to lack of chlorophyll.

'Pendula' ('Sargentii'). Broad-spreading weeping form that graces many estates from Boston to North Carolina. Grows 10 to 15(20)′ high and 1½ to 2 times as wide. Quite a magnificent

Tsuga canadensis

'Albospica'

'Summer Snow'

Tsuga caroliniana

Tsuga caroliniana
Carolina hemlock

Evergreen conifer. Splendid needle evergreen, perhaps more compact than *T. canadensis*, certainly equal in beauty. Stately, evenly pyramidal, spire-like top. Trees in the wild approach 100′ in height; under cultivation 40 to 60′ by 20 to 25′ is a realistic range. Growth is slower than *T. canadensis*. Bark is reddish brown, deeply fissured, scaly.

Foliage: Needles, quite distinct from *T. canadensis*; spirally arranged, but radiating around the stem in a bottlebrush fashion, linear, flattened, entire, ¼ to ¾″ long, 1/12″ wide, glossy green above, with 2 whitish bands below. **Flowers/ seeds/fruits/cones**: Monoecious. Male yellow, female green. Cones are oblong-cylindrical, short-stalked, 1 to 1½″ long, about as wide, cone scales opening wide, perpendicular to central axis, green initially, brown at maturity. **Native range**: Virginia, Tennessee, North Carolina, South Carolina, and Georgia in the mountains on dry slopes, cliffs, bluffs,

weeping conifer when sited in an expanse of lawn, either alone or in multiples. Additional weeping hemlock cultivars include 'Elmwood Cascade' and 'Forest Fountain'.

'Summer Snow'. Larger than 'Albospica', 15 to 20′ high, 8 to 10′ wide, with white new growth maturing green.

'Pendula'

Tsuga caroliniana

Tsuga chinensis

rocky ridges, and occasionally moist soils from 2,000 to 4,000′ elevation. In north Georgia, large trees grow from the sides of Tallulah Gorge, descending from the rim to the river 1,000′ below. **Adaptability**: Based on where it grows in nature, the species should prove better adapted to stressful environments. There is little proof of this supposition because so few trees have left a cultivated footprint. Zones 4 to 7. **Landscape use**: Authors observed magnificent trees in the wild and in several arboreta. The landscape uses are many and similar to those of *T. canadensis*. Unfortunately, it too is susceptible to the hemlock woolly adelgid, though perhaps not to the degree of *T. canadensis*. When infested by the adelgid, the tree often dies in a 4- to 6-year window. **Street tree use**: No. **In the trade**: Several selections are known, with 'Arnold Pyramid', a pyramidal form, 25 to 35′ tall. At the U.S. National Arboretum, this species was successfully crossed with *T. chinensis* to produce adelgid-resistant hybrids; in the near future these hybrids will grace our gardens and landscapes.

Tsuga chinensis
Chinese hemlock

Evergreen conifer. Quite difficult to wrap our arms around this species since so few specimens exist and all are young. The several small trees at the Morris Arboretum are plumpish pyramidal-oval in habit, densely foliated, with graceful arching shoots. Trees over 100′ high are reported in the wild, developing broad-conical habit, the crown flat-topped with age. From a distance it is difficult to separate from *T. canadensis* and, at close range, not much easier. Bark is gray-brown to cinnamon-brown, blocky. The USDA-ARS germplasm repository in Beltsville, MD, has grown numerous plants from wild-collected seed; the variation is phenomenal, with the best as described herein. The seedlings range from 15 to 25′ high, one-half to two-thirds as wide.

Authors studied them during three visits from November 2015 to June 2016. They were beautiful. The species is resistant to the adelgid, and the hybrids with *T. caroliniana*, *T. diversifolia*, and *T. sieboldii* are resistant. Growth is moderate, some seedlings with 1 to 2′ of terminal growth per year.

Foliage: Needles spirally arranged, irregularly spreading, linear, flattened, emarginated apex, entire, ½ to ¾″ long, $\frac{1}{12}$″ wide, glossy medium to dark green above, green underside without 2 obvious silver bands; based on the numerous seedlings at Beltsville, needle color is variable. **Flowers/seeds/fruits/cones**: Monoecious. Male yellow; female green. Cones are ovoid, ½ to 1(1½)″ long, about as wide, lustrous light brown, each scale orbicular and beveled. **Native range**: China, Taiwan, Vietnam. The most widely distributed hemlock in China in mountain forests with hardwoods and conifers. **Adaptability**: Zones 5 to 7(8). **Landscape use**: We believe this species will serve the same landscape functions as *T. canadensis*. It is not fussy about soils as long as well drained. Exposures from full sun (Beltsville, MD) to oak shade (Dirr garden) are acceptable. Numerous articles recount the introduction of *T. chinensis* from many

Tsuga chinensis

Tsuga diversifolia

locations in the wild and subsequent evaluations for adelgid resistance (high); these early reports led to the breeding program at the U.S. National Arboretum. **Street tree use**: No. **In the trade**: Rare. A limiting factor for *T. chinensis* may be its difficulty in propagation. The Arnold Arboretum reported successful rooting from a century-old E. H. Wilson collection, and the U.S. National Arboretum has successfully propagated their selections via cuttings.

Tsuga diversifolia
northern Japanese hemlock

Evergreen conifer. Develops a most graceful, dignified pyramidal habit, the branches arching at their extremities. Landscape size approximates 40 to 60′, one-half to two-thirds that in width; in the great garden at Mount Congreve, Ireland, 30 to 40′ high trees raised our horticultural blood pressure. Growth is slow. Bark is gray-brown to cinnamon-brown, scaly, furrowed. This is the first of the

hemlocks discussed herein to produce new spring growth, and references note it is less troubled by insects that affect *T. canadensis* and *T. caroliniana*.

Foliage: Needles spirally arranged, more or less distichously, linear, entire, notched at apex, furrowed above, ¼ to ⅝″ long, 1/10″ wide, glossy dark green, 2 chalk-white bands below. **Flowers/seeds/fruits/cones**: Monoecious. Male yellow-orange; female green. Cones are ovoid, ¾ to 1″ long, green ripening light brown, scales flat and striated. **Native range**: Japan, where it grows on moist slopes and ridges of mixed montane and subalpine forests to timberline, 8,000′. **Adaptability**: Zones (4)5 to 6(7). **Landscape use**: Another hemlock with minimal presence in North American gardens yet worthy of pursuit and consideration. Authors witnessed beautiful plants at Millcreek Valley Park, Youngstown, OH, and Hoyt Arboretum, Portland. Except for these and the trees at Mount Congreve, it's rarely seen. Why? We lament its paucity in cultivation and wonder if perhaps the American nursery industry is fixated and satiated with *T. canadensis* to the exclusion of the other species. It is safer and easier to grow and design with tried and true; however, nature threw a curve ball with the advent of the hemlock woolly adelgid. **Street tree use**: No. **In the trade**: Uncommon, available seed-grown. Hybrids with *T. chinensis* courtesy of USDA-ARS researchers are resistant to the adelgid, but we have not seen tree-sized cultivars.

Tsuga heterophylla
western hemlock

Evergreen conifer. A large, narrowly pyramidal tree with graceful, down-sweeping branches. It grows with a very straight central trunk, but the tip is always weeping. Fine-textured, medium fast growth rate, to 100′ high and 25′ wide; the National Champion is 237′. Bark is brownish gray, lightly fissured into flattened ridges and small plates.

Tsuga heterophylla

Tsuga heterophylla

'Iron Springs'

Foliage: Dark green needles are ¼ to ¾″ long and ¹⁄₁₆″ wide, held flatly along both sides of the branches. Twigs finely pubescent. Fine branches tend to weep slightly. New growth is a particularly soft, light green and contrasts nicely with the darkness of the older foliage. **Flowers/seeds/fruits/ cones**: Monoecious. Pollen cones are tiny and inconspicuous. The seed cones are so small for such a large tree that you just have to call them cute. They first appear, like tiny green eggs, in early summer, maturing to brown in the fall, pendulous and elliptical, ¾ to 1″ long, hanging from branch tips. **Native range**: Pacific coastal strip from Alaska to northern California within 100 miles of the water, with a second distribution in the western valleys of the Rockies from British Columbia to northern Idaho. **Adaptability**: Likes cooler temperatures, moist soil, and moist air. At home in climates of the Pacific Northwest and northern Europe. Suffers from too much heat and dryness farther inland. Will grow in shade or full sun. Shows good resistance to the hemlock woolly adelgid. Zones (4)5, with the right seed source, to 8 on the West Coast. **Landscape use**: Wonderful in woodland and naturalistic plantings, but use it only in the cool areas where it is well adapted. **Street tree use**: Generally not recommended, doesn't like reflected heat. **In the trade**: Sold as seed-grown and as at least one, more compact cultivar, 'Iron Springs', with an upright irregular pyramidal habit and an alpine look. Its dark foliage is slightly blue-green, with greater density along the branches than the species, and its slow growth projects a height of 20′ and a width of 10′. A favorite of the authors.

Tsuga mertensiana
mountain hemlock

Evergreen conifer. Very narrowly pyramidal, a small alpine spire when growing in the mountains near timberline but much taller at lower elevations; native forest trees can exceed 100′. Fine-textured, slow-growing to a garden size of 20′ by 8′ with time. Bark as shown.

Foliage: Color varies from rich medium green to silvery green to distinctly blue-green. Most trees carry a lovely blue tint. Needles are arranged radially around the branches,

unlike most hemlocks, densely and stiffly bristling forward and outward. Needles ¼ to ¾″ long, ¹⁄₁₆″ or less in width, but thickened, more round in profile than other hemlocks. **Flowers/seeds/fruits/cones**: Monoecious. Pollen cones are small, about ⅓″ long, purplish at first then yellow-green. Seed cones are the largest of the hemlocks, oblong to cylindrical, 2 to 3″ long and ¾″ in diameter; they are a lovely violet and quite attractive before maturing to brown. They typically hold on the tree for a second year, and after opening, resemble a spruce cone. **Native range**: Western

Tsuga mertensiana

Tsuga mertensiana

Tsuga mertensiana

North America, from sea level in coastal Alaska to higher elevations moving south through the coastal mountains to the Sierra Nevada of California, and the western Rockies in British Columbia and northern Idaho. **Adaptability**: Prefers cool weather, damp air, moist soil with good drainage. Well adapted to the Pacific Northwest and northern Europe. Not happy in the heat of eastern states. Resists hemlock woolly adelgid. Zones (4)5 to 8 in the cool coastal West. **Landscape use**: In the Pacific Northwest, this is the perfect tree for creating an alpine garden look. In lowland cities there, its growth rate slows considerably, and it maintains an ideal, somewhat dwarf size. Whereas many alpine tree species, when brought to a lower elevation, grow faster and lose their characteristic habit, mountain hemlock remains true to form. It's a wonderful experience to ride the ski lifts of the Northwest through the mountain hemlocks, their lovely little cones hanging from snow-laden branches. A favorite species of the authors. **Street tree use**: Not for traditional use, but in a cool enough climate, perhaps for mountain villages. Its growth rate and shape are certainly compatible. **In the trade**: Sold as seed-grown. Grafted cultivars provide consistent color.

'Blue Star'. A narrower form, tall and sparse when young then filling in nicely, with perhaps the bluest foliage of the cultivars, as intense in color as many blue spruce. 15 to 20′ tall, 6 to 8′ wide.

'Glacier Peak'. Consistently upright pyramidal, beautifully irregular and alpine-looking, like the species; selected for the silvery blue-green needles, almost as blue as 'Blue Star', but form is a little denser at an earlier age. 15 to 20′ tall, 6 to 8′ wide.

'Glacier Peak'

'Glacier Peak'

U

Ulmus alata
winged elm

Deciduous. With two opposing (opposite) corky wings along the stem, the winged elm is appropriately named. This characteristic is variable and often minimized on slow-growing and mature trees, yet prominent on fast-growing seedlings and young trees. Habit is similar to *U. americana*, with more refined, pendent branches, forming an oval-rounded outline. Becomes a medium to large tree, 50 to 60′ high and two-thirds this in spread. Bark is gray-brown, shallowly ridged and furrowed. Unfortunately, Dutch elm disease and elm yellows infect the species, and many trees are covered with gray powdery mildew in late summer–fall. With that said, it must be moderately resistant to both diseases because numerous healthy specimens dot the native range.

Foliage: Ovate-oblong to oblong-lanceolate, unequal leaf base, doubly serrate, 1½ to 3″ long, half as wide, smooth or rough above, leathery, dark green; occasionally with uniform yellow fall color. **Flowers/seeds/fruits/cones**: Flowers in clusters before the leaves (February-March) on previous year's stems, greenish red. The winged samara is oval-rounded, ⅓″ wide, the margins finely hairy, deeply notched with 2 incurving beaks at the apex. **Native range**: Virginia to Florida, west to Illinois, Oklahoma, and Texas, growing in upland soils in abandoned fields, woods, fence-rows, on any spot of soil. **Adaptability**: Might be termed a weedy native. Abundant in the Piedmont of Georgia, growing in miserable, acid, heavy clay soils, yet prospering with neglect. Authors sighted trees in slight soil pockets among boulders in Piedmont rivers. Zones 6 to 9. **Landscape use**: Truly a species worth considering for miserable urban sites and dry, compacted, acid or neutral soils. We

Ulmus alata

Ulmus alata

'Lace Parasol'

Ulmus americana

believe greater use is warranted assuming uniform habit and mildew-resistant clones are available. Has a mystical quality when the early flowers and, particularly, the hairy fruits are backlighted by the morning and setting sun. Easily identified by this trait, for fruits mature in February-March, before the leaves. In Oregon trials, we found the species extremely slow-growing, especially compared to the other, normally fast-growing elm species, developing little stem caliper. Apparently it needs more summer heat. **Street tree use**: No. **In the trade**: Available.

'Lace Parasol'. Stiffly weeping form with broad, corky wings; the original plant easily 20′ by 30′ in the JC Raulston Arboretum; discovered in Chapel Hill, NC, by Charles Keith and shared with the world. Makes an impressive specimen, a conversation starter.

'Woodland'. Pyramidal in youth, vase-like and spreading with age, estimated 45′ by 40′. The dark green, mildew-resistant leaves turn yellow in fall and, upon abscission, the corky winged stems are showcased.

Ulmus americana
American elm

Deciduous. If trees carried a nostalgia rating, this would be in first place. It was the most widely planted street tree in the United States during the first half of the 20th century, the fabled urban tree of yesteryear—gone from our cities but now making a comeback. Strongly upright, with a sturdy trunk; form is variable, typically with branches arching overhead and forming a vase-shaped canopy, sometimes more broadly spreading and oak-like. Moderately coarse texture, fast-growing, 80′ tall and 70′ wide. Bark is dark gray, ridged and furrowed.

Foliage: Leaves ovate to elliptic or broadly elliptic, 3 to 6″ long and 1 to 3″ wide, doubly serrate, with an oblique base and an acuminate tip. Medium to dark green, dull satiny to slightly lustrous, surface smooth to moderately rough. Fall color yellow. **Flowers/seeds/fruits/cones**: Flowers in spring before the leaves emerge, very small and without petals, green with a reddish tint, in 1″ long clusters, not showy. Fruit a paper-thin, disc-shaped samara, ciliate, ½″ wide, with a central seed, light green, ripening in May to June. **Native range**: Eastern North America, from Nova Scotia to southern Manitoba and Florida to central Texas. **Adaptability**: Highly adaptable, tolerates wet soil and acid to high pH soils, climatic extremes, and difficult city street environments. Extreme susceptibility to Dutch elm disease had made the species unusable as a landscape plant until the recent introduction of resistant cultivars; however, these cultivars are still susceptible to elm yellows and other disease and insect problems. Zones 3 to 9. **Landscape use**:

Ulmus americana

Ulmus americana

Ulmus americana

On campuses and in parks, for historic buildings and boulevards, nothing compared to the tall cathedral archways provided by American elms. These urban forests dominated U.S. street tree plantings—until they were destroyed by Dutch elm disease. Those old enough to have experienced them remember them fondly, but don't let your nostalgia be too selective, remembering the beautiful overhead canopies while forgetting the fogging DDT trucks that kept the foliage clean. Though it is susceptible to more pests and diseases than the vast majority of trees, American elm creates a sense of place like no other, and new introductions with resistance to Dutch elm disease offer hope. But realize that this fungus has mutated before, and may once again. How do we balance the majesty of this great tree and the wish for its place in our towns and cities with real-world concerns for its health and compatibility with modern expectations? As always in the world of urban forestry, choose carefully, use in the right place, and diversify. Biology does not carry guarantees. **Street tree use**: Resistant cultivars are bringing it back to selected streets, where the living green cathedral feel is of the highest priority and maintenance will be assured. It definitely has its place, and tree professionals need to relearn its idiosyncrasies. **In the trade**: Use only resistant cultivars. Specify own-root plants, because trees budded or grafted onto seedling rootstock could be susceptible to root graft infection. Dutch elm disease (DED) testing status or resistance varies and is indicated.

'American Liberty Multiclone'. We suggest avoiding these, a group of six selections that are not individually identified; they vary in their tolerance of DED and generally are not up to the standards set by newer cultivars. 'Independence', the one clone that has been named, is probably the best. 75′ tall, 70′ wide.

COLONIAL SPIRIT 'JFS-Prince II'. Quite upright, with evenly spaced ascending branches, widening and arching with age to form a classic vase shape. We think it's one of the best for form. Selected from a mature survivor in New Jersey and subsequently tested for DED tolerance. Yellow fall color. 75′ tall, 50′ wide.

U

'Independence'

CREOLE QUEEN 'UASNZ'. Upright oval and symmetrical with good form, becoming rounded. Heat tolerant, introduced from a tree growing near New Orleans. Attractive, but not yet tested for DED susceptibility, and we can't recommend until that is known.

'Jefferson'. Selected from the Washington Mall, then named and released by the National Park Service. The original tree has vase-shaped main structural branches with a high, broadly rounded crown, forming an overhead canopy. Young trees are nicely upright in form with wide, strong crotch angles. Very dark green foliage. Has been mixed in the trade with 'Princeton'; true 'Jefferson' has wider branch angles and leafs out earlier. Tested well for DED tolerance. We like it and recommend. 70′ tall and 60′ wide.

'New Harmony'. Fast-growing and a little hard to maintain when young because of its vigor. Grows into a broad oval at first, widely vase-shaped with time. The more we see its mature form develop, the fonder we are of this cultivar. One of the best in testing for DED tolerance. 75′ tall, 70′ wide.

PRAIRIE EXPEDITION 'Lewis & Clark'. Selected in North Dakota, it is of the "prairie form," maturing lower and wider-spreading than other cultivars, 60′ tall, 65′ wide. Very nice dark green foliage. Tested for DED. Proven cold hardiness to zone 3, possibly into 2.

'Princeton'. The most widely planted of the new elm cultivars because of handsome, dark green foliage and symmetrical outline, but its branching habit has proven problematic:

COLONIAL SPIRIT

COLONIAL SPIRIT

'Jefferson'

'Jefferson'

CREOLE QUEEN

'Princeton'

'New Harmony'

U

PRAIRIE EXPEDITION

PRAIRIE EXPEDITION

'Princeton'

'Valley Forge'

crowding and narrow crotches lead to storm breakage. Very nice oval to vase shape, a good tree if you commit to proper thinning periodically at a young age. Tested well for DED tolerance, but occasional infected trees have been seen. 75′ tall, 50′ wide.

'St. Croix'. A patented (PP20,097) cold hardy selection from Minnesota. Tested for DED. A broadly vase-shaped tree with a slightly open crown, the original tree is 75′ tall and 110′ wide, zone 3.

'Valley Forge'. Extremely vigorous, challenging for the nursery to keep pruned for shape, and needing follow-up pruning in the landscape until it reaches a more mature age and growth slows. In short, a bit wild when young, especially in a warm climate where growth is especially fast. In cooler climates, growth is slower and more controlled. But with proper pruning, it makes a fine tree. Lush new growth is light green, then matures medium green. Has the best testing record of proven DED tolerance of all the cultivars. 75′ tall, 80′ wide.

Ulmus crassifolia

cedar elm

Deciduous. Upright-growing to an irregularly oval to rounded shape. Fine-textured, moderate growth rate to 50′ tall and 40′ wide. Bark is light brown to gray-brown, furrowed and scaly.

Foliage: Leaves rather small, 1 to 2″ long, half as wide, oval with a bluntly acute tip, serrate, lustrous dark green, thick, with a rough surface. Yellow fall color. **Flowers/ seeds/fruits/cones**: Small inconspicuous flowers, no petals, greenish with purple anthers, in late summer to early fall. Seed develops quickly, ripening in October, as greenish oval samaras with a single central seed. **Native range**: Western Mississippi to eastern Texas and northeastern Mexico. **Adaptability**: Adapted to high temperatures and tolerant

Ulmus crassifolia

of drought, poor drainage, compaction, and alkaline soils. It is susceptible to Dutch elm disease but seems less so than American elm. Zones 6 to 9. **Landscape use**: Used as a tough, drought-tolerant native tree in Texas and Oklahoma. Its small leaves and late flowering are similar to *U. parvifolia*, which it resembles. Cedar elm is less ornamental but can claim the high ground of being native. Although Dutch elm disease can be fatal, it seems to be a manageable risk. The species has enough resistance in its native range to function as a landscape tree, although we would caution against its use in areas where the disease is known to be active. **Street tree use**: It is tough, tolerant of all the bad things streets throw at a tree, and it can be pruned up for proper form. Just watch out for DED. **In the trade**: Sold as seed-grown.

Ulmus crassifolia

Ulmus davidiana

David elm

Nomenclatural note: Traditionally, four closely related Asian species made up the *U. davidiana* species complex: *U. davidiana*, *U. japonica*, *U. propinqua*, and *U. wilsoniana*. The Flora of China and GRIN have now lumped all these into one species, *U. davidiana*. Although we are not able to evaluate these in their native ranges, we see distinct differences and so maintain the four as separate entries. Horticulturally, it is the cultivars derived from these species that are used in landscaping (and they have differences that align with the four original species designations); therefore, all cultivars of the *U. davidiana* group are grouped together here for convenience and comparison.

Deciduous. A large tree with ascending then arching branches forming a vase-shaped crown, similar to American elm but on a slightly smaller scale. Bark gray, rough, ridged and furrowed. Young branches may have corky bark ridges. Medium texture, moderate growth rate to 60′ tall, 50′ wide.

U

Foliage: Dark green, 2 to 5″ long, one-half to two-thirds as wide, elliptic to obovate with an acuminate tip and prominent parallel veins, margin serrate. Leaf sheen varies from dull-satiny to moderately glossy; pubescence is variable. **Flowers/seeds/fruits/cones**: Small flowers in early spring before the leaves, purplish stamens, apetalous and not showy, in small, tight clusters. Paper-thin samara, ½ to ¾″ wide, obovate with a central seed, green, ripening tan in late spring. **Native range**: The species complex is native to China, Korea, Japan. *U. davidiana* (*U. davidiana* var. *davidiana* per GRIN) is found in very cold areas of northeastern China. **Adaptability**: Resistant to Dutch elm disease. Very adaptable, tolerant of wet soil and reasonable drought, acid to higher pH soils. Native habitat includes disturbed and heavy river bottom soils. Tough and cold hardy, zones (3)4 to 7, 8 in the West. **Landscape use**: Use where a high overhead canopy is desired, as a shade tree, in parking lots, plazas, and campuses. Its vase shape is as close as it comes to the classic form of American elm. Intermediate in size between American elm and zelkova but better adapted to tough Midwest and Plains conditions than zelkova. Elms are susceptible to a variety of insects—elm leaf beetle, Japanese beetle, flea weevil, leaf miner, and aphids. No elm is resistant to all, but the *U. davidiana* group generally fares a little better than most. **Street tree use**: A proven good performer in urban street situations. Its form, disease resistance, and adaptability make it a great choice. **In the trade**: Rarely sold as the species, which is variable from seed. Recent introductions, both hybrids involving it as well as selections from the *U. davidiana* species complex, are predictable and reliable, and have been well received by city foresters and landscape architects. Many of the finest new elm introductions are in this group, utilizing the Dutch elm resistance genetics of the *U. davidiana* complex. We believe that this group carries the strongest level of resistance to the disease. These introductions also carry some resistance to elm yellows and better insect resistance than most of the genus. As a group, these are practical trees and probably the closest you can get to reliable, trouble-free American elm look-alikes. Hats off to George Ware of the Morton Arboretum for championing this species complex and introducing the cultivars that popularized it. Most make excellent street trees; look for the more upright or vase-shaped forms. Again, hybrids and selections of the *U. davidiana* complex are listed here together.

ACCOLADE 'Morton'. A wonderful recreation of the classic American elm vase-shaped form in a slightly smaller size, 60′ tall and 50′ wide. It adds the advantage of very dark green glossy foliage, resistance to elm yellows, and less insect susceptibility. It forms a graceful, street-compatible vase shape. It is stiffer and harder to train when young, and nurseries in the South have found it wild and awkward. Slightly slower growing in the North, it is easier to maintain. It improves with time and when mature, it is a beautiful tree. Landscape performance and classic shape in the

ACCOLADE

ACCOLADE

ACCOLADE

'Discovery'

North have made it Warren's favorite of the group. Yellow fall color. *U. japonica* × *U. wilsoniana*.

'Cathedral'. Extremely vigorous, wide-spreading and rangy, it forms a broadly vase-shaped, open form, often with weeping tips. A little too wild, and being half *U. pumila*, we see little to recommend in it. 50′ by 50′. *U. pumila* × *U. japonica*.

COMMENDATION 'Morton Stalwart'. Hybrid of *U. wilsoniana*, *U. japonica*, *U. pumila*, and *U. minor*. The most rounded form of the Morton introductions, it is full and more formal in appearance and less vase-shaped than others. Foliage is not as glossy, but still smooth and attractive. Branching is even, and the form is quite symmetrical, easy to grow in the nursery. Nice yellow fall color. 55′ by 50′.

DANADA CHARM 'Morton Red Tip'. A fine tree with a broad vase shape similar to an American elm, it would no doubt be more popular if ACCOLADE and TRIUMPH hadn't been introduced at the same time and eclipsed it, partly from appearance and partly because they have more comprehensible names. "Danada" honors Dan and Ada Rice, benefactors

'Cathedral'

U

COMMENDATION

'Discovery'

COMMENDATION

GREENSTONE

EMERALD SUNSHINE

GREENSTONE

EMERALD SUNSHINE

of the Morton Arboretum elm improvement efforts. Dark green with red-tipped new growth. 60′ tall, 50′ wide. *U. japonica* × *U. wilsoniana*.

'Discovery'. Introduced in Manitoba and of known cold hardiness. In our trials, it has been a more rounded vase shape, slower growing and symmetrical. It can be a bit low-branched unless pruned. Foliage a little rough, less glossy, but dark green. 40′ tall, 30′ wide. *U. japonica*.

EMERALD SUNSHINE 'JFS-Bieberich'. Derived from *U. pro-pinqua*, the species that grows into the harsh climate of Mongolia, and selected in equally harsh western Oklahoma. Drought resistant, remaining dark green in the summer heat when others turn dull. It features highly pubescent foliage that could be called warm and fuzzy but has the function of providing improved resistance to flea weevil, elm leaf beetle, and Japanese beetle. Sometimes seeds heavily; samaras are more visible than on most cultivars but briefly held. Upright and narrow oval at first, it develops an upright oval to tightly vase-shaped form, to 45′ tall and 25′ wide. Good yellow fall color.

GREENSTONE 'JFS-KW2UD'. Selected from seed picked from cold hardy native trees at the upper end of the range of classic *U. davidiana* var. *davidiana* in northeastern China, this cultivar has cold and difficult climates in mind. From the 2,000 seedling trees in the evaluation, it was chosen as the most attractive and most similar to American elm. Good branching structure, excellent upright arching vase shape, and yellow fall color, to 50′ tall and 40′ wide.

U

'New Horizon'

'Patriot'

'Patriot'

'New Horizon'. A strong grower with a dominant central leader and a symmetrical, pyramidal form, it is the easiest of the group to grow in the nursery. But its *U. pumila* heritage makes it the most susceptible to elm leaf beetle. It becomes a broader pyramid with age, slightly rounded on top, a handsome form, but more linden-like than elm-like in shape. 55′ tall and 40′ wide. *U. japonica* × *U. pumila*.

'Patriot'. Upright with a strong leader and a stiff oval form when young, it fills in nicely, gains height, and becomes more vase-shaped with age, 55′ tall and 30′ wide. Attractive foliage is neatly formed and dark green in summer; the canopy is more finely textured and slighty open, casting filtered shade. One of the best elms for fall color, a clear yellow, which we have observed consistently in both Oregon and South Carolina sites. A favorite of ours. Hybrid of *U. wilsoniana*, *U. ×hollandica*, and *U. minor*.

'Prospector'. Selected from *U. wilsoniana*, the species that is shorter and more broadly vase-shaped, this cultivar is true to form. Spreading as wide or wider than tall, it may reach 30 to 40′ in height with at least an equal width, a graceful vase shape with weeping tips. Needs pruning to raise canopy

'Prospector'

'Sapporo Autumn Gold'

TRIUMPH

if street use in planned. New growth is slightly red-tinted and pubescent, summer leaves are bright green and glossy.

'Sapporo Autumn Gold'. A decent street tree form, introduced by the University of Wisconsin program; it has gained significant use in Europe. Its wider vase shape is a bit open and less refined, reflecting the *U. pumila* in its parentage, 40′ by 40′. *U. japonica* × *U. pumila*.

TRIUMPH 'Morton Glossy'. Currently the most popular tree in this cultivar group, it combines easy nursery production, attractive initial landscape appearance, and good long-term form and performance, making everyone happy. Initially symmetrical and upright oval, it becomes more vase-shaped with time, but never as much so as related ACCOLADE. Moderately glossy deep green foliage, decent yellow in the fall. Dirr's favorite of the group, and the best performer in the South. 60′ tall and 50′ wide. Hybrid of *U. japonica*, *U. wilsoniana*, and *U. pumila*.

U

TRIUMPH

TRIUMPH

VANGUARD

Ulmus glabra
Scotch elm, Wych elm

Deciduous. Upright-spreading, usually low-branched with a heavy trunk and stout structural branches, forming a broadly rounded crown. Bark gray-brown and fissured. Coarse-textured, moderately fast-growing to 80′ tall and 60′ wide.

Foliage: Leaves dark green, 3 to 6½″ long, half that or a little more in width, obovate, with an oblique leaf base and an acuminate tip. Surface usually rough, margin coarsely serrate, sometimes with 1 or 2 very small pointed lobes looking like serrations gone wild. Dull yellow fall color. **Flowers/seeds/fruits/cones**: Small flowers in early spring before the leaves, greenish with red-purple stamens, apetalous and not showy, in clusters of 10 to 20. Light green, oval to obovate samaras ripen to tan in May, paper-thin, ¾″ long with a

VANGUARD 'Morton Plainsman'. A nice broad vase shape with handsome glossy medium green foliage. It looks quite good when young, but the *U. pumila* in its parentage eventually shows with more open form over time and attractiveness to elm leaf beetle. Useful for tougher climates of the Northern Plains, but we prefer other cultivars. 45′ tall, 40′ wide. *U. japonica* × *U. pumila*.

886

Ulmus glabra

Ulmus glabra

'Camperdownii'

'Camperdownii'

'Horizontalis'

central seed. **Native range**: Europe and western Asia, from Ireland east to the Urals. **Adaptability**: Quite cold hardy but also quite susceptible to Dutch elm disease. Zones 4 to 7. **Landscape use**: Rarely used as a species; important as a parent in hybridization and for its cultivars of unique form. **Street tree use**: No. **In the trade**: In the United States, the wonderful 'Camperdownii' (Camperdown elm) might as well wear a sign saying "historic site," as it is so closely associated with fine old buildings and landscapes. It definitely sets a mood. Dark green, broadly mounded, with curtains of foliage gracefully weeping to the ground, 15′ tall and 20 to 30′ wide. Few seeds. 'Horizontalis' (tabletop elm) is similar but flat-spreading, growing horizontally in layers, branch tips drooping but not weeping to the ground, 15′ tall and 30′ wide. Seeds heavily.

U

Ulmus ×hollandica
Dutch elm

Deciduous. This hybrid species, derived from *U. glabra* and *U. minor*, is represented by selected cultivars that are best described individually. The cross has occurred both naturally and in breeding programs for disease resistance.

Adaptability: The cultivars tend to be urban-tolerant. They have been selected for resistance to Dutch elm disease, but they are not immune. Zones 5 to 7. **Landscape use**: Large shade trees. **Street tree use**: Common as such in Europe, where most were developed. The upright forms with highest disease resistance are good choices. **In the trade**: We have grouped here a few more complex hybrids that are primarily of this parentage.

'Clusius'. Upright-growing with a good central leader, quite dense, forming a pyramidal canopy with a rounded top, 50′ tall and 35′ wide.

'Dodoens'. Upright and moderately oval when young, becoming broadly oval to rounded with age, 50′ tall and 40′ wide.

'Homestead'. Upright with a good central leader, becoming pyramidal and eventually a moderately narrow oval, dark green, 55′ tall, 35′ wide. Hybrid of *U. ×hollandica*, *U. pumila*, and *U. minor*.

'Lobel'. Tall with a good central leader and ascending branches, very narrow at first, broadening to a moderate upright oval form. A good form for streets, 50′ tall and 20′ wide. Hybrid of *U. minor*, *U. ×hollandica*, and *U. wallichiana*.

'Pioneer'. Vigorous growing, broadly pyramidal when young, more spreading and nearly round with age, a good shade tree form for parks, big and broad, to at least 50′ by 50′.

'Pioneer'

'Pioneer'

'Homestead'

'Regal'

'Wredei'

'Plantijn'. Upright oval when young, staying narrower below and flaring slightly wider on top with age, fast-growing, a good street form, 50′ tall and 25′ wide.

'Regal'. Strongly upright with a good central leader, pyramidal to oval, rather stiff and a bit open in form, a functional tree but not the prettiest. 55′ tall and 45′ wide. Hybrid of *U. ×hollandica*, *U. pumila*, and *U. minor*.

'Wredei'. Bright yellow foliage, intense in spring, more yellow-green in summer. Columnar when young, broadly oval to round with age, a smaller tree to 30′ tall, 25′ wide. Less resistant to disease but planted for its color.

Ulmus japonica
Japanese elm

Deciduous. Tallest member of the *U. davidiana* complex; now considered *U. davidiana* var. *japonica* by GRIN. A 91′ by 73′ specimen at UMass Amherst, planted in 1890, is the largest and oldest representative of the species in North America; it survived DED. **Native range**: Northeast Asia and Japan, growing in forests on well-drained slopes. **Adaptability**: At Morton Arboretum, it showed a preference for well-drained soil, hardy to zone 4. **In the trade**: 'Discovery'. See *U. davidiana*.

Ulmus japonica

U

Ulmus minor (U. carpinifolia)
smoothleaf elm, field elm

Deciduous. Upright with ascending branches and a broadly pyramidal to broadly oval crown. Bark gray-brown, smooth when young then ridged and furrowed. Medium texture, moderately fast growth, 70′ tall and 50′ wide.

Foliage: Leaves lustrous dark green, 1½ to 4″ long, half as wide, long ovate, elliptic, or long obovate with an offset, very oblique leaf base and an acuminate tip, doubly serrate, usually with a smooth surface. **Flowers/seeds/fruits/cones**: Small flowers, reddish purple from exserted stamens, apetalous, provide color but not really showy, in small clusters in early spring before the leaves. Light green samaras are obovate, ⅝″ long, paper-thin, ripen to light tan. **Native range**: Europe, east to the Caucasus. **Adaptability**: Susceptible to Dutch elm disease. Zones 5 to 7. **Landscape use**: No longer used in landscaping. **Street tree use**: No. **In the trade**: Uncommon, of importance in breeding resistant elm cultivars. See U. ×hollandica.

Ulmus minor

Ulmus parvifolia
lacebark elm

Deciduous, tardily so in Deep South. With resistances to both Dutch elm disease and elm leaf beetle, this species has received significant attention from selectors/breeders, designers, and landscape architects in the past 25 years. Rounded in outline, with a dense canopy; averages 40 to 50′ high and wide. Bark is its heart and soul, 2″ and larger branches/trunks exfoliating into puzzle-shaped pieces, creating a mosaic of gray, green, orange, and brown; seedling variation is maddening, so utilize cultivars with the proven bark characteristics.

Foliage: Elliptic to ovate or obovate, unequally rounded at base, simply or nearly simply serrate, with 10 to 12 vein pairs, ¾ to 2½″ long and 1½″ wide, leathery, lustrous dark green and smooth above, yellow to burgundy fall color. **Flowers/seeds/fruits/cones**: Greenish red flowers in axillary clusters during late summer; lost among the

Ulmus parvifolia

foliage and seldom noticed. Fruit is winged, elliptic-ovate samara, notched at apex, ⅓″ long, glabrous, maturing October-November; produced in great quantities even on young trees, and stray seedlings occur; observed areas where the species has seeded in to the exclusion of other vegetation. **Native range:** China, Korea, Japan, Taiwan. **Adaptability:** Universal soil adaptability. Literally any soil, except permanently wet, wide pH range, and full sun are the basic expectations. Zones 5 to 9. Authors recorded trees on the Iowa State campus, Ames, and University of Maine, Orono, which equates with the northern limit for successful culture. Trees were observed in central Florida, Texas, and California. We speculate the species has the most diverse cultivated range of an exotic introduction, excepting *Ailanthus altissima*. **Landscape use:** One of the most serviceable, adaptable species for stressful urban landscapes, and, in the Southeast, is prevalent along streets, in parking lots, campuses, parks, and residential sites. In Nashville, TN, trees were pleached into a continuous green box on stilts of exfoliating trunks. Easy to transplant and propagate. The southeastern universities and nursery industry were active in the 1990s and early 2000s, selecting and testing clones of various habits, from somewhat columnar (EVERCLEAR) to vase-shaped (ALLÉE) to broad-rounded (ATHENA Classic) to compact ('Small Frye'). **Street tree use:** Common, durable, and successful. **In the trade:** Restrained presentation herein, since many cultivars have fallen by the wayside.

ALLÉE 'Emer II'. Superior selection from the University of Georgia campus. Arguably, the bark is the most spectacular of all the introductions. Similar to *U. americana* in habit, branches not as arching, original tree was 70′ by 50′ with a

Ulmus parvifolia

Ulmus parvifolia

ALLÉE

U

ALLÉE

ATHENA

ALLÉE

ATHENA

fluted trunk and broad-flaring root collar. In Oregon, where late dormancy combined with the possibility of an early freeze limits the use of the species, this cultivar has proven the most reliable of true *U. parvifolia* selections.

ATHENA / ATHENA Classic 'Emer I'. One and the same, except the current ATHENA Classic is a reconstitution via cuttings (instead of tissue culture like ATHENA) of the original tree. Tissue culture had caused a phase change resulting in more shrubby growth for the first 10 years before reverting to normal. Beautiful, broad, mushroom-shaped crown; 40 to 45' high, 50 to 60' wide; superb exfoliating bark.

BOSQUE 'UPMTF'. Described as pyramidal-columnar form with strongly ascending branches; the original seedling tree was 18' high and 8' wide, with time developing an oval-rounded habit; however, authors recorded 25' by 25' trees in Wilmington, NC, and estimate 40 to 50' by 20 to 30'. Bark is beautiful. Two trees in the Dirr garden were 25'

by 20' in 7 years; West Coast growers report snow and ice damage on this cultivar.

'Burgundy'. Kicked to the curb in its early days, but keeps surfacing in nurseries from Kentucky to Georgia. A seedling found in a parking island on the University of Georgia campus. Extremely leathery, dark green summer foliage and consistent burgundy fall color give it an edge over the majority of cultivars; outstanding exfoliating bark. Goes dormant earlier than most, avoiding fall freeze damage, and less susceptible to ice weight. Habit is graceful and rounded; we estimate 30 to 40' high and wide at landscape maturity.

'Drake'. Evergreen in warm southern climates and briefly deciduous to the north, probably best suited to warm portions of zones 8 and 9, where it holds foliage year-round. Rounded in form with arching, pendulous branches. The similar 'True Green' is semi-evergreen and also only minimally hardy.

BOSQUE

'Drake'

'Burgundy'

ATHENA

'Drake'

U

'Dynasty'

'Dynasty'

EMERALD FLAIR

'Emerald Prairie'

'Dynasty'. Broadly rounded with leaves slightly larger than most cultivars, among the best for cold hardiness, but lacks the colorful mosaic bark of our favorite cultivars. Yellow-orange fall color, 40′ by 40′. Has lost popularity due to the infusion of superior exfoliating bark cultivars.

EMERALD FLAIR 'JFS-Barrett'. Upright, broadly spreading vase-shape, deep dark green leaves hold green color better in the heat of summer, orange-red to red fall color, 40′ by 35′. Attractive orange-tan-brown exfoliating bark.

'Emerald Prairie'. Upright-spreading, arching vase shape, glossy dark green leaves, yellow fall color, excellent bark, resistant to black leafspot, 40′ by 30′, proven in the prairie climate, a Kansas State University introduction.

EVERCLEAR 'BSNUPF'. The first true columnar selection; the original tree 35′ high, 7 to 8′ wide. We observed fast-growing trees with slight splaying branches (and note 2017 literature that lists the size as 40′ high, 25′ wide). It still ranks as the narrowest in width among commercial cultivars. Bark is outstanding.

EMERALD FLAIR

EVERCLEAR

EVERCLEAR

'Frontier'. A hybrid between *U. minor* and *U. parvifolia*, vase-shaped in youth, broad-oval at maturity, lustrous dark green foliage, red fall color excellent in the North but does not hold in the Southeast. Never once developed red fall color in University of Georgia trials, although trees grew well over a 15-year period. In Oregon, we see one full month of fall color, starting out deep burgundy and slowly intensifying to bright, deep red. Moderate resistance to elm leaf beetle; bark is similar to *U. minor* without the exfoliating nature of *U. parvifolia*. More reliable cold hardiness than true *U. parvifolia* cultivars and very popular. 50′ tall, 30′ wide.

'Golden Rey' ('Golden Ray'). Dome-shaped habit; foliage yellow, and, as seen in Oklahoma City, still yellow in October; gray-orange-brown exfoliating bark; 20 to 30′ high, slightly wider.

'Hope'. Broad-rounded form with arching branches and a more graceful habit similar to 'Burgundy'; 40′ tall and 45′ wide; with larger medium green leaves than typical, yellow fall color, and outstanding bark.

'Small Frye'. Rounded to perfect mushroom-shaped outline, the branches and foliage densely borne, creating a solid dome of green. Only 20 to 25′ high and wide after 30 years in an east Athens, GA, neighborhood that was thickly planted with *U. parvifolia* seedlings. Most were woody trash except the *one*. The need for a smaller lacebark elm is genuine. It has been easy to root from cuttings and is also being budded. Outstanding bark.

U

'Frontier'

'Golden Rey'

'Small Frye'

'Frontier'

Ulmus propinqua
chalkbark elm

Deciduous. Part of the *U. davidiana* complex; now considered *U. davidiana* var. *japonica* by GRIN. Slightly smaller, to 40′. Branches often quite corky. Leaves are pubescent on both surfaces with no glossiness. **Native range**: Inner Mongolia and the drier areas close to the grasslands, west of the other species in the complex. **Adaptability**: Zone 5, possibly 4b. **In the trade**: EMERALD SUNSHINE. See *U. davidiana*.

Ulmus pumila

Siberian elm

Deciduous. Branches ascending and upright-spreading, form varies from moderately vase-shaped to rounded, usually slightly open and irregular. Bark gray to gray-brown, rough, ridged and furrowed. Medium coarse in texture, scruffy-looking, fast-growing, 50′ high and 40′ wide. Invasive across North America and in many other parts of the world.

Foliage: Leaves medium to dark green, 1 to 3″ long, half as wide, elliptic to elongated elliptic, with an acuminate tip, serrate. Leaf base is symmetrical to slightly oblique, less so than most elms. Surface smooth, dull to satiny. No real fall color, yellowish green. **Flowers/seeds/fruits/cones**: Small flowers with purplish stamens, apetalous and not showy, in small, tight clusters in early spring before the leaves. Paper-thin samara, ½″ wide, round to obovate with a central seed, ripening to tan in May. Unlike most elms, it can self-pollinate and usually produces heavy seed crops. **Native range**: Eastern Siberia and northern China to Korea. **Adaptability**: Unfortunately, very adaptable, or should we say terribly adaptable, making it terribly invasive. Tolerates heat, cold, drought, and alkalinity. A very tough tree. Resistant to Dutch elm disease but highly susceptible to elm leaf beetle. Zones 3 to 9. **Landscape use**: You may think the authors guilty of praising every tree, but not so. This tree deserves to be firewood. Extensively planted in the Plains during the Dust Bowl years, it was at first valued then widely despised for its brittleness and weediness. **Street tree use**: No. **In the trade**: Should not be sold or planted. Of value only in breeding because of its Dutch elm disease resistance, but this is offset by its susceptibility to the elm leaf beetle; both characteristics tend to carry through to progeny.

Ulmus wilsoniana

Wilson elm

Deciduous. Part of the *U. davidiana* complex; now considered *U. davidiana* var. *japonica* by GRIN. It is shorter and more wide-spreading in form than the other species, with reddish new growth. **Native range**: The more central portion of China, south of the other members of the complex, thus a little less hardy. **Adaptability**: Zone (4)5. **In the trade**: 'Prospector'. See *U. davidiana*.

Ulmus pumila

V

Vernicia fordii

Vernicia fordii

Vernicia fordii (*Aleurites fordii*)
tung-oil tree

Evergreen to deciduous, depending on temperature. This pyramidal to round-headed, coarse-textured, 20 to 40′ high and wide tree is occasionally found in the Deep South. Initially, it was planted for the fruits, the seeds of which yield a valuable oil utilized in the paint and varnish industry. Both seeds and leaves are poisonous so, if present, be aware. Fast-growing.

Foliage: Lustrous dark green leaves, to 10″ long and wide, are evergreen in frost-free zones. In Athens, GA, trees defoliate after the first freeze. Foliage lends a semi-tropical appearance to the plant. Leaves are late to emerge. **Flowers/seeds/fruits/cones:** Flowers open before the leaves in 6 to 8″ long panicles. Each campanulate flower is white, maturing to rose in the center. Full flower in April in zone 8. The fruit is a 2 to 3″ wide globose drupe with 3 to 5 large seeds. **Native range:** Middle Asia. **Adaptability:** Zones 8 to 10. Trees have been killed to ground at 10 to 15°F. **Landscape use:** Interesting from a historical perspective. Attempts were made in the Deep South to establish commercial orchards, and remnant trees show up in various locales, including Louisiana State University campus, Wight Nurseries, Cairo, GA, and the Grand Hotel, Point Clear, AL. Logically, for safety reasons, a sterile cultivar is the best choice for landscape use. **Street tree use:** No. **In the trade:** 'Anna Bella', to the author's knowledge, is the first sterile introduction. It was developed by Tim Rinehart, USDA-ARS, Poplarville, MS.

Viburnum lentago
nannyberry viburnum, sheepberry, wild raisin

Deciduous. Small tree or large shrub, with slender arching branches and an open habit. Authors recorded pretty tree-type specimens in both the wild and cultivation, with a notable 25′ tree at the Biltmore Estate, Asheville, NC. Expect 15 to 20′ in height, similar spread. The species may develop suckers, forming large colonies. Growth is slow to moderate. Bark is blackish, patterned scaly to blocky, a distinct identification characteristic. Fruits are edible and can be used for jams and jellies; they provide sustenance for birds as well.

Foliage: Ovate to elliptic-obovate, finely and regularly serrated, 2 to 4″ long, half as wide, thin-textured, soft yellow-green when emerging, then glossy dark green, and at its best red-purple in autumn; fall color is maddeningly variable and selection for superior coloration and mildew resistance is needed. **Flowers/seeds/fruits/cones:** Delicate, agreeably fragrant white flowers with raised yellow stamens, in 3 to 4½″ wide flat-topped cymes in April-May, opening with the developing leaves. Fruit is a drupe, oval,

Viburnum lentago

Viburnum lentago

Viburnum lentago

a pretty native species useful for naturalizing, woodland edges, and borders, offering multi-season beauty. It performs best in moist, acid to neutral, well-drained soil in sun to moderate shade. Quite drought tolerant once established. **Street tree use**: No. **In the trade**: Available. Enthusiasm for the species would increase if reliable cultivars were available. 'Prairie Classic' is a hybrid (*V. lentago* × *V. rufidulum*) with excellent vigor, leathery dark green leaves, red-yellow-green fall color; forms a broad, compact, dense, oval outline with minimal suckering, 15 to 18′ by 12 to 15′.

Viburnum odoratissimum var. *awabuki* (*V. awabuki*)
awabuki sweet viburnum

Nomenclatural note: Authors consider *V. odoratissimum* a distinctly different entity and not at all close to var. *awabuki* in affinities, apart from similar flowers and fruits. Var. *awabuki* is described herein. *V. odoratissimum* differs from it in size (to 40′), habit (oval-rounded), foliage (2 to 4″ long, ovate-oval, dull olive-green on both surfaces), and odor when bruised (fetid green pepper). It's also killed outright in zone 7, while var. *awabuki* is not even damaged. What's more, the taxonomic literature is a messy Mulligan stew with no clear agreement. Our best advice is assess leaf shape, color, and smell before installing.

Broadleaf evergreen. Pyramidal-oval in habit, most often grown as a large, multi-stemmed shrub but could be fashioned into a single-stemmed tree, much like an *Ilex latifolia*. It reaches 15 to 25′ in height, two-thirds as wide. Growth is fast, and suckers develop from the base, extending 3 to 5′ in a season. Bark is gray-brown, dotted with abundant gray lenticels. A beautiful glossy-leaf viburnum, essentially unknown in U.S. garden culture until J. C. Raulston introduced 'Chindo'.

Viburnum odoratissimum var. *awabuki*

⅓ to ½″ long, bluish black, bloomy; color initiates green, then degrees of yellow, rose, and pinks before maturing; aging-rotting fruits smell like wet sheep wool and will persist into winter. **Native range**: New Brunswick to Georgia, west to Manitoba and Nebraska, also North Dakota, South Dakota, Wyoming, and Colorado. Grows in moist soils in rich woods and along streams, often in shady habitats. **Adaptability**: Zones 3 to 7. **Landscape use**: At its best,

V

Foliage: Ovate-lanceolate, remotely serrate toward apex, 3 to 7″ long, 1½ to 2½″ wide, leathery, lustrous green above, dull olive-green below, holding color in winter. Odor when bruised is minimal. **Flowers/seeds/fruits/cones**: White, borne in rounded 6 to 10″ high and wide, cymose panicles; flowers are produced on mature plants, often in the top portions, in June. Fruit is an ovoid drupe, ¼ to ⅓″ long, red, seldom in appreciable quantities. Many viburnums require outcrossing for heavy fruit set, so two seedlings or different clones (cultivars) must be present; thinking is that most cultivated plants descended from the original Raulston clone, which he described as having "large pendulous masses of bright red fruits hanging...like ornaments on a Christmas tree." Authors observed a few fruits on isolated plants and noted them turning red to black. **Native range**: India, Taiwan, Philippines, Japan, Korea. Found in evergreen forests on hills and in valleys in warm coastal areas, at 30 to 2,500′ elevation. **Adaptability**: Adapts to any well-drained, moist, acid soil and once established requires nothing but appreciation. Zones 7 to 9. **Landscape use**: A popular specimen evergreen and a staple in warm zones for screening, massing, and even hedging, its large leaves notwithstanding. Thrives in full sun and moderate to heavy shade. Extremely fast-growing, which necessitates butcher-shop pruning with

COPPERTOP

Viburnum odoratissimum var. *awabuki*

Viburnum odoratissimum

Viburnum odoratissimum var. *awabuki*

'Variegata'

Viburnum prunifolium

subsequent arrow-shaft regrowth, resulting in an aesthetic boondoggle. Ideally, plant and leave alone, or feather prune to shape and keep in bounds. Large specimens are dense and beautiful without any intervention. **Street tree use**: No. **In the trade**: 'Chindo', the basis for the description just given, is available, as is COPPERTOP 'Brant01', a 2017 introduction with bronze-copper new growth, becoming lustrous dark green at maturity; listed as 6 to 8' high, 5 to 6' wide, but we estimate larger with age; defoliated at 10°F in Athens ('Chindo' was untouched). 'Variegata' has green-centered, white-margined leaves and will revert; requires moderate shade to be at its best.

Viburnum prunifolium
blackhaw viburnum

Deciduous. Small tree or large shrub, often suckering, 15 to 20' high and wide. Co-national champions are 33' by 40' and 31' by 37', the first single-trunked, the latter multiple. Develops a stiff, rigid, rounded patchwork of intersecting branches, not unlike that of a hawthorn. Growth is slow to moderate. Bark is black and blocky. Fruits, which are similar to those of *V. lentago*, are used for preserves. In fact, the storyline for *V. lentago* could be overlain here. A major difference is that *V. prunifolium* blankets all eastern North America; *V. lentago* only the northern tier. The leaf of *V. prunifolium* is generally smaller, the petiole with no wing, and its winter flower and vegetative buds are half the length of *V. lentago*.

Foliage: Broad elliptic, ovate to obovate, finely serrate (more so than *V. lentago*); 1½ to 3½" long, 1 to 2" wide, dull to lustrous dark green, shades of red to red-purple in fall; leaves emerge early in spring; no mildew. **Flowers/seeds/fruits/cones**: White with raised yellow stamens, no fragrance, in 2 to 4" wide, flat-topped cymes with the

Viburnum prunifolium

emerging leaves, April-May; similar in effect to *V. lentago*. Fruit is an ovoid drupe to ½" long, green, pink, rose, to glaucous bluish black at maturity, sweetish, palatable; ripening in October, persisting into winter. **Native range**: Connecticut to Georgia, west to Wisconsin, Kansas,

V

Viburnum prunifolium

Oklahoma, Texas, in moist soils or rich soils of slopes/hill-sides. **Adaptability**: Zones 3 to 9. **Landscape use**: Valuable for naturalistic woodland plantings. Its stiff, dense branches make a great and impenetrable barrier or hedge. As a specimen, accent, or screen it functions admirably. Prefers moist, acid to neutral, well-drained soils in full sun to partial shade, and once established is drought and heat tolerant. **Street tree use**: No. **In the trade**: Limited and generally shrub forms. FOREST ROUGE 'McKRouge' is a small single-stemmed tree or multi-stemmed shrub with dense, upright oval habit. The maroon fall color comes early and persists; 12 to 15′ by 8 to 10′.

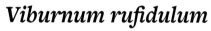

Viburnum rufidulum
rusty blackhaw viburnum

Deciduous. Somewhat similar to *V. lentago* and *V. prunifolium* in features, but possessing thicker, more lustrous, mirror-surfaced leaves and rusty brown hairs on buds, young stems, and petioles. In the wild, it is often single-stemmed, sometimes multi-stemmed, upright-spreading, with stiff, twiggy branches, and can exceed 30′ in height. We estimate 10 to 20′ high, two-thirds as wide, under cultivation. Growth is slow to moderate. Bark is black and blocky.

Foliage: Oval, ovate to obovate, leathery, serrulate (fine-toothed), 2 to 4″ long to 2″ wide, lustrous dark green, rich burgundy to yellow-orange-red fall color. **Flowers/seeds/fruits/cones**: White with raised yellow stamens, slight to no fragrance, each ⅓″ across, borne in 3 to 5″ wide, flat-topped cymes, April-May, after the leaves have matured. Fruit is a drupe, ellipsoidal, ½ to ⅔″ long, bloomy dark blue, October and persisting. **Native range**: Virginia

Viburnum rufidulum

Viburnum rufidulum

Viburnum rufidulum

to Florida, west to Kansas and Texas. Definitely an upland species, most often found in shady woodlands in relatively dry soil situations, in well-drained hedgerows and fence-rows. **Adaptability**: Offers pretty, ornamental features and iron-clad adaptability. We believe it is more drought and heat tolerant than V. *lentago* and V. *prunifolium*. Although southeastern in distribution, plants have thrived from Boston to Chicago, withstanding -25°F in the Midwest. Zones 5 to 9. **Landscape use**: Beautiful and worthy native species for naturalizing, woodland edges, even understory planting with rhododendrons and azaleas. Often develops an open canopy in shade environments. On the University of Georgia campus, plants sited under large pines are densely foliated. Excellent choice for dry soil areas, acid to neutral, full sun to partial shade. **Street tree use**: Potential. **In the trade**: The species could use an infusion of superior cultivars, as row-run seedlings are often disappointing. 'Royal Guard' has the glossy green foliage of the type and burgundy fall color; will reach 15' in height, 10' in width; a 10' high plant at the JC Raulston Arboretum was less than impressive.

Viburnum sieboldii
Siebold viburnum

Deciduous. Oval-rounded, single- to multi-stemmed, with stiff, stout, rigid branches. Grows 15 to 20(30)' high, variable width, although we recorded a 25' by 30' tree in England. Moderate growth rate. Bark is gray, nothing spectacular. The authors have always considered V. *sieboldii* among the best tree-statured viburnums and, indeed, Warren continues to breed for superior selections.

Foliage: Elliptic or obovate to oblong, coarsely serrate, with 7 to 10 pairs of deeply impressed veins, 2 to 6″ long, 1½ to 3″ wide, lustrous dark green, variable fall color, yellow-green to dull red and burgundy (seldom), holding late; fetid odor when bruised. **Flowers/seeds/fruits/cones**: Cream-white, fragrant (sweet lemony), borne in long-stalked, 3 to 6″ long

and wide, cymose panicles, in May-June after leaves have matured; beautiful and abundant at their best. Fruit is an oval drupe, ⅓ to ½″ long, rose-red, red, eventually black if birds do not devour, effective for weeks from August to October; even after fruits abscise or are eaten, the inflorescence (peduncle and pedicels) remain rose-red for 2 to 4 weeks. **Native range**: Japan. **Adaptability**: The greatest concentration of honorable specimens reside in the

Viburnum sieboldii

Viburnum sieboldii

Viburnum sieboldii

V

Northeast, Midwest, and Pacific Northwest. It languishes in the heat of the South. Zones 4 to 7, 8 in the coastal West. **Landscape use**: Superb as a specimen or in groupings; at the University of Massachusetts, it was used to soften the dull red brick expanses of campus buildings. Prefers a cooler climate, moist, acid to neutral soils, and full sun to light shade. Selections for uniform upright-columnar habits would prove useful in urban and restricted areas. Cultivars are produced by cuttings. **Street tree use**: Potential. **In the trade**: Seldom available, alas. Our retail industry is focused on "wow in a bucket." If a plant does not "pop" in a 3-gallon container, chances are it won't sell in the current instant-gratification atmosphere. In fact, all viburnums discussed in the book may suffer the fate. 'Seneca' is a tree form, 25 to 30′ high, 15′ wide, with large pendent clusters of red, changing to black fruit; fruits stay firm and birds supposedly do not eat; beautiful introduction from the U.S. National Arboretum. Just one example of the prize justifying the pursuit.

Vitex agnus-castus
chastetree

Deciduous. Small low-branched tree or large multi-stemmed shrub, 15 to 20′ high and wide, with a rounded, fine-textured foliage canopy. Growth is extremely fast. Bark is gray-brown; blocky on larger trunks. Chastetree is used in various herbal medicines, particularly for women's health issues, including acne, migraines, joint conditions, and overactive libido. Its flowers are an important summer nectar source for butterflies, hummingbirds, and bees; vitex honey is highly prized.

Foliage: Leaves are compound palmate, 5 to 7(9) finger-like leaflets, each narrow-elliptic to lanceolate; 2 to 5″ long, ½ to 1″ wide, tapering at apex and base, either entire or toothed toward apex, dark gray-green, almost blue-green;

aromatic when crushed; no fall color; sensitive to early fall and spring freezes. **Flowers/seeds/fruits/cones**: Slightly fragrant lavender to blue-purple flowers borne on 3 to 6″ long racemes from the ends and leaf axils of the current season's growth, resulting in a racemose-panicle, eventually 12 to 18″ long, two-thirds as wide, June-July into September. Fruit is a rounded drupe, $\frac{1}{12}$″ wide, persisting through winter. Removal of spent flowers and developing fruit promotes new vegetative growth and the development of additional flowers. **Native range**: Central Asia to Mediterranean region, where it grows in river beds with *Tamarix* and *Nerium*. **Adaptability**: Prospers in any well-drained soil, sand, clay, acid, alkaline. Tolerates salt, heat, and drought and, in fact, flowers best with ample warmth. We have recorded choice specimens from coast to coast and into the Deep South. Zones 7 to 9; serviceable in zone 6 as a dieback shrub, where it regrows and flowers in late summer. Leaves are killed at 28°F. **Landscape use**: Over the past decade, the species has left the wings and taken center stage, becoming a common landscape element in the Southeast and particularly the Southwest, where it is referred to as the

Vitex agnus-castus

Vitex agnus-castus

DELTA BLUES

"Texas lilac." Use as a specimen, in groupings and borders, or espalier. A well-groomed chastetree, in full flower, has few competitors. Requires tidying of dead branches, and old, dried fruits should be removed. If a plant has become overgrown to the point of no redemption, simply cut it back to 6 to 12″ above ground. The following year all will again be right. **Street tree use**: Potential but rather low and wide. **In the trade**: Breeders from Georgia, Louisiana, and Texas have been at their work benches, cobbling dwarf, intermediate, and large cultivars with disease-resistant foliage and white, pink, deep purple, and blue flowers. Like rabbits, cultivars keep showing up in the literature and nursery production. We have recorded over 30, with the best of the tree-types described here.

'Abbeville Blue', 'Le Compte', and 'Mississippi Blues'. All are 15′ in height, with deep blue-purple flowers.

f. *alba* 'Silver Spire'. Pure white flowers.

'Cooke's Blue', 'Cooke's Pink', 'Cooke's Purple', 'Cooke's White'. All described as growing 15 to 25′ high and wide. Introduced by L. E. Cooke Co., Visalia, CA.

DELTA BLUES 'PIIVAC-I'. More compact, 10′ by 8′, with rich blue flowers in dense panicles and leafspot-resistant foliage. Easily fashioned into a small tree. Discovered by Dirr's son Matt.

'Flora Ann' and 'Salinas Pink'. The best pink-flowered forms, 'Flora Ann' with deeper pink petals.

'Shoal Creek'. One of the best old-timers, with lilac flowers in 12 to 18″ long panicles on a 15 to 20′ high framework. Foliage is more resistant to leafspot. Originated near Athens, GA.

'Flora Ann'

'Le Compte'

'Salinas Pink'

Vitex agnus-castus

V

'Shoal Creek'

'Shoal Creek'

W

Washingtonia filifera
California fan palm, desert fan palm

Evergreen. The two *Washingtonia* species are not the easiest palms to identify; in fact, they hybridize, thus compounding the issue. This forms a more open crown than *W. robusta*, the older leaf bases persistent and forming a dense skirt (as in *W. robusta*). The leaflets are pendulous, loosely swaying, with cottony threads persisting, compared to stiff leaflets and dehiscing cottony threads in *W. robusta*. Landscape size is 40 to 60′ high, 15 to 20′ wide. Growth is slow to moderate. Trunk is gray, thick, barrel-shaped, to 3′ at its widest point.

Foliage: Palmate, divided into numerous segments, leaves 3 to 6′ long held on a petiole to 6′ long, gray-green, drooping at their tips, edged with white threads, petiole armed with curved spines. **Flowers/seeds/fruits/cones**: White-yellow, borne in inflorescences up to 15′ long. Fruit is an oblong-rounded drupe, ¼″ wide, dark brown to red-black. **Native range**: Arizona, Baja California, in desert and arid regions, along streams, in canyons, and in open areas where ground water is present. **Adaptability**: Reported to grow in soils with pH of 9.2. Zones 8 to 11, hardy to 15°F. **Landscape use**: Similar to *W. robusta* in landscape attributes but not as drought tolerant. A better choice for Arizona and California. Grown in warm-climate countries around the world. **Street tree use**: Yes. **In the trade**: Sold as seed-grown.

Washingtonia filifera

Washingtonia robusta

Mexican fan palm

Evergreen. This and *W. filifera* are common in landscapes in the southern tier of the United States from California to Florida, where it develops a rounded crown, with proximate leaf bases persisting in a skirt-like fashion. Growth is fast in youth, up to 6′ per year, maturing at 40 to 80′ high, with potential to 100′, spread 12′. The slender trunk is smooth toward the swollen gray base; it tapers from 2′ wide at the base to as little as 8″ near the top.

Foliage: Palmate, somewhat rounded, divided halfway to the base, 3 to 5′ across, the tips slightly drooping, glossy bright green, the petiole is 3 to 4′ long, reddish brown, armed with prominent reddish brown spines. **Flowers/seeds/fruits/cones**: White, slightly fragrant, in 7 to 10′ long pendulous inflorescences, spring. Fruit is a drupe, ⅓″ wide, black, summer. **Native range**: Mexican state of Sonora. **Adaptability**: Considered less cold hardy than *W. filifera*; 20°F and below results in leaf injury. Zones 8 to 11. **Landscape use**: Stately, elegant palm reaching significant height and useful for urban plantings. It prospers in dry, sandy, well-drained soil and full sun. Easily transplanted and extremely drought tolerant. **Street tree use**: Yes. **In the trade**: Sold as seed-grown. It hybridizes readily with *W. filifera*, so intermediates occur.

Washingtonia robusta

Washingtonia robusta

Wollemia nobilis

Wollemi pine

Evergreen conifer. Narrowly pyramidal with a strong single leader and primary branches that radiate, closely spaced, from the trunk and don't fork, the lower ones slightly drooping. Medium coarse texture, moderately slow-growing, reaching 100′ tall in the wild. Individual single-trunked trees are narrow, but may produce multiple parallel trunks from a single base. Dark brown, knobby or bubbly-looking bark. Known only in the fossil record from the age of the dinosaurs, until a remnant population was discovered in 1994.

Foliage: Needles are flat with a slight curve and a pointed tip, soft lime-green to deep green, 1 to 3″ long and about ⅛″ wide, held in a slightly droopy plane along the branch. **Flowers/seeds/fruits/cones**: Monoecious. Pollen cones occur lower on the tree than female cones, cylindrical, 2 to 4″ long. Female cones grow on the tips of upper branches, broadly ovoid, 2½ to 5″ long, green. **Native range**: Restricted to an isolated canyon in Wollemi National Park in southeastern Australia. **Adaptability**: Considering that when found, 40 mature trees and a couple hundred seedlings in a single rainforest gorge separated it from extinction, you can hardly call it adaptable. Too new to know for sure, but probably best suited to mild to warm coastal areas with some humidity and not too much temperature fluctuation, zones 8 to 10. **Landscape use**: The very definition of a collector plant. A tree with a story straight out of *Jurassic Park*, with a lush, tropical, prehistoric look to match. It's related to *Araucaria*, with a similar primitive appearance. **Street tree use**: Probably not. **In the trade**: Sold as seed- or cutting-grown.

Wollemia nobilis

Wollemia nobilis

X

Xanthoceras sorbifolium

Xanthoceras sorbifolium
yellowhorn

Deciduous. Low-branched or multi-stem shrubby tree, open below and rounded to irregularly spreading above. The foliage is fine-textured; the form is more coarse. Slow growth rate, to 15 to 20′ tall and wide. The seeds are edible and consumed in China, said to be nut-like in flavor.

Foliage: Pinnately compound, very bright glossy green. Leaves are 5 to 9″ long with 9 to 17 leaflets, each 1½ to 2½″ long, finely serrate with acute tips. Yellow fall color. **Flowers/seeds/fruits/cones**: Flowers are held in 6 to 10″ long, many-flowered racemes, spray-like, appearing in May with the emerging foliage. Individual flowers are ¾ to 1″ in diameter with 5 white petals and a central blotch, yellow at first, then changing to bright crimson-red. The fruit is a 2 to 3″ wide capsule, green and rounded, 3-chambered, each chamber holding several dark brown, ½″ wide, round seeds. **Native range**: Northern China. **Adaptability**: Needs full sun. Tolerant of higher pH soils and moderate drought. Takes the tough climate of the High Plains. Has grown well in the Northeast, but failed in Georgia. In Oregon nursery trials, it proved a weak grower with slender stems, probably needing a hotter, sunnier, climate. Zones (3)4 to 7. **Landscape use**: Valued for its bright spring flower display and glossy foliage. It makes an unusual accent plant or specimen, or use as a background plant with small shrubs or perennials in front, as the lower portion is often rather bare. **Street tree use**: No. **In the trade**: Usually sold as seed-grown, as it is difficult to propagate vegetatively. The one cultivar, CLEAR CREEK 'Psgan', a cold hardy selection from Colorado, is hard to find.

Xanthoceras sorbifolium

Xanthoceras sorbifolium

Z

seeds/fruits/cones: Monoecious. Male, bisexual, and female flowers in leaf axils along the shoots, small and not showy, flowering with the emerging foliage. Fruit is a dry ⅛″ wide drupe, ripening in the fall. **Native range:** Southeast to central China. **Adaptability:** Its native range overlaps with that of *Z. serrata*, but it extends farther to the south, suggesting slightly less cold hardiness but better heat tolerance, both of which we have observed in the United States. Good pH tolerance. Zones 6 to 9. **Landscape use:** A tree with promise but still not ready for prime time. It brings the potential of deep red fall color to the genus, along with expanded heat tolerance. Use as you would *Z. serrata*. **Street tree use:** Yes, especially if breeding and selection bring us improved

Zelkova schneideriana
Schneider zelkova

Deciduous. Upward-spreading branches form a rounded to vase-shaped crown. Quite similar to *Z. serrata*, perhaps slightly wider and more open, but the comparison is difficult because *Z. schneideriana* is uncommon and represented by seedling trees, while in *Z. serrata*, we are used to looking at refined cultivars. Bark is attractively exfoliating, mosaic-like, orange, tan, and green. Medium texture, moderate growth rate, 50 to 60′ tall and wide.

Foliage: Leaves dark green, ovate to long ovate with an acuminate tip, sharply serrate, with parallel veins, 2 to 5″ long, a third to half as wide. Upper leaf scabrous, rougher than *Z. serrata*. The underside is quite pubescent, as are the new shoots. Fall color yellow to orange-red and burgundy-red, more often red than *Z. serrata*. **Flowers/**

Zelkova schneideriana

Zelkova schneideriana

'Wine Me Up'

cultivars. **In the trade**: You will have a hard time finding the species. 'Wine Me Up' is wider-spreading and more open than *Z. serrata* 'Green Vase', with weeping tips, but more susceptible to early fall freezes. Nice burgundy-red fall color. Selected in Georgia and probably a good choice for the South. 40 to 45′ or more in height and width.

Zelkova serrata
Japanese zelkova

Deciduous. Upward-spreading or arching, decurrent branch structure, usually without a leader above 10′, forming a vase-shaped canopy. Young bark is smooth and gray-green with prominent horizontal lenticels, with age exfoliating in patches, revealing an inner bark of greens, oranges, and tans. Medium fine texture, moderate growth rate, 50 to 60′ tall and wide.

Foliage: Leaves dark green, ovate to long ovate with an acuminate tip, sharply serrate, with neatly parallel veins, 2 to 5″ long, a third to half as wide, glabrous above and below except in vein axils; upper leaf surface slightly rough to the touch. Fall color usually good, yellow to orange, occasionally red. **Flowers/seeds/fruits/cones**: Monoecious. Male, bisexual, and female flowers in leaf axils along the shoots, small and not showy, flowering with the emerging foliage. Fruit is a dry ⅛″ wide drupe, ripening in the fall, green to tan. **Native range**: Japan, Korea, Manchuria, China, Taiwan. **Adaptability**: Quite adaptable and one of the most commonly used street and landscape trees across the country with the exception of arid parts of the West and the cold north-central states. Good soil adaptability and pH tolerance, but needs adequate moisture and favors some humidity. Zones 5 to 8, 9 in the West. **Landscape use**: Widely used as a residential shade tree, in parking lots, offices complexes, parks, and campuses. When a tree gets this much use, some will say it is overused. But when a tree seems overused,

there is probably a good reason—in this case, several. It imitates the classic vase shape of the American elm, on a slightly smaller scale and perhaps with less grace; but the smaller scale fits our cities well. Its shape is ideal for traffic below, both vehicles and pedestrians, and in a garden it provides maximum shade with a minimum footprint. It is highly resistant to Dutch elm disease. It shares some insect

Zelkova serrata

Zelkova serrata

Zelkova serrata

CITY SPRITE

'Goshiki'

CITY SPRITE

'Goshiki'

GREEN VASE

GREEN VASE

GREEN VASE

problems with elm, but generally seems less troubled by these pests. Narrow crotch angles can be concerning in the narrower cultivars, but the wood seems very strong, so breakage is not very common. Still, we suggest structural pruning of the narrow cultivars; thin them for proper branch spacing at a young age. **Street tree use**: Ideal for the purpose. **In the trade**: The species itself is a little unpredictable in form, but cultivars, which we recommend, give a complete choice of shapes, from tall and skinny to low and wide, plus semi-dwarf and color variations. Choose primarily on form.

CITY SPRITE 'JFS-KW1'. Compact, dense, and semi-dwarf. Short internodes carry smaller leaves on a fine, self-branching structure, creating a more delicate tree of about half the size of the species, perfect for small urban spaces. Fine-textured appearance, yellow fall color, expect slower growth to maturity of 24′ high, 18′ wide.

'Goshiki'. Variegated foliage, leaves mostly green in the center and cream-white along the margin, with a speckled transition in between. New growth shows a fleeting pink tint. In summer, the tree presents an overall cream to light green appearance from a distance. Foliage burned in the sun in our Oregon testing; looks better in partial shade or East Coast humidity. It is slender and weak-stemmed when young, a little weepy, but grows to a nice vase form. A garden tree, not a street tree, 25′ tall and 20′ wide.

914

GREEN VASE. The standard of comparison among the cultivars. Upright narrow vase shape, between the very narrow 'Musashino' and the wider 'Village Green'. An ideal elm-like street tree form with good clearance for people and traffic below, and narrow enough for business signage to be visible. Watch for and prune out narrow crowded crotch angles. Nice fall color, glowing orange at its best. 45′ high and 25 to 30′ wide, widest at the top.

'Green Veil'. At a younger age, it tends to weep and sprawl, but a fully grown tree is very handsome, a tall, upright, vase-shaped form with fountain-like weeping tips, to 50′ tall and 35′ wide. We have seen the original tree at Brookside Gardens, MD, and it is impressive.

'Halka'. Vase-shaped, slightly wider than 'Green Vase', and more informal in appearance, looser, not overly dense, and quite similar to a small American elm. Yellow to yellow-orange fall color, to 50′ tall and 40′ wide.

'Kiwi Sunset'. Spring foliage is soft yellowish, with pink new growth as shoot tips unfold; new growth is lax, weeping slightly; summer foliage is lime-green. Tree form is vase-shaped, a little broader-spreading than most, 45′ by 40′. Yellow to red-bronze fall color.

'Green Veil'

'Halka'

Z

'Ogon'

'Urban Ruby'

'Variegata'

'Musashino'. The narrowest cultivar, a tight vase shape that is almost columnar, ideal for narrower streets and urban downtowns with limited setbacks to businesses. This is one of the most useful trees for cramped city settings, as there is hardly a place it can't fit. Yellow fall color. Grows to 45' high and 15' wide.

MYRIMAR 'ZSFKF'. A wider-spreading vase-shaped tree with dark green foliage, selected in Georgia for better heat adaptation in the South. 45' tall, 40' wide.

'Ogon'. Foliage emerges yellowish in spring but becomes more yellow-green as the season progresses, often with yellowish new growth against a green interior. Some burning has been noticed, and it is not the brightest of yellow-foliaged trees. Winter stems attractive amber-orange. Performs well in the South. 30' by 30'.

'Urban Ruby'. Upright-spreading, but a little wider than most, similar to 'Village Green' in overall shape but with tips more weeping, giving less traffic clearance. Very dark green foliage is especially handsome in summer, reddish fall color. Probably will reach 40' tall and 45' wide.

'Variegata'. Variegation similar to 'Goshiki', but the plants we have seen appear whiter and variegation seems more marginal. Foliage tends to be wrinkled and distorted, and burned badly in our Oregon trials. We prefer 'Goshiki'. 20' by 20'.

VILLAGE GREEN. The most popular cultivar before the introduction of the narrower 'Green Vase'. A formal-looking, dense, broad vase shape with very dark green foliage. Casts dense shade. Rusty red fall color. 40' tall and wide.

WIRELESS

WIRELESS 'Schmidtlow'. Low and flat-topped, wide-spreading, shorter than most cultivars, named with use below utility wires in mind. Train upright as high as desired, then growth will mainly spread outward. Best red fall color we have seen in a zelkova. Reaches 20' tall and 35' wide.

'Musashino'

VILLAGE GREEN

VILLAGE GREEN

WIRELESS

Z

Zelkova sinica
Chinese zelkova

Deciduous. Upright-spreading, usually low-branched, forming a rounded to somewhat vase-shaped canopy. Fine-textured, moderate growth rate, to 40′ tall and 35′ wide in cultivation, but 100′ trees are known. Bark is an attractive, exfoliating mosaic of gray-green, orange, and tan.

Foliage: Leaves dark green, 1 to 2½″ long, half as wide, ovate with an acuminate tip, sharply serrate. Surface rough, underside gray-green and pubescent. Yellow to orange fall color. **Flowers/seeds/fruits/cones:** Monoecious. Male, bisexual, and female flowers in leaf axils along the shoots, small and not showy, flowering with the emerging foliage. Fruit large for a zelkova, a dry ¼″ wide drupe. **Native range:** Central China. **Adaptability:** Little tested but seems similar to or better than other species of the genus. Heat tolerant, and it may prove to have better cold hardiness than *Z. serrata*. Zones 5 to 8. **Landscape use:** Use where a slightly smaller, more rounded, finer-textured version of *Z. serrata* is desired. Site where the bark of the mature tree will be appreciated. **Street tree use:** Has potential, will need to be pruned up for clearance. **In the trade:** Sold as seed-grown, not common.

Zelkova sinica

Zelkova sinica

Zelkova sinica

Ziziphus jujuba
Chinese date, jujube

Deciduous. Usually a low-branched tree with an upright-spreading rounded crown. Grows 1 to 2′ per year in youth, slowing with age, reaching 20 to 30′ high and wide. The largest tree recorded in the United States, 61′ by 51′, grew on the Capitol grounds in Washington, DC. Bark is gray-brown, scaly, blocky, alligator-hide in pattern. Rare garden tree in the United States but has been grown in China for over 4,000 years, prized as one of the five most popular fruits. There are 704 cultivars in China: 224 for dry-fruit production, 261 for fresh, 159 for dry and fresh, 56 for special products (medicinal), and 4 for ornamental. The fresh fruits we sampled had a spongy, dried-apple texture without the sugar, but when fruits were dried, Warren found them quite tasty.

Foliage: Oval, ovate to ovate-lanceolate, with 3 distinct impressed veins originating at base, crenate-serrulate, 1 to 2½″ long, two-thirds as wide, lustrous polished bright green, pretty yellow fall color. **Flowers/seeds/fruits/cones**: Self-fertile, yellow, 2 or 3 together in the leaf axils of the current season's growth, each flower ¼ to ⅓″ wide, fragrant (grape soda), May-June, after leaves have developed. Fruits plum- to egg-shaped, ½ to 1″ long, shiny brown, red to black when ripe, September-October. **Native range**: Southeastern Europe to southern and eastern Asia. **Adaptability**: Adaptable and will grow in any well-drained, acid or alkaline soil and full sun. At the University of Georgia Horticulture Farm, a row of Chinese dates were growing in soil so poor that even weeds would not colonize. Zones 6 to 9. Trees have survived -15°F with no injury; -24°F beat up an old planting. **Landscape use**: Certainly fits the collector's modus operandi of "What is it?" Or perhaps a plant for those who enjoy exotic fruits. Perhaps the biggest liability is the thorny nature of the stems with paired, decurved spines at the nodes and larger straighter ones to 1¼″ long. Even year-old seedlings assume the posture of a barbed-wire fence. For the squeamish, var. *inermis* does not produce thorns. **Street tree use**: No. **In the trade**: 'Lang' is a popular cultivar that produces 1½ to 2″ long, pear-shaped fruits; 'Li' produces more rounded, 2″ long fruits. Both fruited with reckless abandon, and no one cared or dared (spines) enough to pick at the University of Georgia Horticulture Farm.

Ziziphus jujuba

Ziziphus jujuba

Ziziphus jujuba

Z

Photo Credits

All photos are by the authors, with the exception of the following, which we gratefully acknowledge.

James R. Ault, page 149 (top right)

Kris R. Bachtell, page 635 (bottom left)

Bailey Nurseries, pages 112 (top left), 515 (top left), 717 (top left, top right), 822 (bottom right)

Bold Springs Nursery, pages 162 (middle right, bottom right), 550 (bottom right), 551 (middle left), 725 (top right, bottom right), 738 (bottom left), 739 (bottom left, top right), 750 (top right), 751 (top left), 751 (middle left), 752 (top left), 758 (bottom right)

Nancy Buley, pages 260 (middle left), 359 (left), 378 (bottom left), 432 (top right, bottom right), 527 (top center), 549 (top right), 559 (top left), 784 (bottom right), 833 (bottom left), 852 (bottom left), 915 (bottom)

Carlton Plants, page 822 (middle left)

Michael Hayman, page 379 (top right)

James Hines, page 547 (bottom left)

Jackson Nursery, pages 241 (top right), 245 (bottom right), 279 (bottom left), 501 (top right)

Jeffries Nurseries, pages 115 (top left), 190 (bottom left), 512 (top left), 528 (top left), 529 (bottom left), 670 (bottom right), 671 (top right, bottom center), 853 (top left, bottom left)

Jeff Lafrenz, pages 108 (bottom left), 299 (bottom left), 477 (top right), 686 (top left)

Guy Meacham, pages 291 (bottom right), 346 (bottom right)

Thomas Molnar, pages 286 (top right), 287 (bottom left)

Plants Nouveau, pages 525 (top right), 536 (bottom left), 559 (top right), 560 (top left)

Tom Ranney, pages 273 (bottom left, top right), 284 (top left), 288 (bottom right), 289 (top left), 494 (bottom left, bottom right), 710 (bottom left)

J. Frank Schmidt III, page 206 (left)

Select Trees, pages 108 (top left), 258 (bottom right), 261 (bottom left), 409 (bottom), 424 (top left, bottom left), 536 (bottom right), 740 (top left, top right, bottom left), 750 (bottom), 751 (top right), 756 (top right)

Michael D. Yanny, pages 204 (bottom left, top right), 205 (top left)

Index

A

Abies alba, 'PENDULA', 36
Abies balsamea, 37
Abies cilicica, 37
Abies concolor, 'Candicans', 38
Abies firma, 39
Abies fraseri, 39–40
Abies grandis, 40
Abies homolepis, 41
Abies koreana, 41–42
  'Silberlocke', 42
Abies lasiocarpa, 43–44
  var. *arizonica*, 44
  'Compacta', 44
Abies nordmanniana, 44
  subsp. *bornmuelleriana*, 44
  subsp. *equi-trojani*, 44
Abies pinsapo, 45
  'Aurea', 45
  'Glauca', 45
Abies procera, 46
  'Glauca', 46
  'Glauca Prostrata', 46
Abies ×umbellata, 41
Acer, 16–17
Acer barbatum. See *Acer saccharum* subsp.
  barbatum
Acer buergerianum, 47–49
  AERYN 'ABMTF', 49
  'Angyo Weeping', 49
  BLOOD MOON 'Rusty Allen', 49
  VALYNOR 'ABFSS', 49
Acer campestre, 50–53
  'Carnival', 50
  'Elsrijk', 51
  JADE PATINA 'Bailee', 51
  METRO GOLD 'Panacek', 51
  'Nanum', 52
  QUEEN ELIZABETH 'Evelyn', 53
  ST. GREGORY 'Stgrezam', 53
  STREETSIDE 'JFS-Schichtel2', 53
Acer capillipes, 53–54
Acer circinatum, 54–55
  'Monroe', 54
  'Pacific Fire', 54
  PACIFIC PURPLE 'JFS-Purple', 55

  'Sunny Sister', 55
  THREE CHEERS 'HSI2', 55
Acer cissifolium, 56, 68
Acer davidii, 56–57, 137
  'George Forrest', 57
  'Serpentine', 57
Acer ×freemanii, 57–58, 102, 103, 109, 110, 116
Acer ginnala, 58–60
  'Flame', 59
  RED NOVEMBER 'JFS-UGA', 60
  'Ruby Slippers', 60
Acer glabrum, 61
  var. *diffusum*, 61
  var. *douglasii*, 61
  var. *glabrum*, 61
Acer grandidentatum, 61–63, 121
  CANYON TREASURE 'Orbit', 62
  HIGHLAND PARK 'Hipzam', 62
  'Manzano', 62
  MESA GLOW 'JFS-NuMex 3', 62
  ROCKY MOUNTAIN GLOW 'Schmidt', 62
Acer griseum, 64–67, 73, 138
  BRONZE TABLET 'AROY', 65
  'Cinnamon Flake', 65
  CINNAMON GIRL 'Molly Fordham', 66
  FIREBURST 'JFS-KW8', 66
  GINGERBREAD 'Ginzam', 66
  'Girard's Hybrid', 66
  SHAVED CHOCOLATE 'KLMEE', 66
Acer henryi, 68
Acer japonicum, 69–70
  'Aconitifolium', 69
  'Aureum', 69
  'Ed Wood #2', 69
  'Vitifolium', 69
Acer leucoderme. See *Acer saccharum* subsp.
  leucoderme
Acer macrophyllum, 70–71
  'Seattle Sentinel', 71
Acer mandshuricum, 72
Acer maximowiczianum, 65, 73, 138
Acer miyabei, 74–75
  RUGGED RIDGE 'JFS-KW3AMI', 74
  STATE STREET 'Morton', 74
Acer mono, 90
Acer negundo, 68, 76–78
  'Aureomarginatum', 78

  'Aureovariegatum', 78
  var. *californicum*, 77
  'Flamingo', 77
  'Kelly's Gold', 77
  'Sensation', 77
  'Variegatum', 78
Acer nigrum. See *Acer saccharum* subsp.
  nigrum, 121
Acer nikoense, 73
Acer palmatum, 54, 79–88, 100
  'Arakawa', 80
  'Bihou', 80
  'Bloodgood', 80
  'Butterfly', 80
  'Crimson Prince', 80
  'Emperor I', 83
  'Fireglow', 83
  'Glowing Embers', 83
  'Hefner's Red', 83
  'Katsura', 83
  'Koto No Ito', 83
  'Moonfire', 83
  'Nishiki-gawa', 84
  'Nuresagi', 84
  'Osakazuki', 84
  'Oshio-Beni', 85
  'Ryusen', 85
  'Sango-kaku', 80, 85
  'Seiryu', 86
  'Shishigashira', 86
  'Suminagashi', 86
  'Trompenburg', 88
  'Tsukasa Silhouette', 88
  'Twombly's Red Sentinel', 80, 88
Acer pensylvanicum, 'Erythrocladum', 89
Acer pictum, 90
  CANYON SUNSET 'KLMSS', 90
  'Usugumo', 90
Acer platanoides, 90–97
  'Cleveland', 92
  'Columnare', 92
  CONQUEST 'Conzam', 92
  'Crimson King', 20, 21, 92, 140
  'Crimson Sentry', 93
  'Deborah', 93
  'Drummondii', 93
  EMERALD LUSTRE 'Pond', 95

Acer platanoides [*continued*]
‘Emerald Queen’, 95
‘Eurostar’, 95
‘Fairview’, 95
‘Globosum’, 95
PARKWAY ‘Columnarbroad’, 96
PRINCETON GOLD ‘Prigo’, 96
‘Royal Red’, 96
‘Schwedleri’, 20, 21, 97
‘Silver Variegated’. *See* ‘Drummondii’
‘Summershade’, 97
‘Superform’, 97
Acer pseudoplatanus, 98
‘Atropurpureum’, 98, 99
‘Brilliantissimum’, 99
‘Esk Sunset’, 99
Acer pseudosieboldianum, 79, 99–101
ARCTIC JADE ‘IslAJ’, 100
NORTHERN GLOW ‘Hasselkus’, 100
NORTHERN SPOTLIGHT ‘KorDak’, 100
NORTH WIND ‘IslNW’, 100
Acer rubrum, 58, 102–118
‘Armstrong’, 103
ARMSTRONG GOLD ‘JFS-KW78’, 104
AUTUMN BLAZE ‘Jeffersred’, 104, 110
AUTUMN FANTASY ‘DTR 102’, 105
‘Autumn Flame’, 105, 117, 118
AUTUMN RADIANCE, 106
‘Autumn Spire’, 22, 106, 109
‘Bowhall’, 104, 106, 115
‘Brandywine’, 107
BUILT TO LAST ‘ARNOG’, 109
BURGUNDY BELLE ‘Magnificent Magenta’,
    22, 109
CELEBRATION ‘Celzam’, 109
‘Columnare’, 109
‘Fairview Flame’, 109
FIREFALL ‘AF#1’, 109
‘Florida Flame’, 109
‘Halka’, 109
‘Karpick’, 22, 109
‘Marmo’, 110
MATADOR ‘Bailston’, 110
‘Morgan’, 110
‘New World’, 111
NORTHFIRE ‘Olsen’, 22, 111
‘Northwood’, 22, 112
‘October Brilliance’, 113
OCTOBER GLORY ‘PNI 0268’, 21, 22, 112,
    113, 117
REDPOINTE ‘Frank Jr.’, 16, 114
‘Red Rocket’, 114
RED SUNSET ‘Franksred’, 115
REGAL CELEBRATION ‘Jefcel’, 115
‘Scanlon’, 115
SCARLET JEWEL ‘Bailcraig’, 22, 115
SCARLET SENTINEL ‘Scarsen’, 115

‘Schlesingeri’, 22, 116
SIENNA GLEN ‘Sienna’, 116
‘Somerset’, 117
SUMMER RED ‘HOSR’, 22, 113, 117
SUMMER SENSATION ‘Katiecole’, 117
‘Sun Valley’, 118
Acer saccharinum, 119–120
‘Silver Cloud’, 119
‘Silver Queen’, 119
‘Skinner’, 120
Acer saccharum, 121–131
APOLLO ‘Barrett Cole’, 122
‘Arrowhead’, 122
AUTUMN FAITH ‘Hawkersmith 1’, 122
AUTUMN FEST ‘JFS-KW8’, 122
‘Autumn Splendor’, 122
BELLE TOWER ‘Reba’, 122
‘Bonfire’, 122
“Caddo”, 121, 124, 134
COMMEMORATION, 124, 134
CRESCENDO ‘Morton’, 124
‘Endowment’, 124
FALL FIESTA ‘Bailsta’, 124
FLASHFIRE ‘JFS-Caddo2’, 33, 124, 126
‘Green Mountain’, 126
HARVEST MOON ‘Sandersville’, 126
HIGHLAND PARK. See *Acer grandidentatum*
‘John Pair’, 126
LEGACY, 128, 134
MAJESTY ‘Flax Mill’, 128
‘Newton Sentry’, 128
NORTHERN FLARE ‘Sisseton’, 33, 128
OREGON TRAIL ‘Hiawatha 1’, 128
POWDER KEG ‘Whit XLIX’, 128
STEEPLE ‘Astis’, 130
‘Sugar Cone’, 130
‘Sweet Shadow’, 130
‘Temple’s Upright’, 128, 130
UNITY ‘Jefcan’, 33, 130
‘Wright Brothers’, 131
Acer saccharum subsp. *barbatum*, 26, 132
Acer saccharum subsp. *floridanum*, 132
Acer saccharum subsp. *leucoderme*, 121, 133
Acer saccharum subsp. *nigrum*,
    ‘Greencolumn’, 134
Acer tataricum, 134–136
BEETHOVEN ‘Betzam’, 59, 135
HOT WINGS ‘GarAnn’, 135
PATTERN PERFECT ‘Patdell’, 135
RUGGED CHARM ‘JFS-KW2’, 136
Acer tegmentosum, 136–137
‘Joe Witt’, 137
‘White Tigress’, 137
Acer triflorum, 137–138
ARTIST ETCHING ‘CROY’, 138
‘Jack-o-Lantern’, 138
Acer truncatum, 139–143

‘Akikaze Nishiki’, 140
CRIMSON SUNSET ‘JFS-KW202’, 140
‘Fire Dragon’, 141
‘Golden Dragon’, 141
MAIN STREET ‘WF-AT1’, 141
NORWEGIAN SUNSET ‘Keithsform’, 141
PACIFIC SUNSET ‘Warrenred’, 142
RUBY SUNSET ‘JFS-KW249’, 142
URBAN SUNSET ‘JFS-KW187’, 142
Aesculus, 28
Aesculus californica, 143–144
‘Blue Haze’, 144
‘Canyon Pink’, 144
Aesculus ×*carnea*, 144–145
‘Briotii’, 145
‘Fort McNair’, 145
‘O’Neil’s Red’, 145
Aesculus flava, 28, 31, 146–147, 153
‘Homestead’, 147
Aesculus glabra, 138, 147–149, 153
var. *arguta*, 149
‘Autumn Splendor’, 149
EARLY GLOW ‘J. N. Select’, 149
LAVABURST ‘LavaDak’, 149
PRAIRIE TORCH ‘Bergeson’, 149
Aesculus hippocastanum, 149–151
‘Baumannii’, 151
Aesculus indica, 151–152
‘Sydney Pearce’, 152
Aesculus octandra, 146–147
Aesculus parviflora, 153
Aesculus pavia, 144, 152–153
‘Atrosanguinea’, 153
‘Humilis’, 153
‘Splendens’, 153
Aesculus sylvatica, 153
Aesculus turbinata, 153–154
Ailanthus altissima, 154, 531
Alaska yellow cedar, 322–325
Albizia julibrissin, 155–156
CHOCOLATE FOUNTAIN ‘NCAJ1’, 155
‘Flame’, 156
MERLOT MAJIK ‘Nurcan 10’, 156
OMBRELLA ‘Boubri’, 156
‘Pendula’, 156
f. *rosea*, 156
‘Summer Chocolate’, 156
Aleppo pine, 605
Aleurites fordii. See *Vernicia fordii*
Alice Holt cypress, 326
Allegheny serviceberry, 165–167
Alnus cordata, 156–157
Alnus glutinosa, 157–158
Alnus incana, 159–160
subsp. *incana*, 159
subsp. *rugosa*, 159
subsp. *tenuifolia*, 160

Alnus japonica, 161
Alnus rubra, 160
Alnus rugosa. See *Alnus incana*
Alnus ×spaethii, 161
Alnus subcordata, 161
Alnus tenuifolia. See *Alnus incana*
alpine goldenchain, 430
Amelanchier arborea, 161–162
   PINK DAMSEL 'Tift County', 162
Amelanchier ×grandiflora, 162, 163–164, 165,
   168
   'Autumn Brilliance', 163
   'Ballerina', 164
   'Cole's Select', 164
   'Princess Diana', 164
   'Robin Hill', 164
Amelanchier laevis, 165–167
   'Cumulus', 165
   LUSTRE 'Rogers', 165
   'Snowcloud', 165, 166, 167
   SPRING FLURRY 'JFS-Arb', 165
Amelanchier lamarckii, 168
American beech, 350–351
American chestnut, 22, 29, 212–213
American elm, 16, 22, 102, 874–878
American holly, 411–413
American hophornbeam, 555–556
American hornbeam, 203–206, 555
American linden, 846–849
American mountain ash, 803
American planetree, 637–638
American smoketree, 302–303
American sweetgum, 451–457
American yellowwood, 264–265
Amur chokecherry, 670–671
Amur corktree, 565
Amur maackia, 464–465
Amur maple, 58–60
anise magnolia, 482, 489
apple, 505–530
apple serviceberry, 163–164
Araucaria, 909
Araucaria araucana, 168–169
arborvitae, 418
Arbutus ×andrachnoides, 169–170
   'Marina', 170
Arbutus menziesii, 170
Arbutus unedo, 171
Arizona ash, 374
Arizona cypress, 315–317
Arizona sycamore, 640–641
arolla pine, 597–598
ash, 361
Asian white birch, 189–190
Asimina triloba, 172–173
   ALLEGHENY '2-9', 173
   'Overleese', 173

POTOMAC '4-2', 173
RAPPAHANNOCK 'Aidfievate', 173
SHENANDOAH 'Wanserwan', 173
'Sunflower', 173
SUSQUEHANNA 'LERfiv', 173
WABASH '1-7-2', 173
Atlantic white cedar, 255
Atlas cedar, 227–229
Austrian pine, 611–613
awabuki sweet viburnum, 899–901
Azara microphylla, 173–174
   'Variegata', 174

B

balsam fir, 37
basket oak, 744–745
basswood, 846–849
Bauhinia ×blakeana, 175
Bauhinia variegata, 175
bead tree, 530–531
beebee tree, 838–839
bell-flowered cherry, 657
Betula albosinensis, 176–177
   'Bowling Green', 177
   'China Rose', 177
   'China Ruby', 177
   'Chinese Garden', 177
   'Fascination', 177
   'Kansu', 177
   'Pink Champagne', 177
   'Red Panda', 177
   var. *septentrionalis*, 177
Betula alleghaniensis, 177–178
Betula jacquemontii, 193
Betula lenta, 178–179
   subsp. *uber*, 178
Betula nigra, 179–183, 191
   CITY SLICKER 'Whit XXV', 180
   DURA-HEAT 'BNMTF', 180
   FOX VALLEY 'Little King', 180
   HERITAGE 'Cully', 180
   HERITAGE IMPROVED 'Cully Improved',
      183
   NORTHERN TRIBUTE 'Dickinson', 183
   'Shiloh Splash', 183
   'Summer Cascade', 183
   TECUMSEH COMPACT 'Studetec', 183
Betula occidentalis, 183
Betula papyrifera, 183–185, 186, 191
   PRAIRIE DREAM 'Varen', 185
   RENAISSANCE OASIS 'Oenci', 185
   RENAISSANCE REFLECTION 'Renci', 185
   RENAISSANCE UPRIGHT 'Uenci', 185
Betula pendula, 186–188, 191
   'Dalecarlica', 187
   'Fastigiata', 187

PURPLE RAIN 'Monle', 187
'Purpurea', 187
'Youngii', 187
Betula platyphylla, 189–190
   'Crimson Frost', 189
   DAKOTA PINNACLE 'Fargo', 190
   PARKLAND PILLAR 'Jefpark', 190
   PRAIRIE VISION 'VerDale', 190
   ROYAL FROST 'Penci 2', 190
   'Whitespire', 189
Betula populifolia, 189, 191–192
   'Whitespire', 191
   'Whitespire Senior', 191
Betula utilis, 192–194
   'Doorenbos', 193
   'Grayswood Ghost', 193
   'Jacquemontii'. *See* 'Doorenbos'
   subsp. *jacquemontii*, 192–193
   'Jermyns', 194
   'Silver Shadow', 194
   'Snow Queen'. *See* 'Doorenbos'
   WHITE SATIN 'Madison', 194
bigleaf linden, 857–858
bigleaf magnolia, 486–487
bigleaf maple, 70–71
bigleaf podocarp, 642–643
bigtooth aspen, 651
bigtooth maple, 61–63
birchbark cherry, 683
black alder, 157–158
black ash, 367
black birch, 178–179
black cherry, 682–683
black gum, 544–551
blackhaw viburnum, 901–902
black locust, 778–781
black maple, 134
black mulberry, 539
black oak, 773–774
black poplar, 652–653
black tupelo, 544–551
black walnut, 414–416
blue ash, 372
blueberry tree, 336
blue gum, 341–342
Bolleana poplar, 644
Bosnian pine, 606–607
boxelder, 76–78
Brewer weeping spruce, 574
broadleaf kindlingbark, 340–341
broadpetal lily-tree, 481, 488
bronze loquat, 339
bud wood, 31
bur oak, 740–743
Butia capitata, 194
×*Butyagrus*, 194
button-ball tree, 637–638

C

cabbage palm, 782
Caddo sugar maple, 62
California buckeye, 143–144
California fan palm, 907
California nutmeg, 862–863
California redbud, 246–247
California sycamore, 640
Callery pear, 28, 661, 705–713
Callistemon viminalis, 195
  'Boyette', 195
  'Red Cascade', 195
Calocedrus decurrens, 196–197
  'Aureavariegata', 196
  'Berrima Gold', 196
  'Maupin Glow', 196
Camellia japonica, 198
  'High Fragrance', 198
  'Kumagai', 198
  'Lady Clare', 198
  'Lavender Prince II', 198
  'Professor Sargent', 198
  'Rose Twilight', 198
  'Royal Velvet', 198
  'Scarlet Temptation', 198
  'Tama no Ura', 198
  'Tiny Princess', 198
Campbell magnolia, 471–473
Camperdown elm, 887
camphor tree, 263
Canadian hemlock, 22, 865–867
Canadian poplar, 646
Canadian redbud, 238–246
Canary Island date palm, 567–568
Canary Island pine, 596–597
Carolina buckthorn, 358
Carolina cherrylaurel, 660–661
Carolina hemlock, 867–868
Carolina poplar, 646
Carolina silverbell, 390–391
Carpinus betulus, 199–202
  'Columnaris Nana', 199
  'Cornerstone', 199
  EMERALD AVENUE 'JFS-KW1CB', 199
  'Fastigiata', 199–201
  'Frans Fontaine', 201
  'Globosa', 201
  'Pendula', 202
  'Pinocchio', 202
Carpinus caroliniana, 203–206, 555, 810
  FIRE KING 'JN Select A', 204
  FIRESPIRE 'J. N. Upright', 204
  NATIVE FLAME 'JFS-KW6', 204
  PALISADE 'CCSQU', 205
  RISING FIRE 'Uxbridge', 206
Carpinus japonica, 206

Carya, 207
Carya aquatica, 207, 209
Carya glabra, 208, 210
Carya illinoinensis, 209
  'Elliott', 209
  'Gloria Grande', 209
  'Green River', 209
  'Huffman', 209
  'Major', 209
  'Peruque', 209
  'Striking Hardy Giant', 209
  'Sumner', 209
  'Tanner', 209
  'Tom', 209
  'Whiddon', 209
Carya laciniosa, 211, 212
Carya ovata, 210–212
Caryopteris, 595
cascara, 359
Castanea dentata, 22, 212–213, 215
  'Darling 54', 29
Castanea mollissima, 22, 214
Castanea sativa, 'Albo-marginata', 215
castor-aralia, 425
Catalpa, 27
Catalpa bignonioides, 215–216, 217, 218
  'Aurea', 216
  'Kohnei', 216
  'Nana', 216
  'Variegata', 216
Catalpa bungei, 216
Catalpa ×erubescens, 'Purpurea', 217
Catalpa ovata, 217
Catalpa speciosa, 217–219
  HEARTLAND 'Hiawatha 2', 219
Caucasian fir, 44
Caucasian wingnut, 702–703
cedar elm, 879
cedar of Lebanon, 225–226
Cedrus atlantica. See *Cedrus libani* subsp.
    atlantica
Cedrus deodara, 219–225
  'Albospica', 220
  'Aurea', 220
  'Bill's Blue', 221
  'Blue Ice', 221
  'Bracken's Best Cedar', 222
  'Bush's Electra', 222
  'Crystal Falls', 222
  'Devinely Blue', 222
  'Eisregen', 222
  'Gold Cone', 222
  'Karl Fuchs', 222
  'Kashmir', 224
  'Mountain Aire', 224
  MYSTIC ICE 'CDMTF1', 224
  'Sander's Blue', 224

  'Shalimar', 224
  'Silver Mist', 224
  'Snow Sprite', 224
  STERLING FROST 'Grester', 224
  WYNDIMERE 'CDMTF2', 225
Cedrus libani, 37, 225–226
  subsp. *atlantica*, 227–229
  subsp. *atlantica* 'Aurea', 228
  subsp. *atlantica* 'Glauca', 228
  subsp. *atlantica* 'Glauca Fastigiata', 228
  subsp. *atlantica* 'Glauca Pendula', 228
  subsp. *atlantica* 'Horstmann', 228
  'Glauca Pendula', 226
  subsp. *stenocoma*, 226
Celtis laevigata, 229–230
  'All Seasons', 230
  'Magnifica', 230
  ULTRA 'Ulzam', 230
Celtis occidentalis, 230–231
  'Chicagoland', 231
  'Delta', 231
  'Magnifica', 231
  'Prairie Pride', 231
  PRAIRIE SENTINEL 'JFS-KSU1', 231
Celtis sinensis, 232–233
  'Green Cascade', 233
Cephalotaxus, 836
Cercidiphyllum japonicum, 233–238
  'Amazing Grace', 235
  'Boyd's Dwarf', 235
  CLAIM JUMPER 'HSI1', 235
  HANNAH'S HEART 'Biringer', 235
  'Heronswood Globe', 235
  'Morioka Weeping', 236
  f. *pendulum*, 236
  'Rotfuchs', 236
  'Strawberry', 237
  'Tidal Wave', 238
Cercis, 349
Cercis canadensis, 238–246, 247, 391
  'Ace of Hearts', 246
  'Alley Cat', 241
  'Appalachian Red', 239
  BLACK PEARL 'JN16', 240
  BURGUNDY HEARTS 'Greswan', 240
  CAROLINA SWEETHEART 'NCCC1', 243
  'Floating Clouds', 241
  'Forest Pansy', 240
  'Hearts of Gold', 242
  LAVENDER TWIST 'Covey', 243
  'Little Woody', 246
  'Merlot', 27, 240
  'Minnesota Hardy', 243
  NORTHERN HERALD 'Pink Trim', 243
  PINK HEARTBREAKER 'Pennsylvania Pride
    Pink Heartbreaker', 243
  'Pink Pom Poms', 27, 239

'Royal White', 240
'Ruby Falls', 27, 244
'Silver Cloud', 241
SUMMER'S TOWER 'JN7', 246
'Tennessee Pink', 240
THE RISING SUN 'JN2', 242
subsp. *texensis* 'Oklahoma', 240
subsp. *texensis* 'Texas White', 240–241
subsp. *texensis* 'Traveller', 244
'Vanilla Twist', 244
WHITEWATER 'NC2007-8', 243
Cercis occidentalis, 246–247
Cercis siliquastrum, 247
f. *albida*, 247
'Bodnant', 247
'White Swan', 247
Chaenomeles, 695
Chaenomeles sinensis, 695
Chaenomeles speciosa, 696
chalkbark elm, 896
chalkbark maple, 133
Chamaecyparis lawsoniana, 248–249
'Oregon Blue', 248
'Sullivan', 248
Chamaecyparis nootkatensis. See *Cupressus nootkatensis*
Chamaecyparis obtusa, 249–252, 255
'Aurea', 250, 251
'Compacta', 251
'Crippsii', 250–251
'Fernspray Gold', 251
'Filicoides', 252
'Gracilis', 250, 252
'Graciosa', 252
'Verdoni', 252
Chamaecyparis pisifera, 250, 253–254, 255
'Boulevard', 254
'Filifera', 253
'Filifera Aurea', 253
'Plumosa', 253
'Plumosa Aurea', 253
'Squarrosa', 254
Chamaecyparis thyoides, 255
'Rachael', 255
'Rubicon', 255
'Variegata', 255
Chang sweetgum, 449
chastetree, 904–906
cherry birch, 178–179
cherry laurel, 668
cherry plum, 661–664
chestnut oak, 744–745
Chilean myrtle, 463
Chilopsis, 27
Chilopsis linearis, 256–257
'Alpine', 257
ART'S SEEDLESS 'Shelly's Nuts', 257

'Barranco', 257
'Bubba', 257
'Burgundy', 257
'Dark Storm', 257
'Desert Amethyst', 257
'Hopi', 257
'Lois Adams', 257
LUCRETIA HAMILTON, 257
'Marfa Lace', 257
'Mesquite Valley Pink', 257
'Regal', 257
'Rio Salado', 257
ROYAL PURPLE, 257
'Tejas', 257
TIMELESS BEAUTY, 257
WARREN JONES, 257
'White Star', 257
'White Storm', 257
Chinaberry, 530–531
China-fir, 314–315
Chinese chestnut, 214
Chinese crabapple, 506
Chinese date, 919
Chinese evergreen oak, 746–747
Chinese flametree, 426–427
Chinese fringetree, 257–259
Chinese hackberry, 232–233
Chinese hemlock, 868–869
Chinese holly, 410
Chinese juniper, 417–419
Chinese maackia, 466
Chinese paper birch, 176–177
Chinese parasol tree, 357–358
Chinese parrotia, 563
Chinese pearltree, 643–644
Chinese photinia, 568–569
Chinese pistache, 630–631
Chinese podocarpus, 642–643
Chinese privet, 448
Chinese quince, 695–696
Chinese stewartia, 812–813
Chinese tamarisk, 827
Chinese toon, 861–862
Chinese tuliptree, 458
Chinese tupelo, 543–544
Chinese windmill palm, 864
Chinese wingnut, 703–704
Chinese witch-hazel, 397
Chinese yellowwood, 264
Chinese zelkova, 918
chinquapin oak, 745–746
Chionanthus pubescens, 257
Chionanthus retusus, 257–259
'Arnold's Pride', 257
'Ashford', 258
'China Snow', 258
'Confucius', 258

SPIRIT 'CRN10', 258
'Tokyo Tower', 258
Chionanthus virginicus, 257, 259–261
Dirr Clone, 260
'Emerald Knight', 260, 261
PRODIGY 'CVSTF', 260
SERENITY, 260
SERENITY 'CV1049', 261
'Spring Fleecing', 261
'White Knight', 261
×*Chitalpa tashkentensis*, 262
'Morning Cloud', 262
'Pink Dawn', 262
SUMMER BELLS 'Minsum', 262
chokecherry, 692–693
Chusan palm, 864
cider gum, 342
Cilician fir, 37
Cinnamomum camphora, 263
MAJESTIC BEAUTY 'MonProud', 263
Cladrastis delavayi, 'China Rose', 264
Cladrastis kentukea, 264–265
'Perkins Pink', 265
'Summer Shade', 265
Cladrastis lutea, 264–265
Cladrastis sinensis, 264
Clerodendrum trichotomum, 266
'Carnival', 266
'Purple Haze', 266
Clethra barbinervis, 'Variegata', 267
Clethra fargesii, 267
coast live oak, 720–721
coast redwood, 794–796
cockspur coral-tree, 339–340
cockspur hawthorn, 304–305
coffin tree, 826–827
Colorado blue spruce, 583–589
Colorado redcedar, 420
common alder, 157–158
common baldcypress, 827–835
common crapemyrtle, 433–434
common hackberry, 230–231
common horsechestnut, 149–151
common laburnum, 431
common lime, 855–857
common mulberry, 538
common pawpaw, 172–173
common peach, 676–678
common persimmon, 333–334
common sassafras, 791–792
common spindle-tree, 348–349
common witch-hazel, 399
common yew, 836–837
Compton oak, 738
cork oak, 772–773
corkscrew willow, 789
corneliancherry dogwood, 290–293

Cornus, 268, 349
Cornus alternifolia, 268–270, 865
   'Argentea', 269
   BIG CHOCOLATE CHIP 'Bichozam', 270
   'Black Stem', 270
   GOLDEN SHADOWS 'Wstackman', 270
   PISTACHIO 'Piszam', 270
Cornus angustata, 272–274
Cornus capitata, 273, 274
   subsp. *omeiensis*, 273
Cornus controversa, 270–272
   'Janine', 271
   JUNE SNOW 'June Snow-JFS', 271
   'Variegata', 272
Cornus elliptica, 272–274
   EMPRESS OF CHINA 'Elsbury', 273
   LITTLE RUBY 'NCCH1', 273
   'Mountain Moon', 274
   'Summer Passion', 274
Cornus ×*elwinortonii*, 268, 298–299
   ROSY TEACUPS 'KN144-2', 298
   STARLIGHT 'KN4-43', 298
   VENUS 'KN30-8', 299
Cornus florida, 274–280, 295, 391
   Appalachian series, 275–276
   CHEROKEE BRAVE 'Comco No. 1', 22, 268,
      277, 278
   'Cherokee Chief', 277, 278
   CHEROKEE DAYBREAK 'Daybreak', 279
   'Cherokee Princess', 268, 276
   CHEROKEE SUNSET 'Sunset', 279
   'Cloud 9', 277
   FIREBIRD 'Fircom 2', 280
   'First Lady', 280
   'Pluribracteata', 277
   'Prairie Pink', 277, 278
   RAGIN' RED 'JN13', 279
   f. *rubra*, 278, 279
   SPRING GROVE 'Grovflor', 277
   'Welch's Bay Beauty', 277
Cornus hongkongensis, 273
Cornus kousa, 25, 27, 268, 281–289, 295
   'Akatsuki', 282
   var. *angustata*, 272–274
   'Big Apple', 282
   CHAMPION'S GOLD 'Losely', 282
   'China Girl', 282
   subsp. *chinensis*, 282
   CROWN JEWEL 'Madison', 283
   'Empire', 283
   GALILEAN 'Galzam', 283
   'Gold Star', 283
   'Greensleeves', 283, 284
   HEART THROB 'Schmred', 285
   'Lustgarten Weeping', 285
   MANDARIN JEWEL 'Madi II', 285
   'Milky Way', 285

'Milky Way Select', 285
'National', 286
'Pam's Mountain Bouquet', 286
PROPHET 'Propzam', 286
RADIANT ROSE 'Hanros', 286
'Red Steeple', 286
SAMARITAN 'Samzam', 286–287
'Satomi', 287
SCARLET FIRE 'Rutpink', 286, 287
'Snow Tower', 287
'Summer Fun', 287
'Summer Gold', 288
'Summer Stars', 288
'Sunsplash', 288
'Temple Jewel', 283, 288
'Teutonia', 288
'Tri-Splendor', 288, 289
'Weisse Fontaine', 288
'Wisley Queen', 289
'Wolf Eyes', 289
Cornus mas, 27, 290–293
   'Golden Glory', 292
   SAFFRON SENTINEL 'JFS PN4Legacy',
      292
   'Spring Glow', 291, 293
   'Variegata', 291
Cornus nuttallii, 268, 294–295
   'Colrigo Giant', 294
   'Eddie's White Wonder', 295
   'Goldspot', 295
Cornus officinalis, 27, 290, 293
   'Kintoki', 293
Cornus omeiensis, 273
Cornus ×*rutgersensis*, 268, 295–298
   AURORA 'Rutban', 295
   CELESTIAL 'Rutdan', 296
   'Celestial Shadow', 296
   CONSTELLATION 'Rutcan', 296
   HYPERION 'KF111-1', 297
   RUTH ELLEN 'Rutlan', 297
   SATURN 'KF1-1', 297
   STARDUST 'Rutfan', 297
   STELLAR PINK 'Rutgan', 297
   VARIEGATED STELLAR PINK 'KV10-105v1',
      298
Corylus avellana, 'Burgundy Lace', 300
Corylus colurna, 300–301
   'Te Terra Red', 301
Corylus fargesii, 301–302
Corymbia citriodora, 302
Cotinus coggygria, 595
Cotinus obovatus, 302–303
   'Candy Floss', 302
   COTTON CANDY 'Northstar', 302
   'Flame', 302
   'Grace', 302
crabapple, 505–530

crack willow, 783
crapemyrtle, 28, 435–441
Crataegus crus-galli, 304–305, 307
   'Inermis', 304, 305
Crataegus laevigata, 305–306
   'Crimson Cloud', 306
   'Paul's Scarlet', 306
   'Rosea Flore Pleno', 306
Crataegus ×*lavalleei*, 'Carrierei', 307
Crataegus macracantha, 305
Crataegus mexicana, 307
Crataegus ×*mordenensis*, 307–308
   'Snowbird', 307
   'Toba', 308
Crataegus phaenopyrum, 308–309
   WASHINGTON LUSTRE 'Westwood I',
      309
   "Washington Tree", 309
Crataegus ×*prunifolia* 'Splendens', 305
Crataegus viridis, 'Winter King', 309
Crimean linden, 855
Cryptomeria japonica, 310–314
   'Araucarioides', 311
   'Black Dragon', 311
   'Cristata', 311
   'Gyokuryu', 311
   'Radicans', 311
   'Rein's Dense Jade', 312
   'Sekkan', 314
   'Yoshino', 314
cucumbertree magnolia, 468–471
Cunninghamia lanceolata, 'Glauca', 314–315
Cunninghamia unicanaliculata, 315
×*Cupressocyparis leylandii*. See *Cupressus*
      ×*leylandii*
×*Cupressocyparis notabilis*. See *Cupressus*
      ×*notabilis*
×*Cupressocyparis ovensii*. See *Cupressus*
      ×*ovensii*
Cupressus arizonica var. *glabra*, 315–317
   'Blue Ice', 316
   'Blue Pyramid', 316
   'Carolina Sapphire', 317
   'Limelight', 317
   'Raywood's Weeping', 317
   'Silver Smoke', 317
Cupressus ×*leylandii*, 318–320, 327
   'Castlewellan', 319
   EMERALD ISLE 'Moncal', 319
   'Fern Gold', 319
   'Goldconda', 319
   'Gold Rider', 319
   'Green Spire', 319, 326
   'Haggerston Grey', 320, 326
   'Leighton Green', 320
   'Naylor's Blue', 320, 326
   'Robinson's Gold', 319

'Silver Dust', 320
Cupressus macrocarpa, 318, 320–321
  'Aurea', 321
  'Conybearii', 321
  'Donard Gold', 321
  'Goldcrest', 321
  'Golden Cone', 321
  'Golden Pillar', 321
  'Lutea', 321
  'Wilma', 321
Cupressus ×murrayana, 327
Cupressus nootkatensis, 318, 322–325
  'Glauca', 323
  'Glauca Pendula', 323
  'Green Arrow', 323
  'Pendula', 323
  'Strict Weeping', 323
  'Van den Akker', 323
  'Variegata', 323
Cupressus ×notabilis, 326
Cupressus ×ovensii, 326–327
Cupressus sempervirens Stricta Group,
    327–329
  'Glauca', 329
  'Stricta', 329
  'Swane's Gold', 329
  TINY TOWER 'Monshel', 329
custard apple, 172–173
cutleaf weeping birch, 187
Cydonia sinensis. See *Pseudocydonia sinensis*

D

David elm, 879–886
Davidia involucrata, 330–331
  'Aya Nishiki', 331
  'Iseli Fastigiate', 331
  'Lady Dahlia', 331
  'Lady Sunshine', 331
  'Sonoma', 331
David keteleeria, 426
David's maple, 56–57
dawn redwood, 533–537
deodar cedar, 219–225
Dermatophyllum secundiflorum, 'Silver Peso',
    332
desert fan palm, 907
desert willow, 256–257
Diospyros virginiana, 333–334
  'Early Golden', 334
  'John Rick', 334
  'Killen', 334
  MAGIC FOUNTAIN 'JN5', 334
Distylium, 776
dogwood, 22, 27, 268
Douglas fir, 698–701
dove-tree, 330–331

downy serviceberry, 161–162
dragon's eye pine, 602
Dutch elm, 888–889
dwarf Alberta spruce, 576

E

eastern arborvitae, 839–842
eastern cottonwood, 647–649
eastern hemlock, 865–867
eastern larch, 446
eastern redbud, 238–246
eastern redcedar, 422–424
eastern white pine, 620–623
Elaeagnus angustifolia, 335
Elaeocarpus decipiens, 336
Elaeocarpus sylvestris, 336
Emily Bruner holly, 407, 411
Emmenopterys henryi, 337
empress tree, 564
Engelmann spruce, 574–575
English hawthorn, 305–306
English holly, 404–405
English laurel, 668
English oak, 760–767
English walnut, 416
English yew, 836–837
Eriobotrya deflexa, 339
Eriobotrya japonica, 338–339
  'Golden Nugget', 339
  'Hatsushimo', 339
  'Variegata', 339
Erythrina crista-galli, 339–340
  'Red Lights', 340
Eucalyptus cinerea, 340
Eucalyptus citriodora. See *Corymbia citriodora*
Eucalyptus dalrympleana, 340–341
Eucalyptus globulus, 341–342
  'Compacta', 342
Eucalyptus gunnii, 342
Eucalyptus neglecta, 342
Eucalyptus nicholii, 343
Eucalyptus parvifolia. See *Eucalyptus parvula*
Eucalyptus parvula, 344
Eucalyptus pauciflora subsp. *niphophila*,
    344–345
Eucalyptus polyanthemos, 345
Eucommia ulmoides, 345–346
  EMERALD POINTE, 346
Eucryphia ×nymansensis, 346–347
  'Mount Usher', 347
  'Nymansay', 347
  'Nymans Silver', 347
Euodia daniellii. See *Tetradium daniellii*
Euonymus bungeanus, 347–348, 349
  'Pink Lady', 347
  PRAIRIE RADIANCE 'Verona, 347–348

Euonymus europaeus, 348–349
  'Red Caps', 349
  'Red Cascade', 349
European ash, 364–365
European beech, 351–357
European birdcherry, 674–676
European chestnut, 215
European euonymus, 348–349
European gray alder, 159
European hazelnut, 300
European larch, 442–443
European linden, 855–857
European mountain ash, 805–806
European silver fir, 36
European white birch, 186–188
Euscaphis japonica, 349
evergreen ash, 373
evergreen pear, 715
evodia, 838–839

F

Fagus grandifolia, 350–351
  'Cameron', 351
  'Diamond Bark', 351
  'Mr. Tee', 351
Fagus sylvatica, 351–357
  'Aspleniifolia', 353
  Atropurpurea Group, 353
  'Aurea Pendula', 353
  'Dawyck', 353
  'Dawyck Gold', 353
  'Dawyck Purple', 353, 354
  'Pendula', 354
  'Purple Fountain', 355
  'Purpurea Pendula', 355
  'Purpurea Tricolor', 355
  'Red Obelisk', 356
  'Riversii', 356
  'Rohan Gold', 356
  'Rohanii', 356
  'Rohan Obelisk', 356
  'Rohan Trompenburg', 356
  'Spaethiana', 356
  'Tricolor', 355
  f. *tortuosa*, 357
  'Zlatia', 357
Farges filbert, 301–302
fernspray falsecypress, 252
fevertree, 337
field elm, 890
field maple, 50–53
filbert, 300
Firmiana simplex, 357–358
flamegold, 427
Florida nutmeg, 863
Florida sugar maple, 132

flowering ash, 367–368
flowering dogwood, 274–280
flowering peach, 676–678
Formosan cherry, 657
Formosan sweetgum, 450
Fothergilla ×intermedia, 'Mt. Airy', 302
fragrant epaulette-tree, 704–705
fragrant snowbell, 820–821
fragrant tea-olive, 553–555
Frangula caroliniana, 358
Frangula purshiana, 359
Franklinia alatamaha, 360–361
Fraser fir, 39–40
Fraxinus, 22, 361
Fraxinus americana, 361–363
  AUTUMN APPLAUSE 'Appldell', 362
  AUTUMN PURPLE 'Junginger', 362
  NORTHERN BLAZE 'Jefnor', 363
Fraxinus angustifolia, 363
  'Flame', 363
  'Raywood', 363
Fraxinus excelsior, 364–365
  'Globosa', 364
  GOLDEN DESERT 'Aureafolia', 364
  'Hessei', 364
  'Jaspidea', 364
Fraxinus mandshurica, 'Mancana', 366
Fraxinus nigra, 367
  'Fallgold', 367
  'Northern Gem', 367
  'Northern Treasure', 367
Fraxinus ornus, 367–368
  'Meczek', 368
  'Obelisk', 368
  URBAN BOUQUET 'JFS-Coate', 368
Fraxinus oxycarpa, 363
Fraxinus pennsylvanica, 23, 369–372
  CIMMARON 'Cimmzam', 370
  'Marshall's Seedless', 370
  'Patmore', 370
  PRAIRIE SPIRE 'Rugby', 370
  'Summit', 371
  URBANITE 'Urbdell', 372
Fraxinus quadrangulata, 372
Fraxinus uhdei, 373
  MAJESTIC BEAUTY 'Monus', 373
Fraxinus velutina, 374
  'Bonita', 374
  FAN-TEX 'Rio Grande', 374
  'Modesto', 374
Freeman maple, 57
Fremont cottonwood, 650
Fuji cherry, 665–666
fullmoon maple, 69–70

G

Garry oak, 731–732
giant arborvitae, 318, 843–846
giant dogwood, 270–272
giant sequoia, 797–799
Ginkgo biloba, 375–379, 697
  'Autumn Gold', 376
  EMPEROR 'Woodstock', 377
  GOLDEN COLONNADE 'JFS-UGA2', 377
  'Golden Globe', 377
  GOLDSPIRE 'Blagon', 377
  'Magyar', 377
  PRESIDENTIAL GOLD 'The President', 377
  PRINCETON SENTRY 'PNI 2720', 379
  'Samurai', 379
  'Saratoga', 379
  'Shangri-La', 379
  SKY TOWER 'JN9', 379
ginnala maple, 58–60
Gleditsia triacanthos, 380–385
  'Emerald Kascade', 381
  HALKA 'Christie', 381
  IMPERIAL 'Impcole', 382
  'Moraine', 382
  NORTHERN ACCLAIM 'Harve', 382
  PERFECTION 'Wandell', 382
  'Ruby Lace', 383
  'Shademaster', 383
  SKYLINE 'Skycole', 384
  SPECTRUM 'Speczam', 384
  STREETKEEPER 'Draves', 384
  SUNBURST 'Suncole', 385
  SUNSET GOLD 'Sungolzam', 385
  'True Shade', 385
globe locust, 781
glossy privet, 448
goat willow, 783
goldenchain, 431
golden larch, 696–697
goldenrain tree, 427–429
golden weeping willow, 784
×Gordlinia grandiflora, 361, 386
  'Sweet Tea', 386
grand fir, 40
gray alder, 159–160
gray birch, 191
Great Basin bristlecone pine, 591–592
great white cherry, 688
green ash, 16, 369–372
green hawthorn, 309
Gymnocladus dioicus, 387–389
  DECAF 'McKBranched', 388
  ESPRESSO 'Espresso-JFS', 388
  PRAIRIE TITAN 'J. C. McDaniel', 388
  SKINNY LATTE 'Morton', 388
  'Stately Manor', 388
  TRUE NORTH 'UMNSynergy', 388

H

Halesia carolina, 390–391
  'Arnold Pink', 391
  CRUSHED VELVET 'JFS-PN2-Legacy', 391
  'Emily Marie', 391
  'James Laubach', 391
  'Jersey Belle', 391, 392
  'Lady Catherine', 391
  'Rosea', 391, 392
  'Rosy Ridge', 391
  'UConn Wedding Bells', 391, 392
  Vestita Group, 391
Halesia diptera, 392–393
  Magniflora Group, 392
  'PRN Snowstorm', 393
  'Southern Snow', 393
  'Yellow Leaf Selection', 393
Halesia monticola. See *Halesia carolina*
Halesia tetraptera. See *Halesia carolina*
Hamamelis, 394
Hamamelis ×intermedia, 394–396, 397
  'Arnold Promise', 394
  'Diane', 395
  'Feuerzauber', 395
  'Jelena', 395
  'Pallida', 396
  'Primavera', 396
  'Sunburst', 396
  'Westerstede', 396
Hamamelis japonica, 397
  'Superba', 397
  'Zuccariniana', 397
Hamamelis mollis, 397–398
  'Boskoop', 397
  'Coombe Wood', 397
  'Early Bright', 397
Hamamelis virginiana, 'Harvest Moon', 399
hardy rubber tree, 345–346
harlequin glorybower, 266
hazelnut, 301–302
hedge maple, 50–53
Henry emmenopterys, 337
Henry maple, 68
Henry's rose tree, 776
Henry tanbark oak, 462
Henry Wilson tree, 801
Heptacodium miconioides, 400
higan cherry, 689–691
Himalayan evergreen dogwood, 273
Himalayan pine, 629–630
Himalayan white birch, 192
hinoki falsecypress, 249–252
Hippophae rhamnoides, 401

'Leikora', 401
TITAN, 401
holly, 404
honeylocust, 380–385
Hong Kong dogwood, 273
Hong Kong orchid tree, 175
hop-tree, 701–702
hornbeam, 199–202
Hovenia dulcis, 402
Hungarian oak, 730–731
hybrid catalpa, 217
hybrid goldenchain, 431
hybrid mountain ash, 806–807
hybrid strawberry tree, 169–170
hybrid witch-hazel, 394–396
Hydrangea macrophylla, 705

I

Idesia polycarpa, 403–404
Igiri tree, 403–404
Ilex, 404
  'Emily Bruner', 407, 411
  'Golden Nellie', 410
  'Nellie R. Stevens', 410
Ilex ×altaclerensis, 404
Ilex aquifolium, 404–405, 408, 410, 411
  'Argentea Marginata', 405
  'Aurea Marginata', 405
Ilex ×aquipernyi, 404
Ilex ×attenuata, 405–407, 411
  'East Palatka', 407
  'Foster No. 2', 407
  'Savannah', 407
Ilex cassine, 405
Ilex cornuta, 410
Ilex ×koehneana, 408
  'Agena', 408
  'Ajax', 408
  'San Jose', 408
  'Wirt L. Winn', 408
Ilex latifolia, 408–409
  'Alva', 408
  COOL FENCES 'ILDG', 408
  'Fusmu', 408
Ilex ×meserveae, 404
Ilex opaca, 405, 411–413, 553
  'Canary', 412
  'Carolina No. 2', 412
  'Croonenburg', 412
  'Goldie', 412
  'Jersey Princess', 412
  'Miss Helen', 412
  'Princeton Gold', 412
  'Satyr Hill', 412
incense cedar, 196–197
Indian horsechestnut, 151–152

India quassiawood, 590
Irish yew, 836
ironwood, 203–206, 555–556
Italian alder, 156–157
Italian cypress, 327–329
Italian stone pine, 616
ivy-leaved maple, 56

J

Jacaranda mimosifolia, 414
jack pine, 594
jacktree, 800–801
Japanese apricot, 672–674
Japanese black pine, 627
Japanese blueberry tree, 336
Japanese camellia, 198
Japanese cedar, 310–314
Japanese clethra, 267
Japanese cornel dogwood, 293
Japanese evergreen oak, 732–733
Japanese falsecypress, 253–254
Japanese flowering cherry, 684–688
Japanese flowering crabapple, 506
Japanese hackberry, 232–233
Japanese hornbeam, 206
Japanese horsechestnut, 153–154
Japanese larch, 444–445
Japanese maple, 79–88, 100
Japanese momi fir, 39
Japanese pagodatree, 813–814
Japanese raisintree, 402
Japanese red pine, 601–603
Japanese snowbell, 815–820
Japanese stewartia, 810–811
Japanese tree lilac, 821–823
Japanese white pine, 614–615
Japanese witch-hazel, 397
Japanese zelkova, 912–917
Jeffrey pine, 608
jelly palm, 194
Judas-tree, 247
Juglans major, 415
Juglans nigra, 414–416
  'Laciniata', 416
  'Sauber', 416
  'Sparrow', 416
Juglans regia, 416
  'Broadview', 416
  'Buccaneer', 416
  'Carpathian', 416
  'Hansen', 416
  'Laciniata', 416
  'Pendula', 416
  'Purpurea', 416
jujube, 919
juneberry, 161–162, 168

Juniperus chinensis, 417–419
  'Hetzii Columnaris', 418
  'Kaizuka', 418
  'Keteleeri', 418
  'Pyramidalis', 418
  'Robusta Green', 418
  'Spartan', 418
  STAR POWER 'JN Select Blue', 418
  'Trautman', 418
Juniperus horizontalis, 420
Juniperus scopulorum, 420–421
  'Blue Arrow', 420
  'Blue Heaven', 420
  'Gray's Gleam', 420
  'Moonglow', 420
  'Pathfinder', 420
  SKY HIGH 'Bailigh', 420
  'Skyrocket', 420
  'Wichita Blue', 420
Juniperus virginiana, 420, 422–424
  'Brodie', 422
  'Burkii', 423
  'Canaertii', 423
  EMERALD SENTINEL 'Corcorcor', 423
  PROVIDENCE 'JVBP3', 423
  TAPESTRY 'JVADR', 423
  'Taylor', 424

K

Kalopanax pictus. See *Kalopanax septemlobus*
Kalopanax septemlobus, 425
katsura, 233–238
Kentucky coffeetree, 387–389
Keteleeria davidiana, 426
Keteleeria evelyniana, 426
Keteleeria fortunei, 426
Kobus magnolia, 482
Koehne holly, 408
Koelreuteria bipinnata, 426–427
Koelreuteria elegans, 427
Koelreuteria paniculata, 427–429
  'Coral Sun', 428
  'Fastigiata', 428
  GOLDEN CANDLE 'Golcanzam', 428
  'Rose Lantern', 428
  'September', 428
  SUMMERBURST 'Sunleaf', 429
Korean fir, 41–42
Korean maple, 99–101
Korean mountain ash, 802
Korean pear, 714
Korean pine, 609–610
Korean sweetheart tree, 349
kousa dogwood, 281–289

L

Laburnum alpinum, 'Pendulum', 430
Laburnum anagyroides, 431
Laburnum ×watereri, 430, 431–432
 'Columnaris', 431
 'Vossii', 431
lacebark elm, 28, 890–896
lacebark pine, 595–596
Lagerstroemia indica, 433–434, 437
 DOUBLE DYNAMITE 'Whit X', 434
 DYNAMITE 'Whit II', 434
 PINK VELOUR 'Whit III', 434
 RED ROCKET 'Whit IV', 434
Lagerstroemia limii, 437
Lagerstroemia speciosa, 434–435
Lagerstroemia subcostata var. *fauriei*, 435–441,
  438–439
 'Apalachee', 437
 'Arapaho', 437
 BLACK DIAMOND series, 28, 437
 'Choctaw', 437
 DELTA JAZZ 'Chocolate Mocha', 28, 437,
  438
 Ebony series, 437
 'Fantasy', 435
 HIGH COTTON 'Worthington's Upright',
  435
 'Kiowa', 435
 'Miami', 437
 MOONLIGHT MAGIC, 28, 437
 'Muskogee', 437
 'Natchez', 437
 'Sarah's Favorite', 439
 'Sioux', 439
 'Townhouse', 437
 'Tuscarora', 439
 'Tuskegee', 439
 TWILIGHT MAGIC, 28, 437
 'Wichita', 439
 'Woodlander's Chocolate', 437
large-leaved lime, 857–858
Larix decidua, 442–443, 444, 446
 'Horstmann's Recurva', 443
 'Pendula', 443
 'Varied Directions', 443
Larix kaempferi, 444–445, 446
 'Diana', 444
 'Pendula', 444
Larix laricina, 446
laurel oak, 733–734
laurel willow, 783
Laurus nobilis, 447
 'Angustifolia', 447
 'Aurea', 447
 EMERALD WAVE 'Monem', 447
 'Saratoga', 447

Lavalle hawthorn, 307
Lawson falsecypress, 248
lemon-scented gum, 302
Leyland cypress, 248, 310, 318–320, 418
Libocedrus decurrens. See *Calocedrus
  decurrens*, 196–197
Ligustrum lucidum, 448
 'Excelsum Superbum', 448
 'Excelsum Variegatum', 448
 'Tricolor', 448
limber pine, 603–604
Liquidambar acalycina, 449, 450
 'Burgundy Flush', 449
Liquidambar formosana, 449, 450
 'Afterglow', 450
 Monticola Group, 450
Liquidambar styraciflua, 451–457
 'Burgundy', 452
 'Cherokee', 452
 EMERALD SENTINEL 'Clydesform', 452
 'Festival', 452
 GOLD DUST 'Goduzam', 453
 'Golden Treasure', 453
 HAPPIDAZE 'Hapdell', 453
 'Lane Roberts', 455
 'Moraine', 455
 'Palo Alto', 455
 'Rotundiloba', 455
 'Silver King', 455
 'Slender Silhouette', 456
 'Variegata', 457
 'Worplesdon', 457
Liriodendron chinense, 'Chapel Hill', 458
Liriodendron tulipifera, 458–462, 811
 'Ardis', 460
 'Aureomarginatum', 460
 EMERALD CITY 'JFS-Oz', 25, 26, 460
 'Fastigiatum' ('Arnold'), 25, 460, 462
 'Little Volunteer', 25, 26, 462
Lithocarpus henryi, 462
little epaulette-tree, 705
little-leaf azara, 173–174
littleleaf linden, 850–854
loblolly pine, 625–626
lodgepole pine, 599–601
Loebner magnolia, 483–486
Lombardy poplar, 653
London planetree, 632–637
longleaf pine, 613
loquat, 338–339
Loropetalum, 776
lost gordonia, 360–361
Lucombe oak, 773
Luma apiculata, 463
lusterleaf holly, 408–409

M

Maackia amurensis, 464–465, 466
 MAACNIFICENT 'JFS-Schichtel1', 464
 'Starburst', 465
 'Summertime', 465
Maackia chinensis, 466
Maackia hupehensis. See *Maackia chinensis*
Maclura pomifera, 466–467
 'Cannonball', 466
 'White Shield', 467
 'Wichita', 467
Magnolia, 468
Magnolia acuminata, 468–471
 'Anilou', 470
 'Butterbowl', 470
 'Butterflies', 470
 'Elizabeth', 471
 'Fertile Myrtle', 469
 'Gold Star', 471
 'Honey Flower', 471
 'Judy Zuk', 471
 'Lois', 471
 'Petit Chicon', 471
 'Philo', 469
 'Urbana', 469
 'Yellow Bird', 471
 'Yellow Lantern', 471
Magnolia campbellii, 471–473
 Alba Group, 472
 'Black Tulip', 472
 BURGUNDY STAR 'JURmag4', 473
 'Charles Rafill', 472
 'Felix Jury', 473
 'Frank's Masterpiece', 473
 'Genie', 473
 'Grant David', 473
 'Ian's Giant Red', 473
 'Ian's Red', 473
 'Lanarth', 472
 'Margaret Helen', 473
 'Purple Sensation', 473
 'Red Is Red', 473
 'Ruth', 473
 'Shirazz', 473
 'Strawberry Fields', 473
 'Vulcan', 473
Magnolia denudata, 471, 473, 474–475, 475,
  492, 504
 'Forrest's Pink', 475
 'Purpurascens', 475
 'Sawada', 475
 'Swarthmore Sentinel', 475
Magnolia doltsopa, 481
Magnolia grandiflora, 408, 468, 475–479, 490,
  744
 'Bracken's Brown Beauty', 476

'Claudia Wannamaker', 476
'D. D. Blanchard', 477
'Edith Bogue', 477
GREENBACK 'Mgtig', 477
'Hasse', 477
'Kay Parris', 477
'Little Gem', 479
TEDDY BEAR 'Southern Charm', 479
'Victoria', 479
Magnolia insignis, 480–481
'Anita Figlar', 480
Magnolia ×kewensis 'Wada's Memory', 482, 483
Magnolia kobus, 482–483
Magnolia liliiflora, 475, 492, 496
'Nigra', 473, 495
Magnolia ×loebneri, 483–486
'Ballerina', 485
'Donna', 485
'Leonard Messel', 485
'Merrill', 485
'Spring Snow', 486
SPRING WELCOME 'Ruth', 486
'White Rose', 486
'Wildcat', 486
Magnolia macrophylla, 486–487, 499
subsp. *ashei*, 487, 490, 500
'Julian Hill', 487
Magnolia maudiae, 481
Magnolia platypetala, 481, 488
'Spring Bouquet', 488
'Touch of Pink', 488
Magnolia salicifolia, 482, 489–490
'Else Frye', 490
'Grape Expectations', 490
'Iufer', 490
'Jermyns', 490
'Miss Jack', 490
'W. B. Clarke', 490
Magnolia sieboldii, 468, 490, 490–491, 500
'Charles Coates', 490
'Colossus', 490
'Exotic Star', 490
Magnolia ×soulangeana, 492–495
'Alexandrina', 493
'Amabilis', 493
'Brozzonii', 493
'Lennei', 494
'Lennei Alba', 494
MERCURY 'NCMX1', 494
'Rustica Rubra', 495
'Verbanica', 495
Magnolia sprengeri, 495–496
'Burncoose Purple', 496
'Copeland Court', 496
'Dark Diva', 496
'Diva', 496

'Galaxy', 495, 496
'Lanhydrock', 496
'Spectrum', 495, 496
Magnolia stellata, 483, 497–499, 504
'Centennial', 497, 498
'Centennial Blush', 497, 498
'Chrysanthemumiflora', 498
'Pink Stardust', 499
'Royal Star', 497, 499
'Waterlily', 497, 499
Magnolia tripetala, 499–500, 500
Magnolia virginiana, 500–503, 744
var. *australis*, 500
EMERALD TOWER 'JN8', 501
'Green Mile', 501
'Green Shadow', 501
'Henry Hicks', 502
KELTYK 'MVMTF', 502
'Mardi Gras', 502
MOONGLOW 'Jim Wilson', 502
'Northern Belle', 502
'Santa Rosa', 503
'Satellite', 503
Magnolia yuyuanensis, 481
Magnolia zenii, 'Pink Parchment', 504–505
maidenhair tree, 375–379
Malus, 505–530, 526
'Adams', 513
'Adirondack', 507
APRIL SHOWERS 'Uebo', 525
BRANDYWINE 'Branzam', 513
CAMELOT 'Camzam', 523
'Candymint', 513
'Cardinal', 514
CENTURION 'Centzam', 514
CORALBURST 'Coralcole', 523
'Dolgo', 506, 508
'Donald Wyman', 508
EMERALD SPIRE 'Jefgreen', 528
FIREBIRD 'Select A', 523
'Floribunda', 509
GLADIATOR 'Durleo', 514
GOLDEN RAINDROPS 'Schmidtcutleaf', 509
HARVEST GOLD 'Hargozam', 509
'Indian Magic', 515
'Indian Summer', 515
IVORY SPEAR 'JFS KW214MX', 528
'Klehm's Improved Bechte', 515
LANCELOT 'Lanzam', 523
LOLLIPOP 'Lollizam', 523
'Louisa', 526
'Luwick', 526
MARILEE 'Jarmin', 530
'Mary Potter', 510
MOLTEN LAVA 'Molazam', 526
'Morning Princess', 515

'Orange Crush', 516
PERFECT PURPLE, 516
PINK PRINCESS 'Parrsi', 516
PINK SPARKLES 'Malusquest', 516
'Pink Spires', 517
'Prairie Rose', 530
'Prairifire', 517
'Profusion', 518
'Purple Prince', 518
PURPLE SPIRE 'Jefspire', 528
'Radiant', 518
RASPBERRY SPEAR 'JFS KW213MX', 528
'Red Barron', 519
'Red Jade', 526
RED JEWEL 'Jewelcole', 510
'Red Splendor', 519
REJOICE 'Rejzam', 519
'Robinson', 518, 521
'Royal Beauty', 526
ROYAL RAINDROPS 'JFS-KW5', 521
'Royalty', 521
RUBY DAYZE 'JFS KW139MX', 521
RUBY TEARS 'Bailears', 526
'Satin Cloud', 511
SCARLET BRANDYWINE 'Scbrazam', 521
SHOW TIME 'Shotizam', 521
'Snowdrift', 511
SPARKLING SPRITE 'JFS-KW207', 525
'Spring Snow', 530
STARLITE 'Jeflite', 511
SUGAR TYME 'Sutyzam', 513
'Thunderchild', 521
VELVET PILLAR 'Velvetcole', 521
Malus angustifolia, 505, 507
Malus baccata, 505
'Jackii', 508
Malus coronaria, 506
Malus floribunda, 506
Malus hupehensis, 506, 510
Malus ioensis, 506
BRANDYWINE, 506
'Klehm's Improved Bechtel', 506, 515, 516
'Prairie Rose', 506
Malus pumila var. *niedzwetzkyana*, 506
Malus sargentii, 506, 523
'Tina', 524
'Tina's Charm', 524
'Tina's Ruby', 525
'Tina's Weeper', 526
Malus sieboldii, 506
Malus spectabilis, 506
Malus toringo, 506
Malus tschonoskii, 506, 513
Malus zumi, 506
'Calocarpa', 513
Manchurian ash, 366
Manchurian maple, 72

Manchurian striped maple, 136–137
Manglietia, 468
Manglietia insignis. See *Magnolia insignis*
Manglietia yuyuanensis. See *Magnolia yuyuanensis*
Mayday tree, 674–676
Mediterranean redbud, 247
medlar tree, 532
Melia azedarach, 530–531
   'Jade Snowflake', 531
   'Umbraculifera', 531
Mespilus germanica, 532
Metasequoia glyptostroboides, 533–537
   AMBERGLOW 'Wah-08AG', 534
   'Golden Guusje', 535
   'Goldrush', 533, 535
   'Jack Frost', 535
   JADE PRINCE 'JFS-PN3Legacy', 533, 535
   'Miss Grace', 533, 537
   'National', 537
   PALATIAL 'MG1042', 537
   SHAW'S LEGACY 'Raven', 537
   'Urban Spire', 537
   'Waasland', 537
Mexican baldcypress, 832
Mexican fan palm, 908
Mexican loquat-leaved oak, 769–770
Mexican white pine, 593
Michelia, 468
mimosa, 155–156
mitsumine fir, 41
Miyabe maple, 74
Mongolian linden, 857
monkey puzzle tree, 168–169
Monterey cypress, 320–321
Monterey pine, 617–618
moosewood, 89
Morden hawthorn, 307–308
Morus alba, 538–539
   'Chaparral', 538
   'Fruitless', 538
   'Kingan', 538
   'Pendula', 538
   var. *tatarica*, 538
Morus nigra, 539
   'Black Beauty', 539
   'Persian', 539
Morus rubra, 540
moss falsecypress, 254
mossy-cup oak, 740–743
mountain gum, 340–341
mountain hemlock, 871–872
Murray cypress, 326–327
musclewood, 203–206
Myrtus luma. See *Luma apiculata*

N
nannyberry viburnum, 898–899
narrowleaf ash, 363
narrow-leaf black peppermint, 343
narrowleaf cottonwood, 646
Nellie R. Stevens holly, 410, 411
Niedzwetzky apple, 506
Nikko fir, 41
Nikko maple, 73
noble fir, 46
Nootka falsecypress, 322–325
Nordmann fir, 44
North American tanoak, 462
northern catalpa, 217–219
northern Japanese hemlock, 869
northern pin oak, 728–729
Norway maple, 28, 90–97, 98
Norway spruce, 570–573
Notholithocarpus, 462
Nuttall oak, 748–752
Nyman eucryphia, 346–347
Nyssa, 27
Nyssa aquatica, 541
Nyssa biflora, 542
Nyssa ogeche, 542–543
Nyssa sinensis, 543–544
Nyssa sylvatica, 542, 544–551, 792
   AFTERBURNER 'David Odom', 545
   'Autumn Cascades', 546
   FIREMASTER 'PRP1', 546
   FIRESTARTER 'JFS-red', 546
   FOREST FIRE 'TheJames', 546
   FORUM 'NXSXF', 546
   GREEN GABLE 'NSUHH', 546
   GUM DROP 'JFS-PN Legacy1', 546
   NORTHERN SPLENDOR, 546
   'Penwood Weeper', 549
   RED RAGE 'Haymanred', 549
   RED SPLYNDOR 'NSMTF', 549
   'Sheri's Cloud', 549
   TUPELO TOWER 'WFH1', 551
   WHITE CHAPEL 'Cherry Pie', 551
   'Wildfire', 551
   'Wisley Bonfire', 551
   'Zydeco Twist', 551
Nyssa sylvatica var. *biflora*, 542

O
oak, 9, 718–719
oakleaf mountain ash, 806–807
Ogeechee-lime, 542–543
Ogeechee tupelo, 542–543
Ohio buckeye, 147–149
Olea europaea, 552–553
   'Arbequina', 553

   'Swan Hill', 553
olive, 552–553
omeo gum, 342
orchid tree, 175
Oregon white oak, 731–732
oriental arborvitae, 641–642
oriental photinia, 569–570
oriental spruce, 581–583
Osage-orange, 466–467
Osmanthus fragrans, 553–555
   'Aurantiacus', 554
   'Nanjing's Beauty', 554
Osmanthus yunnanensis, 555
Ostrya virginiana, 555–556
   AUTUMN TREASURE 'JFS-KW5', 556
   SUN BEAM 'Camdale', 556
overcup oak, 737
Oxydendrum arboreum, 556–557, 792
   'Chaemeleon', 557

P
Pacific dogwood, 294–295
Pacific madrone, 170
Pacific yew, 837–838
pagoda dogwood, 268–270
painted maple, 90
paperbark cherry, 683
paperbark maple, 64–67
paper birch, 183–185
Parrotia, 776
Parrotia persica, 27–28, 558–562, 563
   'Lamplighter', 560
   'Pendula', 560
   PERSIAN SPIRE 'JLColumnar', 560
   RUBY VASE 'Inge', 560
   STREETWISE 'PPS551', 560
   'Vanessa', 560
Parrotia subaequalis, 27–28, 563
Paulownia tomentosa, 564
pear, 513
pecan, 209
Peking lilac, 824–825
Persea borbonia, 565
Persian parrotia, 558–562
Persian walnut, 416
Phellodendron amurense, 565–567
   EYE STOPPER 'Longenecker', 566
   'His Majesty', 566
   'Macho', 567
   SUPERFECTION 'Supzam', 567
Phellodendron lavalleei, 565
Phellodendron sachalinense, 565
Phoenix canariensis, 567–568, 782
Phoenix reclinata, 568
Photinia ×fraseri, 569
Photinia glabra, 569

Photinia serratifolia, 568–569
  CURLY FANTASY 'Kolcurl', 569
  'Green Giant', 569
  'Jenny', 569
  'Marwood Hill', 569
Photinia serrulata, 568–569
Photinia villosa, 569–570
  var. *laevis*, 570
  'Village Shade', 570
Picea abies, 570–573
  'Aarburg', 571
  'Acrocona', 571
  'Clanbrassiliana Stricta', 571
  'Cobra', 571
  'Cupressina', 573
  'Hillside Upright', 573
  'Pendula', 573
  'Sherwood Compact', 573
Picea breweriana, 574
Picea engelmannii, 574–575
  'Bush's Lace', 575
  'Fritsche', 575
Picea glauca, 576–577
  'Conica', 576
  'Densata', 576
  var. *densata*, 576
  'Montrose Spire', 576
  'North Star', 576
  'Pendula', 576
  'Yukon Blue', 576
Picea omorika, 578–580
  'Bruns', 579
  'Gotelli Weeping', 579
  'Nana', 579
  'Pendula', 579
  'Pendula Bruns', 580
  'Silberblau', 580
Picea orientalis, 44, 581–583
  'Aureospicata', 581
  'Firefly', 581
  'Nigra Compacta', 583
  'Skylands', 583
Picea pungens, 575, 583–589
  'Avatar', 584
  'Baby Blue', 584
  'Baby Blueyes', 584
  'Bakeri', 584
  'Bizon Blue', 584
  'Blue Diamond', 584
  'Blue Select', 585
  'Bonny Blue', 585
  'Fastigiata'. See 'Iseli Fastigiate'
  'Fat Albert', 585
  'Gebelle's Golden Spring', 585
  'Hoopsii', 587
  'Iseli Fastigiate', 587
  'Koster', 587
  'Montgomery', 588
  'Pendula', 588
  'Sester Dwarf', 588
  'Thomsen', 589
Picea sitchensis, 589–590
Picrasma quassioides, 590
pignut hickory, 208
Pinckneya bracteata, 337
pindo palm, 194
pine bark maple, 84
pin oak, 753–756
Pinus albicaulis, 590–591
Pinus aristata, 591–592
  'Horstmann', 592
Pinus ayacahuite, 593
Pinus banksiana, 'Uncle Fogy', 594
Pinus bungeana, 595–596
  'Great Wall', 596
  'Rowe Arboretum', 596
  'Silver Ghost', 596
Pinus canariensis, 596–597
Pinus cembra, 597–598
  'Chalet', 598
  PRAIRIE STATESMAN 'Herman', 598
  'Stricta', 598
Pinus contorta, 599–601
  'Chief Joseph', 599
  var. *contorta*, 601
  var. *latifolia*, 601
  var. *murrayana*, 601
  'Taylor's Sunburst', 601
Pinus densiflora, 601–603
  'Burke's Red Variegated', 602
  'Golden Ghost', 602
  'Oculus Draconis', 602
  'Umbraculifera', 603
Pinus elliottii, 626
Pinus flexilis, 603–604
  'Extra Blue', 604
  'Vanderwolf's Pyramid', 604
Pinus halepensis, 605
Pinus heldreichii, 606–607
  'Compact Gem', 606
  'Emerald Arrow', 606
  'Indigo Eyes', 606
  'Mint Truffle', 606
  'Satellit', 606
Pinus ×holfordiana, 593
Pinus jeffreyi, 'Joppi', 608
Pinus koraiensis, 609–610
  'Glauca', 609
  'Morris Blue', 609
  'Oculus Draconis', 609
Pinus leucodermis. See *Pinus heldreichii*
Pinus longaeva, 591–592
  'Blue Bear', 592
  'Formal Form', 592
  'Joe's Bess', 592
Pinus monophylla, 610–611
Pinus nigra, 611–613
  'Arnold Sentinel', 613
  'Oregon Green', 613
Pinus palustris, 613, 626
Pinus parviflora, 614–615
  'Aoi', 615
  'Bergman', 615
  'Blue Wave', 615
  'Gimborn's Ideal', 615
  'Glauca', 615
  'Glauca Brevifolia', 615
  'Tempelhof', 615
Pinus pinea, 616
Pinus ponderosa, 616–617
Pinus radiata, 617–618
  Aurea Group, 618
Pinus resinosa, 594
Pinus rigida, 618–619, 626
  'Sherman Eddy', 619
Pinus strobiformis, 620
Pinus strobus, 594, 620–623
  'Angel Falls', 622
  'Contorta', 622
  'Fastigiata', 622
  'Glauca', 622
  'Louie', 622
  'Pendula', 622
  'Stowe Pillar', 622
  'Winter Gold', 622
Pinus sylvestris, 624–625
  Fastigiata Group, 625
  'Gold Coin', 625
  'Watereri', 625
Pinus taeda, 619, 625–626
  JC Raulston Dwarf, 626
Pinus thunbergii, 627
  MAJESTIC BEAUTY 'Monina', 627
  'Thunderhead', 627
Pinus virginiana, 628
  'Ancient Wonder', 628
  'Wate's Golden', 628
Pinus wallichiana, 593, 629–630
  'Prairie Giant', 629
  'Zebrina', 629
Pistacia chinensis, 630–631
  'Keith Davey', 631
  'Pearl Street', 631
  'Sarah's Radiance', 631
  WESTERN SON 'Pair's Choice', 631
pitch pine, 618–619
plains cottonwood, 649
planetree, 27
planetree maple, 98
Platanus ×acerifolia, 632–637, 639
  'Alphen's Globe', 633

Platanus ×*acerifolia* [*continued*]
  'Bloodgood', 633
  'Columbia', 633
  EXCLAMATION! 'Morton Circle', 27, 634
  'Huissen', 634
  'Liberty', 634
  METROSHADE 'Metzam', 634
  MONUMENTAL 'Morton Naper', 27, 634, 635
  'Pyramidalis', 636
  'Suttneri', 636
  'Tremonia', 636
  'Yarwood', 636
Platanus occidentalis, 633, 637–638
  'Howard', 638
  SILVERWOOD 'Grenickel', 638
Platanus orientalis, 'Digitata', 639
Platanus racemosa, 640
Platanus wrightii, 640–641
Platycladus orientalis, 595, 641–642
  'Aurea Nana', 642
  'Van Hoey Smith', 642
Podocarpus, 836
Podocarpus macrophyllus, 642–643
  'Aureus', 642
  'Argenteus', 642
  EMERALD FLAME, 643
  LEMON SPARKLER, 643
  var. *maki*, 643
  'Variegata', 643
Poliothrysis sinensis, 643–644
pond cypress, 832
ponderosa pine, 616–617
Populus acuminata, 652
Populus alba, 644–645, 647
  'Pyramidalis', 644
  'Raket', 644
Populus angustifolia, 646
Populus ×*canadensis*, 646
  'Nor'easter', 646
  'Prairie Sky', 646
  'Robusta', 646
Populus ×*canescens* 'Tower', 647
Populus deltoides, 646, 647–649
  'Jeronimus', 649
  subsp. *monilifera*, 649
  NORTHERN ESTEEM 'Schreiner', 649
  'Purple Tower', 649
  'Siouxland', 649
  'Sparks', 649
  subsp. *wislizeni*, 649
Populus fremontii, 650
Populus grandidentata, 651
Populus 'Highland', 652
Populus nigra, 646, 652–653
  'Afghanica', 653
  'Italica', 653

Populus sargentii, 649, 652
Populus tremula, 653–654
  'Erecta', 654
Populus tremuloides, 654–657
  'Bethel Spire', 655
  DANCING FLAME 'KMN01', 655
  FOREST SILVER 'Drifest', 657
  MOUNTAIN SENTINEL 'JFS-Column', 657
  PRAIRIE GOLD 'Ne Arb', 657
  'Prairie Skyrise', 657
  SUMMER SHIMMER 'Select Klaus', 657
Port Orford cedar, 248
Portuguese laurel, 669
post oak, 771–772
prairie crabapple, 506
pride of India, 427–429
Prunus ×*blireana*, 661–662
Prunus campanulata, 657–659
  'Abigail Adams', 658
  'Dream Catcher', 658
  'Felix Jury', 658
  FIRST BLUSH 'JFS-KW14', 658
  'First Lady', 659
  'Okame', 659
Prunus caroliniana, 660–661
  BRIGHT 'N TIGHT 'Compacta', 661
  CENTRE COURT 'GRECCT', 661
Prunus cerasifera, 661, 661–664
  'Atropurpurea', 661
  CRIMSON POINTE 'Cripoizam', 662
  'Hollywood', 662
  'Krauter Vesuvius', 662, 663
  MT. ST. HELENS 'Frankthrees', 662
  'Newport', 664
  'Purple Pony', 664
  'Thundercloud', 664
Prunus incisa, 659, 665–666
  FRILLY FROCK / LEMON SPLASH 'FPMSPL', 665
  'Hilling's Weeping', 665
  'Kojo-no-mai', 665
  LITTLE TWIST 'CarltonLT', 665
  'Pendula', 667
  PINK CASCADE 'NCPH1', 667
  SNOW FOUNTAINS 'Snofozam', 667
  'Snow Goose', 667
  'Snow Showers', 667
  'Umineko', 667
Prunus laurocerasus, 668
  'Caucasica', 668
  'Magnoliifolia', 668
Prunus lusitanica, 669
  'Angustifolia', 669
  'Myrtifolia', 669
  'Variegata', 669
Prunus maackii, 670–671

  'Amber Beauty', 670
  GOLDSPUR 'Jefspur', 670
  KLONDIKE 'Jefdike', 670
Prunus mume, 661, 672–674
  'Alba Plena', 673
  'Bridal Veil', 673
  'Dawn', 673
  'Fragrant Snow', 673
  'Hokkai-bungo', 673
  'Kanko Bai', 673
  'Kobai', 673
  'Matsurabara Red', 673
  'Nicholas', 674
  'Peggy Clarke', 674
  'Rosemary Clarke', 674
  'W. B. Clarke', 674
  'Yuh-Hwa', 674
Prunus padus, 669, 674–676
  'Albertii', 675
  'Colorata', 675
  MERLOT 'Drietree', 675
  'Nana', 675
  'Pandora', 675
  SUMMER GLOW 'DTR 117', 676
  'Sweetheart', 676
  'Watereri', 676
Prunus pendula, 689
Prunus persica, 676–678
  'Alba', 677
  'Alboplena', 677
  'Alboplena Pendula', 677
  Corinthian series, 677
  'Foliis Rubris', 678
  'Helen Borchers', 678
  'Peppermint Stick', 678
Prunus sargentii, 678–681
  'Accolade', 679
  'Columnaris', 679
  PINK FLAIR 'JFS-KW58', 679
  'Rancho', 679
  'Spire', 679
  SPRING WONDER 'Hokkaido Normandale', 679
  'Tiltstone Hellfire', 679
Prunus serotina, 'Spring Sparkle', 682–683
Prunus serrula, 683
Prunus serrulata, 684–688
  'Amanogawa', 684
  'Hokusai', 684
  'Horinji', 684
  'Ichiyo', 684
  'Kanzan', 684
  'Kiku-shidare-zakura', 687
  'Pink Perfection', 687
  'Royal Burgundy', 687
  'Shirofugen', 687
  'Shirotae', 687

'Shogetsu', 688
'Sunset Boulevard', 688
'Taihaku', 688
'Ukon', 688
Prunus speciosa, 667
Prunus subhirtella, 679, 689–691
  'Accolade'. See *Prunus sargentii*
  'Autumnalis', 689
  'Autumnalis Rosea', 689
  'Fukubana', 689
  'Hally Jolivette', 689
  'Pendula', 690
  'Pendula Plena Rosea', 690
  'Pendula Rubra', 691
  PINK SNOW SHOWERS 'Pisnshzam', 691
  WEEPING PINK INFUSION 'Wepinzam', 690
  'Whitcomb', 691
Prunus virginiana, 692–693
  'Canada Red', 692
  'Canada Red Improved', 692
  'Canada Red Select', 692
  'Schubert', 692
  SUCKER PUNCH 'P002S', 693
Prunus ×yedoensis, 694–695
  'Akebono', 694
  'Helen Taft', 694
  'Pink Shell', 694
  'Shidare Yoshino', 695
  'Yoshino', 695
Pseudocydonia sinensis, 695–696
Pseudolarix amabilis, 696–697
Pseudotsuga menziesii, 698–701
  'Blue', 698
  'Emerald Twister', 698
  'Fastigiata', 701
  var. *glauca*, 701
  'Glauca Pendula', 701
  'Graceful Grace', 701
  GREEN CANYON 'Winterscape', 701
  'Pendula', 701
  'Waggin Tails', 701
Ptelea trifoliata, 701–702
  'Aurea', 702
  'Glauca', 702
Pterocarya fraxinifolia, 702–703
Pterocarya stenoptera, 703–704
  'Fernleaf', 704
Pterostyrax corymbosa, 705
Pterostyrax hispida, 704–705
purpleblow maple, 139–143
purple-leaf crapemyrtle, 28
purple-leaf plum, 661–664
Pyrus betulifolia, 714
Pyrus calleryana, 705–713
  'Aristocrat', 707
  'Autumn Blaze', 707

'Bradford', 17, 707
'Capital', 709
CHANTICLEER 'Glen's Form', 707, 709
CHASTITY 'NCPX2', 28, 709
'Fauriei', 711
JACK 'Jaczam', 711
JAVELIN 'NCPX1', 711
LIL JILL 'Liljilzam', 711
NEW BRADFORD 'Holmford', 711
'Redspire', 712
'Trinity', 712
'Whitehouse', 713
Pyrus fauriei, 714
  KOREAN SUN 'Westwood', 714
  'Silver Ball', 714
Pyrus kawakamii, 715
Pyrus salicifolia, 715–716
  'Pendula', 716
  SILVER FROST 'Silfrozam', 716
Pyrus ussuriensis, 716–717
  MOUNTAIN FROST 'Bailfrost', 717
  PRAIRIE GEM 'MorDak', 717

Q

quaking aspen, 654–657
queen palm, 194
queen's crapemyrtle, 434–435
Quercus, 17, 718–719
Quercus acuta, 747
Quercus acutissima, 719
Quercus agrifolia, 720–721
Quercus alba, 721–722, 737, 741, 760, 774
Quercus ×benderi, 728
Quercus bicolor, 722–725, 741, 760
  AMERICAN DREAM 'JFS-KW12', 24–25, 723
  BEACON 'Bonnie and Mike', 31, 32, 723
  SUN BREAKER 'Green Nova', 725
Quercus ×bimundorum, 760
Quercus cerris, 726, 773
  'Argenteovariegata', 726
Quercus coccinea, 727–728
Quercus ×comptoniae, 738
Quercus ellipsoidalis, 728–729
  'Hemelrijk', 729
  MAJESTIC SKIES 'Bailskies', 729
Quercus falcata, 729–730, 774
  var. *pagodifolia*, 730
  'QXMTF', 730
Quercus frainetto, 730–731
  FOREST GREEN 'Schmidt', 731
  'Trump', 731
Quercus garryana, 731–732
Quercus glauca, 732–733, 747
Quercus hemisphaerica, 733–734
  AVALYN 'QHMTF', 734

Quercus ×hispanica, 726, 773
  'Lucombeana', 773
  'Wageningen', 726
Quercus imbricaria, 735
Quercus lobata, 736
Quercus lyrata, 737–740
  ENDURANCE 'QCE295', 739
  GREEN SPRING 'Dahlonega', 739
  HIGHBEAM 'QLFTB', 739
  MARQUEE 'Hopeulikit', 739
  RESILIENCE 'QLRS10', 739
  STREAMLINE 'QLR552', 739
Quercus ×macdanielii, 760
Quercus macrocarpa, 725, 740–743, 760, 774
  COBBLESTONE 'JFS-KW14', 741
  JORDAN STREET 'Atwood', 743
  URBAN PINNACLE 'JFS-KW3', 743
Quercus michauxii, 743–744, 745, 746
Quercus montana, 744–745, 746
Quercus muehlenbergii, 745–746
Quercus myrsinifolia, 732, 746–747
Quercus nigra, 747–748, 774
Quercus nuttallii, 748–752, 757
  ARCADE 'QNSTG', 749
  BIG BOY 'QNJB', 749
  BREEZEWAY 'Ochlocknee', 749
  CHARISMA 'MonPowe', 749
  ESPLANADE 'QNFTA', 749
  HIGHPOINT 'QNFTA', 749
  ICON 'QNI374', 751
  'New Madrid', 751
  RUBY SPRING 'Betterred', 751
  SANGRIA 'QNSTD', 751
  SOLSHINE 'New Madrid', 751
  TYTLEST 'QNMTF', 751
Quercus pagoda, 730
Quercus palustris, 728, 753–756
  'Crownright', 755
  EPIC 'QREP20', 755
  GREEN PILLAR 'Pringreen', 755
  PACIFIC BRILLIANCE 'PWJR08', 755
  PROMENADE 'QS20', 755
  'Sovereign', 755, 756
  STREETWISE 'QRSW18', 755
Quercus phellos, 733, 756–759
  ABUNDANCE 'QPAB64', 758
  ASCENDOR 'QPSTJ', 758
  FORTITUDE 'QPFT06', 759
  HIGHTOWER 'QPSTA', 759
  KINGPIN 'Greenenvy', 759
  SHIRAZ 'QPSTB', 759
  UPPERTON 'RT3', 759
  WYNSTAR 'QPMTF', 759
Quercus prinus. See *Quercus montana*
Quercus robur, 760–767
  'Birthday Candle', 761
  'Chimney Fire', 761

Quercus robur [*continued*]
CRIMSON SPIRE 'Crimschmidt', 761
'Fastigiata', 761
FOREST KNIGHT 'Tabor', 761
HERITAGE 'Clemons', 763
KINDRED SPIRIT 'Nadler', 763
'Koster', 763
PRAIRIE STATURE 'Midwest', 763
REGAL PRINCE 'Long', 764
ROSEHILL 'Asjes', 764
SKINNY GENES 'JFS-KW2QX', 764
SKYMASTER 'Pyramich', 766
SKYROCKET 'Fastigiata', 766
STREETSPIRE 'JFS-KW1QX', 766
TRIPLE CROWN 'Taylor', 767
WALKENBACH 'Adeline', 767
Quercus rubra, 728, 768–769
'Aurea', 769
Quercus rysophylla, 769–770
'Maya', 770
Quercus salicina, 747
Quercus ×schuettei, 725
Quercus shumardii, 730, 770–771
MADISON 'ACNRT1', 771
PANACHE 'QSFTC', 771
PROMINENCE 'QSSTH', 771
Quercus stellata, 771–772
Quercus suber, 719, 726, 772–773
Quercus texana. See *Quercus nuttallii*
Quercus ×tottentii, 739
Quercus velutina, 773–774
Quercus virginiana, 774–775
BOARDWALK 'FBQV22', 775
'Cannon-Sharp', 775
CATHEDRAL 'SDLN', 775
'Empire', 775
HIGHRISE 'QVTIA', 775
MILLENNIUM 'CLTFZ', 775
PARK SIDE 'FBQV1', 775
'Southern Shade', 775
Quercus ×warei, 760

R

red alder, 160
red ash, 369–372
redbay, 565
red box, 345
red buckeye, 152
redbud, 27
red horsechestnut, 144–145
red lotus tree, 480–481
red maple, 102–118
red mulberry, 540
red oak, 718–719, 768–769
red snakebark maple, 53–54
redwood, 794–796

Rhamnus caroliniana. See *Frangula caroliniana*
Rhamnus purshiana. See *Frangula purshiana*
×*Rhaphiobotrya*, 339
'Coppertone', 339
Rhaphiolepis indica, 339
Rhodoleia championii, 776
Rhodoleia henryi, 'Scarlet Bells', 776
Rhus typhina, 776–777
'Laciniata', 777
TIGER EYES 'Bailtiger', 777
Rio Grande cottonwood, 649
river birch, 179–183
Robinia ×ambigua 'Decaisneana', 778
Robinia hispida, 778
Robinia ×margaretta 'Casque Rouge', 778
Robinia pseudoacacia, 778–781
'Bessoniana', 778
CHICAGO BLUES 'Benjamin', 778
'Frisia', 781
'Idahoensis', 781
'Purple Robe', 781
'Pyramidalis', 781
TWISTY BABY 'Lace Lady', 781
'Umbraculifera', 781
Robinia ×slavinii 'Hillieri', 781
Rocky Mountain bristlecone pine, 591–592
Rocky Mountain juniper, 420
Rocky Mountain maple, 61
roundleaf birch, 178
royal paulownia, 564
Russian mulberry, 538
Russian olive, 335
rusty blackhaw viburnum, 902–903
Rutgers hybrid dogwood, 295–299

S

Sabal palmetto, 782
Salix, 256, 782–789, 784
'Babylon', 784
'Blanda', 784
'Britzensis', 784
'Chrysocoma', 784
'Crispa', 784
'Curly Locks', 784
'Fan Giant', 785
'Flame', 785
'Flamingo', 787
'Globe Navajo', 789
'Golden Curls', 787
'Hakuro-Nishiki', 787
'Pendula', 786, 787
'Prairie Cascade', 787
PRAIRIE REFLECTION 'Silver Lake', 787
SCARLET CURLS 'Scarcuzam', 787
'Snake', 787
'Torulosa', 789

'Umbraculifera', 789
'Vitellina', 789
'Weeping Sally', 789
Salix alba, 783, 784, 789
Salix babylonica, 783, 787, 789
var. *pekinensis*, 783
Salix caprea, 783, 787, 789
Salix euxina, 783
Salix ×fragilis, 783, 784
Salix integra, 783
Salix matsudana, 783
Salix ×pendulina, 783, 785
Salix pentandra, 783
Salix ×salamonii, 783, 784
salt cedar, 827
Sapindus drummondii. See *Sapindus saponaria*
var. *drummondii*
Sapindus saponaria var. *drummondii*, 790–791
Sargent cherry, 678–681
Sargent crabapple, 506, 523
Sargent Tina, 524
Sassafras albidum, 791–792, 865
saucer magnolia, 492–495
Sawara falsecypress, 253–254
sawtooth oak, 719
scarlet oak, 727–728
Schneider zelkova, 911–912
Sciadopitys, 17
Sciadopitys verticillata, 16, 792–794
'Gruene Kugel', 793
'Joe Kozey', 793
'Sternschnuppe', 794
'Wintergreen', 794
scion wood, 31
Scotch elm, 886–887
Scotch laburnum, 430
Scotch pine, 624–625
scrub pine, 628
sea buckthorn, 401
Senegal date palm, 568
sentinel pine, 625
Sequoia sempervirens, 794–796
'Aptos Blue', 795
'Filoli', 796
'Santa Cruz', 796
'Soquel', 796
Sequoiadendron giganteum, 797–799
'Barabit's Requiem', 798
'Glaucum', 798
'Greenpeace', 798
'Hazel Smith', 798
'Pendulum', 798
'Von Martin', 798
Serbian spruce, 578–580
seven-son flower, 400
shagbark hickory, 210–212
shamel ash, 373

Shantung maple, 139–143
sheepberry, 898–899
shellbark hickory, 212
shingle oak, 735
shore pine, 599–601
Shumard oak, 770–771
Siberian crabapple, 505
Siberian elm, 897
Sichuan China fir, 315
Siebold magnolia, 490–491
Siebold viburnum, 903–904
silk-tree, 155–156
silky stewartia, 808
silver birch, 186–188
silver dollar gum, 345
silver dollar tree, 340
silver lime, 859–861
silver linden, 859–861
silver maple, 109, 119–120
single-leaf pinyon pine, 610–611
Sinojackia, 801
Sinojackia rehderiana, 800–801
  'La Grima', 801
  'Linda Carol', 801
Sinowilsonia henryi, 801
Sitka spruce, 589–590
slender hinoki cypress, 252
small-leaved gum, 344
smiling monkey forest tree, 481
smoothleaf elm, 890
snakebark maple, 89
snow gum, 344–345
snowy mespilus, 168
Sophora japonica. See *Styphnolobium japonicum*
Sophora secundiflora. See *Dermatophyllum secundiflorum*
Sorbus alnifolia, 802
Sorbus americana, RED CASCADE 'Dwarfcrown', 803
Sorbus aria, 804–805, 806
  'Lutescens', 805
  'Magnifica', 805
Sorbus aucuparia, 805–806
  'Aspleniifolia', 805
  CARDINAL ROYAL 'Michred', 805
  'Rossica', 806
  'Sheerwater Seedling', 806
Sorbus ×hybrida, 806–807
  'Gibbsii', 807
  'Quercifolia', 807
Sorbus obtusifolia, 806
Sorbus rupicola, 806
Sorbus ×thuringiaca, 806–807
  'Fastigiata', 807
sourwood, 556–557
southern catalpa, 215–216

southern crabapple, 505
southern magnolia, 408, 468, 475–479
southern red oak, 729–730
southern yew, 642–643
southwestern white pine, 620
Spaeth alder, 161
Spanish chestnut, 215
Spanish fir, 45
speckled alder, 159
Sprenger magnolia, 495–496
spring cherry, 689–691
staghorn sumac, 776–777
star magnolia, 483, 497–499
Stewartia ×henryae, 811
Stewartia koreana, 810
Stewartia malacodendron, 808
Stewartia monadelpha, 808–809
  'Harold Hillier', 811
Stewartia ovata var. *grandiflora*, 811
Stewartia pseudocamellia, 810–811
  'Ballet', 811
  'Harold Hillier', 811
  'Milk and Honey', 811
  'Mint Frills', 811
  'Pilar Bella', 811
  'Scarlet Sentinel', 811
Stewartia sinensis, 812–813
stinking-ash, 701–702
stinking cedar, 863
stone pine, 616
strawberry tree, 171
striped maple, 89
Styphnolobium japonicum, 813–814
  'Gold Standard', 814
  MILLSTONE 'Halka', 814
  'Pendula', 814
  'Regent', 814
Styrax japonicus, 815–820
  'Carillon', 816
  'Emerald Pagoda', 816
  'Evening Light', 817
  'Fragrant Fountain', 817
  'Frosted Emerald', 818
  MARLEY'S PINK 'JL Weeping', 818
  'Pink Chimes', 818
  PRYSTINE SPIRE 'MTFSJ', 818
  SNOW CHARM 'JFS-E', 818
  SNOWCONE 'JFS-D', 819
  'Spring Showers', 820
Styrax obassia, 820–821
subalpine fir, 43–44
sugarberry, 229–230
sugar hackberry, 229–230
sugar maple, 33, 121–131
swamp chestnut oak, 743–744
swamp red oak, 770–771
swamp tupelo, 542

swamp white oak, 722–725
sweet bay, 437
sweetbay magnolia, 500–503
sweet birch, 178–179
sweet crabapple, 506
sweetheart tree, 349
Swiss stone pine, 597–598
Syagrus romanzoffiana, 194
sycamore, 637–638
sycamore maple, 98
Sycopsis, 776
Syringa pekinensis. See *Syringa reticulata* subsp. *pekinensis*
Syringa reticulata, 821–823
  'Golden Eclipse', 823
  IVORY PILLAR 'Willamette', 823
  'Ivory Silk', 823
  SNOWCAP 'Elliott', 823
  SNOWDANCE 'Bailnce', 822
  'Summer Storm', 823
Syringa reticulata subsp. *pekinensis*, 824–825
  BEIJING GOLD 'Zhang Zhiming', 824
  CHINA SNOW 'Morton', 825
  COPPER CURLS 'SunDak', 825
  GREAT WALL 'WFH2', 825
  SUMMER CHARM 'DTR 124', 825

T

Taiwanese photinia, 568–569
Taiwania cryptomerioides, 826–827
Taiwan redwood, 826–827
tall stewartia, 808–809
tamarack, 446
Tamarix chinensis, 827
Tamarix ramosissima, 827
Tasmanian bluegum, 341–342
Tatarian maple, 134
Taxodium distichum, 541, 827–835
  AUTUMN GOLD 'Sofine', 830, 831
  'Cascade Falls', 829, 830, 831, 832
  DEBONAIR 'Morris', 829, 831
  'Falling Waters', 829, 831–832
  'Fox Red', 832
  GREENFEATHER 'Carolyn Malone', 832
  GREEN WHISPER 'JFS-SGPN', 832
  var. *imbricarium*, 829, 832, 833, 835
  LINDSEY'S SKYWARD 'Skyward', 832
  var. *mexicanum*, 832
  'Peve Minaret', 829, 833
  'Prairie Sentinel', 829, 831, 833
  SHAWNEE BRAVE 'Michelson', 829, 833
Taxus baccata, 836–837, 838
  'Fastigiata', 836
  Fastigiata Aurea Group, 837
Taxus brevifolia, 837–838
Taxus canadensis, 838

Taxus cuspidata, 838
Taxus floridana, 838
tea crabapple, 506
Tetradium daniellii, 838–839
"Texas lilac", 905
Texas mountain laurel, 332
Texas umbrella-tree, 531
Theves poplar, 653
three-flower maple, 137–138
Thuja occidentalis, 839–842
 'American Pillar', 840
 'Brabant', 840
 'Brandon', 840
 'Degroot's Spire', 841
 'Emerald', 841
 'Jantar', 841
 'Nigra', 841
 NORDIC SPIRE 'Rebild', 841
 NORTH POLE 'Art Boe', 841
 'Pyramidalis', 841
 'Rushmore', 842
 'Skybound', 842
 'Sunkist', 842
 'Techny', 842
 'Wintergreen', 842
Thuja orientalis. See *Platycladus orientalis*
Thuja plicata, 843–846
 'Atrovirens', 844
 'Excelsa', 844
 'Fastigiata', 844
 'Golden Spire', 844
 'Green Giant', 310, 318, 844
 'Hogan', 844
 SPRING GROVE 'Grovepli', 846
 'Virescens', 846
 VIRGINIAN 'BFC68', 846
 'Zebrina', 846
 'Zebrina Extra Gold', 846
Thuja standishii, 844
Tibetan cherry, 683
Tilia americana, 846–849
 AMERICAN SENTRY 'McKSentry', 847
 'Boulevard', 847
 'Continental Appeal', 847
 FRONTYARD 'Bailyard', 848
 LEGEND 'DTR 123', 848
 'Redmond', 848
 TRUE NORTH 'Duros', 849
Tilia cordata, 850–854, 855, 856, 858
 'Akira Gold', 850
 'Böhlje', 850
 CORINTHIAN 'Corzam', 851
 'Glenleven', 851
 'Golden Cascade', 851
 GREENSPIRE 'PNI 6025', 851
 'Harvest Gold', 853, 857
 NORLIN 'Ronald', 853

 'Rancho', 853
 SHAMROCK 'Baileyi', 853
 SUMMER SPRITE 'Halka', 853
Tilia dasystyla, 855
Tilia ×euchlora, 848, 855
Tilia ×europaea, 855–857
 'Euchlora', 855
 'Pallida', 857
 'Pallida Typ Lappen', 857
Tilia heterophylla, 846
Tilia mongolica, 857
Tilia petiolaris. See *Tilia tomentosa*
Tilia platyphyllos, 856, 857–858
 'Delft', 858
 'Laciniata', 858
 'Örebro', 858
 'Rubra', 858
Tilia tomentosa, 859–861
 'Brabant', 859
 GREEN MOUNTAIN 'PNI 6051', 860
 'Petiolaris', 860
 SATIN SHADOW 'Sashazam', 860
 'Silver Lining', 860
 'Sterling', 861
Toona sinensis, 861–862
 'Flamingo', 862
topal holly, 405–407
Toringo crabapple, 506
Torreya, 836
Torreya californica, 862–863
Torreya taxifolia, 863
Tower poplar, 647
Trachycarpus fortunei, 864
tree-of-heaven, 154
trident maple, 47–49
Trochodendron aralioides, 864–865
true laurel, 437
Tsuga, 24, 27, 836
Tsuga canadensis, 22, 811, 865–867
 'Albospica', 866
 GOLDEN DUCHESS 'MonKinn', 866
 GOLDEN DUKE 'Monjers', 866
 'New Gold', 866
 'Pendula', 866
 'Summer Snow', 867
Tsuga caroliniana, 867–868
 'Arnold Pyramid', 868
Tsuga chinensis, 22, 868–869
Tsuga diversifolia, 22, 868, 869
Tsuga heterophylla, 869–871
 'Iron Springs', 870, 871
Tsuga mertensiana, 871–872, 872
 'Blue Star', 872
 'Glacier Peak', 872
Tsuga sieboldii, 22, 868
tuliptree, 458–462

tung-oil tree, 898
turkey oak, 726
Turkish filbert, 300–301
two-winged silverbell, 392–393

U

Ulmus alata, 873–874
 'Lace Parasol', 874
 'Woodland', 874
Ulmus americana, 874–878
 'American Liberty Multiclone', 875
 COLONIAL SPIRIT 'JFS-Prince II', 22, 875
 CREOLE QUEEN 'UASNZ', 876
 'Independence', 875
 'Jefferson', 22, 876
 'New Harmony', 22, 876
 PRAIRIE EXPEDITION 'Lewis & Clark', 22, 876
 'Princeton', 22, 23, 876
 'St. Croix', 22, 878
 'Valley Forge', 22, 878
Ulmus carpinifolia. See *Ulmus minor*
Ulmus crassifolia, 879
Ulmus davidiana, 879–886, 897
 ACCOLADE 'Morton', 880
 'Cathedral', 881
 COMMENDATION 'Morton Stalwart', 881
 DANADA CHARM 'Morton Red Tip', 881–883
 'Discovery', 883
 EMERALD SUNSHINE 'JFS-Bieberich', 883
 GREENSTONE 'JFS-KW2UD', 883
 var. *japonica*, 897
 'New Horizon', 884
 'Patriot', 884
 'Prospector', 884, 897
 'Sapporo Autumn Gold', 885
 TRIUMPH 'Morton Glossy', 885
 VANGUARD 'Morton Plainsman', 886
Ulmus glabra, 886–887
 'Camperdownii', 887
 'Horizontalis', 887
Ulmus ×hollandica, 884, 888–889
 'Clusius', 888
 'Dodoens', 888
 'Homestead', 888
 'Lobel', 888
 'Pioneer', 888
 'Plantijn', 889
 'Regal', 889
 'Wredei', 889
Ulmus japonica, 879, 881, 883, 884, 885, 889
Ulmus minor, 881, 888, 889, 890
Ulmus parvifolia, 890–896
 ALLÉE 'Emer II', 891
 ATHENA / ATHENA Classic 'Emer I', 892

BOSQUE 'UPMTF', 892
'Burgundy', 892
'Drake', 892
'Dynasty', 894
EMERALD FLAIR 'JFS-Barrett', 894
'Emerald Prairie', 894
EVERCLEAR 'BSNUPF', 894
'Frontier', 895
'Golden Rey', 895
'Hope', 895
'Small Frye', 895, 896
Ulmus propinqua, 883, 896
Ulmus pumila, 881, 884, 885, 889, 897
Ulmus wallichiana, 888
Ulmus wilsoniana, 879, 881, 884, 885, 897
umbrella magnolia, 499–500
umbrella pine, 792–794
Ussurian pear, 716–717

V

valley oak, 736
velvet ash, 374
Vernicia fordii, 'Anna Bella', 898
*Viburnum awabuki. See Viburnum
    odoratissimum* var. *awabuki*
Viburnum lentago, 898–899, 903
    'Prairie Classic', 899
Viburnum odoratissimum var. *awabuki*,
    899–901
    'Chindo', 899–901
    COPPERTOP 'Brant01', 901
Viburnum prunifolium, 901–902, 903
    FOREST ROUGE 'McKRouge', 902
Viburnum rufidulum, 899, 902–903
    'Royal Guard', 903
Viburnum sieboldii, 903–904
    'Seneca', 904
vine maple, 54–55
Virginia pine, 628
Vitex agnus-castus, 904–906
    'Abbeville Blue', 905
    f. *alba* 'Silver Spire', 905
    Cooke's series, 905
    DELTA BLUES 'PIIVAC-I', 905

'Flora Ann', 905
'Le Compte', 905
'Mississippi Blues', 905
'Salinas Pink', 905
'Shoal Creek', 905

W

wafer-ash, 701–702
Wasatch maple, 61–63
Washington hawthorn, 308–309
Washingtonia filifera, 907, 908
Washingtonia robusta, 908
water birch, 183
water hickory, 207
water oak, 747–748
water tupelo, 541
waxleaf privet, 448
wedding cake tree, 272
weeping bottlebrush, 195
western cottonwood, 650
western hemlock, 869–871
western redbud, 246–247
western red cedar, 843–846
western soapberry, 790–791
Westonbirt cypress, 326
wheel tree, 864–865
white alder, 159–160
white ash, 361–363
whitebark pine, 590–591
whitebeam, 804–805
white fir, 38
white fringetree, 259–261
white mulberry, 538
white oak, 718–719, 721–722
white poplar, 644–645
white spruce, 576–577
white willow, 783
wild raisin, 898–899
willow, 256, 782–789
willow-leafed magnolia, 482, 489
willowleaf pear, 715–716
willow-leaf peppermint, 343
willow oak, 756–759
Wilson elm, 897

winged elm, 873–874
winterberry euonymus, 347–348
Wisconsin weeping willow, 784
witch-hazel, 394
Wollemia nobilis, 909
Wollemi pine, 909
Wych elm, 886–887

X

Xanthoceras sorbifolium, CLEAR CREEK
    'Psgan', 910

Y

yellow birch, 177–178
yellow buckeye, 28, 146
yellowhorn, 910
Yoshino cherry, 694–695
Yulan magnolia, 474–475

Z

Zelkova schneideriana, 911–912
    'Wine Me Up', 912
Zelkova serrata, 912–917, 918
    CITY SPRITE 'JFS-KW1', 914
    'Goshiki', 914
    GREEN VASE, 915
    'Green Veil', 915
    'Halka', 915
    'Kiwi Sunset', 915
    'Musashino', 916
    MYRIMAR 'ZSFKF', 916
    'Ogon', 916
    'Urban Ruby', 916
    'Variegata', 916
    VILLAGE GREEN, 916
    WIRELESS 'Schmidtlow', 916
Zelkova sinica, 918
Zen magnolia, 504–505
Ziziphus jujuba, 919
    var. *inermis*, 919
    'Lang', 919
    'Li', 919
Zumi Calocarpa, 513